Studien zum ausländischen und internationalen Privatrecht

511

Herausgegeben vom

Max-Planck-Institut für ausländisches und internationales Privatrecht

Direktoren:

Holger Fleischer und Ralf Michaels

Biset Sena Güneş

Succession Upon Death: A Comparison of European and Turkish Private International Law

Mohr Siebeck

Biset Sena Güneş, born 1987; legal studies at Istanbul University; LL.M. (Queen Mary University London); 2021 doctorate (University of Regensburg); since 2020 Senior Research Fellow and Head of the Centre of Expertise on Turkey at the Max Planck Institute for Comparative and International Private Law, Hamburg.
orcid.org/0000-0001-8390-6761

ISBN 978-3-16-161352-4 / eISBN 978-3-16-161353-1
DOI 10.1628/978-3-16-161353-1

ISSN 0720-1141 / eISSN 2568-7441
(Studien zum ausländischen und internationalen Privatrecht)

The Deutsche Nationalbibliothek lists this publication in the Deutsche Nationalbibliographie; detailed bibliographic data are available at *http://dnb.dnb.de*.

The book was printed and bound on non-aging paper by Gulde Druck in Tübingen.

Printed in Germany.

To my family…

Preface

This study was accepted by the Faculty of Law of the University of Regensburg as a dissertation for the degree of doctor juris in September 2021. Revisions of the literature and case law cited were made until April 2022.

It is often said that writing a doctoral thesis is a rather lonely but rewarding experience. I am fortunate enough to say that I received a great degree of academic and personal support from many people in this highly rewarding journey, which did not leave me feeling lonely. Therefore, I would like to use this occasion to thank all of them here.

First and foremost, I would like to express my sincere gratitude to my doctoral supervisor, Prof. Dr. Anatol Dutta, M. Jur. (Oxford), for his invaluable advice and continuous support during the entire process. Even from the very early days of this process, he always encouraged me and offered his help whenever I had difficulty drafting my work. I have indeed benefited greatly from his extensive knowledge and experience both professionally and personally, and for this I will always be grateful to him. I would like to extend my thanks also to the second examiner of my thesis, Prof. Dr. Martin Löhnig, for his prompt submission of the examination report and for the supportive comments in his report.

This study is in fact a product of time I spent in Ankara, Regensburg, and Hamburg. The idea of pursuing a doctorate in Germany originated in Ankara, where I previously worked as a research assistant at the department of international private and procedural law at Ankara Yıldırım Beyazıt University. I would like to express my deepest appreciation to Prof. Dr. Musa Aygül and Prof. Dr. M. Fatih Uşan for their tireless support and encouragement at every phase of my doctorate, even when I decided to continue my career in Germany. I also thank my colleagues from Ankara, Dr. iur. Belkıs Vural Çelenk, Dr. Canan Erdoğan, Assoc. Prof. Dr. Ersin Erdoğan, and Dr. Elif Hande Altıntaş Açıkgöz, for their support and help throughout all the years I worked there; and all my other colleagues from the department for their many collaborative efforts and assistance in finding resources.

Most of the foundational research on which this book is based was conducted in Regensburg and Hamburg. I would like to acknowledge the assistance that was provided by the staff of the chair of Prof. Dutta at the University of Regensburg with the doctoral procedures and to thank them for the friendly exchange we had during the time I spent there. I would also like to extend my special thanks to my colleagues from the Max Planck Institute for Comparative and International Private Law in Hamburg, which I first visited as a guest researcher and where I now have the privilege of being employed as a senior research fellow and head of the Centre of Expertise on Turkey. First of all, I am very grateful to Prof. Dr. Ralf Michaels, LL.M. (Cambridge), under whom I work at the Institute, for his steady reassurance during both the final phase of my doctorate and the publishing process of this book. From the Institute, I would also like to express my thanks to Priv.-Doz. Dr. Jan Peter Schmidt for the enlightening discussions on different parts of my thesis; to Prof. Dr. Nadjma Yassari, LL.M. (London), Dr. Dörthe Engelcke, Dr. Jennifer Trinks, Maître en droit (Paris II), LL.M. (Yale), Dr. Mateusz Grochowski, LL.M. (Yale), Dr. Antonia Sommerfeld, Dr. Denise Wiedemann, LL. M. (Lissabon), and all my other colleagues from 'Team Michaels' for the moral support and friendly exchange at the Institute; to Claudia Holland and her entire team for their help with research in the library; to Elke Halsen-Raffel for kindly arranging my previous visits to the library; to Dr. Christian Eckl, Michael Friedman, A.B. Economics (USC), Juris Doctor (Berkeley), Janina Jentz, LL.M. (oec), M.A., and David Schröder-Micheel, M.A., for their editorial support during the publication process of this book; and to my student assistants, Ruth Sander and Luiz Florian Wimmer, for their help on the revision of the bibliography and for the final proofreading.

Various stages of my doctoral studies in Germany have been financially supported by the Jean Monnet Scholarship, the DAAD Scholarship, and the research scholarship of the Max Planck Institute for Comparative and International Private Law. The generous financial backing from the granting institutions is truly appreciated. My dissertation was honoured by the Alumni Association of the Law Faculty at the University of Regensburg with the Juratisbona-Prize recognizing exceptional doctoral dissertations. I am truly thankful to the Alumni Association for the accolade and the financial support. I also gratefully acknowledge the generous financial support of the Johanna und Fritz Buch Gedächtnis-Stiftung, Hamburg, for the publication costs of this book.

During this journey, I am highly indebted to my dear friends, Dr. iur. Merve Ürem Çetinel, Dr. Büşra Cömert Akbay, Dr. Zahide Altunbaş Sancak, Dr. Anıl Güven Yüksel, Dr. Ekin Korkmaz, Assoc. Prof. Dr. Müge Ürem, Dr. Nurten Kansu Okyay, Hüseyin Coşgun, LL. M. (London), and Cansu Sinem Eden. I thank each and every one of them wholeheartedly for their continuous support, praise, and truly invaluable friendship.

Last but not least, this endeavour would of course not have been possible without the support of my beloved family. I am deeply thankful to my mother, Nalan Güneş, my father, Dr. Ahmet Güneş, and my brother, İsmet Serhan Güneş, not only for their never-ending belief in me, encouragement, and patience during the process, but also for their unconditional love and for all the things they have taught me throughout my entire life. I would also like to thank my uncles, Hüseyin Kadir İleri and Mustafa Sadık İleri, my grandfather, Halil İbrahim İleri, and my late grandmother, Zekavet İleri, for their deeply appreciated support and love during my whole life. Lastly, I would like to recognize the moral support of my sister-in-law, Nevin Güneş who joined our family during the last phase of this study.

Hamburg, December 2022 *Biset Sena Güneş*

Summary of Contents

Table of Contents

Table of Abbreviations

AB	Ausschussbericht (Committee Report)
ABD	Ankara Barosu Dergisi (Journal/Turkey)
Abs	Absatz
AcP	Archiv für die civilistische Praxis (Journal/Germany)
AD	Adalet Dergisi (Journal/Turkey)
aF	alte Fassung
AG	Amtsgericht (Local Courts of Germany)/Advocate General of the CJEU
AGORA Int'l J Jurid Sci	AGORA International Journal of Juridical Sciences
AJCL	American Journal of Comparative Law
AJIL	American Journal of International Law
AJP	Aktuelle Juristische Praxis (Journal/Switzerland)
AkdHFD	Akdeniz Üniversitesi Hukuk Fakültesi Dergisi (Journal/Turkey)
Am U L Rev	American University Law Review
Anali PFZE	Anali Pravnog fakulteta Univerziteta u Zenici (Journal/Bosnia and Herzegovina)
Ankara L Rev	Ankara Law Review
Anm.	Anmerkung
Art/Arts	Article/Articles
AS	Amtliche Sammlung des Bundesrechts (The Official Compilation of Federal Legislation in Switzerland)
AußStrG	Außerstreitgesetz (Austrian Non-Contentious Proceedings Act)
AÜEHFD	Atatürk Üniversitesi Erzincan Hukuk Fakültesi Dergisi (Journal/Turkey)
AÜHFD	Ankara Üniversitesi Hukuk Fakültesi Dergisi (Journal/Turkey)
AÜSBFD	Ankara Üniversitesi Siyasal Bilgiler Fakültesi Dergisi (Journal/Turkey)
AYM	Anayasa Mahkemesi (Constitutional Court of Turkey)
BAÜHFD	Bahçeşehir Üniversitesi Hukuk Fakültesi Dergisi (Journal/Turkey)
BBl	Bundesblatt (Federal Law Gazette of Switzerland)
BeckFormB ErbR	Beck'sches Formularbuch Erbrecht (Form Book/Germany)
BeckOK	Beck'scher Online-Kommentar (Legal Commentary/Germany)
BeckOGK	Beck-online Großkommentar zum Zivilrecht (Legal Commentary/Germany)
BeckRS	Beck-Rechtsprechung (Journal/Germany)
BerGesVR	Berichte der Deutschen Gesellschaft für Völkerrecht (Journal/Germany)

BGB	Bürgerliches Gesetzbuch (Civil Code of Germany)
BGBl.	Bundesgesetzblatt (Federal Law Gazette of Germany and Austria)
BGH	Bundesgerichtshof (German Federal Court of Justice)
BGHZ	Entscheidungen des Bundesgerichtshofes in Zivilsachen (Collection of Judgments of the German Federal Court of Justice in Civil Matters)
Bing	Bingham's Reports, Common Pleas
BÜHFD	Başkent Üniversitesi Hukuk Fakültesi Dergisi (Journal/Turkey)
BVerfG	Bundesverfassungsgericht (German Federal Constitutional Court)
BvR	Aktenzeichen einer Verfassungsbeschwerde zum Bundesverfassungsgericht (File number of a Constitutional Complaint to the German Federal Constitutional Court)
BWNotZ	Zeitschrift für das Notariat in Baden-Württemberg (Journal/Germany)
BYIL	British Yearbook of International Law
C	Information and Notices (of the European Union)
Case W Res J Int'l L	Case Western Reserve Journal of International Law
Cass.	Cour de cassation (French Court of Cassation)
CESifo Econ Stud	CESifo Economic Studies
cf.	confer/conferatur (meaning compare)
ch.	chapter/chambre
civ.	civile (Civil Chamber of the French Court of Cassation)
CJEU/ECJ	Court of Justice of the European Union/European Court of Justice
CML Rev	Common Market Law Review
COM	Commission (of the European Union)
contra	against/conflicting/opposite
Cornell LQ	Cornell Law Quarterly
ÇSGB	T.C. Çalışma ve Sosyal Güvenlik Bakanlığı (Turkish Ministry of Labour and Social Security)
ÇTTAD	Çağdaş Türkiye Tarihi Araştırmaları Dergisi (Journal/Turkey)
Destatis	Statistisches Bundesamt (Federal Statistical Office of Germany)
DEÜHFD	Dokuz Eylül Üniversitesi Hukuk Fakültesi Dergisi (Journal/Turkey)
div.	division
DNotI	Deutsches Notarinstitut (The German Notarial Institute)
DNotZ	Deutsche Notar-Zeitschrift (Journal/Germany)
Doc	Document
DStR	Deutsches Steuerrecht (Journal/Germany)
DTJV	Deutsch-türkische Juristenvereinigung (German-Turkish Lawyers Association)
DÜHFD	Dicle Üniversitesi Hukuk Fakültesi Dergisi (Journal/Turkey)
E	Esas Sayısı (File number for judgments of Turkish Courts)
EC	European Community
ECR	European Court Reports
ed/eds	editor/editors
Edinburgh L Rev	Edinburgh Law Review
edn	edition

EEC	European Economic Community
EFTA	European Free Trade Association
EG	Europäische Gemeinschaft
EGBGB	Einführungsgesetz zum Bürgerlichen Gesetzbuche (Introductory Act to the Civil Code – Private International Law Code of Germany)
EJIL	European Journal of International Law
ELI	European Law Institute
Emory Int'l L Rev	Emory International Law Review
EPLJ	European Property Law Journal
ErbR	Zeitschrift für die gesamte erbrechtliche Praxis (Journal/Germany)
ErbStB	Der Erbschaft-Steuerberater (Journal/Germany)
ERPL	European Review of Private Law
ESR	European Succession Regulation
esp.	especially
et seq.	et sequentes (and the following)
EU	European Union
EuErbVO	Europäische Erbrechtsverordnung (European Succession Regulation)
EuGVVO	Brüssel I Verordnung (Brussels I Regulation)
EuGüVO	Europäische Güterrechtsverordnung (European Matrimonial Property Regulation)
EuR	Europarecht (Journal/Germany)
Eur J L Reform	European Journal of Law Reform
Eur Rev	European Review
EUV/AEUV	Der Vertrag über die Europäische Union/Der Vertrag über die Arbeitsweise der Europäischen Union (Treaty of the European Union/Treaty on the Functioning of the European Union)
EuZPR/EuIPR	Europäisches Zivilprozess- und Kollisionsrecht (European Civil Procedural Law and Conflict-of-Laws)
EWCA Civ	England and Wales Court of Appeal Civil Division
EWHC (Ch/Comm/Fam)	England and Wales High Court (Chancery Division/Commercial Division/Family Division)
FamFG	Gesetz über das Verfahren in Familiensachen und in den Angelegenheiten der freiwilligen Gerichtsbarkeit (German Act on Court Procedure in Family and Non-litigious Matters)
FamRZ	Zeitschrift für das gesamte Familienrecht (Journal/Germany)
ff	and the following
FGPrax	Praxis der freiwilligen Gerichtsbarkeit (Journal/Germany)
FLR	Family Law Reports
fn	footnote
Form.	Formular
FORUM	International Law FORUM du droit international
FuR	Familie und Recht (Journal/Germany)
GBO	Grundbuchordnung (German Real Estate Registry Act)
Geo Wash Int'l L Rev	George Washington International Law Review
GKG	Gerichtskommisärsgesetz (Austrian Act on Court Commissioners)

GP	Gesetzgebungsperiode (des Nationalrates) (Legislative Period of Austrian National Council)
GPR	Zeitschrift für das Privatrecht der Europäischen Union (Journal/Germany)
GSÜHFD	Galatasaray Üniversitesi Hukuk Fakültesi Dergisi (Journal/Turkey)
GÜHFD	Gazi Üniversitesi Hukuk Fakültesi Dergisi (Journal/Turkey)
Harv L Rev	Harvard Law Review
Hg.	Herausgeber
HL	House of Lords
HmbGVBl	Hamburgisches Gesetz- und Verordnungsblatt (Hamburg Law and Ordinance Gazette)
HmbWBG	Hamburgisches Wohn- und Betreuungsqualitätsgesetz (Hamburg Quality of Housing and Care Law)
HTestFormÜ	Haager Testamentsformübereinkommen (Hague Form of Wills Convention)
IAS	Iustum Aequum Salutare (Journal/Hungary)
ICJ	International Court of Justice
ICLQ	International and Comparative Law Quarterly
IESC	Supreme Court of Ireland
IJPL	International Journal of Procedural Law
ILPr	International Litigation Procedure
InfAuslR	Informationsbrief Ausländerrecht (Journal/Germany)
InsO	Insolvenzordnung (Insolvency Statute of Germany)
IntErbRVG	Internationales Erbrechtsverfahrensgesetz (Act on International Procedure in Succession Matters)
IntGüRVGEG	Gesetz zum Internationalen Güterrecht und zur Änderung von Vorschriften des Internationalen Privatrechts (German Law on International Matrimonional Property Law and Reform of International Private Law Provisions)
Iowa L Rev	Iowa Law Review
IPR	Internationales Privatrecht
IPRax	Praxis des Internationalen Privat- und Verfahrensrechts (Journal/Germany)
IPRG	Bundesgesetz über das Internationale Privatrecht (Swiss Federal Act on Private International Law)
IPRspr	Die deutsche Rechtsprechung auf dem Gebiet des Internationalen Privatrechts (Collection of Court Rulings/Germany)
İBD	İstanbul Barosu Dergisi (Journal/Turkey)
İKÜHFD	İstanbul Kültür Üniversitesi Hukuk Fakültesi Dergisi (Journal/Turkey)
İMÜHFD	İstanbul Medipol Üniversitesi Hukuk Fakültesi Dergisi (Journal/Turkey)
İnÜHFD	İnönü Üniversitesi Hukuk Fakültesi Dergisi (Journal/Turkey)
İÜHFM	İstanbul Üniversitesi Hukuk Fakültesi Mecmuası (Journal/Turkey)
İTİCÜSBD	İstanbul Ticaret Üniversitesi Sosyal Bilimler Dergisi (Journal/Turkey)

J	Justice
JbItalR	Jahrbuch für Italienisches Recht (Yearbook/Germany)
JDI	Journal du Droit International (Journal/France)
JHA	Justice and Home Affairs
J Islam Stud	Journal of Islamic Studies
JN	Jurisdiktionsnorm (Austrian Act on Court Jurisdiction in Civil Matters)
J Priv Int L	Journal of Private International Law
JT	Journal des tribunaux (Journal/Belgium)
JURA	Juristische Ausbildung (Journal/Germany)
jurisPK-BGB	juris PraxisKommentar BGB (Legal Commentary/Germany)
JZ	Juristenzeitung (Journal/Germany)
K	Karar Sayısı (Decree number for judgments of Turkish Courts)
KG	Kammergericht (Court of Appeal in Berlin)
KHASHFD	Kadir Has Üniversitesi Hukuk Fakültesi Dergisi (Journal/Turkey)
L	Legislation (of the European Union)
La L Rev	Louisiana Law Review
Law & Contemp Probs	Law and Contemporary Problems
Leiden J Int Law	Leiden Journal of International Law
LG	Landgericht (Regional Courts of Germany)
Lloyd's Rep	Lloyd's Law Reports
LugÜ	Lugano-Übereinkommen (Lugano Convention)
LPartG	Gesetz über die Eingetragene Lebenspartnerschaft (German Law on Registered Partnerships)
LQR	The Law Quarterly Review
Maast J Eur & Comp L	Maastricht Journal of European and Comparative Law
MB	Moniteur Belge (Official Gazette of Belgium)
MHAD	Mukayeseli Hukuk Araştırmaları Dergisi (Journal/Turkey)
MHB	Milletlerarası Hukuk ve Milletlerarası Özel Hukuk Bülteni (Journal/Turkey)
MHFD	Maltepe Üniversitesi Hukuk Fakültesi Dergisi (Journal/Turkey)
MİHDER	Medeni Usul ve İcra İflas Hukuku Dergisi (Journal/Turkey)
MittBayNot	Mitteilungen des Bayerischen Notarvereins, der Notarkasse und der Landesnotarkammer Bayern (Journal/Germany)
MittRhNotK	Mitteilungen der Rheinischen Notarkammer (Journal/Germany)
MÖHUK	Milletlerarası Özel Hukuk ve Usul Hukuku Hakkında Kanun (Turkish Private International and Procedural Law Act)
MÜHF-HAD	Marmara Üniversitesi Hukuk Fakültesi Hukuk Araştırmaları Dergisi (Journal/Turkey)
MüKoBGB	Münchener Kommentar zum BGB (Legal Commentary/Germany)
MüKoZPO	Münchener Kommentar zur Zivilprozessordnung (Legal Commentary/Germany)
n	note

NA	Nachlassabkommen
NK-BGB	Nomos-Kommentar zum BGB (Legal Commentary/Germany)
No/no/Nr.	Number/Nummer
NR	Nationalrat (The National Council of Austria)
NILR	Netherlands International Law Review
NIPR	Nederlands Internationaal Privaatrecht (Journal/Netherlands)
NJW	Neue Juristische Wochenschrift (Journal/Germany)
NZ	Österreichische Notariats-Zeitung (Journal/Austria)
OFK	Orell Füssli Kommentar (Legal Commentary/Switzerland)
OGH	Oberster Gerichtshof der Republik Österreich (Supreme Court of Justice of the Republic of Austria)
OJ	Official Journal of the European Union
OLG	Oberlandesgericht (Higher Regional Courts of Germany)
Osgoode Hall LJ	Osgoode Hall Law Journal
OUP	Oxford University Press
p/pp	page/pages
para/paras	paragraph/paragraphs
PIL	Private International Law
PILA	Private International Law Act
Pol Int Eur Law	Polish Review of International and European Law
PPPM	Problemy Prawa Prywatnego Międzynarodowego (Journal/Poland)
Q	Question
RabelsZ	Rabels Zeitschrift für ausländisches und internationales Privatrecht (Journal/Germany)
RdC	Recueil des Cours (Collected Courses of The Hague Academy of International Law)
RDIPP	Rivista di diritto internazionale privato e processuale (Journal/Italy)
Rev crit dr int privé	Revue critique de droit international privé (Journal/France)
RGBl.	Reichsgesetzblatt (Official Gazette of the German and Austrian Empires)
RIW	Recht der Internationalen Wirtschaft (Journal/Germany)
RNotZ	Rheinische Notar-Zeitschrift (Journal/Germany)
Roman LT	Roman Legal Tradition
RPflG	Rechtspflegergesetz (Act on Senior Judicial Officers)
S/S.	Section/Seite/Satz
SJZ	Schweizerische Juristen-Zeitung (Journal/Switzerland)
SIG	Special Interest Group (of ELI)
soFid	Sozialwissenschaftlicher Fachinformationsdienst (Social Science Information Service)
StAZ	Das Standesamt (Journal/Germany)
Stb.	Staatsblad van het Koninkrijk der Nederlanden (Official Gazette of the Kingdom of the Netherlands)
subpara	subparagraph

SÜHFD	Selçuk Üniversitesi Hukuk Fakültesi Dergisi (Journal/Turkey)
Sydney L Rev	Sydney Law Review
T	Tarih (Date for the judgments of Turkish Courts)
TBB	Türkiye Barolar Birliği (Union of Turkish Bar Associations)
TBMM	Türkiye Büyük Millet Meclisi (The Grand National Assembly of Turkey)
T.C.	Türkiye Cumhuriyeti (Republic of Türkiye)
TFEU	Treaty on the Functioning of the European Union
TIL	The International Lawyer
TLQ	The Lawyer Quarterly
Tru L I	Trust Law International
TÜİK	Türkiye İstatistik Kurumu (Turkish Statistical Institute)
U Colo L Rev	University of Colorado Law Review
UINL	Union Internationale du Notariat (International Union of Latin Notaries)
UMD	Uyuşmazlık Mahkemesi Dergisi (Journal/Turkey)
U Miami L Review	University of Miami Law Review
UNIDROIT	International Institute for the Unification of Private Law
Urt	Urteil
UTTDER	Uluslararası Ticaret ve Tahkim Hukuku Dergisi (Journal/Turkey)
UYAP	Ulusal Yargı Ağı Projesi (National Judiciary Informatics System in Turkey)
v	von/vom
Ves & Beames	Vesey & Beames' Reports
VO	Verordnung
vol	volume
Vorb.	Vorbemerkungen
VwGH	Verwaltungsgerichtshof (Administrative Court of Austria)
WPNR	Weekblad voor Privaatrecht, Notariaat en Registratie (Journal/Netherlands)
YbPIL	Yearbook of Private International Law
YD	Yargıtay Dergisi (Journal/Turkey)
YKD	Yargıtay Kararları Dergisi (Journal/Turkey)
YLJ	Yale Law Journal
YÜHFD	Yeditepe Üniversitesi Hukuk Fakültesi Dergisi (Journal/Turkey)
ZEuP	Zeitschrift für Europäisches Privatrecht (Journal/Germany)
ZEV	Zeitschrift für Erbrecht und Vermögensnachfolge (Journal/Germany)
ZGBR	Schweizerische Zeitschrift für Beurkundungs- und Grundbuchrecht (Journal/Switzerland)
ZPO	Zivilprozessordnung (German Code of Civil Procedure)
ZVglRWiss	Zeitschrift für Vergleichende Rechtswissenschaft (Journal/Germany)
ZZPInt	Zeitschrift für Zivilprozess International (Journal/Germany)

Introduction

As the Turkish poet *Turgut Uyar* famously wrote: 'Death is like a memory in man; / sometimes [it is] remembered, sometimes [it is] forgotten. / Yet one day, one day finally, / [it becomes] visible, tangible…'.[1] Indeed, when this tragic yet inevitable fact of life becomes 'visible' and 'tangible' for a person, there are a number of legal issues to be dealt with by the surviving relatives. One of these issues, undoubtedly, is how property will devolve. The answer to this question is considered part of the 'legal DNA'[2] of a country, whereby cultural and social customs play an important role and the rights of family members and third parties are involved;[3] hence, the national rules of States often differ in this field. Such variety does not usually pose a problem in a purely domestic case, since courts will resolve the dispute in line with their own laws. This unproblematic posture was generally the case in former times, when international succession cases were exceptional rather than common practice. Yet in today's world there is an ever-increasing mobility of people. This has a direct effect on the perception, content, and application of the law in many fields.[4] And this is especially true for the law of succession, a legal field which, compared to others, will frequently feature international elements.[5]

Despite the likelihood of cross-border succession cases, the diversity of national rules in this area presents certain challenges in practice.[6] In the first place, such a diversity negatively affects foreseeability and legal certainty for

---

1 Turgut Uyar, 'Ölüme Dair Konuşmalar 2' in Bedirhan Toprak (ed), *Büyük Saat* (11th edn, Yapı Kredi Yayınları 2011) 25 (author translation from Turkish original).

2 House of Lords European Union Committee, 'Minutes of Evidence on the EU's Regulation on Succession – 6th Report of Session' 2009–2010 HL 75 18-Q8 <https://publications.parliament.uk/pa/ld200910/ldselect/ldeucom/75/75.pdf> accessed 22 June 2021.

3 Eva Lein, 'A Further Step Towards a European Code of Private International Law – The Commission Proposal for a Regulation on Succession' (2009) XI YbPIL 107, 108–109.

4 Walter Schwimmer, 'The Effects of Globalisation on Law: The Impact on the Council of Europe' (2000) 2 FORUM 227, 227.

5 Eduard Maurits Meijers, 'Erfrechtelijke moeilijkheden op het gebied van het internationaal privaatrecht' (1936) 67 WPNR 609, 645.

6 Heinrich Dörner and others, 'Auf dem Weg zu einem europäischen Internationalen Erb- und Erbverfahrensrecht' [2005] IPRax 1, 2; Anatol Dutta, in Franz Jürgen Säcker and others (eds), *MüKoBGB*, vol 12 (8th edn, C.H. Beck 2020) EuErbVO Vorb. Art 1 para 16.

estate planning.[7] It is difficult for individuals operating in such a diversity to know in advance which court will have jurisdiction or which law will be applicable to their succession.[8] Furthermore, the wide variety of rules also complicates the situation for the individuals entitled to the succession in terms of the cross-border administration of an estate and the enforcement of succession rights. This is because judgments or authentic instruments relating to a succession may not be easily recognised in other States where some parts of the estate are located, in other words, in those places where succession rights are ultimately to be asserted.[9] In addition, divergent or sometimes overlapping jurisdictional rules in this area can trigger *forum shopping*[10] for the involved individuals and also confront them with jurisdiction conflicts, be they of a negative or positive nature. There is also the risk of their receiving inconsistent judgments as a result of different conflict-of-laws rules being applicable.[11]

The European legislature, considering the frequency of cross-border cases in this area and aiming to eliminate such difficulties within the European Union (hereinafter also referred to as 'the EU' or simply 'the Union'),[12] enacted the European Succession Regulation (hereinafter 'the Regulation'),[13] which has been applicable in the Member States[14] since 17 August 2015 (Article 84). Although not binding on third States,[15] the Regulation has nevertheless great significance for them since its application may be triggered in various ways. First and foremost, the Regulation's conflict-of-laws rules extend

[7] Dutta, *MüKoBGB* (2020) EuErbVO Vorb. Art 1 para 16; cf. Dörner and others, [2005] IPRax 1, 2. See also Recital 37 of the Regulation.

[8] Dutta, *MüKoBGB* (2020) EuErbVO Vorb. Art 1 para 16; cf. Dörner and others, [2005] IPRax 1, 2.

[9] Dutta, *MüKoBGB* (2020) EuErbVO Vorb. Art 1 para 16.

[10] Forum shopping could be described as a phenomenon in transnational litigation in which there are multiple fora available to hear the case and the claimant chooses the one that is most favourable to him. For detailed information, see Andrew S. Bell, *Forum Shopping and Venue in Transnational Litigation* (OUP 2003).

[11] Dutta, *MüKoBGB* (2020) EuErbVO Vorb. Art 1 para 16; cf. Dörner and others, [2005] IPRax 1, 2.

[12] Dörner and others, [2005] IPRax 1, 2; Dutta, *MüKoBGB* (2020) EuErbVO Vorb. Art 1 para 16. See also Recital 7 of the Regulation.

[13] Regulation (EU) No 650/2012 of the European Parliament and of the Council of 4 July 2012 on jurisdiction, applicable law, recognition and enforcement of decisions and acceptance and enforcement of authentic instruments in matters of succession and on the creation of a European Certificate of Succession [2012] OJ L 201/107.

[14] The Regulation is not applicable in Ireland and Denmark due to the special status they have since the Treaty of Amsterdam (Treaty of Amsterdam amending the Treaty on European Union, the Treaties establishing the European Communities and certain related acts [1997] OJ C 340/01). See, in this regard, Protocols no 21 and 22 annexed to the TFEU and also Recitals 82 and 83 of the Regulation.

[15] This work uses the term 'third State' in order to refer to the States which are not Member States of the European Union.

to cases having a connection with third States. It provides that the law applicable to succession covers the entire estate regardless of the fact that some of the assets are located in a third State (Article 21(1)). Moreover, unlike most other legal regimes, the Regulation gives a right to the deceased to choose the law applicable to the succession as a whole, and this law could be the national law of the deceased (Article 22). For third State nationals, this would be the law of a third State whose nationality they possess at the time of making the choice or at the time of death.[16] Additionally, the Regulation provides uniform jurisdiction rules for the courts of Member States, allowing them to rule on succession as a whole regardless of the fact that some assets of the estate may be located in third States (esp. Article 4) or that the last habitual residence of the deceased was in a third State (Article 10).[17]

When this is the case, the Regulation, which binds only its participating Member States but not third States, distorts the outcome of the cases between Member States and third States which possibly adopted the same connecting factors and/or non-conflicting jurisdiction rules before the entry into force of the Regulation.[18] If, for example, both sides applied the law of nationality or domicile to the succession, or both accepted the dualist approach,[19] or both rejected choice of law as regards to succession, there could have been a decisional harmony between those States. The Regulation, by introducing uniform conflict-of-laws rules to be applicable within the EU (Article 20 et seq.), precludes such a possibility.[20] Furthermore, as the rules of the Regulation allow Member State courts to assert jurisdiction even in cases which are more closely connected to third States (see esp. Article 10), further jurisdiction conflicts could result between Member State courts and third State courts.[21]

One might think that succession issues in relation to third States are only a rare occurrence. Yet their practical relevance cannot be underestimated when the number of foreign nationals residing in the EU or the potential number of EU nationals who have assets in third States is taken into consideration. According to figures published by the official statistical institute of the Europe-

---

[16] Eva Lein, 'Die Erbrechtsverordnung aus Sicht der Drittstaaten' in Anatol Dutta and Sebastian Herrler (eds), *Die Europäische Erbrechtsverordnung, 20 Jahre DNotI 1993–2013* (C.H. Beck 2014) 200; cf. Andrea Bonomi and Azadi Öztürk, 'Auswirkungen der Europäischen Erbrechtsverordnung auf die Schweiz unter besonderer Berücksichtigung deutsch-schweizerischer Erbfälle' (2015) 114 ZVglRWiss 4, 5.

[17] Lein, 'Die Erbrechtsverordnung aus Sicht der Drittstaaten' (2014) 200; Bonomi and Öztürk, (2015) 114 ZVglRWiss 4, 5–6; Fabrizio Marongiu Buonaiuti, 'The EU Succession Regulation and Third Country Courts' (2016) 12 J Priv Int L 545, 545–549.

[18] Lein, 'Die Erbrechtsverordnung aus Sicht der Drittstaaten' (2014) 200.

[19] On monist and dualist approaches, see pp 55ff.

[20] Lein, 'Die Erbrechtsverordnung aus Sicht der Drittstaaten' (2014) 200.

[21] Lein, 'Die Erbrechtsverordnung aus Sicht der Drittstaaten' (2014) 200; cf. Buonaiuti, (2016) 12 J Priv Int L 545, 545–549.

an Union (Eurostat), there were 23 million non-Member State nationals residing in the EU at the beginning of 2020. From the Member States, the largest number of non-EU nationals were living in Germany (10.4 million), Spain (5.2 million), France (5.1 million), and Italy (5.0 million).[22] A similar statistic illustrating the number of EU nationals owning assets in third countries seemingly does not exist. Nevertheless, it is likely that their numbers are considerable, given the Union's policy of encouraging free movement of capital not only between EU countries, but also between EU and non-EU countries (Article 63 of the Treaty on the Functioning of the European Union (hereinafter 'TFEU')).[23] Both of these groups increase the likelihood of a third country element being involved in succession cases arising in the EU. The analysis of the Regulation also from a third State perspective is thus of foremost significance for legal practice.

Among the succession cases which are closely related to third States, the cases connected to Turkey are of substantial relevance for the EU by virtue of their potential frequency. The significant size of the migrant population of Turkey in Member States – which includes EU residents with Turkish origin who hold the nationality of a Member State and who sometimes still retain their Turkish nationality – makes it likely that these residents will be involved in succession cases.[24] In addition, there are also individuals, either EU or non-EU citizens, who are resident in Turkey on a permanent or a temporary basis, some of them as a result of the phenomena of 'international retirement migration'[25] or 'return migration'.[26] These groups of people create a potential for

[22] Eurostat, 'Migration and Migrant Population Statistics – Statistics Explained' <https://ec.europa.eu/eurostat/statistics-explained/index.php/Migration_and_migrant_population_statistics#Migrant_population:_21.8_million_non-EU-27_citizens_living_in_the_EU-27_on_1_January_2019> accessed 30 July 2020.

[23] Consolidated Version of the Treaty on the Functioning of the European Union [2012] OJ C 326/47.

[24] Although studies reveal that the previously extensive migration flow from Turkey to the EU has decelerated in recent years, it is beyond dispute that a sizeable Turkish community is still present in the Union, this being the result of both the guest-worker schemes adopted by some Member States in earlier decades and also the mobility intrinsic to the contemporary era: Heinz Fassmann and Ahmet İçduygu, 'Turks in Europe: Migration Flows, Migrant Stocks and Demographic Structure' (2013) 21 Eur Rev 349, 350. For figures and more information, see below under Chapter 1 – A: Turkish-EU Successions.

[25] International retirement migration refers to the cross-border mobility of older people which sees them relocate to destinations offering advantages such as more favourable environmental conditions or a pleasant lifestyle: Canan Balkır and Berna Kırkulak, 'Turkey, the New Destination for International Retirement Migration' in Heinz Fassmann, Max Haller and David Lane (eds), *Migration and Mobility in Europe: Trends, Patterns and Control* (Edward Elgar Publishing 2009) 123.

[26] Return migration is a term used for the 'return' of persons to their country of origin after living a significant time outside this country: Edda Currle, 'Theorieansätze zur Er-

cross-border succession cases between Turkey and the EU, particularly when there are assets located in both territories.

The Turkey-EU-related succession cases may be of paramount importance in practice also due to consular treaties that exist between Turkey and individual Member States, namely the Turkish-German Consular Treaty of 1929,[27] the Turkish-Hungarian Consular Treaty of 1938,[28] and the Turkish-Italian Consular Treaty of 1929.[29] In addition to covering other legal matters, these Treaties address private international law issues of succession,[30] a fact that assumes considerable significance given that Article 75(1) (1) reiterates the well-established international law principle of *pacta sunt servanda* and provides that the Treaties should enjoy priority of application over the Regulation.[31] This article has been described as the 'Achilles' heel'[32] of the Regulation given its potential to vitiate the desired uniformity.[33] Consequently, some of the Turkish-EU succession cases will be governed by these Treaties and not by the Regulation nor, conversely, by the private international law (hereinafter also referred

---

klärung von Rückkehr und Remigration' [2006] soFid – Migration und ethnische Minderheiten 7, 7; Esma Durugönül, 'Turkish Return Migration from Europe' (2013) 21 Eur Rev 412, 413.

Turkey is apparently a country characterised by both return and international retirement migration, see below, under Chapter 1 – A: Turkish-EU Successions.

[27] *Resmi Gazete* of 8.6.1930, no 1514

[28] *Resmi Gazete* of 27.12.1939, no 4395.

[29] *Resmi Gazete* of 7.4.1931, no 1768.

[30] Turkey signed a similar consular treaty which also addresses conflict-of-laws and jurisdiction issues of succession in 1927 with Poland (*Düstur*, Tertip III, Cilt VIII, 1258 (583); Protocol of 19.1.1938 amending the Treaty: *Düstur*, Tertip III, Cilt XIX, 1340 (553)). However, the Treaty never entered into force. See, in this regard, Hakkı Yaşar, 'Konsoloslara İlişkin Adli Ayrıcalıklar ve Bağışıklıklar (I)' (1982) 8 YD 37, 42; Paweł Czubik, 'Polish Consular Law and Practice after Regaining Independence in 1918 – the Selected Key Issues of the Interwar Period' (2020) 9 Pol Int Eur Law 49, 54.

[31] See, for comments on the effect of such treaties of Member States on the Regulation, Max Planck Institute for Comparative and International Private Law, 'Comments on the European Commission's Proposal for a Regulation of the European Parliament and of the Council on Jurisdiction, Applicable Law, Recognition and Enforcement of Decisions and Authentic Instruments in Matters of Succession and the Creation of a European Certificate of Succession' (2010) 74 RabelsZ 522, 532; Walter Pintens, 'Foreword' in Anatol Dutta and Wolfgang Wurmnest (eds), *European Private International Law and Member State Treaties with Third States – The Case of the European Succession Regulation* (Intersentia 2019) v.

[32] Anatol Dutta, 'Das neue internationale Erbrecht der Europäischen Union – Eine erste Lektüre der Erbrechtsverordnung' [2013] FamRZ 4, 15; Anatol Dutta and Wolfgang Wurmnest, 'Introduction' in Anatol Dutta and Wolfgang Wurmnest (eds), *European Private International Law and Member State Treaties with Third States – The Case of the European Succession Regulation* (Intersentia 2019) 1.

[33] Dutta and Wurmnest, 'Introduction' (2019) 1.

to as 'PIL') rules of Turkey. These consular treaties were, however, concluded in the 20th century with the underlying legal and political ideas of that period of time, and hence have rules based on the needs of that era.[34] This obviously adds another dimension to Turkish-EU successions.

The aim of this book is, therefore, to examine the regime of both the Regulation and the treaties from the Turkish PIL perspective as a third State for the EU. It is hoped that a third State perspective on the Regulation and the regime of existing treaties will be an important contribution to the literature; while the Regulation has been extensively covered in numerous scholarly works, it has not received the same depth of treatment from the third State perspective.[35]

It is important to clarify here at the outset that whereas the Regulation is of an 'all-inclusive'[36] nature, covering all aspects of private international law issues relating to succession, including the European Certificate of Succession (hereinafter also referred to as 'the ECS'), this book will concentrate exclusively on the issues which might have practical relevance from the Turkish perspective: the rules on the applicable law and on jurisdiction as well as

---

[34] Max Planck Institute for Comparative and International Private Law, (2010) 74 RabelsZ 522, 532–533; cf. Dutta and Wurmnest, 'Introduction' (2019) 1. See also Biset Sena Güneş, 'The Relations of Turkey with EU Member States' in Anatol Dutta and Wolfgang Wurmnest (eds), *European Private International Law and Member State Treaties with Third States – The Case of the European Succession Regulation* (Intersentia 2019) 285.

[35] Examples of scholarly works adopting a third State perspective exists for Switzerland: Michelle Kalt and Matthias Uhl, 'Die EU-Erbrechtsverordnung und die Schweiz' in Lukas Fahrländer and Reto A. Heizmann (eds), *Europäisierung der schweizerischen Rechtsordnung* (Dike 2013); Agnes Dormann, 'Das schweizerische internationale Privatrecht und die europäische Erbrechtsverordnung im Vergleich' in DACH Europäischen Anwaltsvereinigung e.V. (ed), *Die EU-Erbrechtsverordnung Nr. 650/2012 und deren Auswirkungen auf diverse Länder* (Schulthess 2014); Bonomi and Öztürk, (2015) 114 ZVglRWiss 4; Gian Paolo Romano, 'Remarks on the Impact of the Regulation No 650/2012 on the Swiss-EU Successions' (2015–2016) XVII YbPIL 253.

Exemplary studies can also be found in regards to the UK, which initially decided not to opt into the Regulation and later decided to leave the EU entirely, thus becoming a 'third State' as the term is used in this study: Jonathan Harris, 'The Proposed EU Regulation on Succession and Wills: Prospects and Challenges' (2008) 22 Tru L I 181; Paul Beaumont and Jayne Holliday, 'Some Aspects of Scots Private International Law of Succession Taking Account of the Impact of the EU Succession Regulation' (2015) <https://www.abdn.ac.uk/law/documents/CPIL_Working_Paper_No_6_Beaumont_and_Holliday.pdf> accessed 22 June 2021; James A. McLean, 'The UK and the European Succession Regulation: Fog over the Channel – Potential Pitfalls for the Unwary?' (2018) 22 Edinburgh L Rev 86.

For a paper comparing some aspects of the Regulation with the situation in both Switzerland and England and Wales, see Lein, 'Die Erbrechtsverordnung aus Sicht der Drittstaaten' (2014).

[36] Harris, (2008) 22 Tru L I 181, 188.

certain issues regarding the ECS. The topic of recognition and enforcement of judgments and other instruments falls mostly outside the scope of this study, and it is discussed only in the context of the ECS. Moreover, although certain rules in the Regulation are of particular interest for this book, the present study does not intend to offer detailed comments on the Regulation from a purely European perspective. The Regulation and its rules are discussed within this book in relation to those succession matters which are likely to arise in the Turkish-EU context.

As to the scope of the book, it should be further highlighted that of the three similarly formulated treaties between Turkey and individual Member States, the Turkish-German Treaty – which presumably has the greatest impact on legal practice by virtue of the fact that Germany is home to the majority of the Turkish nationals living within the borders of the Union[37] – will be focused on as exemplary. Further clarifications as regards the Turkish-Italian and Turkish-Hungarian treaties will be made only where dissimilarities appear. It should be also noted that the purpose of this study is not to scrutinise all the provisions of the Turkish-Germany Consular Treaty, but instead to focus on the succession provisions which are annexed to Article 20 of the Treaty ('Terekeye Ait Ahkâm'/ 'Nachlassabkommen').

Except where there are uniform rules applicable, such as the rules of the Treaty, it could be seen as quite normal that the European Union (a community driven by supranational interests) and Turkey (a single State) would have different private international law rules and different civil procedure provisions. This may, however, result in inconsistent judgments, and hence, would run counter to the *raison d'être* of private international law as introduced by *Savigny*.[38] Admittedly, decisional harmony – an equivocal and debated concept[39] and one sometimes referred to as the 'Holy Grail'[40] – requires that like cases should be decided in like way regardless of the forum in which they are brought.[41] Such an outcome will only be achieved when there is a certain degree of coordination between the private international law rules and civil procedure of different jurisdictions.[42]

---

[37] See below p 19.

[38] Friedrich Carl von Savigny, *System des heutigen Römischen Rechts*, vol 8 (Veit & Comp. 1849) 27.

[39] In this regard, see authors cited in Sarah Nietner, *Internationaler Entscheidungseinklang im europäischen Kollisionsrecht* (Mohr Siebeck 2016) 12–13.

[40] Friedrich K. Juenger, 'Jurisdiction, Choice of Law and the Elusive Goal of Decisional Harmony' (1992) 39 NILR 137, 138.

[41] Savigny, *System des heutigen Römischen Rechts* (1849) 27.

[42] Under *Savigny*'s approach, a complete harmony between the laws of different States is required to reach decisional harmony. However, as rightly argued, such a far-reaching harmony is not achievable. Therefore, the aim of the decisional harmony should be only a certain degree of coordination between the laws of different States: Nietner, *Interna-*

Despite being an abstract concept, international harmony of decisions would bring practical benefits in cross-border cases. First and foremost, it provides for the free movement of a right or status.[43] When a legal relationship is recognised in one State and not in another,[44] legal certainty is undermined and the enforcement of rights is problematic.[45] In this sense, the harmony of decisions would also safeguard legal certainty. What is more, the coordination of private international law, i.e. ensuring that different States apply the same rules in transnational cases, precludes forum shopping,[46] which for its part is mostly[47] seen as undesirable in transnational litigation.

In this sense, the quest for international harmony of decisions is also of paramount importance with regards to cross-border succession cases. Every legal institute is believed to safeguard certain interests. In the law of succession, among other things, two salient but sometimes contradicting interests are mostly at the forefront: first, the execution of the last wishes of the deceased as regards an estate and, second, the protection of the surviving family members.[48] At the PIL level, these are safeguarded when the deceased is able to plan his succession without problems and when succession rights of the beneficiaries are easily enforceable in different jurisdictions. A certain level of coordination between the private international rules and civil procedure of different States – and the resulting decisional harmony – would help to achieve these two aims of succession law. The purpose of this book is, therefore, to comparatively analyse the machinery of the Regulation and of Turk-

---

tionaler Entscheidungseinklang (2016) 8. This is referred as the statutory harmony ('Gesetzesharmonie'). The term is believed to have first been used by *Kahn*: Franz M. Kahn, *Ueber Inhalt, Natur und Methode des internationalen Privatrechts* (G Fischer 1899) 76ff.

[43] Erik Jayme, 'Identité Culturelle et Intégration: Le Droit International Privé Postmoderne' (1995) 251 RdC 9, 89; Nietner, *Internationaler Entscheidungseinklang* (2016) 2.

[44] A so-called 'limping' legal relationships: Michael Bogdan, *Private International Law as Component of the Law of the Forum* (Ail-Pocket 2012) 72.

[45] Arthur Taylor von Mehren, 'Special Substantive Rules for Multistate Problems: Their Role and Significance in Contemporary Choice of Law Methodology' (1974) 88 Harv L Rev 347, 358.

[46] Paul Heinrich Neuhaus, 'Legal Certainty versus Equity in the Conflict of Laws' (1963) 28 Law & Contemp Probs 795, 806; von Mehren, (1974) 88 Harv L Rev 347, 358; Nietner, *Internationaler Entscheidungseinklang* (2016) 21.

[47] For a different view on forum shopping, see, for example, Friedrich K. Juenger, 'What's Wrong with Forum Shopping?' (1994) 16 Sydney L Rev 5.

[48] See, for example, Rona Serozan and Baki İlkay Engin, *Miras Hukuku ve Uygulama Çalışmaları* (7th edn, Seçkin 2021) § 1 paras 6–7.

There is undoubtedly much to be written and discussed on the legal values underlying (substantive) succession law. These, however, would go beyond the aim and scope of this book, which limits itself to the private international law aspects of succession in the Turkish-EU context. For a detailed discussion on the functions of succession law, see, for example, Anatol Dutta, *Warum Erbrecht?* (Mohr Siebeck 2014).

ish PIL with an eye to decisional harmony. Although a level of decisional harmony is generally present under the Treaty because of its simultaneous application in Turkey and Germany – the exception being those instances when the Contracting States adopt different interpretations of the same text – its 'outdated'[49] rules should still be considered in the comparative analysis in order to describe the interplay between these rules and modern approaches.

In the light of these objectives, Chapter 1 of this book first focuses on the potential consequences of Turkish-EU successions for legal practice and gives an overview on, as well as the background of, the three legal sources which are at issue: the Regulation, Turkish private international law on succession, and the Turkish-German Treaty. Chapter 2 then comparatively analyses the conflict-of-laws rules in these three legal sources and discusses, particularly, the approaches of them (monist or dualist) towards succession, their connecting factors (including, if possible, the option for *professio iuris*), the scope of succession matters, the PIL approach towards dispositions of property upon death, and also the topics of *renvoi*, overriding mandatory provisions, and *ordre public*. Finally, Chapter 3 focuses on procedural issues in Turkish-EU successions. This chapter examines the main jurisdiction rules and, where applicable, the subsidiary jurisdiction rules of the three legal sources, considering their nature (exclusive or non-exclusive) and the potential for conflicts. In addition, the function of the ECS for Turkish nationals in Germany and the recognition of the ECS in Turkey are discussed.

---

[49] Max Planck Institute for Comparative and International Private Law, (2010) 74 RabelsZ 522, 532.

Chapter 1

General Overview and Background

Today, succession matters in cross-border context are not rare. This seems to be especially true for cases that arise between the European Union and Turkey. Despite the likelihood of their occurrence, matters of succession are still said to be amongst the most elusive subjects confronted by private international law, particularly because the law of succession, on the cross-border level as well as on the domestic level, is subject to divergent regulations in each jurisdiction, probably because of the close link between the law of succession and the political, social, and legal atmosphere existing in a State.[1] Therefore, the aim of this chapter is to identify the potential frequency of Turkish-EU successions and to give a general overview and background of the three relevant legal texts in order to set the scene at the outset for the rest of the book.

A. Turkish-EU Successions

Although the Regulation is applicable only within the Union, it may also have significant consequences from an external perspective. This is, firstly, because the deceased or the beneficiaries who are involved in succession proceedings are not always individuals who have ties solely with the Union. The Union indeed hosts more than 20 million third country nationals, as explained earlier.[2] Within this pool of persons, Turkish nationals constitute one of the biggest groups. The most recent figures which were published in 2011 indicated that Turkish citizens are the second largest group of third country nationals residing in the Union, with approximately 2.1 million nationals.[3]

---

[1] Vedat Raşit Seviğ, *Mirasla İlgili Devletler Hususi Hukuku Kaideleri* (Sulhi Garan Matbaası 1963) 1–2.

[2] See above pp 3–4.

[3] Eurostat, *People in the EU: Who Are We and How Do We Live?* (Publications Office of the European Union 2015) 90, Table 1 <http://ec.europa.eu/eurostat/documents/3217494/7089681/KS-04-15-567-EN-N.pdf/8b2459fe-0e4e-4bb7-bca7-7522999c3bfd> accessed 22 June 2021.

It is noteworthy that the numbers indicated by the Turkish Ministry of Foreign Affairs are even bigger. According to the Ministry, there were around 4 million Turkish citizens residing in EU countries at the beginning of 2019 and half of them were living in Germany. See <https://www2.tbmm.gov.tr/d27/7/7-2838sgc.pdf> accessed 22 June 2021.

These numbers have seemingly not changed much since then.[4] It is believed that the figure is even bigger if the number of former Turkish nationals who have already acquired citizenship in one of the Member States is also considered.[5] This prominence of Turkish diaspora in the Union is certainly the outcome of the migration flow.

Turkish migration into European countries started after the Second World War mostly for the purposes of employment. The post-war reconstruction efforts required European States to import labour to boost productivity and to enable the upward mobility of their own workforce. Turkey, meanwhile, was facing economic problems which it believed could be solved with the export of surplus manpower, as this could remediate the high rate of unemployment and, in turn, provide the country experienced employees (upon their return from abroad) as well as foreign currency.[6] This 'win-win' situation between Turkey and European States paved the way for Turkish migration to Europe. Especially in the 1960s, with the help of bilateral agreements[7] and the poli-

---

[4] For the statistics published more recently, see Eurostat, 'Population on 1 January by Age Group, Sex and Citizenship (Migr_pop1ctz)' <https://ec.europa.eu/eurostat/databrowser/view/MIGR_POP1CTZ__custom_2278307/default/table?lang=en> (selecting EU Member States as the reporting Geopolitical Entity and Türkiye as the Country of Citizenship), accessed 14 March 2022.

[5] According to a statistic published in 2010, the total number of Turks having EU citizenship was over 1.2 million in that year: House of Commons – Home Affairs Committee, *Implications for the Justice and Home Affairs Area of the Accession of Turkey to the European Union: Tenth Report of Session 2010–12* (The Stationery Office 2011) 43.

For the exact number of Turkish nationals who acquired citizenship between 2010 and 2019 on a Member State basis, see Eurostat, 'Acquisition of Citizenship by Age Group, Sex and Former Citizenship (Migr_acq)' <https://ec.europa.eu/eurostat/databrowser/view/migr_acq/default/table?lang=en> (by selecting EU Member States as the reporting Geopolitical Entity and Türkiye as the Country of Citizenship), accessed 14 March 2022.

[6] Nermin Abadan Unat, *Turks in Europe: From Guest Worker to Transnational Citizen* (Berghahn Books 2011) xxi–xxiv.

[7] The first agreement in this regard was the Turkish-German Recruitment Treaty which was signed on 31 October 1961 (it was signed through the exchange of notes between the States and was not officially published). During the same period, such agreements were also signed with certain other Member States of today's EU, namely with Austria (1964 – *Resmi Gazete* of 17.9.1964, no 11809), Belgium (1964 – *Resmi Gazete* of 13.7.1965, no 12047), France (1965 – *Resmi Gazete* of 2.10.1965, no 121165, no 12116), the Netherlands (1964 – *Resmi Gazete* of 22.6.1965, no 12029), and Sweden (1967 – *Resmi Gazete* of 31.10.1967, no 12738). Apart from this, Denmark (starting from the 1970s) also recruited Turkish workers without a recruitment agreement. All of these recruitment actions were also supported by Social Security Agreements: Abadan Unat, *Turks in Europe* (2011) 11.

The well-known Ankara Agreement with the EU (Agreement establishing an Association between the European Economic Community and Turkey [1963] OJ 1977 L 361/29) was also signed in the same period; the Agreement aims, *inter alia*, to increase the level of employment of Turks in the Union (Art 2(1)).

cies of the States, the population of the Turkish workers in Europe increased by a substantial number.[8] During this time, however, the idea was that the workers would come to the European States only on a temporary basis (as 'Gastarbeiter') without their families.[9]

The phenomenon continued in the 1970s, but with the realisation that it was no longer a transient process. The workers, consequently, received more social rights from the governments and started to bring their families as a result of integration policies. Whilst the economic recession faced by the States, especially by Germany, in the middle of the 1970s resulted in a short period of decline in the growth of the number of Turkish migrants who were able to obtain a work permit, the number of Turkish citizens in European States has always been substantial.[10] This resulted in Turkish nationals gaining more rights at the EU level. Since the initial migration flow from Turkey to European countries and the formalisation of links between the EU and Turkey in the 1960s, the rights of Turkish nationals in the EU have been expanded with the help of international arrangements. Turkish migrant workers and their families are provided with the most extensive legal protection among third country nationals at the EU level,[11] particularly with the Ankara Agreement between Turkey and the EU.[12] Although these rights are not unrestricted,[13] the Agreement provides, *inter alia*, that the Contracting Parties

---

[8] In the years 1968–1969, there were 192,476 Turks in the EEC countries. This number reached 711,671 in the year 1980. See, in this regard, Nermin Abadan Unat, 'Turkey: Late Entrant into Europe's Work Force' in Daniel Kubat (ed), *The Politics of Migration Policies: Settlement and Integration – The First World into the 1990s* (2nd edn, Center for Migration Studies 1993) 308–309. In addition, as the largest group of immigrants went to Germany, the numbers with regards to Europe can be estimated based on the figures in Germany. According to the statistics of *Destatis*, there were only 6,700 Turkish nationals in Germany in the year 1961. This number rose to 429,400 in 1970 and to 1,275,900 at the end of 1988. See, in this regard, Statistisches Bundesamt (Destatis) (ed), *Statistisches Jahrbuch 1990 für die Bundesrepublik Deutschland* (Metzler-Poeschel Verlag 1990) 59, Table 3.19.

[9] Abadan Unat, *Turks in Europe* (2011) 12.

[10] See, in general, Abadan Unat, *Turks in Europe* (2011) 13 ff.

[11] Catherine Barnard, *The Substantive Law of the EU: The Four Freedoms* (6th edn, OUP 2019) 393.

[12] The rights of Turkish immigrants were also reinforced with the 1970 Additional Protocol (Additional Protocol and Financial Protocol signed on 23 November 1970, Annexed to the Agreement Establishing the Association between the European Economic Community and Turkey and On Measures to be Taken for Their Entry into Force – Final Act – Declarations [1977] OJ L 361/59).

[13] For more information on this issue, see Martin Hedemann-Robinson, 'An Overview of Recent Legal Developments at Community Level in Relation to Third Country Nationals Resident within the European Union, with Particular Reference to the Case Law of the European Court of Justice' (2001) 38 CML Rev 525, 541 ff; Barnard, *EU Substantive Law* (2019) 393 ff.

would be guided by the TFEU in terms of removing restrictions as regards the free movement of workers (Article 12), the freedom of establishment (Article 13), and the freedom to provide services (Article 14).

This policy of guest-worker migration which started individually between Turkey and some European States and then continued at the EU level obviously consolidated the existence of Turks, especially guest-workers and their families, in the EU. Even though the labour migration flow from Turkey to Europe has considerably slowed down from the late 1990s due to a change of policy in both sides in favour of restricting migration,[14] mobility from Turkey to the EU Member States has not stopped due to globalisation. Statistics of the EU indicate that there are hundred thousands of residence permits issued every year by Member States to Turkish nationals.[15] In addition to family reasons, they are also issued for educational and professional purposes.[16] Hence the Turkish community in the EU today consists not only of Turkish workers and their families, but also of students and professionals.[17] These individuals often continue to have strong ties with Turkey, e.g. they may live there part of the year or they may still have heirs[18] or properties in Turkey,[19]

---

[14] Fassmann and İçduygu, (2013) 21 Eur Rev 349, 352.

[15] For exact numbers, see Eurostat, 'All Valid Permits by Age, Sex and Citizenship on 31 December of Each Year (MIGR_RESVAS)' <https://ec.europa.eu/eurostat/databrowser/view/MIGR_RESVAS__custom_2278646/default/table?lang=en> (selecting EU Member States as the reporting Geopolitical Entity and Türkiye as the Country of Citizenship), accessed 14 March 2022.

[16] See, in this regard Eurostat, 'First Permits by Reason, Length of Validity and Citizenship (MIGR_RESFIRST)' <https://ec.europa.eu/eurostat/databrowser/view/MIGR_RESFIRST__custom_2279549/default/table?lang=en> (selecting EU Member States as the reporting Geopolitical Entity and Türkiye as the Country of Citizenship), accessed 14 March 2022.

[17] It should be also noted that a further big migration flow from Turkey to the EU is expected in the event of Turkey's accession to the EU. See, for an assumption regarding Turkish migration to Germany by 2030, Harry Flam, 'Turkey and the EU: Politics and Economics of Accession' (2004) 50 CESifo Econ Stud 171, 186, Figure 2.

[18] According to the tourism statistics provided by the Turkish Statistical Institute (*Turkstat*), around 18% of people who came to Turkey in the year of 2021 were Turkish nationals residing abroad. Their main purpose of visit, again pursuant to numbers provided by *Turkstat*, is reunion with family members and friends. This may be considered as a significant indicator of their strong ties with Turkey. See, in this regard, Turkstat, 'Tourism Statistics, Quarter IV: October-December and Annual, 2021' <https://data.tuik.gov.tr/Bulten/Index?p=Tourism-Statistics-Quarter-IV:-October-December-and-Annual,-2021-45785> accessed 14 March 2022.

[19] The statistics of *Turkstat* regarding house sales indicate that German nationals are each year in the top ten of foreign nationals acquiring houses in Turkey. In the year of 2021, around 2,350 houses were sold to German citizens. Considering the fact that the biggest Turkish community in the EU is resident in Germany, it is highly probable that some of the German nationals buying properties in Turkey may be migrants of Turkish origin in Germany. This may also be seen as an indication of maintaining strong ties with Turkey. See,

while, at the same time, they may also be well integrated in their current or former EU Member State of residence.[20]

The circle of people who may be involved in Turkish-EU successions grows much wider when one takes into account EU nationals – either people who reside in Turkey for various reasons[21] or 'international retirement migrants'[22] – and migrant Turks who returned to Turkey after living and working in a Member State for a certain time (known as 'return migrants').[23] Having such situations in mind, it is highly likely that a significant number of transnational succession cases involving these individuals will arise in the EU[24] and, conversely, in Turkey. In such cases, rules in the Regulation, rules

---

in this regard, Turkstat, 'House Sales Statistics, December 2021' <https://data.tuik.gov.tr/Bulten/Index?p=House-Sales-Statistics-December-2021-45672> accessed 14 March 2022.

[20] From the succession perspective, this can be assumed from property ownership. Based on the numbers given by *Destatis* in the year of 2008, the German Federal Office for Migration and Refugees (Bundesamt für Migration und Flüchtlinge) found that 27.1% of Turks in Germany have their own apartments in Germany. See BAMF, 'Wohnen und innerstädtische Segregation von Migranten in Deutschland – Working Paper 21' 30 <https://www.bamf.de/SharedDocs/Anlagen/DE/Forschung/WorkingPapers/wp21-wohnen-innerstaedtische-segregation.pdf?__blob=publicationFile&v=12> accessed 22 June 2021.

For other indicators of integration, such as education, employment, and the integration level of Turkish migrants in Germany, please refer to the Statistisches Bundesamt (Destatis), *Migration und Integration – Integrationsindikatoren* (Statistisches Bundesamt (Destatis) 2019) <https://www.destatis.de/DE/Themen/Gesellschaft-Umwelt/Bevoelkerung/Migration-Integration/_inhalt.html#sprg228898> accessed 22 June 2021.

[21] Even though the numbers of EU nationals in Turkey are not comparable to the number of Turkish nationals in the EU, they are still a group of people which may be involved in Turkish-EU successions. According to the statistics of 2021, there were more than 180,000 EU-27 nationals – which seemingly does not include Turkish nationals with multiple nationalities – in Turkey: Turkstat, 'Foreign Population by Country of Citizenship' <https://data.tuik.gov.tr/Bulten/Index?p=The-Results-of-Address-Based-Population-Registration-System-2021-45500> accessed 14 March 2022.

[22] The coastal part of Turkey is one of the destinations for international retirement migration. Statistics indicate that in the year of 2012, more than 100,000 EU and non-EU Schengen area nationals owned properties in Turkey: İlkay Südaş, 'Lifestyle Migration to Turkey: EU Citizens Living on the Turkish Sunbelt' 4 <https://lifestylemigrationhub.files.wordpress.com/2012/09/lifestyle_migration_turkey.pdf> accessed 22 June 2021. Although this number includes the UK and non-EU Schengen States, it nevertheless strongly suggests that sizable numbers of EU nationals are also retiring in Turkey. On this, see below p 199.

[23] The Turkish Ministry of Foreign Affairs states that there are approximately 3 million returnees in Turkey: <http://www.mfa.gov.tr/yurtdisinda-yasayan-turkler_.tr.mfa> accessed 14 March 2021.

[24] According to the statistics of *Destatis*, 5,445 Turkish citizens died in Germany in the year of 2015 alone. This constituted the biggest group of foreigners who died that year. See, for the statistics of *Destatis*, Statistisches Bundesamt (Destatis), *Bevölkerung und Erwerbstätigkeit: Natürliche Bevölkerungsbewegung 2015 (Fachserie 1, Reihe 1.1)* (Statistisches

in Turkish law, and also PIL rules occasioned through *renvoi* under Article 34(1) of the Regulation[25] may become applicable before EU courts.

In Turkey, on the other hand, Turkish courts have to refer to the relevant provisions of the Turkish Private International and Procedural Law Act (hereinafter 'the Turkish PILA')[26] and of the governing foreign law, which is to be determined pursuant to the Turkish PILA (Article 2(1)) when dealing with cross-border matters of succession, unless there is an international treaty which has priority of application pursuant to Article 1(2) of the Turkish PILA. The Regulation is not binding on Turkey, and hence does not directly apply before the Turkish courts. It is also clarified by the legislature under Article 2(3) of the Turkish PILA that *renvoi* is applicable only for issues of personal status and family law. Even though there seems to be different opinions on the subject, the prevailing view holds that succession matters, as being part of neither area, do not fall within the scope of application of the *renvoi* doctrine.[27] This means that the provisions of the Regulation will never become directly applicable before the courts of Turkey.[28] For these reasons, it could be asserted that the Regulation is of no great importance in the eyes of Turkey.

Such a perspective is, nonetheless, not appropriate, especially in consideration of the Turkish migrants in the EU who are likely to be involved in Turkish-EU successions. The regime of the Regulation is still important for the decedents, for persons entitled to succession, and for legal practitioners who advise these parties on estate planning and/or claiming rights over the estate in such cases.[29] The adoption of the Regulation appears, at first sight, to have a positive effect in cases which may potentially arise in the Turkish-European context, as

---

Bundesamt 2017) 92, Table 3.4 <https://www.destatis.de/DE/Themen/Gesellschaft-Umwelt/Bevoelkerung/Geburten/Publikationen/Downloads-Geburten/bevoelkerungsbewegung-2010110157004.pdf;jsessionid=67375A0636B645667895767CFE2B7D90.live722?__blob=publicationFile> accessed 5 March 2022.

This suggests that minimum of 7,000 annual deaths of Turkish nationals can be estimated within the EU. The numbers may be even higher if one considers former Turkish citizens who acquired the citizenship of an EU Member State. Therefore, the amount of succession cases regarding Turks within the EU cannot be underestimated.

[25] See below pp 154 ff.

[26] *Resmi Gazete* of 12.12.2007, no 26728. An authoritative English translation of the Act does not exist. The English translations used in this book are taken from NA Odman Boztosun, 'The 2007 Turkish Code on Private International Law and International Civil Procedure' (2007) IX YbPIL 583, sometimes as slightly modified by the author.

[27] For more on this, see below pp 80–81.

[28] Cf. Faruk Kerem Giray, 'Possible Impacts of EU Succession Regulation No 650/2012 on Turkish Private International Law' (2016) 9 Anali PFZE 235, 238.

[29] For an article arguing that the rules of EU Regulations may be relevant for Turkish parties, even though they are not directly applicable in Turkey, see: Ceyda Süral, 'Avrupa Birliği'nin Milletlerarası Özel Hukuka İlişkin Düzenlemelerinin Türk Hukukuna Etkileri' (2013) 12 MHFD 31.

the persons involved or interested in those cases now do not have to examine the private international and procedural law rules on succession of each Member State having a connection with the case, their needing instead to check only one legal system, the one that the Regulation has laid down. Notwithstanding this fact, the extent to which the system of the Regulation and the Turkish PILA are similar or different is likely to affect the outcome in those cases.[30]

Moreover, though it is already a long-winded story[31] and one which will most probably not come to fruition in the near future,[32] Turkey's candidate

---

[30] See for similar remarks as regards to the Swiss-EU context, Bonomi and Öztürk, (2015) 114 ZVglRWiss 4, 7; Romano, (2015–2016) XVII YbPIL 253, 264.

[31] A brief history of Turkey's candidate status in the EU should be given here. Turkey made its first application to join the EEC in 1959, only one year after its creation in 1958. The EEC suggested an accession agreement until the conditions for the accession were met (<http://www.ab.gov.tr/index.php?p=4&l=2> accessed 22 June 2021). In this regard, the parties reached an association agreement (the well-known Ankara Agreement) in 1963. This was the official beginning of the Turkey-EU relationship regarding the membership of Turkey. Almost two decades after this agreement, in 1987, Turkey made its application for membership. Later in 1999, it acquired 'candidate country' status ('Helsinki European Council 10 and 11 December 1999 – Presidency Conclusions' <http://www.europarl.europa.eu/summits/hel1_en.htm> accessed 22 June 2021) and in 2005, accession negotiations between Turkey and the EU officially started ('Copenhagen European Council 12 and 13 December 2002 – Presidency Conclusions' <http://www.consilium.europa.eu/en/european-council/conclusions/pdf-1993-2003/presidency-conclusions_copenhagen-european-council_-12-and-13-december-2002/> accessed 22 June 2021). See, for a general overview of Turkey's accession process, Sanem Baykal, 'Turkey's EU Accession Process: Current State of Play in Accession Negotiations' in Paul Beaumont and Burcu Yüksel (eds), *Turkish and EU Private International Law – A Comparison* (On İki Levha 2014).

[32] It should be observed that the hope of Turkish society for Turkey's membership in the EU is not very high. Pursuant to a study conducted in 2019, although 60% of Turkish population supported Turkey's accession to the EU, only 23% believe that Turkey will ultimately become a Member State: İktisadi Kalkınma Vakfı, 'Türkiye Kamuoyunda Avrupa Birliği Desteği ve Avrupa Algısı Araştırması' (Anadolu Basın Merkezi 2019) 31 ff and 40 ff <https://www.ikv.org.tr/images/files/%C4%B0KV%20Kamuoyu%20ara%C5%9Ft%C4%B1rmas%C4%B1(1).pdf> accessed 22 June 2021.

On the EU side also, hope and willingness for Turkey's accession to the EU do not seem to exist. This is evident from the declarations of the General Affairs Council made in 2018 and 2019. The Council declared in 2018 that '[...] Turkey has been moving further away from the European Union. Turkey's accession negotiations have therefore effectively come to a standstill and no further chapters can be considered for opening or closing [...]': General Affairs Council, 'Council Conclusions on Enlargement and Stabilisation and Association Process as adopted by the Council on 26 June 2018 – No 10374/18' 13 no 35 <https://www.consilium.europa.eu/media/35863/st10555-en18.pdf> accessed 22 June 2021.

This was reiterated later in 2019: General Affairs Council, 'Council Conclusions on Enlargement and Stabilisation and Association Process from 18 June 2019' <http://www.consilium.europa.eu/en/press/press-releases/2019/06/18/council-conclusions-on-enlargement-and-stabilisation-and-association-process/> accessed 22 June 2021.

status in the EU cannot be entirely disregarded. An important condition of membership for all candidate countries is compliance with the rules and standards of the European Union, which is known as the *acquis communautaire*. This undoubtedly applies also to Turkey.[33] One of the chapters of the *acquis* relates to freedom, security, and justice (Chapter 24).[34] Private international law rules of the European Union, as a component of judicial cooperation in civil matters, fall under the scope of this chapter, and, hence, Turkey needs to bring its private international law into compliance with those rules to be considered for full membership.

As a preparatory phase for accession negotiations regarding the *acquis,* the EU started screening processes with candidate countries, including Turkey. In these processes, Member States decide on whether a chapter will be opened with a candidate country. The screening process for Turkey was completed in 2006. Regarding the chapter on freedom, security, and justice, it was observed in the screening report that the Turkish PILA at that time (the former Turkish PILA, Law no 2675)[35] was not in line with EU requirements. Whilst there was no need for the full adaption of EU Regulations in this regard – because they would automatically apply in Turkey after the membership – there was a need for a number of important changes in the Turkish PILA in order to achieve a certain level of compliance.[36] After the chapters have been screened, it is for the Member States to decide whether a chapter will be opened for negotiation, and, hence, no decision in this regard has been made until now. The chapter on freedom, security, and justice remains unopened. Notwithstanding, in line with the comments made in the screening report of 2006, one of the most significant policy incentives for the last amendment of the Turkish PILA has been compliance with the European private internation-

Recently, on 19 May 2021, members of the EU Parliament also noted that Turkish-EU relations are 'at a historic low point' and called on the EU Commission to formally suspend the accession negotiations with Turkey: <https://www.europarl.europa.eu/delegations/en/d-tr/documents/ep-resolutions> accessed 22 June 2021.

Under these circumstances, it seems that Turkey's membership to the EU will not become a reality in the near future.

[33] See, in this regard, Council of the European Union, 'Negotiating Framework (Luxembourg, 3 October 2005)' principle 10 <http://ec.europa.eu/enlargement/pdf/turkey/st20002_05_tr_framedoc_en.pdf> accessed 22 June 2021.

[34] See Council of the European Union, 'Negotiating Framework' principle 15.

[35] *Resmi Gazete* of 22.5.1982, no 17701. For a general overview and for an English translation of the Act, see Tuğrul Ansay and Eric Schneider, 'The New Private International Law of Turkey' (1990) XXXVII NILR 139.

[36] 'Screening Report Turkey, Chapter 24 – Justice, Freedom and Security (6 June 2006)' 9 <http://www.ab.gov.tr/files/ardb/evt/2_turkiye_ab_iliskileri/2_2_adaylik_sureci/2_2_6_muzakere_sureci/2_2_6_2_tarama_raporlari/Screening_Report-Chapter_24_-_Justice_Freedom_and_Security-TR.pdf> accessed 22 June 2021.

al law rules.[37] Even without considering the never-ending admission process of Turkey, the Regulation may constitute a model for a future reform of the PILA regarding succession.[38] Although succession may be one of the fields in which the legislature is reluctant to change the current state of the law, the rules of the Regulation may at least open up discussion in the process of a future reform. Developments in the European legal area and the alignment process have generally been an impetus for legal reforms in Turkey.

Thus, it is important to examine how well both systems get along with each other and the degree to which they collide, particularly as regards scenarios which, from the perspective of the EU, fall within the scope of the Regulation and, by contrast, are covered by the Turkish PILA from the viewpoint of Turkey.[39]

Another significant dimension of Turkish-EU successions, as mentioned earlier,[40] is the potential number of cases which are covered by the bilateral treaties between Turkey and EU countries of Germany, Italy, and Hungary. Thanks to Article 75(1) (1) of the Regulation, the treaty regimes continue to govern succession issues faced by nationals of the Contracting States who live in each other's land. Of these treaties, the one with Germany – which has been chosen as the main focus in this study – has the highest practical relevance, since Germany is host to the highest number of Turkish citizens within the EU, totalling roughly 1.5 million citizens.[41] Although the Treaty was enacted almost a century ago, at the end of the 1920s, it has always held an important place in

---

[37] See, in this regard, '5718 Sayılı Milletlerarası Özel Hukuk ve Usul Hukuku Hakkında Kanun Tasarısı ve Gerekçe' <http://www2.tbmm.gov.tr/d23/1/1-0337.pdf> accessed 22 June 2021.

[38] It is argued that the adoption of the residence principle in the Regulation, which is applicable in the entire Union (except for Ireland and Denmark), may place pressure on third States to change their laws: Anatol Dutta, 'Succession and Wills in the Conflict of Laws on the Eve of Europeanisation' (2009) 73 RabelsZ 547, 564. This has actually happened in Switzerland. The succession rules in the Swiss PILA (AS 1988, 1776) have been subject to an ongoing reform process which takes the Regulation as a model. See, for the draft rules, Änderung vom Bundesgesetz über das Internationale Privatrecht (IPRG) (Entwurf), BGBl. 2019, 3353. See, for the report of Federal Council on the draft rules, Botschaft zur Änderung des Bundesgesetzes über das Internationale Privatrecht (Erbrecht), BGBl. 2019, 3309. Yet this may not be surprising for Switzerland as it is a country which is seen as sharing more similarities with the Union than with any other non-EU legal system as a result of its multinational structure. See, in this regard, Romano, (2015–2016) XVII YbPIL 253, 264.

[39] In the same direction for the EU-Swiss Successions, see Romano, (2015–2016) XVII YbPIL 253, 264.

[40] See above pp 5–6.

[41] Statistisches Bundesamt (Destatis), *Bevölkerung und Erwerbstätigkeit: Ausländische Bevölkerung Ergebnisse des Ausländerzentralregisters 2020 (Fachserie 1, Reihe 2)* (Statistisches Bundesamt (Destatis) 2021) 23 <https://www.destatis.de/DE/Themen/Gesellschaft-Umwelt/Bevoelkerung/Migration-Integration/Publikationen/Downloads-Migration/auslaend-bevoelkerung-2010200207004.pdf?__blob=publicationFile> accessed 14 March 2022.

German legal practice and academia due to the large Turkish community in Germany.[42] With the entry into force of the Regulation and its deferral to the application of the Treaty (Article 75(1) (1)), a large number of Turkey-related succession cases fall outside the Regulation and remain governed by this Treaty, which is a rather exceptional one in the field of succession and which has rules completely different than the Regulation, their reflecting the political and legal concerns of the previous century.[43] Consequently, the Treaty has a significant impact on how the Regulation plays out in practice.

The practical significance of the Treaty in Turkey is not comparable to Germany or to the EU. Turkey, once an immigrant-sending country, does not host a large group of German nationals. In the year of 2021, only around 102,500 German nationals were resident in Turkey.[44] Probably as a consequence of this, the Treaty also seems to have been forgotten in practice.[45]

---

[42] There are a number of cases in which the provisions of the Turkish-German Treaty have been discussed before the German courts. See, for instance, LG München I 26.9.2006 – 6 O 15963/05 (rkr.), FamRZ 2007, 1250; LG Braunschweig 18.5.2009 – 8 T 344/09, IPRax 2010, 255; LG München I 25.10.2011 – 28 O 243/10, ZEV 2012, 596; LG Karlsruhe 17.12.2014 – 9 S 24/14, ZEV 2015, 588; OLG Karlsruhe 21.4.2015 – 11 Wx 82/14, BWNotZ 2015, 81; BGH 21.10.2015 – IV ZR 68/15, FamRZ 2016, 122; OLG Karlsruhe 27.2.2018 – 14 W 113/16 (Wx), ZEV 2018, 330.

The same could not be said for other Treaties of Turkey. In Italy, for example, it is reported that there is no published judgment on the Turkish-Italian Treaty: Pietro Franzina, 'The External Relations of Italy' in Anatol Dutta and Wolfgang Wurmnest (eds), *European Private International Law and Member State Treaties with Third States – The Case of the European Succession Regulation* (Intersentia 2019) 192.

[43] Max Planck Institute for Comparative and International Private Law, (2010) 74 RabelsZ 522, 532–533; Güneş, 'The Relations of Turkey with EU Member States' (2019) 285, 312 and 315; cf. Frank Bauer, 'Anmerkung zur Entscheidung LG München v. 26.9.2006 – 6 O 15963/05' [2007] FamRZ 1250, 1255; Hilmar Krüger, 'Erbrechtliche Probleme in den deutsch-türkischen Beziehungen' in Hilmar Krüger and Yasemin Körtek (eds), *Beiträge zum türkischen Recht – Erbrecht und Sozialrecht* (BWV 2010) 141 ff.

[44] Turkstat, 'Foreign Population by Country of Citizenship'. It should be noted that this figure does not cover people having dual or multiple nationalities, one of which is Turkish.

[45] It appears that there is only one published judgment of the Turkish Court of Cassation (hereinafter referred in the judgment references in footnotes with its original name: *Yargıtay*) in which the rules of the Turkish-German Treaty were applied: Yargıtay 2. Hukuk Dairesi, T. 27.1.1977, E. 401 K. 665. The case is published and commented on in Ergin Nomer, 'Ehliyetsizlik Sebebi ile Almanya'daki Gayrimenkul Mallar İçin Vasiyetin İptali' (1981) 1 MHB 61.

On the other hand, there are a number of cases in which the Turkish Court of Cassation did not refer to rules of Treaty. See, for example, Yargıtay 2. Hukuk Dairesi, T. 19.7.2006, E. 2006/4387 K. 2006/11476 <http://www.kazanci.com > accessed 20 April 2020; Yargıtay 7. Hukuk Dairesi, T. 17.7.2008, E. 2008/3686 K. 2008/3210 <https://www.lexpera.com.tr/> accessed 20 April 2020.

The same could also be said for the Turkish-Italian Treaty. See, for example, Temyiz Mahkemesi 2. Hukuk Dairesi, T. 17.11.1939, E. 1377 K. 3687 commented on in Osman

Notwithstanding this, the Treaty could still be considered crucial for Turkey from the perspective of its nationals in Germany. In addition, although not as significant as the differences between the Regulation and the Treaty regime in terms of a unitary vs. a dualist approach, nationality vs. habitual residence as a connecting factor, and the approach towards *professio iuris*, the rules of the Turkish PILA on the conflict of laws and jurisdiction in matters of succession also differ from the provisions of the Treaty in some aspects. Furthermore, as with the Regulation, wherever the Treaty is applicable, the rules of Turkish PILA are not applicable. The cases falling within the scope of the Treaty and, hence, potential conflicts between the Regulation and Turkish PILA should, thus, also be regarded as significant from the Turkish perspective, just as from that of the European Union. Consequently, a detailed analysis of the rules of the Treaty in comparison with the ones of Turkish PILA and the Regulation are important for Turkish-EU Successions. Before moving into this analysis, however, the background of each legal source should be examined, along with a consideration of how this background affected the formulation of the approaches. This will be done with a general overview in the next part.

B. Background of the Regulation and its Four Pillars

I. A Brief History of the Regulation

One might think at first sight that the law of succession falls outside the original remit of the European Union,[46] as it emerged mainly due to economic considerations.[47] The idea of drafting European conflict rules on succession is, however, not a new phenomenon, contrary to the general belief.[48] It was opined, long ago, that a diversity of national conflict rules on succession

---

Fazıl Berki, 10 AÜHFD 1953 792; Temyiz Mahkemesi 2. Hukuk Dairesi, T. 9.11.1951, E. 6788 K. 7012 commented on in Osman Fazıl Berki and Hilmi Ergüney, *Yabancılar Hukuku ve Kanun İhtilafları ile İlgili Yargıtay Kararlarının Tahlil ve İzahı* (Banka ve Ticaret Hukuku Araştırma Enstitüsü 1963) 121–122; Yargıtay 8. Hukuk Dairesi, T. 20.6.2014, E. 2013/13351 K. 2014/13084 <http://www.kazanci.com > accessed 12 August 2020.

[46] Even though the European Union was previously named the European Economic Community (EEC) and later the European Community (EC), this book prefers the term 'the European Union (or the EU)', which needs to be understood as a reference to its original name in the relevant period.

[47] Alain-Laurent Verbeke and Yves-Henri Leleu, 'Harmonisation of the Law of Succession in Europe' in Arthur S. Hartkamp and Others (eds), *Towards A European Civil Code* (4th edn, Kluwer Law International 2011) 475; Jacqueline Gray, 'Identifying the Impetus behind the Europeanization of the Private International Law Rules on Family Matters and Succession' (2015) 17 Eur J L Reform 341, 342.

[48] Paul Terner, 'Perspectives of a European Law of Succession' (2007) 14 Maast J Eur & Comp L 147, 157.

would have negative effects on the desired integration within the EU.[49] This was also acknowledged by the Union impliedly in the Jenard Report on the Brussels Convention.[50]

Succession is indeed a crucial part of European integration due to its impact on the freedom of movement, as one of the fundamental freedoms of the EU. Cross-border transfer of succession rights within the Union is, firstly, an issue related to the free movement of capital (Article 63(1) of the TFEU). This is well settled by the case law of the Court of Justice of the European Union (hereinafter also referred to as 'CJEU').[51] Hence, when there is a restriction on succession rights, it might amount to a violation of the free movement of capital. Moreover, the diversity of PIL rules in relation to succession affects estate planning of the deceased and thus, his/her freedom of movement within the Union (Article 21 of the TFEU).[52] Within a legal environment where divergent rules are applicable, not only the deceased, but also the heirs, executors, and other beneficiaries may face difficulties, especially

---

[49] Konrad Zweigert, 'Einige Auswirkungen des Gemeinsamen Marktes auf das internationale Privatrecht der Mitgliedstaaten' in Ernst von Caemmerer, Hans-Jürgen Schlochauer and Ernst Steindorff (eds), *Probleme des europäischen Rechts, Festschrift für Walter Hallstein zu seinem 65. Geburtstag* (Klostermann 1966) 558–559.

[50] Paul Jenard, 'Report on the Convention on Jurisdiction and the Enforcement of Judgments in Civil and Commercial Matters (Signed at Brussels, 27 September 1968)' (1979) OJ C 59/1 11. As described in the Jenard Report, the International Union of Latin Notaries (UINL), when consulted by the Commission, stated that a convention on the recognition and enforcement of judgments in respect to succession issues was desirable due to the growing importance of the issue for the EU. However, the EU was of the opinion that priority should be given to the unification of conflict rules. For criticism of this view, see, Andreas F. Lowenfeld, 'International Litigation and the Quest for Reasonableness' (1994) 245 RdC 9, 165.

[51] See, in this regard, C-513/03 Heirs of M.E.A. van Hilten-van der Heijden v. Inspecteur van de Belastingdienst/Particulieren/Ondernemingen buitenland te Heerlen [2006] ECR I-1957 [42]; C-256/06 Theodor Jäger v. Finanzamt Kusel-Landstuhl [2008] ECR I-123 [25]; C-11/07 Eckelkamp v. Belgische Staat [2008] ECR I–6845 [39]; C-43/07 D. M. M. A. Arens-Sikken v. Staatssecretaris van Financiën [2008] ECR I-6887 [30]; C-318/07 Hein Persche v. Finanzamt Lüdenscheid [2009] ECR I-359 [26]; C-67/08 Margarete Block v. Finanzamt Kaufbeuren [2009] ECR I-883 [20]; C-35/08 Grundstücksgemeinschaft Busley and Cibrian Fernandez v. Finanzamt Stuttgart-Körperschaften [2009] ECR I-9807 [18]; C-25/10 Missionswerk Werner Heukelbach e.V. v. État belge [2011] ECR I-497 [16]; C-132/10 Halley v. Belgische Staat [2011] ECR I-8353 [19]; C-181/12 Yvon Welte v. Finanzamt Velbert EU:C:2013:662 [20]; C-133/13 Staatssecretaris van Economische Zaken, Staatssecretaris van Financiën v. Q. EU:C:2014:2460 [20]; C-559/13 Finanzamt Dortmund-Unna v. Josef Grünewald EU:C:2015:109 [18].

[52] Recital 7 of the Regulation. For views on the relevance of succession matters to the free movement of persons, see, for example, Erik Jayme and Christian Kohler, 'Europäisches Kollisionsrecht 1997 – Vergemeinschaftung durch "Säulenwechsel"?' [1997] IPRax 385, 386; Bernd von Hoffmann, 'The Relevance of European Community Law' in Bernd von Hoffmann (ed), *European Private International Law* (Ars Aequi Libri 1998) 30.

with regards to the recognition and enforcement of their rights. This would harm legal certainty and predictability, as the key elements of a European judicial area,[53] and it would result in complex proceedings. It was, therefore, inevitable that the European Union – a political entity which guarantees free movement for its citizens in general as well as for their capital – would at some point have to deal with cross-border succession cases.[54]

The entry into force of the Treaty of Amsterdam, which created the area of freedom, security and justice, paved the way for the desired harmonisation in this field. In line with the aims of the Treaty – namely 'to maintain and develop the Union as an area of freedom, security and justice, in which the free movement of persons is assured [...]' – the European Council and Commission published the Vienna Action Plan,[55] therein identifying the areas for harmonisation allowing for the best implementation of the Treaty. The Union, hence, made its first official declaration on the need for harmonisation in the field of succession.

In the following years, it was reiterated on different occasions that particularly mutual recognition in matters of succession is of utmost importance for the Union.[56] The Commission was then invited to submit a Green Paper on the conflict of laws in the area of succession, including procedural issues, mutual recognition, and enforcement of decisions concerning matters of succession and the creation of a European Certificate of Succession.[57] In line with this endeavour, and based on a study prepared by German Notaries Institute (DNotI),[58] the Commission published a Green Paper in 2005.[59] The Green

53 This is evidenced by the express references to these concepts in major European private international law instruments. See, for example, Recital 6 of the Rome I and II Regulations and Recital 15 of the Brussels I (recast) Regulation. See also Recital 37 of the Succession Regulation.

54 Christoph A. Kern and Daniela Glücker, 'Das neue Europäische Erbstatut und seine Aufnahme in der deutschen Literatur' (2014) 78 RabelsZ 294, 294–295; Dutta, *MüKoBGB* (2020) EuErbVO Vorb. Art 1 para 20.

55 Action Plan of the Council and the Commission on how best to implement the provisions of the Treaty of Amsterdam on an area of freedom, security and justice [1998] OJ C 19/1.

56 Draft programme of measures for implementation of the principle of mutual recognition of decisions in civil and commercial matters [2001] OJ C 12/1; Communication from the Commission to the Council and the European Parliament Area of Freedom, Security and Justice: Assessment of the Tampere programme and future orientations COM(2004) 401 Final.

57 The Hague Programme: Strengthening Freedom, Security and Justice in the European Union [2005] OJ C 53/1; Communication from the Commission to the Council and the European Parliament COM(2005) 184 Final.

58 DNotI (in collaboration with Heinrich Dörner and Paul Lagarde), 'Rechtsvergleichende Studie der erbrechtlichen Regelungen des Internationalen Verfahrensrechtes und Internationalen Privatrechts der Mitgliedsstaaten der Europäischen Union (2002)' in DNotI (ed), *Les Successions Internationales dans l'UE* (DNotI 2004).

Paper mainly received support from the Member States.[60] Hence, in 2009 the Commission published its proposal,[61] covering most of the issues addressed in the Green Paper, alongside a Staff Working Document.[62] Even though the subject is considered to be one of the most technical and difficult issues of action in the field of judicial cooperation in civil matters,[63] the Proposal successfully navigated the legislative procedures in the European Parliament and the Council in 2012[64] and became applicable in 2015.

II. Four Pillars of the Regulation

The brief history of the Regulation as described above demonstrates that the harmonisation of the rules applicable to cross-border succession matters has been driven by the integration policy and the policy of safeguarding free movement within the Union. The same concerns also affected the choices of the legislature when drafting the rules of the Regulation. There are seemingly four fundamental principles which characterise the Regulation and reflect the policy incentives of the legislature.[65]

First and foremost, the legislature, as with every harmonisation attempt in the field of conflict of laws, had to decide whether movable and immovable properties should be subject to the same regime.[66] A dilemma between monist and dualist approaches has existed among legal systems for a long time. Countries following the monist approach regard the estate as a unity and do

---

[59] The Green Paper Succession and Wills COM(2005) 65 Final.

[60] For the responses to the Green Paper see <http://europa.eu.int/comm/justice_home/news/consulting_public/successions/news_contributions_successions_en.htm> accessed 21 September 2016. For an overview of the responses, see, for example, Daniel Lehmann, 'Internationale Reaktionen auf das Grünbuch zum Erb- und Testamentsrecht' [2006] IPRax 204.

[61] Proposal for a Regulation of the European Parliament and of the Council on jurisdiction, applicable law, recognition and enforcement of decisions and authentic instruments in matters of succession and the creation of a European Certificate of Succession COM(2009) 154 Final.

[62] Commission Staff Working Document Accompanying the Proposal for a Regulation of the European Parliament and of the Council on Jurisdiction, Applicable Law, Recognition and Enforcement of Decisions and Authentic Instruments in Matters of Successions and on the Introduction of a European Certificate of Succession – Summary of the Impact Assessment [2009] SEC (2009) 411 Final C7-0236/09 2009.

[63] Rolf Wagner, 'Der Kommissionsvorschlag vom 14.10.2009 zum internationalen Erbrecht: Stand und Perspektiven des Gesetzgebungsverfahrens' [2010] DNotZ 506, 519; Rolf Wagner, 'Aktuelle Entwicklungen in der justiziellen Zusammenarbeit in Zivilsachen' [2012] NJW 1333, 1334.

[64] 'P7_TA(2012)0068' <http://www.europarl.europa.eu/sides/getDoc.do?type=TA&reference=P7-TA-2012-0068&language=EN> accessed 21 September 2016.

[65] Johannes Weber, in Anatol Dutta and Johannes Weber (eds), *Internationales Erbrecht* (2nd edn, C.H. Beck 2021) Einleitung paras 33 ff.

[66] Dutta, (2009) 73 RabelsZ 547, 554.

not distinguish movable and immovable parts thereof. As a consequence, the whole of the estate is governed by a single law, which is, depending on the legal system, the law of the nationality, domicile, or habitual residence of the deceased. In the dualist approach, on the other hand, scission is inevitable if the deceased left behind assets in more than one State. This is because the dualistic approach makes a distinction between movable and immovable parts of the estate and submits each part to different laws.[67] Under this approach, the *lex rei sitae* – considered by some jurisdictions as the sole authority based on the strong territorial ties between the property and its *situs*[68] – applies to succession in immovable property, whereas a law which is connected to the deceased governs matters of succession as regards movables. The two antagonistic stances were also seen in the European Union before harmonisation.[69] Arguments can be made to support or reject each system.[70] The Regulation, however, opted for the unity principle for the sake of its policy objectives (Article 4 and Article 10(1) for jurisdiction, Articles 21–23 for the purposes of conflict of laws). Splitting movable and immovable parts of the estate would, first of all, have presented challenges for cross-border estate planning and administration due to the legal costs which may have been incurred when dealing with these procedures as a consequence of considering multiple legal systems at the same time. Furthermore, application of these two conflicting systems in a single succession case may have caused problems in respect of the distribution of assets and forced heirship or reserved shares.[71] Following

---

[67] Dutta, (2009) 73 RabelsZ 547, 554–555; Max Planck Institute for Comparative and International Private Law, (2010) 74 RabelsZ 522, 602; Lajos Vékás, 'Objektive Anknüpfung des Erbstatuts' in Gerte Reichelt and Walter H. Rechberger (eds), *Europäisches Erbrecht: Zum Verordnungsvorschlag der Europäischen Kommission zum Erb- und Testamentsrecht* (Jan Sramek Verlag 2011) 42.

[68] Cf. Sjef van Erp, 'The New Succession Regulation: The Lex Rei Sitae Rule in Need of Reappraisal?' (2012) 1 EPLJ 187, 187; Bram Akkermans, 'Lex Rei Sitae and the EU Internal Market – Towards Mutual Recognition of Property Relations' (Social Science Research Network 2018) SSRN Scholarly Paper ID 3289625 4 <https://papers.ssrn.com/abstract=3289625> accessed 5 September 2020.

[69] For details, see Dutta, (2009) 73 RabelsZ 547, 554–555 and fn 42–43; Vékás, 'Objektive Anknüpfung des Erbstatuts' (2011) 42–43.

[70] See, for more information on this, below at pp 55 ff.

[71] It should be clarified here that there are different approaches as regards to mandatory protection of family members against the testamentary freedom of the deceased in different legal systems. There seems to be two main models in this regard: forced heirship ('Noterbenrecht') and reserved share/compulsory portion ('Pflichtteil'). The former originally refers to the model where forced heirs are entitled to proprietary rights over a part of the deceased's estate, which should be paid *in natura*. The latter, on the other hand, means that entitled heirs will only have a monetary claim (or in better words: *jus in personam*) over a part of the deceased's estate. See, for a short explanation in this regard, e.g. Cécile Pérès, 'Compulsory Portion in France' in Kenneth G. C. Reid, Marius J. de Waal and Reinhard Zimmermann (eds), *Comparative Succession Law – Volume III: Mandatory Family Protec-*

the monist approach, thus, was seen as the better option which best suited the objectives of the Union.[72]

Second, the Regulation, in accordance with the general trend in international[73] and EU private international law instruments,[74] espoused the last habitual residence of the deceased as the main connecting factor for determining both jurisdiction and applicable law. Until the harmonisation in this field, there was diversity in the laws of Member States. Nationality was the prevalent connecting factor for determining the law applicable to succession matters in many of the Member States.[75] The European legislature, however, preferred habitual residence, which is based on the assumption that a significant portion of a deceased's estate and a deceased's heirs or beneficiaries are often located in the country of residence, whereby a deceased's connection to the national State is somewhat limited in comparison,[76] with the caveat that a person's level of connection to the home State or to the residence will be contingent upon multiple factors and is hard to determine.[77] The principle of habitual residence is believed to contribute the integrative policy of the European Union concerning individuals living outside their State of origin.[78]

---

tion (OUP 2020) 98–99. See, for detailed explanations on these concepts with a comparison of different legal systems, Reinhard Zimmermann, 'Pflichtteil und Noterbenrecht in historisch-vergleichender Perspektive' (2020) 84 RabelsZ 465.

[72] Dörner and others, [2005] IPRax 1, 4; Heinz-Peter Mansel, 'Vereinheitlichung des Internationalen Erbrechts in der Europäischen Gemeinschaft – Kompetenzfragen und Regelungsgrundsätze' in Sabih Arkan and Aynur Yongalık (eds), *Prof. Dr. Tuğrul Ansay'a Armağan* (Turhan Kitabevi 2006) 205–206; Dutta, (2009) 73 RabelsZ 547, 555–557; Max Planck Institute for Comparative and International Private Law, (2010) 74 RabelsZ 522, 602–603; Vékás, 'Objektive Anknüpfung des Erbstatuts' (2011) 43; Weber, *Dutta/Weber* (2021) Einleitung para 38.

[73] See, for instance, Art 5(1) and Art 15(1) of The Hague Convention on Jurisdiction, Applicable Law, Recognition, Enforcement and Co-operation in Respect of Parental Responsibility and Measures for the Protection of Children of 19.10.1996. For more examples, see Dutta, (2009) 73 RabelsZ 547, 563 fn 90.

[74] For references to habitual residence, see, for example, Art 4(1) (a), (b), (d), (e), (f) and (2), Art 5(1) and (2), Art 6(1), Art 7(2) and, Art 11(2), (3) and (4) of the Rome I Regulation as well as Art 4(2), Art 5(1) (a) and (1) subpara 2, Art 10(2), Art 11(2) and Art 12(2) (b) of the Rome II Regulation. For more specific references and further examples, see Dutta, (2009) 73 RabelsZ 547, 563 fn 91–97.

[75] For an overview in this regard, see Mansel, 'Vereinheitlichung des Internationalen Erbrechts in der EG' (2006) 186–187; Dutta, (2009) 73 RabelsZ 547, 561–562; Vékás, 'Objektive Anknüpfung des Erbstatuts' (2011) 51; Stephan Lorenz, 'Erbrecht in Europa – Auf dem Weg zu kollisionsrechtlicher Rechtseinheit' [2012] ErbR 39, 40.

[76] Vékás, 'Objektive Anknüpfung des Erbstatuts' (2011) 52; Lorenz, [2012] ErbR 39, 43.

[77] Dutta, (2009) 73 RabelsZ 547, 564. For more details, see Cornelia Herweg, *Die Vereinheitlichung des Internationalen Erbrechts im Europäischen Binnenmarkt* (Nomos 2004) 51 ff; Daniel Lehmann, *Die Reform des Internationalen Erb- und Erbprozessrechts im Rahmen der geplanten Brüssel – IV Verordnung* (zerb verlag 2006) 76 ff.

Another significant pillar of the Regulation is the notion referred to as 'Gleichlauf', i.e. a parallelism between forum and *ius*. The European legislature does not limit the use of the habitual residence connecting factor for conflict-of-laws issues (Article 21(1)); rather extends it for procedural issues (Article 4). As a consequence, courts of Member States often apply their own laws when dealing with succession matters.[79] This was again a political decision taking into account the increasing mobility of persons within the Union.[80] With this parallelism, the legislature prevents a potential increase of legal costs and contributes to the quality of legal practice in cases involving more than one State, as the courts seised will no longer have to determine the scope of a foreign law and apply it.[81]

Lastly, the legislature also had to make a decision regarding party autonomy in the context of successions. As mentioned above, by giving priority to habitual residence as the main connecting factor in this field, the Regulation determined that the integration interests of the deceased should prevail. Such a rule could, however, trigger practical problems when the ties of the deceased to his/her home State are still stronger than to the State of residence. In such situations, in order to allow the deceased to plan the succession with a degree of legal certainty and in a manner consistent with stability interests, the Regulation allows a deceased to choose his/her national law at the time of making the choice or at the time of death (Article 22).[82] This is also in line with the current approach adopted in major European private international texts.[83]

All these principles, as the idea of harmonisation itself, are shaped in accordance with the political considerations of the Union. This Union-wide harmony may, however, create friction with the outside world given that the laws and policy objectives of non-Member States may not be aligned with those of the Regulation.[84] As regards both procedural rules and conflict-of-laws rules, this potential for friction will be examined in detail from the Turkish perspective in Chapters 2 and 3, below. However, before analysing these issues, the background and general overview of the rules of the Turkish PILA is set out in the following section.

---

[78] Mansel, 'Vereinheitlichung des Internationalen Erbrechts in der EG' (2006) 210; Dutta, (2009) 73 RabelsZ 547, 565; Vékás, 'Objektive Anknüpfung des Erbstatuts' (2011) 53; Lorenz, [2012] ErbR 39, 43; Weber, *Dutta/Weber* (2021) Einleitung para 34.

[79] Weber, *Dutta/Weber* (2021) Einleitung para 40.

[80] Lena Kunz, 'Die neue Europäische Erbrechtsverordnung – ein Überblick (Teil I)' [2012] GPR 208, 209.

[81] Peter Mankowski, 'Der gewöhnliche Aufenthalt des Erblassers unter Art. 21 Abs. 1 EuErbVO' [2015] IPRax 39, 41; Weber, *Dutta/Weber* (2021) Einleitung para 40.

[82] Dutta, (2009) 73 RabelsZ 547, 569ff; Weber, *Dutta/Weber* (2021) Einleitung para 36.

[83] See, for example, Art 3 of the Rome I Regulation, Art 14 of the Rome II Regulation.

[84] Dutta, (2009) 73 RabelsZ 547, 564.

C. Background of Turkish Private International Law on Succession and a General Overview of the Rules

Unlike certain other civil law legal systems having separate legislation on different issues,[85] all aspects of PIL issues related to succession, i.e. jurisdiction, applicable law, and recognition and enforcement, are regulated under the Turkish PILA in the Turkish legal system. As every system developed its own approach in the field of cross-border successions based on its historical background, the brief history of the Turkish PILA and its general rules in the field of succession should, respectively, be examined here.

I. A Brief History of the Turkish Private International Law on Succession

Under the Turkish legal system, the application of foreign law by virtue of private international law became possible only after the Turkish War of Independence and the 1923 Treaty of Lausanne[86] signed in its aftermath.[87] Up to that point, the Ottoman Empire's judicial power over foreigners, i.e. non-Muslims,[88] was circumscribed by virtue of the capitulations[89] granted by the

---

[85] In Germany, for example, conflict-of-laws issues in the field of succession law are regulated in the EGBGB (particularly Art 25 and Art 26), whereas procedural issues are regulated in the FamFG (particularly Art 105 and Art 108 et seq.) and in the ZPO (particularly Art 328 and Arts 722–723). EGBGB: BGBl. I 1994, 2494; the articles were amended after the Regulation in BGBl. I 2015, 1042. FamFG: BGBl. I 2008, 2586–2587. ZPO: BGBl. I 2005, 3202.

[86] *Düstur*, Tertip III, Cilt V, 13. For the text of the Treaty, see <http://www.mfa.gov.tr/lausanne-peace-treaty.en.mfa> accessed 20 September 2020.

[87] Muammer Raşit Seviğ, *Devletler Hususi Hukuku: Tabiiyet – Yabancılar Hukuku – Kanunlar İhtilafı*, vol I (Bozkurt Basımevi 1937) 334.

[88] In States following classical Islamic law, the world is divided into two parts: '*Dâr'al Islam*' and '*Dâr'al Harb*'. The first refers to the territory of Islam, i.e. parts of the world ruled under Islamic law, whereas the second means the territory of war, i.e. lands ruled by other religions. See, in this regard, Yılmaz Altuğ, *Yabancıların Hukukî Durumu* (3rd edn, Sermet Matbaası 1968) 39; Belkıs Konan, *Osmanlı Devleti'nde Yabancıların Hukuki Statüsü* (Statü Yayıncılık 2013) 5–6; Bahadır Apaydın, *Kapitülasyonların Osmanlı-Türk Adli ve İdari Modernleşmesine Etkisi* (3rd edn, Adalet Yayınevi 2017) 133–134.

This was also the case in the Ottoman Empire, and it affected the meaning of the term 'foreigner' in the Empire: Yasemin Saner Gönen, 'Osmanlı İmparatorluğunda Yabancıların Adli Ayrıcalıkları' (DPhil thesis, Marmara University 1998) 19; Apaydın, *Kapitülasyonlar* (2017) 133–134.

Particularly before the *Tanzimat*, i.e. the reform period of the Ottoman Empire in the 19th Century, there was an understanding of a nation based on religion. All non-Muslims were referred to as '*harbî*' – meaning literally people from non-Islamic countries – which also consisted of two groups: '*dhimmi*', who were non-Muslim subjects of the Ottoman Empire and '*musta'min*', who were staying in the territories of the Empire with a residence permit. Therefore, during this time, there was no law governing foreigners formulated

Ottoman Empire in favour of these individuals' home States.[90] Although capitulations were initiated for commercial purposes, they often encroached on the judicial arena. Consequently, based on the principle of 'personality of law' (an idea which originated in the Medieval Period)[91], consular officers gained extraterritorial powers over private or, sometimes, public law matters arising in their community.[92] This extraterritorial judicial authority of consuls, which could be exercised in accordance with the laws as well as the customs of their

---

based on nationality, as in today's understanding; rather there was the law of non-Muslims, which changed for each nation according to their beliefs. It was only after the *Tanzimat*, especially with the Ottoman Nationality Law of 1869 ('Tâbiiyet-i Osmaniye Kanunnamesi', 11 Kânunsani 1284, *Takvim-i Vekâyi*, no 1044; *Düstur*, Tertip I, Cilt I, 16; for the text of the law, see İlhan Unat, *Türk Vatandaşlık Hukuku (Metinler – Mahkeme Kararları)* (Sevinç Matbaası 1966)), that an understanding of nationality irrespective of religion was developed: Konan, *Yabancıların Hukuki Statüsü* (2013) 6–7; Apaydın, *Kapitülasyonlar* (2017) 133–137; Rona Aybay, Nimet Özbek and Gizem Ersen Perçin, *Vatandaşlık Hukuku* (Siyasal Kitabevi 2019) 59–62.

89 Capitulations referred to and were defined as the rights and privileges regardıng commercial, social, and judicial matters conferred by Muslim States to non-Muslim individuals in their territories: John Wansbrough, 'Imtiyāzāt' in Bernard Lewis and others (eds), *The Encyclopaedia of Islam*, vol III (H-Iram) (2nd edn, J. Brill 1986) 1178–1179; Zeki Arıkan, 'Mahmut Esat Bozkurt ve Kapitülasyonlar' (1994) 2 ÇTTAD 217, 217. See, for more information on capitulations in the Ottoman Empire, Halil İnalcık, 'Imtiyazat – The Ottoman Empire' in Bernard Lewis and others (eds), *The Encyclopaedia of Islam*, vol III (H-Iram) (2nd edn, J. Brill 1986) 1179 ff.

90 M. R. Seviğ, *Tabiiyet – Yabancılar Hukuku – Kanunlar İhtilafı* (1937) 334.

91 The principle of personality of law can be briefly explained as a principle where people continue to be subject to the legal system of their own nation or tribe irrespective of territoriality and, hence, of their place of domicile. See, for more information, Simeon L. Guterman, 'The Principle of the Personality of Law in the Early Middle Ages: A Chapter in the Evolution of Western Legal Institutions and Ideas' (1966) 21 U Miami L Rev 259.

Even though this understanding of the Medieval Period yielded to the principle of territoriality after the 15th Century, it continued to apply in the capitulary regime. This is because the Ottoman Empire, which followed Islamic Law, found it difficult to conceive of the application of any law to its community other than the Islamic one, especially for matters of personal status: Gotthard Jaeschke, 'Türk Hukukunda Evlenme Aktinin Şekli: Devletler Hususi Hukukunda bir Araştırma' (1953) 19 İÜHFM 400, 409–410. Other States enjoying capitulations were also happy to keep this system in place for their subjects, since they mistrusted Islamic law: Hilmar Krüger, 'Studien über Probleme des türkischen Internationalen Erbrechts' in Sabih Arkan and Aynur Yongalık (eds), *Festschrift Liber Amicorum Tuğrul Ansay – Zum 75. Geburtstag/in Honour of his 75th Birthday* (Kluwer Law International 2006) 144 fn 62; cf. Walther Lehmann, *Die Kapitulationen* (Kiepenheuer 1917) 15–17.

92 Wansbrough, 'Imtiyāzāt' (1986) 1179; cf. Tahir Taner, 'Lozan Muahedesi ve Kapitülasyonların İlgası', *Devletler Hususi Hukuku Ordinaryüs Profesörü Muammer Raşit Seviğ'e Armağan* (İsmail Akgün Matbaası 1956) 724; İnalcık, 'Imtiyāzāt' (1986) 1180.

home States, covered, above all, matters of family and succession law,[93] as such issues were of great importance at the time especially for merchants.[94]

The effect of the capitulary regime in the field of succession is mostly seen with reference to movables. Pursuant to this regime, foreign consular courts in the Ottoman Empire had jurisdiction over the movable estate of its own subjects. When the estate was left without a claimant, the Ottoman Empire was not able to claim any rights over it; instead, only the national State of the deceased had such rights.[95] The law applicable in such cases was, in principle, the national law of the deceased.[96] With regards to immovable properties, there was no special regime provided by the capitulations in light of the fact that foreign nationals did not have any right to acquire real estate in the Ottoman Empire until the 19th century.[97] It was only after the adoption of the

---

[93] Altuğ, *Yabancıların Hukukî Durumu* (1968) 66–67; İnalcık, 'Imtiyāzāt' (1986) 1181–1182; Saner Gönen, 'Osmanlı İmparatorluğunda Yabancıların Adli Ayrıcalıkları' (1998) 21, 30 and 69; Konan, *Yabancıların Hukuki Statüsü* (2013) 121 ff; Apaydın, *Kapitülasyonlar* (2017) 139 ff.

It is important to clarify that succession between nationals of different countries and different religious groups was not possible according to the principles of Islamic law. Therefore, succession issues as discussed here should be understood in this sense: Altuğ, *Yabancıların Hukukî Durumu* (1968) 250–251; Vedat Raşit Seviğ, 'Yabancı Gerçek Kişilerin Türkiye'de Miras Hakları', *Prof. Dr. Hıfzı Timur'un Anısına Armağan* (Fakülteler Matbaası 1979) 783; Gülören Tekinalp, *Türk Yabancılar Hukuku* (8th edn, Beta 2003) 201 fn 1.

[94] Wansbrough, 'Imtiyāzāt' (1986) 1178–1179.

[95] Konan, *Yabancıların Hukuki Statüsü* (2013) 121–123. See, in the same regard for disputes concerning movables, M. R. Seviğ, *Tabiiyet – Yabancılar Hukuku – Kanunlar İhtilafı* (1937) 336; Altuğ, *Yabancıların Hukukî Durumu* (1968) 66; Saner Gönen, 'Osmanlı İmparatorluğunda Yabancıların Adli Ayrıcalıkları' (1998) 68–69; Apaydın, *Kapitülasyonlar* (2017) 190–191. One provision of the capitulations granted in favour of France in 1740 reads as follows (in translation by author): 'When a French national dies, no one shall intervene (in the estate proceedings regarding his clothes and other movable estates). The estate shall be given to whom he bequeathed and when he has died intestate to heirs of the same nationality through the consuls. The public treasury ('Beyt'ül mal') or public administrators ('qassams') shall not intervene'. For the original text of the 1740 capitulations, see *Mecmua-i Muahedat*, vol 1 (Hakikat Matbaası 1294) 14–35. For the Turkish translation of the Article, see Konan, *Yabancıların Hukuki Statüsü* (2013) 121. Similar provisions can be found in the capitulations issued in favour of some other current EU States, particularly Austria and Denmark among others. See, in this regard, Konan, *Yabancıların Hukuki Statüsü* (2013) 122.

[96] M. R. Seviğ, *Tabiiyet – Yabancılar Hukuku – Kanunlar İhtilafı* (1937) 336; Saner Gönen, 'Osmanlı İmparatorluğunda Yabancıların Adli Ayrıcalıkları' (1998) 68–72; Apaydın, *Kapitülasyonlar* (2017) 195–196.

[97] M. R. Seviğ, *Tabiiyet – Yabancılar Hukuku – Kanunlar İhtilafı* (1937) 335; Saner Gönen, 'Osmanlı İmparatorluğunda Yabancıların Adli Ayrıcalıkları' (1998) 69; Apaydın, *Kapitülasyonlar* (2017) 190–191.

Safer Law[98] that foreigners became entitled to acquire real estate in Ottoman territories, with certain restrictions. Under this law, Ottoman courts had jurisdiction over any disputes regarding immovables, and the law of the Ottoman Empire was applicable.[99]

Whilst capitulations had a long history in the Empire,[100] they became a tool for Western States to politically, economically, or even judicially subordinate the Ottoman State once the empire had weakened. The privileges, which were mostly not reciprocal, had been excessively exploited by the Europeans. The abuses were manifold. In the first place, the scope of concessions and the circle of people enjoying them had been widened. Through a protection system which at times encompassed bribery,[101] they were extended even to nationals of other foreign States (some of them being the Empire's own non-Muslim subjects). As a result of this, a group which was entitled to more rights and privileges than other Ottoman subjects was created. Foreigners were exempted from Ottoman law and Ottoman jurisdiction, even sometimes for criminal matters. Furthermore, consuls used extraterritorial powers and interfered in matters before Ottoman Courts. Moreover, translators accompanying foreign parties at court influenced the decisions of Ottoman courts.[102] These practices were contrary to the very terms of the capitulations; more importantly, they ran counter to recognised principles of international law, particularly the sovereign equality of States, and to the independence and

---

[98] The Law on the Rights of Foreign Nationals to Acquire Real Estate of 8 June 1868 ('7 Safer 1284 Tarihli Tebaa-i Ecnebiyenin Emlâke Mutasarrıf Olmaları Hakkında Kanun'), *Düstur*, Tertip I, Cilt I, 230. The Law is usually referred to as the 'Safer Law' due to the month it was enacted in. For the text of the Law, see Yılmaz Altuğ, *Yabancıların Arazi İktisabı Meselesi* (4th edn, Sulhi Garan Matbaası 1976) 169–170. For an English translation of the Law, see F. Ongley, *The Ottoman Land Code* (W. Clowes 1892) 168–171.

[99] M. R. Seviğ, *Tabiiyet – Yabancılar Hukuku – Kanunlar İhtilafı* (1937) 336; Altuğ, *Yabancıların Hukukî Durumu* (1968) 66; Saner Gönen, 'Osmanlı İmparatorluğunda Yabancıların Adli Ayrıcalıkları' (1998) 69; Konan, *Yabancıların Hukuki Statüsü* (2013) 127–128; Apaydın, *Kapitülasyonlar* (2017) 191. However, it should be kept in mind that there were different categories of land in the Ottoman Empire, and, thus, the applicability of rules to all categories of lands was a matter of discussion. Consular courts claimed jurisdiction for particular categories of land. See, in this regard, Konan, *Yabancıların Hukuki Statüsü* (2013) 126–127.

[100] See, in this regard, İnalcık, 'Imtiyāzāt' (1986) 1182–1188; Konan, *Yabancıların Hukuki Statüsü* (2013) 9–17; Apaydın, *Kapitülasyonlar* (2017) 38–53.

[101] This is known as the 'protégé system'. For example, through a number of capitulary arrangements, the French took Christian Ottoman subjects into their protection. Such kind of a protection was sometimes gained by wealthy (non-Muslim) Ottoman subjects by means of bribery. Through this system, the subjects of the Ottoman Empire could themselves enjoy the priviliges of the capitulatory system. See, in this regard, Salahi R. Sonyel, 'The Protégé System in the Ottoman Empire' (1991) 2 J Islam Stud 56; Belkıs Konan, 'Osmanlı Devletinde Protégé (Koruma) Sistemi' (2009) 58 AÜHFD 169.

[102] İnalcık, 'Imtiyāzāt' (1986) 1187–1188.

national dignity of the Empire.[103] There was a need for the Ottoman side to stop the legal deterioration and to take fundamental steps toward the replacement of this onerous regime with a modern system compatible with recognised tenets of international law. The outbreak of the First World War created an important opportunity for the Ottoman side.[104] Seizing upon this chance, the Ottoman Empire abolished capitulations[105] and initiated reforms in order to regulate the legal status as well as the rights and duties of foreigners.[106]

The most important of these reforms was undoubtedly the enactment of what is known as the Temporary Act.[107] Adopted in 1915, only a short time before the official foundation of the Turkish Republic in 1923, the legislation could be considered the first private international law legislation of Turkey. Unlike modern private international law legislation, the Temporary Act did not cover all cross-border legal disputes, instead covering only the ones involving foreign nationals. It also did not address procedural and conflict-of-laws matters for different subjects with separate rules; rather it laid down a general rule which included most of the matters under Article 4.[108] The Article was also applicable for matters of succession. The dualist approach toward succession during the capitulary regime, i.e. the different treatment of movable and immovable property, had not been changed. Disputes concerning immovable property situated in the territories of the Ottoman State were subject to the sole authority of Ottoman courts and to the laws of the Empire. Although a unilateral conflict-of-laws rule, it was considered[109] and applied[110]

---

[103] İnalcık, 'Imtiyāzāt' (1986) 1186–1188.

[104] Denkschrift zu dem Konsularvertrag von 1917, Reichstagsdrucksache Nr. 755, 13. Legislaturperiode, 11. Session (1914–1917) 171; Tahir Taner, *Kapitülasyonlar Nasıl İlga Edildi?* (İsmail Akgün Matbaası 1956) 9; İnalcık, 'Imtiyāzāt' (1986) 1188.

[105] The complete abolition of capitulations ultimately took longer than the Ottoman government expected. Although the Empire declared the unilateral abolition of capitulations in 1914 with an imperial decree ('İmtiyazat-ı Ecnebiyyenin (Kapitülasyon) İlgası Hakkında İrade-i Seniyye', *Takvim-i Vekayi* of 17.9.1914, no 1938) and sent diplomatic notes to concerned States declaring this step (*Düstur*, Tertip II, Cilt VI, 1273; for the text of the notes, see also Cemil Bilsel, *Lozan*, vol 2 (Sosyal Yayınlar 1998) 65–67), there were protests by the States enjoying capitulations in the Empire due to the fact that they had a contractual nature and could not be terminated by a unilateral declaration. Thus, it was only in 1923 with Article 28 of the Treaty of Lausanne that capitulations were completely abolished. For more information on the abolition of capitulations, see Taner, *Kapitülasyonlar Nasıl İlga Edildi?* (1956).

[106] Taner, *Kapitülasyonlar Nasıl İlga Edildi?* (1956) 11–12; Apaydın, *Kapitülasyonlar* (2017) 289–295.

[107] The Temporary Act on Rights and Duties of Foreigners in Ottoman Lands of 23 February 1915 ('23 Şubat 1330 Tarihli Memalik-i Osmaniyede Bulunan Ecnebilerin Hukuk ve Vezaifi Hakkında Kanun-u Muvakkat'), *Düstur*, Tertip II, Cilt VII, 458.

[108] M. R. Seviğ, *Tabiiyet – Yabancılar Hukuku – Kanunlar İhtilafı* (1937) 338.

[109] Şakir Berki, *Tatbîkî Devletler Hususî Hukuku* (Nur Matbaası 1950) 60; Osman Fazıl Berki, *Kanuni Miras ve Ölüme Bağlı Tasarruflardan Doğan Kanun İhtilafları* (Güzel Sana-

as a multilateral one, adopting the *lex rei sitae* as regards immovable assets. Succession matters concerning movable property, on the other hand, could only be heard before the courts of the Ottoman State, where the parties started proceedings before them or where the case also involved Ottoman subjects, i.e. where either the deceased or one of the beneficiaries was a national of the Empire,[111] or where there was already a related proceeding pending before the Ottoman courts. Though the law was silent on the issue, it was argued that Ottoman courts might rule on succession, on an exceptional basis, if proceedings could not be brought before the competent court due to a situation such as war[112] or when required by *ordre public*;[113] in such cases it was asserted that the court could act as a *forum necessitatis*. Except for these circumstances, Ottoman courts could not assume jurisdiction over the succession of foreigners to movable property. This was consistent with the legal developments of that era in which courts of States other than the courts of the national State of the person in question declined to exercise jurisdiction in matters of personal status.[114] In accordance with this understanding, the governing law in matters of succession as regards movables was the national law of the deceased under Article 4.

The Temporary Act continued to be applicable also in the Turkish Republic as the successor of the Ottoman Empire. This is because Turkey was then following a closed economic policy, and hence, cross-border cases were rare instances and were mostly issues of personal status, family, and succession law.

---

tlar Matbaası 1960) 18; Nihal Uluocak, *Kanunlar İhtilafı (Yasama Yetkisi Kuralları)* (Fakülteler Matbaası 1971) 111; Vedat Raşit Seviğ, *Kanunlar İhtilafı (Yasama ve Yargılama Çatışmaları)* (2nd edn, Sulhi Garan Matbaası 1974) 88; Erdoğan Göğer, *Devletler Hususi Hukuku (Kanunlar İhtilafı)* (4th edn, Ankara Üniversitesi Hukuk Fakültesi Yayınları 1977) 273.

[110] See, for instance, some judgments from the Turkish Court of Cassation, Yargıtay 2. Hukuk Dairesi, T. 20.11.1958, E. 5762 K. 5476; Yargıtay 2. Hukuk Dairesi, T. 3.2.1959, E. 6846 K. 584; Yargıtay 2. Hukuk Dairesi, T. 21.3.1963, E. 1638 K. 1687. For the texts of the judgments, see Hilmi Yazıcı and Hasan Atasoy, *Şahıs, Aile ve Miras Hukuku ile İlgili Yargıtay Tatbikatı 1952–1970* (Kardeş Matbaası 1970) 795–797.

[111] O. F. Berki, *Miras* (1960) 84.

[112] The Turkish Court of Cassation held in one decision that a divorce case between two German nationals during the Second World War could be heard before Turkish courts, as it was impossible for the claimant to initiate proceedings in Germany by virtue of the fact that diplomatic relations between Turkey and Germany were severed at that time: Temyiz Mahkemesi 2. Hukuk Dairesi, T. 6.4.1945, E. 37 K. 1922 published and commented on in Berki and Ergüney, *Yabancılar Hukuku ve Kanun İhtilafları ile İlgili Yargıtay Kararlarının Tahlil ve İzahı* (1963) 81–82.

[113] Muammer Raşit Seviğ, *Türkiye Cumhuriyeti Kanunlar İhtilafı Kaidelerinin Sentezi* (Fakülteler Matbaası 1941) 35; O. F. Berki, *Miras* (1960) 85; V. R. Seviğ, *Mirasla İlgili Devletler Hususi Hukuku Kaideleri* (1963) 196.

[114] Vedat Raşit Seviğ, *Ahkâmı Şahsiye Davalarında Türk Mahkemesinin Yetkisi* (Sermet Matbaası 1964) 8; cf. O. F. Berki, *Miras* (1960) 85.

The Temporary Act was considered sufficient to provide guidance for the judges in such rare instances. The situation changed somewhat with the ensuing effect of the migration flow from Turkey to European States in the 1960s and with the growth of transnational trade in the 1980s. These two historic developments triggered a considerable increase in conflict-of-laws matters. Thus, the Turkish legislator enacted the former Turkish PILA numbered 2675 in 1982.[115]

The former Turkish PILA of 1982 dealt with succession issues in two different articles: Article 22 designated the law applicable in succession matters and Article 30 dealt with the issue of jurisdiction. In terms of applicable law, there was a small change in the dualist approach. This time, the national law of the deceased was authorised for all matters of succession. The only exception to this was succession to immovable properties located in Turkey, which was governed by Turkish law (Article 22(1)). On the other hand, the system of scission was completely altered as regards to jurisdiction in the Act. Article 30 provided that Turkish courts situated in the place where the deceased had his last domicile should have jurisdiction to rule on succession. If the last domicile of the deceased was located outside Turkey, then the Turkish court at the place where the asset was located should be competent. In 2007, as a consequence of both transnational developments and problems experienced at the time, the legislature felt the need for a reform in the area of private international law, after more than twenty years of application of the former Act.[116] The start of Turkey's accession process to the EU and, more specifically, the drafting of rules in alignment with the Rome and Brussels Regulations were the main policy incentives of the private international law reform undertaken in 2007.[117] In the field of succession, however, only certain minimal changes in the wording of the former Act were made. This is not surprising, as the idea of reform in this field in the EU was also in its early stages.

II. The Private International Law of Turkey in the Field of Succession: A Brief Overview of the Rules

The Turkish PILA of 2007, as the former version, regulates succession issues in two different articles. Whereas the designation of the applicable law is regulated in Article 20, the international jurisdiction of Turkish courts as regards succession is determined under Article 43. Article 20(1), once again, provides that the law applicable to succession is the national law of the de-

---

115 Nuray Ekşi, *Yargıtay Kararları Işığında Milletlerarası Miras Hukuku* (Beta 2013) 5.

116 '5718 Sayılı Milletlerarası Özel Hukuk ve Usul Hukuku Hakkında Kanun Tasarısı ve Gerekçe' 1. For a brief history of the Turkish PILA of 2007 and a general overview on its rules, see Gülören Tekinalp, 'The 2007 Turkish Code Concerning Private International Law and International Civil Procedure' (2007) IX YbPIL 313.

117 '5718 Sayılı Milletlerarası Özel Hukuk ve Usul Hukuku Hakkında Kanun Tasarısı ve Gerekçe' 2.

ceased, but Turkish law applies for immovable property situated in Turkey. This means that when the deceased is a Turkish national, Turkish law would govern the succession as a whole regardless of the nature and the *situs* of assets. Although the outcome would not change for movables and immovables located elsewhere in the event that the deceased was a non-Turkish national, succession to his/her immovable property in Turkey would be under the sole authority of Turkish law.[118] It is undoubted that succession is, on the one hand, closely related to the property ownership regime in a country, and on the other hand, that is also connected with the family structure in that country. This double-sided nature of succession, therefore, is decisive for the determination of the *lex successionis* in a legal system.[119] It seems that the family law nature of succession has always predominated in the Turkish system, and thus the *lex successionis* has been the national law of the deceased. By contrast, immovable property ownership and its inheritance by way of succession have a political system dimension that cannot be disregarded. Hence, for immovable property found in Turkey, *lex successionis* has been chosen as the Turkish law, in other words, the law of the *situs*.[120]

This system should normally govern all issues of intestate succession. The legislature, however, has restricted the scope of it – based on practical concerns[121] – in the second paragraph by providing that provisions pertaining to the grounds for opening succession as well as the acquisition and distribution of succession should be governed by the law of the country where the estate is located. Due to these exceptions as to the material scope of the rule, the Turkish system cannot be regarded as a legal system adopting a unitary approach to succession.[122]

Article 20 also has a provision as regards an heirless estate in Turkey. In order to prevent other States from claiming succession rights on it,[123] it is prescribed that an estate left without a claimant in Turkey should belong to the (Turkish) State (Article 20(3)).

---

118 Ekşi, *Milletlerarası Miras Hukuku* (2013) 34; Ali Gümrah Toker and Ahmet Cemal Ruhi, *Milletlerarası Özel Hukuk ve Usul Hukuku Hakkında Kanun – Gerekçeli, Açıklamalı, İçtihatlı* (On İki Levha 2019) 148; Gülören Tekinalp, *Milletlerarası Özel Hukuk: Bağlama ve Usul Hukuku Kuralları* (13th edn, Beta 2020) 234; Aysel Çelikel and Bahadır Erdem, *Milletlerarası Özel Hukuk* (17th edn, Beta 2021) 348; Ergin Nomer, *Devletler Hususî Hukuku* (23rd edn, Beta 2021) 297; Cemal Şanlı, Emre Esen and İnci Ataman Figanmeşe, *Milletlerarası Özel Hukuk* (9th edn, Beta 2021) 263; Vahit Doğan, *Milletlerarası Özel Hukuk* (8th edn, Savaş Yayınevi 2022) 368–369.

119 V. R. Seviğ, *Mirasla İlgili Devletler Hususi Hukuku Kaideleri* (1963) 81.

120 Cf. V. R. Seviğ, *Mirasla İlgili Devletler Hususi Hukuku Kaideleri* (1963) 84.

121 Tekinalp, *Milletlerarası Özel Hukuk* (2020) 234. For details, see p 88, below.

122 See pp 58–59, below.

123 Nomer, *Devletler Hususî Hukuku* (2021) 300.

The legislature has also laid down specific conflict-of-laws rules over testamentary dispositions upon death. Article 20(4) provides that Article 7 – the general rule dealing with the law applicable to formalities of legal acts – applies in terms of the form of testamentary dispositions. Such dispositions made in accordance with the national law of the deceased will also be valid. Hence, testamentary dispositions will be valid if they are made in accordance with the law of the place where they are concluded (*locus regit actum*) or with the law applicable to their substance (*lex causae*) (Article 7) or with the national law of the deceased (*lex patriae*). The capacity to make testamentary dispositions upon death, on the other hand, should be governed by the national law of the testator at the time of making the disposition (Article 20(5)).

In terms of the rule of jurisdiction, no change has been made in Article 43. As formulated in the previous version, (Turkish) courts at the place where the deceased had his/her last domicile should have jurisdiction on succession, and when the deceased died with a last domicile outside Turkey, the (Turkish) courts at the place where the estate is located should be competent on the matter.

It is apparent that the understanding of succession in Turkey and concerns inherited from the past shaped these rules. This does not mean, however, that every system is without flaws, especially when cases arise in which more than one legal system is involved. As such cases are highly likely in the Turkish-EU context, these rules should be examined in detail in the following chapters by way of comparison to the rules of the Regulation. However, as mentioned in the beginning, there is also a third leg to this context, this being the bilateral treaties concluded between Member States and Turkey. As the most practically relevant among them, the background of the Turkish-German Treaty and a general overview of it should also be provided in the following part.

D. Background of the Turkish-German Treaty and a General Overview of its Rules as well as its Scope of Application

The idea of drafting uniform transnational rules in the field of private international law has always been appealing. It seems that, above all, the works and already concluded instruments of the Hague Conference on Private International Law prove this. Nonetheless, in certain fields it is an onerous task to reach an international agreement that includes rules which should be mutually applicable in different States and which are perfectly suitable to divergent legal traditions and policy incentives. There is no doubt that succession law – even at the cross-border level – is one of these areas.[124] International instruments in this field have thus been mostly rare. However, bilateral treaties

[124] Gareth Miller, *International Aspects of Succession* (Ashgate 2000) 285.

covering procedural and conflict-of-laws rules on succession have existed between Turkey and, from the EU, the Member States of Germany, Hungary, and Italy for almost a century.

Even the substantial change made as regards cross-border successions with the Union's adoption of the Regulation did not render these treaties obsolete. Reflecting the well-established principle of *pacta sunt servanda*, Article 75(1)(1) of the Regulation provides that international conventions concluded between Member States and third States prior to the Regulation's entry into force will continue to be primarily applicable between Contracting States. With this provision – similar versions of which can be found in other European private international law texts, e.g. Article 25(1) of the Rome I Regulation, Article 28(1) of the Rome II Regulation and, more recently, in Article 62(1) of the European Matrimonial Property Regulation and European Registered Partnerships Regulation – the European legislature is following the rationale of Article 351 of the TFEU and allowing Member States to fulfil their obligations *vis-à-vis* third States as arising out of international agreements even after the entry into force of the Regulation.[125]

Yet this means that a substantial number of cases will be beyond the reach of the Regulation, since the European Union hosts over two million Turkish nationals who are – as will be seen below – subject to the treaties. Although one cannot ascribe the same level of practical relevance to those treaties for Turkey, they are – and particularly the Turkish-German Treaty examined in this book – of significance for the migrant community of Turkey within the EU. Therefore, it is important to present the background and a general overview of the Treaty here. Unlike the previous parts, the scope of the Treaty should also be examined in this part to demonstrate in which situations it becomes applicable.

I. *A Brief History of the Turkish-German Treaty*

The capitulary regime which was briefly explained above[126] was also applicable in the history of Turkish-German relationships. The privileges granted in favour of Germany date back to the Amity and Commerce Treaty of 22 March 1761 between the Kingdom of Prussia and the Ottoman Empire. This Treaty was extended for fifty years in 1790 and later replaced with a new agreement based on the same rules on behalf of the States of the *Zollverein* on 10 and 20 October 1840. The rules of the Treaty remained applicable also in the relationships with the German Empire.[127] According to this regime, like the arrangements concluded with other States, German consular courts had juris-

[125] Dutta, *MüKoBGB* (2020) EuErbVO Art 75 para 1.

[126] See above pp 28–32.

[127] This is explicitly stated in Art XXIV of the Amity, Commerce and Shipping Treaty of 26 August 1890 between the German and Ottoman Empires (RGBl. I 1891, 117). See generally on this issue, Denkschrift zu dem Konsularvertrag von 1917.

diction over civil and commercial matters, including the succession[128] of German nationals and other individuals under the protection of German Empire.[129] Nonetheless, Ottoman judicial authorities were to be competent over such cases when Ottoman subjects were involved, but the hearings were to be held with the participation of the consul or an agent of the consulate and with the translator from the consulate.[130] The only group of civil and commercial cases over which Ottoman Courts had exclusive jurisdiction without any interference of consuls were those involving immovable properties located in the territories of the Empire.[131]

Capitulations, which also included judicial privileges as exemplified here through Turkish-German relationships, had been an important part of the policy of the Ottoman Empire for political and economic reasons, as explained above. At the time when the State was powerful, they were mostly on a reciprocal basis and provided crucial benefits for the Empire. Over time, however, and especially in the 18th century when the Ottoman State started to lose power, the States enjoying capitulations began to exploit these privileges in a non-reciprocal and extensive way. As a consequence of this, the Empire fell under the subordination of Western powers, losing its dignity along with its sovereign right to adjudicate within its own territories. In order to put an end to this burdensome regime and to make a new start, the Ottoman Empire seized upon the opportunity presented by the start of the First World War and abolished capitulations. The new regime replacing the capitulations, which was to be more consistent with the international law standards, was consequently introduced with new legislation concerning, in particular, the legal status, rights, and duties of foreign nationals in the Empire.[132]

Together with the internal legal reforms, there was a need to conclude international conventions with other States on the conditions of residence as well as on commercial and consular relations, conditions which were, unlike the capitulary system, to follow the canons of public international law.[133] At that time,

---

[128] See, for the scope of authority of the German consuls over succession matters of German nationals, the edited version of Article 6 of the Amity and Commerce Treaty of 1761 between the Kingdom of Prussia and the Ottoman Empire, Necdet Kurdakul, *Osmanlı Devleti'nde Ticaret Anlaşmaları ve Kapitülasyonlar* (Döler Neşriyat 1981) 155. See, for the German version, W. Lehmann, *Die Kapitulationen* (1917) 73–74.

[129] See above n 101, p 31.

[130] Denkschrift zu dem Konsularvertrag von 1917. See, for more information on the issue, Saner Gönen, 'Osmanlı İmparatorluğunda Yabancıların Adli Ayrıcalıkları' (1998) 82ff; Apaydın, *Kapitülasyonlar* (2017) 222ff.

[131] Denkschrift zu dem Konsularvertrag von 1917 171.

[132] See, general on this, İnalcık, 'Imtiyāzāt' (1986).

[133] Taner, *Kapitülasyonlar Nasıl İlga Edildi?* (1956) 12. See also the speech of the Minister of Foreign Affairs in the Parliament after the conclusion of the Treaty, *Meclis-i Mebusan Zabıt Ceridesi,* Cilt 1 [1916 – Devre: 3 İçtima Senesi: 3] (T.B.M.M. Basımevi 1991) 362–364.

however, the First World War was still ongoing and the Empire was also fighting in the war alongside the Central Powers. Consequently, the conclusion of such agreements proved possible only with the Empire's allies.[134] These States, for their part, had doubts about the Ottoman judicial system – despite the new legislation – and a mutually agreed transnational order was seen as highly desirable particularly for their nationals residing in the Ottoman Empire.[135]

Thanks to these two-sided concerns of the parties at that time, a series of agreements were concluded between Turkey and the German and Austro-Hungarian Empires. Whilst the treaties with the Austro-Hungarian Empire could never enter into force given that the Austro-Hungarian Empire collapsed during the unexpectedly long drafting process, the treaties entered into with Germany became effective.[136] One of the treaties was the Consular Treaty between the German and Ottoman Empires of 1917, which included as an annex an Agreement on Succession.[137] The Treaty, which became effective on 10 July 1918 (Article 29), gave consuls of each State a reciprocal position, this unlike the system of capitulations where only German consuls enjoyed rights and privileges.[138] This reconstituted system between the States could not remain in force for a lengthy period of time as a result of the defeat of the Central Powers in the war. Nevertheless, the newly founded Turkish Republic, as the successor of the Ottoman Empire, was determined not to repeat the same mis-

---

134 Taner, *Kapitülasyonlar Nasıl İlga Edildi?* (1956) 12–13.

135 Ergin Nomer, 'Yabancıların "Ahkamı Şahsiyesi" (Statut Personnel) ve Terekesi ile İlgili İhtilaflarda Türk Kanunlar İhtilafı Sisteminin Gelişimi', *İstanbul Üniversitesi Hukuk Fakültesi'nin 50. Yıl Armağanı: Cumhuriyet Döneminde Hukuk* (Fakülteler Matbaası 1973) 500–501; cf. Denkschrift zu dem Konsularvertrag von 1917.

136 Taner, *Kapitülasyonlar Nasıl İlga Edildi?* (1956) 12–13. Regarding the Treaties with the Austro-Hungarian Empire, see also Yasemin Saner Gönen, 'Osmanlı Konsolosluk Sözleşmeleri – II' [1999] Toplumsal Tarih 36, 37.

It should be noted that the Treaty on the Conditions of Establishment of Austrian Nationals in Turkey and Turkish Nationals in Austria ('Übereinkommen zwischen der Republik Österreich und der Türkischen Republik über die Bedingungen der Niederlassung österreichischer Staatsangehöriger in der Türkei und türkischer Staatsangehöriger in Österreich') was signed between Austria and Turkey on 24 January 1924 in Istanbul. Art 10 of this Treaty provides that courts or authorities of the national State of the person in question should exclusively be competent for matters of personal status including matters of testamentary and intestate succession on movable property. For the text of the Treaty, see *T.B.M.M. Zabıt Ceridesi,* Cilt 8 & 8/1 [1924 – Devre: II İçtima Senesi: 2] (T.B.M.M. Matbaası 1975) 960–963 (Ratification law: *Resmi Gazete* of 24.5.1924, no 71)/BGBl. Nr. 392/1924 (NR: GP II 105 AB 131 S. 45).

As a result of the mutual agreement of both States, the Treaty has been out of force since 20 November 1959: <https://www.ris.bka.gv.at/GeltendeFassung.wxe?Abfrage=Bundesnormen&Gesetzesnummer=10000075> accessed 5 March 2021. See also VwGH 16.2.1982 – 81/07/0158.

137 *Düstur*, Tertip II, Cilt IX, 467–486/RGBl. 1918 I, 55.

138 Denkschrift zu dem Konsularvertrag von 1917 172.

takes and sought to establish relationships with other States through the help of international agreements based on the principle of the sovereign equality of States.[139] Once again, the realisation of this policy was possible with countries to which Turkey was politically close. Germany was obviously one of these States, and hence, a series of treaties were concluded with Germany, including the Consular Treaty of 1929, which was signed on 28 May 1929 in Ankara and which entered into force on 18 September 1931 in accordance with Article 30. This Treaty, like the former one, includes an Agreement on Succession as an annex to its Article 20.[140] The application of the Treaty experienced a short period of suspension, after Turkey declared war against Germany in 1945 during the Second World War;[141] however, it became effective again on 1 March 1952,[142] and it is still in force between both States.

II. Private International Law and Procedural Law in the Treaty: A General Overview

As the Treaty is actually a consular treaty, it regulates the privileges, immunities, and authorities of consuls, vice consuls, and consular officers as regards different topics. One of the legal matters specifically addressed in the Treaty is the estate administration process, because of the domestic interests involved in this area.[143] To this end, Article 20 of the Treaty, as the source of the Agreement on Succession, provides (in translation): 'As regards the estate of the nationals of one of the Contracting Parties found in the territory of other, Consuls shall have the powers mentioned in this Treaty.' The extent of these powers as well as the private international law regime and the procedural rules applicable to succession is regulated under the Agreement on Succession annexed to this Article.

The Contracting Parties sought to draft the Treaty's private international law provisions and procedural rules in such a way as to secure the interests of both sides. A balance should be achieved between the interests of the country

---

[139] See, for the preamble of the Treaty of 1929, <https://www.tbmm.gov.tr/tutanaklar/TUTANAK/TBMM/d03/c019/tbmm03019062ss0163.pdf> accessed 7 October 2020.

[140] An authoritative English translation of the Treaty does not exist. The English translations used in this book are taken from Dirk Looschelders, 'Treaty 19: Germany-Turkey' in Anatol Dutta and Wolfgang Wurmnest (eds), *European Private International Law and Member State Treaties with Third States – The Case of the European Succession Regulation* (Intersentia 2019) 427–429, sometimes as slightly modified by the author particularly because differences apply between the German and Turkish texts of the Treaty.

[141] See in this regard, Decision of the Grand National Assembly of Turkey ('TBMM Kararı') of 23.2.1945, *Resmi Gazete* of 24.2.1945, no 5940.

[142] See in this regard, Decree of the Cabinet of Ministers ('Bakanlar Kurulu Kararı') of 29.5.1952, no 3/14511, *Resmi Gazete* of 3.5.1952, no 8100.

[143] Denkschrift zu dem Konsularvertrag von 1929, Reichstagsdrucksache Nr. 1584, 4. Wahlperiode (1928) 29.

represented by the consul and the beneficiaries of succession from this State, having in mind the sovereign rights of the country where the estate is located and the creditors in this country.[144] At the time, however, Germany and Turkey had different approaches with respect to the law governing succession matters as concerning immovable assets. Whereas Germany applied the *lex patriae defuncti* to the succession as a whole without making a distinction between the movable and immovable parts of an estate (Article 24 of the EGBGB in 1896),[145] Turkey followed the principle of territoriality, i.e. the *lex rei sitae* principle, as regards any immovable property (Article 4 of the Temporary Act). With the only concession of the German side in the Treaty,[146] a dualist approach was adopted in the end. According to Article 20(14), the law applicable to succession issues concerning the movable estate is the national law of the deceased at the time of death (subparagraph (1)); succession with regards to immovable property, on the other hand, is governed by the law of the State where the property is located (subparagraph (2)). The determination of the nature of a property as movable or immovable is under the authority of the *lex rei sitae* (Article 20(12) (3)).

The scission of movable and immovable property was also accepted in the field of jurisdiction. Article 20(15) of the Treaty provides that all legal claims regarding any entitlement to the estate, the recovery of inheritance ('hereditatis petitio/vindicatio hereditatis' or 'miras sebebiyle istihkak davası'), dispositions of property upon death, and the reserved share should be subject to the jurisdiction of the courts of the national State of the deceased at the time of death as long as they are related to the movable estate, and to the courts of the Contracting State where the property is located as long as they are related to the immovable estate.[147] As to claims of creditors of the deceased against the estate, however, only the courts of the State where the estate is located should be competent (Article 20(8)).

---

[144] Denkschrift zu dem Konsularvertrag von 1917 179.

[145] RGBl. 1896 I, 604.

[146] H. Krüger, 'Studien über Probleme des türkischen Internationalen Erbrechts' (2006) 146 fn 80.

[147] It has been held that this list is exhaustive and that the provision covers only disputes between the heirs concerning their status as heirs and entitlement to the estate: BGH 21.10.2015 – IV ZR 68/15, FamRZ 2016, 122. For a similar opinion, see also Heinrich Dörner, in Jan Kropholler (ed), *Staudinger BGB – EGBGB/IPR Einführungsgesetz zum Bürgerlichen Gesetzbuche – Art 25, 26 EGBGB (Internationales Erbrecht)* (Sellier & de Gruyter 2007) EGBGB Vorb. zu Art 25 f para 181; Dirk Looschelders, 'The External Relations of Germany' in Anatol Dutta and Wolfgang Wurmnest (eds), *European Private International Law and Member State Treaties with Third States – The Case of the European Succession Regulation* (Intersentia 2019) 167; Dutta, *MüKoBGB* (2020) EuErbVO Art 75 para 27.

The provision does not cover succession claims against third parties: Dörner, *Staudinger BGB* (2007) EGBGB Vorb. zu Art 25 f para 181; Looschelders, 'The External Relations of Germany' (2019) 168; Dutta, *MüKoBGB* (2020) EuErbVO Art 75 para 27.

These two provisions of the Treaty, which reflect the legal and political circumstances of the early 20th century, are different from the current private international law of both sides, though the degree of difference is not the same for each. An examination of these rules is thus important for an understanding of Turkish-EU successions. Yet before discussing those rules, the personal and territorial scope of application of the Treaty will be analysed in the following part.

III. Personal and Territorial Scope of Application of the Treaty

1. Ratione personae

The Treaty is applicable to the succession of a national of one of the Contracting States who died in the territory of the other State, i.e. a German national who died in Turkey or a Turkish national who died in Germany (Article 20 of the Consular Treaty and paragraph (1)). Its rules will apply by analogy also to cases in which a national of one of the Contracting States has died in another (non-Contracting) country, i.e. a German or a Turkish national who died in France (Article 20(18)). This means that it is not important if the deceased has died in one of the Contracting States or in a third State. In the same vein, it is not important if he was a resident or domiciliary of one of the Contracting States or of a non-Contracting State.[148] Therefore, based on the sole condition of application, i.e. the nationality of the deceased, one can ask whether the Treaty governs succession issues for persons having dual or multiple citizenships. There may be two scenarios in this regard: a person may hold the nationalities of both States or he/she may be a citizen of one of the Contracting Parties and of another Country.

It is certainly the case that, as a side effect of growing transnational relations, a not insignificant number of people today possess dual or multiple nationalities. Yet such instances may trigger practical problems in the field of private international law by virtue of the fact that nationality is one of the most common connecting factors.[149] As the Treaty also adopts the *lex patriae* for succession matters concerning movable property and as it is silent on the

[148] Ullrich Spelsberg-Korspeter, in Walter Zimmermann (ed), *Praxiskommentar Erbrechtliche Nebengesetze* (2nd edn, zerb verlag 2017) Deutsch-türkisches Nachlassabkommen para 12; Looschelders, 'The External Relations of Germany' (2019) 157; Felix Odersky, in Rainer Hausmann and Felix Odersky (eds), *Internationales Privatrecht in der Notar- und Gestaltungspraxis* (4th edn, C.H. Beck 2021) § 15 para 352; Stephan Lorenz, in Wolfgang Hau and Roman Poseck (eds), *BeckOK BGB (Stand: 1.2.2022)* (61st edn, C.H. Beck 2022) EGBGB Art 25 aF para 6; cf. Kurt Lechner, in Reinhold Geimer, Rolf A. Schütze and Wolfgang Hau (eds), *Internationaler Rechtsverkehr in Zivil- und Handelssachen* (63rd edn, C.H. Beck 2021) EuErbVO Art 75 paras 42 ff. As regards the Turkish-Italian Treaty, see Franzina, 'The External Relations of Italy' (2019) 196.

situation of dual and/or multiple nationals, such a problem may also arise when applying the Treaty.[150]

In the first place, it has been argued that the Treaty was laid down with the underlying policy of protecting the citizens from each Contracting Party against discriminatory treatment in the other party's territory on account of their nationality. However, if the deceased holds the citizenship of both States, he/she would not need special treatment from the consuls as he/she is not a foreigner in either of the countries. Hence, the Treaty does not cover situations where the deceased is a Turkish-German dual national.[151] Such cases will be handled by the judges in accordance with the domestic conflict-of-laws rules and the procedural law of the States.[152] With this interpretation, there will therefore be much room for application of the Regulation in Germany,[153] and, *vice versa*, of the Turkish PILA in Turkey.

---

[149] İnci Ataman Figanmeşe, 'Çifte Vatandaşlık Halinde MÖHUK'un 4. Maddesinin b ve c Bentlerinin Uygulama Alanı' (2000) 19–20 MHB 95, 95–96; Bilgin Tiryakioğlu, 'Multiple Citizenship and its Consequences in Turkish Law' (2006) 3 Ankara L Rev 1, 13.

[150] Zekiye Kaya, 'Der Nachlass eines deutsch-türkischen Doppelstaaters' [2015] ZEV 208, 209.

[151] Klaus Schurig, in Gerhard Kegel (ed), *Soergel BGB*, vol 10 (Einführungsgesetz) (12th edn, Kohlhammer 1996) EGBGB Art 25 para 108; H. Krüger, 'Studien über Probleme des türkischen Internationalen Erbrechts' (2006) 150 ff; Bauer, [2007] FamRZ 1250, 1255; Christian Friedrich Majer, 'Das deutsch-türkische Nachlassabkommen: ein Anachronismus' [2012] ZEV 182, 183–184; Spelsberg-Korspeter, (2017) Deutsch-türkisches Nachlassabkommen para 11; Looschelders, 'The External Relations of Germany' (2019) 158–159; Dutta, *MüKoBGB* (2020) EuErbVO Art 75 para 20; Frank Bauer and Rembert Süß, in Anatol Dutta and Johannes Weber (eds), *Internationales Erbrecht* (2nd edn, C.H. Beck 2021) EuErbVO Art 75 Anhang II-deutsch-türkisches NA para 3.

See also Franzina, 'The External Relations of Italy' (2019) 194–195 (in the context of the Turkish-Italian Consular Treaty of 1929).

The *lex rei sitae* rule governing immovables under Article 20(14) (2) of the Treaty would, of course, be applicable for Turkish-German dual nationals: Günther Schotten and Cornelia Schmellenkamp, *Das Internationale Privatrecht in der notariellen Praxis* (2nd edn, C.H. Beck 2007) para 264; Andreas Köhler, in Ludwig Kroiß, Claus-Henrik Horn and Dennis Solomon (eds), *NK/Nachfolgerecht: Erbrechtliche Spezialgesetze* (2nd edn, Nomos 2019) EuErbVO Vorb. Art 20–38: Einleitung IPR para 52; cf. Heinrich Dörner, 'Das deutsch-türkische Nachlaßabkommen' [1996] ZEV 90, 91; Dörner, *Staudinger BGB* (2007) EGBGB Vorb. zu Art 25 f para 173; contra Majer, [2012] ZEV 182, 183; Spelsberg-Korspeter, (2017) Deutsch-türkisches Nachlassabkommen para 11; Looschelders, 'The External Relations of Germany' (2019) 158.

[152] Feriha Bilge Tanrıbilir, *Kanuni Mirasçılıktan Doğan Kanunlar İhtilafı* (Gazi Üniversitesi İletişim Fakültesi Basımevi 2000) 193; H. Krüger, 'Studien über Probleme des türkischen Internationalen Erbrechts' (2006) 151.

[153] Looschelders, 'The External Relations of Germany' (2019) 158; cf. Martin Gebauer, 'Das deutsch-türkische Nachlassabkommen im Sog des Europäischen Kollisionsrechts' [2018] IPRax 345, 349–350.

Another view, by contrast, asserts that the Contracting States' domestic conflict-of-laws rules – namely, Article 5(1) EGBGB and Article 4(b) and (c) of the Turkish PILA – should apply with respect to persons having more than one nationality such that problems are solved within the scope of the Treaty.[154] These provisions are drafted in a similar manner and both make a distinction between a situation where one of the persons in question is a citizen of the forum State and a situation where the individual does not hold the nationality of the forum State. In the first scenario, the nationality of the forum State would prevail regardless of the other nationalities he/she holds (Article 4(b) of Turkish PILA and Article 5(1) EGBGB). When this is not the case, however, the law of the State which the person has the closest connection to should be applied (Article 4(c) of the Turkish PILA, Article 5(1) EGBGB). This means that the Treaty would not be applicable for individuals who hold the nationality of the forum State but could be applicable to persons holding only the nationality of one of the Contracting States (in addition to that of another State or States) if this nationality is the effective one.

Some scholars, on the other hand, reject the application of domestic rules in the context of international conventions and, hence, maintain that only the effective nationality test – without differentiating the cases whether one of the nationalities of the deceased is of that of forum or not – could provide guidance for such situations.[155] Such a solution, in their opinion, seems to be more consistent with the desired decisional harmony within the Treaty[156] and also

---

[154] Hans-Peter Schömmer and Nebi Kesen, *Internationales Erbrecht Türkei* (C.H. Beck 2004) 242; Schotten and Schmellenkamp, *Das Internationale Privatrecht in der notariellen Praxis* (2007) para 264; Nicole Emmerling de Oliveira and Marc Heggen, 'Türkische Mandanten im Notariat' [2011] Notar 39, 44; Lorenz, *BeckOK BGB* (2022) EGBGB Art 25 aF para 6; cf. Looschelders, 'The External Relations of Germany' (2019) 159; Dutta, *MüKoBGB* (2020) EuErbVO Art 75 para 20; contra Bauer and Süß, *Dutta/Weber* (2021) EuErbVO Art 75 Anhang II-deutsch-türkisches NA para 3. See also AG Bad Homburg 13.7.1977 – 4 VI 517/76, IPRspr 1977 Nr. 103, 292.

[155] Dörner, [1996] ZEV 90, 92; Johannes Fetsch, 'Auslandsvermögen im Internationalen Erbrecht – Testamente und Erbverträge, Erbschein und Ausschlagung bei Auslandsvermögen –' [2006] RNotZ 77, 115; contra Franzina, 'The External Relations of Italy' (2019) 195 and fn 66 (as regards to the Turkish-Italian Treaty of 1929). Unlike the use of national rules, there is a need for a treaty-autonomous solution: Dörner, [1996] ZEV 90, 92. For general information on treaty-autonomous gap filling, see Jan Kropholler, *Internationales Einheitsrecht* (Mohr Siebeck 1975) 292ff.

[156] Dörner, [1996] ZEV 90, 92; Fetsch, [2006] RNotZ 77, 115; cf. H. Krüger, 'Studien über Probleme des türkischen Internationalen Erbrechts' (2006) 151.

See also Heinz-Peter Mansel, *Personalstatut, Staatsangehörigkeit und Effektivität* (C.H. Beck 1988) paras 480ff; Hans Jürgen Sonnenberger, 'Anerkennung der Staatsangehörigkeit und effektive Staatsangehörigkeit natürlicher Personen im Völkerrecht und im internationalen Privatrecht' (1988) 29 BerGesVR 9, 21–22; Wolfgang Meyer-Sparenberg, *Staatsvertragliche Kollisionsnormen* (Duncker & Humblot 1990) 135ff; Ataman Figanmeşe, (2000) 19–20 MHB 95, 101–102.

with the rules regarding reciprocal recognition of judgments as well as certificates of succession.[157]

Whereas the effective nationality test is often used in public international law for the purposes of diplomatic protection,[158] it also has a long history in the private international law codes of many States.[159] This is because when a conflict rule adopts citizenship as a connecting factor and the person in question holds the citizenship of different States, there is a need to treat this person as if he/she had only one nationality in order to determine the governing law.[160] To this end, the effective nationality test offers a practical solution[161] and serves the interest of the parties.[162] It seems that the use of effective nationality test would be the best solution also within the context of the Treaty to ensure harmonious application in both Contracting States.[163]

Yet from the Turkish perspective, its applicability to dual and multiple nationals who are also citizens of Turkey does not appear to be likely. It is maintained that Turkish nationals should be subject to Turkish law based on the sovereign rights of the State,[164] even in the absence of an explicit provision providing that the nationality of the forum State will prevail.[165] Turkish nationality, therefore, should always prevail for individuals having dual/multiple nationality irrespective of how effective the bond with the other State or States

[157] Fetsch, [2006] RNotZ 77, 115.

[158] See particularly the landmark case of Nottebohm (Liechtenstein v. Guatemala) [1955] ICJ Reports 1955 4.

[159] Cf. Franzina, 'The External Relations of Italy' (2019) 195 fn 66.

[160] Berk Demirkol, 'Uluslararası Hukukta Dikkate Alınan Vatandaşlık: Gerçek Kişilerde "Etkin Vatandaşlık" Sorunsalı' [2015] GSÜHFD 159, 183–184.

[161] Cf. Demirkol, [2015] GSÜHFD 159, 183.

[162] See, in this regard, Gülüm Bayraktaroğlu Özçelik, 'Kanunlar İhtilafı Hukukunda Olumlu Vatandaşlık İhtilaflarının Çözümü ve MÖHUK m. 4(1)(b) ve (c) Hükümlerinin Değerlendirilmesi' (2015) 19 GÜHFD 111, 125–126; Şanlı, Esen and Ataman Figanmeşe, *Milletlerarası Özel Hukuk* (2021) 37 fn 66; Doğan, *Milletlerarası Özel Hukuk* (2022) 215–216; cf. Demirkol, [2015] GSÜHFD 159, 184.

[163] Ataman Figanmeşe, (2000) 19–20 MHB 95, 105; Martin Gebauer, 'Erbrechtliche Fragen im deutsch-türkischen Rechtsverkehr' (2018) 27 Informationsbrief der DTJV 18, 23; cf. Güneş, 'The Relations of Turkey with EU Member States' (2019) 296–297. There is no doubt that one of the purposes of the Treaty is to ensure that both States apply the same law to succession issues: Hanno Naumann, 'Grundzüge des neuen türkischen Ehegüter- und Erbrechts' [2003] RNotZ 344, 345.

[164] Erdoğan Göğer, 'Çifte Vatandaşlık' (1995) 44 AÜHFD 127, 163; Gülin Güngör, *Tâbiiyet Hukuku: Gerçek Kişiler – Tüzel Kişiler – Şeyler* (9th edn, Yetkin 2021) 30; Ergin Nomer, *Türk Vatandaşlık Hukuku* (29th edn, Filiz Kitabevi 2021) 37 ff. For similar remarks at the time of the Temporary Act, see also O. F. Berki, *Miras* (1960) 20; V. R. Seviğ, *Mirasla İlgili Devletler Hususi Hukuku Kaideleri* (1963) 91.

[165] Güngör, *Tâbiiyet Hukuku* (2021) 30.

may be.[166] The result would be the same also within the context of the Treaty, and, hence, the Treaty would not be applicable for dual and/or multiple nationals holding the citizenship of Turkey, e.g. for a Turkish-German national. It is believed that this interpretation would be consistent with the *ratio legis* of the Treaty, i.e. preventing the discriminatory treatment of nationals of Contracting States in each other's territories. When the deceased is a national of the forum State, it is hard to speak about such a risk of discrimination.[167]

It can be argued that the Treaty should be applied to persons who have dual or multiple nationalities, one of which is that of a Contracting State but which is not the State of the forum (e.g. the succession case of a German-Swiss national who died in Turkey), regardless of the nature of the link with the Contracting State on the grounds that the Treaty is in fact a consular treaty giving special protection to nationals of both States and any contrary practice could amount to the violation of promises made to the opposing Treaty party.[168] Nevertheless, it is believed that when the deceased has no genuine link with the Contracting State in question, there would be no need for such a special protection and, hence, for a departure from the national rules in favour of rather exceptional conflict-of-laws and procedural rules. The application of the Treaty for such persons, therefore, remains possible only through the effective nationality test.[169]

2. *Ratione loci*

The language used in different provisions of the Treaty lacks the required degree of clarity and creates doubts as to the territorial scope of application of the Treaty. The main concern here is whether the Treaty solely covers assets which are located in Contracting States or whether it may also become applicable for assets located outside these States.

Article 20(14) (2) of the Treaty prescribes that succession matters regarding immovable property should be settled according to the law of the 'State' where this property is situated, and in the same way as if the deceased had been a national of the forum State. The rather unclear terminology in this provision, especially the reference to the 'State' without an identifier – i.e. the 'Contracting' State – resulted in some commentators concluding that the

---

[166] Ergin Nomer, 'Türk Devletler Özel Hukukunda Çifte Vatandaşlık' (1994) 14 MHB 55, 58. This principle is applied under the Turkish PILA without any exceptions. For a brief explanation in this regard, see Güneş, 'The Relations of Turkey with EU Member States' (2019) 297 fn 89. It is, however, argued that international treaties which Turkey is a party may be an exception to the application of this, see Gülin Güngör, *Türk Milletlerarası Özel Hukuku* (2nd edn, Yetkin 2021) 57.

[167] Güneş, 'The Relations of Turkey with EU Member States' (2019) 297.

[168] Franzina, 'The External Relations of Italy' (2019) 195 fn 66 (in the context of the Turkish-Italian Treaty of 1929); cf. Bauer and Süß, *Dutta/Weber* (2021) EuErbVO Art 75 Anhang II-deutsch-türkisches NA para 3.

[169] Güneş, 'The Relations of Turkey with EU Member States' (2019) 297.

Treaty is also applicable to estates located outside the territories of the Contracting States.[170] Whilst Article 20(1) of the Treaty requires consular staff and local authorities to inform each other 'in the event of the death of a national of one Contracting State in the territory of the other', and hence clarifies that the Treaty is applicable for persons who died in one of the Contracting States. Article 20(18) expands its scope of application so as to include instances where the death occurs in a third State. This, in the view of these same commentators, also seems to support an extensive interpretation.[171] The proponents of this view contend that such an interpretation would limit the scission of an estate to a minimum and hence is more in line with the aim of the Regulation to treat the succession as a unity.[172]

Such an interpretation, however, would run counter to the bilateral and consular nature of the Treaty. With this 'bilateral' Treaty, Germany and Turkey provide a different and unique regime that is to be applicable in a succession case involving the two Contracting States. Assets located elsewhere than these two States and the legal issues attached to them are of no interest to the contracting parties.[173] As a 'consular' Treaty vesting consular staff with broad powers over any portion of the deceased's estate located in the Contracting States, it would be illogical to embrace a broad interpretation favouring application of the Treaty also for estate items located in third States as neither Germany nor Turkey would have the same powers there.[174] For these reasons, a restrictive interpretation should be adopted whereby the Treaty covers only assets located in the Contracting States.[175] The Treaty should not, however, also find application for property

---

[170] H. Krüger, 'Studien über Probleme des türkischen Internationalen Erbrechts' (2006) 150; Peter Mankowski, 'Gelten die bilateralen Staatsverträge der Bundesrepublik Deutschland im Internationalen Erbrecht nach dem Wirksamwerden der EuErbVO weiter?' [2013] ZEV 529, 530; Dutta, *MüKoBGB* (2020) EuErbVO Art 75 para 21; cf. Fetsch, [2006] RNotZ 77, 114; Bauer and Süß, *Dutta/Weber* (2021) EuErbVO Art 75 Anhang II-deutsch-türkisches NA para 4.

[171] Bauer and Süß, *Dutta/Weber* (2021) EuErbVO Art 75 Anhang II-deutsch-türkisches NA para 4.

[172] Dutta, *MüKoBGB* (2020) EuErbVO Art 75 para 21. See, however, Rembert Süß, 'Erste Konsequenzen aus der Mahnkopf-Entscheidung des EuGH – und Rechtsermittlung zweiter Klasse für türkische Witwen? Anmerkungen zur Entscheidung des OLG Hamm vom 21. März 2019' [2019] ZErb 249, 249 fn 7.

[173] Majer, [2012] ZEV 182, 184; Christian Hertel, in Thomas Rauscher (ed), *EuZPR/EuIPR*, vol V (4th edn, Otto Schmidt 2016) EuErbVO Art 75 para 13.

[174] Rembert Süß, 'Der Vorbehalt zugunsten bilateraler Abkommen mit Drittstaaten' in Anatol Dutta and Sebastian Herrler (eds), *Die Europäische Erbrechtsverordnung, 20 Jahre DNotI 1993–2013* (C.H. Beck 2014) 187–188; Linus Konvalin, *Das Europäische Nachlasszeugnis ohne europäischen Entscheidungseinklang* (Wolfgang Metzner Verlag 2018) 76; contra Dutta, *MüKoBGB* (2020) EuErbVO Art 75 para 21.

[175] Dörner, [1996] ZEV 90, 94; Dörner, *Staudinger BGB* (2007) EGBGB Vorb. zu Art 25 f paras 163 and 171; Schotten and Schmellenkamp, *Das Internationale Privatrecht*

of the deceased located in his home State since that would – again – not be in line with the logic behind a bilateral consular treaty.[176]

A restrictive interpretation has also the advantage of creating more room for the applicability of the Turkish PILA and the Regulation. This can be illustrated with the help of a short example. Imagine, for example, a Turkish guest worker who had been living with his family in Germany for many years; with his death, movable as well as immovable assets were left in Turkey, Germany, and France.

In this case, if a restrictive interpretation were followed, the movable assets of the deceased in Germany would be governed by Turkish law as the national law of the deceased and immovable assets of the deceased in Germany would be governed by German law (Article 20(14) of the Treaty). For the assets in Turkey and in France, on the other hand, the Turkish PILA or the Regulation would become applicable. When the matter is pending before Turkish courts, Turkish law will eventually govern also those assets pursuant to Article 20(1) of the Turkish PILA, as the national law of the deceased. From the Regulation's perspective, however, succession to assets in France and Turkey will be subject to German law under Article 21(1) of the Regulation. Hence, the departure from the Turkish PILA and from the Regulation is limited to a minimum. This is more favourable from the Turkish perspective and probably from the European perspective as well.

---

in der notariellen Praxis (2007) para 264; Majer, [2012] ZEV 182, 184; Süß, 'Der Vorbehalt zugunsten bilateraler Abkommen mit Drittstaaten' (2014) 187ff; Kurt Lechner, 'EU Regulation 650/2012 on successions and the creation of a European Certificate of Succession' in European Parliament, Directorate General for Internal Policies, Policy Department C: Citizens' Rights and Constitutional Affairs – Legal Affairs (ed), *Cross-border activities in the EU Making life easier for citizens – Workshop for the JURI Committee – PE 510.003* (2015) 144 <http://www.europarl.europa.eu/RegData/etudes/STUD/2015/510003/IPOL_STU(2015)510003_EN.pdf> accessed 17 January 2017; DNotI, 'Deutsch-türkisches Nachlassabkommen; EUErbVO, Türkei: Gesetzliche Erbfolge nach einem türkischen Staatsangehörigen' [2016] DNotI-Report 103, 104; Kurt Lechner, 'Die Europäische Erbrechtsverordnung' [2016] DNotZ-Sonderheft 102, 113; Spelsberg-Korspeter, (2017) Deutsch-türkisches Nachlassabkommen para 8; Gebauer, [2018] IPRax 345, 347; Konvalin, *Das Europäische Nachlasszeugnis* (2018) 78–79; Güneş, 'The Relations of Turkey with EU Member States' (2019) 294–295; Köhler, *NK/Nachfolgerecht* (2019) EuErbVO Vorb. Art 20–38: Einleitung IPR para 52; Looschelders, 'The External Relations of Germany' (2019) 157–158; Süß, [2019] ZErb 249, 249; Lorenz, *BeckOK BGB* (2022) EGBGB Art 25 aF para 6. See also V. R. Seviğ, *Ahkâmı Şahsiye Davaları – Yetki* (1964) 15–16. For a similar interpretation with respect to the Turkish-Italian Treaty of 1929, which has parallel rules and wording, see Franzina, 'The External Relations of Italy' (2019) 194.

[176] Emmerling de Oliveira and Heggen, [2011] Notar 39, 44; Süß, 'Der Vorbehalt zugunsten bilateraler Abkommen mit Drittstaaten' (2014) 187–188; Spelsberg-Korspeter, (2017) Deutsch-türkisches Nachlassabkommen para 8; Looschelders, 'The External Relations of Germany' (2019) 157–158.

E. Concluding Remarks as to General Overview and Background

Turkish-EU successions are likely to have significant practical relevance for the European side due to the large migrant Turkish community in the Member States of the Union. Although that it is a third State from the Regulation's perspective, the rules of the Turkish PILA may also become relevant in such cases. Another dimension of Turkish-EU successions are cases in which the bilateral Treaty between Germany with Turkey finds application, since the European legislature left this Treaty, together with other such treaties involving Member States, intact under Article 75 of the Regulation with deference to the international commitments of its Member States made prior to the forming of the European Union. The Turkish-German Treaty is undoubtedly the most significant of these treaties for Turkish-EU successions given that Germany hosts the majority of the Turkish community within the EU. As these cases will be governed by the Treaty, the harmonised system of the Regulation is seriously undermined.

For Turkey, the practical relevance of the Regulation and the Treaty is not comparable to its European counterpart. The first reason for this is that the number of EU citizens – and particularly German citizens – in Turkey is not as high as the Turkish nationals in the EU. In addition, as *renvoi* is not applicable in succession matters, the rules of the Regulation will not become directly applicable in Turkey. The Treaty, on the other hand, should normally find application in Turkey, even if it is in a small number of cases. However, the Turkish presence in the Member States – and especially in Germany – makes the rules of the Regulation and the Treaty worthy of consideration for Turkish scholars and legal practitioners working in this area. Furthermore, even though it could be seen as a 'never ending story', Turkey's candidate status in the European Union means that the Regulation, as with all other European private international and procedural law instruments, may at least in some aspects serve as a model for future legal reform, one not specifically limited to the field of succession but rather related to the reform of some general parts which could also cover succession matters in Turkey. The Treaty would, of course, still be applicable between Turkey and Germany, but in the event of such reform the gap between the Treaty and the Turkish PILA would be extended and take on a dimension similar to the gap presently existing between the Treaty and the Regulation.

The practical and academic relevance of Turkish-EU successions invites an inquiry into the policy considerations that shaped the pertinent rules of each legal text. The above analysis obviously reveals that each legal text has been drafted in the light of different concerns and the applicable historical background. As a further step towards full Europeanisation, the Regulation accomplishes the long-awaited unification of the private international law and procedural rules of Member States in the field of succession. With regards to European policy considerations, the mechanism of the Regulation is based on four pillars: the unitary approach in the field of succession, habitual residence as the connecting factor at the centre of the system, a parallelism of forum and *ius*, and party autonomy. By contrast, for a very long time Turkey adhered in its domestic conflict-of-laws rules to a scissionist and traditional approach based on nationality, this no doubt being attributable to its traumatic historical experience and the lessons learned especially in the capitulary era, but also in its aftermath. The evolving understanding gained throughout the years had an important impact when drafting the current rules on jurisdiction and the applicable law. Nevertheless, the legislature was still guided by the important role of realty for the State and by the idea that succession matters should be governed by the national law of the deceased. The trauma encountered by Turkey, at the time, in fact the Ottoman Empire, during the capitulary regime is also a reason behind the conclusion of the Treaty with Germany. The understanding of cross-border succession cases that was prevalent in those times resulted in a strong dualist approach, not only in the Treaty's conflict-of-laws rules but also in the procedural rules. This remains unchanged even today, in the different circumstances of the modern world, and it is manifested in the different legal approaches of both sides. The historical setting behind the Treaty also requires us to conclude that the Treaty has a limited scope of application. It applies only to the property of a Turkish deceased located in Germany or, *vice versa*, the property of a German deceased located in Turkey. Succession matters concerning the properties located in his home State or in any other State will not be covered by the Treaty. Further, the Treaty does not find application if the deceased holds the nationalities of both Contracting States, i.e. to Turkish-German nationals.

As they are all driven by different policies, it is likely that the rules of these three legal instruments may result in conflict-of-laws issues as well as procedural problems in Turkish-EU successions. It is thus appropriate that each of these rules be analysed in turn from a comparative perspective, an examination that occurs in the following chapters.

Chapter 2

Conflict of Laws in Turkish-EU Successions

Haruki Murakami, a famous author, wrote in one of his novels that '[d]eath exists, not as the opposite but as a part of life'.[1] As 'a part of life', we indeed think about the death of our own and beloved ones from time to time. Devolution of property upon a death admittedly may not often play a role in this unpleasant thought. Nonetheless, in the same way that death is 'a part of life', how properties will devolve is one of those things which should be dealt with in the event of a death. Particularly when there are cross-border elements involved, this process will be dependent on the law applicable to succession. Even though it would be desirable to have a single answer to the question of which law is applicable regardless of the concerned State where the case is pending, such a worldwide unification of the private international law on succession still seems to be 'an ideal which is very far from being realised',[2] if, in particular, previous attempts of the Hague Conference on the matter are considered.[3] Every system has its own dynamics and rules when dealing with succession matters, thereby creating divergence in the outcomes reached. The same, as briefly indicated in the previous chapter, also applies in the Turkish European context.

The Regulation lays down conflict rules, as the core of its system,[4] to be applicable in succession matters throughout the Union under Articles 20–38. The main purpose of the European legislature with these rules is obviously to ensure a decisional harmony on matters of succession within the European Union and to provide legal certainty for its citizens – be they deceased, beneficiaries, creditors or other third parties – over the law governing the succession irrespective of the forum.[5] In addition, uniform conflict rules are im-

---

1 Haruki Murakami, *Norwegian Wood* (English translation Jay Rubin, The Harvill Press 2001) 31.

2 William E. Beckett, 'The Question of Classification (Qualification) in Private International Law' (1934) 15 BYIL 46, 47.

3 See, for details, Dutta, *MüKoBGB* (2020) EuErbVO Vorb. Art 1 paras 3 ff.

4 Dutta, *MüKoBGB* (2020) EuErbVO Vorb. Art 20 para 1.

5 Recital 37 of the Regulation (see esp. the 1st sentence). See also Andrea Bonomi, in Andrea Bonomi and Patrick Wautelet (eds), *Le droit européen des successions-Commentaire du Règlement n°650/2012 du 4 juillet 2012* (2nd edn, Bruylant 2016) Introduction au Chapitre III para 1; Dutta, *MüKoBGB* (2020) EuErbVO Vorb. Art 20 para 2.

portant to avoid any contradictions between the Member States as regards decisions,[6] thereby creating a significant ground for a well-functioning recognition and enforcement system of decisions and hereditary titles as well as other related documents.[7] Based on these objectives and the two cardinal principles, i.e. *Gleichlauf* and the unity of succession, Article 21 of the Regulation prescribes that the law applicable to succession as a whole is, in principle, the law of the State where the deceased has his habitual residence at the time of death. The deceased has also a right to choose his national law to govern the succession as a whole under Article 22. The principle of the unity of succession, which underlies the machinery of the Regulation, is reiterated in these provisions, but it is derogated from in Articles 24–27 on the admissibility and validity of testamentary dispositions for the sake of a well-established principle in the field of testamentary dispositions, namely the principle of *favor testamenti*.[8] The Regulation also provides rules on overriding mandatory law (Article 30), estates without a claimant (Article 33), *renvoi* (Article 34) and public policy (Article 35), all of which may also result in scenarios where a scission occurs.[9]

From the Turkish perspective as a third State, an important feature of the conflict rules of the Regulation is the *loi uniforme* nature of these rules as provided under Article 20.[10] This means that the law specified in the Regulation to govern the succession will be applied in the Member States' courts irrespective of its being Member State law or third State law. This, at the same time, clarifies that the Regulation also covers succession cases related to third States, and Member State courts are not allowed to refer to their domestic conflict rules in such cases; rather, they are bound by the rules of the Regulation.[11] This undoubtedly contributes to the aimed uniform application of the Regulation by

---

[6] Recital 37 of the Regulation (see esp. the 2nd sentence).

[7] Dutta, *MüKoBGB* (2020) EuErbVO Vorb. Art 20 para 2; cf. Bonomi, *Bonomi/Wautelet* (2016) Introduction au Chapitre III para 1.

[8] Bonomi, *Bonomi/Wautelet* (2016) Introduction au Chapitre III para 2. The principle of *favor testamenti* attempts to avoid situations where a testamentary disposition is declared invalid with respect to form so as to give effect to the last wishes of the testator: Donald G. Casswell, 'The Conflict of Laws Rules Governing the Formal Validity of Wills: Past Developments and Suggested Reform' (1977) 15 Osgoode Hall LJ 165, 174; Haopei Li, 'Some Recent Developments in the Conflict of Laws of Succession' (1990) 224 RdC 9, 109.

[9] Dutta, *MüKoBGB* (2020) EuErbVO Vorb. Art 20 paras 7–8.

[10] This universal approach is in fact not new for private international law instruments. Similar rules could also be found in Hague conventions and in European private international law instruments on the issue of the applicable law. See, for example, Art 6 of the Hague Form Convention (Convention of 5 October 1961 on the Conflicts of Laws Relating to the Form of Testamentary Dispositions); Art 2 of the Rome I Regulation and Art 3 of the Rome II Regulation.

[11] Frank Bauer and Matteo Fornasier, in Anatol Dutta and Johannes Weber (eds), *Internationales Erbrecht* (2nd edn, C.H. Beck 2021) EuErbVO Art 20 paras 1–2.

the Member State courts, as they are consequently not under the burdensome duty of differentiating between 'European' and 'non-European' cases and, hence, applying two different set of rules.[12] Furthermore, it reinforces once again the object of legal certainty and unity. Such an approach may also be seen as advantageous from a third State perspective at first glance, since the laws of Member States and third States seem to be equally treated at the Union level. Nevertheless, the reality is that the Regulation, as with other European private international law instruments, aims to provide uniformity, albeit only within the Union and giving little regard to the outside world.[13] When this is the case, it is highly likely that problems arising as a result of the differences in approach would occur with the outer world even to the extent that would not have been the case between some Member States and third States before the adoption of the Regulation. This is to say that there were instances before the adoption of the Regulation where a third State and a Member State had adopted the same connecting factors with respect to the law applicable to succession, i.e. the nationality or the last domicile of the deceased, or where they had the same system, be it monist or dualist.

This was the case, for example, between Austria[14] and Turkey[15] for movables, since both States applied, in principle, the law of nationality of the deceased; it was also true as between Belgium[16] and Turkey[17] for immovables located in Tur-

[12] Alfonso-Luis Calvo Caravaca, in Alfonso-Luis Calvo Caravaca, Angelo Davì and Heinz-Peter Mansel (eds), *The EU Succession Regulation – A Commentary* (Cambridge University Press 2016) ESR Art 20 para 9.

[13] Etienne Pataut, 'International Jurisdiction and Third States: A View from the EC in Family Matters' in Alberto Malatesta, Stefania Bariatti and Fausto Pocar (eds), *The External Dimension of EC Private International Law in Family and Succession Matters* (CEDAM 2008) 123.

[14] Bundesgesetz vom 15. Juni 1978 über das internationale Privatrecht (IPR-Gesetz) StF: BGBl. Nr. 304/1978 (NR: GP XIV RV 784 AB 945 S. 96. BR: AB 1841 S. 377) § 28. Consistent with the rules of the Regulation, this paragraph, together with some other paragraphs, was repealed in 2015. See BGBl. I Nr. 87/2015 (NR: GP XXV RV 688 AB 718 S. 83. BR: AB 9419 S. 844).

[15] The same example could also be formulated for Albania instead of Turkey. See Article 33 of the Albanian Private International Law Act – No 10 428, Official Gazette of Albania of 17.6.2011 No 82. For a general introduction on the law, see, Aida Gugu Bushati, 'The Albanian Private International Law of 2011' (2013–2014) XV YbPIL 509.

[16] See Art 78 of Loi portant le Code de droit international privé, Loi du 16 juillet 2004, MB 27 juillet 2004, 5734. Consistent with the rules of the Regulation, this provision, together with other relevant articles, was modified in 2017. See, Loi portant simplification, harmonisation, informatisation et modernisation de dispositions de droit civil et de procédure civile ainsi que du notariat, et portant diverses mesures en matière de justice, MB 27 julliet 2017, 75168.

[17] This was also the case between Belgium and England as regards immovables, as they both had adopted the dualist approach and applied the *lex situs* for succession matters on

key given that both applied Turkish law as the law of *situs*. Under such circumstances, decisions rendered from the courts could have been, at least to a certain degree, in conformity with each other. The Regulation, therefore, does not only disregard the situation with third States but also affects the possible harmony of decisions or, in general, outcomes which could have been established between EU and non-EU States prior to the entry into force of the Regulation.[18]

The difference between the Regulation and the Turkish PILA is obvious upon examination of Article 20 of the Turkish PILA, which consists of five paragraphs. The Article provides under paragraph (1) that matters of succession are to be governed by the national law of the deceased. Immovable assets located in Turkey, however, are to be governed by Turkish law. Exceptions to this main rule are laid down under the following paragraphs for certain specific matters of succession (paragraph (2)), for an estate located in Turkey without a claimant (paragraph (3)), and for testamentary dispositions, particularly as to their formal validity (paragraph (4)) and the capacity to make such dispositions (paragraph (5)).

The rules of both systems should also be compared with the provisions of the Treaty. The Treaty adopts the nationality connecting factor for movable property and the *situs* connecting factor for immovable property in determining the law applicable for issues of succession (Article 20(14)). The Treaty also regulates the law applicable to the formal validity of dispositions of property upon death under Article 20(16), which is applicable for both movable and immovable property.[19] In accord with the circumstances of the time it was concluded, a *professio iuris* is not allowed under the Treaty.[20] As it is a bilateral treaty, the law applicable to succession, for both testamentary and intestate succession, will ultimately be the substantive law of the States. In other words, *renvoi* is not allowed under the Treaty.[21] Likewise, there is no provision on the *ordre public* since mutual trust is the basis for concluding such a bilateral treaty.[22]

---

immovables. For England, see Lawrence Collins (ed), *Dicey, Morris & Collins the Conflict of Laws*, vol 2 (15th edn, Sweet & Maxwell 2012) Rule 134 and 135.

[18] Lein, 'Die Erbrechtsverordnung aus Sicht der Drittstaaten' (2014) 200.

[19] Nomer, 'Yabancıların "Ahkamı Şahsiyesi"' (1973) 525.

[20] H. Krüger, 'Studien über Probleme des türkischen Internationalen Erbrechts' (2006) 148.

[21] Naumann, [2003] RNotZ 344, 345; H. Krüger, 'Studien über Probleme des türkischen Internationalen Erbrechts' (2006) 148; Emmerling de Oliveira and Heggen, [2011] Notar 39, 44; Ludwig Kroiß, in Thomas Heidel and others (eds), *NK-BGB/EGBGB*, vol 1 (3rd edn, Nomos 2016) EGBGB Art 25 para 8; Bauer and Süß, *Dutta/Weber* (2021) EuErbVO Art 75 Anhang II: deutsch-türkisches NA para 16; Lorenz, *BeckOK BGB* (2022) EGBGB Art 25 aF para 6.

[22] H. Krüger, 'Studien über Probleme des türkischen Internationalen Erbrechts' (2006) 148. However, see below, pp 166–169.

It is obvious from this general outline that divergences apply between these three bodies of law with respect to the law governing succession issues. This is unsurprising given that each source was concluded at a different period of time in different geographical settings, and with the political and legal sentiments of the time and place in which they were drafted. Complete harmony between them, therefore, does not seem to be realistic in the near future. Regardless, the tension between them may cause numerous problems in cross-border cases, particularly when the assets belonging to an estate are located in different States. In the first place, conflicting decisions may arise, and this would impair the desired decisional harmony for international succession cases. Furthermore, conflicting decisions would also mean that both the deceased and the beneficiaries would be affected. From the deceased's perspective, different conflict rules – particularly when the estate is comprised of assets located in different States and when there is no pre-arranged estate planning – may result in undesirable and problematic consequences for the different parts of the estate. The deceased may of course be well prepared for such circumstances and wish to perfect estate planning prior to his death in order to avoid the risk that his estate is governed by an unforeseeable legal system. This, however, is not an easy task when differences apply between the systems.[23] Furthermore, the deceased's potential beneficiaries would also be affected. For them, different applicable laws would be decisive for their claim and, if they are entitled, for the enforcement of their succession rights. It is, for example, highly likely that a beneficiary would be entitled to receive a different succession share in different States.[24] Thus, the main differences between the three bodies of law should be examined in detail, as is undertaken below.

A. Monist vs. Dualist Approach

It is well known that there is an old but still unsettled dichotomy pertaining to the monist or dualist approaches in the conflict of laws in matters of succession. This duality also existed within the European Union before the Regulation's entry into force. Some Member States[25] had adopted the principle of unity, thereby treating movable and immovable property belonging to the

[23] Detlev J. Piltz, in Hans Flick and Detlev J. Piltz (eds), *Der internationale Erbfall: Erbrecht, Internationales Privatrecht, Erbschaftssteuerrecht* (2nd edn, C.H. Beck 2008) paras 60ff.

[24] See, from the European perspective, Dutta, *MüKoBGB* (2020) EuErbVO Vorb. Art 1 para 16.

[25] See the Member States referred in Mireia Artigot i Golobardes, 'Will Regulation 650/2012 Simplify Cross-Border Successions in Europe?' (2015) 4 EPLJ 22, 30–31. See also Art 7(1) of the Hague Succession Convention.

estate equally and submitting them to the authority of a single law regardless of the place where these properties were situated (the monist approach or the principle of universality). Other Member States,[26] by contrast, distinguished between movable and immovable property belonging to an estate and applied different laws to them in matters of succession (the dualist approach or the principle of scission). The Regulation, at least on the general level, ends this disparity between Member States and regards the estate as a unity under Article 21 by prescribing that the succession should be governed as a whole by the law of the State where the deceased had his habitual residence at the time of death or, exceptionally, by the law of the State which is, on the face of all circumstances of the case, most closely connected to the case.

The reasons for such a unitary system are manifold. First of all, treating movables and immovables of the same estate differently may increase legal costs, particularly for estate planning or administration or for succession actions. In a scission system, the deceased may have to arrange his estate planning for different groups of assets; and after death, those assets will, based on their nature, be administered or handled in a succession-related action pursuant to different legal systems.[27] Moreover, when the succession is not perceived as a unity, the characterisation of an estate asset as movable or immovable may be different under the *lex fori* and the *lex rei sitae*.[28] More importantly, a system of scission may create difficult adaptation ('intibak' or 'Anpassung')[29] problems in practice. The application of different laws to the same estate may be problematic with respect to the distribution of an estate or a reserved portion.[30] Therefore, it has been contended that such problems may be eliminated in the monist approach.[31]

The classic textbook example where the deceased considered only a fair partition of his estate among his children but did not pay attention to fragmentation may illustrate problems of the dualist approach.[32] If, for instance, the testator owning two items of immovable property having the same value, e.g. a villa in Paris and a penthouse in London, bequeaths the villa in Paris to his daughter and the penthouse in London to his son, a succession conflict regarding the reserved portion between the siblings may occur under a dualist approach,[33] namely the children of the testator may file a forced heirship claim

---

[26] See the Member States referred in Artigot i Golobardes, (2015) 4 EPLJ 22, 31.

[27] Max Planck Institute for Comparative and International Private Law, (2010) 74 RabelsZ 522, 602; Dutta, (2009) 73 RabelsZ 547, 555; cf. Dörner and others, [2005] IPRax 1, 5.

[28] Dörner and others, [2005] IPRax 1, 5; Dutta, (2009) 73 RabelsZ 547, 555.

[29] See, on this issue, below, p 119.

[30] See, for example, § 1922 of the BGB.

[31] Dörner and others, [2005] IPRax 1, 5; Dutta, (2009) 73 RabelsZ 547, 555–556.

[32] Dörner and others, [2005] IPRax 1, 5.

[33] Dörner and others, [2005] IPRax 1, 5; Dutta, (2009) 73 RabelsZ 547, 556.

under French law.[34] That is to say that the testator's son in the example given above is entitled to such a claim under French law for the villa in Paris which was bequeathed to his sister. The same, however, may not come into play for the penthouse in London by virtue of the fact that family members of the deceased may only claim provision *vis-à-vis* estate items found in England under certain circumstances.[35] In this example, the problem is not that there are different levels of protection for family members in the same succession case; rather, the question is whether there is any protection at all when different laws govern the same case. If one law governs the succession as a whole in this example, be it that of England or France, a problem of protection would not arise.[36] Thus, it has been advocated that a conflict rule should avoid such problems associated with a scission system, which have long been identified by scholars[37] and the legal practitioners,[38] at least within the Union.[39]

Whereas the unity of succession is adopted in the European Union for the above-mentioned reasons, the attitude of the Turkish PILA towards this classical question of whether or not to perceive succession as a unity is different from the Regulation. As mentioned earlier, Article 20(1) of the Turkish PILA provides that the law applicable to succession is the national law of the deceased. For the immovable assets located in Turkey, however, Turkish law is to be applicable. This rule has been in existence in the Turkish legal system since the adoption of Article 4 of the Temporary Act. Article 4 of the Temporary Act, as mentioned before, provided that the law applicable to succession to personal property is the national law of the deceased, whereas succession to real property found in Turkey (or at the time of enactment, in the Ottoman Empire) was to be governed by Turkish law. This unilateral rule for immovable property in Turkey was interpreted as a multilateral conflict rule, thereby resulting in the *lex rei sitae* being applicable to immovable properties and a dualist approach to succession. This approach, with some changes, was main-

---

34 See Art 912 et seq. of the French Civil Code.

35 See Inheritance (Provision for Family and Dependants) Act 1975.

36 Dörner and others, [2005] IPRax 1, 5; Dutta, (2009) 73 RabelsZ 547, 556.

37 See, for example, John Humphrey Carlile Morris, 'Intestate Succession to Land in the Conflict of Laws' (1969) 85 LQR 339.

38 See, for example, Brodie v. Barry [1813] 2 Ves. & Beames 127, 130–131 (*Sir William Grant*): 'Where land and personal property are situated in different countries, and governed by different laws, and a question arises upon the combined effect of those laws, it is often very difficult to determine what portion of each law is to enter into the decision of the question. It is not easy to say how much is to be considered as depending on the law of real property, which must be taken from the country where the land lies, how much upon the law of personal property, which must be taken from the law of domicil, and to blend both together so as to from a rule applicable to the mixed question which neither law separately furnishes sufficient materials to decide.'

39 Dörner and others, [2005] IPRax 1, 5; Dutta, (2009) 73 RabelsZ 547, 556.

tained in Article 22 of the former Turkish PILA (Law no 2675) and in Article 20 of the current Turkish PILA (Law no 5718).

At the time of enactment of Article 22 of the former Turkish PILA, which is still applicable as Article 20 of the current Turkish PILA, the drafters discussed the option of a monist approach, which was a rising trend in respect of the law applicable to succession matters in most of the jurisdictions in Europe. Nonetheless, considering the Turkish court practice and the fact that succession certificates issued by Turkish courts which involve immovables located outside Turkey may not be recognisable/enforceable in the States where these immovable assets are located, they decided to keep the long-standing dualist approach with an important change.[40] Instead of applying the *lex rei sitae* as a multilateral conflict rule to govern all the deceased's immovables irrespective of their location, they adopted it as a unilateral conflict rule to cover only immovables situated in Turkey. In this version of the rule, hence, the law applicable to succession as a whole irrespective of the nature of assets is the *lex patriae*, but succession on immovables located in Turkey will be governed by Turkish law as the *lex rei sitae*. A further exception is provided in the second paragraph, which states, without making a distinction between movable and immovable assets, that issues pertaining to the grounds for the opening of succession as well as acquisition and the sharing-out of succession should be subject to the *lex rei sitae*.

This formulation of Article 20 has caused much discussion among scholars on the nature of the system adopted as regards to succession. Some argue that notwithstanding the exception provided for immovable properties in Turkey, it could be regarded as a unity system,[41] as fragmentation will only come into play if the deceased leaves an immovable estate asset in Turkey.[42] A second

---

[40] İstanbul Üniversitesi Hukuk Fakültesi – Milletlerarası Hukuk ve Milletlerarası Münasebetler Enstitüsü, *Milletlerarası Özel Hukuk ve Milletlerarası Usul Hukuku Kanunu Öntasarı Sempozyumu, 22–24 Kasım 1976* (Fakülteler Matbaası 1978) 17 and 138–139 (*Nihal Uluocak*); Tanrıbilir, *Kanuni Mirasçılıktan Doğan Kanunlar İhtilafı* (2000) 93–95; A. Elif Ulusu Karataş, 'Türk Miras Hukukunda Mirasın Kazanılmasında Halefiyet Türleri ve Türk Milletlerarası Özel Hukukundaki Yansımaları' (2015) 73 İÜHFM 357, 384–385; cf. Gülören Tekinalp, 'Türk "Milletlerarası Özel Hukuk ve Milletlerarası Usul Hukuku Tasarısı"' (1978) 44 İÜHFM 91, 110. See also 'Danışma Meclisi Tutanakları – Milletlerarası Özel Hukuk ve Usul Hukuku Hakkında Kanun Tasarısı ve Adalet Komisyonu Raporu (1/5)' 7 <https://www.tbmm.gov.tr/tutanaklar/TUTANAK/DM__/d02/c004/dm__02004071ss0100.pdf> accessed 29 November 2020.

[41] Tekinalp, (1978) 44 İÜHFM 91, 110; Rona Aybay and Esra Dardağan, *Uluslararası Düzeyde Yasaların Çatışması (Kanunlar İhtilafı)* (2nd edn, İstanbul Bilgi Üniversitesi Yayınları 2008) 232; Tekinalp, *Milletlerarası Özel Hukuk* (2020) 234; Çelikel and Erdem, *Milletlerarası Özel Hukuk* (2021) 348; Güngör, *Türk Milletlerarası Özel Hukuku* (2021) 166; Nomer, *Devletler Hususî Hukuku* (2021) 296–297; cf. Doğan, *Milletlerarası Özel Hukuk* (2022) 368–369.

[42] Tanrıbilir, *Kanuni Mirasçılıktan Doğan Kanunlar İhtilafı* (2000) 90; Giray, (2016) 9 Anali PFZE 235, 237; Doğan, *Milletlerarası Özel Hukuk* (2022) 369.

view, however, contends that the rule still takes the movable and immovable nature of an asset into consideration and, hence, keeps the scission system adopted in the Temporary Act.[43] For some commentators, the *lex rei sitae* rule should indeed be interpreted and applied – like in the old system – as a multilateral one which would then mean that succession issues concerning immovables should be subject to the *lex rei sitae.*[44]

Despite these views asserting that the rule should be classified as a system of unity or scission, the system adopted in the Turkish PILA can only be considered as a mix of both systems.[45] It is true that a scission will only come into play in cases where the deceased leaves estate assets in Turkey and that it will have a very limited scope of application in some cases.[46] If, for instance, a Dutch national leaves a number of movable and immovable properties in France and a holiday home in Turkey (where he spent the summer months), only the succession on this holiday home will be governed by Turkish law, whereas the rest of the assets will be governed by Dutch law regardless of their nature. Notwithstanding the number of immovable estate assets falling into the scope of the exception in each case, it should be accepted that Article 20(1) could not be regarded as a monist or dualist approach; it is rather a mix of both systems, which may lead to a scission of succession in some cases, e.g. in instances where the deceased's only immovable property was located in Turkey, and unity of succession in others, e.g. in a case where the deceased leaves only movable property in Turkey but immovable property outside Turkey or for issues falling within the scope of the second paragraph of Article 20.

The approach of the Treaty to the issue is also different from both the Regulation and the Turkish PILA. Under the Treaty, for succession matters on movable estate, the national law of the deceased at the time of death will be applicable (Article 20(14) (1)). Succession issues with regards to immovable

[43] İstanbul Üniversitesi Hukuk Fakültesi – Milletlerarası Hukuk ve Milletlerarası Münasebetler Enstitüsü, *MÖHUK Öntasarı Sempozyumu* (1978) 141 (*Necip Kocayusufpaşaoğlu*).

[44] Vahit Doğan, 'Miras Hukukundan Doğan Kanunlar İhtilafı' (1990) 3 SÜHFD 181, 185; Tanrıbilir, *Kanuni Mirasçılıktan Doğan Kanunlar İhtilafı* (2000) 98–100.

[45] Nihal Uluocak, *Milletlerarası Özel Hukuk Dersleri (Kişisel Statü – Miras Statüsü)* (Filiz Kitabevi 1987) 112; Neşe Baran Çelik, *Milletlerarası Unsurlu Ölüme Bağlı Tasarruflara Uygulanacak Hukukun Tayini* (Yetkin 2011) 107; Ekşi, *Milletlerarası Miras Hukuku* (2013) 33; Nuray Ekşi, 'Comparison of Articles 20 and 43 of the Turkish Private International Law and Procedural Law Act ('PILA') with the EU Succession Regulation' in Paul Beaumont and Burcu Yüksel (eds), *Turkish and EU Private International Law – A Comparison* (On İki Levha 2014) 122; Ulusu Karataş, (2015) 73 İÜHFM 357, 383; Ayşe Kübra Altıparmak, *İngiliz, Avrupa Birliği ve Türk Hukukunda Mirasa Uygulanacak Hukuk* (On İki Levha 2017) 20 and 105; Şanlı, Esen and Ataman Figanmeşe, *Milletlerarası Özel Hukuk* (2021) 263–264 fn 296; cf. Necla Öztürk, 'Miras Statüsünün Belirlenmesinde İrade Muhtariyetinin Rolü' (2015) 5 AkdHFD 177, 185.

[46] Tanrıbilir, *Kanuni Mirasçılıktan Doğan Kanunlar İhtilafı* (2000) 90.

estate, however, are to be governed by the law of the State where the assets are located and 'as [if] the deceased was a national of this State at the time of death' (Article 20(14) (2)). Thus, the Treaty makes a clear distinction between movable and immovable parts of the estate and espouses the system of scission that is consistent with the Article 4 of the Temporary Act which was in force at the time of conclusion of the Treaty.

This obviously contradicts with the unitary approach adopted in the Regulation and thus will result in an exception to the desired unity of succession within the borders of Europe in cases arising between Germany and Turkey that are in the scope of the Treaty. Had the Treaty not been applicable, a succession matter involving a Turkish national who resided in Berlin and died there intestate, leaving movable and immovable assets in each of the two States, would have been settled pursuant to German law, as the law of the State of habitual residence at the time of death (Article 21 of the Regulation), no matter whether the issue relates to a movable or immovable part of the estate and no matter where the assets are located. Nevertheless, since the Treaty continues to be applicable under Article 75(1) (1) of the Regulation, German courts would have to make a distinction between the assets in Germany and in Turkey. For the movable and immovable assets of the Turkish deceased in Germany, they will apply the Treaty and determine the law applicable to each group of assets differently. This causes a fragmentation of succession, which the Regulation is principally determined to avoid in the entirety of Europe.

The rule of the Treaty, on the other hand, is only slightly different from Article 20 of the Turkish PILA. In the succession case involving, for example, a German citizen who was habitually resident/domiciled in Istanbul and who dies there intestate by leaving some amount of money in a bank account and a house in Istanbul behind, German law would govern the succession claim on the money, whereas Turkish law will be applicable for the succession to the house, if the Treaty is applicable. When the Turkish PILA applies to the case, the result would be the same, as German law is the national law of the deceased and applicable on the money in the bank account, and Turkish law is the law governing the house found in Istanbul pursuant to Article 20(1). In such a case, the result will be a scission, regardless of whether the Turkish PILA or the Treaty apply.

The results which would be reached by the application of the Turkish PILA or the Treaty may be different based on the disputed matter in the case. If, for instance, there is a claim of estate creditors against the heirs,[47] the matter will be solved in accordance with German law, for the money, and with Turkish law, for the house (Article 20(14) of the Treaty). Had the Treaty not been

[47] For the material scope of Art 20(1) and (2) of the Turkish PILA and of Art 20(14) of the Treaty, see pp 90–97 and 97–98, below.

applicable, the issue would have been settled pursuant to Turkish law – as the *lex rei sitae* – for both assets (Article 20(2) of the Turkish PILA). In such a situation, whereas the application of the Treaty results in a scission, the Turkish PILA results in a unitary approach.

B. Different Connecting Factors: Last Habitual Residence vs. Nationality + Forum/*situs*

One of the fundamental decisions for legislators when drafting conflict rules is to find the appropriate connecting factor. A sole connecting factor in the realm of succession should guide practitioners to find – in the easiest way possible – the law applicable to the devolution of the deceased's patrimony to his kin or other beneficiaries. In the vast majority of jurisdictions, therefore, this law is the one, as in matters of personal status and family law, with which the decedent has a close and personal connection through his nationality, domicile, or habitual residence.[48] Due to the diversity of traditions and policies,[49] there has been a longstanding controversy among the legal systems in terms of adhering to the principle of nationality or that of domicile in the field of personal law and, as a part of it, of succession.[50] This opposition, which has not yet universally been settled, has gained another dimension with the use of the domicile principle's next of kin, the principle of habitual residence. The divergence of connecting factors in the realm of succession does not obviously increase the number of conflict-of-laws cases we come across,[51] but it does cause instances where multiple laws claim applicability in the same case. Such a conflict then results in limping legal relationships and problems in terms of efficiency in the realm of succession.[52] These may also come into play in the Turkish-EU context, since there are divergent connecting factors.

The Regulation's 'universally applicable' conflict rules adopt, like the jurisdictional rules, the habitual residence of the deceased at the time of death as the main connecting factor to be applicable on succession as a whole, unless otherwise provided in the Regulation (Article 21(1)). If, however, there are exceptional circumstances in which the deceased was manifestly more closely

[48] David Hayton, 'Determination of the Objectively Applicable Law Governing Succession to Deceaseds' Estates' in DNotI (ed), *Les Successions Internationales dans l'UE* (DNotI 2004) 362; Dutta, (2009) 73 RabelsZ 547, 560.

[49] Ernst Rabel, *The Conflict of Laws: A Comparative Study*, vol I (Callaghan & Company 1945) 155.

[50] Rabel, *The Conflict of Laws* (1945) 101.

[51] Louis I. de Winter, 'Nationality or Domicile? The Present State of Affairs' (1969) 128 RdC 346, 357.

[52] de Winter, (1969) 128 RdC 346, 357.

connected with a State other than the State of his habitual residence, succession would be governed by the law of that other State (Article 21(2)). The rule designates the objectively applicable law governing the succession as a whole; further, in addition to the general rationales of the system, i.e. legal certainty, decisional harmony, unity, and *Gleichlauf*,[53] it aims to find, from the perspective of the deceased, the legal system which is closely connected to the case.[54]

There was a consensus between the Member States before the Regulation that conflict rules should place the deceased at the centre,[55] since he assumes that the law of the country which he is closely connected will be applicable to succession after his death.[56] Such a harmony, however, did not exist when determining this 'most closely connected law'. Likewise, at the universal level, Member States were divided into two groups, between following the principle of nationality and that of residence.[57] The European legislature, therefore, tried to find a compromise between these connecting factors[58] and adhered to the approach of other European private international law instruments as well as Hague conventions.

The choice of habitual residence as the main connecting factor to be applicable on succession may be defensible from the European Union's perspective for a number of reasons. In the first place, habitual residence is, in the words of *Graveson*, perceived as 'the most appropriate available concept to meet the demands of a fluid, modern society'.[59] The Union is indeed, or at least is determined to be, a place where the free movement of persons is guaranteed and an integrative policy is supported.[60] It is undoubted that 'getting into the mind

---

[53] Recital 37 of the Regulation.

[54] Recital 37 of the Regulation.

[55] *Dutta* refers to Latvia as the only exception amongst the Member States which did not place the deceased at the centre of conflict rules: Dutta, (2009) 73 RabelsZ 547, 560.

[56] Dutta, (2009) 73 RabelsZ 547, 561.

[57] Max Planck Institute for Comparative and International Private Law, (2010) 74 RabelsZ 522, 600–601, esp. fn 147 and 148.

[58] Haris P. Pamboukis, in Haris P. Pamboukis (ed), *EU Succession Regulation No 650/2012 – A Commentary* (Nomiki Bibliothiki & C.H. Beck & Hart & Nomos 2017) ESR Art 21 para 2.

[59] Ronald Harry Graveson, *The Conflict of Laws* (7th edn, Sweet & Maxwell 1974) 194.

[60] See Title IV of the TFEU and also Art 18 of the TFEU. See also Dieter Leipold, 'Europa und das Erbrecht' in Gerhard Köbler, Meinhard Heinze and Wolfgang Hromadka (eds), *Europas universale rechtsordnungspolitische Aufgabe im Recht des dritten Jahrtausends – Festschrift für Alfred Söllner zum 70. Geburtstag* (C.H. Beck 2000) 664ff; DNotI (in collaboration with Heinrich Dörner and Paul Lagarde), 'DNotI Report' (2004) 261; Brigitta Jud, 'Rechtswahl im Erbrecht: Das Grünbuch der Europäischen Kommission zum Erb- und Testamentsrecht' [2005] GPR 133, 135; Jan Kropholler, *Internationales Privatrecht* (6th edn, Mohr Siebeck 2006) 270, 277 and 291; Mansel, 'Vereinheitlichung des Internationalen Erbrechts in der EG' (2006) 209ff; Dutta, (2009) 73 RabelsZ 547, 564–565; Max Planck Institute for Comparative and International Private Law, (2010) 74 RabelsZ 522,

of the deceased'[61] and assessing his integration in the State of habitual residence or his adherence to the origin State is not an easy task for the Member States in a succession case.[62] Taking this into consideration, the European legislature followed the presumption that a person resident, not merely present,[63] in a State different from his origin State feels himself at 'home' in this State and therefore adopted the habitual residence principle. This supports, from a European point of view, the integrative policy of the Union.[64]

Moreover, the European legislature considered that the application of the nationality principle could have caused divergent practices between the Member States, thereby impairing the desired autonomous application within the Union.[65] The European Union, in principle, lacks the competence to make decisions on the acquisition or loss of citizenship on behalf of Member States.[66] Therefore, choosing the nationality principle to be applicable in European private international law could not have ensured an autonomous solution; rather, it could have been affected by national policies of Member States.[67]

Furthermore, though nationality as a connecting factor would be easier to determine in some cases, it may not provide for application of the most closely connected law in cases where the deceased lived in a State different than his origin State, which is often the situation in cases having international elements. The place of residence in these cases is frequently the place where the assets of the estate and the main creditors are located. In such cases, the application of the nationality principle, however, could not establish the necessary factual link between the case and the State whose law is applicable.[68] The use of the

---

604; Dutta, *MüKoBGB* (2020) EuErbVO Art 21 para 1; Maksymilian Pazdan and Maciej Zachariasiewicz, 'The EU Succession Regulation: Achievements, Ambiguities, and Challenges for the Future' (2021) 17 J Priv Int L 74, 82; Ferenc Szilágyi, 'The Option to Choose the Law Applicable to Succession Under the EU Succession Regulation' (2021) XVII IAS 149, 150.

[61] Cf. Pippa Rogerson, 'Habitual Residence: The New Domicile?' (2000) 49 ICLQ 86, 90.

[62] Herweg, *Die Vereinheitlichung des Internationalen Erbrechts* (2004) 56ff; D. Lehmann, *Die Reform des Internationalen Erb- und Erbprozessrechts* (2006) 77ff; Dutta, (2009) 73 RabelsZ 547, 564.

[63] Cf. Rogerson, (2000) 49 ICLQ 86, 90.

[64] Mansel, 'Vereinheitlichung des Internationalen Erbrechts in der EG' (2006) 210; Dutta, (2009) 73 RabelsZ 547, 564–565; Peter Kindler, 'Vom Staatsangehörigkeits- zum Domizilprinzip: das künftige internationale Erbrecht der Europäischen Union' [2010] IPRax 44, 46ff; Kern and Glücker, (2014) 78 RabelsZ 294, 302.

[65] Dutta, (2009) 73 RabelsZ 547, 566–567.

[66] This has been made clear since the Treaty of Maastricht (The Treaty on European Union [1992] OJ C 191). See Declaration 2 annexed to the Treaty.

[67] Dutta, (2009) 73 RabelsZ 547, 567.

[68] DNotI (in collaboration with Heinrich Dörner and Paul Lagarde), 'DNotI Report' (2004) 261; Hayton, 'Determination of the Objectively Applicable Law Governing Succession' (2004) 362–363; Dutta, (2009) 73 RabelsZ 547, 567; Max Planck Institute for Com-

nationality approach may also result in the application of different, and probably, conflicting succession laws within the same household in cases where family members hold different nationalities. As the foreign population within the Union is considerably high,[69] such instances are not unlikely. In a migrant family where the first generation kept the nationality of the home State, but the second and third generations acquired the citizenship of their Member State of residence, for example, the succession law applicable to the father and the son will be different under the nationality principle. Under the residence principle, however, there will be no such situation and the succession will be governed by the same law regardless of their nationalities.[70]

Last but not least, the choice of the residence principle as being applicable to the succession as a whole attempts to establish a *Gleichlauf* between the forum and *ius*, which is time and cost efficient for succession cases as the Member State courts having jurisdiction will apply their own laws to the case, which is the law they will be most familiar with.[71]

Notwithstanding these advantages from the Union's perspective, the habitual residence rule has also an important drawback – and that is its uncertain character. The last habitual residence of the deceased is not defined in the Regulation and will be decided by the courts on the circumstances of the case (Recital 23). In each case, the courts will try to locate the centre of life and social interests of the deceased, or in other words the place where the person in question feels himself 'at home' and where he actually is 'at home'.[72] This brings a level of uncertainty to the concept of habitual residence, particularly in complex cases, and hence it may undermine the two chief traits of European Union law, namely foreseeability and legal certainty. Nevertheless, it may be argued that

---

parative and International Private Law, (2010) 74 RabelsZ 522, 604; Dennis Solomon, 'Die allgemeine Kollisionsnorm (Art 21, 22 EuErbVO)' in Anatol Dutta and Sebastian Herrler (eds), *Die Europäische Erbrechtsverordnung, 20 Jahre DNotI 1993–2013* (C.H. Beck 2014) 21; Szilágyi, (2021) XVII IAS 149, 150. See, however, Mariusz Załucki, 'The Future of Succession Law in the EU. A Proposal' in Catarina Santos Botelho and Fábio da Silva Veiga (eds), *Future Law* (Universidade Católica Editora 2018) 581.

[69] In the year 2010, the number of foreign nationals in the Union was 32.5 million, which was equal to 6.5% of the total population in that year: Katya Vasileva, 'Population and Social Conditions' (2011) 34 Eurostat-Statistics in Focus <https://ec.europa.eu/eurostat/documents/3433488/5579176/KS-SF-11-034-EN.PDF/63cebff3-f7ac-4ca6-ab33-4e8792c5f30c> accessed 27 November 2020. For the most recent numbers on a Member State basis, see Eurostat, 'Population on 1 January by Age Group, Sex and Citizenship (Migr_pop1ctz)'.

[70] Dutta, (2009) 73 RabelsZ 547, 567–568; cf. Max Planck Institute for Comparative and International Private Law, (2010) 74 RabelsZ 522, 604–605.

[71] Dutta, (2009) 73 RabelsZ 547, 568; Solomon, 'Die allgemeine Kollisionsnorm' (2014) 21.

[72] Michael Stürner, in Harm Peter Westermann, Barbara Grunewald and Georg Maier-Reimer (eds), *Erman BGB*, vol 2 (16th edn, Otto Schmidt 2020) EuErbVo Art 21 para 2.

the guidance given by the CJEU – not specifically on the matter of succession, but in other fields – may be helpful for the courts in case-by-case analysis.[73]

The Regulation makes reference to the law of the last habitual residence of the deceased but still takes the possibility into consideration that this law may not realise the desired principle of proximity in some cases, and thus it fortifies this main rule with an 'escape clause'.[74] It will be used in cases where, for example, the habitual residence of the deceased changes shortly before death, but all the other circumstances of the case suggest that the deceased was manifestly more closely connected to the previous State of habitual residence.[75]

Although the escape clause had been much criticised during the drafting process of the Regulation on account of its alleged redundancy (as it requires courts to analyse all circumstances of the case in a way similar to ascertaining the habitual residence) and because of its risk of impairing the legal security and *Gleichlauf* intended by the Regulation,[76] it is justified for a number of reasons. It is argued that it allows courts to take the factual circumstances of the case into account and, for the sake of justice in individual cases,[77] apply a foreign law without requiring them to decline the jurisdiction established pursuant to Article 4 of the Regulation.[78] It is also found helpful in cases where there is no valid *professio iuris* under Article 22 of the Regulation, e.g. a choice made by the deceased in favour of the law of previous habitual residence,[79] and in cases where, on the face of the circumstances, the application of the law of the State of habitual residence of the deceased seems unreason-

[73] Dutta, (2009) 73 RabelsZ 547, 568.

[74] Calvo Caravaca, *Calvo Caravaca/Davì/Mansel* (2016) ESR Art 21 para 2; Pamboukis, *Pamboukis* (2017) ESR Art 21 para 1; Dirk Looschelders, in Rainer Hüßtege and Heinz-Peter Mansel (eds), *NK-BGB/Rom-Verordnungen*, vol 6 (3rd edn, Nomos 2019) EuErbVO Art 21 paras 1–2; Köhler, *NK/Nachfolgerecht* (2019) EuErbVO Art 21 para 1.

[75] Recital 25 of the Regulation.

[76] Daniel Lehmann, 'Die EU-Erbrechtsverordnung zur Abwicklung grenzüberschreitender Nachlässe' [2012] DStR 2085, 2086; Felix M. Wilke, 'Das internationale Erbrecht nach der neuen EU-Erbrechtsverordnung' [2012] RIW 601, 605; Wolfgang Burandt, 'Die EU-ErbVO – Das europäische Erbrecht im Wandel (Teil 2)' [2013] FuR 377, 382; Christoph Döbereiner, 'Das internationale Erbrecht nach der EU-Erbrechtsverordnung (Teil I)' [2013] MittBayNot 358, 362; Felix Odersky, 'Die Europäische Erbrechtsverordnung in der Gestaltungspraxis' [2013] Notar 3, 5 fn 11; Solomon, 'Die allgemeine Kollisionsnorm' (2014) 34; Jutta Müller-Lukoschek, *Die neue EU-Erbrechtsverordnung: Leitfaden mit Erläuterungen für die notarielle Praxis* (2nd edn, Deutscher NotarVerlag 2015) §2 paras 148–150; Calvo Caravaca, *Calvo Caravaca/Davì/Mansel* (2016) ESR Art 21 paras 12 ff; Magdalena Pfeiffer, 'Legal Certainty and Predictability in International Succession Law' (2016) 12 J Priv Int L 566, 575 ff.

[77] Dutta, *MüKoBGB* (2020) EuErbVO Art 21 para 6.

[78] Heinrich Dörner, 'Die Verordnung zum Internationalen Erb- und Erbverfahrensrecht ist in Kraft!' [2012] ZEV 505, 511; Dutta, *MüKoBGB* (2020) EuErbVO Art 21 para 6; cf. D. Lehmann, [2012] DStR 2085, 2086; Pfeiffer, (2016) 12 J Priv Int L 566, 577.

[79] Dutta, *MüKoBGB* (2020) EuErbVO Art 21 para 6.

able, such as instances where the deceased has no other connection to the State of habitual residence.[80]

The approach of the Turkish PILA on the law applicable to succession is different from the Regulation, which, as seen above, takes the 'vague' concept of the habitual residence of the deceased as the central element of the law governing succession matters and complements it with an escape clause which gives a further measure of flexibility to the Member State courts to apply the law different than the forum. From the Union's perspective, the 'well-justified' and 'fashionable'[81] connecting factor of the habitual residence is not applicable in Turkey. Article 20(1) of the Turkish PILA chooses nationality as the main connecting factor to be applicable to the succession but excludes immovable assets located in Turkey from the scope of the rule. The law applicable to succession issues concerning immovable assets found in Turkey, according to the second sentence of the provision, is Turkish law. Article 20(2) of the Turkish PILA, in the same vein, articulates that issues concerning the grounds for opening succession, acquisition, and partition of succession should be subject to the *lex rei sitae*. By doing so, the Turkish PILA adopts the nationality principle and – for immovable property in Turkey and for the opening of succession, acquisition, and distribution of succession – the principle of *lex rei sitae* as the law governing cross-border succession matters. This means that if the deceased is a Turkish national, the law applicable to the succession as whole – except the issues falling into the scope of Article 20(2) – would be Turkish law; and if he is a national of a State other than Turkey the law applicable to succession would be his national law, with the exception of immovable estate assets found in Turkey, which will ultimately be governed by Turkish law.[82]

The Turkish legislature's main motive for choosing nationality and *situs* as connecting factors to find the law governing succession upon death is the twofold nature of the law of succession. Succession law, on the one hand, deals with the transfer of property upon death, and, hence, technically belongs to property law.[83] On the other hand, it has family law aspects which require, from the deceased's perspective, that succession matters should be governed by a law which also takes into consideration his cultural considerations and

[80] Odersky, [2013] Notar 3, 5; Dutta, *MüKoBGB* (2020) EuErbVO Art 21 para 6.

[81] The Green Paper Succession and Wills COM(2005) 65 Final 3.

[82] Tanrıbilir, *Kanuni Mirasçılıktan Doğan Kanunlar İhtilafı* (2000) 89; Baran Çelik, *Ölüme Bağlı Tasarruflar* (2011) 106; Ekşi, *Milletlerarası Miras Hukuku* (2013) 34; Tekinalp, *Milletlerarası Özel Hukuk* (2020) 234; Çelikel and Erdem, *Milletlerarası Özel Hukuk* (2021) 348; Nomer, *Devletler Hususî Hukuku* (2021) 297; Şanlı, Esen and Ataman Figanmeşe, *Milletlerarası Özel Hukuk* (2021) 263; Doğan, *Milletlerarası Özel Hukuk* (2022) 368–369.

[83] Bilge Öztan, *Miras Hukuku (Tablolar ve Örneklerle)* (12th edn, Yetkin 2021) 3; Serozan and Engin, *Miras Hukuku* (2021) § 1 para 1.

personal values.[84] Therefore, it is assumed that the deceased, regardless of the place of residence, is most closely connected to his national law, and that this law is the most familiar law to him and meets his interests better than any other law.[85] The application of the *lex rei sitae* for immovable property in Turkey – as well as for the opening of succession, acquisition and distribution of succession – is justified on the grounds that it is much more practical for the courts and assures that the rights of third parties, such as the creditors or the possessors of the estate, are respected.[86] In addition, restrictions on the acquisition of immovable property by foreigners in Turkey require that the law applicable to immovable property located in Turkey should be Turkish law.[87] Moreover, there are also political reasons underlying the choice of nationality, and of *situs* for immovable assets situated in Turkey. In accordance with the policy of immigrant-sending States, it is important for Turkey that its nationals outside the country should keep their close ties with Turkish law, particularly in matters of family and personal status.[88] For this reason, succession matters are, in principle, governed by the national law of the deceased. The political importance that Turkey has attached to immovable estate assets since the time of the Ottoman Empire explains the application of Turkish law to succession matters involving immovable assets in Turkey under Article 20(1) of the Turkish PILA.[89] Even though foreigners are also entitled to acquire immovable property, the matters concerning such property should be under the ultimate authority of the Turkish courts and Turkish law.[90]

In addition to the many aspects relating to family and personal status, other advantages associated with nationality – as compared to residence –[91] might have also affected the Turkish legislature in its decision to adopt nationality as the general connecting factor for cross-border successions. The dichotomy between nationality and residence is obviously one of the classic issues of

---

[84] Şanlı, Esen and Ataman Figanmeşe, *Milletlerarası Özel Hukuk* (2021) 33–34.

[85] Tekinalp, *Milletlerarası Özel Hukuk* (2020) 33; Çelikel and Erdem, *Milletlerarası Özel Hukuk* (2021) 63–64; Nomer, *Devletler Hususî Hukuku* (2021) 114; Şanlı, Esen and Ataman Figanmeşe, *Milletlerarası Özel Hukuk* (2021) 33; Doğan, *Milletlerarası Özel Hukuk* (2022) 213.

[86] İstanbul Üniversitesi Hukuk Fakültesi – Milletlerarası Hukuk ve Milletlerarası Münasebetler Enstitüsü, *MÖHUK Öntasarı Sempozyumu* (1978) 140 and 144 ff; 'Danışma Meclisi Tutanakları – Milletlerarası Özel Hukuk ve Usul Hukuku Hakkında Kanun Tasarısı ve Adalet Komisyonu Raporu (1/5)', (1981) 7–8; Uluocak, *Milletlerarası Özel Hukuk Dersleri* (1987) 121; Tanrıbilir, *Kanuni Mirasçılıktan Doğan Kanunlar İhtilafi* (2000) 87; Tekinalp, *Milletlerarası Özel Hukuk* (2020) 234.

[87] Ekşi, *Milletlerarası Miras Hukuku* (2013) 40.

[88] Nomer, *Devletler Hususî Hukuku* (2021) 113; Şanlı, Esen and Ataman Figanmeşe, *Milletlerarası Özel Hukuk* (2021) 33–34.

[89] Cf. Nomer, *Devletler Hususî Hukuku* (2021) 296.

[90] V. R. Seviğ, *Mirasla İlgili Devletler Hususi Hukuku Kaideleri* (1963) 85.

[91] See Arts 9–18 of the Turkish PILA.

private international law.[92] There has been indeed much discussion on the merits and demerits of each connecting factor.[93] It has been held that one of the advantages of nationality is its easily ascertainable character.[94] The question of whether a person is a national of a State will be determined by the State whose nationality is in dispute, and hence, the determination of the nationality will not be problematic in most of the cases.[95] Furthermore, it also has a stable nature which means that it can be changed only through naturalisation and, hence, that it does not depend entirely on the intention of the person in question.[96] Therefore, the problems arising in cases of *conflit mobile* are less likely to occur when the law applicable to a matter is the national law of the relevant person.[97] These advantages of nationality may also have affected the decision of the Turkish legislature regarding the law applicable to personal and family law matters including succession.

Whereas the rule provided under Article 20(1) of the Turkish PILA is not clear on the question of which moment of time the nationality of the deceased should be taken into account in order to determine the law governing succession, it should be understood that the nationality of the deceased at the time of death determines the law governing succession.[98]

In an approach similar to the Turkish PILA but one completely different from the approach of the Regulation, the Treaty also adopts the nationality

---

[92] Dutta, (2009) 73 RabelsZ 547, 562–563; Max Planck Institute for Comparative and International Private Law, (2010) 74 RabelsZ 522, 603.

[93] See, for example, Christian von Bar and Peter Mankowski, *Internationales Privatrecht: Allgemeine Lehren*, vol 1 (2nd edn, C.H. Beck 2003) § 7 paras 18 ff; Kropholler, *Internationales Privatrecht* (2006) 269 ff; Lawrence Collins, *Dicey, Morris & Collins the Conflict of Laws*, vol 1 (15th edn, Sweet & Maxwell 2012) paras 6-167 ff; Paul Torremans and James J. Fawcett (eds), *Cheshire, North and Fawcett Private International Law* (15th edn, OUP 2017) 170–171; Nomer, *Devletler Hususî Hukuku* (2021) 114; Şanlı, Esen and Ataman Figanmeşe, *Milletlerarası Özel Hukuk* (2021) 33 ff.

[94] Collins, *Dicey, Morris & Collins the Conflict of Laws* (2012) para 6-170; Torremans and Fawcett, *Cheshire, North and Fawcett PIL* (2017) 171.

[95] Şanlı, Esen and Ataman Figanmeşe, *Milletlerarası Özel Hukuk* (2021) 35; Doğan, *Milletlerarası Özel Hukuk* (2022) 213.

[96] Collins, *Dicey, Morris & Collins the Conflict of Laws* (2012) paras 6-169–170.

[97] Nomer, *Devletler Hususî Hukuku* (2021) 114.

[98] Uluocak, *Milletlerarası Özel Hukuk Dersleri* (1987) 114; Ekşi, *Milletlerarası Miras Hukuku* (2013) 35; Altıparmak, *Mirasa Uygulanacak Hukuk* (2017) 104; Feriha Bilge Tanrıbilir, 'MÖHUK ve Mirasa İlişkin Bağlama Kuralının Uygulanmasında Öne Çıkan Hususlar' in Feriha Bilge Tanrıbilir and Gülce Gümüşlü Tunçağıl (eds), *10. Yılında MÖHUK Sempozyumu – 7–8 Aralık 2017, Ankara* (Adalet Yayınevi 2018) 134; Tekinalp, *Milletlerarası Özel Hukuk* (2020) 235; Güngör, *Türk Milletlerarası Özel Hukuku* (2021) 167. The Turkish Court of Cassation also held that the nationality of the deceased at the time of death should be taken into consideration in succession cases regarding foreign nationals: Yargıtay 2. Hukuk Dairesi, T. 11.2.1992, E. 1992/1217 K. 1992/1514 <http://www.kazanci.com> accessed 21 February 2017.

and the *situs* as general connecting factors to be applicable in the field of succession. Article 20(14) (1) of the Treaty prescribes that the law applicable to succession matters regarding movable estate is the national law of the deceased at the time of death. With respect to immovable estate, on the other hand, succession issues are to be governed by the law of the State where the assets are located (Article 20(14) (2)). This rule is influenced by the political and legal background of the time at which the Treaty was concluded. It indeed merely reflects Article 4 of the then-current Temporary Act. Thus, it can be explained with the reasons underlying the approach of Article 4 of the Temporary Act.

The difference between the approaches of the three legal texts can be illustrated by way of two examples. Imagine that Turkish guest worker *(T)*, who was habitually resident with his family for many years in Dortmund/Germany, dies there intestate and leaves behind 50,000 euros in an account held in the Dortmund branch of a well-known German bank, a car, and an apartment in an old building in the centre of Dortmund.

When the Regulation is applied to this hypothetical scenario, succession matters relating to all assets, irrespective of their being movable or immovable, would be governed by German law as the law of the State of habitual residence of *(T)* at the time of death (Article 21(1)). If, however, the Turkish PILA becomes applicable, the law governing succession issues in connection with these assets will be Turkish law since it is the national law of *(T)* at the time of death (Article 20(1)). In the same hypothetical example, the Treaty will provide a different outcome from both the Turkish PILA and the Regulation. Pursuant to Article 20(14) of the Treaty, succession to *(T)*'s 50,000 euros cash in the bank account and car is to be governed by Turkish law, as his national law. Succession to the apartment of *(T)*, on the other hand, will be under the sole authority of German law for conflict-of-laws purposes as the law of the *situs* of the apartment.

Another hypothetical scenario could be that a German businessperson *(G)* resides and runs a German chemical company in Izmir/Turkey for more than ten years. After facing some financial problems, however, he moves his company to Sofia/Bulgaria and starts living there with his family. As he always liked Izmir, which is the city where his mother originally comes from, he keeps his waterside luxury apartment in Alsancak (Izmir) and spends the summer months there every year with his family. In one of his visits to Izmir – three years after moving to Sofia – he dies there intestate. He leaves behind his company, a car, a house, some amount of money in a bank account in Sofia, and his apartment in Izmir.

This second scenario is another example where the divergent approaches of Turkey, the European Union, and the Treaty to cross-border successions can be illustrated. In this example, when the Regulation becomes applicable, the deceased's entire estate, irrespective of its locations and nature, will be governed by Bulgarian law since the Bulgarian courts will mostly likely conclude that *(G)* was habitually resident in Sofia at the time of death (Article 21(1)). On the other hand, the Turkish PILA provides for a different outcome to the case. On *(G)*'s movable and immovable assets found in Sofia, his national law (German law) will be applicable. The apartment in Izmir, however, will be governed by Turkish law (Article 20(1)). The Treaty's approach to the issue also differs. The Treaty only covers assets located in the Contracting States.[99] This means that it is only applicable for the apartment in Izmir; it will be governed by Turkish law pursuant to Article 20(14) (2).

C. *Professio iuris?*

Professio iuris – a kind of freedom required in pluralistic democracies, a useful tool for parties to effectively organise their economic activities, and an important opportunity for individuals to safeguard their personal interests in the best way possible in the modern world where migration, mobility, and transnational cases are not rare[100] – is undoubtedly a widely accepted principles in the fields of contract law[101] and non-contractual relations.[102] In recent years, it has even gained a place in the field of family and succession law, areas where cultural and traditional sentiments of the States have played an important role and left them as disciplines perceived until now as unsuitable for *professio iuris*.[103]

This is indeed the case for the Regulation. The reasons behind allowing *professio iuris* in the Regulation may be explained from different perspectives. On the one hand, it could be argued that the fundamental principles of the European Union, such as the freedom of movement, legal certainty, and, more generally, the respect for human rights, compel Member States to recognise a legal status that has already been obtained in other Member States. In the light of these principles and in the face of growing mobility of individuals, it has no longer been possible to resist a choice of law in the field of family and succession law.[104] On the other hand, it could be contended that with the help

---

[99] See, for the discussion on this issue, above pp 46–48.

[100] Cf. Karin Dreher, *Die Rechtswahl im internationalen Erbrecht* (Peter Lang 1999) 1; Erik Jayme, 'Party Autonomy in International Family and Succession Law: New Tendencies' (2009) XI YbPIL 1, 1–2.

[101] See, for example, Art 3 of the Rome I Regulation and Art 24(1) of the Turkish PILA.

[102] See, for example, Art 14 of the Rome II Regulation and Art 34(5) of the Turkish PILA.

[103] Jayme, (2009) XI YbPIL 1, 2–3; Magdalena Pfeiffer, 'Choice of Law in International Family and Succession Law' (2012) 2 TLQ 291, 292.

[104] Toni Marzal Yetano, 'The Constitutionalisation of Party Autonomy in European Family Law' (2010) 6 J Priv Int L 155, 155–156.

of *professio iuris*, the European legislature is attempting to find a compromise for the longstanding 'deadlock'[105] between the Member States on the question of whether the nationality or the domicile is the right connecting factor in the field of family and succession law. In other words, it has been argued that the introduction of the *professio iuris* to this field was driven by the unifying policy that the European Union has adopted towards differences between legal systems.[106]

In any event, the right to choose the law applicable to succession has certain advantages. This is true in the first place as regards the interests of the deceased. Whereas habitual residence has been adopted as the cornerstone of the Regulation's conflict-of-laws and procedural rules, it impedes the desired legal certainty in certain cases. The aim of habitual residence, from a choice-of-law perspective, is to ensure the application of the law of the State which the deceased is most closely connected. Nonetheless, in cases where the deceased is connected with more than one State, the determination of habitual residence and, hence, the law applicable to succession may prove complex. In such cases, *professio iuris* is of paramount importance to ensure legal certainty from the deceased's perspective.[107]

In addition, habitual residence as the main connecting factor also disregards the connection of the deceased to his national State. Put differently, it may not always reflect reality to assume that the deceased is most closely connected to the legal system of his State of habitual residence, on the purported rational that he is or should be well integrated in this State. Habitual residence is justified on the grounds of the European Union's integrative policy not only for its own citizens but also for non-EU citizens. This understanding, which places integration interests before the stability interests of the deceased, may lead to the application of a law which is in fact not closely connected to the deceased. Thus, the *professio iuris* would serve the stability

105 Yetano, (2010) 6 J Priv Int L 155, 155.

106 Jayme, (2009) XI YbPIL 1, 3.

107 Dörner and others, [2005] IPRax 1, 5; Dutta, (2009) 73 RabelsZ 547, 571; Lein, (2009) XI YbPIL 107, 131 ff; Rembert Süß, 'Der Vorschlag der EG-Kommission zu einer Erbrechtsverordnung (Rom IV Verordnung) vom 14. Oktober 2009' [2009] ZErb 342, 344; Anatol Dutta, 'Die Rechtswahlfreiheit im Künftigen internationalen Erbrecht der Europäischen Union' in Gerte Reichelt and Walter H. Rechberger (eds), *Europäisches Erbrecht: Zum Verordnungsvorschlag der Europäischen Kommission zum Erb- und Testamentsrecht* (Jan Sramek Verlag 2011) 61; Pfeiffer, (2012) 2 TLQ 291, 300; Bonomi, *Bonomi/Wautelet* (2016) ESR Art 22 para 8; Esperanza Castellanos Ruiz, in Alfonso-Luis Calvo Caravaca, Angelo Davì and Heinz-Peter Mansel (eds), *The EU Succession Regulation – A Commentary* (Cambridge University Press 2016) ESR Art 22 para 4; Dimitrios Stamatiadis, in Haris P. Pamboukis (ed), *EU Succession Regulation No 650/2012 – A Commentary* (Nomiki Bibliothiki & C.H. Beck & Hart & Nomos 2017) ESR Art 22 paras 25–26; Bauer and Fornasier, *Dutta/Weber* (2021) EuErbVO Art 22 para 2; Szilágyi, (2021) XVII IAS 149, 159–160; cf. Jud, [2005] GPR 133, 136–137.

interests of the deceased in such cases where he has stronger ties with a law other than the law of his State of habitual residence.[108]

Another important advantage of the *professio iuris* in the field of succession law is that it also serves public interests. The problems attached to the determination of the habitual residence in complex cases will not come into play when the deceased makes a choice of law. Hence, succession proceedings would be cost and time efficient not only for the courts but also for notaries or other relevant authorities and even for the heirs.[109]

Finally, *professio iuris* in the field of cross-border successions could be seen as an extension of the prominent principle of testamentary freedom intrinsic to domestic succession laws.[110] It is true that limits apply on testamentary freedom due to the interests of family members of the testator who are entitled to a reserved share or due to the interests of the States regarding *ordre public*. Such restrictions, however, cannot be a counter-argument for the *professio iuris* as regards conflict rules. This is because the deceased-centred objective connecting factor, be it his habitual residence or nationality, is also not able to fully safeguard those interests on the international level. In the vast majority of the cases, it is a mere coincidence that the State of nationality or habitual residence of the deceased has protective rules for the family members, since the rights of beneficiaries often do not play a role in the legislature's choice for the objective connecting factor.[111] In addition, particularly in the case of habitual residence but sometimes even in the case of nationality, these relatives cannot prevent the testator from changing the objectively applicable law specifically in order to avoid the protection attributed to them under that law. To be more precise, the possibility of changing habitual residence or even nationality is always open to the testator. Thus, the protection of family members may not always be a good justification for protesting against *professio iuris*.[112] In the same vein, the desire of the States to safeguard their *ordre public* in the field of succession law might not justify a

[108] Dutta, (2009) 73 RabelsZ 547, 571; Dutta, 'Die Rechtswahlfreiheit in der EuErbVO' (2011) 63 ff; Castellanos Ruiz, *Calvo Caravaca/Davì/Mansel* (2016) ESR Art 22 para 4; Szilágyi, (2021) XVII IAS 149, 151 and 160.

[109] Dörner and others, [2005] IPRax 1, 5; cf. Jud, [2005] GPR 133, 137.

[110] Dörner and others, [2005] IPRax 1, 5; Dutta, (2009) 73 RabelsZ 547, 574; Dutta, 'Die Rechtswahlfreiheit in der EuErbVO' (2011) 67; cf. Hans Dölle, 'Die Rechtswahl im Internationalen Erbrecht' (1966) 30 RabelsZ 205, 222.

[111] Dölle, (1966) 30 RabelsZ 205, 217; Gunther Kühne, *Die Parteiautonomie im internationalen Erbrecht* (Gieseking 1973) 77 ff; Dutta, (2009) 73 RabelsZ 547, 574; cf. Jud, [2005] GPR 133, 137 ff; Neşe Baran Çelik, 'Milletlerarası Özel Hukuk Alanındaki Gelişmeler Işığında Mirasa Uygulanacak Hukuk Bağlamında İrade Muhtariyeti İlkesinin Değerlendirilmesi', *Prof. Dr. İlhan Unat'a Armağan* (Mülkiyeliler Birliği Vakfı Yayınları 2012) 119.

[112] DNotI (in collaboration with Heinrich Dörner and Paul Lagarde), 'DNotI Report' (2004) 269; Dutta, (2009) 73 RabelsZ 547, 574. See also Baran Çelik, 'Miras–İrade Muhtariyeti' (2012) 118.

hostility towards the choice of law. The underlying reason for this is that there are always tools available to States to protect their legal order against foreign law in international cases, such as overriding mandatory provisions or the *ordre public* exception.[113]

Owing to these advantages, *professio iuris* had found support starting in the early stages of the drafting process of the Regulation.[114] The European legislature, accordingly, granted the deceased a limited right to choose the law applicable to succession under Article 22 of the Regulation. Even though *professio iuris* in the field of succession is a novelty for most of the Member States,[115] it is found in the Hague Succession Convention[116] which guided the European legislature when formulating the Regulation's choice-of-law rules.[117] Article 22 prescribes under its first paragraph that the deceased may choose the law of the State whose nationality he possesses at the time of making the choice or at the time of death as applicable to the succession as a whole. By doing this, it strikes a balance between the competing connecting factors in succession matters, i.e. habitual residence and nationality,[118] and allows the persons to arrange their succession in advance.[119]

Even though the academic literature called for a wider choice-of-law rule,[120] the choice of the deceased is limited to the national law. This limited choice is justified for two main reasons. In the first place, the chosen law

---

[113] Dutta, (2009) 73 RabelsZ 547, 575. See also Baran Çelik, 'Miras–İrade Muhtariyeti' (2012) 119.

[114] Dörner and others, [2005] IPRax 1, 5; Jud, [2005] GPR 133, 139; Daniel Lehmann, 'Stellungnahme zum Grünbuch der Kommission der Europäischen Gemeinschaften zum Erb- und Testamentsrecht' [2005] ZErb 320, 323; Mansel, 'Vereinheitlichung des Internationalen Erbrechts in der EG' (2006) 208ff; Harris, (2008) 22 Tru L I 181, 212–213; Dutta, (2009) 73 RabelsZ 547, 571; Lein, (2009) XI YbPIL 107, 131; Kindler, [2010] IPRax 44, 49; Wagner, [2010] DNotZ 506, 515; Dutta, 'Die Rechtswahlfreiheit in der EuErbVO' (2011) 60ff; Julia Remde, 'Die Europäische Erbrechtsverordnung nach dem Vorschlag der Kommission vom 14. Oktober 2009' [2012] RNotZ 65, 73ff.

[115] Dutta, (2009) 73 RabelsZ 547, 569; Anna Wysocka, 'How Can a Valid Professio Iuris Be Made under the EU Succession Regulation?' [2012] NIPR 569, 569; Marion Greeske, *Die Kollisionsnormen der neuen EU-Erbrechtsverordnung* (Peter Lang 2014) 100; Castellanos Ruiz, *Calvo Caravaca/Davì/Mansel* (2016) ESR Art 22 para 2.

[116] See Arts 5 and 6 of the Convention (Convention of 1 August 1989 on the Law Applicable to Succession to the Estates of Deceased Persons). It should be noted that the Convention is not yet in force.

[117] Max Planck Institute for Comparative and International Private Law, (2010) 74 RabelsZ 522, 525.

[118] Stamatiadis, *Pamboukis* (2017) ESR Art 22 para 1.

[119] Recital 38 of the Regulation.

[120] Dutta, (2009) 73 RabelsZ 547, 576–577; Lein, (2009) XI YbPIL 107, 132ff; Kindler, [2010] IPRax 44, 49; Max Planck Institute for Comparative and International Private Law, (2010) 74 RabelsZ 522, 607ff; Dutta, 'Die Rechtswahlfreiheit in der EuErbVO' (2011) 71ff; cf. Pazdan and Zachariasiewicz, (2021) 17 J Priv Int L 74, 90.

should have a close connection with the deceased. Second, the law chosen should not deprive heirs entitled to reserved share of their legitimate expectations.[121] Nevertheless, it has been argued that these justifications are unsatisfactory by virtue of the fact that a person in the EU – a geopolitical system based on mutual trust – may well be closely connected to more than one legal system, such as when the deceased holds a passport from a Member State but has his habitual residence in another Member State and his heirs or properties are located in a different Member State than the State of habitual residence or nationality. Further, contrary to the social policy of States calling upon ancestors to protect their offspring – a notion arguably belonging to a bygone era – people may now have different reasons to disinherit heirs otherwise entitled to a reserved share.[122] It has been contended that a broader rule allowing the deceased also to choose the law of the State in which he or she is then, or was previously habitually resident, the law applicable to matrimonial property regimes, or the law of the State where the assets are located could have been desirable in the Regulation, instead of such a restrictive choice-of-law rule.[123] Notwithstanding this, the Regulation allows for a *professio iuris* only in favour of the national law of the deceased.

In the event that the deceased possesses more than one nationality at the same time, he may choose the law of any of his national States at the time of making the choice or at the time of death. This means that the question of whether the nationality of the State whose law has been chosen is an effective one or not is irrelevant.[124] Such an approach is justified by the fact that in the case of a *professio iuris,* the choice of the deceased who holds multiple nationalities should be trusted.[125] This has a practical advantage for the Member State courts in that they would not have to endure the difficulty of determining which nationality is effective and, hence, should prevail over another.[126] What is more important from a third State perspective is that no differentia-

---

[121] Recital 38 of the Regulation.

[122] Lein, (2009) XI YbPIL 107, 132–133; Szilágyi, (2021) XVII IAS 149, 162–163.

[123] Max Planck Institute for Comparative and International Private Law, (2010) 74 RabelsZ 522, 609ff; Dutta, 'Die Rechtswahlfreiheit in der EuErbVO' (2011) 70ff.

[124] Döbereiner, [2013] MittBayNot 358, 362; Odersky, [2013] Notar 3, 5; Jens Heinig, 'Rechtswahlen in Verfügungen von Todes wegen nach der EU-Erbrechts-Verordnung' [2014] RNotZ 197, 203; Solomon, 'Die allgemeine Kollisionsnorm' (2014) 39; Castellanos Ruiz, *Calvo Caravaca/Davì/Mansel* (2016) ESR Art 22 para 15; Stamatiadis, *Pamboukis* (2017) ESR Art 22 para 40; Köhler, *NK/Nachfolgerecht* (2019) EuErbVO Art 22 para 6; Looschelders, *NK-BGB/Rom-Verordnungen* (2019) EuErbVO Art 22 para 20; Dutta, *MüKo-BGB* (2020) EuErbVO Art 22 para 3; Martin Schauer, in Astrid Deixler-Hübner and Martin Schauer (eds), *Kommentar zur EU-Erbrechtsverordnung* (2nd edn, Manz 2020) EuErbVO Art 22 para 23.

[125] Solomon, 'Die allgemeine Kollisionsnorm' (2014) 39.

[126] Castellanos Ruiz, *Calvo Caravaca/Davì/Mansel* (2016) ESR Art 22 para 15.

tion is made between the nationality of a third State and a Member State in accordance with the universal nature of the conflict rules of the Regulation.[127]

The preliminary question of whether a person is or is not a national of a State will be decided by the law of the State whose nationality is in question.[128] Thus, a court dealing with a matter of succession where a choice of law has been made by the deceased in favour of his national law – be it that of a Member State or a third State – will have to refer to the rules of the State whose nationality is contended.

Another important issue for a *professio iuris*, regardless of the chosen law, is the form of the choice.[129] This is dealt with under the second paragraph of Article 22. Pursuant to this, the choice could be either express or implied. An express choice could be made in a declaration in the form of a testamentary disposition, i.e. a will, joint will, or an agreement as to succession.[130] An implied choice of law, on the other hand, could be inferred by the terms of such dispositions. Any revocation or modification of the choice of law should be made in the form of a revocation or modification of the relevant disposition of property upon death in which the choice was expressed or demonstrated by the terms (Article 22(4)).

For the *professio iuris* – 'as a judicial act of private international law'[131] – to be effective, it should be both formally and substantively valid. The substantive validity in the context of *professio iuris* refers to the understanding and consent of the deceased as to the act of choice of law.[132] Article 22(3) of the Regulation provides that the substantive validity of the act whereby the choice is made will be governed by the chosen law (Article 22(3)), regardless of whether the chosen law does or does not recognise such a choice.[133] That is to say that when a Turkish deceased habitually resident in a Member State makes a testament and chooses Turkish law to be applicable to his succession after his death, the substantive validity of this declaration of intent will be governed by Turkish law, irrespective of whether Turkish law permits a choice of law for succession matters. Nevertheless, when a choice of law is not allowed in this field, it is questionable whether the chosen law will have specific rules on the understanding of the consequences of the choice or the consent to the choice in matters of succession.[134] Guidance in this regard can, however, be found in Article 26(1) of the Regulation on the substantive valid-

---

[127] Castellanos Ruiz, *Calvo Caravaca/Davì/Mansel* (2016) ESR Art 22 para 15.

[128] Recital 41 of the Regulation.

[129] Greeske, *Kollisionsnormen der EU-Erbrechtsverordnung* (2014) 142.

[130] Art 3(1) (d) of the Regulation.

[131] Wysocka, [2012] NIPR 569, 573.

[132] Wysocka, [2012] NIPR 569, 573. See Recital 40 of the Regulation.

[133] Wysocka, [2012] NIPR 569, 573; Castellanos Ruiz, *Calvo Caravaca/Davì/Mansel* (2016) ESR Art 22 para 17; Stamatiadis, *Pamboukis* (2017) ESR Art 22 para 69; Dutta, *MüKoBGB* (2020) EuErbVO Art 22 para 17. See Recital 40 of the Regulation.

ity of dispositions of property upon death; given that a choice of law could only be made in instances of such a disposition, it is suggested that an analogous process should apply in assessing the substantive validity of the choice.[135] Accordingly, the following elements should be subject to consideration: the capacity to make a choice of law (Article 26(1) (a)), the admissibility of representation for the choice of law (Article 26(1) (c)), the interpretation of the choice of law (Article 26(1) (d)), and the situations affecting the consent or intention of the deceased (Article 26(1) (e)). All these matters will be governed by the chosen law.[136]

Whereas the European legislature allows the deceased to make a *professio iuris*, neither the Turkish PILA[137] nor the Treaty includes such an option for the deceased. Hence, there are a number of issues which should be considered in the Turkish-European context.

One issue is that problems may arise when the deceased makes a choice of law pursuant to Article 22 of the Regulation in a case related to Turkey, as the choice will not be recognised under the Turkish PILA.[138] There are a number of scenarios which are conceivable. First, a national of a Member State may make a *professio iuris* in favour of his national law under Article 22 of the Regulation but later move to Turkey, where his choice of law would have no effect.[139] This would be the case, for example, when a French national who is habitually resident in Berlin/Germany makes a disposition of property upon death to share out his estate, which consists of a villa in Antalya/Turkey and

---

[134] Carl Friedrich Nordmeier, 'Grundfragen der Rechtswahl in der neuen EU-Erbrechtsverordnung – Eine Untersuchung des Art 22 ErbRVO' [2013] GPR 148, 153; Stamatiadis, *Pamboukis* (2017) ESR Art 22 para 70.

[135] Nordmeier, [2013] GPR 148, 153; Christoph Döbereiner, '(Bindende?) Rechtswahlen nach der EU-Erbrechtsverordnung' [2014] DNotZ 323, 325; Dutta, *MüKoBGB* (2020) EuErbVO Art 22 para 19; Schauer, *Deixler-Hübner/Schauer* (2020) EuErbVO Art 22 para 13.

[136] Nordmeier, [2013] GPR 148, 153; Dutta, *MüKoBGB* (2020) EuErbVO Art 22 para 19; Schauer, *Deixler-Hübner/Schauer* (2020) EuErbVO Art 22 para 14.

[137] Although Article 20 of the Turkish PILA does not allow the deceased to choose the law applicable to succession, there are scholars who argue that *professio iuris* in the field of succession should also be allowed in Turkish law as part of a future reform. See, in this regard, Baran Çelik, *Ölüme Bağlı Tasarruflar* (2011) 77–81; Baran Çelik, 'Miras–İrade Muhtariyeti' (2012) 128–130; Öztürk, (2015) 5 AkdHFD 177, 202; Mesut Aygün and Ayşe Kübra Altıparmak, '650/2012 Sayılı Avrupa Birliği Miras Tüzüğü'nde Mirasa Uygulanacak Hukukun Tespiti' (2016) 11 BAÜHFD 29, 52–53; Altıparmak, *Mirasa Uygulanacak Hukuk* (2017) 155–156; contra Tanrıbilir, 'MÖHUK ve Mirasa İlişkin Bağlama Kuralının Uygulanmasında Öne Çıkan Hususlar' (2018) 226–227.

[138] See, more general on the cases in relation to third States, Lein, 'Die Erbrechtsverordnung aus Sicht der Drittstaaten' (2014) 212.

[139] See, in this regard, Lein, 'Die Erbrechtsverordnung aus Sicht der Drittstaaten' (2014) 212.

an apartment in Paris/France, among his three nephews and a friend and states the law applicable to his succession should be the law of France. He later starts living in Antalya and dies there after eight years of residency. In this case, the choice in favour of French law is valid under Article 22 of the Regulation but invalid under the Turkish PILA. The solution of the Turkish PILA (Article 20(1)) – unlike the Regulation which would apply French law to both of the assets – would be that the apartment in Paris is governed by French law, as the national law of the deceased, and that the villa in Antalya is governed by Turkish law.

Second, there may be a case where a Turkish national who is habitually resident/domiciled in Turkey or in one of the Member States chooses Turkish law to govern his succession pursuant to Article 22 of the Regulation. Such a choice would again not be effective in Turkey, since Article 20 of the Turkish PILA does not grant the deceased the right to designate the law applicable to succession. This can be demonstrated with a simple example. Assume, for instance, that a Turkish citizen who is habitually resident/domiciled in Istanbul/Turkey and who owns, in addition to the assets found in Istanbul, a holiday house in Mallorca/Spain and a flat in the Hague/Netherlands, chooses Turkish law to govern his succession in the holographic will he drafted in his last days. The *professio iuris* made in the will would be declared valid by the European courts if it were made in accordance with the formal and substantive validity requirements. Such a choice, on the other hand, could not be recognised in Turkey.[140] Nevertheless, the non-recognition of the choice of law clause in Turkey would not make any difference on the law applicable to succession in this case. This is because the deceased is a Turkish national and the law governing his succession as a whole, except for certain matters, is Turkish law (Article 20(1)).

A third scenario could come into play when a person who is habitually resident in a Member State and who holds the nationality of Turkey in addition to the State of his habitual residence makes a choice of law in favour of Turkish law in accordance with Article 22 of the Regulation.[141] In such a case, the choice of law would once again be valid in the Member State but invalid in Turkey. The following example illustrates this: A Turkish-Belgian national habitually resident in Ghent/Belgium has assets in Ghent as well as in his hometown, Bursa/Turkey. If he makes a testamentary disposition and chooses Belgian law to be applicable to his succession, such a choice will be valid in the Union thanks to Article 22(1) of the Regulation, which allows multiple nationals to choose one of their national laws, irrespective of whether the chosen law is that of the State whose nationality is effective. The choice of Bel-

[140] See, in this regard, Lein, 'Die Erbrechtsverordnung aus Sicht der Drittstaaten' (2014) 212.

[141] See, in this regard, Lein, 'Die Erbrechtsverordnung aus Sicht der Drittstaaten' (2014) 212.

gian law, however, would not be recognised in Turkey, and instead Turkish law would be applicable to the succession as a whole pursuant to Article 20(1) of the Turkish PILA. This is because the Turkish nationality of a person holding dual and/or multiple citizenships would prevail in a case where the law applicable to a matter is determined on the basis of nationality (Article 4(b) of the Turkish PILA). Only in the case where the deceased had chosen Turkish law could the law applicable to succession have been the same (Turkish law) in both jurisdictions, even though the *professio iuris* has no effect in Turkey.

This third scenario could of course be formulated differently such that the deceased has not Turkish nationality but the dual nationality of two different Member States. Assume, for instance, the deceased holds the citizenship of Belgium as well as of the Netherlands and he chooses Dutch law to govern succession pursuant to Article 22 of the Regulation. Regardless of the *situs* of the assets and regardless of Dutch nationality being the effective one, his choice will be valid in the Union if it is consistent with other conditions of validity. In Turkey, on the other hand, no effect would be given to the *professio iuris*; rather, the law applicable would be determined according to Article 20 of the Turkish PILA. Since the deceased has multiple nationalities none of which is the nationality of Turkey, Article 4(c) of the Turkish PILA is to be applied. Article 4(c) of the Turkish PILA prescribes that in such instances the law of the State to which the person has the closer connection is to be applicable. This means that the effective nationality test is employed by the Turkish PILA to find the law applicable for persons holding more than one nationality of States other than Turkey wherever the law applicable is determined on the basis of nationality. The Turkish judge, therefore, would assess the circumstances of the case, find the effective nationality of the deceased, and apply the law of this State to the dispute. The result reached by the Turkish judge may not necessarily be the same as within the EU. The courts on the European side will be bound by the *professio iuris* of the deceased and apply Dutch law to the succession as a whole, whereas the Turkish courts may come to the conclusion that the effective nationality of the deceased is that of Belgium and apply Belgian law to the succession, except for any immovable property located in Turkey that should ultimately be under the authority of Turkish law.

The number of examples could always be increased. These are, however, enough to indicate that availability of the *professio iuris* option for the deceased on only the EU side may give rise to problems in the Turkish-European context. It is true that on some occasions the law applicable to succession would be the same in both jurisdictions, even though the choice of law made by the deceased has no effect in Turkey. This is because the national law of the deceased is already the objectively applicable law in matters of succession under the Turkish PILA. Notwithstanding this, a valid *professio iuris* under Turkish law could have guaranteed that the estate would be governed by the same law in the Turkish-EU context.

One could question whether a choice of law could have been effective through a *renvoi* in these cases.[142] Although no *renvoi* is applicable in a case of *professio iuris* made in accordance with Article 22 of the Regulation (Article 34(2) of the Regulation), its application in a third State may carry the result that the choice made by the deceased will be effective in that State.[143] This was the case in the former Turkish PILA (Law no 2675) which allowed for single (partial) *renvoi*[144] in all matters, including succession, under Article 2(3).[145] In that case, a choice of law could have been given an indirect effect under the Turkish PILA. Imagine, for example, a Portuguese national who is habitually resident in Madrid/Spain and who has movable and immovable assets in Madrid as well as a significant amount of money in a bank account in Istanbul/Turkey, where he used to live for a couple of years. This individual drafts a testament and chooses Portuguese law to be applicable to his succession. Had this case been brought before the Turkish courts at the time when the former Turkish PILA was in force, Portuguese law would have been applicable not because it was the objectively applicable law under Article 22 of the former Turkish PILA, but because of the choice of law made by the deceased in accordance with Article 22 of the Regulation. The underlying reason for this is that Article 22(1) of the former Turkish PILA, like Article 20(1) of the current Turkish PILA, required the Turkish judge to apply the national law of the deceased to the dispute. Article 2(3) of the former Turkish PILA, however, provided for a single (partial) *renvoi* system. Thus, the Turkish judge should have taken the private international rules of Portugal into account and given effect to the choice of law made by the deceased in accordance with Article 22 of the Regulation as the Portuguese private international law on succession.[146] A Turkish judge has to apply a foreign law consistent with the way it is applied

[142] Lein, 'Die Erbrechtsverordnung aus Sicht der Drittstaaten' (2014) 212.

[143] See, in this regard, Tanrıbilir, *Kanuni Mirasçılıktan Doğan Kanunlar İhtilafı* (2000) 62–63.

[144] On the meaning of single (partial) *renvoi*, see pp 153, below.

[145] Uluocak, *Milletlerarası Özel Hukuk Dersleri* (1987) 113; Vahit Doğan, 'Atıf Teorisindeki Gelişmeler ve Türk Hukuku' (1998) 6 SÜHFD 821, 842; Tanrıbilir, *Kanuni Mirasçılıktan Doğan Kanunlar İhtilafı* (2000) 10ff; Ekşi, *Milletlerarası Miras Hukuku* (2013) 84; Süheyla Balkar Bozkurt, 'Uluslararası Özel Hukukta Bitmeyen Tartışma: Atıf (Renvoi) Teorisi, Uygulaması ve Değerlendirilmesi' [2014] GSÜHFD 795, 846; Altıparmak, *Mirasa Uygulanacak Hukuk* (2017) 100; Barış Mesci, 'Milletlerarası Özel Hukukta Atıf (Renvoi)' (2017) 16 İKÜHFD 311, 353; Tekinalp, *Milletlerarası Özel Hukuk* (2020) 39; Çelikel and Erdem, *Milletlerarası Özel Hukuk* (2021) 123; contra Aybay and Dardağan, *Kanunlar İhtlilafı* (2008) 169–171; Esra Dardağan Kibar, 'Güncel Gelişmeler Işığında Atıf Sorununa Bakış Denemesi' in Feriha Bilge Tanrıbilir and Gülce Gümüşlü Tunçağıl (eds), *10. Yılında MÖHUK Sempozyumu – 7–8 Aralık 2017, Ankara* (Adalet Yayınevi 2018) 37–38. See also Yargıtay 2. Hukuk Dairesi, T. 15.4.2002, E. 2002/4651 K. 2002/5612 published in Ahmet Cemal Ruhi, 'Mirasçılık Belgesi ve Yabancı Ülke Mahkemelerinden Verilen Mirasçılık Belgelerinin Türkiye'de Tanınması' (2006), 32 YD 265, 279–280 fn 50.

and interpreted in the State of origin.[147] Accordingly, a choice of law made by the deceased which is permitted under the regulation should not be ignored by the judge, despite the fact that *professio iuris* is not allowed in the field of cross-border successions under Turkish law.[148]

Yet this possibility may not come into play under the current Turkish PILA, as Article 2(3) allows *renvoi* only for issues of personal status and family law. It is, however, questionable, at least for certain commentators, whether this also covers succession. It is contended that in determining whether *renvoi* becomes applicable, a distinction should be made between succession matters relating to movables and immovables. Under this line of thought, *renvoi* should be accepted for succession matters on movable estate. On succession issues involving immovable estate, conversely, *renvoi* could only be applicable when reference is made to the *lex rei sitae* by the private international law rules of the State whose law is applied.[149] This would be the case, for example, upon the intestate death of an English national living in Didim/Turkey who has a flat in London/England, a house in Provence/France, and a house in Didim.[150] The Turkish judge would apply English law, as the national law of the deceased, to all the properties located outside Turkey. English law applies the *lex rei sitae* for immovables,[151] which would be French law for the house in Provence. It is maintained that this reference to the *lex rei sitae* should be taken into account by the Turkish courts,[152] as the *lex rei sitae* contributes to the international harmony of decisions and is practical for the local authorities.[153] The prevailing opinion, however, rightly holds that *renvoi* is not applicable for succession matters, since they are not considered to be

---

146 For a similar example, see Tanrıbilir, *Kanuni Mirasçılıktan Doğan Kanunlar İhtilafı* (2000) 62–63.

147 Tuğçe Nimet Yaşar, 'Türk Mahkemelerinde Yabancı Hukukun Uygulanması' (2013) 33 MHB 75, 95–96; Mustafa Erkan, 'Türk Milletlerarası Özel Hukuk Sisteminde Yabancı Hukukun Tatbiki: Olan vs. Olması Gereken' in Bilgin Tiryakioğlu and others (eds), *Milletlerarası Özel Hukukta Güncel Konular Sempozyumu* (Yetkin 2016) 543; Can Yöney, *Yabancı Hukukun Uygulanması* (On İki Levha 2018) 65–67; Çelikel and Erdem, *Milletlerarası Özel Hukuk* (2021) 179; Nomer, *Devletler Hususî Hukuku* (2021) 198; Şanlı, Esen and Ataman Figanmeşe, *Milletlerarası Özel Hukuk* (2021) 69–70.

148 Tanrıbilir, *Kanuni Mirasçılıktan Doğan Kanunlar İhtilafı* (2000) 63.

149 Balkar Bozkurt, [2014] GSÜHFD 795, 828; Çelikel and Erdem, *Milletlerarası Özel Hukuk* (2021) 120.

150 This example is inspired by Lein, 'Die Erbrechtsverordnung aus Sicht der Drittstaaten' (2014) 212.

151 See above n 17, p 53.

152 Balkar Bozkurt, [2014] GSÜHFD 795, 828; Çelikel and Erdem, *Milletlerarası Özel Hukuk* (2021) 120.

153 Balkar Bozkurt, [2014] GSÜHFD 795, 828; cf. Tekinalp, *Milletlerarası Özel Hukuk* (2020) 39.

issues relating to personal status and family law.[154] Thus, the choice of law made by the deceased may not become effective through *renvoi* under the current Turkish PILA.

Though it may be the case that a choice of law is not permitted by the Turkish PILA and problems may be attached to such a choice in the Turkish-EU context, the Regulation's approach to *professio iuris* should be evaluated from the Turkish perspective. As mentioned earlier, although it has a limited scope, the availability of *professio iuris* for the deceased in favour of the national law has been appreciated by European scholars. It should also be welcomed from the Turkish perspective. This is due to the considerable number of Turkish nationals resident in the EU. These individuals may guarantee the application of Turkish law – which is the law applicable to succession under Article 20(1) of the Turkish PILA – by way of a *professio iuris* within the Union. Choosing Turkish law to be applicable to succession could eliminate for them the risk that different laws become applicable for the same estate, i.e. Turkish law as the national law of the deceased in Turkey (Article 20(1) of the Turkish PILA) and a Member State law as the law of the last habitual residence of the deceased (Article 21(1) of the Regulation). This is of particular practical importance in cases where the deceased has heirs or assets, especially movable assets,[155] in Turkey. If, for instance, a Turkish national habitually resident in Ghent/Belgium – who has some of his heirs and assets in both States – makes a testament and chooses Turkish law to be applicable to succession pursuant to Article 22 of the Regulation, the succession will be governed by Turkish law regardless of the State before whose courts the case is brought.

In addition, *professio iuris* in favour of the national law is also important from the Turkish perspective, as the European legislature also took into consideration the stability interests of Turkish nationals as third country residents in the EU. There is of course no data indicating the integration or stability levels of third country nationals, including Turkish nationals, at the Union level, its being a detail which is impossible to establish.[156] Therefore, it is

[154] Faruk Kerem Giray, 'Milletlerarası Özel Hukuk Hakkaniyetinin 5718 Sayılı MÖHUK Kapsamında Değerlendirilmesi' (2012) IX YÜHFD 555, 562; Ekşi, *Milletlerarası Miras Hukuku* (2013) 84–85; Altıparmak, *Mirasa Uygulanacak Hukuk* (2017) 100–101; Burcu İrge Erdoğan, '5718 Sayılı MÖHUK Uyarınca Tenkis Davasında Uygulanacak Hukukun Kamu Düzeni Bakımından Değerlendirilmesi ve Yetkili Mahkeme' (2018) 20 DEÜHFD 397, 414; Tekinalp, *Milletlerarası Özel Hukuk* (2020) 39; Güngör, *Türk Milletlerarası Özel Hukuku* (2021) 167.

[155] As the jurisdiction of Turkish courts in matters of succession involving immovable assets is considered exclusive, there may be recognition and enforcement issues for the judgments or certificates of succession which are rendered/issued by the Member State courts, in spite of the fact that Turkish law has been applied.

[156] Herweg, *Die Vereinheitlichung des Internationalen Erbrechts* (2004) 56ff; D. Lehmann, *Die Reform des Internationalen Erb- und Erbprozessrechts* (2006) 77ff; Dutta,

questionable whether Turkish nationals in the EU, particularly guest workers and their offspring who live for almost their entire life in the EU are still most closely connected to Turkey, or whether Turkish law is the law which they are more familiar with. One might argue that the application of national law may not ensure the application of the most closely connected law.[157] Nevertheless, there might still be instances where they are not well integrated, or cases where they simply still do not feel well connected to their State of habitual residence, and they might desire the application of their national law in matters of succession. Thus, the potential for a *professio iuris* in favour of the national law under the Regulation seems to be advantageous from the Turkish point of view, despite *professio iuris* not being allowed in succession matters in Turkey.

Notwithstanding this, it is disputable whether the same is true for cases falling within the scope of the Treaty. There is obviously no provision allowing for *professio iuris* in the Treaty, this being in accord with the circumstances in place at the time it was drafted.[158] A further issue in relation to cases involving Turkey and the EU is, therefore, whether a *professio iuris* pursuant to Article 22 of the Regulation could be made by Turkish nationals in cases falling within the scope of the Treaty. This was discussed in a case[159]

(2009) 73 RabelsZ 547, 564. For some statistics from Germany, see Jürgen Basedow and Barbara Diehl-Leistner, 'Das Staatsangehörigkeitsprinzip im Einwanderungsland' in Erik Jayme and Heinz-Peter Mansel (eds), *Nation und Staat im Internationalen Privatrecht* (C.F. Müller 1990).

[157] Doğan, *Milletlerarası Özel Hukuk* (2022) 213–214. See, for a general view questioning the familiarity of a person with his national law, Basedow and Diehl-Leistner, 'Das Staatsangehörigkeitsprinzip' (1990) 16.

It has even been concluded that a choice of law in favour of a national law would be fraudulent in cases where the person has, except for the nationality, no other connection to his national State: Bonomi, *Bonomi/Wautelet* (2016) ESR Art 22 para 22; Castellanos Ruiz, *Calvo Caravaca/Davì/Mansel* (2016) ESR Art 22 para 6.

[158] H. Krüger, 'Studien über Probleme des türkischen Internationalen Erbrechts' (2006) 148.

[159] LG Hamburg 12.2.1991 – 302 T 88/90, IPRspr 1991 Nr. 142, 264, 272 ff. Even though the case falls within the scope of the Treaty, the LG Hamburg did not refer to the Treaty. Therefore, the case is in fact not particularly helpful for legal practice but is important for the scholarly debate.

Another relevant case in this regard was decided by the OLG Hamm: OLG Hamm 29.4.1992 – 15 W 114/91, IPRax 1994, 49. The court in that case dealt with the question of whether the differences applicable between the husband and the wife on entitlement to an estate, particularly the fact that the wife was not entitled to succession on the immovable property of her husband, violated German *ordre public*. The court held that such a situation indeed violates German *ordre public* as the deceased could have chosen German law to govern immovables located in Germany pursuant to (then-current) Art 25(2) EGBGB. Unlike the LG Hamburg, the court articulated the priority of application of the German-Iranian Treaty. However, it similarly did not address the relationship between the Treaty and the possibility of *professio iuris* under Art 25(2) EGBGB. See, on these cases, Ingo

relating to the German-Iranian Treaty on Establishment of 17 February 1929.[160] The court held in that case that Iranian nationals were allowed to choose German law pursuant to former Article 25(2) EGBGB, which was in force at the time, to govern succession issues on their immovable property located in Germany;[161] this was a departure from Article 8(3) of the German-Iranian Treaty, which provides that the law applicable to issues of succession is the national law of the deceased. The underlying justification behind this ruling, one that also found support from certain commentators,[162] was the general rule on interpretation of treaties enshrined in Article 31(1) of the Vienna Convention on the Law of Treaties. This provision requires that a treaty be interpreted in the light of its objective and purpose. Therefore, it was argued that the gap in the Treaty regarding the *professio iuris* should be filled based on this. Article 8(1) and (2) of the Treaty aims that the nationals of each Contracting State will be granted equal treatment in the territory of the other Contracting Party. In parallel to this purpose, Article 8(3) refers to the national law of the person in question for matters of personal status, including succession, in order to prevent that the relevant person is subject to the rules of another legal culture for such matters. It was, thus, argued that those aims would be realised when the deceased was given the right to choose German law pursuant to former Article 25(2) EGBGB.[163] Such an interpretation, however, was criticised by many scholars.[164]

Ludwig, in Maximilian Herberger and others (eds), *jurisPK-BGB*, vol 6 (7th edn, juris 2015) EGBGB Art 25, 26 para 18.

[160] RGBl. 1930 II, 1002. The Treaty became applicable on 11.1.1931, RGBl. 1931 II 9. The application of the Treaty was suspended between 9.9.1943 (Iran's declaration of war against Germany) and 8.5.1945 (German surrender in World War II). It was put into force again with a protocol on 4.11.1954 (BGBl. II 1955, 829) and is still applicable. See, for more information on the issue, Dörner, *Staudinger BGB* (2007) EGBGB Vorb. zu Art 25 f para 149.

[161] The provision read as follows: 'The deceased may choose, in the form of a disposition of property upon death, German law for immovable estate assets located in Germany'.

[162] Dörner, *Staudinger BGB* (2007) EGBGB Vorb. zu Art 25 f para 151; cf. Schotten and Schmellenkamp, *Das Internationale Privatrecht in der notariellen Praxis* (2007) paras 134 and 263.

[163] Dörner, *Staudinger BGB* (2007) EGBGB Vorb. zu Art 25 f para 151; cf. Schotten and Schmellenkamp, *Das Internationale Privatrecht in der notariellen Praxis* (2007) paras 134 and 263.

[164] Günther Schotten and Ralf Wittkowski, 'Das deutsch-iranische Niederlassungsabkommen im Familien- und Erbrecht' [1995] FamRZ 264, 269; Rembert Süß, 'Notarieller Gestaltungsbedarf bei Eingetragenen Lebenspartnerschaften mit Ausländern' [2001] DNotZ 168, 174; Gerhard Hohloch, in Harm Peter Westermann, Barbara Grunewald and Georg Maier-Reimer (eds), *Erman BGB*, vol 2 (14th edn, Otto Schmidt 2014) EGBGB Art 25 para 4a; Ludwig, *jurisPK-BGB* (2015) EGBGB Art 25, 26 para 21. See also Christian von Bar and Peter Mankowski, *Internationales Privatrecht: Besonderer Teil*, vol 2

This discussion may be seen as irrelevant for the Turkish-German Treaty. This is because Article 20(14) of the Turkish-German Treaty, unlike the German-Iranian Treaty, makes a distinction between movables and immovables and subjects immovables to the *lex rei sitae*. Therefore, under the Turkish-German Treaty, immovables located in Germany are already governed by German law, and the application of the former Article 25(2) EGBGB, which allowed the deceased to make a choice of law in favour of German law only for immovable properties found in Germany, could not have come into play.[165] The same contention, however, is now relevant for the Turkish-German Treaty, as Article 22 of the Regulation affords the deceased a *professio iuris* in favour of his national law. When this is the case, the question arises whether a Turkish deceased is allowed to choose Turkish law also to govern immovable properties located in Germany. The prevailing view in this regard maintains that a choice of law is not possible in cases falling in the scope of the treaties, including the Turkish-German Treaty, as they enjoy a priority of application under Article 75(1) of the Regulation.[166]

Considering the lack of a specific *professio iuris* rule in the Treaty, this could be seen as a matter of interpretation.[167] On the one hand, it is argued that a restrictive teleological interpretation should be made here, as the treaties intend to provide uniform rules that should be applicable in all of the States party to them, and a departure from those rules should only come into play when the rules are in contradiction with the aim intended by the drafters.[168] Therefore, it is contended that the aim of the respective State's drafters to ensure a level of protection for their nationals against discriminative treatment in the other State's territory is already safeguarded with the objectively applicable rules of the Treaty. Hence a choice of law, which is not even applicable in Turkey, has no particular advantage for the deceased.[169] On the other hand, this could be seen as a matter of interpretation, wherein one needs to

---

(2nd edn, C.H. Beck 2019) § 5 para 598; Dutta, *MüKoBGB* (2020) EuErbVO Art 75 para 12; Lorenz, *BeckOK BGB* (2022) EGBGB Art 25 aF para 11.

165 Looschelders, 'The External Relations of Germany' (2019) 164–165 fn 90.

166 Mario Leitzen, 'Die Rechtswahl nach der EuErbVO' [2013] ZEV 128, 128; Heinig, [2014] RNotZ 197, 203; Looschelders, 'The External Relations of Germany' (2019) 164–165; Martin T. Schwab, in Christopher Keim and Daniel Lehmann (eds), *BeckFormB ErbR* (4th edn, C.H. Beck 2019) Form. K.VI.1 Anm. 4; Dutta, *MüKoBGB* (2020) EuErbVO Art 75 para 12; Stürner, *Erman BGB* (2020) EuErbVO Art 75 para 10; Bauer and Süß, *Dutta/Weber* (2021) EuErbVO Art 75 Anhang II-deutsch-türkisches NA para 12.

167 Ludwig, *jurisPK-BGB* (2015) EGBGB Art 25, 26 para 21; Dutta, *MüKoBGB* (2020) EuErbVO Art 75 para 12; cf. Dörner, *Staudinger BGB* (2007) EGBGB Vorb. zu Art 25 f para 151.

168 Meyer-Sparenberg, *Staatsvertragliche Kollisionsnormen* (1990) 122; Ludwig, *jurisPK-BGB* (2015) EGBGB Art 25, 26 para 21.

169 Ludwig, *jurisPK-BGB* (2015) EGBGB Art 25, 26 para 21 (in relation to the German-Iranian Treaty).

examine whether a Treaty rule could be replaced by a later national rule (such as former Article 25(2) EGBGB) or a Union rule (Article 22 of the Regulation). With respect to this question, it is argued that allowing the deceased to make a *professio iuris* – a later-enacted device which was unknown and unforeseeable for the drafters at the time of the Treaty's conclusion and something which is still not prevalent among all legal systems – would be a substantial change to the rules of the Treaty and is thus unacceptable.[170]

As it has already been argued above, a choice of law under Article 22 of the Regulation seems advantageous for Turkish nationals resident in the Union so as to avoid problems that are likely to arise when different laws become applicable to the same estate depending on the jurisdiction where the case is brought. Taking into consideration that the majority of Turkish nationals who are resident in the Union are actually resident in Germany, one might argue that such an advantage is far more evident in cases within a Turkish-German context. Nevertheless, the Treaty already provides harmonised rules that should be applicable to succession matters in both of the Contracting States, and thus a *professio iuris* would not be of much help in the Treaty also from the perspective of such Turkish nationals. Furthermore, the *professio iuris*, as argued by its proponents, is neither relevant for the realisation of the drafter's intention nor in accord with the legal circumstances of the time it was concluded, when a choice of law for cross-border succession issues was unfamiliar to the vast majority of legal systems.[171] The lack of a *professio iuris* in the field of succession under the Turkish PILA also makes it difficult to defend such a possibility under the Treaty, since the opposite solution would be a 'unilateral'[172] one which is beneficial only for Turkish nationals residing in Germany but not for German nationals residing in Turkey. It seems, therefore, that a *professio iuris* pursuant to Article 22 of the Regulation – at least until a clarification is made by the European side[173] – is not possible in cases covered by the Treaty.

---

170 Dutta, *MüKoBGB* (2020) EuErbVO Art 75 para 12 (in relation to the German-Iranian Treaty).

171 See, in this regard, O. F. Berki, *Miras* (1960) 8 ff.

172 See, in the same direction with respect to the German-Iranian Treaty, Ludwig, *juris-PK-BGB* (2015) EGBGB Art 25, 26 para 21.

173 The question of whether a *professio iuris* is possible for a deceased in cases falling within the scope of treaties between Member States and third States that remain applicable under Article 75 of the Regulation was recently referred to the CJEU by a notary in Krapkowice/Poland in case C-387/20. The Court, however, found the application of the notary inadmissible, as the notary is not a 'court or tribunal' within the meaning of Art 267 TFEU, and hence, did not answer the question. See, for the order of the Court, C-387/20 OKR [2021] ECLI:EU:C:2021:751.

D. The Scope of the Applicable Laws

Determining which matters are characterised as matters of succession is crucial in determining the material scope of the *lex successionis* in each of the legal instruments. The Regulation, with the intention of guaranteeing legal certainty and avoiding any kind of fragmentation with respect to succession among Member States, provides that the law applicable to succession governs the succession as a whole (Article 23(1)). This intends, in the first place, that any 'territorial scission',[174] i.e. the possibility that different parts of the estate are governed by different laws due to their locations or nature, should be eschewed.[175] Furthermore, with the unity of succession, the Regulation aims to avoid also a 'substantial scission' of succession. That is to say that the law governing succession should be applied to any aspect of succession from its opening to transfer of the assets to the beneficiaries.[176] In the light of these aims, the Regulation enumerates exemplary issues[177] under Article 23 which are characterised as matters of succession in order to avoid conflicting interpretations from the Member States.[178] This 'positive list'[179] which clarifies the ambit of the *lex successionis* should be considered together with the 'negative list' under Article 1(2).

Article 1(2) of the Regulation gives guidance on the issues which are excluded from the scope of the Regulation. According to this, the following issues are not covered by the Regulation: the status of natural persons as well as family relationships or other kinds of similar relationships; the legal capacity of natural persons, except the capacity to inherit and testamentary capacity; questions with respect to the disappearance, absence, or presumed death of natural persons; issues relating to matrimonial property regimes or property regimes that are applicable in the course of other types of relationships which have comparable effects to marriage; maintenance obligations other than those aris-

---

174 For the use of the terms 'territorial' and 'substantive' scission, see Murad Ferid, 'Le Rattachement Autonome de la Transmission Successorale en Droit International Privé' (1974) 142 RdC 71, 110; Alexander S. Metallinos, in Haris P. Pamboukis (ed), *EU Succession Regulation No 650/2012 – A Commentary* (Nomiki Bibliothiki & C.H. Beck & Hart & Nomos 2017) ESR Art 23 para 2 (also citing *Ferid*).

175 Recital 37 of the Regulation.

176 Recital 42 of the Regulation. See, in this regard, Castellanos Ruiz, *Calvo Caravaca/ Davì/Mansel* (2016) ESR Art 23 paras 1–2; Metallinos, *Pamboukis* (2017) ESR Art 23 paras 1–8; Jan Peter Schmidt, in Anatol Dutta and Johannes Weber (eds), *Internationales Erbrecht* (2nd edn, C.H. Beck 2021) EuErbVO Art 23 para 1.

177 The Article uses the word 'in particular', and therefore, the issues listed in this provision are not exhaustive: Castellanos Ruiz, *Calvo Caravaca/Davì/Mansel* (2016) ESR Art 23 para 3; J. P. Schmidt, *Dutta/Weber* (2021) EuErbVO Art 23 para 10.

178 Dutta, *MüKoBGB* (2020) EuErbVO Vorb. Art 20 ff para 49 and Art 23 para 1.

179 For the use of terms 'positive' and 'negative' list, see Dutta, *MüKoBGB* (2020) EuErbVO Art 23 paras 1 and 5.

ing by reason of death; the formal validity of oral dispositions of property upon death; property rights, interests, and assets created or transferred for reasons other than succession; questions governed by the law of companies and other similar corporate or incorporate bodies which determine what will happen to members' shares upon death; the dissolution, extinction, or merger of companies and other corporate or unincorporated bodies; matters related to trusts; the nature of rights *in rem*; and issues with respect to the registration of rights in movable or immovable property. These matters, which are listed exhaustively,[180] may well give rise to preliminary questions in succession cases. They are, however, left outside the ambit of the Regulation and will be determined by the courts of Member States according to either, if applicable, other international conventions or European legal instruments, or domestic laws of the States.[181] By doing so, the Regulation draws a line between the law applicable to succession and the law applicable to other related areas.[182]

The material scope of the *lex successionis* is further elucidated under Article 23(2). Under the Regulation, the *lex successionis* encompasses: the causes and the time and place of the opening of succession; the determination of the beneficiaries, their respective shares, and the obligations which may be imposed them by the deceased, and the determination of any other succession rights, including those of the surviving spouse or partner; the capacity to inherit; disinheritance and disqualification by conduct; the transfer of the assets, rights, or obligations forming part of the estate to the heirs or legatees, including the conditions or effects of a waiver or acceptance of the succession or of a legacy, the powers of the heirs, administrators, or testamentary executors, particularly with respect to the sale of the property or the payment of creditors; liability for the deceased's debts; the disposable part of the estate, the reserved shares and other restrictions on the freedom of the testator to dispose of his property upon death as well as claims which persons close to the deceased may have against the estate or the heirs; any obligation to restore or account for gifts, advancements, or legacies in the process of determining the shares of the beneficiaries; and the sharing-out of the estate.

When it comes to Turkish law, Article 20(1) of the Turkish PILA laying out the general *lex successionis* should be applied to all matters regarding succession, including those arising out of dispositions of property upon death unless the issue falls within the scope of the exceptions provided under the subsequent paragraphs.[183] Indeed, other paragraphs of the article restrict the

[180] Bonomi, *Bonomi/Wautelet* (2016) ESR Art 1 para 10; Matthias Weller, in Alfonso-Luis Calvo Caravaca, Angelo Davì and Heinz-Peter Mansel (eds), *The EU Succession Regulation – A Commentary* (Cambridge University Press 2016) ESR Art 1 para 10.

[181] Weller, *Calvo Caravaca/Davì/Mansel* (2016) ESR Art 1 para 6.

[182] Dutta, *MüKoBGB* (2020) EuErbVO Art 23 para 2.

[183] Uluocak, *Milletlerarası Özel Hukuk Dersleri* (1987) 115; Tanrıbilir, *Kanuni Mirasçılıktan Doğan Kanunlar İhtilafı* (2000) 121; Tekinalp, *Milletlerarası Özel Hukuk* (2020)

ambit of the general rule. Paragraphs 4 and 5 of the rule relate, respectively, to the law applicable to the formal validity of dispositions of property upon death and the capacity of the testator to make such dispositions. As these are discussed below,[184] they are not examined here. However, the second and third paragraphs of the article are important, since they exclude some issues from the scope of the general *lex successionis* and submit them to different laws.

The first exception to the general rule is rendered in the second paragraph, holding that provisions pertaining to the grounds for the opening, acquisition, and sharing-out of the succession should be governed by the law of the place where the estate is located. This stipulates that succession matters relating to these particular subjects will not be governed by the national law of the deceased but rather by the law of the State where those assets are found. As mentioned earlier,[185] such an exception is justified, above all, for practical reasons.[186] The legislature considered that judges might have faced potential difficulties when taking into account the grounds for the opening of succession which are not regulated under Turkish law and when applying the provisions regarding the acquisition and the sharing-out of succession of a foreign law, and it thus submitted these issues to the authority of *lex rei sitae.*[187] Furthermore, there was also a concern that the rights of legatees could have been affected and problems regarding the possessory interests in properties forming the estate could have arisen when different laws govern the movable and immovable parts of the estate. This is because in cases where a non-Turkish deceased has movable property outside Turkey and immovable property in Turkey, different laws would be applicable to them under Article 20(1) of the Turkish PILA, which may result in such problems. Therefore, the legislature provided that such matters should be governed by the law of the States where those assets are located.[188] Notwithstanding this, it is obvious that this excep-

---

236; Güngör, *Türk Milletlerarası Özel Hukuku* (2021) 167–168; Şanlı, Esen and Ataman Figanmeşe, *Milletlerarası Özel Hukuk* (2021) 266–267; Doğan, *Milletlerarası Özel Hukuk* (2022) 370 ff.

[184] See below under E. pp 126–153.

[185] See above p 35.

[186] Tekinalp, (1978) 44 İÜHFM 91, 111; Aybay and Dardağan, *Kanunlar İhtlilafı* (2008) 234; Tekinalp, *Milletlerarası Özel Hukuk* (2020) 234; Şanlı, Esen and Ataman Figanmeşe, *Milletlerarası Özel Hukuk* (2021) 269. See also, for views in favour of and against this justification, İstanbul Üniversitesi Hukuk Fakültesi – Milletlerarası Hukuk ve Milletlerarası Münasebetler Enstitüsü, *MÖHUK Öntasarı Sempozyumu* (1978) 141 ff.

[187] Uluocak, *Milletlerarası Özel Hukuk Dersleri* (1987) 121; Aybay and Dardağan, *Kanunlar İhtlilafı* (2008) 234; Tekinalp, *Milletlerarası Özel Hukuk* (2020) 234; Şanlı, Esen and Ataman Figanmeşe, *Milletlerarası Özel Hukuk* (2021) 269.

[188] İstanbul Üniversitesi Hukuk Fakültesi – Milletlerarası Hukuk ve Milletlerarası Münasebetler Enstitüsü, *MÖHUK Öntasarı Sempozyumu* (1978) 139 and 144 ff; 'Danışma Meclisi Tutanakları – Milletlerarası Özel Hukuk ve Usul Hukuku Hakkında Kanun Tasarısı ve Adalet Komisyonu Raporu (1/5)', (1981) 7–8.

tion further impairs the advantages of the unitary system which may come into play when the deceased has no immovable property in Turkey.[189] Moreover, in cases where the assets of the estate are located in more than one State, each property will be governed by a different law. This would prove difficult for the judges and would still result in problems regarding the possessory interests or rights of the legatees in contrast to the aim of the rule.[190] Thus, it is argued that the scope of this rule should be interpreted restrictively.[191]

Another exception to the general rule is provided in the third paragraph of the article with a substantive provision (of private international law):[192] the State acquires an heirless estate located in Turkey. This means that the State acquires the estate located in Turkey to the extent that it has no claimant in accordance with the law applicable to succession, i.e. the national law of the deceased for movables and Turkish law for immovables. It is a well-known principle that States claim rights over an heirless estate found in their territories. There are, however, two divergent approaches in this regard. In certain jurisdictions, the right of the State over estates without a claimant is of a public law nature. That is to say that the State seizes an estate having no statutory or testamentary claimant based on its sovereign rights.[193] Under this approach, the State would exercise its right only over estate assets situated in its territory and not over estate assets located outside this territory. In other legal systems, by contrast, the issue is considered a private law matter and the State inherits such an estate as the final heir.[194] Turkey is also in this group.[195] Conflicts might arise in cross-border cases as a result of this divergence. The

[189] Tekinalp, *Milletlerarası Özel Hukuk* (2020) 234.

[190] Baran Çelik, *Ölüme Bağlı Tasarruflar* (2011) 108; cf. Tanrıbilir, *Kanuni Mirasçılıktan Doğan Kanunlar İhtilafı* (2000) 123 fn 5.

[191] Tanrıbilir, *Kanuni Mirasçılıktan Doğan Kanunlar İhtilafı* (2000) 129–131 and 151; Baran Çelik, *Ölüme Bağlı Tasarruflar* (2011) 108; Tekinalp, *Milletlerarası Özel Hukuk* (2020) 235.

[192] İstanbul Üniversitesi Hukuk Fakültesi – Milletlerarası Hukuk ve Milletlerarası Münasebetler Enstitüsü, *MÖHUK Öntasarı Sempozyumu* (1978) 152–154; Uluocak, *Milletlerarası Özel Hukuk Dersleri* (1987) 138; Tanrıbilir, *Kanuni Mirasçılıktan Doğan Kanunlar İhtilafı* (2000) 186; Baran Çelik, *Ölüme Bağlı Tasarruflar* (2011); Ekşi, 'Comparison of the Turkish PILA with the ESR' (2014) 126; Hacı Can and Ekin Tuna, *Milletlerarası Özel Hukuk* (5th edn, Adalet Yayınevi 2021) 429; Güngör, *Türk Milletlerarası Özel Hukuku* (2021) 59 and 168; Şanlı, Esen and Ataman Figanmeşe, *Milletlerarası Özel Hukuk* (2021) 268 and 276; cf. Tekinalp, *Milletlerarası Özel Hukuk* (2020) 244; Nomer, *Devletler Hususî Hukuku* (2021) 300. However, *Çelikel/Erdem* states that it is an overriding mandatory rule: Çelikel and Erdem, *Milletlerarası Özel Hukuk* (2021) 355.

[193] This is the case, for example, in Austria (§ 760 of Austrian Civil Code) or in the UK (§ 46(1) (vi) of the UK Administration of Estates Act).

[194] Max Planck Institute for Comparative and International Private Law, (2010) 74 RabelsZ 522, 653–654. This is the case, for example, in Germany (BGB § 1936).

[195] See Art 501 of the Turkish Civil Code.

underlying reason for including such a paragraph in the Turkish PILA was, therefore, to counter other States' claims as the final heir over estate assets found in Turkey.[196]

In the light of these exceptions, it is crucial to determine the scope of the general *lex successionis* under Article 20(1) of the Turkish PILA as well as the issues which are not governed by the *lex successionis* but by the *lex rei sitae* under the second paragraph. Unlike the Regulation, which attempts to eliminate the characterisation problems in the Union as much as possible and hence provides clear rules on the scope of the rules, the Turkish PILA does not have a specific provision giving guidance to the courts on this issue. This is, of course, understandable, since the need to define the scope of national PIL rules is rather small. Therefore, although there are different views on characterisation, the *lex fori* characterisation, i.e. the definition of the ambit of PIL rules with respect to the substantive law of Turkey, should be the initial starting point,[197] unless there is a need for otherwise, such as the case where a legal institute is unknown to Turkish law.[198]

In the light of this, the issues covered by the general *lex successionis* under Article 20(1) are: the determination of the beneficiaries and their respective shares,[199] including the succession rights of the surviving spouse,[200] the un-

---

[196] Nomer, *Devletler Hususî Hukuku* (2021) 300. *Nomer* (*ibid* fn 144) also cites a decision of the Turkish Constitutional Court which held that the acquisition of real estate in Turkey by foreign States is unconstitutional, except in certain situations. See Anayasa Mahkemesi, T. 9.10.1986, E. 1986/18 K. 1986/24, *Resmi Gazete* of 31.1.1987, no 19358. Due to this policy incentive, it has been argued that the system adopted in Turkish private international law is different from the domestic law in the sense that here the State claims the heirless estate in accordance with its regalian rights: Tanrıbilir, *Kanuni Mirasçılıktan Doğan Kanunlar İhtilafı* (2000) 186–187.

[197] V. R. Seviğ, *Kanunlar İhtilafı* (1974) 143; Uluocak, *Milletlerarası Özel Hukuk Dersleri* (1987) 201–202; Çelikel and Erdem, *Milletlerarası Özel Hukuk* (2021) 86–88; Nomer, *Devletler Hususî Hukuku* (2021) 100 and 104; Doğan, *Milletlerarası Özel Hukuk* (2022) 223–224; cf. Göğer, *Devletler Hususi Hukuku* (1977) 87–88; Şanlı, Esen and Ataman Figanmeşe, *Milletlerarası Özel Hukuk* (2021) 58.

[198] On the issue of characterisation, see below, pp 121–122.

[199] O. F. Berki, *Miras* (1960) 30ff; Uluocak, *Milletlerarası Özel Hukuk Dersleri* (1987) 115 and 125; Tanrıbilir, *Kanuni Mirasçılıktan Doğan Kanunlar İhtilafı* (2000) 133; Aybay and Dardağan, *Kanunlar İhtlilafı* (2008) 232; Baran Çelik, *Ölüme Bağlı Tasarruflar* (2011) 116; Altıparmak, *Mirasa Uygulanacak Hukuk* (2017) 107; Toker and Ruhi, *Milletlerarası Özel Hukuk ve Usul Hukuku Hakkında Kanun* (2019) 148; Tekinalp, *Milletlerarası Özel Hukuk* (2020) 236; Can and Tuna, *Milletlerarası Özel Hukuk* (2021) 426; Çelikel and Erdem, *Milletlerarası Özel Hukuk* (2021) 352; Güngör, *Türk Milletlerarası Özel Hukuku* (2021) 168; Nomer, *Devletler Hususî Hukuku* (2021) 298; Şanlı, Esen and Ataman Figanmeşe, *Milletlerarası Özel Hukuk* (2021) 266; Doğan, *Milletlerarası Özel Hukuk* (2022) 370.

[200] O. F. Berki, *Miras* (1960) 34–35; V. R. Seviğ, *Mirasla İlgili Devletler Hususi Hukuku Kaideleri* (1963) 109; Göğer, *Devletler Hususi Hukuku* (1977) 278–279; Uluocak,

born child,[201] or the State (except where Article 20(3) of the Turkish PILA applies);[202] the determination of the disposable part of the estate[203] and matters relating to the reserved share;[204] the determination of the assets, rights, and obligations forming parts of the estate,[205] the capacity to inherit,[206] dis-

---

Milletlerarası Özel Hukuk Dersleri (1987) 129; Doğan, *Milletlerarası Özel Hukuk* (2022) 371–372.

[201] Uluocak, *Milletlerarası Özel Hukuk Dersleri* (1987) 125; Aybay and Dardağan, *Kanunlar İhtlilafı* (2008) 233; Baran Çelik, *Ölüme Bağlı Tasarruflar* (2011) 122–123; Ekşi, *Milletlerarası Miras Hukuku* (2013) 39; Altıparmak, *Mirasa Uygulanacak Hukuk* (2017) 107; Toker and Ruhi, *Milletlerarası Özel Hukuk ve Usul Hukuku Hakkında Kanun* (2019) 148; Tekinalp, *Milletlerarası Özel Hukuk* (2020) 236; Can and Tuna, *Milletlerarası Özel Hukuk* (2021) 426; Çelikel and Erdem, *Milletlerarası Özel Hukuk* (2021) 352–353; Güngör, *Türk Milletlerarası Özel Hukuku* (2021) 168; Şanlı, Esen and Ataman Figanmeşe, *Milletlerarası Özel Hukuk* (2021) 266 and 269; Doğan, *Milletlerarası Özel Hukuk* (2022) 370 and 374; contra Abdülhak Kemal Yörük, *Nazari ve Ameli Devletler Hususi Hukuku* (2nd edn, İsmail Akgün Matbaası 1950) 428; Göğer, *Devletler Hususi Hukuku* (1977) 275.

[202] O. F. Berki, *Miras* (1960) 36; V. R. Seviğ, *Mirasla İlgili Devletler Hususi Hukuku Kaideleri* (1963) 109ff; Göğer, *Devletler Hususi Hukuku* (1977) 281–283; Baran Çelik, *Ölüme Bağlı Tasarruflar* (2011) 134ff; Toker and Ruhi, *Milletlerarası Ozel Hukuk ve Usul Hukuku Hakkında Kanun* (2019) 148; Tekinalp, *Milletlerarası Özel Hukuk* (2020) 237; Can and Tuna, *Milletlerarası Özel Hukuk* (2021) 426; Çelikel and Erdem, *Milletlerarası Özel Hukuk* (2021) 352; Doğan, *Milletlerarası Özel Hukuk* (2022) 372–373.

[203] Uluocak, *Milletlerarası Özel Hukuk Dersleri* (1987) 115; Tanrıbilir, *Kanuni Mirasçılıktan Doğan Kanunlar İhtilafı* (2000) 144–145; Aybay and Dardağan, *Kanunlar İhtlilafı* (2008) 233; Baran Çelik, *Ölüme Bağlı Tasarruflar* (2011) 116; Çelikel and Erdem, *Milletlerarası Özel Hukuk* (2021) 353; Güngör, *Türk Milletlerarası Özel Hukuku* (2021) 168; Doğan, *Milletlerarası Özel Hukuk* (2022) 374.

[204] Uluocak, *Milletlerarası Özel Hukuk Dersleri* (1987) 116; Tanrıbilir, *Kanuni Mirasçılıktan Doğan Kanunlar İhtilafı* (2000) 144–145; Aybay and Dardağan, *Kanunlar İhtlilafı* (2008) 233; Baran Çelik, *Ölüme Bağlı Tasarruflar* (2011) 116; Ekşi, *Milletlerarası Miras Hukuku* (2013) 39; Altıparmak, *Mirasa Uygulanacak Hukuk* (2017) 107; Tekinalp, *Milletlerarası Özel Hukuk* (2020) 236; Güngör, *Türk Milletlerarası Özel Hukuku* (2021) 168; Şanlı, Esen and Ataman Figanmeşe, *Milletlerarası Özel Hukuk* (2021) 266.

[205] Uluocak, *Milletlerarası Özel Hukuk Dersleri* (1987) 115; Tanrıbilir, *Kanuni Mirasçılıktan Doğan Kanunlar İhtilafı* (2000) 145; Aybay and Dardağan, *Kanunlar İhtlilafı* (2008) 233; Ekşi, *Milletlerarası Miras Hukuku* (2013) 39; Altıparmak, *Mirasa Uygulanacak Hukuk* (2017) 107–108; Tekinalp, *Milletlerarası Özel Hukuk* (2020) 237; Çelikel and Erdem, *Milletlerarası Özel Hukuk* (2021) 352; Güngör, *Türk Milletlerarası Özel Hukuku* (2021) 168; Doğan, *Milletlerarası Özel Hukuk* (2022) 374.

Here, a distinction should be made between the scope of the debts and obligations of the estate and the liability of the beneficiaries for these debts and obligations *vis-à-vis* estate creditors. The former issue should be governed by the general *lex successionis* under Article 20(1) of the Turkish PILA, whereas the latter is an issue regarding the sharing-out of succession, which falls under the scope of Article 20(2) of the Turkish PILA: Şanlı, Esen and Ataman Figanmeşe, *Milletlerarası Özel Hukuk* (2021) 275 fn 321. See, however, for the view holding that the liability of beneficiaries should also be governed by the general *lex successionis*, V. R. Seviğ, *Mirasla İlgili Devletler Hususi Hukuku Kaideleri* (1963)

qualification ('mirastan mahrumiyet'),[207] disinheritance ('mirasçılıktan çıkarma')[208] and the renunciation of inheritance ('mirasın reddi');[209] *com-*

129; Göğer, *Devletler Hususi Hukuku* (1977) 277; Ekşi, *Milletlerarası Miras Hukuku* (2013) 39; cf. Can and Tuna, *Milletlerarası Özel Hukuk* (2021) 426. *Berki*, on the other hand, contends that the liability of the beneficiaries towards estate creditors should be governed by the *lex fori*: O. F. Berki, *Miras* (1960) 59.

[206] Uluocak, *Milletlerarası Özel Hukuk Dersleri* (1987) 125; Tanrıbilir, *Kanuni Mirasçılıktan Doğan Kanunlar İhtilafı* (2000) 140–141; Baran Çelik, *Ölüme Bağlı Tasarruflar* (2011) 122; Tekinalp, *Milletlerarası Özel Hukuk* (2020) 236; Güngör, *Türk Milletlerarası Özel Hukuku* (2021) 168; Nomer, *Devletler Hususî Hukuku* (2021) 298; Doğan, *Milletlerarası Özel Hukuk* (2022) 373; contra Yörük, *Devletler Hususi Hukuku* (1950) 428; Göğer, *Devletler Hususi Hukuku* (1977) 275.

[207] V. R. Seviğ, *Mirasla İlgili Devletler Hususi Hukuku Kaideleri* (1963) 435; Göğer, *Devletler Hususi Hukuku* (1977) 278; Uluocak, *Milletlerarası Özel Hukuk Dersleri* (1987) 134; Tanrıbilir, *Kanuni Mirasçılıktan Doğan Kanunlar İhtilafı* (2000) 144; Aybay and Dardağan, *Kanunlar İhtlilafı* (2008) 233; Baran Çelik, *Ölüme Bağlı Tasarruflar* (2011) 128 ff; Altıparmak, *Mirasa Uygulanacak Hukuk* (2017) 107; Toker and Ruhi, *Milletlerarası Özel Hukuk ve Usul Hukuku Hakkında Kanun* (2019) 148; Tekinalp, *Milletlerarası Özel Hukuk* (2020) 237; Can and Tuna, *Milletlerarası Özel Hukuk* (2021) 426; Çelikel and Erdem, *Milletlerarası Özel Hukuk* (2021) 352–353; Güngör, *Türk Milletlerarası Özel Hukuku* (2021) 168; Nomer, *Devletler Hususî Hukuku* (2021) 298; contra Ş. Berki, *Devletler Hususî Hukuku* (1950) 64; Yörük, *Devletler Hususi Hukuku* (1950) 428–429; O. F. Berki, *Miras* (1960) 41.

[208] V. R. Seviğ, *Mirasla İlgili Devletler Hususi Hukuku Kaideleri* (1963) 126; Göğer, *Devletler Hususi Hukuku* (1977) 277; Uluocak, *Milletlerarası Özel Hukuk Dersleri* (1987) 147; Tanrıbilir, *Kanuni Mirasçılıktan Doğan Kanunlar İhtilafı* (2000) 148; Aybay and Dardağan, *Kanunlar İhtlilafı* (2008) 233; Ekşi, *Milletlerarası Miras Hukuku* (2013) 39; Altıparmak, *Mirasa Uygulanacak Hukuk* (2017) 107; Toker and Ruhi, *Milletlerarası Özel Hukuk ve Usul Hukuku Hakkında Kanun* (2019) 148; Tekinalp, *Milletlerarası Özel Hukuk* (2020) 239; Can and Tuna, *Milletlerarası Özel Hukuk* (2021) 426; Çelikel and Erdem, *Milletlerarası Özel Hukuk* (2021) 352; Güngör, *Türk Milletlerarası Özel Hukuku* (2021) 168; Nomer, *Devletler Hususî Hukuku* (2021) 298; Şanlı, Esen and Ataman Figanmeşe, *Milletlerarası Özel Hukuk* (2021) 266. For a different view, see Ş. Berki, *Devletler Hususî Hukuku* (1950) 64; O. F. Berki, *Miras* (1960) 48.

[209] V. R. Seviğ, *Mirasla İlgili Devletler Hususi Hukuku Kaideleri* (1963) 127; Göğer, *Devletler Hususi Hukuku* (1977) 277; Baran Çelik, *Ölüme Bağlı Tasarruflar* (2011) 126 ff; Ekşi, *Milletlerarası Miras Hukuku* (2013) 39; Altıparmak, *Mirasa Uygulanacak Hukuk* (2017) 107; Tekinalp, *Milletlerarası Özel Hukuk* (2020) 236; Can and Tuna, *Milletlerarası Özel Hukuk* (2021) 427–428; Çelikel and Erdem, *Milletlerarası Özel Hukuk* (2021) 352–354; Güngör, *Türk Milletlerarası Özel Hukuku* (2021) 168. For a different view, see Uluocak, *Milletlerarası Özel Hukuk Dersleri* (1987) 135; Tanrıbilir, *Kanuni Mirasçılıktan Doğan Kanunlar İhtilafı* (2000) 160; Aybay and Dardağan, *Kanunlar İhtlilafı* (2008) 236; Sema Çörtoğlu Koca and İpek Yücer Aktürk, 'Yabancı Unsurlu Miras İlişkilerinden Doğan Uyuşmazlıklarda Mirasın Reddine Uygulanacak Hukuk' (2018) 4 BÜHFD 11, 15–16; Nomer, *Devletler Hususî Hukuku* (2021) 298; Şanlı, Esen and Ataman Figanmeşe, *Milletlerarası Özel Hukuk* (2021) 272–273 fn 318; Doğan, *Milletlerarası Özel Hukuk* (2022) 377.

morientes;[210] matters relating to an action for reduction ('tenkis davası')[211] and to an action for the recovery of inheritance;[212] and the substantive validity and effects of dispositions of property upon death ('ölüme bağlı tasarrufların maddi geçerliliği ve etkileri').[213]

The issues pertaining to the grounds for the opening of succession as well as for the acquisition and the sharing-out of succession are outside the scope of the general *lex successionis* (Article 20(2) of the Turkish PILA). The question of just which matters fall under these topics is a characterisation issue. There seems to be two possible approaches which could be applicable here. In the first place, it could be argued that the ambit of the terms should be determined in line with the *lex fori*. In such a case, a Turkish judge dealing with the question of whether a specific dispute should be governed by the *lex successionis* under Article 20(1) of the Turkish PILA or the *lex rei sitae* pursuant to Article 20(2) of the Turkish PILA should take guidance only from the Turkish Civil Code.[214] When the *lex fori* approach is adopted, disqualification, for instance, should be characterised as a matter related to the opening of succession in accordance with the Turkish Civil Code[215] and hence will be governed by the *lex rei sitae*

---

210 V. R. Seviğ, *Mirasla İlgili Devletler Hususi Hukuku Kaideleri* (1963) 87–88; Aybay and Dardağan, *Kanunlar İhtlilafı* (2008) 233; Ekşi, *Milletlerarası Miras Hukuku* (2013) 39; Altıparmak, *Mirasa Uygulanacak Hukuk* (2017) 107; Tekinalp, *Milletlerarası Özel Hukuk* (2020) 236 and 241–242; Şanlı, Esen and Ataman Figanmeşe, *Milletlerarası Özel Hukuk* (2021) 266; Doğan, *Milletlerarası Özel Hukuk* (2022) 374. For different views, see O. F. Berkı, *Mıras* (1960) 50–51; Göğer, *Devletler Hususi Hukuku* (1977) 275–276; Uluocak, *Milletlerarası Özel Hukuk Dersleri* (1987) 133; Tanrıbilir, *Kanuni Mirasçılıktan Doğan Kanunlar İhtilafı* (2000) 143; Baran Çelik, *Ölüme Bağlı Tasarruflar* (2011) 123 ff.

211 O. F. Berki, *Miras* (1960) 45; Uluocak, *Milletlerarası Özel Hukuk Dersleri* (1987) 115; Tanrıbilir, *Kanuni Mirasçılıktan Doğan Kanunlar İhtilafı* (2000) 146; Baran Çelik, *Ölüme Bağlı Tasarruflar* (2011) 116; Altıparmak, *Mirasa Uygulanacak Hukuk* (2017) 107; İrge Erdoğan, (2018) 20 DEÜHFD 397, 404; Güngör, *Türk Milletlerarası Özel Hukuku* (2021) 168.

212 For a different view, see V. R. Seviğ, *Mirasla İlgili Devletler Hususi Hukuku Kaideleri* (1963) 129.

213 O. F. Berki, *Miras* (1960) 45 ff; V. R. Seviğ, *Mirasla İlgili Devletler Hususi Hukuku Kaideleri* (1963) 116 and 124; Uluocak, *Milletlerarası Özel Hukuk Dersleri* (1987) 115; Tanrıbilir, *Kanuni Mirasçılıktan Doğan Kanunlar İhtilafı* (2000) 121 and 145 ff; Pelin Güven, 'Yabancıların Vasiyetname Yapma Ehliyetine, Vasiyetin Şekline ve Esasına Uygulanacak Hukuk ile Bu Kapsamda Yabancı Gerçek Kişilerin Miras Hakkı' (2006) X AÜEHFD 341, 347 ff; Aybay and Dardağan, *Kanunlar İhtlilafı* (2008) 234; Baran Çelik, *Ölüme Bağlı Tasarruflar* (2011) 154 ff; Altıparmak, *Mirasa Uygulanacak Hukuk* (2017) 107; Tekinalp, *Milletlerarası Özel Hukuk* (2020) 238–239; Çelikel and Erdem, *Milletlerarası Özel Hukuk* (2021) 358; Güngör, *Türk Milletlerarası Özel Hukuku* (2021) 168; Şanlı, Esen and Ataman Figanmeşe, *Milletlerarası Özel Hukuk* (2021) 277–278; Doğan, *Milletlerarası Özel Hukuk* (2022) 374. See, on this issue, below, under E.I. pp 128–142.

214 Uluocak, *Milletlerarası Özel Hukuk Dersleri* (1987) 117 ff.

215 The issue is regulated under Arts 578–579 of the Turkish Civil Code under the title of the opening of succession.

under Article 20(2) of the Turkish PILA.[216] The second approach, on the other hand, suggests that whereas the judges are inclined to take guidance from the *lex fori* in the characterisation process, these terms should be understood in the light of the interests involved in private international law. This is because every legal system might have different regulations, and, therefore, the legal character of the matter – or, in other words, the *ratio legis* of the matter – should be decisive for the characterisation.[217] Pursuant to this, therefore, the example of disqualification would be considered as being within the scope of the general *lex successionis* under Article 20(1) of the Turkish PILA, since it is in fact a matter relating to the capacity to inherit.[218] This would also be more in line with the exceptional nature of Article 20(2).

As a consequence, the grounds for the opening of succession cover the question of whether the succession is opened upon the death or upon the disappearance, absence, or presumed death of the deceased.[219] In the vast majority of the jurisdictions, the succession is opened upon the death of the deceased.[220] However, there may be instances where the death or the survival of a person is uncertain. In such cases, depending on the circumstances of the case, absence[221] or the presumed death[222] of the person in question may be declared by the courts, and this may result in the opening of succession.[223] These rules may differ in different legal systems, and hence they will be governed by the *lex rei sitae* pursuant to Article 20(2) of the Turkish PILA.

---

216 Cf. Çelikel and Erdem, *Milletlerarası Özel Hukuk* (2021) 352–353 (only referring to this problem).

217 Tanrıbilir, *Kanuni Mirasçılıktan Doğan Kanunlar İhtilafı* (2000) 129–131; Aybay and Dardağan, *Kanunlar İhtlilafı* (2008) 235–237; Baran Çelik, *Ölüme Bağlı Tasarruflar* (2011) 185–186; Ekşi, *Milletlerarası Miras Hukuku* (2013) 43; Tekinalp, *Milletlerarası Özel Hukuk* (2020) 234–235; Çelikel and Erdem, *Milletlerarası Özel Hukuk* (2021) 351; Şanlı, Esen and Ataman Figanmeşe, *Milletlerarası Özel Hukuk* (2021) 269; Doğan, *Milletlerarası Özel Hukuk* (2022) 369–370; cf. Güngör, *Türk Milletlerarası Özel Hukuku* (2021) 167.

218 Ekşi, *Milletlerarası Miras Hukuku* (2013) 43; Tekinalp, *Milletlerarası Özel Hukuk* (2020) 235. See also explanations concerning Art 20 of the Turkish PILA, '5718 Sayılı Milletlerarası Özel Hukuk ve Usul Hukuku Hakkında Kanun Tasarısı ve Gerekçe' 7.

219 Tanrıbilir, *Kanuni Mirasçılıktan Doğan Kanunlar İhtilafı* (2000) 152–154; Aybay and Dardağan, *Kanunlar İhtlilafı* (2008) 236; Baran Çelik, *Ölüme Bağlı Tasarruflar* (2011) 186–187; Ekşi, *Milletlerarası Miras Hukuku* (2013) 43–45; Tekinalp, *Milletlerarası Özel Hukuk* (2020) 241; Çelikel and Erdem, *Milletlerarası Özel Hukuk* (2021) 353; Güngör, *Türk Milletlerarası Özel Hukuku* (2021) 167–168; Nomer, *Devletler Hususî Hukuku* (2021) 297; Şanlı, Esen and Ataman Figanmeşe, *Milletlerarası Özel Hukuk* (2021) 270; Doğan, *Milletlerarası Özel Hukuk* (2022) 375–376.

220 Marcello Maggiolo, 'The Decedent' in Ulrich Drobnig and Karl Heinz Neumayer (eds), *International Encyclopedia of Comparative Law – Vol V: Succession* (Mohr Siebeck & Martinus Nijhoff Publishers 1992) para 6. For Turkey, see Art 575 of the Turkish Civil Code.

221 See Arts 32–35 of the Turkish Civil Code.

222 See Art 31 of the Turkish Civil Code.

The acquisition of succession refers, in the first place, to the procedure of transferring succession to the beneficiaries. It is well known that there are two main systems regarding this in jurisdictions. In most of the civilian legal traditions, including Turkey,[224] the succession passes to the beneficiaries directly and immediately upon death. By contrast, in common law jurisdictions, the transfer of succession does not occur directly but through an executor or representative who is in charge of the winding up of the estate, i.e. the determination, collection and, where necessary, the protection of the deceased's assets and the payment of debts. The succession is transferred to the beneficiaries only after this process.[225] This matter is governed by the *lex rei sitae* under Article 20(2) of the Turkish PILA, as it is related to the title to or possession of the assets forming a part of the estate.[226] Furthermore, the transfer of succession may be in the form of 'universal' or 'singular' succession. Universal succession refers to the transfer of the totality of assets together with all rights, debts, and liabilities to the beneficiaries, whereas singular succession means the individual transfer of the things, such as gifts, legacies, or purchases. Differences in this regard also apply among the jurisdictions.[227] Therefore, this question should also be governed by the *lex rei sitae* according to Article 20(2) of the Turkish PILA.[228]

---

[223] Maggiolo, 'The Decedent' (1992) paras 24ff. For the effect of absence and presumed death on the opening of succession under Turkish law, see Arts 35 and 44 of the Turkish Civil Code.

[224] See Art 599(1) of the Turkish Civil Code.

[225] Miller, *International Aspects of Succession* (2000) 2–3; Marius J. de Waal, 'A Comparative Overview' in Kenneth G. C. Reid, Marius J. de Waal and Reinhard Zimmermann (eds), *Exploring the Law of Succession* (Edinburgh University Press 2007) 23; Verbeke and Leleu, 'Harmonisation of the Law of Succession in Europe' (2011) 463; Manfred Wenckstern, 'Inheritance, Acceptance and Disclaimer' in Jürgen Basedow and others (eds), *The Max Planck Encyclopedia of European Private Law*, vol I (OUP 2012) 884–887; Jan Peter Schmidt, 'Transfer of Property on Death and Creditor Protection: The Meaning and Role of "Universal Succession"' in Andrew J. M. Steven, Ross Gilbert Anderson and John Keith Macleod (eds), *Nothing so Practical as a Good Theory: Festschrift for George L Gretton* (Avizandum 2017) 324.

[226] O. F. Berki, *Miras* (1960) 53; V. R. Seviğ, *Mirasla İlgili Devletler Hususi Hukuku Kaideleri* (1963) 127; Uluocak, *Milletlerarası Özel Hukuk Dersleri* (1987) 121; Tanrıbilir, *Kanuni Mirasçılıktan Doğan Kanunlar İhtilafı* (2000) 158; Aybay and Dardağan, *Kanunlar İhtlilafı* (2008) 236; Ekşi, *Milletlerarası Miras Hukuku* (2013) 45–46; Çelikel and Erdem, *Milletlerarası Özel Hukuk* (2021) 353; Güngör, *Türk Milletlerarası Özel Hukuku* (2021) 168; Nomer, *Devletler Hususî Hukuku* (2021) 298; Şanlı, Esen and Ataman Figanmeşe, *Milletlerarası Özel Hukuk* (2021) 271–272; Doğan, *Milletlerarası Özel Hukuk* (2022) 376–377.

[227] William Warwick Buckland and Arnold Duncan McNair, *Roman Law and Common Law* (2nd edn, Cambridge University Press 1965) 143–144; J. P. Schmidt, 'Transfer of Property on Death and Creditor Protection' (2017) 325.

[228] V. R. Seviğ, *Mirasla İlgili Devletler Hususi Hukuku Kaideleri* (1963) 127; Tanrıbilir, *Kanuni Mirasçılıktan Doğan Kanunlar İhtilafı* (2000) 161; Aybay and Dardağan, *Kanunlar*

Matters regarding the sharing-out of the succession will also be governed by the *lex rei sitae* under Article 20(2) of the Turkish PILA. The term 'sharing-out of the succession' first covers the relationship between the co-heirs and the liability they owe to estate creditors where the estate is not inherited by a single heir. This is because diversity once again exists between different legal systems on these issues. In certain systems belonging to the civilian law realm, including Turkey,[229] a community of co-heirs ('miras ortaklığı' or 'Erbengemeinschaft') arises and the estate devolves to them in its entirety under the Germanic principle of 'joint tenancy' ('elbirliğiyle haksahipliği' or 'Gesamthand').[230] This also affects the liability of heirs against estate creditors. The co-heirs, unlike in the Roman law tradition, remain jointly and severally liable to estate creditors. In other words, their liability for debts and obligations of the estate is not limited to their respective shares.[231] Nevertheless, in some legal systems based on the common law, in England for instance, the estate devolves to the personal representative who is responsible for the winding up of the estate, and the creditors must bring an action against him to collect their debts.[232] The question of which of these systems would be applicable for an estate asset is one related to the sharing-out of the succession, and, hence, it is dealt with pursuant to the law of the State where that asset is located.[233] Moreover, other matters regarding the sharing-out of succession,

---

İhtlilafı (2008) 236; Tekinalp, *Milletlerarası Özel Hukuk* (2020) 242; Çelikel and Erdem, *Milletlerarası Özel Hukuk* (2021) 353; Güngör, *Türk Milletlerarası Özel Hukuku* (2021) 168; Şanlı, Esen and Ataman Figanmeşe, *Milletlerarası Özel Hukuk* (2021) 271 fn 312; Doğan, *Milletlerarası Özel Hukuk* (2022) 376–377; contra Nomer, *Devletler Hususî Hukuku* (2021) 298.

[229] See Arts 640–641 of the Turkish Civil Code.

[230] Max Rheinstein, 'European Methods for the Liquidation of the Debts of the Deceased Persons' (1935) 20 Iowa L Rev 431, 453; J. P. Schmidt, 'Transfer of Property on Death and Creditor Protection' (2017) 330. For Turkey, see Mustafa Dural and Turgut Öz, *Türk Özel Hukuku Cilt IV – Miras Hukuku* (17th edn, Filiz Kitabevi 2021) paras 1863 ff; Serozan and Engin, *Miras Hukuku* (2021) § 7 paras 1 ff; Sezer Çabri, *Miras Hukuku Şerhi (TMK m. 495–574)*, vol I (2nd edn, On İki Levha, 2022) paras 13 ff.

[231] Rheinstein, (1935) 20 Iowa L Rev 431, 453; J. P. Schmidt, 'Transfer of Property on Death and Creditor Protection' (2017) 330. For Turkey, see Art 641 of the Turkish Civil Code; for more details in this regard, see Dural and Öz, *Miras Hukuku* (2021) paras 1890 ff; Serozan and Engin, *Miras Hukuku* (2021) § 7 paras 28a ff.

[232] J. P. Schmidt, 'Transfer of Property on Death and Creditor Protection' (2017) 328–329.

[233] Uluocak, *Milletlerarası Özel Hukuk Dersleri* (1987) 122–123; Tanrıbilir, *Kanuni Mirasçılıktan Doğan Kanunlar İhtilafı* (2000) 168; Aybay and Dardağan, *Kanunlar İhtlilafı* (2008) 237; Baran Çelik, *Ölüme Bağlı Tasarruflar* (2011) 196–200; Altıparmak, *Mirasa Uygulanacak Hukuk* (2017) 128–129; Tekinalp, *Milletlerarası Özel Hukuk* (2020) 242; Çelikel and Erdem, *Milletlerarası Özel Hukuk* (2021) 354; Nomer, *Devletler Hususî Hukuku* (2021) 298; Şanlı, Esen and Ataman Figanmeşe, *Milletlerarası Özel Hukuk* (2021) 274–

such as the procedure regarding the sharing-out of succession, the transfer of the succession shares between the heirs or between heirs and third parties, restrictions regarding the sharing-out of some assets[234] (e.g. the right of the surviving spouse over the matrimonial home and household goods[235]), and a partial division of the assets will also be governed by the *lex rei sitae* pursuant to Article 20(2) of the Turkish PILA.[236]

After determining the scope of the law applicable to succession under the Regulation and under the Turkish PILA, it is also important to focus on this issue under the Treaty. The Treaty is applicable both for intestate and testamentary succession. Article 20(14) uses a general wording of 'issues related to succession' ('hakkı verasete müteallik/müteferri mesail' or 'Die erbrechtlichen Verhältnisse'). Which issues would be considered as the 'issues related to succession', however, remains unclear.[237]

The German preamble to the Treaty clarifies that this should be interpreted as all the issues which are connected to the succession; this would include the issues not only with respect to succession rights or the order of succession but also the liability of the heirs for the debts and obligations of the deceased *vis-à vis* creditors.[238] As court practice on the Treaty in Turkey is very limited, some guidance could be taken from the scope of the *lex successionis* adopted by the Temporary Act – as applicable at the time the Treaty was entered into – in order to illustrate the issues which are encompassed by the Treaty. Accordingly, this comprises issues such as the determination of the beneficiaries and their respective shares, including the succession rights of the surviving spouse; the determination of the reserved portion; the determination of the succession rights of the State to an heirless estate; and the determination of succession rights in a case of *commorientes* or renunciation of inheritance. Since no exception is provided under the provision, nor under Article 4 of the Temporary Act, most of the issues related to the opening of succession and to the acquisition and sharing-out of the succession would also be governed by

---

275; Doğan, *Milletlerarası Özel Hukuk* (2022) 378. On the liability of heirs to estate creditors, see also above n 205, p 91.

234 Arts 652–658 of the Turkish Civil Code. See, for views in this regard, V. R. Seviğ, *Mirasla İlgili Devletler Hususi Hukuku Kaideleri* (1963) 129; Ekşi, *Milletlerarası Miras Hukuku* (2013) 46–47.

235 Art 652 of the Turkish Civil Code.

236 See, in this regard, Tanrıbilir, *Kanuni Mirasçılıktan Doğan Kanunlar İhtilafı* (2000) 169; Aybay and Dardağan, *Kanunlar İhtilafı* (2008) 237; Baran Çelik, *Ölüme Bağlı Tasarruflar* (2011) 200–201; Altıparmak, *Mirasa Uygulanacak Hukuk* (2017) 128–129; Tekinalp, *Milletlerarası Özel Hukuk* (2020) 242; Güngör, *Türk Milletlerarası Özel Hukuku* (2021) 168; Nomer, *Devletler Hususî Hukuku* (2021) 298; Şanlı, Esen and Ataman Figanmeşe, *Milletlerarası Özel Hukuk* (2021) 274; Doğan, *Milletlerarası Özel Hukuk* (2022) 378.

237 Dörner, [1996] ZEV 90, 91; H. Krüger, 'Studien über Probleme des türkischen Internationalen Erbrechts' (2006) 149.

238 Denkschrift zu dem Konsularvertrag von 1929 29.

the *lex successionis* under the Treaty.[239] Against its drafting background, however, questions regarding the applicable matrimonial property regime[240] or issues related to the status of natural persons, such as family status or the status of an adoptive child, would fall outside the scope of the Treaty, even though they are closely connected with succession.[241]

Whereas the scope of the law applicable to succession is to some extent determinable in each legal instrument with the help of either express provisions in this regard, as in the Regulation, or by way of interpretation as in the Turkish PILA and the Treaty, scholarly views, problems may still arise given that the law of succession is often closely intertwined with other areas of law, such as the law on the status of natural persons (including issues regarding adoption and marriage), property law, and matrimonial property regimes. Two exemplary issues which have already given rise to academic discussions in Germany[242] could be particularly important in the Turkish-European context: the effect of *legatum per vindicationem* and BGB § 1371(1).

I. The Interplay between the Law Applicable to Succession and The Law Applicable to Property Law Matters: The Effect of legatum per vindicationem?

One of the issues which has been widely discussed among scholars since the drafting process of the Regulation is the delineation between the *lex successionis* and the *lex rei sitae*.[243] This would come into play especially when a so-called *legatum per vindicationem* has been drawn up for an item of property located in a jurisdiction which does not recognise such a legacy. The question will then arise whether this legacy would be given effect in the State of *situs* where legacies of this kind are not allowed. This question was even dealt with by

---

[239] O. F. Berki, *Miras* (1960) 30ff; V. R. Seviğ, *Mirasla İlgili Devletler Hususi Hukuku Kaideleri* (1963) 86ff; Uluocak, *Kanunlar İhtilafı* (1971) 91–99; Tanrıbilir, *Kanuni Mirasçılıktan Doğan Kanunlar İhtilafı* (2000) 122; Filiz Sütçü, 'Deutsch-türkische Erbrechtsfälle in der Anwaltspraxis' [2015] ZErb 43, 45; Güneş, 'The Relations of Turkey with EU Member States' (2019) 293.

[240] H. Krüger, 'Studien über Probleme des türkischen Internationalen Erbrechts' (2006) 148; Gebauer, (2018) 27 Informationsbrief der DTJV 18, 21ff; Memet Kılıç, 'Türkei' in Rembert Süß (ed), *Erbrecht in Europa* (4th edn, zerb verlag 2020) paras 10–12.

[241] See, in this regard, also Güneş, 'The Relations of Turkey with EU Member States' (2019) 292–293.

[242] See, for example, Franz Gärtner, *Die Behandlung ausländischer Vindikationslegate im deutschen Recht* (C.H. Beck 2014); Peter Mankowski, 'Das erbrechtliche Viertel nach § 1371 Abs. 1 BGB im deutschen und europäischen Internationalen Privatrecht' [2014] ZEV 121.

[243] See, for instance, Markus Buschbaum and Marius Kohler, 'Vereinheitlichung des Erbkollisionsrechts in Europa Eine kritische Würdigung des Kommissionsvorschlags zur Erbrechtsverordnung Erster Teil' [2010] GPR 106, 108ff.

the CJEU in the case of *Kubicka*.[244] The discussion within the EU Member States is, of course, of little practical significance for Turkey as a third State. A legacy with such effect may, however, also be made by a non-Turkish deceased for movable or immovable property located in Turkey. For such cases, it is appropriate to discuss whether this would lead to a problem before the Turkish courts.

In modern succession laws, testators are allowed to bequeath not only their entire property or a part thereof but also specific gifts to the persons they wish.[245] When the testator states, for instance, that 'my daughter-in-law shall have the jewels in my safe box' or '*(A)* shall have my antique mosaic vase', the daughter-in-law of the testator and *(A)* subsequently become particular legatees of the jewels and the vase.[246] Such legacies may have different legal effects in different legal systems, as there were two types of *legatum* in the classical period of Roman law, namely the *legatum per vindicationem* (legacy by vindication) and the *legatum per damnationem* (legacy by damnation). *Legatum per vindicationem* is a legacy with direct real effect and transfers the title of the property that is object of the legacy to the legatee automatically upon the death of the testator. These types of legacies still exist in some legal systems following Roman legal tradition.[247] On the other hand, in other legal systems, for example in Turkey,[248] the ownership of the property which was bequeathed to the legatee is not automatically transferred to him; rather, he is only entitled to raise a personal claim for that property against the heirs. This is called a *legatum per damnationem*.[249]

Given this diversity among the legal systems, it might be questionable whether a *legatum per vindicationem* may also lead to a problem in succession cases arising in Turkey. This could first be the case under the Turkish

---

244 C-218/16 Kubicka [2017] ECLI:EU:C:2017:755.

245 Jan Peter Schmidt, 'Challenged Legacies – First Decision of the European Court of Justice on the EU Succession Regulation (ECJ, 12 October 2017, C-218/16 (Kubicka))' (2018) 7 EPLJ 4, 5.

246 Serozan and Engin, *Miras Hukuku* (2021) § 4 para 133.

247 Such a type of legacy exists, for example, in France (Art 1014 of the French Civil Code), Belgium (Art 1014 Belgian Civil Code), Italy (Art 649(2) of the Italian Civil Code), Poland (Art 981 of the Polish Civil Code) and Greece (Art 1996 of the Greek Civil Code) laws: Christoph Döbereiner, 'Vindikationslegate unter Geltung der EU-Erbrechtsverordnung: Praktische Anmerkungen aus notarieller Sicht' [2014] GPR 42; J. P. Schmidt, (2018) 7 EPLJ 4, 6 fn 10–14.

248 Art 600 of the Turkish Civil Code. See, in this regard, Serozan and Engin, *Miras Hukuku* (2021) § 4 paras 133 and 135, § 6 para 16.

249 Lourdes Salomon, 'The Acquisition of Possession in Legacies per vindicationem in Classical Roman Law and Its Influence in the Modern Civil Codes' (2006) 3 Roman LT 65; Mariusz Załucki, 'Attempts to Harmonize the Inheritance Law in Europe: Past, Present, and Future' (2018) 103 Iowa L Rev 2318, 2335–2336; Piotr Tereszkiewicz and Anna Wysocka-Bar, 'Legacy by Vindication Under the EU Succession Regulation No 650/2012 Following the Kubicka Judgment of the ECJ' (2019) 27 ERPL 875, 878–881.

PILA. If, for example, a Greek national *(G)* who owns a number of items of movable and immovable property in Turkey draws up a will and states therein that 'my best friend, *(B)*, shall have my black car, my wife *(W)* shall have my apartment situated on the Bosphorus; the rest of my properties shall belong to my children', the question would arise whether *(B)* and *(W)* may exercise *rei vindicatio* against heirs because of the direct effects of *legatum per vindicationem* that exist in Greek law, as the national law of the deceased.[250]

The first issue which may be discussed here is whether such effects of the legacies regarding the ownership of the bequeathed property should be characterised as a matter of succession or property law. It is undoubted that the *legatum per vindicationem* has obligations and property law aspects, although the extent of it varies in different legal systems.[251] This is because it is considered a 'title legacy'[252] and accordingly has a real effect in favour of the legatee on the bequeathed property. Therefore, one might question whether it should be qualified as a matter belonging to the property law.

Under Turkish law, whereas succession matters on movable and immovable property are governed by the *lex successionis* under Article 20 of the Turkish PILA, title to movable and immovable property and other rights *in rem* on these properties should be governed by the *lex rei sitae* under Article 21(1).[253] In some cases it does not seem straightforward to draw a line between these two statutes, as in the case of the *legatum per vindicationem.*[254]

It could be argued that when there is an entire transfer of rights and obligations, as in universal succession, the matter should be governed by the *lex successionis.* In the case of legacies, however, there is no entire transfer but rather a singular transfer of rights – with either real or personal effect – over a particular property or properties. It is subsequently contended that this transfer should be governed by the *lex rei sitae* as the general conflict-of-laws rule of property law. Hence, under this view, the drawing up of a legacy would be considered as an issue of succession law, but its property law effects would be considered as matters of property law as in the case of donations.[255] If this

[250] J. P. Schmidt, (2018) 7 EPLJ 4, 7.

[251] Rembert Süß, 'Das Vindikationslegat im Internationalen Privatrecht' (2001) 65 RabelsZ 245, 253 ff.

[252] Erkan Küçükgüngör, 'Roma ve Türk Hukukunda Muayyen Mal Vasiyeti' (1996) 45 AÜHFD 505, 517.

[253] Tekinalp, *Milletlerarası Özel Hukuk* (2020) 271.

[254] For a recent book discussing the issue from the German perspective before and after the entry into force of the Regulation, see Elena Gubenko, *Die Abgrenzung des Erbstatuts vom Sachstatut in der EuErbVO* (Mohr Siebeck 2021) 62 ff and 222 ff.

[255] Süß, (2001) 65 RabelsZ 245, 255–256. This was apparently the prevailing view in Poland in earlier times when the *legatum per vindicationem* was also foreign to the Polish system, which now recognises such legacies, see Tereszkiewicz and Wysocka-Bar, (2019) 27 ERPL 875, 882–883.

line of thought finds application in Turkey, Article 21(1) of the Turkish PILA, i.e. the provision calling for the application of Turkish law as the *lex rei sitae*, would be applied and thus a *legatum per vindicationem* could not have real effects in Turkey.

Notwithstanding this, the succession law aspects of legacies appear to predominate. This is because the difference between these two types of legacies in fact stems from the distinction between the systems of 'universal' and 'singular' succession. Their aim, however, seems to be the same. In the first place, they do not deal with the distribution of the assets forming part of the estate among the beneficiaries; in other words, they do not attempt to answer the question of 'who gets what?' but instead look to determine the manner in which the distribution takes place, i.e. 'how do the beneficiaries get the assets?'.[256] Furthermore, their effects cannot be seen as isolated from the whole succession process but instead should be seen as a part of a broader policy dealing with the estate administration, whereby each system strikes a different balance between testamentary freedom and the protection of the creditors. In jurisdictions which do not permit the testator to make a testament with a real effect, the disposed property is not allowed to pass into the hands of the legatee in order to protect the deceased's creditors, and hence the last wishes of the testator are respected to only a certain degree. Nevertheless, legal systems which give the testator a right to transfer the title of a bequeathed object directly to the legatee upon his death are obviously more focused on realising such wishes. The protection of creditors is still important, since the legatee becomes liable for the debts of the estate.[257] This may, however, be very complex for the creditors since they have to pursue different individuals and various estate assets.[258] Regardless of the attitude of the legal systems in favour of or against legacies with real effect and regardless of the drawbacks and merits of each system, it appears that both types of legacies are by-products of the succession policy of the States, and, hence, they should be characterised as matters of succession. Indeed, under the Turkish Civil Code, not only types of legacies (Article 517) but also their effects (Article 600) are regulated under succession provisions. It is only in cases where the object of the legacy is a usufruct, annuity, or other recurring benefit that the provisions of the law of obligations and

---

[256] J. P. Schmidt, (2018) 7 EPLJ 4, 8.

'The legacy by vindication does not create a new right *in rem*' (Pazdan and Zachariasiewicz, (2021) 17 J Priv Int L 74, 93) rather it 'concerns the arrangement by which that right *in rem* is transferred at the time of the testator's death' (C-218/16 Kubicka [2017] ECLI:EU:C:2017:755 [49]).

[257] J. P. Schmidt, (2018) 7 EPLJ 4, 7–10.

[258] Michael A. Schwind, 'Liability for Obligations of the Inheritance' in Ulrich Drobnig and Karl Heinz Neumayer (eds), *International Encyclopedia of Comparative Law – Vol V: Succession* (Mohr Siebeck & Martinus Nijhoff Publishers 1995) para 17; J. P. Schmidt, (2018) 7 EPLJ 4, 10.

property law will find application. Thus, such legacies and their effects should be characterised as succession matters, and the law applicable to them should be determined pursuant to Article 20 of the Turkish PILA.

Another issue here would be whether this matter should be governed by the general *lex successionis* under Article 20(1) of the Turkish PILA or as one of the exceptions under Article 20(2) of the Turkish PILA. One view could be that issues regarding the specific bequests normally fall under the scope of substantive validity of dispositions of property upon death, which are normally governed by the general *lex successionis* under Article 20(1) of the Turkish PILA.[259] When this is the case, the desired real effects of the legacy made by *(G)* in the above example would not be recognised over the apartment left to *(W)*, as the law applicable to immovable properties located in Turkey is Turkish law and specific bequests do not have such effects under Turkish law. It may be questionable, however, whether *(A)* will directly become the owner of the car of *(G)*, since succession rights on movable properties are governed by the national law of the deceased. Notwithstanding this, such a result may not be accepted due to the main principles of Turkish succession law. Particularly, the *numerus clausus* principle which is applicable for dispositions of property upon death prevents other types of dispositions *mortis causa*. This means that the testator is allowed neither to make other forms of dispositions of property upon death other than those provided in the law nor to change the singular succession system of the specific bequeaths.[260] Therefore, *legatum per vindicationem* would not be allowed in Turkish law. Such a legacy made by the deceased, in this line of thought, will only be accepted in Turkey as *legatum per damnationem* by way of adaptation,[261] i.e. the legatee will not directly have the title of the bequeathed property but will have a personal claim over it against the heirs. In other words, the legacy by vindication will be 'downgraded'[262] to a legacy by damnation in Turkey.

Another view could be that the effects of legacies are in fact issues related to the acquisition of succession under the Turkish Civil Code and that the difference between the two types of legacies stems originally from the dilemma of the legal systems regarding universal and singular succession. Therefore, such effects seem to be in the scope of the exception under Article 20(2) of the Turkish PILA. Turkish law, as the *lex rei sitae*, would govern this question and *(A)* would not have the title over the car of *(G)*, having

---

[259] *Baran Çelik*, for example, states that the general *lex successionis* under Article 20(1) of the Turkish PILA governs whether a deceased is allowed to make a specific bequest with a legacy, which assets or rights may be specifically bequeathed under a legacy, the rights or obligations of the legatee in such legacies, and the invalidity of such legacies: Baran Çelik, *Ölüme Bağlı Tasarruflar* (2011) 161.

[260] Serozan and Engin, *Miras Hukuku* (2021) § 1 para 76, § 4 para 135.

[261] For further explanations on the doctrine of adaptation, see below p 119.

[262] J. P. Schmidt, (2018) 7 EPLJ 4, 11.

instead only a personal claim against heirs. This latter view seems to be more in line with the Turkish Civil Code.

A similar scenario of the example given above could also come into play in the context of the Treaties. Although the focus of this study is the Turkish-German Treaty, the Turkish-Italian Treaty serves as an illustrative example here. Imagine, for instance, that *(G)* in our example above is an Italian national. Once again, *(A)* and *(W)* may have *rei vindicatio* claims against the heirs under Italian law. As regards movable property, the law applicable to testamentary or intestate succession under the Treaty is the national law of the deceased; as regards immovable property it is the *lex rei sitae* (Article 21(15)(3) of the Treaty). Such a conflict would not arise for the apartment, as the law applicable to it is Turkish law. A conflict of this nature would normally not arise for the car either, as the jurisdictional rule of the Treaty (Article 21(11) of the Treaty) confers jurisdiction to the courts of the national State of the deceased for succession matters in respect of movable property. Imagine, however, that the dispute is somehow brought before the Turkish courts.[263] Here the question once again arises whether the real effects of the legacy would be allowed. The answer to this question would be the same as in the scope of the Turkish PILA, and by virtue of the fundamental principles of Turkish succession law, such an effect would not be accepted.

II. The Interplay between the Law Applicable to Succession and the Law Applicable to Matrimonial Property Regimes: The Effect of the Additional Quarter of the Surviving Spouse under BGB § 1371(1) in Turkish-German Successions

An issue in the law of succession which probably has the most practical relevance and, at the same time, creates the greatest difficulty for any legislature is a determination of the rights of spouses *vis-à-vis* property in the event of death.[264] The approach of jurisdictions to this issue is often divergent in many

[263] On the face of the Treaty's historical background, it is believed that the jurisdiction rule is exclusive: Güneş, 'The Relations of Turkey with EU Member States' (2019) 307–310. For this reason, it is highly likely that the Turkish court would decline jurisdiction in such a case and would not find the opportunity to discuss the effect of a *legatum per vindicationem* made in accordance with Italian law. For a different interpretation of the jurisdiction rule in the Turkish-Italian Treaty, however, see Franzina, 'The External Relations of Italy' (2019) 197–198.

[264] Jan Peter Schmidt, 'Trying to Square the Circle: Comparative Remarks on the Rights of the Surviving Spouse on Intestacy' (2020) 24 Edinburgh L Rev 123, 123. For similar statements, see also Reinhard Zimmermann, 'Intestate Succession in Germany' in Kenneth G. C. Reid, Marius J. de Waal and Reinhard Zimmermann (eds), *Comparative Succession Law – Volume II: Intestate Succession* (OUP 2015) 209; Dieter Leipold, in Franz Jürgen Säcker and others (eds), *MüKoBGB*, vol 11 (8th edn, C.H. Beck 2020) BGB § 1931 para 2.

aspects.[265] In cases with foreign elements, therefore, the clash of rules belonging to different systems may give rise to characterisation problems and require the use of coordination tools,[266] such as substitution[267] or adaptation,[268] from a PIL perspective.[269]

Such issues may also arise in the Turkish-German context due to BGB § 1371(1), the characterisation of which has already given rise to divergent academic opinions and judgments in Germany.[270] Although the characterisation of this provision seems to be settled now within the scope of the Regulation,[271] there may be substitution or adaptation problems before the German courts when Turkish law becomes applicable – as the law of succession or the law of matrimonial property – together with German law. The issue of characterisation and its possible consequences (the need for substitution or adaptation) could, however, still be relevant from the Turkish perspective in Turkish-German cases falling within the scope of the Treaty or the Turkish PILA and where Turkish and German laws become applicable together. These possibilities should be analysed here. The analysis should start with a brief overview of the law applicable to matrimonial property in Turkey and Germany as well as both jurisdictions' substantive law approaches in terms of statutory matrimonial property regimes.

1. Legal Framework Regarding Matrimonial Property Regimes in Germany and in Turkey

Before analysing possible problems attached with BGB § 1371(1) in Turkish-German successions, the legal framework in both States concerning matrimo-

---

265 For a comparative analysis on this issue concerning certain legal systems, see Kenneth G. C. Reid, Marius J. de Waal and Reinhard Zimmermann, 'Intestate Succession in Historical and Comparative Perspective' in Kenneth G. C. Reid, Marius J. de Waal and Reinhard Zimmermann (eds), *Comparative Succession Law – Volume II: Intestate Succession* (OUP 2015) 489 ff; Reinhard Zimmermann, 'Das Ehegattenerbrecht in historisch-vergleichender Perspektive' (2016) 80 RabelsZ 39; J. P. Schmidt, (2020) 24 Edinburgh L Rev 123.

266 See, for a short note on the different tools of coordination found in different laws, Ralf Michaels, 'Comparative Law and Private International Law' in Jürgen Basedow and others (eds), *Encyclopedia of Private International Law* (Edward Elgar Publishing 2017) 422.

267 For explanation, see below p 115 ff.

268 For explanation, see below p 117 ff.

269 Jeffrey A. Schoenblum, *Multistate and Multinational Estate Planning*, vol 1 (CCH 2008) ch 10.24 [H]; Jan Peter Schmidt, 'The Interplay between Succession and Matrimonial Property Regimes from a Comparative Perspective – Abstract', *ELI The Family and Succession Law SIG* (2020) <https://www.europeanlawinstitute.eu/fileadmin/user_upload/p_eli/SIGs/Family_Law/Webinar_2020/JP_Schmidt.pdf> accessed 4 January 2021.

270 For examples, see below pp 112 ff.

271 See, for judgments of BGH and the CJEU, below pp 112 ff.

nial property regimes in private international law and in substantive law should first be explained to set the scene for the reader. In the light of this, the following remarks will first briefly address the PIL context for marital property before then explaining the basics of statutory matrimonial property regimes and the dissolution of marriage upon death in both jurisdictions.

a) The Law Applicable to Matrimonial Property in Germany and in Turkey

The Treaty, as indicated above,[272] does not cover the law applicable to matrimonial property regimes. Therefore, the private international law rules of States will become applicable. In Germany, 'questions related to matrimonial property regimes' are outside the scope of the Succession Regulation (Article 1(2) (d)) and are rather governed by the European Matrimonial Property Regulation.[273] The European legislature, upon consideration of the possible negative consequences resulting from the diversity of Member State laws in this area for the free movement of its nationals,[274] harmonised the private international and procedural rules of Member States also in the field of matrimonial property regimes with this Regulation. The Regulation's conflict-of-laws rules, which are laid down under Chapter III (Articles 20–35),[275] will be applicable for matrimonial property regimes even where a marriage ends by death of one of the spouses.[276]

According to the Regulation, spouses (or future spouses) are allowed to make a *professio iuris* in favour of the law of the State in which they are, or one of them is, habitually resident, or, of which they, or one of them, hold the nationality at the time of the conclusion of the agreement (Article 22(1)). When they do not use their autonomy in this regard, the law applicable to the matrimonial property regime is the law of the State of the spouses' first common habitual residence after the conclusion of the marriage, or failing that the common nationality at the time of the conclusion of the marriage (Article 26(1) (a) and (b)). If they do not have a common habitual residence or nationality at those times, the law of the State to which the spouses together have the closest con-

---

[272] See above p 98.

[273] Regulation (EU) No 2016/1103 of 24 June 2016 implementing enhanced cooperation in the area of jurisdiction, applicable law and the recognition and enforcement of decisions in matters of matrimonial property regimes [2016] OJ L 183.

[274] Christian Kohler and Walter Pintens, 'Entwicklungen im Europäischen Personen- und Familienrecht 2010–2011' [2011] FamRZ 1433, 1435; Rainer Hausmann, *Internationales und Europäisches Familienrecht* (2nd edn, C.H. Beck 2018) B. Güterrechtssachen para 9; Dirk Looschelders, in Franz Jürgen Säcker and others (eds), *MüKoBGB*, vol 11 (8th edn, C.H. Beck 2020) EuGüVO Vorb. Art 1 para 1.

[275] For detailed comments on the rules of the Regulation, see Looschelders, *MüKoBGB* (2020) EuGüVO.

[276] Recital 18 of the Regulation.

nection at the time of the conclusion of the marriage may become applicable upon consideration of all relevant circumstances (Article 26(1) (c)).

The European Legislature also drafted an escape clause in the Regulation. In cases where the law governing the matrimonial property regime is that of the State of first common habitual residence of them after the conclusion of the marriage (under Article 26(1) (a)), one of the spouses may ask the court seised of the matter to apply another State law upon demonstrating that they were last habitually resident together in that State for a significantly longer period of time than in their first common habitual residence and that they relied on the law of this State for their plans and arrangements concerning their marital property (Article 26(3)). *Renvoi* is excluded, and hence the substantive law of the relevant State will ultimately be applied (Article 32).

These rules are now also applicable in Germany but only for spouses who marry or who make a choice of law as regards to marital property relations after 29 January 2019 (Article 69(3)). Therefore, former German national conflict-of-laws rules are still applicable for spouses married before this date or for those who did not specify the law applicable to this matter after this date (Article 229 § 47(2) EGBGB).[277] In particular, former Article 15 EGBGB, which was repealed after the adoption of the European Matrimonial Property Regulation,[278] is relevant for matrimonial property regimes. According to Article 15(2) EGBGB, spouses had a right to designate the law that would govern their matrimonial property. They could choose one of the following laws: the law of the national State or the law of the habitual residence of one of the spouses, or, for immovable property, the law of *situs*. Article 15(1) EGBGB deals with the law applicable to matrimonial property regimes in the absence of a *professio iuris*. It provides that the law applicable to general effects of the marriage, i.e. Article 14 EGBGB, should also govern matrimonial property relations between the spouses. Article 14 EGBGB was also amended after the Matrimonial Property Regulation,[279] but the old version should still be applicable in light of Article 15(1) EGBGB.[280] Pursuant to

---

[277] Anatol Dutta, 'Das neue internationale Güterrecht der Europäischen Union – ein Abriss der europäischen Güterrechtsverordnungen' [2016] FamRZ 1973, 1985; Johannes Weber, 'Die Europäischen Güterrechtsverordnungen: Eine erste Annäherung' [2016] DNotZ 659, 663; Robert Magnus, in Rainer Hüßtege and Heinz-Peter Mansel (eds), *NK-BGB/Rom-Verordnungen*, vol 6 (3rd edn, Nomos 2019) EuGüVO Art 1 para 12; Looschelders, *MüKoBGB* (2020) EuGüVO Art 69 para 8.

See also the explanations accompanying the reform of Article 14 EGBGB in the Deutscher Bundestag, 19. Wahlperiode, Drucksache 19/4852 (10.10.2018) p 37.

[278] See Art 2 IntGüRVGEG, BGBl. I 2018, 2573.

[279] See Art 2 IntGüRVGEG.

[280] R. Magnus, *NK-BGB/Rom-Verordnungen* (2019) EuGüVO Art 69 para 16; Looschelders, *MüKoBGB* (2020) EGBGB Art 14 para 8. See also BGH 26.6.2019 – XII ZB 299/18, NJW 2019, 2935 paras 26ff.

Article 14(1) EGBGB (old version), matrimonial property matters are subject to the law of the State of their common nationality or their last common nationality during the marriage if at least one of the spouses still holds this nationality; or, failing that, to the law of the State of their common habitual residence or last common habitual residence during the marriage, if at least one of them still has his habitual residence in that State; or, failing that, to the law of the State to which they are closely connected otherwise. *Renvoi* is not excluded,[281] and hence PIL rules of one of these States will be applied. If, however, these rules refer the matter to back to German law, German (substantive law) rules will be ultimately applicable (Article 4(1) EGBGB).

In Turkey, when the marriage terminates upon death of one of the spouses, first, the matrimonial property rights of the surviving spouse should be determined pursuant to the law applicable under Article 15 of the Turkish PILA. Only after this process should succession matters be handled consistent with the law indicated under Article 20 of the Turkish PILA.[282]

Article 15 of the Turkish PILA gives spouses a right to choose the governing law. This choice could be made in favour of the law of the State of habitual residence or the law of the State of nationality at the time of marriage. When the spouses do not make a choice in this regard, the law of the State of their common nationality at the time of marriage; or failing that, the law of the State of their common habitual residence at the time of marriage; or failing that, Turkish law would be applicable to matrimonial property regimes (paragraph 1). In the process of liquidation, the *lex rei sitae* will apply for immovables (paragraph 2).[283] If spouses acquire a common nationality after their marriage,

---

[281] Looschelders, *MüKoBGB* (2020) EuGüVO Art 32 para 2.

[282] Uluocak, *Milletlerarası Özel Hukuk Dersleri* (1987) 71–72; Aybay and Dardağan, *Kanunlar İhtlilafı* (2008) 211; Ebru Şensöz, '27.11.2007 Tarih ve 5718 Sayılı MÖHUK Uyarınca Yabancılık Unsuru Taşıyan Evlilik Mallarına İlişkin İhtilaflarda Uygulanacak Hukuk' (2009) 8 İTİCÜSBD 173, 204; Tekinalp, *Milletlerarası Özel Hukuk* (2020) 165; Çelikel and Erdem, *Milletlerarası Özel Hukuk* (2021) 269.

[283] There is a discussion over this provision as to whether it provides a dualist system in the context of matrimonial property regimes. Certain authors argue that this provision should not be regarded as an adoption of a general dualist approach for movables and immovables. According to them, two different laws become applicable only when the matrimonial assets should be physically divided between the spouses: Mustafa Alper Gümüş, 'Edinilmiş Mallara Katılma Rejiminin Tasfiyesinden Kaç Tane "Katılma Alacağı" Doğar? – TMK m.236/I Kapsamında Bir İnceleme' (2009) VI YÜHFD 91, 92 fn 1; Şensöz, (2009) 8 İTİCÜSBD 173, 200–203; Şükran Şıpka, *Türk Hukukunda Edinilmiş Mallara Katılma Rejimi ve Uygulamaya İlişkin Sorunlar* (3rd edn, On İki Levha 2013) 358–359; Gizem Ersen Perçin, *Milletlerarası Özel Hukuk Bakımından Mal Rejimleri: Uygulanacak Hukuk, Milletlerarası Yetki, Tanıma ve Tenfiz* (On İki Levha 2014) 191–192; Şükran Şıpka and Ayça Özdoğan, *Yargı Kararları Işığında Soru ve Cevaplarla Eşler Arasındaki Malvarlığı Davaları* (2nd edn, On İki Levha 2017) 387–390; Tekinalp, *Milletlerarası Özel Hukuk* (2020) 164; Şanlı, Esen and Ataman Figanmeşe, *Milletlerarası Özel Hukuk* (2021) 161 fn 83; cf.

they could also be subject to the law of that State for matrimonial property relations, without prejudice to the rights of third parties (paragraph 3).

Matrimonial property regimes, however, are matters of family law where single (partial) *renvoi*[284] finds application pursuant to Article 2(3) of the Turkish PILA.[285] This means that the Turkish judge would first look at the conflict-of-laws rules of the State referred to in Article 15 of the Turkish PILA and apply the domestic provisions of the State whose law has been indicated there as the law applicable to matrimonial property regimes.

b) Statutory Matrimonial Property Regimes, and Dissolution of Marriage Upon Death in Germany and in Turkey

In Germany, the statutory marital property regime, which applies unless the spouses make any other arrangements to this effect, is the community of accrued gains ('Zugewinngemeinschaft'). Although the name seems to imply so, there is no community of property in this system.[286] The mechanism requires the equalisation of the accrued gains that are acquired during the marriage upon the dissolution of marriage as per the prescribed calculations (BGB § 1363). In this system, by looking at each spouse's initial assets (at the time of marriage) and final assets (at the time of divorce), the accrued gains of the spouses are calculated. The main idea behind the statutory regime is that accrued gains in the course of marriage should be equally shared between the spouses at the end of marriage. If, for instance, *(A)* has an accrued gain of 100,000 euros and *(B)* has gains of 80,000 euros, *(A)* has to pay 10,000 euros to *(B)* in order to provide that they end their marriage with an equal amount of accrued gains.[287]

The death of one of the spouses, in principle, also terminates this regime and the succession of the deceased spouse is determined according to general

---

Nomer, *Devletler Hususî Hukuku* (2021) 268–269; contra Ziya Akıncı and Cemile Demir Gökyayla, *Milletlerarası Aile Hukuku* (Vedat Kitapçılık 2010) 76; Zeynep Derya Tarman, 'Die eherechtlichen Kollisionsnormen im türkischen Recht' [2013] StAZ 206, 210.

For a detailed overview of literature on the issue, see Hanswerner Odendahl, *Die Auseinandersetzung der Errungenschaftsbeteiligung in der Rechtsprechung des türkischen Kassationshofs* (Peter Lang 2020) 163 ff.

[284] On *renvoi*, see below pp 153 ff.

[285] Şensöz, (2009) 8 İTİCÜSBD 173, 197–198; Akıncı and Demir Gökyayla, *Milletlerarası Aile Hukuku* (2010) 77; Ersen Perçin, *Milletlerarası Özel Hukuk Bakımından Mal Rejimleri* (2014) 189–190; Hanswerner Odendahl, 'Die Bedeutung neuer internationaler IPR-Normen im Familien- und Erbrecht für Fälle mit Türkeibezug' [2018] IPRax 450, 453; Tekinalp, *Milletlerarası Özel Hukuk* (2020) 162; contra Giray, (2012) IX YÜHFD 555, 562.

[286] Jens M. Scherpe, 'The Financial Consequences of Divorce in a European Perspective' in Jens M. Scherpe (ed), *European Family Law Volume III – Family Law in a European Perspective* (Edward Elgar Publishing 2016) 158.

[287] Scherpe, 'The Financial Consequences of Divorce in a European Perspective' (2016) 158–159.

principles (BGB § 1371(1)). Succession rights of the surviving spouse in cases of intestacy are regulated under BGB § 1931. This provides that the surviving spouse is entitled to 1/4 of the estate together with the first group of statutory heirs, i.e. the descendants of the deceased, unless there was a separation of property between the spouses (paragraph 4); and 1/2 of the estate together with the second group of statutory heirs (parents and siblings of the deceased) and grandparents of the deceased (paragraph 1). When there is no surviving heir in the first or second group and none of the grandparents are alive, the surviving spouse receives the entire estate (paragraph 2).

The main solution offered for equalising the accrued gains of one of the spouses upon death is not to have resort to the mathematical liquidation process but rather to make a payment to the surviving spouse in the form of an additional fixed succession share of one quarter (the so-called 'succession law solution' or 'integration model' under BGB § 1371(1)).[288] The provision should serve the purposes of avoiding complex calculations regarding marital property, and, as attached to this process of calculation, avoiding conflicts between the surviving spouse and the children or other heirs of the decedent.[289] One of the original ideas underlying this model was to protect the

---

[288] See, in this regard, Burkhard Thiele, in Christian von Bar (ed), *Staudinger BGB – Buch 4: Familienrecht – §§ 1363–1407 (Eheliches Güterrecht 1 – Gesetzliches Güterrecht)* (Sellier & de Gruyter 2017) BGB § 1371 paras 1–10; Olaf Werner, in Gerhard Otte (ed), *Staudinger BGB – Buch 4: Erbrecht – §§ 1922–1966 (Einleitung zum Erbrecht – Erbfolge)* (Sellier & de Gruyter 2017) BGB § 1931 paras 20ff; Martin Löhnig, in Dagmar Kaiser and others (eds), *NK-BGB/Familienrecht*, vol 4 (4th edn, Nomos 2021) BGB § 1371 paras 1–7; Ludwig Kroiß, in Ludwig Kroiß and Claus-Henrik Horn (eds), *NK-BGB/Erbrecht*, vol 5 (6th edn, Nomos 2022) BGB § 1931 paras 10–12.

For a short explanation of the 'integration model' and BGB § 1371(1), see also Eugen Dietrich Graue, 'The Rights of Surviving Spouses under Private International Law' (1966) 15 AJCL 164, 186ff; Christian Kohler, 'Application of the Succession Regulation by German Courts – Selected Issues' (2020) 26 PPPM 27, 29–30; J. P. Schmidt, 'The Interplay between Succession and Matrimonial Property Regimes from a Comparative Perspective – Abstract' (2020).

[289] Johannes Bärmann, 'Das neue Ehegüterrecht' (1958–1959) 157 AcP 145, 181ff; R. Zimmermann, 'Intestate Succession in Germany' (2015) 212–213; Elisabeth Koch, in Franz Jürgen Säcker and others (eds), *MüKoBGB*, vol 9 (8th edn, C.H. Beck 2019) BGB § 1371 paras 1–2.

For a view supporting the introduction of a similar solution to Turkish law to eliminate problems of two distinct procedures in practice, see Zafer Zeytin, *Edinilmiş Mallara Katılma Rejimi ve Tasfiyesi* (5th edn, Seçkin 2021) paras 959ff; contra Mesut Serdar Çekin, 'Mal Rejimi Hukukunda Gerçekleştirilen Tasarrufların Miras Hukukuna Etkisi' (2017) 4 İMÜHFD 189, 203–204.

It is also argued that the German system, which takes the close relationship between matrimonial property law and succession law and removes the barrier between the two, is more in line with the life interests and desired goals of the involved parties. However, its application may be complex and may cause problems in some cases. It can, however, still

contribution of surviving housewives to marital gains through household activities in the event of the death of the husband, who, in the conception of previous decades, would have made all the marital gain by working but who, at least statistically,[290] would have predeceased his wife.[291] Today, this rule is often criticised on the ground that it creates injustice and distorts equality between the spouses by disregarding their individual gains. This is especially the case if the surviving spouse is the one who made most of the marital gains during the marriage. If the marriage ended by divorce, the predeceased spouse would have a claim against the surviving spouse for the equalisation of gains. Yet where the marriage ends upon death, the surviving spouse keeps all the gains made in the course of marriage and is entitled to 1/2 of the succession share from the predeceased spouse.[292] Such a solution, therefore, does not make the things easier but rather 'entangles matrimonial property law and the law of succession in an illogical and confusing manner.'[293]

The default matrimonial property regime in Turkey is participation in acquired property ('edinilmiş mallara katılma rejimi' or 'Errungenschaftsbeteiligung') under Article 202(1) of the Turkish Civil Code.[294] Like the

---

be useful for the Turkish legislature as an exemplary model to be examined: Muammer Aksoy, *Mukayeseli Hukuk Açısından Karı Koca Mal Rejimi ve Miras Hukuku İle Bağı* (Ankara Üniversitesi Basımevi 1964) 125 and 176ff.

290 The statistics do not seem to have changed over the years. The average life expectancy at birth in Germany in 2020 was 78,9 years for men and 83,6 years for women: Statistisches Bundesamt (Destatis), 'Entwicklung der Lebenserwartung bei Geburt in Deutschland nach Geschlecht in den Jahren von 1950 bis 2060' <https://www-genesis.destatis.de/genesis/online?operation=ergebnistabelleDownload&levelindex=3&levelid=1622738269859&option=xml> accessed 3 June 2021.

291 Bärmann, (1958–1959) 157 AcP 145, 182.

292 See, for example, Wolfram Müller-Freienfels, 'Kernfragen des Gleichberechtigungsgesetzes' [1957] JZ 685, 686ff; Bärmann, (1958–1959) 157 AcP 145, 182ff; Dieter Leipold, 'Wandlungen in den Grundlagen des Erbrechts?' (1980) 180 AcP 160, 176; Uwe Diederichsen, 'Teilhabegerechtigkeit in der Ehe' [1992] FamRZ 1, 9; Dieter Leipold, 'Ist der Wegfall des Zugewinnausgleichs bei Vorversterben des Ehegatten mit dem geringeren Zugewinn verfassungsgemäß?' [2011] NJW 1179; R. Zimmermann, 'Intestate Succession in Germany' (2015) 213; Koch, *MüKoBGB* (2019) BGB § 1371 para 5; Löhnig, *NK-BGB/Familienrecht* (2021) BGB § 1371 para 1;.

293 R. Zimmermann, 'Intestate Succession in Germany' (2015) 221.

294 The Turkish Civil Code is drafted in accord with the Swiss model. Therefore, most of the rules are largely identical between the two systems. This also encompasses the default matrimonial property regime. For short explanations on the Swiss system (as the source and identical model of the Turkish system), see Scherpe, 'The Financial Consequences of Divorce in a European Perspective' (2016) 160–161; Ingeborg Schwenzer and Tomie Keller, 'The Changing Concept of "Family" and Challenges for Family Law in Switzerland' in Jens M. Scherpe (ed), *European Family Law Volume II – The Changing Concept of 'Family' and Challenges for Domestic Family Law* (Edward Elgar Publishing 2016) 314–316.

German system,[295] there is no community of property between the spouses. Each spouse has two types of assets: individual property and acquired property (Article 218 of the Turkish Civil Code). The death of one of the spouses causes the dissolution of the marriage and the termination of the statutory matrimonial property regime between the spouses also in Turkish law (Article 225(1) of the Turkish Civil Code). In such instances, the succession share of the surviving spouse, unlike in German law, is not increased; rather, a two-stage liquidation process takes place. At the first stage, the matrimonial property is liquidated in the calculative way, and this is followed by the liquidation of succession (the so-called 'separation model', examples of which exist in legal orders following Roman family law and in some European legal systems).[296] In the liquidation process, the judge should determine the group to which each asset belongs (husband's individual property or acquired property, or wife's individual property and acquired property). If there are contributions from one group to another or there is an increase/decrease of value, all of these should be considered in the liquidation process. At the end of the process, the surplus of the acquired property of each spouse should be found on which the other spouse would have a claim of one half (Article 236(1) of the Turkish Civil Code). If, for example, *(A)* has a surplus of 100,000 TL and *(B)* has 80,000 TL, *(A)* will be entitled to 40,000 TL from *(B)*'s surplus (=80,000 TL/2); *(B)* will be entitled to 50,000 TL from (A)'s surplus (=100,000 TL/2). This would mean that *(B)* would have a participation claim for 10,000 TL from *(A)* (=50,000 TL – 40,000 TL). After the liquidation process, the worth of the estate and the succession share of the surviving spouse will be clear. The succession share of a surviving spouse is enshrined under Article 499 of the Turkish Civil Code. This provides that the surviving spouse receives 1/4 of the estate with the first group of statutory heirs (the descendants of the deceased), 1/2 of the estate with the second group (parents and

On the adoption of the Swiss Civil Code by Turkey, see, for example, Yeşim M. Atamer, 'Rezeption und Weiterentwicklung des schweizerischen Zivilgesetzbuches in der Türkei' (2008) 72 RabelsZ 723.

[295] For a comparison of the Turkish and German statutory matrimonial property regimes, see Hanswerner Odendahl, 'Edinilmiş Mallara Katılma Rejiminin Alman Yasal Mal Rejimi ile Karşılaştırılması ve Alman Milletlerarası Özel Hukukunda Mal Rejimi' in Şükran Şıpka, Barış Özbilen and Ebru Şensöz (eds), *Uygulamalı Aile Hukuku Sertifika Programı III. Dönem 17–18 Kasım 2006 – Edinilmiş Mallara Katılma Rejimi ve Uygulama Sorunları* (İstanbul Ticaret Üniversitesi Yayınları 2007) 113 ff.

[296] Şıpka, *Türk Hukukunda Edinilmiş Mallara Katılma Rejimi* (2013) 347 ff; Şıpka and Özdoğan, *Yargı Kararları Işığında Eşler Arasındaki Malvarlığı Davaları* (2017) 483 ff; Faruk Acar, *Aile Konutu, Mal Rejimleri, Eşin Yasal Miras Payı* (6th edn, Seçkin 2021) paras 551 ff; Zeytin, *Edinilmiş Mallara Katılma* (2021) paras 613–617 and 952–958.

For a brief introduction of the 'separation model', see J. P. Schmidt, 'The Interplay between Succession and Matrimonial Property Regimes from a Comparative Perspective – Abstract' (2020).

siblings of the deceased), 3/4 of estate with the third group of statutory heirs (grandparents of the deceased and their descendants), and the entire estate when there is no surviving heir in any of the groups.[297]

2. *Characterisation of BGB § 1371(1) from the German (and the European) Perspective and Possible Consequences for Turkish-German Successions*

Before the well-known *Mahnkopf* judgment of the CJEU dealing with the characterisation of BGB § 1371 from the Regulation's perspective,[298] three main points of view were identifiable among the commentators and in court practice in Germany. The prevailing view was that the provision should be characterised as a rule concerning the matrimonial property regime, and hence it finds application only in cases where German law is the law governing the matrimonial property regime, regardless of the fact that a foreign law is applicable to succession matters.[299] There were two main arguments justifying this view. In the first place, the provision is regulated under the part of the fourth book on family law of the BGB that covers matrimonial property regimes (title 6). Its systematic position in the Code thus makes it difficult to argue against its matrimonial property regime character. Furthermore, the aim of the provision is to liquidate assets which were gained by the spouses during and because of the marriage, and this is obviously one of the functions of matrimonial property law.[300]

---

[297] See, in this regard, Dural and Öz, *Miras Hukuku* (2021) paras 180 ff; Serozan and Engin, *Miras Hukuku* (2021) § 2 paras 59 ff; Çabri, *Miras Hukuku Şerhi (TMK m. 495–574)* (2022) paras 171 ff. For details on the liquidation of the matrimonial property under the statutory regime, see Şıpka and Özdoğan, *Yargı Kararları Işığında Eşler Arasındaki Malvarlığı Davaları* (2017) 161 ff; Acar, *Aile Konutu* (2021) paras 903 ff; Zeytin, *Edinilmiş Mallara Katılma* (2021) paras 594 ff; Mustafa Dural, Tufan Öğüz and Mustafa Alper Gümüş, *Türk Özel Hukuku Cilt III – Aile Hukuku* (17th edn, Filiz Kitabevi 2022) paras 1119 ff.

[298] C-558/16 Mahnkopf [2018] ECLI:EU:C:2018:138.

[299] See, for example, Schurig, *Soergel BGB* (1996) EGBGB Art 15 paras 38 ff; Dörner, *Staudinger BGB* (2007) EGBGB Art 25 paras 32 ff; Dirk Looschelders, 'Anwendbarkeit des § 1371 Abs. 1 BGB nach Korrektur einer ausländischen Erbquote wegen Unvereinbarkeit mit dem ordre public' [2009] IPRax 505, 509; Peter Mankowski, in Dieter Henrich (ed), *Staudinger BGB – EGBGB/IPR Einführungsgesetz zum Bürgerlichen Gesetzbuche – Art 13–17b EGBGB (Internationales Eherecht)* (Sellier & de Gruyter 2010) EGBGB Art 15 paras 346–348; Mankowski, [2014] ZEV 121; Michael Stürner and Christoph Wendelstein, 'Eine deutsch-türkische Erbschaft mit Tücken' [2014] JURA 707, 713. See also LG Bonn 19.12.1984 – 5 T 195/84, MittRhNotK 1985, 106; OLG Karlsruhe 29.6.1989 – 11 W 86/89, NJW 1990, 1420; LG Mosbach 18.3.1997 – 2 T 177/96, ZEV 1998, 489; OLG Stuttgart 8.3.2005 – 8 W 96/04, ZEV 2005, 443; OLG München 16.4.2012 – 31 Wx 45/12, ZEV 2012, 591; OLG Schleswig 19.8.2013 – 3 Wx 60/13, NJW 2014, 88.

[300] Christoph Jeremias and Eva Schäper, 'Zugewinnausgleich nach § 1371 BGB bei Geltung ausländischen Erbrechts (zu OLG Stuttgart, 8.3.2005 – 8 W 96/04)' [2005] IPRax

The German Federal Court of Justice ('BGH') also supported this view with its judgment from 2015 prior to the entry into force of the Regulation.[301] The case was about a succession conflict between the widower and the son of a Greek deceased. The law applicable to succession was Greek law, as the national law of the deceased (former Article 25(1) EGBGB), whereas the matrimonial property statute was German law in line with the *professio iuris* made by the spouses in the scope of (then-current) Article 15(2) EGBGB. The characterisation of BGB § 1371(1) would have determined whether the surviving husband would be entitled to another quarter of the succession of his wife. The Court held that the rule aims at the winding up of the matrimonial property regime, i.e. a special property regime applicable between the spouses on the basis of marriage. Furthermore, the surviving spouse's rights in marital property are not based on his close relationship with the deceased, as is the case in the law of succession. This means that the logic behind these two legal matters and their aims are different. Hence, the provision should be characterised as one of a matrimonial property regime, and it is applicable when the German law governs this matter. There may still be cases where the foreign *lex successionis* and German law as the law applicable to the matrimonial property regimes result in discrepancies. Such cases could, however, be handled with the help of the doctrine of adaptation.[302]

A number of commentators, on the other hand, considered this provision as a succession provision and thus as inapplicable in cases where the *lex successionis* is a foreign law.[303] This is because, in their view, it is only applicable in a succession case, and it increases the succession share of the surviving spouse without an additional claim for the matrimonial property regime.[304] In addition, it has lost its function related to the equal distribution of matrimonial property, as it is applicable in succession cases even where there is actually no matrimonial property owned by the spouses[305] or where one of the spouses in fact earned the (vast) majority of the matrimonial property.[306]

521, 524–525; Schotten and Schmellenkamp, *Das Internationale Privatrecht in der notariellen Praxis* (2007) para 285; Mankowski, *Staudinger BGB* (2010) EGBGB Art 15 paras 346–347; Stürner and Wendelstein, [2014] JURA 707, 712.

301 BGH 13.5.2015 – IV ZB 30/14, FamRZ 2015, 1180.

302 BGH 13.5.2015 – IV ZB 30/14, FamRZ 2015, 1180 paras 24 ff.

303 See, for example, Alexander Knur, 'Zugewinngemeinschaft, Ehevertrag und Verfügung von Todes wegen' [1957] DNotZ 451, 455; Fritz Rittner, 'Zur Auslegung des § 1371 Abs. 2 BGB n. F.' [1958] DNotZ 181, 189 ff; Karl Firsching, *Deutsch-Amerikanische Erbfälle* (C.H. Beck 1965) 63.

304 Schotten and Schmellenkamp, *Das Internationale Privatrecht in der notariellen Praxis* (2007) para 286.

305 Stürner and Wendelstein, [2014] JURA 707, 712; cf. Firsching, *Deutsch-Amerikanische Erbfälle* (1965) 63.

306 Schotten and Schmellenkamp, *Das Internationale Privatrecht in der notariellen Praxis* (2007) para 286.

Last but not least, as an alternative, so-called 'double characterisation' was also proposed. According to this, the provision could only become applicable in cases where both the law applicable to succession and the law applicable to matrimonial property regimes was German law.[307] The view has been justified on the ground that although the increase of the succession share of the surviving spouse through this provision supports succession law characterisation, the provision itself is a property law provision, and therefore it needs to be characterised as a provision having both a succession law and matrimonial property law nature.[308]

This question, which provoked divergent opinions in German legal scholarship and jurisprudence, is also relevant for the Regulation. Thus, it was referred to the CJEU from the Higher Regional Court of Berlin ('Kammergericht') in the succession case of Mr. *Mahnkopf* (a German national) who died intestate, thereby leaving his German national wife and son as heirs in respect of assets in Germany as well as a half share in property that the deceased had co-owned in Sweden. The spouses were both habitually resident in Berlin and made no marital agreement choosing the matrimonial property regime. Upon the application of Mrs. *Mahnkopf*, the Local Court ('Amtsgericht') of Schöneberg issued a German national succession certificate ('Erbschein') indicating that she and her son each inherited half of the estate. The half share of the wife was based on one quarter coming from the German rules of intestacy (Article 21 of the Regulation) and the other quarter coming from the BGB § 1371(1). Mrs. *Mahnkopf* subsequently sought to acquire a similar European Certificate of Succession in order to use it in connection with the property located in Sweden, and she contacted a notary who submitted her application once again to the Local Court of Schöneberg. This time, however, the Court rejected the application on the grounds that the additional quarter of her succession share was based on the matrimonial property regime, which falls outside the scope of the Regulation. When Mrs. *Mahnkopf* appealed to the Higher Regional Court of Berlin, the Court referred the question to the CJEU for a preliminary ruling, asking whether succession within the meaning of the Regulation also covers national provisions such as BGB § 1371(1).[309]

In answer to this question, both the Advocate General[310] and the Court stated that the provision does not deal with the division of assets between

---

[307] See, for example, Graue, (1966) 15 AJCL 164, 189; Lajos Vékás, 'Zur Konkurrenz zwischen Erbstatut und Güterrechtsstatut' [1985] IPRax 24, 24; Rembert Süß, 'Die Wahl deutschen Güterrechts für inländische Grundstücke' [1999] ZNotP 385, 392; Schotten and Schmellenkamp, *Das Internationale Privatrecht in der notariellen Praxis* (2007) paras 288ff; Kohler, (2020) 26 PPPM 27, 30–31. See also OLG Düsseldorf 3.8.1987 – 3 Wx 207/87, MittRhNotK 1988, 68; OLG Köln 5.8.2011 – 2 Wx 115/11, ZEV 2012, 205.

[308] Schotten and Schmellenkamp, *Das Internationale Privatrecht in der notariellen Praxis* (2007) para 287; Stürner and Wendelstein, [2014] JURA 707, 712.

[309] C-558/16 Mahnkopf [2018] ECLI:EU:C:2018:138 [20–30].

spouses but concerns succession rights of the surviving spouse as to assets forming part of the estate. Accordingly, its purpose is not to determine the issue of how assets are to be allocated or liquidated in the matrimonial property regime; rather, it indicates the succession share of the widowed spouse *vis-à-vis* other heirs. It is, therefore, a succession law provision which could be properly applied under the Regulation.[311]

This ruling of the CJEU – which in fact attracted much criticism in Germany[312] – generally ends the discussion from the Regulation's perspective.[313] There may, however, still be need for substitution or adaptation in individual cases. These issues should, accordingly, be examined here with the help of illustrative Turkish-German succession cases.

a) German Law as the Succession Statute and Turkish Law as the Matrimonial Property Statute: The Problem of Substitution?

Case No 1: German national (G) dies in 2020 in Düsseldorf/Germany, where he was habitually resident. He leaves behind his Turkish wife (W), whom he married in 2008 in Germany. They entered into a prenuptial agreement[314] which includes a clause that the law applicable to the marital property regime would be Turkish law as the national law of (W) (within the scope of (then-current) Article 15(2) EGBGB). Also left behind was his only child, (A). His entire estate consists of a flat in Düsseldorf and a bank account, both of which were acquired in the course of marriage. The combined worth of the two assets is 4,000,000 euros.

In this scenario, the law applicable to succession pursuant to Article 21(1) of the Regulation is German law. *(W)* is entitled to a 1/4 succession share in accordance with BGB § 1931(1). The law governing the matrimonial property

---

[310] C-558/16 Mahnkopf [2018] ECLI:EU:C:2017:965, Opinion of *AG Szpunar* [78 and 93].

[311] C-558/16 Mahnkopf [2018] ECLI:EU:C:2018:138 [40].

[312] See, for example, Peter Mankowski, 'Europäische Reversion: Das erbrechtliche Viertel ist im europäischen IPR Erbrecht! – Kritik, Umschau und Folgen zur EuGH-Entscheidung Mahnkopf' [2018] ErbR 295; Johannes Weber, 'Ein Klassiker neu aufgelegt Die Qualifikation des § 1371 BGB unter dem Regime der Europäischen Erbrechtsverordnung' [2018] NJW 1356; Michael Sonnentag, 'Die erbrechtliche Qualifikation des güterrechtlichen Viertels durch den EuGH und ihre Konsequenzen' [2019] JZ 657; cf. Karsten Thorn and Karen Varón Romero, 'Die Qualifikation des pauschalisierten Zugewinnausgleichs im Todesfall gemäß § 1371 Abs. 1 BGB nach der EuErbVO' [2020] IPRax 316.

[313] A case concerning an intra-EU situation actually came before the Higher Regional Court of Munich recently in 2019; the court, however, declined to adopt the succession characterisation, as the deceased had died before the entry into force of the Regulation: OLG München 24.9.2019 – 31 Wx 326/18, FGPrax 2019, 278.

Yet in another case, the Higher Regional Court of Frankfurt am Main provided that the succession characterisation made by the CJEU should be adopted but found BGB § 1371(1) inapplicable in the case: OLG Frankfurt am Main 14.9.2020 – 21 W 59/20, openJur 2020, 74330 paras 82 ff.

[314] For the rules governing marriage agreements, see particularly BGB §§ 1408–1410.

regime is, by contrast, Turkish law as a result of the *professio iuris* made in accordance with Article 15(2) EGBGB. Therefore, participation in acquired property becomes applicable as the statutory regime (Article 202(1) of the Turkish Civil Code). The question that arises here is whether the flat-rate equalisation offered by BGB 1371(1) could still be applicable without engaging in the liquidation process and mathematical calculation in accordance with the Turkish regime. This is related to the question of substitution. In more precise terms, the question would be whether the German courts can apply the Turkish statutory matrimonial property regime as a functional substitution of the German statutory regime of a community of accrued gains.

Substitution refers to the problem of whether an instrument or element associated with the applicable law and its legal system can be employed or satisfied in another legal system, typically in the law of the forum.[315] The substantive rules of States are indeed formulated to be used in cases with purely internal elements. In the drafting process, cases with foreign elements typically do not come into question. When non-domestic elements are also involved in cases, however, the question arises whether solely domestic legal instruments should be used for the specific question or whether the same (or similar) result could be reached with the use of instruments of a foreign legal system. Substitution is, therefore, a tool of private international law that can be helpful in such situations.[316] For substitution, two important questions should be examined. The first question is whether the applicable substantive norm of the forum, according to its meaning and purpose, excludes substitution. In addition, the equivalency (in terms of function) of the foreign legal institution with the domestic one should be examined.[317]

In the case example above, German succession provisions should be applied together with the Turkish matrimonial property regime. As BGB § 1371(1) – according to the *Mahnkopf* judgment – is a succession provision, it should also be applicable. This provision, however, normally applies only when the spouses lived under the German statutory matrimonial property regime (the community of accrued gains). The question thus arises whether the approach of the Turkish statutory matrimonial property regime (the participation in acquired property) can, in a case of death, substitute for the German regime such that *(W)* would still be entitled to an additional one quarter of succession share pursuant to BGB § 1371(1) without the mathematical

[315] Kropholler, *Internationales Privatrecht* (2006) 231; Jan D. Lüttringhaus, 'Substitution' in Jürgen Basedow and others (eds), *Encyclopedia of Private International Law* (Edward Elgar Publishing 2017) 1675.

[316] von Bar and Mankowski, *Internationales Privatrecht: Allgemeine Lehren* (2003) § 7 paras 239–240.

[317] von Bar and Mankowski, *Internationales Privatrecht: Allgemeine Lehren* (2003) § 7 para 243; Kropholler, *Internationales Privatrecht* (2006) 231–232.

calculations as regards matrimonial property.[318] It is argued that Turkish matrimonial property regime could not functionally substitute the German matrimonial property regime in a case of dissolution of marriage upon death of one of the spouses. This is because under the Turkish system, unlike in BGB § 1371(1), there is no lump-sum increase in the succession share of the surviving spouse, there being instead a mathematical calculation of the acquests needed.[319] Therefore, although the CJEU classified BGB § 1371(1) as a succession law provision, this provision could not be applicable in cases where the matrimonial property statute is a foreign law which does not have a solution that is amenable to substitution – like in the Turkish system – as regards the interplay between succession law and matrimonial property law. This results in a *de facto* double characterisation of BGB § 1371(1).[320]

In the light of this, matrimonial property as between *(G)* and *(W)* will be first liquidated according to Turkish law and *(W)* will be entitled to a participation claim for 2,000,000 euros from *(G)* (=4,000,000 euros/2 according to Article 236(1) of the Turkish Civil Code). The succession share of *(W)*, then, would be determined in accordance with German law (BGB § 1931(1)), and it will be 500,000 euros (=2,000,000 euros/4).

b) Turkish Law as the Succession Statute and German Law as the Matrimonial Property Statute: The Need for Adaptation?

Case No 2: Turkish national (T) dies in 2020 in Istanbul/Turkey, where she was then habitually resident. She leaves behind her German husband (H), whom she married in 2008 in Germany, where they were habitually resident together for many years, and her only

---

[318] Anatol Dutta, 'Pauschalierter Zugewinnausgleich nach § 1371 Abs. 1 BGB bei ausländischem Güterstatut? – Vom praktischen Nutzen der funktionalen Rechtsvergleichung' [2020] ErbR 304, 305.

[319] OLG Hamm 21.3.2019 – 10 W 31/17, ZEV 2019, 343 paras 30–32. See also DNotI, 'BGB § 1371 Abs. 1; EuErbVO Art. 1 Abs. 1 Erbrechtliche Qualifikation des zusätzlichen Erbteils des überlebenden Ehegatten aus § 1371 Abs. 1 BGB' [2018] DNotI-Report 54, 55; Sonnentag, [2019] JZ 657, 663 fn 119; cf. Heinrich Dörner, 'Erbrechtliche Qualifikation des § 1371 Abs. 1 BGB durch den EuGH: Konsequenzen und neue Fragen' [2018] ZEV 305, 307; Matteo Fornasier, 'Anmerkung – EuGH 1.3.2018, Art 1 I EUErbVO, § 1371 I BGB: Erbrechtl. Qualifikation des güterrechtl. Viertels' [2018] FamRZ 634, 635; Jens Kleinschmidt, 'Anmerkung – § 1371 Abs. 1 BGB ist erbrechtlich zu qualifizieren' [2018] ErbR 327, 328; Mankowski, [2018] ErbR 295, 302–303; Weber, [2018] NJW 1356, 1357–1358; Felix Aiwanger, 'Alte Lieder auf neuen Instrumenten: Die europäischen Güterrechtsverordnungen und das Erbrecht' [2019] ErbR 202, 207; Dutta, [2020] ErbR 304, 305; contra Samy Sakka, 'Der pauschalierte Zugewinnausgleich und das Europäische Nachlasszeugnis' [2018] MittBayNot 4, 7 (with respect to a similar statutory matrimonial property regime in Italian law).

[320] Rembert Süß, 'Die Entscheidung des EuGH in der Rechtssache Mahnkopf: Folgen für das gesetzliche Erbrecht des überlebenden Ehegatten in internationalen Ehen und neue Gestaltungsmöglichkeiten' [2018] DNotZ 742, 751; Aiwanger, [2019] ErbR 202, 207; Dutta, [2020] ErbR 304, 305.

child, (A). Her remaining assets – all acquired after the marriage – are a nice flat in Düsseldorf/Germany and a bank account in Turkey, with a total value of 4,000,000 euros.

In this slightly different scenario, the law applicable to succession is Turkish law, as the law of the State of the last habitual residence of *(T)* (Article 21(1) of the Regulation). As regards the matrimonial property regime, the marriage was concluded before the entry into force of the European Matrimonial Property Regulation, and, hence, the governing law should be determined in accord with the rules of the EGBGB. There was no *professio iuris* made by the spouses. With the reference of Article 15(1) EGBGB (old version), Article 14(1) EGBGB (old version) will be applicable. The couple had no common nationality but had a common habitual residence in Germany. Therefore, German law should be applicable according to Article 14(1) (2) EGBGB (old version).

As BGB § 1371(1) is a succession provision from the Regulation's perspective (according to the *Mahnkopf* judgment) and the law applicable to succession is Turkish law, it will not become applicable in this case. The succession share of the surviving spouse should be determined in accordance with Turkish rules. The matrimonial property regime is, however, subject to German law. As no arrangement was made prior to marriage, the statutory matrimonial property regime (community of accrued gains) is applicable. The relevant provision is again BGB § 1371, which regulates the liquidation of the community of accrued gains in the event of death. BGB § 1371 allows a mathematical equalisation, instead of a lump-sum solution, only in two circumstances: when the survived spouse is not an heir or a legatee of the deceased (paragraph 2) and when the surviving spouse renounces the inheritance (paragraph 3). It is only in these cases that a mathematical equalisation of accrued gains is made in accordance with BGB § 1373 et seq. In the present case, neither of these situations is present. It is, nonetheless, argued that BGB § 1373 et seq. should be used to fill the gap also in cases where German law is not the law applicable to succession and that, hence, the surviving spouse is not entitled to a lump-sum amount according to BGB §1371(1).[321] In the light of this, in the above example *(H)* will be entitled to a 2,000,000 euros claim for equalisation of accrued gains (BGB § 1378(1)). He then will

---

[321] Fornasier, [2018] FamRZ 634, 635; Mankowski, [2018] ErbR 295, 301; Süß, [2018] DNotZ 742, 747; Weber, [2018] NJW 1356, 1358; Aiwanger, [2019] ErbR 202, 207; Thorn and Varón Romero, [2020] IPRax 316, 320–321. See also Deutscher Notarverein, 'Stellungnahme – Entwurf eines Gesetzes zum Internationalen Güterrecht und zur Änderung von Vorschriften des Internationalen Privatrechts' 4 <https://www.bmjv.de/SharedDocs/Gesetzgebungsverfahren/Stellungnahmen/2018/Downloads/070618_Stellungnahme_Notarverein_RefE_Intern.Gueterrecht_intern.Privatrecht.pdf;jsessionid=47C4BB3655C2B0237A9C997515C8C1D7.2_cid324?__blob=publicationFile&v=4> accessed 7 June 2021.

For similar comments in the German-Swiss context, see Oliver Fröhler, 'Die erbrechtliche Stellung des längstlebenden Ehegatten in deutsch-schweizerischen Erbfällen' [2008] BWNotZ 38, 47.

be entitled to a one-quarter succession share in respect of the remaining amount, which equals 500,000 euros (Article 499 of the Turkish Civil Code). In such a case, one can ask whether there is a need for the use of another coordination tool, namely adaptation.[322]

The doctrine of adaptation (or adjustment) comes into play when unintended results arise as a consequence of the fragmentation of the applicable law, as the dispute is connected to more than one legal system. Under this doctrine, the court may modify or disregard the legal norms applicable to the dispute under the rules of private international law.[323] This fragmentation may be in the form of a lack of norms ('Normenmangel') or an abundance of norms ('Normenhäufung').[324] When the surviving spouse is in a better or worse position as a result of the fact that different laws govern succession and the matrimonial property regime, adaptation may be needed.[325] In order to understand this, the result of the application of different laws – especially as regards a question of whether there is an abundance of norms – and the same law (Turkish or German law) should be examined in respect of the given example.

If Turkish law had governed both the matrimonial property regime and succession, *(H)* would have been entitled to 2,500,000 euros (2,000,000 euros as half of the acquired property pursuant to Article 236(1) of the Turkish Civil Code and 500,000 euros as one quarter of the remaining estate pursuant to Article 499(1) of the Turkish Civil Code).

However, if German law had governed both legal questions, *(H)* would have been entitled to 2,000,000 euros (1,000,000 euros as one quarter according to BGB § 1371(1) and 1,000,000 euros as one quarter according to BGB § 1931(1)).

The result of the cumulative application of Turkish succession law and German matrimonial property law is, as shown in the previous page, that *(H)* receives 2,500,000 euros. This falls within the range of results that would be reached upon application of the same legal system, and hence there seems to be no need for adaptation.[326]

---

322 Kleinschmidt, [2018] ErbR 327, 329; Mankowski, [2018] ErbR 295, 303–304.

323 Kropholler, *Internationales Privatrecht* (2006) 234–235; Gerhard Dannemann, 'Adjustment/Adaptation (Anpassung)' in Jürgen Basedow and others (eds), *Encyclopedia of Private International Law* (Edward Elgar Publishing 2017) 8. On the issue of adaptation in general, see also Tekinalp, *Milletlerarası Özel Hukuk* (2020) 40–42; Nomer, *Devletler Hususî Hukuku* (2021) 134 ff; Şanlı, Esen and Ataman Figanmeşe, *Milletlerarası Özel Hukuk* (2021) 57–58 fn 102; Doğan, *Milletlerarası Özel Hukuk* (2022) 255 ff.

324 Martin Wolff, *Das internationale Privatrecht Deutschlands* (3rd edn, Springer 1954) 58–60.

325 See, for another example in the Turkish-German context, Stürner and Wendelstein, [2014] JURA 707, 712–713.

326 Cf. Mankowski, [2018] ErbR 295, 303.

3. *Characterisation of BGB § 1371(1) from the Turkish Perspective (the Turkish PILA and the Treaty) and Possible Consequences for Turkish-German Successions*

Although the characterisation problem is in principle no longer relevant in the Regulation context, the issue still remains open from the Turkish perspective in cases where the Turkish PILA or the Treaty finds application. Hypothetical scenarios similar to the ones above could also be formulated here.

The Treaty perspective is in fact also relevant in Germany. The approach of the German courts to the characterisation of BGB § 1371(1) in the Treaty context has never been uniform. There were three cases before the entry into force of the Regulation in relation to Turkish nationals where the application of BGB § 1371(1) was disputed. Two of these cases came before the Higher Regional Court ('Oberlandesgericht') of Cologne. In the earlier case, the Court adopted the 'double characterisation' view and held that the provision could become applicable only where both the law applicable to succession and to the matrimonial property regime was German law.[327] Notwithstanding this, in a later case, the Court did not take a stance on the question of whether the provision is one of matrimonial property law or of a dual nature, but it implied that it is not a pure succession provision.[328] The German Federal Court of Justice ('BGH') also had the opportunity to answer the question but declined to do so.[329]

It is doubtful whether the CJEU's decision in relation to the Regulation would have any effect in cases falling within the scope of the Turkish-German Treaty. One might think that German courts would be inclined to adopt the same approach also in that context and decide in favour of the application of the provision in cases where German law governs succession.[330] Such a solution may provide legal clarity for the interplay between the succession statute and the matrimonial property statute in the scope of not only the Regulation but also the Treaty. By doing so, the friction between the Regulation and the bilateral treaties would be reduced, and decisional harmony on this issue within the EU would be guaranteed.[331] In fact, this issue recently

[327] OLG Köln 5.8.2011 – 2 Wx 115/11, ZEV 2012, 205.

[328] OLG Köln 11.2.2014 – 2 Wx 245/13, FamRZ 2015, 172.

[329] BGH 12.9.2012 – IV ZB 12/12, FamRZ 2012, 1871.

[330] Martin Gebauer, '§ 1371 Abs. 1 BGB und das deutsch-türkische Nachlassabkommen im Sog der erbrechtlichen Qualifikation' [2018] IPRax 586; cf. Matteo Fornasier, '§ 1371 I BGB: Qualifikation des güterrechtl. Viertels in deutsch-türk. Erbfällen – Anmerkung – OLG Karlsruhe 27.02.2018 – 14 W 113/16 (Wx)' [2018] FamRZ 860, 861; Süß, [2019] ZErb 249, 254.

[331] Fornasier, [2018] FamRZ 860, 861; cf. Gebauer, [2018] IPRax 586, 588.

It is, however, argued that the succession law characterisation of the CJEU could be considered as only a 'pyrrhic victory' for decisional harmony even within the Union and that it actually complicates cross-border estate administration rather than simplifying it:

came before the Higher Regional Court of Hamm in a case where the Treaty was applied. The Court discussed the application of the provision but ultimately found it inapplicable – as the conditions for application were not met from both the succession perspective and the matrimonial property perspective – thereby declining to take a stance on the characterisation despite the CJEU's succession law characterisation.[332] This proves that the issue has not been settled in Germany for cases where the Treaty becomes applicable. The analysis of the Treaty on the matter of characterisation under BGB § 1371 (1) must, however, also be considered from the Turkish viewpoint.

For this discussion, we first need to go to the basics of the issue of characterisation. It is well known that there are different doctrinal streams in the process of characterisation. The first and probably most widely accepted view is characterisation by the *lex fori*. According to this approach, the judge should give meanings to foreign legal concepts or rules in line with the law of the forum. This is because the first point of departure to find the law applicable in a cross-border case is, in fact, the private international law of the forum. This approach is, however, criticised particularly on the grounds that it may lead to conflicting results in different legal orders and might be problematic in cases where such a concept or rule does not exist in the law of the forum.[333]

The opponents of the *lex fori* approach have propounded the *lex cause* approach, which requires that the law governing the legal relationship should decide also on the characterisation of that concept or rule before the courts that are seated in other countries and applying them. This would be particularly helpful for judges in cases where the forum has no legal institution or rule as in the applicable foreign law. The weaknesses of this system, as argued, can especially be seen in two points. First, it seems to be a circular argument that the characterisation process would be governed by foreign law before the judge selects the appropriate legal system that is applicable in a case. In addition, in the instances where there are more than one legal order

---

Jan Peter Schmidt, 'Abschied von alten Gewissheiten: Die EU-Erbrechtsverordnung in der Rechtsprechung' [2020] ErbR 91, 96. See also, for criticism of the decision, Konvalin, *Das Europäische Nachlasszeugnis* (2018) 107–108; Mankowski, [2018] ErbR 295; Weber, [2018] NJW 1356; Dutta, [2020] ErbR 304, 304; Kohler, (2020) 26 PPPM 27, 30–31.

332 OLG Hamm 21.3.2019 – 10 W 31/17, ZEV 2019, 343. For a commentary on the case, see Süß, [2019] ZErb 249.

A similar case also came before the Higher Regional Court of Karlsruhe. The Court did not discuss the characterisation problem in this case either; rather, it found the BGB § 1371(1) inapplicable as the spouses (both Turkish nationals) were married in Turkey and were subject to the Turkish statutory matrimonial property regime: OLG Karlsruhe 27.2.2018 – 14 W 113/16 (Wx), ZEV 2018, 330.

333 Veronique Allarousse, 'A Comparative Approach to the Conflict of Characterization in Private International Law' (1991) 23 Case W Res J Int'l L 479, 481–485; Çelikel and Erdem, *Milletlerarası Özel Hukuk* (2021) 79–81.

governing a case, the characterisation of each system may be different and this would lead to contradictory results.[334]

As a third view, characterisation by reference to universal and independent concepts has been advocated. This argues that the characterisation process should be made in the light of comparative law and jurisprudence. This theory might have the advantage of ensuring a uniform characterisation regardless of the court applying it. It would again be useful where the forum does not recognise a foreign legal institution. Notwithstanding this, it is too ideal and extremely difficult for the judges to apply. Furthermore, it is also vague, as there are no generally applicable principles on an international level.[335]

From these approaches, which one the Turkish judge will employ depends on the case. The *lex fori* approach does not seem to be of much help here, as, in line with the criticism of this approach, such a rule does not exist in the Turkish legal system. Therefore, either the *lex causae* approach or the third approach may be used here. Particularly after the *Mahnkopf* judgment, both of them may result in Turkish courts adopting the succession law characterisation of BGB § 1371(1). This may provide a degree of decisional harmony with Germany, at least in cases which are governed by the Regulation in Germany and, *vice versa*, by the Turkish PILA in Turkey. Nevertheless, the impact, if any, of the approach of the Court of Justice of the European Union may not be at the same level for Turkish courts as for German courts by virtue of the outsider position of Turkey in the Union. This would also be true in the context of the Treaty. Therefore, a Turkish judge may still consider all three options in line with the discussions in Germany as the origin State of the rule.

As every legal system finds its own equilibrium between matrimonial property law and succession law, the combined application of 'flat-rate equalisation'[336] in accord with BGB § 1371(1) alongside the succession share as dictated by the Turkish legal system may be seen as problematic by Turkish judges.[337] From the Turkish perspective, therefore, the 'clean solution'[338] would be to follow the double characterisation view and allow the use of BGB § 1371(1) only in cases where German law governs both the succession and the property regime. This is because when one of these questions is governed by Turkish law and the other by German law, coordination problems may occur which require the use of instruments such as substitution or adaptation.[339] This will

[334] Allarousse, (1991) 23 Case W Res J Int'l L 479, 485–487; Çelikel and Erdem, *Milletlerarası Özel Hukuk* (2021) 81–82.

[335] Allarousse, (1991) 23 Case W Res J Int'l L 479, 487–488; Çelikel and Erdem, *Milletlerarası Özel Hukuk* (2021) 83.

[336] Kohler, (2020) 26 PPPM 27, 29.

[337] Rembert Süß, in Rembert Süß (ed), *Erbrecht in Europa* (3rd edn, zerb verlag 2015) § 3 para 90; Mankowski, [2018] ErbR 295, 301.

[338] Kohler, (2020) 26 PPPM 27, 30.

[339] Cf. Kohler, (2020) 26 PPPM 27, 30–31.

also be true in a reverse scenario in which Turkish law governs the matrimonial property regime but German law governs succession.[340]

Nevertheless, the *ratio legis* of the provision speaks for the matrimonial property law characterisation. Although it technically affects the succession share of the surviving spouse, the German legislature considered the fact that the majority of marriages end upon death of one of the spouses (as was common at least at the time of drafting) and intended to provide a simple, practical, legally certain solution for those instances. It subsequently introduced a particular type of dissolution of the matrimonial property regime with an additional one quarter succession share of the surviving spouse under BGB § 1371(1).[341] Therefore, characterisation of the provision as matrimonial property law and its application whenever – within the scope of the Turkish PILA or the Treaty – German law governs the matrimonial property regime appear to be considerably in line with its *ratio legis*, whereas it may be possible that Turkish law is applicable to succession and such an increase of the succession share of the surviving spouse does not exist under Turkish law.[342] Such a characterisation of the provision will also not be problematic for a reverse scenario where Turkish law governs the matrimonial property regime and German law governs the matter of succession as the provision will not become applicable in such a case.[343]

The adoption of the matrimonial property law characterisation of the provision, as is also the case in pure succession law characterisation, may require the use of substitution or adaptation before Turkish courts.[344] These should be explained again with the help of examples.

Case No 3: Turkish national (T) dies in Istanbul/Turkey, where she had her last domicile/habitual residence. She married her German husband (H) in 1970 in Berlin/Germany, where they were habitually resident at the time. She had never drafted a testament or made an agreement as to succession. Her entire estate consists of 2,000,000 TL cash in a bank account, a car, and two apartments in Istanbul. Upon death of (T), her two children (A) and (B) apply to the competent Istanbul Civil Court of Peace[345] for the issue of a succession certificate and receive the certificate in line with their requests. On the other hand, (H) files a

---

[340] Fröhler, [2008] BWNotZ 38, 47.

[341] Aksoy, *Mal Rejimi ve Miras* (1964) 135–136 and 143. See also BGH 13.5.2015 – IV ZB 30/14, FamRZ 2015, 1180 para 26; contra C-558/16 Mahnkopf [2018] ECLI:EU:C:2017:965, Opinion of *AG Szpunar* [78 and 93]; C-558/16 Mahnkopf [2018] ECLI:EU:C:2018:138 [40].

[342] See, in this regard, Fröhler, [2008] BWNotZ 38, 47; Stürner and Wendelstein, [2014] JURA 707, 713; Kılıç, 'Türkei' (2020) para 12.

[343] Fröhler, [2008] BWNotZ 38, 47.

[344] See, for Turkey, Şanlı, Esen and Ataman Figanmeşe, *Milletlerarası Özel Hukuk* (2021) 267; Doğan, *Milletlerarası Özel Hukuk* (2022) 344 and 371–372.

[345] The competence to issue succession certificates belongs to the civil courts of peace according to Art 598 of the Turkish Civil Code. On the competence to issue succession certificates, see also below pp 304–305 and 316–317.

case before the competent Istanbul Family Court[346] for the liquidation of the matrimonial property regime, and later challenges the validity of the succession certificate, claiming that he is entitled to an additional one quarter of succession share in accordance with BGB § 1371(1).

This exemplary case scenario falls within the scope of the Turkish PILA. The law applicable to succession is Turkish law pursuant to Article 20(1) of the Turkish PILA, whereas the law governing the matrimonial property regime is German law according to Article 15(1) of the Turkish PILA.[347] *(G)* and *(H)* did not make any choice of law and were nationals of different States. They had a common habitual residence, which was Berlin, when they married. Matrimonial property regimes are, however, matters of family law where single (partial) *renvoi* finds application pursuant to Article 2(3) of the Turkish PILA. This means that the Turkish judge would first look at the conflict-of-laws rules of Germany and apply the domestic provisions of the State whose law has been indicated as the law applicable to the matrimonial property regime. Article 15 of the EGBGB (old version) deals with the law governing the matrimonial property regime and is applicable here. It makes a reference to the law applicable to general marriage provisions regulated under Article 14 of the EGBGB, unless the spouses specified the law applicable to the matrimonial property regime. According to Article 14(1) of the EGBGB (old version), the law governing the matrimonial property regime is German law as the spouses had no common nationality and were habitually resident in Germany at the time of marriage. Hence, the result would be that Turkish law is applicable to succession, whereas matters regarding matrimonial property regimes would be governed by German law.

Case No 4: German national (G) dies in Istanbul/Turkey without leaving behind any testamentary dispositions. He has two heirs. The first is his Turkish wife (W), whom he married in Germany and with whom he entered a prenuptial agreement stating their mutual intention of being governed by the statutory matrimonial property regime of a community of accrued gains and choosing German law – as the law of the place where they had their mutual habitual residence at that time – to be the law to govern their matrimonial property regime; his second heir is his only son (A). His entire estate consists of two apartments in Istanbul, which were both acquired during the marriage and which have a total value of 4,000,000 TL. The question in this scenario would once again be whether (W) would be entitled to another one-quarter succession share according to BGB § 1371(1).

---

[346] On competence for the liquidation of the matrimonial property, see Art 214 of the Turkish Civil Code and Art 4(1) of the Law on the Establishment, Duties and Rules of Procedure of Family Courts ('Aile Mahkemelerinin Kuruluş, Görev ve Yargılama Usulleri Hakkında Kanun', *Resmi Gazete* of 18.1.2003, no 24997).

[347] These examples are formulated based on the view explained above that Article 15 of the Turkish PILA adopts a dualist approach by differentiating movable and immovable assets in matrimonial property regimes. This is because Article 15(2), as being different from the first paragraph, provides that immovable properties would be subject to the *lex rei sitae* in the liquidation process. See above n 283, p 107.

This second example falls into the scope of the Turkish-German Treaty, as the deceased is a German national who died in Turkey and left assets there. Therefore, succession matters on the apartments in Istanbul are governed by Turkish law pursuant to Article 20(14) (2) of the Treaty. Issues related to the matrimonial property regime are, however, outside the scope of the Treaty, and the law applicable to it is German law in accordance with their choice of law (Article 15(1) of the Turkish PILA). *Renvoi* will also not be applicable here due to the choice of law (Article 2(4) of the Turkish PILA), and the substantive law of Germany will be applied. In this case, once again, the result is that the law applicable to succession is Turkish law, whilst the law applicable to the matrimonial property regime is German law.

In both cases, the question of whether the deceased would be allowed an additional one-quarter succession share is at stake.

If the Turkish courts consider this provision as related to matrimonial property law, in line with the view held by this present study, the provision becomes applicable due to the fact that the law governing matrimonial property regimes in each case is German law. The Court dealing with the claim regarding the liquidation of matrimonial property should decide that the surviving spouses will receive another 1/4 from the estate. *(H)* in the first case and *(W)* in the second case would be entitled to 1/2 of the estate (1/4 as a succession share arising from Article 499 of the Turkish Civil Code and an additional 1/4 for matrimonial property purposes as arising from the BGB § 1371(1)). Such a result is, of course, only possible with a lump-sum increase of the succession share under BGB § 1371(1), assuming the matrimonial property regime can substitute for the Turkish matrimonial property regime.

In line with the views from the German side as explained above, it can be argued that a flat-rate equalisation pursuant to BGB § 1371(1), in the case of the death of one of the spouses, cannot functionally substitute for the calculative method of the Turkish matrimonial property regime.[348] This would once again lead to a *de facto* double characterisation of BGB § 1371(1), and it could be applied only when German law is both the law applicable to succession and the law applicable to the matrimonial property regime. Instead of BGB § 1371(1), BGB § 1373 et seq. would be used as a gap filler, and the matrimonial property regime would be liquidated in the calculative way in accordance with those provisions. *(H)* and *(W)* would in both examples be entitled to 2,000,000 TL as a claim for accrued gains in the course of marriage (BGB § 1378(1)) and would be entitled to a 500,000 TL succession share from the estate (Article 499(1) of the Turkish Civil Code).

In other scenarios where the law applicable to succession is German law and the law applicable to the matrimonial property regime is Turkish law,

---

[348] Cf. Sütçü, [2015] ZErb 43, 46–47; contra Fröhler, [2008] BWNotZ 38, 47 (as regards to Swiss matrimonial property law); Kılıç, 'Türkei' (2020) para 12.

BGB § 1371(1) will not become applicable due to the preferred matrimonial property characterisation. In the first place, the matrimonial property regime would be liquidated in accordance with Turkish law, and the surviving spouse would have a claim of one half from the surplus (Article 236(1) of the Turkish Civil Code). From the remaining amount which constitutes the estate, he will be entitled to a one-quarter succession share according to BGB § 1931(1). As with the result that was reached above from a German perspective,[349] there will be no need for adaptation in such a case.

E. The Law Applicable to Dispositions of Property Upon Death

Legal experts specialising in the field of succession law quite likely know of the cartoon of *Peter Arno* from *The New Yorker* magazine portraying an old man blissfully saying to his attorney, sitting right beside and drafting his will: 'Now read me the part again where I disinherit everybody'.[350] Whether they are made in order to disinherit statutory heirs, as it would seem to be the case in this cartoon, or to bequeath the estate or a part thereof to specific persons, dispositions of property upon death are the only tools available to us to determine the fate of our estate and to express our last wishes prior to death.[351] As an extension of the civil law principles of party autonomy and protection of property, the freedom of testation is indeed one of the most widely accepted rules in existing legal systems.[352] Whereas the numbers of dispositions of property upon death made each year may be divergent in different States,[353] such dispositions are still of considerable practical relevance, as succession

---

349 See above pp 117–120.

350 Peter Arno, 'Now read me the part again where I disinherit everybody' *The New Yorker* (7 December 1940) 29.

351 Samim Gönensay and Kemalettin Birsen, *Miras Hukuku* (2nd edn, Ahmed Said Matbaası 1963) 39; Nuşin Ayiter and Ahmet Kılıçoğlu, *Miras Hukuku* (3rd edn, Savaş Yayınevi 1993) 72; Dural and Öz, *Miras Hukuku* (2021) para 235.

352 Reinhard Zimmermann (ed), *Freedom of Testation – Testierfreiheit* (Mohr Siebeck 2012) VII.

353 Empirical evidence may not be present for all countries recognising freedom of testation. However, Turkey and Germany could be taken as examples for the purposes of this study. The statistics of 2020 will be examined here. The German Central Register of Wills ('Zentrales Testamentsregister der Bundesnotarkammer') reports that 299,200 testaments were registered in Germany in 2020. See, in this regard, Zentrales Testamentsregister der Bundesnotarkammer, *Jahresbericht 2020* (2020) <https://www.testamentsregister.de/fileadmin/user_upload_ztr/dokumente/Jahresbericht_2020.pdf> accessed 14 March 2022. In Turkey, on the other hand, notaries registered 13,226 testaments in the same year: T.C. Adalet Bakanlığı, Adli Sicil ve İstatistik Genel Müdürlüğü, *Adalet İstatistikleri 2020* (Resmi İstatistik Programı 2020) 41 <https://adlisicil.adalet.gov.tr/Resimler/SayfaDokuman/1692021162011adalet_ist-2020.pdf> accessed 14 March 2022.

issues arising in practice are mostly related to them.[354] Such cases may also arise in the Turkish-EU context. The Regulation, the Turkish PILA, and the Treaty seem to have differences also with respect to the law governing dispositions of property upon death.

The European legislature considered in the Regulation the need of its citizens to benefit from foreseeable estate planning within the Union and laid down specific rules governing the admissibility, substantive validity, and binding effects of dispositions of property upon death as well as their formal validity when made in writing under Article 24 et seq. of the Regulation.[355] The term 'dispositions of property upon death' under the Regulation covers wills, joint wills, and agreements as to succession (Article 3(1) (d)).

Turkish law, on the other hand, only allows wills (in the form of holographic wills, notarial wills, and oral wills) and agreements as to succession (Article 531 et seq. of the Turkish Civil Code), whereas it does not recognise joint wills as a form of testamentary dispositions.[356] The substantive validity of testamentary dispositions is governed by the law applicable to succession in general under Articles 20(1) and 20(2) of the Turkish PILA. There are, however, specific rules on the law applicable to the formal validity of testamentary dispositions (Article 20(4)) and to the capacity to make such dispositions (Article 20(5)).

The main conflict-of-laws rule under the Treaty, i.e. Article 20(14), is also applicable for the admissibility and substantive validity of testamentary dispositions, as the rule does not make a distinction between testamentary and intestate succession and instead uses the broad term of 'issues related to succession', which covers both types of succession conflicts.[357] The law applicable to the formal validity of testamentary dispositions, however, is addressed in a specific provision under Article 20(16) of the Treaty.

The interplay between these rules should be examined here in detail with respect to the admissibility, binding effects, substantive, and formal validity of testamentary dispositions. On the formal validity of such dispositions, the app-

---

[354] In Turkey, for example, almost half of the succession cases before the civil courts were related to dispositions of property upon death in the year 2020. See, in this regard, T.C. Adalet Bakanlığı, Adli Sicil ve İstatistik Genel Müdürlüğü, *Adalet İstatistikleri 2020* (2020) 198.

[355] Recital 48 of the Regulation.

[356] The forms of dispositions of property upon death ('şekli anlamda ölüme bağlı tasarruflar') are listed as *numerus clausus* under the Turkish Civil Code: Dural and Öz, *Miras Hukuku* (2021) para 257; Serozan and Engin, *Miras Hukuku* (2021) § 1 paras 51–52; Çabri, *Miras Hukuku Şerhi (TMK m. 495-574)* (2022) para 529. See especially Art 514 of the Turkish Civil Code.

[357] Güneş, 'The Relations of Turkey with EU Member States' (2019) 292; Looschelders, 'The External Relations of Germany' (2019) 162; Odersky, *Hausmann/Odersky* (2021) § 15 para 350.

lication of the Hague Form Convention may also come into play as Turkey[358] and most of the Member States, including Germany,[359] are party to it. Therefore, the rules of this Convention should also be included in the relevant part.

I. The Law Applicable to Admissibility and the Substantive Validity of Dispositions of Property Upon Death

One of the most important questions regarding dispositions of property upon death which involve cross-border elements is that of which law should govern the admissibility, substantive validity, and binding effects of such dispositions. A possible solution for the European legislature, in this regard, could have been to submit these issues to the law applicable to succession as a whole (*lex successionis*) in accordance with the desired unity of succession within the Regulation. This would obviously have been a simple solution for the courts. This is not only because courts could have applied not only a single law but also their own law (*lex fori*), which coincides with the law applicable to succession in the majority of the cases.[360] In such a case, however, a change of habitual residence or the conclusion of a *professio iuris* after a disposition of property upon death had been validly made by the deceased could have rendered the disposition void under the law of habitual residence at the time of death. Therefore, the Regulation adopts different rules to govern these matters, so that the deceased does not have to worry about the validity of his disposition after making it.[361]

The Regulation makes a distinction between wills and joint wills and agreements as to succession and provides different conflict-of-laws rules for the admissibility, substantive validity, and binding effects of these dispositions. Article 24 of the Regulation covers such matters with respect to wills and joint wills, whereas Article 25 is on agreements as to succession. In addition, Article 26 specifies the issues governed by substantive validity. Before focusing on these rules in detail, the meaning of each type of disposition should be clarified here at the outset.

Wills are not defined in the Regulation. A will could be defined as a unilateral legal act whereby the deceased makes a disposition regarding his proper-

---

[358] See *Resmi Gazete* of 17.1.1983, no 17931. The Convention entered into force in Turkey on 22.10.1983.

[359] The Convention entered into force in Germany on 1.1.1966. See BGBl. II 1966, 11. For the former German Democratic Republic (East Germany), it entered into force 21.9.1974. See BGBl. II 1974, 1461.

[360] Bonomi, *Bonomi/Wautelet* (2016) ESR Art 24 paras 33–34; Metallinos, *Pamboukis* (2017) ESR Art 24 para 1.

[361] Paul Lagarde, in Ulf Bergquist and others (eds), *EU Regulation on Succession and Wills – Commentary* (Otto Schmidt 2015) ESR Art 24 para 5; Bonomi, *Bonomi/Wautelet* (2016) ESR Art 24 paras 29–30; Metallinos, *Pamboukis* (2017) ESR Art 24 para 1; cf. Dutta, [2013] FamRZ 4, 9.

ty which will be effective upon his death.[362] Joint wills, on the other hand, are defined in the Regulation as 'a will drawn up in one instrument by two or more persons' (Article 3(1) (c)). They are the opposite of a 'separate' will. In these types of joint wills, the will (which is a single instrument) is signed and executed by two or more persons. Joint wills may be made as 'mutual' or 'reciprocal' wills, whereby each of the testators makes a disposition in favour of the other side.[363] These type of wills are governed by the 'agreements as to succession' under the Regulation,[364] as the Regulation defines an 'agreement as to succession' as 'including an agreement resulting from mutual wills, which, with or without consideration, creates, modifies or terminates rights to the future estate or estates of one or more persons party to the agreement' (Article 3(1) (b)).

Article 24(1) of the Regulation clarifies that the law governing the admissibility and substantive validity of dispositions of property upon death other than agreements as to succession is the *hypothetical* succession law, i.e. the law which would have been applicable to the succession of the testator who made the disposition if he had died on the day of making the disposition. Thus, the issues of whether a testamentary disposition other than an agreement as to succession is admissible, substantially valid, and binding would normally be governed by the law applicable to succession at the time of making the disposition. This could be either the law of the State where the deceased had his habitual residence (Article 21(1)) or the law of another State with which the deceased by way of an exception, was manifestly more closely connected (Article 21(2)). With this conflict-of-laws rule, the law applicable to admissibility as well as the substantive validity of testamentary dispositions other than agreements as to succession is 'crystallized' at the time of drafting and remains so even in the event of a change of the habitual residence so as to ensure that such a change would not affect the validity of the disposition which has been made.[365]

The testator has also a right to choose his national law on the day of making the disposition or on the day of death to govern these questions pursuant to Article 22 of the Regulation (Article 24(2)). Such a choice, if only made for these matters, would be a partial choice of law, and for other matters the main

---

362 Michael Schmidt, in Harm Peter Westermann, Barbara Grunewald and Georg Maier-Reimer (eds), *Erman BGB*, vol II (16th edn, Otto Schmidt 2020) BGB Vorb. § 2064 para 5; Öztan, *Miras Hukuku* (2021) 188.

363 William L. Eagleton, 'Joint and Mutual Wills Mutual Promises to Devise as a Means of Conveyancing' (1930) 15 Cornell LQ 358, 361; Juliana Rodríguez Rodrigo, in Alfonso-Luis Calvo Caravaca, Angelo Davì and Heinz-Peter Mansel (eds), *The EU Succession Regulation – A Commentary* (Cambridge University Press 2016) ESR Art 24 para 4.

364 Rodríguez Rodrigo, *Calvo Caravaca/Davì/Mansel* (2016) ESR Art 24 para 4; Metallinos, *Pamboukis* (2017) ESR Art 24 para 4.

365 Bonomi, *Bonomi/Wautelet* (2016) ESR Art 24 para 23.

rule applicable to succession under Article 21 would remain applicable.[366] For example,[367] a 16-year-old Turkish national who is habitually resident in Stockholm/Sweden wishes to make a testament that conveys all his assets to a charity in order so as to exclude his parents. As he is under 18, which is the minimum age required to make a testament under Swedish law,[368] he chooses Turkish law, where persons who have reached 15 years of age are allowed to make a testament that should govern the admissibility as well as the substantive validity of his testament,[369] pursuant to Article 24(2) of the Regulation. For the remaining succession matters, however, he wishes that Swedish law, as the law of the State of habitual residence (Article 21(1)), continue to be applicable, which, unlike Turkish law,[370] does not grant a reserved portion to his parents.[371]

The law applicable to the admissibility and substantive validity of testamentary dispositions other than agreements as to succession, whether of an objective (Article 21) or subjective nature (Article 22), will also govern the modifications or revocations of dispositions of property upon death, other than agreements as to succession (Article 24(3)). Here, the question arises as to which time should be taken into account to find the *hypothetical* succession law that will govern the modification and revocation of such dispositions. Recital 51 clarifies this issue by providing that the reference to the *hypothetical* succession law should be understood as the law of the State of habitual residence or the law of nationality on the day of revocation or modification.

As mentioned earlier, the law applicable to agreements as to succession for the issues of admissibility, substantive validity, and binding effects between the parties (including also an agreement's dissolution) is specifically enshrined in Article 25 of the Regulation.[372] Based on the definition of an agreement as to succession under Article 3(1) (b), and in addition to mutual or reciprocal joint wills, agreements on the renunciation of inheritance or a

---

[366] Andrea Bonomi and Azadi Öztürk, 'Das Statut der Verfügung von Todes wegen (Art. 24 ff EuErbVO)' in Anatol Dutta and Sebastian Herrler (eds), *Die Europäische Erbrechtsverordnung, 20 Jahre DNotI 1993–2013* (C.H. Beck 2014) 54–55.

[367] The example is inspired by Bonomi and Öztürk, 'Das Statut der Verfügung von Todes wegen' (2014) 54–55.

[368] Ch. 9 § 1 of the Swedish Inheritance Code (*Ärvdabalk (SFS 1958:637)*). See, for general information on the issue, Lisa Nordlund, 'Sweden' in Lucia Ruggeri, Ivana Kunda and Sandra Winkler (eds), *Family Property and Succession in EU Member States: National Reports on the Collected Data* (Sveučilište u Rijeci, Pravni fakultet 2019) 666ff, esp. p 669 and pp 672–674 <https://www.euro-family.eu/documenti/news/psefs_e_book_compressed.pdf> accessed 14 December 2020.

[369] Art 502 of the Turkish Civil Code.

[370] Art 505 of the Turkish Civil Code.

[371] Ch. 7 of the Swedish Inheritance Code.

[372] A similar rule is found in Art 8 et seq. of the Hague Succession Convention.

reserved portion and *donatio mortis causa* are also considered as agreements as to succession in the Regulation.[373]

An agreement as to succession with respect to those matters would also be governed by the *hypothetical* succession law. This would be either the law of habitual residence (Article 21(1)) or the law of nationality (Article 22) on the day of conclusion of the agreement (Article 25(1) and (3)). The rule, however, distinguishes cases where an agreement as to succession involves the estate of one person and of several persons.

Agreements as to succession involving the estate of more than one person are much important in practice. Spouses often arrange the succession matters of the family, achieving binding effects, in the form of an agreement as to succession which is attached to or included in a prenuptial agreement.[374] Therefore, the question of which law should govern these type of agreements as to succession is provided under the second paragraph of Article 25. According to this provision, the admissibility of such dispositions would be governed by the cumulative application of the law of the States of habitual residences of the deceased (Article 21(1)) or the law of the State(s) whose law has been chosen (Article 22) at the time of the conclusion of the agreement. The cumulative application of these laws could be problematic in cases when, for example, the deceased whose estates are involved in the agreement as to succession have their habitual residences in different States or are nationals of different States; or when, even where they hold the same nationality, one of them made a choice of law whereas the other one did not.[375] The agreement as to succession, therefore, should be admissible under all of the applicable laws.[376] When this is not the case, there would be no agreement as to succession and the succession of each person would be governed by the general rules.[377]

[373] Carl Friedrich Nordmeier, 'Erbverträge und nachlassbezogene Rechtsgeschäfte in der EuErbVO – eine Begriffsklärung' [2013] ZEV 117, 121; Dutta, *MüKoBGB* (2020) EuErbVO Art 25 para 2; cf. Bonomi and Öztürk, 'Das Statut der Verfügung von Todes wegen' (2014) 59.

[374] Bonomi, *Bonomi/Wautelet* (2016) ESR Art 25 para 24; Christos G. Zoumpoulis, in Haris P. Pamboukis (ed), *EU Succession Regulation No 650/2012 – A Commentary* (Nomiki Bibliothiki & C.H. Beck & Hart & Nomos 2017) ESR Art 25 para 22.

[375] Zoumpoulis, *Pamboukis* (2017) ESR Art 25 para 24; Dutta, *MüKoBGB* (2020) EuErbVO Art 25 para 9; cf. Rodríguez Rodrigo, *Calvo Caravaca/Davì/Mansel* (2016) ESR Art 25 para 15.

[376] Christoph Döbereiner, 'Das internationale Erbrecht nach der EU-Erbrechtsverordnung (Teil II)' [2013] MittBayNot 437, 442; Müller-Lukoschek, *Die neue EU-Erbrechtsverordnung* (2015) § 2 para 184; Rodríguez Rodrigo, *Calvo Caravaca/Davì/Mansel* (2016) ESR Art 25 para 15; Dutta, *MüKoBGB* (2020) EuErbVO Art 25 para 9; Constanze Fischer-Czermak, in Astrid Deixler-Hübner and Martin Schauer (eds), *Kommentar zur EU-Erbrechtsverordnung* (2nd edn, Manz 2020) EuErbVO Art 25 para 23; Frank Bauer and Johannes Weber, in Anatol Dutta and Johannes Weber (eds), *Internationales Erbrecht* (2nd edn, C.H. Beck 2021) EuErbVO Art 25 para 28.

[377] Dutta, *MüKoBGB* (2020) EuErbVO Art 25 para 9.

If the agreement as to succession involving the estate of several persons is admissible under the *hypothetical* succession law, matters of substantive validity and *inter partes* effect, including the conditions for the agreement's dissolution, would be governed by the law, from amongst the laws applicable to the admissibility of such an agreement as to succession, which has the closest connection with that agreement. Neither the text of the provision nor a Regulation recital states the criteria which are relevant in determining the law which is most closely connected to the agreement.[378] Thus, the courts should make a careful examination of all circumstances of the case in order to find the law applicable to an agreement as to succession regarding the succession of more than one person.[379] This is indeed not a straightforward process for judges, and it brings uncertainty for the parties.[380]

A choice of law could be made by the parties to govern their agreement as to succession, with respect to the questions of admissibility, substantive validity, and binding effects between the parties (including the requirements for the agreement's dissolution) in order to avoid the problem of inadmissibility when one of the laws applicable does not allow agreements as to succession and also to avoid problems attached to the determination of the law most closely connected to the agreement that should govern matters other than admissibility (Article 25(3)).[381]

In order to understand the scope of these provisions, the meaning of the matters of 'admissibility' and 'substantive validity' should be examined in the context of dispositions of property upon death. From these matters, 'admissibility' is a particular aspect of substantive validity and means whether a disposition of property upon death is in principle allowed in a legal system. Some legal systems may not allow certain types of dispositions of property upon death, such as joint wills or agreements as to succession.[382] In these cases, there may be the issue whether such a prohibition would be characterised as an issue regarding the formal or material validity of the disposition of

[378] Döbereiner, [2013] MittBayNot 437, 442; Müller-Lukoschek, *Die neue EU-Erbrechtsverordnung* (2015) § 2 para 185; Dutta, *MüKoBGB* (2020) EuErbVO Art 25 para 10; Fischer-Czermak, *Deixler-Hübner/Schauer* (2020) EuErbVO Art 25 para 24.

[379] Dutta, *MüKoBGB* (2020) EuErbVO Art 25 para 10; Fischer-Czermak, *Deixler-Hübner/Schauer* (2020) EuErbVO Art 25 para 24.

[380] Bonomi, *Bonomi/Wautelet* (2016) ESR Art 25 para 29; Zoumpoulis, *Pamboukis* (2017) ESR Art 25 para 24.

[381] Bonomi and Öztürk, 'Das Statut der Verfügung von Todes wegen' (2014) 63; Rodríguez Rodrigo, *Calvo Caravaca/Davì/Mansel* (2016) ESR Art 25 para 17; Zoumpoulis, *Pamboukis* (2017) ESR Art 25 para 26; Dutta, *MüKoBGB* (2020) EuErbVO Art 25 para 11.

[382] Dörner, *Staudinger BGB* (2007) EGBGB Art 25 para 246; Döbereiner, [2013] MittBayNot 358, 365; Bonomi and Öztürk, 'Das Statut der Verfügung von Todes wegen' (2014) 55; Dutta, *MüKoBGB* (2020) EuErbVO Art 24 para 3.

property upon death. The Regulation clarifies this issue and provides that the *hypothetical lex successionis* under Article 24 and Article 25 would govern the admissibility of a disposition of property upon death, i.e. the issue of whether a disposition could be made in the form of a disposition of property upon death.[383]

'Substantive validity' has not been defined in the Regulation, but issues falling within the scope of 'substantive validity' have been exemplified under Article 26.[384] Pursuant to this, the capacity of a person to make such a disposition, particular reasons that prevent a person from making a disposition in favour of certain persons or that prevent certain persons from receiving the disposed properties from the testator, the admissibility of representation for the purpose of making such a disposition, the interpretation of dispositions, and defects in consent with respect to such dispositions all relate to substantive validity. With respect to the capacity to modify or revoke a disposition of property upon death, the Article takes the stability interests of the relevant persons into account.[385] It provides that once a person has the capacity to make a disposition of property upon death under the law applicable in the scope of Article 24 or Article 25, subsequent changes of the law applicable, e.g. a change of habitual residence, would not affect the capacity of the person to modify and revoke such disposition (Article 26(2)).

The Turkish PILA, on the other hand, has only two specific provisions on the law applicable to legal matters arising out of dispositions of property upon death which deal with the capacity to make such dispositions and the formal validity of them. Issues of substantive validity other than testamentary capacity are governed by the *lex successionis*, since there is no specific conflict-of-laws rule applicable to these issues in the Turkish PILA.[386] Therefore, from the Turkish perspective it is important to focus on the applicable law for these issues. It should, however, be noted that the question of whether a type of disposition of property upon death which is not allowed under Turkish law would be admissible from the Turkish perspective would require a characterisation, and hence

---

383 Bonomi and Öztürk, 'Das Statut der Verfügung von Todes wegen' (2014) 65–66.

384 This means that the list under this provision does not have an exhaustive nature: Nordmeier, [2013] ZEV 117, 118; Lagarde, *Bergquist and others* (2015) ESR Art 26 para 1; Bonomi, *Bonomi/Wautelet* (2016) ESR Art 26 para 2; Celia M. Caamiña Domínguez, in Alfonso-Luis Calvo Caravaca, Angelo Davì and Heinz-Peter Mansel (eds), *The EU Succession Regulation – A Commentary* (Cambridge University Press 2016) ESR Art 26 para 1; Frank Bauer and Jan Peter Schmidt, in Anatol Dutta and Johannes Weber (eds), *Internationales Erbrecht* (2nd edn, C.H. Beck 2021) EuErbVO Art 26 para 10. See, however, Heinig, [2014] RNotZ 197, 208; Zoumpoulis, *Pamboukis* (2017) ESR Art 26 para 2; Fischer-Czermak, *Deixler-Hübner/Schauer* (2020) EuErbVO Art 26 para 1.

385 Dutta, *MüKoBGB* (2020) EuErbVO Art 26 para 17.

386 See below pp 135–140.

this issue is not examined here but rather analysed below in the context of joint wills, which are of practical importance in cross-border succession cases.

Article 20(5) of the Turkish PILA is on the law governing the capacity of a person to make a disposition of property upon death. The capacity of a person to make a disposition of property upon death means the conditions which are stipulated by law for the testator to express his last wishes in the form of such a disposition.[387] Due to the fact that capacity to make a disposition of property upon death is a matter of personal status, Article 20(5) of the Turkish PILA prescribes that the law applicable to this is the national law of that person at the time of making the disposition.[388] This is in agreement with the general conflict-of-laws rule on capacity (Article 9 of the Turkish PILA), which also provides that capacity – both the capacity to have rights and obligations ('hak ehliyeti') and the capacity to act ('fiil ehliyeti') – should be governed by the national law of the person whose capacity is in question.[389] For a Turkish national, this would then be Turkish law. Under Turkish law, a person who has the capacity of judgment and who has attained 15 years of age has the capacity to make a will (Article 502 of the Turkish Civil Code). As agreements as to succession, including agreements on the renunciation of inheritance, are contracts, the testator needs full capacity to act to draw up a valid agreement as such. This is expressed under Article 503 of the Turkish Civil Code: in order to draw up an agreement as to succession the person whose succession is in question should have the capacity of judgment, have reached the age of majority, and not be under legal guardianship.[390]

Yet from a comparative perspective, the Regulation and the Turkish PILA once again feature the difference regarding the connecting factors of nationality and habitual residence. As in the above example, a 16-year-old Turkish national who is habitually resident in Stockholm would be able to make a testament according to Turkish law, which is applicable as the law of the State of nationality pursuant to Article 20(5) of the Turkish PILA. This is because persons who are over 15 years old have testamentary capacity under Turkish law (Article 502 of the Turkish Civil Code). From the Regulation's perspective, however, this person lacks testamentary capacity, as under Swedish law, i.e. under the law of habitual residence pursuant to Article 24(1) of

---

387 Ayiter and Kılıçoğlu, *Miras Hukuku* (1993) 76.

388 Osman Fazıl Berki, 'Türk Devletler Özel Hukukunda Vasiyet' (1944) 2 AÜHFD 175, 178; V. R. Seviğ, *Mirasla İlgili Devletler Hususi Hukuku Kaideleri* (1963) 118 ff; Tekinalp, *Milletlerarası Özel Hukuk* (2020) 245; Nomer, *Devletler Hususî Hukuku* (2021) 301; Şanlı, Esen and Ataman Figanmeşe, *Milletlerarası Özel Hukuk* (2021) 280. For criticism of the provision, see Baran Çelik, *Ölüme Bağlı Tasarruflar* (2011) 117 ff.

389 Şanlı, Esen and Ataman Figanmeşe, *Milletlerarası Özel Hukuk* (2021) 280.

390 Dural and Öz, *Miras Hukuku* (2021) paras 273 ff; Öztan, *Miras Hukuku* (2021) 179 ff; Serozan and Engin, *Miras Hukuku* (2021) § 4 paras 50 ff; Çabri, *Miras Hukuku Şerhi (TMK m. 495–574)* (2022) paras 259 ff;.

the Regulation, since persons who are under 18 cannot make a testament in principle (ch 9 § 1 of the Swedish Inheritance Law).

The law applicable to the capacity of the testator to modify or revoke a disposition which has already been made is again the national law of the testator.[391] There are, however, divergent views on the issue as to the time at which the nationality of the testator should be taken into account in determining the law governing this matter. Some scholars argue that the nationality of the testator at the time of death should be decisive on the law applicable to capacity for a subsequent modification or revocation of a disposition of property upon death.[392] Nevertheless, there could be cases where the testator, who had the capacity to make such a disposition according to his national law at the time of making the disposition, later changes his nationality and lacks testamentary capacity under the law of the State whose nationality has been acquired. In those instances, the testator will not be able to make any changes to his disposition. It could be argued that this problem may be solved with the general rules on the law applicable to the capacity of persons found in Article 9 of the Turkish PILA. The third paragraph of this rule prescribes that subsequent changes of nationality could not affect a person's reaching the age of majority pursuant to his national law. In line with this, a solution to the problem may be that the subsequent changes of nationality would have no effect on the capacity of the testator to make, modify, or revoke a disposition of property upon death. The difference between the notions of majority and testamentary capacity should, however, be noted here. A person may not reach the age of majority but may still have testamentary capacity.[393] Thus, in order to avoid this problem, the national law of the testator at the time of making the disposition should be applied to the question of capacity to further modify or revoke such a disposition.[394] By doing this, the reference to the national law of the person who made the disposition is, as in the Regulation, 'crystallized' at the time the disposition is drawn up, and further changes of nationality would not render him incapable of modifying or revoking his disposition.

As mentioned earlier, there is no specific rule on the law governing the substantive validity of dispositions of property upon death under the Turkish PILA. The prevailing view in the Turkish legal academia is that they should be under the authority of the general *lex successionis* in the scope of Article 20(1) of the Turkish PILA.[395] This means that the law applicable to the substantive

---

391 Çelikel and Erdem, *Milletlerarası Özel Hukuk* (2021) 355; Şanlı, Esen and Ataman Figanmeşe, *Milletlerarası Özel Hukuk* (2021) 280 fn 3335. See also Uluocak, *Milletlerarası Özel Hukuk Dersleri* (1987) 140.

392 Şanlı, Esen and Ataman Figanmeşe, *Milletlerarası Özel Hukuk* (2021) 280 fn 335.

393 Şanlı, Esen and Ataman Figanmeşe, *Milletlerarası Özel Hukuk* (2021) 280 fn 335.

394 Çelikel and Erdem, *Milletlerarası Özel Hukuk* (2021) 355.

395 Aybay and Dardağan, *Kanunlar İhtilâfı* (2008) 234; Baran Çelik, *Ölüme Bağlı Tasarruflar* (2011) 156; Ekşi, *Milletlerarası Miras Hukuku* (2013) 49; Tekinalp, *Milletlerarası*

validity of dispositions of property upon death is the national law of the testator. Such matters are, however, governed by Turkish law when they are related to immovable property situated in Turkey. The second and third paragraphs of Article 20 of the Turkish PILA limit the scope of the *lex successionis*.

In cases where the national law of the testator governs the substantive validity of a disposition of property upon death made by the deceased (the first sentence of Article 20(1) of the Turkish PILA), here again it is important to decide – with reference to the nationality of the testator – which time period should be taken into consideration in determining the *lex succesionis*. As has already been mentioned, whereas there is no clarity in the text of the rule, it is unanimously accepted by scholars that this should be the nationality at the time of death.[396] Yet this is the interpretation adopted for *intestate succession*, and the approach of applying the national law of the deceased at the time of death could render a *validly made disposition* void or invalid in the event that the testator changed his nationality after making the disposition.[397] In order to prevent such situations, it would have been helpful if the Turkish legislature had included a specific paragraph to address the substantive validity of testamentary dispositions or at least had been much clearer on the time period that should be taken account in determining the law applicable to them.[398] However, in the absence of a specific provision, it is believed that the nationality of the testator at the time of making the disposition, as in Article 20(5) of the Turkish PILA on the law applicable to testamentary capacity, should determine the applicable law regarding the substantive validity of dispositions of property upon death.[399]

In addition to the first paragraph of Article 20, the second and third paragraphs which limit the scope of the *lex successionis* will also find application with respect to dispositions of property upon death. Article 20(2) of the Turk-

---

Özel Hukuk (2020) 238–239; Çelikel and Erdem, *Milletlerarası Özel Hukuk* (2021) 358; Nomer, *Devletler Hususî Hukuku* (2021) 298 and 300; Şanlı, Esen and Ataman Figanmeşe, *Milletlerarası Özel Hukuk* (2021) 277–278; Doğan, *Milletlerarası Özel Hukuk* (2022) 374. See, in the same direction at the time of the former Turkish PILA no 2675, which similarly did not have a specific provision on the law applicable to the substantive validity of dispositions of property upon death, Uluocak, *Milletlerarası Özel Hukuk Dersleri* (1987) 142; Tanrıbilir, *Kanuni Mirasçılıktan Doğan Kanunlar İhtilafı* (2000) 79 and 146; Güven, (2006) X AÜEHFD 341, 347. This view was supported even at the time of the Temporary Act: O. F. Berki, (1944) 2 AÜHFD 175, 183ff; Yörük, *Devletler Hususi Hukuku* (1950) 427; V. R. Seviğ, *Mirasla İlgili Devletler Hususi Hukuku Kaideleri* (1963) 116ff. For a decision of the Turkish Court of Cassation at the time, see Temyiz Mahkemesi 2. Hukuk Dairesi, T. 13.6.1957, E. 2605 K. 3529 published in Berki and Ergüney, *Yabancılar Hukuku ve Kanun İhtilafları ile İlgili Yargıtay Kararlarının Tahlil ve İzahı* (1963) 135.

[396] See above p 68.

[397] Baran Çelik, *Ölüme Bağlı Tasarruflar* (2011) 110–111.

[398] Baran Çelik, *Ölüme Bağlı Tasarruflar* (2011) 110.

[399] Baran Çelik, *Ölüme Bağlı Tasarruflar* (2011) 110–111; Bahar Küpe, *Milletlerarası Özel Hukukta Şekil* (Adalet Yayınevi 2021) 143.

ish PILA, as mentioned above, excludes the provisions pertaining to the grounds for the opening, acquisition, and distribution of succession from the ambit of the main conflict-of-laws rule under the first paragraph and submits them to the law of the State where the estate is located. This provision will also find application whenever the disputed matter concerning a testamentary disposition is relevant to one of these issues.[400]

Article 20(3) of the Turkish PILA, on the other hand, provides that an heirless estate located in Turkey should pass to the Turkish State. The application of this provision in the context of dispositions of property upon death may raise doubts. The determination of heirs and their rights on the estate are normally issues within the scope of the *lex successionis* under Article 20(1) of the Turkish PILA. The question of whether a deceased with no heirs would be allowed to bequeath his entire estate to a State should also be determined in accordance with the *lex successionis*. In some legal systems,[401] the State could also be a universal legatee ('eingesetzter Erbe' or 'atanmış mirasçı').[402] There may be a case, for example, where a foreign national who has movable property in Turkey, but who has no heirs, drafts a testament and bequeaths his estate to his national State. One might ask in such a case whether Article 20(3) of the Turkish PILA would prevent the entitlement of this State – through the testament – to the estate of the deceased.[403] It could be argued that this provision will not find application in such an instance since the scope of testamentary freedom will be decided according to the national law of the deceased and, as long as such a disposition is allowed, the estate will not be without a claimant due to the disposition of property upon death made

[400] Uluocak, *Milletlerarası Özel Hukuk Dersleri* (1987) 145; Güven, (2006) X AÜEHFD 341, 349; Baran Çelik, *Ölüme Bağlı Tasarruflar* (2011) 184 ff.

[401] This is the case under Turkish law: Serozan and Engin, *Miras Hukuku* (2021) § 2 paras 78 ff.

[402] The use of the terms regarding titles and legatees should be clarified here. The deceased may bequeath his entire estate or a part thereof to one or more persons (Art 516(1) of the Turkish Civil Code). In such cases, these persons become legatees under universal title ('külli halefiyet'). On the other hand, the deceased may also make a specific legacy regarding a particular property in favour of a person or persons (Art 517(1) of the Turkish Civil Code). In this case, these persons become legatees under a particular (specific) title ('cüz'i halefiyet'): Dural and Öz, *Miras Hukuku* (2021) paras 663 ff; Serozan and Engin, *Miras Hukuku* (2021) § 4 paras 129 ff; Çabri, *Miras Hukuku Şerhi (TMK m. 495–574)* (2022) paras 80, 576 and 587. Therefore, in this book the term 'universal legatee' is used to refer to 'eingesetzter Erbe' or 'atanmış mirasçı' under Art 516(1) of the Turkish Civil Code, and the term 'particular legatee' is used to refer to '*Vermächtnisnehmer*' or '*vasiyet alacaklısı*' under Art 517(1) of the Turkish Civil Code. See, in this regard, Tuğrul Ansay, 'Law of Succession' in Tuğrul Ansay, Don Wallace Jr and Işık Önay (eds), *Introduction to Turkish Law* (7th edn, Wolters Kluwer 2020) 154.

[403] Baran Çelik, *Ölüme Bağlı Tasarruflar* (2011) 135 ff.

in favour of the national State.[404] Nevertheless, the *ratio legis* of the rule is stated as preventing succession claims of any foreign State over the estate located in Turkey.[405] In line with this clearly stated intention of the legislature, it seems difficult to maintain that Article 20(3) will not find application in such a case,[406] even though the formulation of the provision and the associated limitation of testamentary freedom raises doubts.[407]

The scope of the term 'substantive validity (and effects) of dispositions of property upon death' ('ölüme bağlı tasarrufların maddi geçerliliği ve etkileri') should be examined here. Matters which are related to the substantive validity (and effects) of testamentary dispositions and, hence, which fall within the scope of application of the *lex successionis* include:[408] issues in respect of limitations of the freedom of testation and reserved portions; an action for reduction ('tenkis davası') in cases where the testator made a disposition exceeding the disposable portion;[409] the appointment of a universal[410] and

---

[404] Uluocak, *Milletlerarası Özel Hukuk Dersleri* (1987) 138–139; Tanrıbilir, *Kanuni Mirasçılıktan Doğan Kanunlar İhtilafı* (2000) 188; Baran Çelik, *Ölüme Bağlı Tasarruflar* (2011) 137; cf. Güngör, *Türk Milletlerarası Özel Hukuku* (2021) 169; Şanlı, Esen and Ataman Figanmeşe, *Milletlerarası Özel Hukuk* (2021) 276 fn 327.

[405] İstanbul Üniversitesi Hukuk Fakültesi – Milletlerarası Hukuk ve Milletlerarası Münasebetler Enstitüsü, *MÖHUK Öntasarı Sempozyumu* (1978) 140 and 153–154; 'Danışma Meclisi Tutanakları – Milletlerarası Özel Hukuk ve Usul Hukuku Hakkında Kanun Tasarısı ve Adalet Komisyonu Raporu (1/5)', (1981) 8.

[406] Aybay and Dardağan, *Kanunlar İhtlilafı* (2008) 237; Ekşi, *Milletlerarası Miras Hukuku* (2013) 86; Altıparmak, *Mirasa Uygulanacak Hukuk* (2017) 131; Tekinalp, *Milletlerarası Özel Hukuk* (2020) 244; Can and Tuna, *Milletlerarası Özel Hukuk* (2021) 429; Çelikel and Erdem, *Milletlerarası Özel Hukuk* (2021) 354–355; Nomer, *Devletler Hususî Hukuku* (2021) 300.

[407] See, in this regard, İstanbul Üniversitesi Hukuk Fakültesi – Milletlerarası Hukuk ve Milletlerarası Münasebetler Enstitüsü, *MÖHUK Öntasarı Sempozyumu* (1978) 152–153 (*İlhan Unat*); Uluocak, *Milletlerarası Özel Hukuk Dersleri* (1987) 139; Baran Çelik, *Ölüme Bağlı Tasarruflar* (2011) 137.

[408] See, generally in this regard, O. F. Berki, (1944) 2 AÜHFD 175, 183–188; Uluocak, *Milletlerarası Özel Hukuk Dersleri* (1987) 143–145; Tanrıbilir, *Kanuni Mirasçılıktan Doğan Kanunlar İhtilafı* (2000) 79–82 and 145–148; Güven, (2006) X AÜEHFD 341, 347–348; Aybay and Dardağan, *Kanunlar İhtlilafı* (2008) 234; Baran Çelik, *Ölüme Bağlı Tasarruflar* (2011) 157 ff; Ekşi, *Milletlerarası Miras Hukuku* (2013) 49; Altıparmak, *Mirasa Uygulanacak Hukuk* (2017) 144 ff; Tekinalp, *Milletlerarası Özel Hukuk* (2020) 238–239; Çelikel and Erdem, *Milletlerarası Özel Hukuk* (2021) 358; Güngör, *Türk Milletlerarası Özel Hukuku* (2021) 168; Nomer, *Devletler Hususî Hukuku* (2021) 300 and 303; Şanlı, Esen and Ataman Figanmeşe, *Milletlerarası Özel Hukuk* (2021) 278; Doğan, *Milletlerarası Özel Hukuk* (2022) 374.

[409] Heirs who are entitled to a reserved portion may bring an action for reduction in instances where the testator made dispositions exceeding their reserved portions (Art 560(1) of the Turkish Civil Code). The concept of the reserved portion may have different effects on the validity of the testamentary dispositions under different legal systems. In some legal systems, they may render the disposition invalid: See, for a remark as such, Dutta,

particular legatee[411] as well as a substitute legatee ('Ersatzerbe' or 'yedek mirasçı')[412] and a remainderman ('Nacherbe' or 'artmirasçı');[413] the drawing up of dispositions of property upon death subject to conditions or charges;[414] appointment of a testamentary executor ('Willensvollstrecker' or 'vasiyeti yerine getirme görevlisi');[415] the establishment of a foundation through a will;[416] renunciation of inheritance[417] and disinheritance[418] through a disposition of property upon death, the grounds for which render such a dispositions void[419] or may render it invalid;[420] substantive requirements for the revocation

MüKoBGB (2020) EuErbVO Art 26 para 16. Under Turkish law, this does not effect the validity of the disposition which has been made but rather gives a right to the heirs entitled to the reserved portion to bring an action for reduction: Ayiter and Kılıçoğlu, *Miras Hukuku* (1993) 190–191. When this is the case, this issue could not be regarded as one regarding the substantive validity of dispositions of property upon death from a conflict-of-laws perspective. Notwithstanding this, such a distinction has no practical importance due to the lack of a specific conflict-of-laws provision on the issue.

[410] Art 516 of the Turkish Civil Code.

[411] Art 517 of the Turkish Civil Code.

[412] The deceased may appoint one or more persons to substitute for the universal legatee in cases where this person dies before the deceased or renunciates the inheritance (Art 520 of the Turkish Civil Code).

[413] The testator may stipulate that the provisional legatee ('Vorerbe' or 'önmirasçı') is to transfer the estate to another person (Art 521 of the Turkish Civil Code). This other person to whom the estate will be transferred by the provisonal legatee is the remainderman.

[414] The deceased may draw up dispositions of property upon death subject to conditions or charges. See Art 515 of the Turkish Civil Code.

[415] The deceased may appoint one or more testamentary executors within his testament (Art 550 of the Turkish Civil Code).

[416] The deceased may bequeath all or a part of the disposable portion of his estate to a foundation under a will (Art 526 of the Turkish Civil Code).

[417] Arts 528–530 of the Turkish Civil Code.

[418] Arts 510–513 of the Turkish Civil Code.

[419] Under Turkish law, dispositions of property upon death will be void in cases where the spouses make dispositions of property upon death in each other's favour and where the marriage ends due to reasons other than death or a declaration of absence (Art 159 and 181(1) of the Turkish Civil Code); where the person in whose favour a disposition *mortis causa* has been made dies before the testator (Arts 548(1), 580(2) and 581(3) of the Turkish Civil Code); where the person in whose favour a disposition *mortis causa* has been made is unworthy to inherit (Art 578 of the Turkish Civil Code); and where the resolutive condition has been fulfilled or the suspensive condition has not been fulfilled. See, in this regard, Dural and Öz, *Miras Hukuku* (2021) paras 992–996; Serozan and Engin, *Miras Hukuku* (2021) § 4 paras 98 ff.

[420] Art 557 of the Turkish Civil Code prescribes four different grounds which may render dispositions of property upon death invalid: 1) the lack of capacity of the person making the disposition, 2) mistake, fraud, or duress on the part of the person making the disposition, 3) immorality and illegality of the content of the disposition or as regards conditions and charges to which the disposition is subject to, 4) non-fulfilment of form requirements.

of a will or the termination of an agreement as to succession; the question of whether an agreement as to succession could be made with or without consideration; and the interpretation of a disposition.[421]

When it comes to the Treaty, it includes no specific rule on the law applicable to the capacity of the person making the disposition or to the substantive validity of dispositions of property upon death. National rules of the Contracting States on testamentary capacity, i.e. Article 20(5) of the Turkish PILA or Article 26(1) (a) of the Regulation, should be applied for questions of the capacity.[422] The application of national rules, i.e. Article 20(1) of the Turkish PILA and Article 24 et seq. of the Regulation, could also be arguable for the substantive validity of dispositions of property upon death.[423] Nevertheless, as Article 20(14) of the Treaty does not differentiate between testamentary or intestate succession, there seems to be no gap in this regard. Hence, the substantive validity of dispositions of property upon death are governed by the *lex successionis* under Article 20(14) of the Treaty, i.e. the

---

From these, the first ground relates to testamentary capacity and is governed by the national law of the testator pursuant to Art 20(5) of the Turkish PILA: O. F. Berki, *Miras* (1960) 46; Tanrıbilir, *Kanuni Mirasçılıktan Doğan Kanunlar İhtilafı* (2000) 80 and 147; Baran Çelik, *Ölüme Bağlı Tasarruflar* (2011) 183; Altıparmak, *Mirasa Uygulanacak Hukuk* (2017) 147. The last one is obviously about formal validity and is governed by Art 20(4) of the Turkish PILA or by the Hague Form Convention depending on the type of disposition: Baran Çelik, *Ölüme Bağlı Tasarruflar* (2011) 183; Altıparmak, *Mirasa Uygulanacak Hukuk* (2017) 147. Therefore, only the second and third grounds are matters of substantive validity that are governed by the *lex successionis*: O. F. Berki, *Miras* (1960) 46; Baran Çelik, *Ölüme Bağlı Tasarruflar* (2011) 183; Altıparmak, *Mirasa Uygulanacak Hukuk* (2017) 147. It is argued, however, that matters of invalidity based on defects in consent of the person making the disposition (Art 557(1) subpara 2) should be governed by the national law of this person rather than the *lex successionis*: Çelikel and Erdem, *Milletlerarası Özel Hukuk* (2021) 356 and 358.

[421] The interpretation of dispositions of property upon death is made in order to find the actual intention of the testator, which cannot always be easily understood from the terms of the disposition: Dural and Öz, *Miras Hukuku* (2021) para 968. Thus, the law applicable to the interpretation of such dispositions should be the law chosen by the testator either expressly or impliedly. Nevertheless, as a *professio iuris* is not allowed in the field of succession law under the Turkish PILA, the *lex successionis* should be applied to the issue: Muammer Raşit Seviğ and Vedat Raşit Seviğ, *Devletler Hususi Hukuku* (3rd edn, İsmail Akgün Matbaası 1962) 527; Baran Çelik, *Ölüme Bağlı Tasarruflar* (2011) 177–178. In such a case, however, there would be the problem that different interpretation rules are applicable to different parts of the disposition of property upon death made by the deceased, as the law applicable to succession is the national law of the deceased, but immovables which are located in Turkey are under the authority of Turkish law according to Art 20(1) of the Turkish PILA: Baran Çelik, *Ölüme Bağlı Tasarruflar* (2011) 176–177.

[422] See, in the same direction for the Turkish-Italian Treaty, Franzina, 'The External Relations of Italy' (2019) 178.

[423] Dutta, *MüKoBGB* (2020) EuErbVO Art 75 para 24.

lex patriae of the deceased for movables at the time of death and the *lex rei sitae* for immovables.[424] Such an interpretation seems to be more in line with Turkish law. Article 4 of the Temporary Act, which was in force at the time when the Treaty was drafted, did not distinguish between testamentary and intestate succession and instead submitted both matters to the same law, that being, as in the Treaty, the national law of the testator for movables and the law of the State where the assets are located for immovables.[425] This law was also applicable for the substantive validity of dispositions of property upon death. Even the current Turkish PILA does not provide any specific rule on this matter; rather, it submits it to the *lex successionis*. Such an interpretation should thus be preferred from the Turkish perspective.

In the event that the testator later changes his nationality, however, the part of the disposition of property upon death concerning movable property may become invalid. This is undesirable considering the fact that the aim of such a conflict-of-laws rule is to provide legal certainty and to meet the legitimate expectations of the persons involved in the disposition *mortis causa*.[426] Thus, two alternative solutions are suggested here. The first one is to apply the national law of the testator at the time of making the disposition as in Article 20(16) of the Treaty on the law applicable to the formal validity of such dispositions.[427] Alternatively, it is argued that the issue could be solved with a reference to the domestic rules of the Contracting States (Article 20(1) of the Turkish PILA and Articles 24 and 25 of the Regulation).[428] The latter solution, however, would not be of much help from the Turkish perspective since there is no clarity for the law applicable to the substantive validity of testamentary dispositions on the issue of whether the testator's nationality at the time of death or at the time of making the disposition should be taken into consideration. Hence, the first view seems to be more plausible in order to avoid situations in which the disposition of property upon death made by the testator becomes invalid because of his subsequent change of nationality.

The scope of the substantive validity of testamentary dispositions of property upon death has not been clarified under the Treaty. Given the lack of any significant legal practice in respect of the Treaty in Turkey, a Turkish judge

---

[424] Dörner, [1996] ZEV 90, 93; Looschelders, 'The External Relations of Germany' (2019) 162; Odersky, *Hausmann/Odersky* (2021) § 15 para 350; Lorenz, *BeckOK BGB* (2022) EGBGB Art 25 aF para 7; cf. Bauer and Süß, *Dutta/Weber* (2021) EuErbVO Art 75 Anhang II-deutsch-türkisches NA para 15.

[425] O. F. Berki, *Miras* (1960) 45 ff; V. R. Seviğ, *Mirasla İlgili Devletler Hususi Hukuku Kaideleri* (1963) 116 ff.

[426] Dörner, [1996] ZEV 90, 93; Looschelders, 'The External Relations of Germany' (2019) 162–163.

[427] Dörner, [1996] ZEV 90, 93; Looschelders, 'The External Relations of Germany' (2019) 163.

[428] Looschelders, 'The External Relations of Germany' (2019) 163.

would probably take guidance from the scope of the term under the Turkish PILA.[429]

II. The Law Applicable to the Formal Validity of Dispositions of Property Upon Death

Legal systems often stipulate formal requirements for testamentary dispositions in order to ensure that the deceased adequately considers his decisions before drafting such a disposition, to prevent the alteration or the falsification of such dispositions, or to understand the real intention and the purpose of the deceased upon his death.[430] Under Turkish law, testaments can be made in the form of a notarial will, a holographic will, or an oral will (Article 531 of the Turkish Civil Code). Each form is subject to different requirements as provided by the Article 532 et seq. of the Turkish Civil Code. These requirements, however, may differ among jurisdictions. It is, therefore, highly likely that issues on the formal validity of such dispositions will arise before the courts of States other than those where they were drafted. As a consequence, they might be declared void, and thus the deceased's last wishes cannot be executed. These problems have already been found problematic in the field of cross-border testamentary succession, and harmonisation efforts were started in the 1960s under the auspices of the Hague Conference. These efforts paved the way for the Hague Form Convention, which provided uniform conflict-of-laws rules governing the formal validity of testamentary dispositions.[431] Unlike the other Hague instruments regarding succession, this Convention has been very successful and was ratified by a significant number of States, including Turkey and most EU Member States.

The European legislature considered the success of the Convention during the drafting process of the Regulation and did not provide a conflict-of-laws provision addressing the issue of the law applicable to the formal validity of dispositions of property upon death in the Commission Proposal.[432] This loophole was, however, criticised by scholars on the ground that conflicting practices could have occurred within the Union, as some Member States are not party to the Convention and the scope of the Convention is limited to testaments.[433]

---

[429] For the issues which are argued to be in the scope of the substantive validity of dispositions of property upon death and hence governed by the general *lex successionis* in Turkish private international law, see above pp 138–140.

[430] Dural and Öz, *Miras Hukuku* (2021) paras 303–307; Öztan, *Miras Hukuku* (2021) 188–189; Serozan and Engin, *Miras Hukuku* (2021) § 4 para 21.

[431] Zoumpoulis, *Pamboukis* (2017) ESR Art 27 para 1.

[432] Recital 19 of the Proposal.

[433] Süß, [2009] ZErb 342, 345; Heinrich Dörner, 'Der Entwurf einer europäischen Verordnung zum Internationalen Erb- und Erbverfahrensrecht – Überblick und ausgewählte Probleme' [2010] ZEV 221, 223; Max Planck Institute for Comparative and International Private Law, (2010) 74 RabelsZ 522, 622.

The European legislature, therefore, struck a balance between the Convention and the Regulation by providing under Article 75(1) (2) that the Convention continues to be applicable between the Contracting Member States; further, for non-Contracting Member States as well as for other types of dispositions of property upon death made in writing which are outside the scope of the Convention, i.e. for agreements as to succession, Article 27 of the Regulation (which is consistent with the provisions of the Convention) is applicable.[434]

The Hague Form Convention is also significant from the Turkish perspective. It is applicable to the validity as to the form of testamentary dispositions instead of Article 20(4) of the Turkish PILA, which deals with the same issue.[435] The application of Article 20(4) of the Turkish PILA only comes into play for testamentary dispositions which were concluded before the entry into force of the Convention (Article 13 of the Convention) and which fall within the scope of the reservations made by Turkey,[436] and for agreements as to succession.[437]

On the other hand, the relationship between former bilateral or multilateral treaties of Contracting Member States (covering the same issues) and the Convention is not addressed in the Convention. This is, however, a classical conflict of treaties situation, and it could be handled by general principles in this context. As the Convention entered into force for Turkey at a later time than the Treaty, the issue could be solved by the help of the well-known maxim *lex posterior derogat legi priori*, which is also enshrined under Article 30 of the Vienna Convention on the Law of Treaties. This principle takes subsequent changes in the intention of the Contracting Parties into account and hence favours the later treaty in cases where the conflicting treaties are on the same subject matter and are concluded by the same parties.[438] Based on this, Article 20(16) of the Turkish-German Treaty on the law applicable to the formal validity of dispositions of property upon death was superseded by the

---

434 Müller-Lukoschek, *Die neue EU-Erbrechtsverordnung* (2015) § 2 paras 173–174; Caamiña Domínguez, *Calvo Caravaca/Davì/Mansel* (2016) ESR Art 27 para 2; Rembert Süß, in Anatol Dutta and Johannes Weber (eds), *Internationales Erbrecht* (2nd edn, C.H. Beck 2021) EuErbVO Art 27 para 11. See also Recital 52 of the Regulation.

435 Uluocak, *Milletlerarası Özel Hukuk Dersleri* (1987) 142; Güven, (2006) X AÜEHFD 341, 345; Baran Çelik, *Ölüme Bağlı Tasarruflar* (2011) 148; Ekşi, *Milletlerarası Miras Hukuku* (2013) 55; Toker and Ruhi, *Milletlerarası Özel Hukuk ve Usul Hukuku Hakkında Kanun* (2019) 149; Begüm Süzen, *Milletlerarası Özel Hukukta Hukuki İşlemlerin Şekline Uygulanacak Hukuk* (On İki Levha 2020) 278; Tekinalp, *Milletlerarası Özel Hukuk* (2020) 246; Çelikel and Erdem, *Milletlerarası Özel Hukuk* (2021) 358; Güngör, *Türk Milletlerarası Özel Hukuku* (2021) 123 and 170; Şanlı, Esen and Ataman Figanmeşe, *Milletlerarası Özel Hukuk* (2021) 281; Doğan, *Milletlerarası Özel Hukuk* (2022) 381.

436 See below pp 146–148.

437 Baran Çelik, *Ölüme Bağlı Tasarruflar* (2011) 148; Süzen, *Hukuki İşlemlerin Şekline Uygulanacak Hukuk* (2020) 278; Tekinalp, *Milletlerarası Özel Hukuk* (2020) 251–252.

438 Christopher J. Borgen, 'Resolving Treaty Conflicts' (2005) 37 Geo Wash Int'l L Rev 573, 587.

rules of the Convention for testamentary dispositions and for their revocation with its entry into force in Turkey on 22 October 1983.[439] Article 20(16) of the Treaty remains applicable between Turkey and Germany only for agreements as to succession, and for testamentary dispositions which were drafted before the entry into force of the Convention (Article 13) and which do not fall within the ambit of the Convention by virtue of Turkey's reservations. Therefore, an analysis on the law applicable to the formal validity of dispositions in the Turkish-European context should also include the rules of the Hague Form Convention.

The Convention is applicable to the formal validity of testamentary dispositions, including joint wills (Article 4), as well as to the formal requirements for the revocation of an earlier testamentary disposition (Article 2, also in the same direction Article 27(2) of the Regulation). Unlike the Regulation,[440] it also covers the formal validity of testamentary dispositions made orally. Based on the principle of *favor testamenti,*[441] it provides numerous connecting factors for the law applicable to the formal validity of testamentary dispositions. Pursuant to this, a testamentary disposition, like in Article 27(1) of the Regulation, will be valid as regards form if it is in conformity with the form requirements of the State where it was made; or of the State of nationality; of the State of domicile; or of the State of habitual residence of the testator either at the time the disposition was made or at the time of death; or of the State where the immovable property of the testator is found (Article 1). These connecting factors have an alternative nature. That is to say that a testamentary disposition is formally valid if it is made in accordance with the form requirements of one of these laws. Hence, it is highly unlikely that a testamentary disposition will be declared invalid as regards form under this Convention.[442]

There may be other existing or future laws applicable in the Contracting States which recognise testamentary dispositions that are made in compliance with the formal requirements of another law than a law applicable under Article 1. The Convention does not affect their application (Article 3). By doing so, the Convention extends the *favor testamenti* to the greatest extent possi-

---

[439] Dörner, [1996] ZEV 90, 95; H. Krüger, 'Studien über Probleme des türkischen Internationalen Erbrechts' (2006) 152; Köhler, *NK/Nachfolgerecht* (2019) EuErbVO Vorb. Art 20–38 para 53; Looschelders, 'The External Relations of Germany' (2019) 162; Dutta, *MüKoBGB* (2020) EuErbVO Art 75 para 23; Stürner, *Erman BGB* (2020) EuErbVO Art 75 paras 4 and 10; Bauer and Süß, *Dutta/Weber* (2021) EuErbVO Art 75 Anhang II-deutsch-türkisches NA para 15; Lorenz, *BeckOK BGB* (2022) EGBGB Art 25 aF para 7; Jessica Schmidt, in Christine Budzikiewicz, Marc-Philippe Weller and Wolfgang Wurmnest (eds), *BeckOGK-EuErbVO (Stand: 1.2.2022)* (C.H. Beck 2022) EuErbVO Art 27 para 16.

[440] See Art 1(2) (f) of the Regulation.

[441] Kurt H. Nadelmann, 'The Hague Conference on Private International Law Ninth Session' (1960) 9 AJCL 583, 584; Li, (1990) 224 RdC 9, 110.

[442] Li, (1990) 224 RdC 9, 110.

ble.[443] This principle is reinforced with the *loi uniforme* nature of the Convention, which stipulates, first, that the application of the Convention is independent from any requirement of reciprocity and, second, that the nationality of the testator or the law applicable is the one of a Contracting or non-Contracting State (Article 6). When this is considered together with the various connecting factors provided under Article 1 of the Convention, the Convention should be applied to the formal validity of all the testamentary dispositions with foreign elements regardless of the nationality, domicile, or habitual residence of the testator and the legatees and regardless of the place where the testamentary disposition was made.[444]

The Convention does not define the meaning of 'form' but takes a certain position towards one of the classification problems among the Contracting States under Article 5 in the same manner as Article 27(3) of the Regulation. According to this, restrictions with regards to the age, nationality, or other personal conditions of testators as well as witnesses in relation to certain types of testamentary dispositions should be considered as a matter of form. This article attempts to solve the well-known classification example referred to as the 'will of the Dutchman'[445] and provides that such restrictions should no longer be treated as a matter of capacity in the Contracting States.[446] It must be noted that the article aims to prevent testamentary dispositions from being invalid by virtue of restrictions that are imposed on certain types of testaments in respect of personal qualities of testators, such as age and nationality. It does not, however, intend that the testamentary capacity of minors should be considered as a matter of form.[447] The testamentary capacity of

---

[443] Li, (1990) 224 RdC 9, 111.

[444] Çelikel and Erdem, *Milletlerarası Özel Hukuk* (2021) 358; Şanlı, Esen and Ataman Figanmeşe, *Milletlerarası Özel Hukuk* (2021) 284.

[445] Yvon Loussouarn, 'The IXth Session of the Hague Conference on Private International Law' (1961) 88 JDI 655, 677; Li, (1990) 224 RdC 9, 114. See, for the example, Ernest G. Lorenzen, 'The Qualification, Classification, or Characterization Problem in the Conflict of Laws' (1941) 50 YLJ 743, 755.

[446] The Convention allows Contracting States which have restrictive provisions of the kind defined under Article 5 to make a reservation in order not to recognise certain forms of testamentary dispositions made abroad (Article 11). This is, however, only possible under strict conditions and is effective only on property situated in the State making the reservation. See, for an example with regards to the operation of Art 11, Loussouarn, (1961) 88 JDI 655, 679.

[447] Henri Batiffol, 'Rapport Explicatif' in Le Bureau Permanent de la Conférence de La Haye de droit international privé (HCCH) (ed), *Actes et Documents de la Neuvième Session – TOME III Forme des Testaments* (Imprimerie Nationale 1961) 168; Wilfried von Schack, 'Neue Kollisionsnormen für die Form von Testamenten: Das Haager Übereinkommen über das auf die Form letztwilliger Verfügungen anzuwendende Recht' [1966] DNotZ 131, 135; Dutta, *MüKoBGB* (2020) HTestformÜ Art 5 para 1; Süzen, *Hukuki İşlemlerin*

minors should still be determined in accordance with the law applicable to the capacity to make testamentary dispositions, i.e. Articles 24 and 25 of the Regulation and Article 20(5) of the Turkish PILA.

This could be explained with the help of an example regarding Turkish and German law. Under Article 502 of the Turkish Civil Code, a person who has the capacity of judgment and is 15 years of age or older can make any form of will. On the other hand, under BGB § 2229, a person who is capable of understanding the testamentary disposition and who is 16 or older can make a will. These two regulations define the testamentary capacity of the testator. BGB § 2247(4) further stipulates that a person should be 18 years old[448] to make a holographic will. By doing so, it imposes a restriction on the age of the testator for a holographic will within the meaning of Article 5 of the Convention. This means, for instance, that a holographic will made by a 17-year-old German citizen during a short-term stay in Turkey will not be invalid in Germany. This is because the person has testamentary capacity under German law (Article 26 of the Regulation) and the 18 years of age requirement for holographic wills under this law is a restriction within the scope of Article 5 of the Convention, which should be considered as a matter of form. If, on the other hand, the testator was 15 years old, his testament will be declared invalid in Germany since the testator does not have the testamentary capacity under German law.[449]

The Convention is also applicable in Turkey for the formal validity of testamentary dispositions,[450] but Turkey made some reservations when signing

---

Şekline Uygulanacak Hukuk (2020) 285; Şanlı, Esen and Ataman Figanmeşe, *Milletlerarası Özel Hukuk* (2021) 285. See, in the same direction, Recital 53 of the Regulation.

See, on this topic, also Baran Çelik, *Ölüme Bağlı Tasarruflar* (2011) 121; Ekşi, *Milletlerarası Miras Hukuku* (2013) 50; Tekinalp, *Milletlerarası Özel Hukuk* (2020) 250.

[448] In other words, the person should be of full age in line with BGB § 2.

[449] For a similar example but a different interpretation of Article 5 of the Convention, see Şanlı, Esen and Ataman Figanmeşe, *Milletlerarası Özel Hukuk* (2021) 286 fn 348. For a similar interpretation to the one made in this study based on that example, see Süzen, *Hukuki İşlemlerin Şekline Uygulanacak Hukuk* (2020) 286. See, generally, on the aim of Art 5, Batiffol, 'Rapport Explicatif' (1961) 165–166; Loussouarn, (1961) 88 JDI 655, 677 and 679; Li, (1990) 224 RdC 9, 114–115.

[450] Yargıtay 2. Hukuk Dairesi, T. 10.7.2001, E. 2001/3841 K. 2001/10889 <https://legalbank.net/> accessed 21 June 2019; Yargıtay 3. Hukuk Dairesi, T. 12.3.2015, E. 2015/2397 K. 2015/4054 <https://www.lexpera.com.tr/> accessed 21 June 2019. There are, however, a number of judgments of the Turkish Court of Cassation in which the Convention was not applied. See, for example, Yargıtay 2. Hukuk Dairesi, T. 23.11.1990, E. 1990/4236 K. 1990/11458 published in Atâ Sakmar, Nuray Ekşi and İlhan Yılmaz, *Milletlerarası Özel Hukuk ve Usul Hukuku Hakkında Kanun Mahkeme Kararları* (3rd edn, Beta 2001) 103–104; Yargıtay 2. Hukuk Dairesi, T. 22.2.1994, E. 1488 K. 1887 published in Sakmar, Ekşi and Yılmaz, *Milletlerarası Özel Hukuk ve Usul Hukuku Hakkında Kanun Mahkeme Kararları* (2001) 186–187; Yargıtay 2. Hukuk Dairesi, T. 6.11.2008, E. 2008/13740 K. 2008/14696 <http://www.

the Convention.[451] The first reservation of Turkey was made under Article 9. As mentioned above, one of the alternative applicable laws within the scope of Article 1 is the law of the State of domicile of the testator either at the time of making the disposition or at the time of death (paragraph (1) (c)). Since the notion of domicile may have different meanings in different legal systems, which may lead to the instance that a testamentary disposition is declared invalid when the meaning of the domicile under *lex fori* is different from the one the testator relied on,[452] the Convention itself provides a characterisation rule under Article 1(3), which clarifies that the question of whether a person is domiciled in a place will be decided under the law of that State. Turkey, however, reserved its right to determine whether the testator was domiciled in a place within the scope of Article 1 in accordance with *lex fori*.[453]

Whilst the Convention also covers the formal validity of testamentary dispositions made orally, Turkey made a reservation with regards to such dispositions in line with Article 10 of the Convention. In this regard, oral testamentary dispositions of Turkish nationals who do not hold any other nationality are not subject to recognition in Turkey. This is because under Turkish law oral wills are, as opposed to official and holographic wills, exceptional types of dispositions of property upon death.[454] They can be made only if the testator is not able to make an official or holographic will because of extraordinary circumstances.[455]

Another reservation made by Turkey further restricts the scope of testamentary dispositions. In accordance with the right given to Contracting States under Article 12 of the Convention, Turkey declared that testamentary clauses which are not considered as the matters of succession under Turkish law are excluded from the scope of the Convention. This means, for example, that testamentary clauses recognising children which are born out of wedlock are

---

kazanci.com> accessed 21 June 2019; Yargıtay 3. Hukuk Dairesi, T. 3.2.2014, E. 2013/17015 K. 2014/1384 <https://www.lexpera.com.tr/> accessed 21 June 2019.

[451] See, in this regard, <https://www.hcch.net/en/instruments/conventions/status-table/notifications/?csid=295&disp=resdn> accessed 20 June 2019.

[452] Batiffol, 'Rapport Explicatif' (1961) 164; Loussouarn, (1961) 88 JDI 655, 673; Dörner, *Staudinger BGB* (2007) EGBGB Vorb. zu Art 25 f para 52.

[453] See, for more information, Uluocak, *Milletlerarası Özel Hukuk Dersleri* (1987) 206–207.

[454] Baran Çelik, *Ölüme Bağlı Tasarruflar* (2011) 149. On the exceptional character of oral wills, see Dural and Öz, *Miras Hukuku* (2021) paras 433–444; Serozan and Engin, *Miras Hukuku* (2021) § 4 para 93; Çabri, *Miras Hukuku Şerhi (TMK m. 495–574)* (2022) paras 985–987. See also Yargıtay 2. Hukuk Dairesi, T. 29.9.1992, E. 1992/7372 K. 1992/8705 <http://www.kazanci.com > accessed 18 December 2020.

[455] Art 539 of the Turkish Civil Code.

not considered as matters of succession under Turkish law[456] and thus that they do not fall within the scope of the Convention.[457]

As mentioned earlier, Article 20(4) of the Turkish PILA governs the formal validity of agreements as to succession for dispositions which were drawn up before the entry into force of the Convention and also for testamentary dispositions which are in the scope of the reservations entered by Turkey. The provision, different from the Regulation and the Convention, only prescribes three alternative laws[458] that govern the question of validity as to the form of dispositions of property upon death. It first makes a reference to the general rule on validity as regards the form of legal transactions under Article 7 of the Turkish PILA. Pursuant to Article 7, a disposition of property is formally valid when it is drafted in accordance with the form requirements of the law of the State in which it is made (*locus regit actum*) or with the form requirements of the law applicable to succession (*lex successionis*). A further alternative is enshrined in Article 20(4): dispositions of property upon death which are made in accordance with the national law of the deceased are valid in form. It is noteworthy that the *lex successionis* under Article 20(1) is the national law of the deceased unless the deceased owned immovable property in Turkey, which should be governed by Turkish law according to the exception provided under the second sentence of this provision. Hence, there are actually two alternative laws applicable under Article 20(4), with the third one coming into play only when the testator dies and leaves behind immovable property in Turkey.[459]

As regards this issue of formal validity, the Treaty has also a separate principle which is applicable for agreements as to the succession of nationals of each State who died in the territory of the other. Article 20(16) of the Treaty has a rather limited scope in comparison to the Regulation and the Turkish PILA. The provision stipulates that dispositions of property upon death are

---

[456] Art 295(1) of the Turkish Civil Code provides that a father may recognise his children in a testament. Such a testamentary clause is not, however, considered as a matter of succession. See, in this regard, Serozan and Engin, *Miras Hukuku* (2021) § 4 para 12b; cf. Dural and Öz, *Miras Hukuku* (2021) para 650.

[457] Ekşi, *Milletlerarası Miras Hukuku* (2013) 79; Tekinalp, *Milletlerarası Özel Hukuk* (2020) 251.

[458] Even though the application of the laws under this provision should be alternative to each other so as to give effect to a testamentary disposition reflecting the last wishes of the testator, in one case form requirements led the Turkish Court of Cassation to rule invalid a testamentary disposition made by a Turkish testator in Maryland; the disposition regarding assets that included immovable property in Turkey was made in accordance with the form requirements of the U.S. state, but the court declared the testament invalid because it failed to meet requirements as to form under the Turkish Civil Code: Yargıtay 3. Hukuk Dairesi, T. 29.3.2011, E. 2010/14495 K. 2011/5129 published in Ekşi, *Milletlerarası Miras Hukuku* (2013) 51 ff.

[459] Tekinalp, *Milletlerarası Özel Hukuk* (2020) 245; Şanlı, Esen and Ataman Figanmeşe, *Milletlerarası Özel Hukuk* (2021) 281 fn 338.

valid if they were made in accordance with the law of the State in which they were drafted or the national State of the testator at the time of making the disposition. These laws are also applicable in cases of annulment or revocation of such dispositions. With its overly narrow scope, this rule seems to be disadvantageous for parties when considering the rules of the Regulation and the Turkish PILA. If, for instance, a German national domiciled in Turkey makes an agreement as to succession in France in accordance with the formal requirements of Turkish law concerning his holiday home in Turkey, this agreement would be valid under the Turkish PILA and the Regulation but invalid under the Treaty.[460]

III. An Issue of Characterisation: Joint Wills?

Joint wills, which are not permitted[461] in some jurisdictions but which are of great practical importance in others,[462] are not regulated under Turkish law. Hence, the law applicable to their admissibility would depend on how Turkish judges characterise such wills.[463] An issue of characterisation with respect to them may also arise in the Turkish-European context. This is because the Hague Form Convention which is applicable between the vast majority of Member States and Turkey, clarifies that it also covers joint wills (Article 4); yet it does not take a stance on the question of whether the admissibility of such wills should be characterised as a matter of form or as a matter of substance. It is, therefore, for Turkish courts to decide whether the issue is a matter of form and is thus governed by the Convention.[464] However, before focusing on this issue, the question of which types of joint wills may give rise to characterisation problems should be clarified here at the outset.

---

[460] Güneş, 'The Relations of Turkey with EU Member States' (2019) 305.

[461] They are prohibited, for example, in Dutch, French, Greek, Italian, Portuguese, Slovenian, and Spanish legal systems. See, in this regard, Dutta, (2009) 73 RabelsZ 547, 585. See, for detailed information as regards joint wills in Member States participating in the Regulation, Patricia van Meegen, *Das gemeinschaftliche Testament im europäischen Kontext* (JWV Jenaer Wissenschaftliche Verlagsgesellschaft 2021) 139 ff.

[462] This is, for example, the case in German law: Serozan and Engin, *Miras Hukuku* (2021) § 4 para 6.

[463] Uluocak, *Kanunlar İhtilafı* (1971) 104; Uluocak, *Milletlerarası Özel Hukuk Dersleri* (1987) 146; Tanrıbilir, *Kanuni Mirasçılıktan Doğan Kanunlar İhtilafı* (2000) 82; Baran Çelik, *Ölüme Bağlı Tasarruflar* (2011) 152–153; Ekşi, *Milletlerarası Miras Hukuku* (2013) 62; Tekinalp, *Milletlerarası Özel Hukuk* (2020) 239; Nomer, *Devletler Hususî Hukuku* (2021) 302.

[464] Henri Batiffol, 'La neuvième session de la Conférence de la Haye de droit international privé' [1961] Rev crit dr int privé 461, 468; Loussouarn, (1961) 88 JDI 655, 677; Uluocak, *Milletlerarası Özel Hukuk Dersleri* (1987) 146; Schoenblum, *Multistate and Multinational Estate Planning* (2008) 15–11; Baran Çelik, *Ölüme Bağlı Tasarruflar* (2011) 153.

There are in fact three types of joint wills. The first type of joint wills are objectively joint wills (in Latin: 'testamentum simultaneum'; in Turkish: 'birlikte vasiyetname'; in German: 'gleichzeitiges gemeinschaftliches Testament'). In these kinds of joint wills, testators draft a single document (*uno actu*) to express their last wishes. Another type of joint wills is reciprocal joint wills (in Latin: 'testamentum reciprocum'; in Turkish: 'karşılıklı vasiyetname'; in German: 'gegenseitiges gemeinschaftliches Testament'), in which each testator appoints the other party in the testament, in the event of his prior death, to be his heir. Lastly, joint wills may also be made in the form of mutual wills (in Latin: 'testamentum correspectivum'; in Turkish: 'birbirine bağlı vasiyetname'; in German: 'wechselbezügliches Testament'). This type of joint will refers to wills where each testator drafts a will which is valid only when the other party's will is valid and has not been revoked. The latter two types of testamentary dispositions do not necessarily have to be made in one single document. They could also be made in separate documents.[465] Both the Regulation (Article 3(1) (c)) and the Hague Form Convention (Article 4) define joint wills in a purely formal manner as wills which are made by two or more persons in a single document.[466] Indeed, joint wills which may give rise to characterisation issues in the Turkish-European context are those which are made in one single document regardless of their content.

As there is no specific rule on the characterisation of such wills, the issue is a matter of discussion among scholars in Turkey. It has been strongly opposed by certain authors that joint wills are a matter of substance and, therefore, that the law applicable to succession is also applicable to their admissibility.[467]

---

465 See, in this regard, Frederick J. Tomkins and Henry D. Jencken, *A Compendium of the Modern Roman Law: Founded Upon the Treatises of Puchta, Von Vangerow, Arndts, Franz Moehler, and the Corpus Juris Civilis* (Butterworth 1870) 230–231; Mustafa Dural, 'İsviçre Türk Hukukunda Ortak (Müşterek) Vasiyetnameler' (1969) 3 MHAD 165, 166ff; Necip Kocayusufpaşaoğlu, *Miras Hukuku* (3rd edn, Filiz Kitabevi 1987) 130–131; Rembert Süß, 'The Proposed EU Regulation on Succession and German Law' in European Parliament, Directorate General for Internal Policies, Policy Department C: Citizens' Rights and Constitutional Affairs – Legal Affairs (ed), *Workshop on the Proposal for a Regulation on Succession – Some National Analysis – 22 March 2010 – PE 419.629* (2010) 26–27 <http://www.europarl.europa.eu/RegData/etudes/STUD/2010/419629/IPOL-JURI_DV(2010)419629_EN.pdf> accessed 10 October 2017 (with regards to the German law); Dural and Öz, *Miras Hukuku* (2021) paras 258ff.

466 Ekşi, *Milletlerarası Miras Hukuku* (2013) 60; Dutta, *MüKoBGB* (2020) EuErbVO Art 3 paras 5–7.

467 Uluocak, *Milletlerarası Özel Hukuk Dersleri* (1987) 146; Baran Çelik, *Ölüme Bağlı Tasarruflar* (2011) 153–154; Ekşi, *Milletlerarası Miras Hukuku* (2013) 63; Süzen, *Hukuki İşlemlerin Şekline Uygulanacak Hukuk* (2020) 289–290; cf. Küpe, *Milletlerarası Özel Hukukta Şekil* (2021) 154–155. *Berki* also considers the issue of joint wills as a matter of substance but argues that even though the law applicable to succession allows a testator to

This is firstly because the types of dispositions of property upon death which the testator can make are to be decided by the *lex successionis*.[468] In addition, they differ from other types of dispositions in that it is the intention of testators to make a joint disposition regardless of the form in which they are made.[469]

This could, however, be problematic for the recognition of rights of parties arising out of such wills in cases where the *lex successionis* is Turkish law. According to Article 20(1) of the Turkish PILA, the law applicable to succession is the national law of the deceased. Turkish law, however, is applicable for immovable property situated in Turkey. Consider, for instance, a childless German couple which makes a valid *Berliner Testament*[470] in a single document in Germany; each is appointed as the other's sole heir in respect of each party's movable and immovable estate in Turkey, in the event of a prior death of one of them, and it is agreed that the remaining estate will finally pass to their nephew after the surviving spouse's death. In such a case, their will may not be recognised as governing the immovable estate since the law applicable to the immovable estate is Turkish law.[471]

It therefore seems more plausible to characterise the issue of joint wills as a matter of form[472] and to declare them valid if they are made in accordance with one of the laws provided in Article 1 of the Convention.[473] Under that approach, the *Berliner Testament* made by the German couple in the above example would be valid in Turkey, as it was validly made in Germany.[474] This

draft them, reciprocal and mutual wills will be declared null and void in Turkey based on the *ordre public*: O. F. Berki, (1944) 2 AÜHFD 175, 186.

468 Uluocak, *Kanunlar İhtilafı* (1971) 105; Baran Çelik, *Ölüme Bağlı Tasarruflar* (2011) 153; Ekşi, *Milletlerarası Miras Hukuku* (2013) 63. For a similar view in German Law, see, for instance, Ulrich Drobnig, *American-German Private International Law* (2nd edn, Oceana Publications 1972) 169, especially the decisions cited in fn 99.

469 Uluocak, *Milletlerarası Özel Hukuk Dersleri* (1987) 146. See also Baran Çelik, *Ölüme Bağlı Tasarruflar* (2011) 153.

470 These types of testaments are regulated under BGB § 2269. For more information on the *Berliner Testament*, see Hans-Joachim Musielak, in Franz Jürgen Säcker and others (eds), *MüKoBGB*, vol 11 (8th edn, C.H. Beck 2020) BGB § 2269 paras 1 ff.

471 Uluocak, *Kanunlar İhtilafı* (1971) 105. However, it has been claimed that they could also be declared valid depending on the circumstances of the case: Baran Çelik, *Ölüme Bağlı Tasarruflar* (2011) 154; Ekşi, *Milletlerarası Miras Hukuku* (2013) 63.

472 In the same direction, see Tekinalp, *Milletlerarası Özel Hukuk* (2020) 239; Nomer, *Devletler Hususî Hukuku* (2021) 302.

473 In a judgment from 2013, the 3rd Civil Chamber of the Turkish Court of Cassation held that a joint will may be valid if it is made in accordance with one of the applicable laws under Art 20(4) of the Turkish PILA. Although the Court failed to mention the Hague Form Convention, and instead based its judgment on Art 20(4) of the Turkish PILA, it could be said that it took a stance in favour of the view that joint wills should be characterised as a matter of form. For the judgment, see Yargıtay 3. Hukuk Dairesi, T. 13.6.2013, E. 2013/6447 K. 2013/10116 <https://www.lexpera.com.tr/> accessed 3 March 2022.

474 Baran Çelik, *Ölüme Bağlı Tasarruflar* (2011) 154.

would be more in line with the expectations of the testators when drafting such wills and with the Convention's aim of giving an international effect to the principle of *favor testamenti*.[475] Furthermore, it could be argued that such a classification is also in conformity with the views in Turkish domestic law.[476] The issue of the validity of joint wills has been considered as a matter of form under the domestic law,[477] and it has been argued that only joint wills

---

[475] Batiffol, [1961] Rev crit dr int privé 461, 467; Loussouarn, (1961) 88 JDI 655, 669; Kurt H. Nadelmann, 'The Formal Validity of Wills and the Washington Convention 1973 Providing the Form of an International Will' (1974) 22 AJCL 365, 365; cf. Tanrıbilir, 'MÖHUK ve Mirasa İlişkin Bağlama Kuralının Uygulanmasında Öne Çıkan Hususlar' (2018) 147.

[476] In the same direction, Tekinalp, *Milletlerarası Özel Hukuk* (2020) 239; Nomer, *Devletler Hususî Hukuku* (2021) 302.

[477] Dural, (1969) 3 MHAD 165, 170; Kocayusufpaşaoğlu, *Miras Hukuku* (1987) 351; Dural and Öz, *Miras Hukuku* (2021) paras 258ff; Zahit İmre and Hasan Erman, *Miras Hukuku – Yasal Mirasçılık, Ölüme Bağlı Tasarruflar, Mirasın Geçmesi, Mirasın Taksimi* (15th edn, Der Yayınları 2021) 226–228.

It is argued that the characterisation of the admissibility of joint wills from a private international law perspective depends on the approach in domestic law. Hence, in order to determine whether the admissibility of joint wills will be characterised as a matter of form or substance in private international law, one should examine whether joint wills are not allowed in domestic law because of their form or their content. For views in this regard within the scope of the Regulation, see e.g. Döbereiner, [2013] MittBayNot 437, 440; Heinig, [2014] RNotZ 197, 201ff; Andreas Köhler, 'Teil 1 EuErbVO' in Walter Gierl and others (eds), *Internationales Erbrecht: EuErbVO, IntErbRVG, DurchfVO, Länderberichte* (3rd edn, Nomos & Manz 2020) § 4 Internationales Privatrecht paras 84 and 95. For other views, see van Meegen, *Das gemeinschaftliche Testament* (2021) 184ff.

In the light of this view, one should look into the reason behind the non-regulation of joint wills under Turkish law. In the first draft of the Swiss Civil Code, a translation of which was adopted in Turkey as the Turkish Civil Code, joint wills between the spouses were regulated in Arts 513–515 (under the section addressing types of dispositions ('Die Verfügungsarten') and in Art 528 (under the section addressing the form of dispositions ('Die Verfügungsformen'): *Schweizerisches Civilgesetzbuch, Vorentwurf des Eidgenössischen Justiz- und Polizeidepartements – Code Civil Suisse, Avant-Projet des Département Fédéral de Justice et Police* (Buchdruckerei Büchler & Co. 1900) 123. These provisions were later deleted by the expert commission, as joint wills were likely to give rise complex legal problems and were redundant alongside agreements as to succession. But at the same time no provision prohibiting joint wills was inserted into the text: Eugen Huber, *Schweizerisches Zivilgesetzbuch, Expertenkommission*, vol II (1902) 579ff (Sitzung vom 12. März 1902); Stephan Wolf and Bettina Spichiger, 'Zum Erbvertrag – Einführung und Überblick' in Stephan Wolf and others (eds), *Der Erbvertrag aus rechtsvergleichender Sicht: Rechtsvergleichendes Symposium an der Rechtswissenschaftlichen Fakultät der Universität Bern vom 17./18. Mai 2018 / Il contratto Successorio, aspetti di diritto comparato: Convegno di diritto comparato alla Facoltà di Giurisprudenza dell'Università di Berna, 17/18 maggio 2018* (Stämpfli Verlag 2018) 16 fn 46.

The current approach of the Swiss Civil Code towards joint wills is considered as a formal prohibition ('Formverbot') of joint wills: Martin Gaida, Holger Hille and Patricia

which are made in one document are annullable due to non-compliance with the form requirements of the wills provided under the Turkish Civil Code.[478] In the same vein, the issue of joint wills should also be considered as a matter of form in Turkish private international law and, hence, governed by the Convention.

F. Other Issues Related to the Law Applicable to Succession

I. Renvoi

The doctrine of *renvoi*, which is sometimes labelled as 'over-complicated, unsound and revolutionary'[479] is also important in ascertaining the law applicable to succession. *Renvoi*, which literally means a sending back, refers to the process where the court seised of a dispute requiring the application of a law other than the law of forum applies that law with all its rules, including the conflict-of-laws rules. The conflict-of-laws rules of this State may apply its own domestic rules to the matter or remit the matter to the determination of the *lex fori* (remission) or to the law of another State (transmission).[480]

There are mainly two ways of applying the *renvoi* doctrine. Under 'partial or single *renvoi*', the court employs the conflict rules of the country indicated by its own private international law code and applies the substantive law of the country subsequently referred. This could be either the law of the forum or the law of another country. On the other hand, if 'total or double *renvoi*' is

---

Mendl, *Vermögensnachfolge in der Finanzberatung: Erb-, Steuer- und Gesellschaftsrecht — systematisch, fallorientiert, anlagegerecht* (Gabler 2001) 136–137.

The same then is also true for Turkish Civil Code. Therefore, in line with this approach in the domestic law, the admissibility of joint wills should be characterised as a matter of form from a private international law perspective.

[478] Dural, (1969) 3 MHAD 165, 170; Kocayusufpaşaoğlu, *Miras Hukuku* (1987) 351; Dural and Öz, *Miras Hukuku* (2021) paras 268–270; İmre and Erman, *Miras Hukuku* (2021) 227–228; Serozan and Engin, *Miras Hukuku* (2021) § 4 para 6; cf. Çabri, *Miras Hukuku Şerhi (TMK m. 495–574)* (2022) 862 ff. In the same direction, the Turkish Court of Cassation held in its judgments that joint wills are annullable – not null and void – when the form requirements are not met. See, in this regard, Yargıtay 2. Hukuk Dairesi, T. 30.5.1996, E. 1996/4422 K. 1996/5810 <http://www.kazanci.com> accessed 3 March 2022; Yargıtay 3. Hukuk Dairesi, T. 17.2.2014, E. 2013/18224 K. 2014/2251 <https://www.lexpera.com.tr/> accessed 3 March 2022; Yargıtay 3. Hukuk Dairesi, T. 16.1.2019, E. 2017/12298 K. 2019/146 <https://www.lexpera.com.tr/> accessed 3 March 2022. For other judgments of the Turkish Court of Cassation, see the cases cited in Dural, (1969) 3 MHAD 165, 172–173; Kocayusufpaşaoğlu, *Miras Hukuku* (1987) 133–134; Dural and Öz, *Miras Hukuku* (2021) para 271.

[479] Frederic R. Coudert, 'Some Considerations in the Law of Domicil' (1927) 36 YLJ 949, 953.

[480] Norman Bentwich, *The Law of Domicile in Its Relation to Succession and the Doctrine of Renvoi* (Sweet & Maxwell 1911) 164.

adopted – what is known as 'foreign court theory' in Common law jurisdictions – the court looks at the conflict-of-laws rules of the country referred to by its own private international law code and applies the law indicated there inclusive of that referred to country's doctrine of *renvoi*, thereby ultimately applying whatever substantive law would find application in that country.[481]

The fundamental aim of the *renvoi* doctrine is to ensure decisional harmony on the same issue as between different States.[482] Yet when there are uniform conflict-of-laws rules, *renvoi* is often excluded in order not to vitiate their unifying effect by taking non-unified conflicts rules into account and thus to not to impair the international consistency of decisions aimed at with those harmonised rules.[483] This is normally the case in European private international law instruments.[484] Nonetheless, unlike other instruments, the European legislature allowed *renvoi* in the Regulation for some cases to ensure a certain level of coordination with the private international law of third States whose laws become applicable through the conflicts rules of the Regulation.[485]

Article 34 of the Regulation prescribes that the law of a third State referred to in the Regulation will be applicable, including its private international law rules in so far as they make a *renvoi* to the law of a Member State or the law of a third State which would apply its own law.[486] *Renvoi* is, however, ex-

---

481 Jonathan Hill and Máire Ní Shúilleabháin, *Clarkson & Hill's Conflict of Laws* (5th edn, OUP 2016) para 1.113–1.114.

482 Kropholler, *Internationales Privatrecht* (2006) 165. See also Recital 57 of the Regulation.

483 Dutta, *MüKoBGB* (2020) EuErbVO Art 34 para 1.

484 See, for instance, Art 20 of the Rome I Regulation, Art 24 of the Rome II Regulation, Art 32 of the European Matrimonial Property and Partnership Regulations.

485 Angelo Davì, in Alfonso-Luis Calvo Caravaca, Angelo Davì and Heinz-Peter Mansel (eds), *The EU Succession Regulation – A Commentary* (Cambridge University Press 2016) ESR Art 34 para 1. See also Recital 57 of the Regulation.

486 The application of *renvoi*, however, may be problematic before Member States' courts. There was a recent case rendered by family court of Namur/Belgium which – to some extent – proves this. The case concerned the succession of a person who died in 2019 in South Korea while habitually resident there and while holding passports from Belgium as well as South Korea. He did not have any children and left his assets to a foundation with a testament dated from 2001. The foundation applied to the Court to claim its title as universal legatee. The Court took jurisdiction according to Article 10(1) of the Regulation as the State of *situs* of the assets and found that South Korean law (the law of the State of habitual residence) should be applicable to the case pursuant to Article 21(1) of the Regulation. In line with Article 34(1) of the Regulation, *renvoi* should have to be taken into account. The South Korean PIL Code (Article 49) provides that the national law of the deceased should govern issues of succession. The Court, however, disregarded the fact that the deceased was a dual national and that his effective nationality was Korean, which should have been given priority under Aricle 3(1) of the Korean PIL Code, and applied Belgian law to the case. Although the reference to the law of nationality from the Korean PIL Code was through *renvoi* given effect, this reference was misinterpreted: Tribunal de la

cluded in cases where the escape clause is applicable (Article 21(2)); where the deceased determines the law applicable (Article 22); where the matter is related to the formal validity of dispositions of property upon death (Article 27); where the habitual residence of the person making the declaration governs the acceptance or waiver of succession, of a legacy, of a reserved share, or the limitation of the liability of this person (Article 28 point (b)), and where overriding mandatory provisions are applicable (Article 30).

There is no clarity in the wording of the provision as to whether a 'single or partial *renvoi*' or a 'total or double *renvoi*' is admitted here. This has been a matter of contention among commentators.[487] This doctrinal controversy has no practical importance in cases where the rules of the Turkish PILA find application given that – as explained earlier[488] – the instrument does not accept *renvoi* for matters of succession. Therefore, the issue which should be discussed in the context of these legal instruments is rather whether the desired harmony of decisions is achieved when the law applicable to succession under the Regulation is Turkish law (Article 21(1)).[489]

This could be illustrated with the help of a basic hypothetical example. Assume, for example, that French national *(F)*, who is domiciled/habitually resident in Ankara/Turkey for a long time, dies there intestate and leaves behind movable and immovable assets both in Turkey and in France. In this scenario, French courts will assume jurisdiction in this case pursuant to Article 10(1) (a) of the Regulation and will apply Turkish law to the succession as a whole, as the law of the State of habitual residence under Article 21(1) of the Regulation. This applies for all of his assets regardless of their nature and location. Turkish courts, on the other hand, will also confer their jurisdiction

Famille de Namur (div. Dinant, 3e ch.) from 12.4.2021 commented on in Jean-Louis van Boxstael, 'Succession internationale, double nationalité et renvoi' [2021] JT 339.

[487] Some scholars argue that the provision only allows for a 'single *renvoi*'. See, for example, Ena-Marlis Bajons, 'Internationale Zuständigkeit und anwendbares Recht in Erbsachen' in Martin Schauer and Elisabeth Scheuba (eds), *Europäische Erbrechtsverordnung (2012/650/EU vom 4. Juli 2012)* (Manz 2012) 37; Julian Emmerich, *Probleme der Anknüpfung im Rahmen der EuErbVO* (Duncker&Humblot 2016) 238; Dutta, *MüKoBGB* (2020) EuErbVO Art 34 para 3; Andreas Schwartze, in Astrid Deixler-Hübner and Martin Schauer (eds), *Kommentar zur EU-Erbrechtsverordnung* (2nd edn, Manz 2020) EuErbVO Art 34 para 11; J. Schmidt, *BeckOGK-EuErbVO* (2022) EuErbVO Art 34 para 9. For the opposite view, however, see Rainer Hausmann, in Dieter Henrich (ed), *Staudinger BGB – EGBGB/IPR Einführungsgesetz zum Bürgerlichen Gesetzbuche – Art 3–6 EGBGB (IPR – Allgemeiner Teil)* (Sellier & de Gruyter 2013) EGBGB Art 4 para 165; Davì, *Calvo Caravaca/Davì/Mansel* (2016) ESR Art 34 paras 24 ff.

[488] See above pp 80–81.

[489] See, in the same direction, Kurt Siehr, 'Connecting Factors, Party Autonomy and Renvoi' in Alberto Malatesta, Stefania Bariatti and Fausto Pocar (eds), *The External Dimension of EC Private International Law in Family and Succession Matters* (CEDAM 2008) 262.

as the State of *(F)'s* last domicile (Article 43 of the Turkish PILA). Yet from their perspective, the law governing succession would be different. According to Article 20(1) of the Turkish PILA, French law governs movable and immovable assets located outside Turkey, whereas Turkish law is applicable to immovables situated in Turkey. For matters regarding the grounds for the opening of succession, acquisition, and sharing-out of succession, the *lex situs* is to be applied (Article 20(2) of the Turkish PILA)). This means that the law applicable would be either French law or Turkish law depending on their *situs*. Such a basic example clearly indicates that the habitual residence of the Regulation and the combination of the *lex patriae* and the *lex rei sitae* of the Turkish PILA triggers, at least for assets which are not governed by Turkish law, contradictory results[490] and scission in each legal system.[491]

The Regulation, however, requires judges seated in the Member State courts to take into consideration the private international law of the third State whose law is specified under its own rules in cases where there is a back- or further reference to a Member State law or a further reference to a third State law which accepts this reference and applies its own law. In the case above, the Turkish PILA remits the matter for assets outside Turkey and for specific issues of succession to French law, i.e. the law of a Member State (Article 34(1) (a)), and it ultimately applies Turkish law for other issues. Thus, whilst the scission could not be eliminated, the doctrine of *renvoi* ensures consistency between the practice of the courts in this case.

Another important issue related to *renvoi* in cases arising in the Turkish-EU context is whether *renvoi* under Article 34(1) of the Regulation may enhance decisional harmony also under the treaties, including the Turkish-German Treaty. The Treaty itself does not permit *renvoi* due to the fact that it is an international agreement which brought harmonisation to the private international and procedural rules of Contracting States for matters of succession. Any reference to the law of a Contracting State in the Treaty, therefore, should be understood as the substantive law of that State. An opposite interpretation would go against the harmonisation aim of international agreements.[492] It is obvious that the Treaty already provides decisional harmony for succession cases between Turkey and Germany. Notwithstanding this, *renvoi* under Article 34(1) of the Regulation may be used to extend this effect to other Member States which would in the end not only be advantageous from

---

[490] See, in this regard, Siehr, 'Connecting Factors, Party Autonomy and Renvoi' (2008) 263–266.

[491] See, similar on this issue, Lein, 'Die Erbrechtsverordnung aus Sicht der Drittstaaten' (2014) 209–210.

[492] H. Krüger, 'Studien über Probleme des türkischen Internationalen Erbrechts' (2006) 148; Kroiß, *NK-BGB/EGBGB* (2016) EGBGB Art 25 para 8; Bauer and Süß, *Dutta/Weber* (2021) EuErbVO Art 75 Anhang II-deutsch-türkisches NA para 16; Lorenz, *BeckOK BGB* (2022) EGBGB Art 25 aF para 6.

the Union's perspective but also from the Turkish perspective. This would be the case when Article 34(1) is applied not only in cases where the law applicable is that of a third State but also that of a Member State.[493]

Under such a possibility, when the Regulation's conflict-of-laws rules refer the matter to a Member State law to govern succession, this would not be understood as the substantive law of that State but all private international law rules of that State, including, if any, the rules of a treaty to which this State is still bound and which is still applicable under Article 75 of the Regulation. For example, the law applicable to the succession case of a Turkish national who is habitually resident in Berlin would then be determined, regardless of the Member State where the case is brought, in accordance with the Turkish-German Treaty as part of German law which is the *lex successionis* under Article 21(1) of the Regulation.[494]

This possibility would, of course, allow a derogation from the rules of the Regulation even in EU Member States which are not bound by those treaties. The Turkish-German Treaty would, for example, not only be applied by Germany but also by other Member States. In addition, decisional harmony can still not be completely restored within the Union, as Germany, for example, would always apply the Turkish-German Treaty to the succession of a Turkish national who is habitually resident in another Member State. However, if the case is brought to another Member State court which is not bound by the Treaty, it will determine jurisdiction and the applicable law pursuant to the Regulation.[495] From the Turkish perspective, however, such an application of *renvoi* would contribute to decisional harmony in the context of the Treaty, since the uniform rules of the Treaty would now be effective in more Member States.

---

[493] Arguing in favour of the application of *renvoi* in such a way with respect to treaties of Member States, see, for instance, Köhler, *Gierl and others* (2020) § 4 Internationales Privatrecht para 138; cf. Konvalin, *Das Europäische Nachlasszeugnis* (2018) 81 ff. Most of the commentators, however, firmly oppose any intra-Union effect of *renvoi*. See, in this regard, Dennis Solomon, 'Die Renaissance des Renvoi im Europäischen Internationalen Privatrecht' in Ralf Michaels and Dennis Solomon (eds), *Liber Amicorum Klaus Schurig zum 70. Geburtstag* (Sellier European Law Publishers 2012) 241 ff; Ingo Ludwig, 'Notariat II Villingen: Zuständigkeit deutscher Gerichte im Einantwortungs- und Erbscheinsverfahren nach einem österreichischen Erblasser' [2013] ZEV 150, 152; Dutta, *MüKoBGB* (2020) EuErbVO Art 34 para 13; Bauer and Fornasier, *Dutta/Weber* (2021) EuErbVO Art 34 para 5.

[494] See, for this example, Anatol Dutta, 'The Perspective of the European Union' in Anatol Dutta and Wolfgang Wurmnest (eds), *European Private International Law and Member State Treaties with Third States – The Case of the European Succession Regulation* (Intersentia 2019) 322.

[495] Dutta, 'The Perspective of the European Union' (2019) 322–323.

II. Overriding Mandatory Provisions

Overriding mandatory provisions, often referred to as 'lois de police' or 'lois d'application immediate', are rules which are necessary for the protection of the political, social, and economic organisation of the country[496] and which, hence, become applicable to a matter involving foreign elements regardless of the *lex causae*.[497] It is undoubted that such provisions may also concern or affect succession. Article 30 of the Regulation, therefore, considers this possibility and stipulates that Member States are to apply special rules of the State of *situs* which, for economic, family, and social reasons, restrict succession rights on certain immovable property, enterprises, or other special categories of assets located there irrespective of the *lex successionis*. Even though this presents a deviation from one of the cornerstones of the Regulation, the unity of succession,[498] it aims to ensure a decisional consistency and to prevent instances where the decision rendered by a Member State court would not be enforced in the State where certain assets are located by virtue of the special rules applicable there.[499]

Which rules fall into this category and should be applied regardless of the law applicable to succession is a matter of interpretation given the circumstances of the case.[500] The only clarification in this regard is made by the European legislature respecting different conflict-of-laws rules applicable for immovable property and reserved shares. Recital 54 of the Regulation provides that the rules on these issues are not special rules within the meaning of Article 30.

The importance of the article from a third State perspective is that it does not cover such provisions only of Member States but also of non-Member States.[501] Whilst it is believed that the European courts would apply a high

---

[496] See, in this regard, Phocion Francescakis, 'Quelques précisions sur les "lois d'application immédiate" et leurs rapports avec les règles sur les conflits de lois' [1966] Rev crit dr int privé 1, 13 and 16.

[497] Michael Wilderspin, 'Overriding Mandatory Provisions' in Jürgen Basedow and others (eds), *Encyclopedia of Private International Law* (Edward Elgar Publishing 2017) 1330.

[498] Patrick Wautelet, in Andrea Bonomi and Patrick Wautelet (eds), *Le droit européen des successions-Commentaire du Règlement n°650/2012 du 4 juillet 2012* (2nd edn, Bruylant 2016) ESR Art 30 para 2; J. P. Schmidt, *Dutta/Weber* (2021) EuErbVO Art 30 para 1.

[499] J. P. Schmidt, *Dutta/Weber* (2021) EuErbVO Art 30 para 2.

[500] Dutta, *MüKoBGB* (2020) EuErbVO Art 30 para 6; J. P. Schmidt, *Dutta/Weber* (2021) EuErbVO Art 30 para 10.

[501] Wautelet, *Bonomi/Wautelet* (2016) ESR Art 30 para 2; Köhler, *NK/Nachfolgerecht* (2019) EuErbVO Art 30 para 3; Looschelders, *NK-BGB/Rom-Verordnungen* (2019) EuErbVO Art 30 para 2; Dutta, *MüKoBGB* (2020) EuErbVO Art 30 para 7; J. P. Schmidt, *Dutta/Weber* (2021) EuErbVO Art 30 para 2.

threshold for such rules of third States,[502] as giving effect to such provisions would mean departing from the desired unity of succession to be achieved by the Regulation, two examples from Turkish law which may fall into scope of Article 30 can be provided here.

In the first place, rules that impose restrictions on foreigners regarding the acquisition of immovable property in Turkey may be considered as such provisions.[503] Acquisition of immovable property by foreigners has always been subject to certain conditions and restrictions in Turkish law.[504] Such restrictions, which exist in an important number of legal systems, are justified based on the importance of the land for the State. This is because the acquisition of real estate by foreign nationals is not solely a problem of proprietary rights of foreigners; rather, such acquisition is a primary concern of the State. Had no limitations been imposed, it is considered the acquisition of property by foreigners might pose a threat to the State. Therefore, States, based on their sovereignty, enforce limits on the right of foreigners to acquire real estate within their territories.[505] Restrictions to this effect exist particularly in the Land Registry Law ('Tapu Kanunu'),[506] the Law on the Closed Military and Security Zones ('Askeri Yasak Bölgeler ve Güvenlik Bölgeleri Kanunu'),[507] and in the Equivalent Retaliation Act ('Hudutları Dahilinde Tebaamızın Emlakine Vaziyet Eden Devletlerin Türkiye'deki Tebaaları Emlakine Karşı Mukabelei Bilmisil Tedabiri İttihazi Hakkında Kanun').[508]

In the context of succession, the most important provision in this regard is Article 35 of the Land Registry Law. Under paragraph (6) of the Article, it is clarified that limitations imposed on foreign natural persons concerning the acquisition of title or other rights *in rem* over immovable property outlined under the first paragraph is also applicable in cases of succession. According to Article 35(1), only nationals of the countries determined by the President, in consideration of international bilateral relations and national interests, are

---

502 Köhler, *NK/Nachfolgerecht* (2019) EuErbVO Art 30 paras 9ff; J. P. Schmidt, *Dutta/Weber* (2021) EuErbVO Art 30 para 10.

503 See, for the same comment with respect to Switzerland, Dormann, 'Schweiz und EuErbVO' (2014) 97–98; Dutta, *MüKoBGB* (2020) EuErbVO Art 30 para 8; Pazdan and Zachariasiewicz, (2021) 17 J Priv Int L 74, 96 fn 87; J. P. Schmidt, *Dutta/Weber* (2021) EuErbVO Art 30 para 14.

504 See, on this issue, Altuğ, *Yabancıların Arazi İktisabı* (1976) 54ff; Fügen Sargın, *Yabancı Gerçek Kişilerin Türkiye'de Taşınmaz Mal Edinmeleri ve Sınırlı Aynî Haklardan Yararlanmaları* (Yetkin 1997) 37ff; Nuray Ekşi, *Yabancıların Türkiye'de Taşınmaz İktisabı* (2nd edn, Beta 2012) 9ff; Ayşe Yasemin Aydoğmuş, *AİHS'E Ek 1 No'lu Protokole Göre Yabancıların Türkiye'de Taşınmaz Edinmesi* (On İki Levha 2016) 28ff.

505 Anayasa Mahkemesi, T. 14.3.2005, E. 2003/70 K. 2005/14, *Resmi Gazete* of 26.4.2005, no 25797.

506 *Resmi Gazete* of 29.12.1934, no 2892.

507 *Resmi Gazete* of 22.12.1981, no 2565.

508 *Resmi* Gazete of 15.6.1927, no 608.

allowed to acquire title and other rights *in rem* over immovable property located in Turkey.[509] Under this provision, there is also a limitation regarding the size of the immovable property. Pursuant to this, the total size of the immovable property should exceed neither 10% of the surface area in the district (allowed for private property ownership) where the property is located nor 30 hectares per person in the whole country. This 30-hectare limit could be increased up to 60 hectares by the President. If these limitations are exceeded or if the person is a citizen of a country whose nationals are not allowed to acquire immovable property in Turkey, the beneficiaries of succession will be given up to one year for the liquidation procedures by the Ministry of Treasury and Finance. When the liquidation procedures are not made within this time period, the excessive amount of property will be liquidated and the value will be paid to beneficiaries (Article 35(6) of the Land Registry Law).[510]

This provision is characterised as an overriding mandatory provision under Turkish law,[511] and hence it is believed that it falls under the scope of Article 30 of the Regulation, as it 'concern[s] or affect[s] the succession'. It should then be applied by the Member State courts in cases where immovable property is located in Turkey.

---

[509] It should be noted that there seems to be no list publicly available indicating the countries whose nationals are allowed to acquire immovable property in Turkey.

[510] For details, in this regard, see Ekşi, *Taşınmaz İktisabı* (2012) 149–150; Aydoğmuş, *Yabancıların Türkiye'de Taşınmaz Edinmesi* (2016) 351–353.

It should be noted here that in the original 1934 version of the Land Registry Law, there was, in addition to the other restrictions, a reciprocity condition for the acquisition of immovable property by foreign nationals which was until 2003 also applied for succession rights of foreign nationals. This was based on the idea that land in the territory was an essential element of the State due to political, economic, social, and even military reasons. In those years, this was interpreted as having effect on the heirship of foreign nationals, and such individuals were not indicated as heirs in succession certificates. This changed, however, after 2003 and in the years following under amendments made to the Law. It could be said that there has been a liberalisation in the system as regards the acquisition of immovable property by foreign nationals in general, and, from the succession perspective, the rules are now more in line with the nature of succession rights. See, for details on this issue, Ekşi, *Milletlerarası Miras Hukuku* (2013) 157 ff; Aydoğmuş, *Yabancıların Türkiye'de Taşınmaz Edinmesi* (2016) 265 ff.

[511] Hatice Özdemir Kocasakal, *Doğrudan Uygulanan Kurallar ve Sözleşmeler Üzerindeki Etkileri* (Galatasaray Üniversitesi Yayınları 2001) 147; Cemile Demir Gökyayla, 'Yabancı Mahkemelerden Alınan Mirasçılık Belgelerinin Türkiye'de Hüküm ve Sonuç Doğurması' in Mehmet Ünal (ed), *Prof. Dr. Fikret Eren'e Armağan* (Yetkin 2006) 577–578; Baran Çelik, *Ölüme Bağlı Tasarruflar* (2011) 130 and 205–207; Mustafa Erkan, 'Bir Tabu: Taşınmazın Aynına İlişkin Davalarda Münhasır Yetki' (2012) 20 SÜHFD 11, 45 fn 125; Ekşi, *Milletlerarası Miras Hukuku* (2013) 73–74; Begüm Süzen, *Tanıma ve Tenfiz Davalarında Kararı Veren Mahkemenin Yetkisinin Denetimi* (On İki Levha 2016) 66; Şanlı, Esen and Ataman Figanmeşe, *Milletlerarası Özel Hukuk* (2021) 10.

Another example from Turkish law which would fall under the scope of Article 30 of the Regulation could be relevant provisions of the Law on Soil Preservation and Land Utilization ('Toprak Koruma ve Arazi Kullanımı Kanunu'),[512] enshrining a special succession regime applicable with respect to agricultural lands (Articles 8/B-8/H). The direct transfer of the estate to the community of co-heirs under Turkish succession law causes the fragmentation of agricultural lands. These lands are, however, of paramount importance for agricultural production, economic policy, and the organisation of the State, and thus a special succession regime is applicable to them.[513] The rules in this respect would also fall under the scope of Article 30 of the Regulation.[514]

Moving from European law to Turkish law, Article 6 of the Turkish PILA has a general provision regarding overriding mandatory rules in Turkish law which could be applicable in succession cases too. The Article provides that overriding mandatory provisions of Turkish law should be applied in cases falling under such law's scope of application and regulatory purpose irrespective of the law otherwise applicable to that matter. In a succession case, therefore, where the *lex successionis* is, for instance, that of one of Member States, the rules analysed above will also find application before the Turkish courts. It should, however, be noted that Article 6 of the Turkish PILA, unlike the Regulation, does not specify any type of assets regarding the scope of application of this provision. Thus, it could also be applicable for an item of movable property. This may come into play, for example, if the proprietary rights of a national of one of the Member States, who is resident in Turkey, is restricted or abolished by the Turkish government by presidential decree (in accordance with Article 1 of the Equivalent Retaliation Act).

Another important aspect of the Turkish PILA concerning overriding mandatory rules is that such rules of a third State, i.e. not those of the *lex causae* or Turkish law, cannot be given effect. This means that, unlike Article 30 of the Regulation, special provisions of the *lex rei sitae* concerning or affecting succession for assets located there would not be applicable if the law applicable to

---

512 *Resmi Gazete* of 19.7.2005, no 25880.

513 See, the preamble of Law no 6537 (*Resmi Gazete* of 15.5.2014, no 29001), introducing this regime to the Law on Soil Preservation and Land Utilization, <https://www.tbmm.gov.tr/develop/owa/tasari_teklif_sd.onerge_bilgileri?kanunlar_sira_no=131060> accessed 25 July 2019.

514 See, for a similar opinion concerning provisions of this nature which were previously enshrined under Arts 659–668 of the Turkish Civil Code, Ekşi, *Milletlerarası Miras Hukuku* (2013) 75. See, for the views considering similar provisions of States within the scope of Art 30 of the Regulation, Köhler, *NK/Nachfolgerecht* (2019) EuErbVO Art 30 para 5; Looschelders, *NK-BGB/Rom-Verordnungen* (2019) EuErbVO Art 30 para 9; Dutta, *MüKoBGB* (2020) EuErbVO Art 30 para 8; Stürner, *Erman BGB* (2020) EuErbVO Art 30 para 7; Pazdan and Zachariasiewicz, (2021) 17 J Priv Int L 74, 96; J. P. Schmidt, *Dutta/Weber* (2021) EuErbVO Art 30 para 13.

succession is that of another State. Imagine, for instance, that the succession case of a Portuguese national – who has, in addition to assets in Portugal and in Turkey, movable and immovable assets in Germany – is brought before the Turkish courts. In this case, the law applicable to succession would be Portuguese law except as regards the immovable assets in Turkey, which should be governed by Turkish law. If, for example, the immovable property in Germany is a farm which falls under the scope of the *Höfeordnung*,[515] determination of the heirs for this farm should be made in accordance with § 5 of the *Höfeordnung*. Determination of heirs is an issue falling within the scope of *lex successionis*, i.e. the law of Portugal, according to Article 20(1) of the Turkish PILA. Turkish courts, therefore, cannot give effect to these rules as overriding mandatory provisions. This is because overriding mandatory rules of another State which is closely connected to the case could be given effect only in contractual matters as regulated under Article 31 of the Turkish PILA.

The Treaty, on the other hand, has no specific provision on overriding mandatory rules most probably because the rules of the Treaty, like the Regulation, provides for *Gleichlauf* between forum and *ius*, and hence the law of the forum in its entirety, including the rules which are considered as overriding mandatory provisions for cross-border cases, would be applicable. In other words, no issue would arise with respect to the overriding mandatory provisions of the forum. One might, however, doubt whether overriding mandatory provisions of the *lex rei sitae* should be given effect when the *lex successionis* is the law of the forum. There would again be no problem with respect to immovable properties of the deceased, as these are already governed by the *lex rei sitae* under Article 20(14) (2) of the Treaty. The question is, however, relevant in the context of movable property.

If, for example, a Turkish national living in a *Seniorenheim* (nursing home) in Hamburg draws up a testament to bequeath some amount of money to the nurse who was caring for him during the time he spent there, the question arises whether such a disposition would be valid. Turkish courts would be competent for this matter (Article 20(15) of the Treaty), and the law applicable would be Turkish law pursuant to Article 20(14) (1) of the Treaty, since issues regarding the substantive validity of a disposition of property upon death are also governed by this provision.[516] Nonetheless, § 5a of the *Heimgesetz* of Hamburg ('HmbWGB')[517] forbids such dispositions by residents of nursing homes to staff working there. When this is the case, it could be questionable whether a Turkish judge applying Turkish law would take this rule

---

[515] BGBl. I 1976, 1933. See, for a short explanation on the *Höfeordnung*, Susanne Kalss, *Company Law and the Law of Succession* (Springer 2015) 224–225.

[516] See above pp 140–141.

[517] HmbGVBl. 2009, S. 494.

into account as an overriding mandatory provision of German law,[518] as the *lex rei sitae*.

This is actually a problem not only in relation to the Treaty, as exemplified here, but is rather relevant more generally for the Turkish PILA, as under Article 31 overriding mandatory provisions of a third State which is closely connected to the case may be given effect only in contractual matters. The question would then be whether a Turkish judge, in the context of either the Treaty or the Turkish PILA, may take overriding mandatory rules of another relevant State into account also in matters arising in a field other than contract law.[519]

It could be argued, even in the absence of a particular provision on the issue, that the judge as *modo legislatoris* may still give effect to such rules, as these rules involve public interests for the States where they originate.[520] The above-mentioned provision of Hamburg is indeed considered to serve the public interest in Germany,[521] and, hence, it is seen as applicable even for the foreign residents of these nursing homes.[522] Giving effect to such important legal regulations of a foreign law, i.e. German law in the example, as the law of *lex rei sitae* may be justifiable for manifold policy reasons, such as ensuring decisional harmony, for the sake of the comity principle, or purely for practical reasons, i.e. increasing the possibility that overriding mandatory provisions of Turkish law would also be given effect before foreign courts.[523]

---

518 See, on such a nature of *Heimgesetze*, Dörner, *Staudinger BGB* (2007) EGBGB Art 25 para 131; Lena Kunz, 'Die neue Europäische Erbrechtsverordnung – ein Überblick (Teil II)' [2012] GPR 253, 254–255; Köhler, *NK/Nachfolgerecht* (2019) EuErbVO Art 30 para 14; Looschelders, *NK-BGB/Rom-Verordnungen* (2019) EuErbVO Art 30 para 6; Ingo Ludwig, in Maximilian Herberger and others (eds), *jurisPK-BGB*, vol 6 (9th edn, juris 2020) EuErbVO Art 30 para 10. See also OLG Oldenburg 19.2.1999 – 5 W 29/99, NJW 1999, 2448. See, however, Anatol Dutta, in Franz Jürgen Säcker and others (eds), *MüKoBGB*, vol 11 (6th edn, C.H. Beck 2015) EGBGB Art 25 para 208.

519 See, for such a discussion as regards to delict claims, Belkıs Vural Çelenk, *Application of Third Country Overriding Mandatory Rules – Analytical Comparison of Swiss, Turkish and EU Law* (Schulthess 2018) 203 ff.

520 A similar view is already supported in the context of Art 30 of the Regulation. Even though the scope of the provision is limited to certain assets, it is contended that it has no 'blocking effect' and judges may still give effect to other rules of this kind. See, in this regard, Köhler, *NK/Nachfolgerecht* (2019) EuErbVO Art 30 para 14; Looschelders, *NK-BGB/Rom-Verordnungen* (2019) EuErbVO Art 30 para 6; Ludwig, *jurisPK-BGB* (2020) EuErbVO Art 30 para 10; cf. Pazdan and Zachariasiewicz, (2021) 17 J Priv Int L 74, 99–100. See, for a similar opinion with respect to Art 9 of the Rome I Regulation and Art 16 of the Rome II Regulation, Andreas Köhler, *Eingriffsnormen – Der 'unfertige Teil' des europäischen IPR* (Mohr Siebeck 2013) 264–278.

521 See, on the source of this provision, *i.e.* § 14 of the *Heimgesetz* (BGBl. I 2001, 2970), BVerfG 3.7.1998 – 1 BvR 434/98, NJW 1998, 2964; OLG Oldenburg 19.2.1999 – 5 W 29/99, NJW 1999, 2448.

522 See references above in n 518.

523 Köhler, *Eingriffsnormen* (2013) 272–273.

Notwithstanding this, it should be noted that overriding mandatory provisions are already considered as 'elusive' and 'unruly'.[524] Identifying such provisions of the forum is also extremely difficult for judges.[525] Therefore, in the absence of a specific provision in this regard, determining the overriding mandatory provisions of another State and giving effect to them alongside Turkish law would considerably burden judges. Unless the scope of Article 31 of the Turkish PILA is extended for all matters including succession, as for example under Article 19 of the Swiss PILA,[526] judges cannot be expected to give effect to a third State's rules of overriding nature even though the dispute is closely connected to this State.

One last issue in the scope of the Treaty regarding overriding mandatory provisions is the equal treatment entitled for the citizens of the Contracting State on each other's territory for succession on immovable property referred to under Article 20(14) (2) of the Treaty. The provision provides that succession matters on immovable property should be dealt with in accordance with the law of the Contracting State where the property is located and *as if the deceased was the national of this State*. This last sentence alludes to equal treatment for nationals of one Contracting State in the territory of the other with respect to succession matters regarding immovable property. One might question whether this suggests that overriding mandatory provisions of the *lex rei sitae*, such as the restrictions applicable for the acquisition of real estate by foreigners in Turkey under the Land Registry Law or the rules providing a special succession regime for agricultural lands and enterprises under the *Höfeordnung* in Germany, would still be applicable for the citizens of other Contracting State in succession cases falling under the scope of the Treaty.

The wording of the provision seems to imply, *prima facie*, that such provisions could only be applicable to the nationals of the other Contracting State if they are also applied to the citizens of the State where the relevant immovable property is located. Under this reading, the rules of the *Höfeordnung* would still apply in succession cases regarding Turkish nationals in Germany. German nationals, on the other hand, would be exempted from the restrictions on real estate acquisition by foreign nationals provided under the Land Registry Law in succession cases before Turkish courts. Nonetheless, the aim of this statement is seemingly to guarantee that the nationals of each State would be

---

[524] Jan Kleinheisterkamp, 'Overriding Mandatory Laws in International Arbitration' (2018) 67 ICLQ 903, 905.

[525] On the difficult nature of overriding mandatory provisions in general, see e.g. İbrahim Doğan Takavut, *Milletlerarası Ticari Tahkimde Doğrudan Uygulanan Kurallar* (On İki Levha 2018) 36; Vural Çelenk, *Application of Third Country Overriding Mandatory Rules* (2018) 216.

[526] See, for a comparison of Art 19 of the Swiss PILA and Art 31 of the Turkish PILA in the context of contract and delict, Vural Çelenk, *Application of Third Country Overriding Mandatory Rules* (2018) 145 ff.

entitled to succession rights in the other State and would not be discriminated against there in this respect. The Treaty was indeed concluded in accord with the political sentiment of the time that individuals risked being subject to discrimination outside their national States. The equal treatment emphasis in the provision was most probably made in accordance with the same idea, and, hence, it cannot be interpreted as exempting nationals of the Contracting States from any restrictions imposed generally on foreign nationals in this regard. Such restrictions as part of the *lex rei sitae* would continue to be applicable. This interpretation also appears to be in line with the Treaty of Establishment between the Turkish Republic and Germany of 1927,[527] which specifically addresses the acquisition of movable and immovable property by nationals of each State in the territory of the other State. Article 3 of the Treaty prescribes that nationals of one Contracting State may acquire movable and immovable property by way of succession in the territory of the other Contracting Party subject to the law and regulations applicable there. In addition, Article 1 of the Treaty provides that the provisions of the Treaty are applicable based on the principle of reciprocity. It is clear from these provisions that nationals of Germany are entitled to acquire movable and immovable property by way of succession in Turkey. This is, however, subject to the reciprocity principle (Article 1 of the Treaty) and other restrictions clarified in the Land Registry Law.[528]

III. Ordre public

It is undisputed that conflict-of-laws theory is premised on the application of a foreign law as a means of upholding both the expectations of the parties to a dispute and public interests.[529] The content of the foreign law applicable to the dispute is, however, not known in advance. It is possible that certain provisions of this law will collide with fundamental tenets of the law of the forum.[530] A useful device to escape from such unwanted effects of the applicable

---

[527] *Resmi Gazete* of 8.6.1927, no 605. As in the case of the Turkish-German Consular Treaty of 1929, the Treaty was suspended during the Second World War but became effective again in 1952.

[528] Sargın, *Yabancı Gerçek Kişilerin Türkiye'de Taşınmaz Mal Edinmeleri* (1997) 159; Aydoğmuş, *Yabancıların Türkiye'de Taşınmaz Edinmesi* (2016) 239–240 and 365.

[529] Trevor C. Hartley, *International Commercial Litigation: Text, Cases and Materials on Private International Law* (3rd edn, Cambridge University Press 2020) 575.

[530] Paul Lagarde, 'Public Policy' in Kurt Lipstein (ed), *International Encyclopedia of Comparative Law – Vol III: Private International Law* (Mohr Siebeck & Martinus Nijhoff Publishers 1994) para 1; Etienne Pataut, 'The Public-Policy Exception and the Proposal for a Regulation of the European Parliament and of the Council on Jurisdiction, Applicable Law, Recognition and Enforcement of Decisions and Authentic Instruments in Matters of Succession and the Creation of a European Certificate of Succession (COM(2009)154)' in European Parliament, Directorate-General for Internal Policies, Policy Department C: Citizens' Rights and Constitutional Affairs – Legal Affairs (ed), *Note PE 432.741* (2010) 7

foreign law, in addition to overriding mandatory provisions is the *ordre public* exception. With this exception, the court seised of the dispute may avoid applying foreign law which normally governs the dispute whenever the substantive content of this law is incompatible with the fundamental values of the forum. Thus, whereas overriding mandatory provisions are a positive application of fundamental values the *ordre public* is a negative application.[531] This protection mechanism *vis-à-vis* an applicable foreign law is often enshrined in private international law instruments. This is also the case in the Regulation and the Turkish PILA; the Treaty, by contrast, makes no such reservation.

Article 35 of the Regulation serves as an 'emergency valve' for Member State courts against the substantive law that would otherwise be applicable to succession.[532] If the application of certain provisions of the law specified by the Regulation to govern succession is manifestly incompatible with the *ordre public* of the forum, the court may refuse to apply them. A similar provision also exists in Article 5 of the Turkish PILA. It grants authority to judges not to apply a specific substantive law provision of the foreign law applicable to the dispute and to instead, if necessary, apply Turkish law in cases where the former provision is manifestly incompatible with Turkish law.[533]

The Treaty, on the other hand, does not contemplate an explicit *ordre public* defence authorising judges to reject the application of the law of the Treaty counterparty. One may think that this does not have much practical significance given that the Treaty achieves *Gleichlauf* as regards forum and *ius* such that the courts of Contracting States will not normally apply each other's law. Yet there still may be cases where the *ordre public* exception could come into play. It may be argued, for example, that it would be against *ordre public* to refer the case to the courts of other Contracting Party based on the rules of the Treaty, as the law applicable to the dispute in that country would infringe constitutional rights of the plaintiff in the forum State.[534] The application of the *ordre public* reservation may also come into play in relation to succession certificates, as the jurisdiction to issue such certificates falls outside the scope of the Treaty.[535]

<http://www.europarl.europa.eu/thinktank/en/document.html?reference=IPOL-JURI_NT(2010)432741> accessed 31 July 2019.

[531] Cf. Hartley, *International Commercial Litigation* (2020) 586–587.

[532] Bauer and Fornasier, *Dutta/Weber* (2021) EuErbVO Art 35 para 1.

[533] For a brief review on the use of the *ordre public* reservation by the Turkish Court of Cassation, see Belkıs Vural Çelenk, 'A Promising Shift to Limit Ordre Public Intervention of Applicable Foreign Law Before Turkish Supreme Court' in Juana Vasella (ed), *Von A wie Arbitration über T wie Transport bis Z wie Zivilprozess: Liber discipulorum für Professor Dr. Andreas Furrer zum 55. Geburtstag* (Stämpfli Verlag 2018).

[534] This was the matter disputed in OLG Köln 30.1.1986 – 12 W 79/85, IPRspr 1986 Nr. 109, 248.

[535] See below Chapter 3 under B.I.1. pp 280–286.

Due the lack of a specific provision on the issue, whether the use of the *ordre public* exception remains possible for the Contracting States in such cases is a matter of interpretation.[536] It could be argued that parties implicitly reserved their right to resort to national rules on *ordre public* to preclude the application of the other Contracting Party's law in such instances.[537] It was indeed a rare instance for private international law treaties at the time to include such an exception. It is, therefore, probable that the drafters of the Treaty found it unnecessary to lay down an *ordre public* provision.[538] On the other hand, the silence of the Treaty on the issue could also be interpreted in a way that the parties intended to draft a conclusive agreement on matters covered by the Treaty based on their trust in respect of each other's law and possible amendments to these laws, and it was not desirable for them to prevent the application of the other party's law by means of domestic rules.[539] The bilateral nature of the Treaty supports such an interpretation.[540] When certain aspects of the substantive succession law of the other Contracting Party are incompatible with the law of the forum, the only way for the forum State to avoid them would be termination of the Treaty.[541] Yet based on the general tenets of international law, Contracting Parties may still use the *ordre public* defence in exceptional cases such as when rights protected under the European Convention on Human Rights are violated[542] or when the result would be manifestly contrary to the system of the Contracting State.[543]

---

536 Gerhard Kegel and Klaus Schurig, *Internationales Privatrecht* (9th edn, C.H. Beck 2004) 541.

537 Dutta, *MüKoBGB* (2020) EuErbVO Art 75 para 22. See also Jan von Hein, in Franz Jürgen Säcker and others (eds), *MüKoBGB*, vol 12 (8th edn, C.H. Beck 2020) EGBGB Art 6 para 39.

538 Franzina, 'The External Relations of Italy' (2019) 204 (in the context of the Turkish-Italian Treaty).

539 H. Krüger, 'Studien über Probleme des türkischen Internationalen Erbrechts' (2006) 148; Dörner, [1996] ZEV 90, 91; cf. Bauer and Süß, *Dutta/Weber* (2021) EuErbVO Art 75 Anhang II-deutsch-türkisches NA para 17. See also OLG Köln 30.1.1986 – 12 W 79/85, IPRspr 1986 Nr. 109, 248, 249 ff. More generally on the use of national *ordre public* clauses in the context of international conventions, see Lorenz, *BeckOK BGB* (2022) EGBGB Art 6 para 7.

540 Alexander N. Makarov, *Grundriß des internationalen Privatrechts* (Alfred Metzner Verlag 1970) 102–103; Kropholler, *Internationales Einheitsrecht* (1975) 340 fn 85; H. Krüger, 'Studien über Probleme des türkischen Internationalen Erbrechts' (2006) 148.

541 Dörner, [1996] ZEV 90, 91.

542 For the text of the Convention, see <https://www.echr.coe.int/Documents/Convention_ENG.pdf> accessed 4 August 2019. See, for views in this regard, Dörner, [1996] ZEV 90, 91; Spelsberg-Korspeter, (2017) Deutsch-türkisches Nachlassabkommen para 36; cf. Bauer and Süß, *Dutta/Weber* (2021) EuErbVO Art 75 Anhang II-deutsch-türkisches NA para 17.

543 Franzina, 'The External Relations of Italy' (2019) 204 (in the context of the Turkish-Italian Treaty).

An example of such a use of the *ordre public* defence within the scope of a bilateral Treaty is given by Austria. The Austrian Supreme Court of Justice ('OGH') used the *ordre public* defence in its judgment from 2019[544] to avoid the application of Iranian law in a case falling within the scope of the Treaty between Austria and Persian Empire of 1959.[545] In that case, the deceased was an Iranian national habitually resident in Austria who died in 2013, leaving behind his wife (an Iranian national resident in Austria) and four children (two daughters and two sons; three of them, i.e. one of the sons and two daughters, were residents of Austria and dual nationals of both States, the other son was an Iranian-Belgian dual national resident in Belgium). The deceased also drafted an invalid testament in favour of his wife. The law applicable in this case was Iranian law (the national law of the deceased) pursuant to Article 10(3) of the Austrian-Persian Treaty.[546] Under Iranian law, however, succession rights of heirs are differentiated based on gender. If the surviving spouse is a man, he is entitled to one-fourth of succession share, whereas a woman has a one-eighth succession share. For children, sons of the deceased inherit twice as much as daughters. Further, the immovable property of the deceased could only be inherited by the children, the widowed spouse would have only a compensation claim on it. The Austrian Supreme Court consequently considered the relevance of the case to Austria, as the State of residence of both the deceased and the majority of heirs, and held that such a discriminatory distribution of succession – regardless of the fact the deceased was bettering the situation of others through a disposition of property – would violate Austrian public policy.[547] In other words, the Iranian law which should have been applicable through the rules of the Treaty was found inapplicable. One of the reasons behind this approach is the implied *ordre public* provision under the Treaty, namely Article 10(4), which gives Contracting Parties the right to derogate from the applicable law in exceptional cases and in accordance with the general practice employed against other States.[548] Even in the absence of such a provision, as is the case in the Turkish-German Treaty, the

---

[544] OGH 29.1.2019 – 2 Ob 170/18s, FamRZ 2019, 738.

[545] BGBl. Nr. 45/1966.

[546] For an English translation of the Article, see Anatol Dutta and Wolfgang Wurmnest, *European Private International Law and Member State Treaties with Third States – The Case of the European Succession Regulation* (Intersentia 2019) 359–360 (by *Claudia Rudolf* and *Sarah Kohlweg*).

[547] OGH 29.1.2019 – 2 Ob 170/18s, FamRZ 2019, 738, 739–740.

[548] OGH 29.1.2019 – 2 Ob 170/18s, FamRZ 2019, 738, 739. On this nature of Article 10(4) of the Treaty between Austria and Persian Empire, see Alfred Duchek and Fritz Schwind, *Internationales Privatrecht* (Manz 1979) 178; Claudia Rudolf, 'The External Relations of Austria' in Anatol Dutta and Wolfgang Wurmnest (eds), *European Private International Law and Member State Treaties with Third States – The Case of the European Succession Regulation* (Intersentia 2019) 26.

use of the *ordre public* defence should be possible for the Contracting States in extreme scenarios, like the one in Austria.

As *ordre public* is referred to as an 'unruly horse';[549] it is not always easy to determine issues which could be considered as contrary to the *ordre public* of Turkey in succession cases. One example where the use of *ordre public* exception may come into play is the application of certain laws which have discriminatory provisions in terms of succession rights. For instance, the *ordre public* of Turkey may be violated by legal systems which grant no succession right to female children of the deceased; or which grant different shares to male and female children without any justification; or which discriminate against children who are born out of wedlock with respect to succession; or which discriminate against certain individuals based on their race or religion.[550] Different provisions of other States regarding succession rights of the surviving spouse or reserved shares or forced heirship may also be discussed in the context of *ordre public*. The interrelation of these issues with the *ordre public* would depend the factual circumstances of the case.[551]

The above-mentioned matters are, however, highly unlikely to arise in the Turkish-EU context, as differences applicable between the substantive succession laws of the Member States and Turkey would only infrequently amount to an *ordre public* violation. An exemplary issue in this regard which could be disputed in the Turkish-EU context is the succession of same-sex partners, as Turkish law, unlike the law of some EU Member States,[552] does not legally recognise marriage or any kind of partnership of same-sex couples.[553] This is because marriage is possible only between persons of a different sex.[554] In addition, there is no legal form of partnership even for persons

[549] Richardson v. Mellish [1824] 2 Bing 229, 252 [*Burrough J*].

[550] See, in this regard, Tanrıbilir, *Kanuni Mirasçılıktan Doğan Kanunlar İhtilafı* (2000) 176ff; Baran Çelik, *Ölüme Bağlı Tasarruflar* (2011) 209–210; Ekşi, *Milletlerarası Miras Hukuku* (2013) 66–67; Öztürk, (2015) 5 AkdHFD 177, 203; Tekinalp, *Milletlerarası Özel Hukuk* (2020) 243; Hatice Selin Pürselim, 'Uygulanacak Hukuk, Yetkili Mahkeme ve Tanıma Davası Kapsamında Mirasçılık Belgesinin İncelenmesi' (2021) 9 KHASHFD 179, 184; Doğan, *Milletlerarası Özel Hukuk* (2022) 379–380.

[551] On the succession rights of a surviving spouse, see Tanrıbilir, *Kanuni Mirasçılıktan Doğan Kanunlar İhtilafı* (2000) 177–178; Doğan, *Milletlerarası Özel Hukuk* (2022) 380. On reserved shares or forced heirship, see Baran Çelik, *Ölüme Bağlı Tasarruflar* (2011) 210–211; Ekşi, *Milletlerarası Miras Hukuku* (2013) 67; Öztürk, (2015) 5 AkdHFD 177, 203. See also Pürselim, (2021) 9 KHASHFD 179, 184.

[552] See, for example, <https://fra.europa.eu/en/publication/2017/mapping-minimum-age-requirements/same-sex-marriage> accessed 20 December 2020.

[553] Gülören Tekinalp, Ergin Nomer and Ayşe Odman Boztosun, *Private International Law in Turkey* (Wolters Kluwer 2012) para 614b.

[554] Arts 124, 134 and 136 of the Turkish Civil Code. See, in this regard, Esen Aydın, 'Maddi Hukuk ve Milletlerarası Özel Hukuk Açısından Eşcinsel Evliliklerin Değerlendi-

from different sex. In Member States allowing such a marriage or partnership of same-sex individuals, the surviving registered partner of the deceased would often be entitled to succession in the same way as the surviving spouse.[555] Under Turkish law, on the other hand, the surviving partner will have obviously no statutory succession rights on the estate. This difference between Turkish law and the laws of Member States, including Germany,[556] that recognise such marriages or partnerships and grant succession rights to them may give rise to the use of the *ordre public* exception on both sides.

In a first scenario, consider two Turkish men, *(T)* and *(A)* who are living in Rotterdam and enter into a registered partnership there.[557] They live in Rotterdam for two years and before later going permanently back to Istanbul, where *(T)* dies after four years. He leaves behind a saving account in the Netherlands with 50,000 euros. He has made neither a choice of court nor a choice of law. *(A)* requests a certificate of succession from a court in the Netherlands.[558] In this case, the law applicable to succession before the Dutch courts is Turkish law according to Article 21(1) of the Regulation. There would also be no *renvoi* in line with Article 34(1) of the Regulation, as Article 20(1) of the Turkish PILA refers the matter to the national law of the deceased, which is Turkish law in this case. Thus, *(A)* would not be considered as one of the heirs of *(T)* for the money in the bank account under Turkish law, whereas he would have been an heir pursuant to Dutch law.[559] Under such a scenario, a useful instrument for the Dutch court could be the use of the *ordre public* exception under Article 35 of the Regulation[560] or simply the use of adaptation doctrine.[561]

---

rilmesi' in Günseli Öztekin Gelgel and Faruk Kerem Giray (eds), *Milletlerarası Aile ve Çocuk Hukukuna İlişkin Seçilmiş Makaleler* (Beta 2017) 111–116.

[555] Manfred Bruns, 'Eingetragene Lebenspartnerschaften im Rahmen der EU-Erbrechtsverordnung' [2014] ZErb 181, 182.

[556] See particularly § 10 LPartG (BGBl. I 2001, 266).

[557] See Art 1: 80a-80g of the Civil Code of the Netherlands ('Burgerlijk Wetboek'), Stb. 1822, 10. See, for general information on Dutch family and succession law (also in relation to same-sex couples), Freek Schols and Theo Reijnen, 'The Netherlands' in Lucia Ruggeri, Ivana Kunda and Sandra Winkler (eds), *Family Property and Succession in EU Member States: National Reports on the Collected Data* (Sveučilište u Rijeci, Pravni fakultet 2019) 478 ff <https://www.euro-family.eu/documenti/news/psefs_e_book_compressed.pdf> accessed 20 December 2020.

[558] For a similar example, see Michael Coester, 'Das Erbrecht registrierter Lebenspartner unter der EuErbVO' [2013] ZEV 115, 116.

[559] See Art 4:8 and Art 4:10 of the Civil Code of the Netherlands.

[560] Coester, [2013] ZEV 115, 117; Bruns, [2014] ZErb 181, 182; Michael Stürner, 'Die Bedeutung des ordre public in der EuErbVO' [2014] GPR 317, 323–324; Dirk Looschelders, 'Die allgemeinen Lehren des Internationalen Privatrechts im Rahmen der Europäischen Erbrechtsverordnung' in Katharina Hilbig-Lugani and others (eds), *Zwischenbilanz – Festschrift für Dagmar Coester-Waltjen zum 70. Geburtstag* (Gieseking 2015) 542; Chris-

In an alternative scenario, imagine that *(T)* is a Dutch national and *(A)* is a Turkish national; they are registered as partners in the Netherlands but live together for the last two years in Istanbul. *(T)* dies there intestate, leaving behind a Turkish bank account with a worth of 1,000,000 TL. A succession action is brought before a court in Istanbul. In this case, the law applicable to the matter of succession would be Dutch law under Article 20(1) of the Turkish PILA. Hence, *(A)* would normally have succession rights on the money pursuant to Dutch law. The judge may refuse to apply those provisions of Dutch law granting succession rights to *(A)* as the surviving partner of *(T)* under Article 5 of the Turkish PILA if he considers that the application of such provisions would be contrary to the *ordre public* of Turkey.

This second scenario may also be formulated within the scope of the Treaty. Imagine that *(T)* is a German national in this example. *(A)* applies to Turkish courts to get a certificate of succession.[562] If the Court finds itself competent to issue the succession certificate, it has to apply German law pursuant to Article 20(14) (1) of the Treaty. *(A)*, thus, would be entitled to succession under §10 LPartG. The use of the *ordre public* exception may again be argued to prevent the application of this provision of German law.

The above examples indicate that succession rights granted or, *vice versa*, not granted to same-sex partners by the law applicable to succession might raise issues regarding the *ordre public* in the Turkish-EU context. From these possible hypothetical cases, whether the application of Turkish law – which does not recognise same-sex partnerships and, hence, does not grant statutory succession rights to the surviving partner of the deceased in such a partnership – would be considered as an *ordre public* violation under Article 35 of the Regulation, as in the first example above, would depend on the analysis of the factual circumstances as made by the court of the Member State having jurisdiction over the case. This issue is, therefore, outside the scope of this study. The latter scenarios, however, are examples which may come before the Turkish courts. A discussion in this regard could be undertaken from the Turkish perspective, without differentiating the cases that arise within the ambit of the Turkish PILA and the Treaty. The discussion would also disre-

---

toph Döbereiner, 'Das Gesetz zum Internationalen Erbrecht und zur Änderung von Vorschriften zum Erbschein' [2015] NJW 2449, 2455; Köhler, *NK/Nachfolgerecht* (2019) EuErbVO Art 35 para 8; Karsten Thorn, in Christian Grüneberg (ed), *Grüneberg BGB* (81st edn, C.H. Beck 2022) EuErbVO Art 35 para 2.

[561] For an argument in favour of the use of the doctrine of adaptation in succession cases involving same-sex couples, see Dutta, *MüKoBGB* (2020) EuErbVO Art 23 para 11.

[562] For a more detailed example in this regard, see Hatice Selin Pürselim, 'Almanya'da Tescil Edilmiş Eşcinsel Hayat Ortaklığında Veraset İlamının Alınması ve bu İlama Dayanılarak Türkiye ve Almanya'da Bulunan Terekenin Paylaşılması' (2011) 31 MHB 243, 253.

gard the problem of whether there is any room for the *ordre public* reservation under the Treaty, an aspect which has been explained above.[563]

As mentioned earlier, same-sex couples cannot marry or establish a legal partnership under Turkish law. For this reason, same-sex marriage or partnership may be considered as contrary to the *ordre public* in Turkey.[564] This is because they are contended to be incompatible with Turkish family structures, customs, and morals.[565] In line with this, the application of the provisions of the *lex successionis* establishing the surviving partner as an heir of the deceased would also be seen as contrary to the *ordre public* of Turkey.[566] When this is the case, the surviving partner of the deceased will not be able to enjoy succession rights in Turkey, unless the deceased – of course within the limits of his testamentary freedom – drafts a disposition of property upon death in favour of his partner.[567]

Such a rigid understanding of the *ordre public* reservation, however, would culminate in an unjust situation for same-sex partners who have married or registered their partnerships outside Turkey in accordance with the laws applicable there.[568] The doctrine of *ordre public* should indeed be employed by

---

563 See above pp 166–169.

564 Pürselim, (2011) 31 MHB 243, 260.

565 Pürselim, (2011) 31 MHB 243, 260. Same-sex partners who are foreign nationals cannot marry in Turkey even according to their own national laws. Such a situation would also be considered as a violation of Turkish *ordre public*: Sedat Sirmen, 'Eş Cinsel Birliktelikler ve Bunların Kanunlar İhtilâfı Hukukunda Düzenlenişi' (2009) 58 AÜHFD 825, 857; Çelikel and Erdem, *Milletlerarası Özel Hukuk* (2021) 148.

566 Pürselim, (2011) 31 MHB 243, 261. See, for views against such a rigid understanding of the *ordre public* in cases of same-sex couples, Sirmen, (2009) 58 AÜHFD 825, 871–872; Candan Yasan, *Milletlerarası Özel Hukukta Aynı Cinsiyetten Kişilerin Birliktelikleri* (On İki Levha 2013) 172; Necla Öztürk, *Milletlerarası Özel Hukukta Aile Kurma Amaçlı Evlilik Benzeri Yaşam Modelleri* (Adalet Yayınevi 2016) 288; Cemile Demir Gökyayla, 'Yeniden Kamu Düzeni' in Feriha Bilge Tanrıbilir and Gülce Gümüşlü Tunçağıl (eds), *10. Yılında MÖHUK Sempozyumu – 7–8 Aralık 2017, Ankara* (Adalet Yayınevi 2018) 97–98; Tekinalp, *Milletlerarası Özel Hukuk* (2020) 142.

It is, however, argued that conflict rules on marriage may be applied to registered partnerships by analogy in cases where the Turkish judges are confronted with such questions. This may provide a solution in situations where both of the parties are the nationals of a State where such a partnership is recognised. In cases where one of the parties is a Turkish citizen, as in the latter two examples, or both parties are Turkish citizens as in the first example, it cannot provide a solution, and hence a partnership concluded elsewhere cannot be recognised in Turkey in this manner: Tekinalp, Nomer and Odman Boztosun, *PIL in Turkey* (2012) paras 614b–614c.

567 Pürselim, (2011) 31 MHB 243, 261.

568 Pürselim, (2011) 31 MHB 243, 256, 259 and 261; Yasan, *Aynı Cinsiyetten Kişilerin Birliktelikleri* (2013) 177, 183; Aydın, 'Eşcinsel Evlilikler' (2017) 129–130; Demir Gökyayla, 'Yeniden Kamu Düzeni' (2018) 97–98.

the judges only after a careful scrutiny of the circumstances of the case.[569] This is because *ordre public* has a 'relative character'[570] which has different dimensions. In the first place, *ordre public* is an evolving notion depending on the time, place, or legal matter at issue.[571] Furthermore, use of the *ordre public* defence against the application of certain provisions of foreign law will only come into play when the issue has a sufficient link with the forum.[572] Last but not least, it is often required that the *ordre public* intervention in opposition to foreign law be made only in exceptional circumstances in respect of certain provisions of that law which are *manifestly* incompatible with the fundamental principles and values of the forum. This is also the case under Article 5 of the Turkish PILA. All these require that *ordre public* should be analysed for each legal case separately rather than concluding that any provision of a foreign law recognising the marriage or partnership of same-sex couples would violate Turkish *ordre public*.[573]

Whilst allowing or not allowing same-sex partnerships or marriages under Turkish law is related to the legal policy of the State, it is believed that the *ordre public* reservation under Article 5 of the Turkish PILA should be used only in this context in exceptional circumstances where the case is closely connected to Turkey.[574] In the latter two examples above, even though *(T)* was living with *(A)* in Turkey and owned movable assets there, he established his registered partnership outside Turkey. In addition, whereas *(A)* is a Turkish national and his title to succession on the movable property in Turkey is

---

569 Gündüz Ökçün, *Devletler Hususî Hukukunun Kaynakları ve Kamu Düzeni* (Sevinç Matbaası 1967) 157; Aydanur Gürzumar, 'Türk Devletler Özel Hukuku Açısından Boşanma Davalarında Kamu Düzeninin Etkileri' (1994) 14 MHB 21, 25; Lagarde, 'Public Policy' (1994) para 24; Cemile Demir Gökyayla, *Yabancı Mahkeme Kararlarının Tanınması ve Tenfizde Kamu Düzeni* (Seçkin 2001) 31; Işıl Özkan and Uğur Tütüncübaşı, *Uluslararası Usûl Hukuku* (2nd edn, Adalet Yayınevi 2020) 215; Güngör, *Türk Milletlerarası Özel Hukuku* (2021) 111.

570 Lagarde, 'Public Policy' (1994) para 25.

571 Ökçün, *Kamu Düzeni* (1967) 151–158; Yılmaz Altuğ, 'Âmme İntizamı ve Tesirleri (Bir Özet)' (1972) XXVII AÜSBFD 371, 376; Kemal Dayınlarlı, 'Milletlerarası Özel Hukukta Kamu Düzeni', *Prof. Dr. Yaşar Karayalçın'a 65 inci Yaş Armağanı* (Türkiye İş Bankası Kültür Yayınları 1988) 673; Gürzumar, (1994) 14 MHB 21, 24–26; Demir Gökyayla, *Tanıma ve Tenfiz'de Kamu Düzeni* (2001) 28–32; Özkan and Tütüncübaşı, *Uluslararası Usûl Hukuku* (2020) 215; Güngör, *Türk Milletlerarası Özel Hukuku* (2021) 111.

572 Lagarde, 'Public Policy' (1994) para 25.

573 Sirmen, (2009) 58 AÜHFD 825, 871–872; Yasan, *Aynı Cinsiyetten Kişilerin Birliktelikleri* (2013) 172 and 174ff; Öztürk, *Milletlerarası Özel Hukukta Evlilik Benzeri Yaşam Modelleri* (2016) 288; Aydın, 'Eşcinsel Evlilikler' (2017) 129–130 and 132–133; Tekinalp, *Milletlerarası Özel Hukuk* (2020) 142–143.

574 For a similar view on the use of the public policy exception for the recognition of foreign same-sex unions in China, Yin Liu, 'Recognition of Foreign Same-Sex Unions in China' (2019–2020) XXI YbPIL 425.

disputed, *(T)* was a national of another State which entitles his partner to succession as his surviving spouse. The case, therefore, seems not be closely connected to Turkey. Therefore, *(A)* should not be deprived of his succession rights on the movable property of *(T)*; rather, he should be entitled to succession as the surviving spouse of *(T)* based on the doctrine of adaptation.[575] It appears that a resolution to the contrary would be unjust for *(A)* and, in a more general sense, for same-sex partners in succession cases.[576]

G. Concluding Remarks as Regards the Conflict of Laws in Turkish-EU Successions

In the event of the death of a person who simultaneously has connections to more than one State, one of the questions would be that of which law becomes applicable for the distribution of his estate. Unless there are harmonised rules adopted, like in the Regulation, the answer to this question may vary from country to country. In the Turkish-EU context, too, there are divergent approaches to the question of the law applicable to succession.

The first difference between the rules of the three legal texts is related to the paradox between the unitary and dualist approaches. The Regulation, with the underlying policy of legal certainty and the aim that its citizens should not face difficulties in estate planning and the distribution of assets, treats the estate as a unity without making any distinction as regards the nature of assets. In stark contrast with this system but as an understandable choice for its own era, the Treaty splits the estate in two masses: one mass, comprising movables, is governed by the national law of the deceased, whereas the other mass that consists of immovables should be inherited under the law of the *situs*. The approach of the Turkish PILA, on the other hand, lies between both ends with its mixed solution. The law applicable to succession as a whole is the national law of the deceased, but succession on immovables as well as certain issues is subject to the Turkish regime.

---

[575] Pürselim, (2011) 31 MHB 243, 259.

[576] Pürselim, (2011) 31 MHB 243, 256, 259 and 261; Yasan, *Aynı Cinsiyetten Kişilerin Birliktelikleri* (2013) 177 and 183; cf. Aydın, 'Eşcinsel Evlilikler' (2017) 116 and 128 ff. For a similar view regarding maintenance matters between same-sex partners, see Sirmen, (2009) 58 AÜHFD 825, 872.

For a view as regards to China arguing that there should be some flexibility in the PIL context for same-sex unions even if they are not allowed under the substantive law, see Liu, (2019–2020) XXI YbPIL 425.

It should, however, be noted that the argument supported by *Tekinalp, Nomer and Odman Boztosun* which is referred in above in n 566, p 172 would probably lead us to the result that succession rights of *(A)* will not be recognised in Turkey, as *(A)* is a Turkish national, and hence, there is no valid relationship according to Turkish law.

It is believed that the principle of universal succession will avoid problems of applying different laws to different group of assets or even differentiating between the nature of assets. In the modern world, the deceased's estate comprises not only classical items of property but also other types of assets, such as company or stock shares, digital assets, mortgages, leases, and the like.[577] Determining the nature of assets in such cases may prove difficult for the courts. The unitary approach also serves to provide decisional harmony in cross-border cases.[578] Decisional harmony is undoubtedly more important in today's world than in the past, where cross-border instances were only rare occurrences. Although the adoption of the monist approach in Turkey will not guarantee full harmony between the Member States and Turkey, except where the deceased makes a choice of law for Turkish law, it could – at least to some extent – provide such harmony with many other States which follow a unitary approach.

Today we are obviously not living in a feudalistic policy-driven world where land is the most valuable asset of a State. This is also evident in Turkey, with the changing policy of the State towards real estate ownership by non-Turkish nationals. Although there are still restrictions applicable to foreigners in this regard, the limits are clearly much broader than the past. Furthermore, these restrictions are applicable only for the transfer of inherited property to heirs or beneficiaries; their application is already guaranteed with the *situs* rule under Article 20(2) of the Turkish PILA.[579] Even in the absence of a provision like that found in the second paragraph of Article 20, they could still be applied as overriding mandatory provisions under Article 6 of the Turkish PILA.[580] Therefore, the monist approach in the field of succession should be adopted in Turkey in a future reform, whereas the abandonment of the rule may not occur in the near future due to the long tradition behind the issue.[581]

Another difference between the three legal texts, which exists actually to a lesser degree between the Turkish PILA and the Treaty, concerns the main connecting factors. The European legislature, in considering the frequency of the mobility of persons and its integrative policy towards a migrant population, prefers the last habitual residence of the deceased as the main connecting factor. The Turkish PILA, as the law of an immigrant sending country, submits succession issues to the national law of the deceased. However, in line with its long tradition on immovables, it provides that succession matters

---

[577] Eugene F. Scoles, 'The Hague Convention on Succession' (1994) 42 AJCL 85, 87; Baran Çelik, *Ölüme Bağlı Tasarruflar* (2011) 38.

[578] Cf. Tanrıbilir, *Kanuni Mirasçılıktan Doğan Kanunlar İhtilafı* (2000) 99; Baran Çelik, 'Miras–İrade Muhtariyeti' (2012) 38; Öztürk, (2015) 5 AkdHFD 177, 202.

[579] Tanrıbilir, 'MÖHUK ve Mirasa İlişkin Bağlama Kuralının Uygulanmasında Öne Çıkan Hususlar' (2018) 140.

[580] Demir Gökyayla, 'Mirasçılık Belgeleri' (2006) 577.

[581] Cf. Symeon C. Symeonides, 'Exploring the "Dismal Swamp": The Revision of Louisiana's Conflicts Law on Successions' (1987) 47 La L Rev 1029, 1092.

on immovables in Turkey be governed by Turkish law, as the *lex rei sitae*. Similar policy considerations which were probably much stronger during the time when it was drafted also shaped the connecting factors of the Treaty. It states, adopting a nuance drawn from the Turkish PILA, that the movable part of the estate should be inherited pursuant to the national law of the deceased, while the immovable part should be inherited under the law of the *situs*.

Although it seems that, as explained in the previous paragraph, a monist approach is advisable from the Turkish perspective – to be accomplished by abolishing the *situs* rule – the chance of replacing the nationality principle with other connecting factors, such as the Regulation's habitual residence, remains limited for the time being. While in most cases it may be a mere presumption that the migrant population of Turkey outside the country is still closely connected to Turkey and wishes to be governed by their national law,[582] the nationality principle retains the advantage of an easy application. The habitual residence connecting factor is criticised by some scholars in the Union on the grounds that it may be difficult for courts to determine habitual residence despite the close judicial cooperation between the States.[583] Furthermore, one could also argue that the foreign population in Turkey is not so big as in the Union such that one can expect a change of policy – towards a more integrative one – on this matter. This has, however, changed in recent years, particularly because of the migration flow to Turkey.[584] Such a migration flow has probably increased the number of cross-border cases, perhaps also in the field of succession, before Turkish courts.[585] Even though it still seems too soon to envision a move away from the nationality principle, the frequency of succession cases involving the increasing number of individuals whose lives have a multinational dimension and the problems which may arise in such cases may require us to reconsider the applicable connecting factor in the future.

The approaches of the three legal texts also differ on *professio iuris*. Whereas neither the Turkish PILA nor the Treaty allows for a choice of law, the Regulation allows the deceased to choose his national law to govern his

---

[582] Doğan, *Milletlerarası Özel Hukuk* (2022) 214.

[583] For statements in this regard and a case example from Latvia which proves that the determination of habitual residence may be complex for legal authorities and courts of Member States, see Toms Krūmiņš, 'Application of the EU Succession Regulation in Practice: The Case of Latvia and Beyond' (2019) 15 J Priv Int L 365.

[584] The statistics of *TurkStat*, as explained earlier, indicate that there were around 1.7 million foreign nationals in Turkey in the year of 2021. This, does not, however, include Syrians under temporary protection: Turkstat, 'Foreign Population by Country of Citizenship'. The Turkish Directorate General of Migration Management reports that there are more than 3.5 million Syrians with temporary protection in Turkey: <https://www.goc.gov.tr/gecici-korumamiz-altindaki-suriyeliler> accessed 18 February 2021. It thus seems that there were almost 5 million foreign nationals in Turkey in 2020.

[585] Cf. Doğan, *Milletlerarası Özel Hukuk* (2022) 1–2.

succession as a whole. This is not surprising in light of, first, the tendency of the Union to give parties a degree of autonomy and, second, the two important objectives of the European legal instruments, i.e. legal certainty and foreseeability. Allowing the deceased to choose the law applicable to his succession in a future reform (in Turkey) does not seem to be realistic, as party autonomy is applicable only for contractual and tort matters under the Turkish PILA and has not found any place until now in matters related to personal status, family law, or property law. Given its relation to these areas, choice of law in the field of succession cannot be expected in the near future. This is also not surprising when considering that *professio iuris* for succession matters has also been a novelty for the vast majority of the Member States. Nonetheless, the approach of the Regulation should be seen as a positive development for the sake of Turkish nationals in the Union. When they make a choice of law in favour of Turkish law, decisional harmony will be provided at least to some extent between Turkey and the Union.

Differences apply also as regards the scope of the law applicable to succession. Two issues which might be of practical importance for Turkish-EU successions in this regard are the treatment of *legatum per vindicationem* under Turkish law and the characterisation of BGB § 1371(1). It seems that legacies with real effect will be seen as a matter concerning the acquisition of succession, which will be governed by the *lex rei sitae* in accordance with Article 20(2) of the Turkish PILA; their real effects will thus not be allowed for property located in Turkey, as Turkish law governs the issue as the *lex rei sitae*. With regards to BGB § 1371(1), it is likely that a Turkish judge will consider the provision as relating to matrimonial property given its aim of offering a practical solution for the liquidation of assets where the marriage ends with the death of one of the spouses, even though the CJEU characterised it as a succession rule. The conclusions on these issues are, of course, merely speculative given the lack of similar provisions and case law in Turkey.

As regards the law applicable to the substantive validity of testamentary dispositions, only the Regulation adopts separate and detailed rules. The main connecting factor is again the habitual residence of the testator at the time of making the disposition. The Treaty and the Turkish PILA do not provide different rules for testamentary and intestate succession and submit both to the general *lex successionis*. It is only in terms of testamentary capacity that the Turkish PILA provides that the national law of the testator should be applicable. When it comes to the law applicable to the formal validity of testamentary dispositions, this is one of the areas where there is harmony between the Turkish and the European sides thanks to the Hague Convention on the issue. The Treaty, however, has a separate rule on this matter which has a narrower scope as compared to the Hague Convention, and it is disadvantageous for today's world. One issue of characterisation which could be important for Turkish-EU successions is the characterisation of joint wills. In terms of their admissibility, the characterisation of such wills as an issue of form would be more in line with the principle of *favor testamenti*.

As regards other issues related to the law applicable to succession, the first one to be considered is *renvoi*. In line with its bilateral nature, *renvoi* is not applicable under the Treaty. The Turkish PILA similarly does not apply *renvoi* for succession matters. The Regulation allows *renvoi* in cases which are closely connected to third States, and this may again provide for harmony of decisions in Turkish-EU successions. The same is also true for the approach of the Regulation on overriding mandatory provisions. The Turkish rules on immovable property may become applicable before the European courts, thereby providing a level of harmony between Turkey and the EU, even though such rules of EU States may not become applicable before Turkish courts as there is no provision on the issue in the Turkish PILA. As a result of its bilateral nature, there is also no such provision in the Treaty, but there is also no need as the courts will always apply their own laws in cases falling within the scope of the Treaty. However, in terms of *ordre public*, despite the lack of a provision on the issue, there may be some cases where the Contracting States may have to refer to the *ordre public* exception by way of interpretation. This, however, should be possible only in extreme cases. For Turkish-EU successions, one issue which may have practical significance for *ordre public* in all of the legal instruments could be the succession rights of same-sex couples, cases in which either a Member State or Turkey may choose to use the 'emergency valve' of *ordre public* to depart from the otherwise applicable law. From the Turkish perspective, this should only come into play when the case has a significant connection to Turkey.

The issues which are important in cross-border successions upon death are definitely not limited to conflict-of-laws issues. There are also procedural issues to be discussed. The following chapter, thus, will focus on procedural issues in Turkish-EU successions.

Chapter 3

Procedural Issues in Turkish-EU Successions

Admittedly an unpleasant situation, '[d]eath is not the end; there remains the litigation over the estate'[1] for the surviving relatives and/or friends. There is no doubt that procedure, whose jurisdictional aspect in an international case actually arises as a question prior to the conflict-of-laws issues examined in the previous chapter, defines the rules of this 'elaborate game' known as litigation.[2] Notwithstanding this important role that it has, there is no common international procedural law applicable for all States, just as in the conflict of laws.[3] This is, as briefly mentioned in the first chapter, also the case in Turkish-EU successions. Accordingly, challenges may arise for the deceased in terms of his estate planning, as without the option of a forum selection the deceased cannot foresee which State's courts or authorities will carry out the proceedings related to his succession and whether his plans and arrangements prior to his death will ever be realised. Indeed, neither of the legal sources relevant for Turkish-EU successions allow the deceased to designate the forum prior to his death.[4] The variety of procedural rules causes difficulties also for the litigants who, upon the deceased's death, seek to enforce their succession rights in one of the two legal systems.

In the Turkish-EU context, two particular areas pose potentially significant problems as regards procedure. First and foremost, depending on how differently rules of procedure are drafted, there may be conflicts of jurisdiction between the courts of Member States and Turkey. Given the lack of coordination rules, these conflicts may not be avoidable and may give rise to inconsistent judgments. Moreover, when the beneficiaries of succession are in need of a European Certificate of Succession there may be problems as regards, first, issuance of the Certificate – particularly due to the existence of the

---

[1] Ambrose Bierce, *Complete Works of Ambrose Bierce* (ePUB, Delphi Classics 2013) A Cynic Looks at Life-Epigrams of a Cynic <https://www.delphiclassics.com> accessed 13 January 2021.

[2] Stephen C. Yeazell and Joanna C. Schwartz, *Civil Procedure* (10th edn, Wolters Kluwer 2019) 1–2.

[3] Ergin Nomer, *Milletlerarası Usul Hukuku* (2nd edn, Beta 2018) 2.

[4] For the Regulation, see Dutta, *MüKoBGB* (2020) EuErbVO Vorb. Art 4 para 25. The information provided below on the absence of a possibility to include a choice of court agreement, as considered from the Turkish and the Treaty perspective, also applies for the deceased. See below pp 249 ff.

Turkish-German Treaty, which has a practical significance in the EU by virtue of the number of Turkish nationals in Germany – and, second, recognition of this Certificate in Turkey in cases where the deceased left assets there. These issues will be respectively examined in detail below.

A. Jurisdiction

The Regulation provides harmonised jurisdictional rules under Articles 4–19 that are to be applicable in cross-border successions, with the targeted areas being the facilitation of succession proceedings, minimisation of forum shopping,[5] and the free circulation of judgments.[6] From these provisions, Article 4 is the one laying down the general principle for jurisdiction, and it adopts, in the same way as the conflict-of-laws provisions, habitual residence as the main connecting factor for establishing jurisdiction. The courts of the Member State where the deceased had his habitual residence at the time of death should be competent to rule on the succession as a whole. When this place is, nonetheless, located outside the Union, the courts of Member States in which the assets of the deceased are located will – or should, even *ex officio*[7] – have jurisdiction on a subsidiary basis, provided that certain conditions defined under Article 10 are met.

As with the European Maintenance Regulation[8] and the recently enacted European Matrimonial Property[9] and Partnership Regulations,[10] the Regulation principally adopts *erga omnes* jurisdictional rules that cover also situations in relation to third States.[11] This could be seen as a 'simpler and argua-

[5] Mansel, 'Vereinheitlichung des Internationalen Erbrechts in der EG' (2006) 189.

[6] Christian Kohler, 'Auf dem Weg zu einem europäischen Justizraum für das Familien- und Erbrecht' [2002] FamRZ 709, 710.

[7] In a recent judgment, the CJEU stated that even though Art 10 provides 'subsidiary' jurisdiction in relation to general jurisdiction under Art 4, this does not mean that it is less binding than Art 4. According to the CJEU, Art 10 has also a mandatory nature in the light of Recital 30, which clarifies the aim of the Regulation to 'ensure' that Member State courts will exercise jurisdiction on the same grounds even if the deceased was habitually resident in a third State. Therefore, as the CJEU held, the Member State Court seised with the dispute should, on its own motion, establish its jurisdiction also under Art 10 based on the uncontested facts satisfying the requirements of this provision, even if the parties never relied on this provision (and rather only argued for general jurisdiction under Art 4): C-645/20 V A, Z A v. TP [2022] ECLI:EU:C:2022:267 [29 ff]. For similar remarks, see also C-645/20 V A, Z A v. TP [2021] ECLI:EU:C:2021:977, Opinion of *AG Campos Sánchez-Bordona* [44 ff].

[8] See Arts 3–8 of the Regulation.

[9] See Arts 4–13 of the Regulation.

[10] See Arts 4–13 of the Regulation.

[11] Bonomi, *Bonomi/Wautelet* (2016) Introduction au Chapitre II – Compétence para 3; Davì, *Calvo Caravaca/Davì/Mansel* (2016) Introduction para 23; Eva Lein, in Anatol

bly better'[12] model for the EU, since no room is left for national jurisdictional rules which are divergent and thus might impair the ultimate harmonisation pursued by the Regulation. Outside the EU, however, jurisdiction conflicts may arise particularly in cases where the assets are located in third States,[13] including Turkey. The Regulation indeed espouses a purely *inter partes* perspective for the mechanisms designed to prevent such conflicts. Except for the limitation of proceedings under Article 12, the rules regarding the prorogation of jurisdiction (Article 5), declination of jurisdiction in the event of a choice of law (Article 6), *lis alibi pendens* (Article 17), and related actions (Article 18), which is not discussed in detail in this study, are, in principle,[14] applicable only between Member State courts.[15]

It is no surprise that Turkey, as an outsider to this system, has other rules of jurisdiction based on different considerations. In Turkish law, as in some of the European States,[16] internal jurisdiction rules (on venue) have, in principle, a dual functionality of also determining international jurisdiction. That is to say that when a court is competent to rule on a purely internal matter, it will also have jurisdiction over it when the matter involves foreign elements. Article 40 of the Turkish PILA, i.e. the main provision of international jurisdiction, articulates this as follows: 'the international jurisdiction of Turkish courts is determined by the jurisdiction rules of domestic law'. It is not to be doubted that this system for the allocation of international jurisdiction is easy to apply.[17] Notwithstanding this, domestic rules on venue may sometimes be inadequate or silent for certain international disputes. Therefore, specific rules are provided under Articles 41–46 of the Turkish PILA.[18] Legal suits concerning cross-border successions upon death are also among the issues for

---

Dutta and Johannes Weber (eds), *Internationales Erbrecht* (2nd edn, C.H. Beck 2021) EuErbVO Vorb. Art 4 ff para 40.

[12] Etienne Pataut, 'The External Dimension of Private International Family Law' in Marise Cremona and Hans-W. Micklitz (eds), *Private Law in the External Relations of the EU* (OUP 2016) 120.

[13] Harris, (2008) 22 Tru L I 181, 221; Maria Álvarez Torné, 'Key Points on the Determination of International Jurisdiction in the New EU Regulation on Succession and Wills' (2012–2013) XIV YbPIL 409, 413.

[14] There are, however, views on the reflexive application of these tools for third States. See, in this regard, below pp 246 ff, 256 ff, and 260 ff.

[15] Buonaiuti, (2016) 12 J Priv Int L 545, 548–549.

[16] Frank Vischer, 'General Course on Private International Law at the Hague Academy of International Law' (1992) 232 RdC 9, 205. For EU Member States, see Arnaud Nuyts, 'Study on Residual Jurisdiction – Review of the Member States' Rules concerning the "Residual Jurisdiction" of their courts in Civil and Commercial Matters pursuant to the Brussels I and II Regulations (JLS/C4/2005/07-30-CE)0040309/00-37)' 16–18 <https://gavclaw.files.wordpress.com/2020/05/arnaud-nuyts-study_residual_jurisdiction_en.pdf> accessed 15 January 2021.

[17] Çelikel and Erdem, *Milletlerarası Özel Hukuk* (2021) 566–567.

which the Turkish legislature provided a separate rule of jurisdiction under Article 43 of the Turkish PILA. Based on the underlying idea that natural persons often make their crucial legal transactions and administer their properties from this place,[19] the Article lays down that (Turkish) courts of the place where the deceased had his last domicile should be competent to hear the case. On the other hand, in cases where the last domicile of the deceased was in another State but some of the assets were located in Turkey, there could have been problems as to jurisdiction in practice. In order to clarify the issue, the Turkish legislature inserted a subsidiary jurisdiction rule in the second part of the provision by submitting such situations to the jurisdiction of (Turkish) courts in the place where the assets of the estate are located.[20]

Due the 'mixed approach'[21] of the Turkish PILA regarding international jurisdiction, one might question whether specific provisions under Article 41 et seq. of the Turkish PILA aim to provide merely additional rules of jurisdiction to the internal rules for international cases on the matters in their scope or whether they are rules of special jurisdiction for those matters which do not allow a reference back to domestic jurisdiction rules.[22]

Domestic rules of jurisdiction, particularly concerning succession matters, are found in Article 576 of the Turkish Civil Code and Article 11 of the Turkish Code of Civil Procedure. Article 576(2) of the Turkish Civil Code provides that actions to contest the validity of and for the reduction of dispositions of property upon death, actions for the sharing-out of the estate, and actions for the recovery of inheritance should be heard by the courts of the place where the deceased was domiciled. Article 11 of the Turkish Code of Civil Procedure, on the other hand, stipulates that the courts of the place at the last domicile of the deceased should have *exclusive* jurisdiction over these

---

[18] Nomer, *Milletlerarası Usul Hukuku* (2018) 89–90 and 98 ff; Çelikel and Erdem, *Milletlerarası Özel Hukuk* (2021) 566 ff; Şanlı, Esen and Ataman Figanmeşe, *Milletlerarası Özel Hukuk* (2021) 409–410 and 457 ff; Doğan, *Milletlerarası Özel Hukuk* (2022) 40 and 53 ff. This was the system adopted in Turkish law even in the previous versions of the Turkish PILA: Ergin Nomer, 'Devletler Hususi Hukukunda Milletlerarası Yetki Mefhumu' (1974) 40 İÜHFM 393, 413; Nuray Ekşi, *Türk Mahkemelerinin Milletlerarası Yetkisi* (2nd edn, Beta 2000) 44 ff.

[19] Mine Akkan, in Hakan Pekcanıtez and others (eds), *Pekcanıtez Usûl: Medenî Usûl Hukuku*, vol 1 (15th edn, On İki Levha 2017) § 3. Mahkemeler, 269; Reinhard Patzina, in Wolfgang Krüger and Thomas Rauscher (eds), *MüKoZPO*, vol 1 (6th edn, C.H. Beck 2020) ZPO § 13 para 1.

[20] İstanbul Üniversitesi Hukuk Fakültesi – Milletlerarası Hukuk ve Milletlerarası Münasebetler Enstitüsü, *MÖHUK Öntasarı Sempozyumu* (1978) 195 (*Atâ Sakmar*).

[21] Nuyts, 'Study on Residual Jurisdiction – Review of the Member States' Rules concerning the "Residual Jurisdiction" of their courts in Civil and Commercial Matters pursuant to the Brussels I and II Regulations (JLS/C4/2005/07-30-CE)0040309/00-37)' (2007) 17.

[22] Ekşi, *Milletlerarası Miras Hukuku* (2013) 22–24.

cases as well as cases arising, invalidity claims against agreements as to the sharing-out of the estate, the administration of the estate between the heirs, and all other cases to be filed against heirs until the final sharing-out the estate. It further provides that actions of persons who claim to have title over the assets against their possessors (pursuant to Article 683 of the Turkish Civil Code), e.g. where the asset was in possession of the deceased prior to death and hence passed to the community of heirs,[23] could also be brought before the courts of the place where those assets are found at the time of the estate inventory. The courts of the places where each of the heirs are domiciled are also competent to hear legal suits regarding the challenge of the certificate of succession and the issue of a new certificate to this effect.

In these latter two instances, the jurisdiction of the courts is not exclusive, and thus the cases could be brought before the other courts in accordance with general rules of procedure under Article 6 et seq. of the Turkish Code of Civil Procedure.[24] For instance, an action to contest the validity of a succession certificate could be brought by the claimant in the place where the deceased had his last domicile, in the place where the defendant has his domicile, or in the place where he resides.[25] For other cases which may be relevant to succession, general rules of jurisdiction will again be applicable.[26]

It is obvious that the first sentence of Article 43 of the Turkish PILA giving competence to (Turkish) courts located in the last domicile of the deceased does not represent a novelty and rather is merely a restatement of the jurisdiction rules of domestic law concerning succession under Article 576 of the Turkish Civil Code and Article 11(1) of the Turkish Code of Civil Procedure.[27] The second sentence of Article 43, diverging from these two internal competence rules, confers jurisdiction to the court of the place where the assets of the deceased are located for cases in which he died domiciled elsewhere. On the whole, nevertheless, the domestic rules seem to be broader than Article 43 of the Turkish PILA.[28] For instance, consider a German national who is domiciled in Berlin but who has a number of assets in Istanbul, Izmir, and Antalya and who has heirs not only in these cities but also in other cities; after he dies intestate, and right after his death, one of his heirs in Istanbul obtains a succession certificate which does not name all of the heirs.

---

[23] Baki Kuru, *Hukuk Muhakemeleri Usulü*, vol 1 (6th edn, Demir Demir 2001) 495.

[24] Kuru, *Hukuk Muhakemeleri Usulü/vol 1* (2001) 495–498.

[25] Yargıtay 2. Hukuk Dairesi, T. 5.10.1972, E. 1972/4866 K. 1972/5550 published in Kuru, *Hukuk Muhakemeleri Usulü/vol 1* (2001) 496.

[26] Kuru, *Hukuk Muhakemeleri Usulü/vol 1* (2001) 491. For some examples, see, Mustafa Reşit Belgesay, *Hukuk Muhakemeleri Kanunu Şerhi*, vol I (Güven Basımevi 1939) 42–44; Kuru, *Hukuk Muhakemeleri Usulü/vol 1* (2001) 491 fn 245.

[27] İstanbul Üniversitesi Hukuk Fakültesi – Milletlerarası Hukuk ve Milletlerarası Münasebetler Enstitüsü, *MÖHUK Öntasarı Sempozyumu* (1978) 195 (*Atâ Sakmar*).

[28] Cf. Berk Demirkol, *Milletlerarası Yetki Anlaşmaları* (Vedat Kitapçılık 2018) 23–24.

Those who were not indicated as heirs in the certificate would subsequently like to challenge its validity. If they are not resident in one of the three cities in which the assets are located but elsewhere in Turkey, they will not have the possibility to file a lawsuit in this regard before the courts of their places of residence pursuant to Article 43 of the Turkish PILA, but they will enjoy that possibility within the scope of Article 11(3) of the Turkish Code of Civil Procedure. This short example illustrates that domestic rules open the jurisdiction of more courts than Article 43 of the Turkish PILA. Therefore, the relationship between Article 40 – which makes a reference to domestic rules on venue for international jurisdiction – and Article 43 of the Turkish PILA should be briefly examined here.

In the first place, it could be argued that jurisdiction rules under Articles 41–46 of the Turkish PILA are only supplementary to domestic rules of jurisdiction, and both set of rules could be used to establish international jurisdiction of Turkish courts in cases involving foreign elements.[29] This view may seem to be significantly advantageous for litigants at first sight since the number of courts available would – as demonstrated in the above example – be greater. Nonetheless, since the legislature considered the importance and nature of cross-border disputes for some matters and laid down specific jurisdiction rules for them,[30] the international jurisdiction of Turkish courts should be determined in accordance with these rules in relation to those matters, including succession.[31] Consequently, in this paper, only Article 43 of the Turkish PILA is subjected to a comparative analysis.

---

[29] Kuru, *Hukuk Muhakemeleri Usulü/vol 1* (2001) 638–640; cf. Fügen Sargın, *Milletlerarası Usul Hukukunda Yetki Anlaşmaları* (Yetkin 1996) 154; Ekşi, *Milletlerarası Yetki* (2000) 47; Nomer, *Milletlerarası Usul Hukuku* (2018) 120.

The Turkish Court of Cassation also refers to domestic rules and the rules of the Turkish PILA together in some cases, see, for example, Yargıtay 2. Hukuk Dairesi, T. 24.6.1999, E. 1999/5494 K. 1999/7289 <https://legalbank.net/> accessed 27 January 2021.

[30] İstanbul Üniversitesi Hukuk Fakültesi – Milletlerarası Hukuk ve Milletlerarası Münasebetler Enstitüsü, *MÖHUK Öntasarı Sempozyumu* (1978) 195 (*Atâ Sakmar*).

[31] Uğur Tütüncübaşı, *Yabancı Çekişmesiz Yargı Kararlarının Türk Hukukunda Tanınması* (Adalet Yayınevi 2014) 156; Neşe Baran Çelik, 'Türkiye'de Yabancılık Unsuru İçeren Mirasçılık Belgelerinin Düzenlenmesi' (2019) 24 DÜHFD 439, 448; Özkan and Tütüncübaşı, *Uluslararası Usûl Hukuku* (2020) 85; Tekinalp, *Milletlerarası Özel Hukuk* (2020) 408 and 411; Musab Bilkay, 'Miras Hukukuna İlişkin Dava ve İşlerde Türk Mahkemelerinin Milletlerarası Yetkisi' (2021) 41 MHB 905, 917; Çelikel and Erdem, *Milletlerarası Özel Hukuk* (2021) 567; Güngör, *Türk Milletlerarası Özel Hukuku* (2021) 257; Şanlı, Esen and Ataman Figanmeşe, *Milletlerarası Özel Hukuk* (2021) 458–459; Feriha Bilge Tanrıbilir, 'Kişi Halleri ve Mirasa İlişkin Milletlerarası Yetki Kurallarının Kapsamı' in Sibel Özel and Hatice Selin Pürselim (eds), *Milletlerarası Usul Hukukunda Mahkemelerin Yetkisine İlişkin Güncel Tartışmalar: Ulusal Konferans 20 Şubat 2021* (On İki Levha 2021) 78 and 93 ff; Doğan, *Milletlerarası Özel Hukuk* (2022) 62. As regards to succession, see also Ekşi, *Milletlerarası Yetki* (2000) 161; Ekşi, *Milletlerarası Miras Hukuku* (2013) 23; Tanrıbilir,

Whilst the Turkish PILA and the Regulation appear to adopt similar criteria for the allocation of general jurisdiction – one being based on the last domicile and the other one being based on the last habitual residence of the deceased – the meaning of the terms in each legal system and their interpretation by the courts may not always overlap, and this may give rise to jurisdiction conflicts between the two systems.[32] Similar conflicts can also arise with the exercise of subsidiary jurisdiction by one State court in a situation where a different State – specifically one of its courts – still deems the case closely connected with its territory and, hence, also asserts jurisdiction over it. One can also think of extreme cases with an additional non-EU country involved in which a conflict of jurisdiction between a court of that country, a Member State court and a Turkish court arises as result of their jurisdiction rules. Such possible conflicts would be especially important when immovable properties are present as to which the Turkish side asserts exclusive jurisdiction. When this is the case, as said earlier, the means to avoid jurisdiction conflicts (or at least to stop them at the level of jurisdiction contests before even turning into conflicts,[33] such as by allowing parties to enter into choice of court agreements or by making use of a *lis pendens* objection) are, according to the Regulation, applicable only between the Member States. The issue is also not subject to resolution from the Turkish side since those tools are not available in the Turkish PILA.

There is of course a small subsection of international cases involving the EU and Turkey where such conflicts do not come into play and that is when bilateral treaties existing between Turkey and three Member States – namely Germany, Italy, and Hungary – which also cover the issue of jurisdiction in cross-border succession are applicable. As this study only focuses on the Turkish-German Treaty, its rules on jurisdiction can be briefly mentioned here. Article 20(15) of the Treaty, like the Regulation, adopts a parallel approach to the matter of the applicable law and prescribes that succession issues on movable properties should be subject to the jurisdiction of the courts of the national State of the deceased at the time of death; and, on immovable properties, the courts of the *situs*. Concerning the legal background of the Treaty and the *ratio legis*, these rules seem to have an exclusive nature.

While the existence of the Treaty does to a certain extent provide for uniformity of jurisdiction in Turkish-EU succession cases, the dualist approach that is preferred in the Treaty (also in respect of jurisdiction) as well as its exclusive character even for movables proves that the Treaty has different and, in today's legal world, extraordinary rules in comparison to the Regulation

---

'MÖHUK ve Mirasa İlişkin Bağlama Kuralının Uygulanmasında Öne Çıkan Hususlar' (2018) 129; cf. Demirkol, *Yetki Anlaşmaları* (2018) 22–24.

[32] Cf. Tekinalp, *Milletlerarası Özel Hukuk* (2020) 411.

[33] See, for such remarks, Romano, (2015–2016) XVII YbPIL 253, 268.

and the Turkish PILA. Therefore, the comparative analysis as regards jurisdiction in this part should also include a look at the approach of the Treaty.

I. General Jurisdiction: Habitual Residence, Domicile, and Nationality + situs Compared

Although public international law stipulates the need for the existence of a genuine link to the case,[34] each legal system is, as a manifestation of its regulatory power, free to determine when their courts will exercise jurisdiction over a case. States may, at their own discretion, choose to follow as the required genuine link the principle of personality (i.e. assertion of jurisdiction based on nationality), as was the case in earlier times, or the principle of territoriality (i.e. opening the jurisdiction of a State court for a case when there is a territorial connection of the case to that State). Even the territorial connection, however, may be established differently by the States based on a wide range of policy considerations.[35] This is also the case for the question of general jurisdiction as regards succession in the Regulation, the Turkish PILA, and the Treaty. Both the Regulation and the Turkish PILA adhere to the territoriality principle for general jurisdiction. Nevertheless, the Regulation prefers habitual residence as the main connecting factor, whereas the Turkish PILA gives preference to domicile. The Treaty, on the other hand, combines the principles of territoriality and personality to determine jurisdiction on succession for movable and immovable assets of the deceased. Each of these legal systems has its own policy considerations for these choices. The underlying interests and the interpretation of these connecting factors should be examined here in detail, respectively.

The jurisdictional rules of the Regulation are developed so as to assure that the competent authority, in most of the cases, will apply its own law when dealing with the succession (such that *Gleichlauf* will be realised).[36] This principle attracted praise in the literature given its ability to satisfy procedural and party interests. In succession matters, procedural law and substantive law are often intertwined. When the courts apply their own laws, there is inevitably a reduction in the costs associated with estate administration and the enforcement of succession rights. Furthermore, the problems attached to the application of foreign law, such as issues of adaptation or characterisation, may to a certain extent be averted.[37]

---

[34] Alex Mills, 'Rethinking Jurisdiction in International Law' (2014) 84 BYIL 187, 194.

[35] Mills, (2014) 84 BYIL 187, 200 ff.

[36] See Recommendation 2 of the European Parliament Resolution with Recommendations to the Commission on Succession and Wills (2005/2148(INI), P6_TA(2006)0496) and the first sentence of Recital 27 of the Regulation.

[37] Dörner and others, [2005] IPRax 1, 4; Mansel, 'Vereinheitlichung des Internationalen Erbrechts in der EG' (2006) 201; Max Planck Institute for Comparative and International

In order to achieve such parallelism, Article 4 of the Regulation, as the cornerstone of the jurisdictional rules together with Article 10, prescribes that Member State courts of the place where the deceased had his last habitual residence should have jurisdiction to rule on the succession as a whole. This has indeed been a novelty for the laws of Member States within the field of succession, which had previously adopted divergent connecting factors and focused on different interests when allocating international jurisdiction among their courts.[38] It is, however, consonant with the focal interest of EU law to enhance the mobility and the integration of EU citizens within the Union.[39] In this sense, habitual residence, as the principal connecting factor applicable in all Member States when assuming jurisdiction in succession cases, enables parties to escape from the complex and conflicting domestic provisions of the Member States that yield positive as well as negative jurisdiction conflicts,[40] thus allowing them to easily conduct their estate planning before their death and to foresee which courts will be competent to hear the case.[41] In addition, this place also helps to maintain procedural interests, since the place where the last habitual residence of the deceased is found mostly coincides with the deceased's centre of interests, with the location where the estate of the deceased is located,[42] and the place where the heirs reside.[43]

Private Law, (2010) 74 RabelsZ 522, 605; Dieter Leipold, 'Die internationale Zuständigkeit in erbrechtlichen Verfahren (nach deutschem Recht und nach dem Kommissionsvorschlag für eine Europäische Erbrechtsverordnung)' in Jacek Gudowski and Karol Weitz (eds), *Aurea Praxis Aurea Theoria: Księga Pamiątkowa ku Czci Profesora Tadeusza Erecińskiego*, vol 1 (LexisNexis 2011) 1178 ff; Stefan Georg Seyfarth, 'Wandel der internationalen Zuständigkeit im Erbrecht' (DPhil Thesis, Universität Konstanz 2012) 238 ff <http://kops.uni-konstanz.de/handle/123456789/19299> accessed 17 January 2017; Ulrich Simon and Markus Buschbaum, 'Die neue EU-Erbrechtsverordnung' [2012] NJW 2393, 2394; Döbereiner, [2013] MittBayNot 358, 361; Burkhard Hess, 'Die internationale Zuständigkeit nach der Erbrechtsverordnung' in Anatol Dutta and Sebastian Herrler (eds), *Die Europäische Erbrechtsverordnung, 20 Jahre DNotI 1993–2013* (C.H. Beck 2014) 134; Dutta, *MüKoBGB* (2020) EuErbVO Vorb. Art 4 para 3; Lein, *Dutta/Weber* (2021) EuErbVO Vorb. Art 4 ff para 24.

[38] DNotI (in collaboration with Heinrich Dörner and Paul Lagarde), 'DNotI Report' (2004) 193 ff.

[39] Lein, *Dutta/Weber* (2021) EuErbVO Art 4 para 2. See also, Recital 23 of the Regulation.

[40] Explanatory Memorandum attached to Commission Proposal (COM(2009) 154 Final) under 4.2 in the explanation to Art 4.

[41] Lein, *Dutta/Weber* (2021) EuErbVO Art 4 para 3.

[42] Explanatory Memorandum attached to Commission Proposal (COM(2009) 154 Final) under 4.2 in the explanation to Art 4, under 4.3 in the explanation to Art 16.

[43] See, Point II in Explanatory Statement attached to European Parliament Resolution (2005/2148(INI), P6_TA(2006)0496). For the positive comments in favour of habitual residence also for the purposes of jurisdiction, see, for example, D. Lehmann, [2005] ZErb 320, 321 ff; Kindler, [2010] IPRax 44, 45; Max Planck Institute for Comparative and Inter-

Unlike the European Union – which acts on behalf of a number of States, prioritises community interests, and attempts to reconcile different systems in order to avoid problems – Turkey, as a single State, unsurprisingly drafted the jurisdictional rule for succession in the light of its own domestic interests and experience. As mentioned earlier, domestic rules concerning jurisdiction in succession cases have for a long time espoused the domicile connecting factor[44] with the belief, similar to that of the EU, that this place typically where the majority of a person's legal relationships and transactions are centred. This was reiterated by Article 30 of the former Turkish PILA for cross-border cases, and it was adopted without any amendments also under Article 43 of the Turkish PILA.

On the side of the Treaty, the historical experience of Turkey and the circumstances of the time were major determinants for the formulation of Article 20(15) on jurisdiction. During the capitulary regime, as explained in Chapter 1 above,[45] Ottoman courts had in principle no jurisdiction on *statut personnel* matters of foreign nationals, which included succession on movable property. In the first decades of the 20th century, the Empire began to abolish this unbearable and, from the perspective of sovereignty, demeaning legal order and undertook reforms to remove its traces. The first private international legislation in Turkish history, namely the Temporary Act, was one of the reforms made in this period. However, the reform process concerning the legal order and the judiciary in the Ottoman Empire was only at its early stages,[46] and there was a firm belief that Ottoman judges were not experienced enough with the application of foreign law,[47] which was also articulated during the negotiations of the Treaty of Lausanne.[48] Therefore, Article 4 of the Act retained the nationality connecting factor to establish jurisdiction for movables. According to this rule, the succession issues of foreign nationals concerning movable property was to be dealt with by the courts of their national State, unless the parties brought the case before Turkish courts, or the

---

national Private Law, (2010) 74 RabelsZ 522, 568; Leipold, 'Die Internationale Zuständigkeit in Erbrechtlichen Verfahren' (2011) 1168; Kunz, [2012] GPR 208, 210; Simon and Buschbaum, [2012] NJW 2393, 2395.

[44] See Art 576(2) of the Turkish Civil Code and Art 11(1) of the Turkish Code of Civil Procedure. This was also the rule in earlier versions of both provisions: Art 518 of the former Turkish Civil Code ('743 sayılı Türk Kanunu Medenisi', *Resmi Gazete* of 4.4.1926, no 339) and Art 11(1) of the former Turkish Code of Civil Procedure ('1086 Sayılı Hukuk Usulü Muhakemeleri Kanunu', *Resmi Gazete* of 02,03,4.7.1927, no 622, 623, 624).

[45] See above Chapter 1 under C.I. pp 28–34

[46] M. R. Seviğ, *Sentez* (1941) 34.

[47] Nomer, *Yabancıların "Ahkamı Şahsiyesi"* (1973) 500–501.

[48] *Lausanne Conference on Near Eastern Affairs (1922–1923) – Records of Proceedings and Draft Terms of Peace [With Map]* (His Majesty's Stationery Office 1923) 481 ff (English Translation). For the Turkish Translation of the Records of Proceedings, see Seha L. Meray, *Lozan Barış Konferansı – Tutanaklar, Belgeler* (3rd edn, Yapı Kredi Yayınları 2001) (for the discussion, see specifically, vol. I-1 40–41).

case involved Turkish nationals, or there was a relevant pending case before the Turkish courts. For immovable property, on the other hand, both the rules of the capitulations and Article 4 of the Temporary Act conferred jurisdiction onto Turkish courts due to the importance of this property for the State. In parallel to this background, the Treaty also maintained the twofold system which combines the territorial and personal approaches on jurisdiction with the nationality and *situs* connecting factors under its Article 20(15), but which provided no exception to the jurisdiction of the courts of the home State of the deceased for movables, as opposed to the Temporary Act.

From these three different approaches, the most extraordinary one is undoubtedly the approach of the Treaty. Even though the legal background of the Treaty justifies such a rule, especially its part in relation to movables which result in Turkish courts having no jurisdiction over succession issues concerning movable assets found in their own territories,[49] one should accept that it contrasts with modern rules on international jurisdiction, including Article 43 of the Turkish PILA, and more importantly raises difficulties for nationals of each Contracting State living in the other State, particularly for Turkish immigrants in Germany, whose numbers are considerable.[50]

The outcome of each rule could be illustrated with an example. For example, *(G)*, who is a Greek national married with Turkish national *(T)* and who lived most of his life entirely in his home town, Thessaloniki, apart from the short-term holidays he spent with his wife in different countries – the most frequent of which was Turkey – dies intestate during one of his holidays in Turkey. He leaves behind movable and immovable assets in Greece; and in Turkey he leaves behind a car, which he kept there to use during his holidays,

[49] A similar rule in the field of succession was also found in Article 16 of the Convention Respecting Conditions of Residence and Business and Jurisdiction, adopted for a period of seven years in 1923 between Turkey and the States belonging to the Allied Powers, including Italy, as an annex to the Treaty of Lausanne. This Convention was in its last year in force or was already abolished by the time when Turkey concluded its bilateral treaties with Germany, Italy, and Hungary, and the reform of the succession rules was already accomplished with the adoption of the Turkish Civil Code in 1926. However, it is still noteworthy that the rule has been left unchanged in the bilateral treaties with Germany, Italy, and Hungary: V. R. Seviğ, *Ahkâmı Şahsiye Davaları – Yetki* (1964) 9.

For the text of the Convention mentioned, see (1924) 18(2) AJIL – Supplement: Official Documents 67.

[50] Dörner, [1996] ZEV 90, 96; Bergü Ercan, 'Deutsch-Türkische erbrechtliche Probleme' (1996) 5 Informationsbrief der DTJV 6, 9; Murat Atalı, *Internationale Zuständigkeit im deutsch-türkischen Rechtsverkehr* (Peter Lang 2001) 123; Bauer, [2007] FamRZ 1250, 1256; Majer, [2012] ZEV 182, 186; Hilmar Krüger, 'Neues zum deutsch-türkischen Nachlassabkommen – Zu einer Initiative des nordrhein-westfälischen Justizministers –' (2013) 22 Informationsbrief der DTJV 4, 5; Sütçü, [2015] ZErb 43, 45; cf. Güneş, 'The Relations of Turkey with EU Member States' (2019) 313. See also Göğer, *Devletler Hususi Hukuku* (1977) 335–337 (with regards to the Temporary Act).

as well as a house where he and his wife spent their holidays. Upon his death, his widow and his children from his former marriage have a conflict over the division of inheritance, and they would like to take the matter to court. In such a case, the courts of Thessaloniki, as the courts of the Member State in which the deceased had his last habitual residence (pursuant to Article 4 of the Regulation) will have jurisdiction to rule on the succession as a whole. Whereas the subsidiary jurisdiction of Turkish courts will come into play in this case due to the car and the house in Turkey, Turkish courts lack general jurisdiction according to the first sentence of Article 43 of the Turkish PILA, since *(G)*, also from a Turkish perspective, was not domiciled in Turkey. If, however, *(G)* were a German national and all references to Greece were replaced by references to Germany, the case would be partly governed by the Regulation and partly by the Turkish-German Treaty. For assets in Germany, German courts would have jurisdiction in accordance with Article 4 of the Regulation. Succession on the car and the house in Turkey, however, would fall within the scope of the Turkish-German Treaty. Whereas German courts would be competent for the car, Turkish courts would be competent for the house under the scope of Article 20(15) of the Treaty.

As demonstrated with this simple example, even though the result reached through the application of the Treaty is totally different from the Regulation and the Turkish PILA, it is possible that these latter two legal instruments may sometimes produce at least partly consonant results and may not give rise to jurisdiction conflicts. This is mainly due to the fact that the centre of interests of the deceased should be examined when assessing each of the connecting factors.[51] Notwithstanding this, there might still be instances in which both jurisdictions allege that the last habitual residence or domicile of the deceased is in their territories.[52] European courts have to make an autonomous interpretation of the term habitual residence, taking their guidance from the former cases and from the recital of the Regulation and taking all circumstances of the case into account. Turkish courts, on the other hand, should make their analysis in accordance with Turkish domestic law due to the fact that the *lex fori* applies to the characterisation of the connecting factors under Turkish procedural law[53] as well as under earlier judgments given

[51] Kenan Tunçomağ, 'İkametgâh' (1961) 26 İÜHFM 153, 154; Ivo Schwander, 'Die EU-Erbrechtsverordnung' [2014] AJP 1084, 1090.

[52] Schwander, [2014] AJP 1084, 1090.

[53] Atâ Sakmar, *Devletler Hususi Hukukunda Boşanma* (İstanbul Üniversitesi Hukuk Fakültesi Yayınları 1976) 67; Ekşi, *Milletlerarası Yetki* (2000) 35–36; Nomer, *Milletlerarası Usul Hukuku* (2018) 38; Çelikel and Erdem, *Milletlerarası Özel Hukuk* (2021) 507; Şanlı, Esen and Ataman Figanmeşe, *Milletlerarası Özel Hukuk* (2021) 465; Doğan, *Milletlerarası Özel Hukuk* (2022) 55. See also Yargıtay 2. Hukuk Dairesi, T. 27.5.1998, E. 1998/4842 K. 1998/6521 <http://www.kazanci.com> accessed 20 January 2021.

on the issue. The meaning of the terms, therefore, should be examined in both of the jurisdictions.

1. The Concept of Habitual Residence under the Regulation

The use of habitual residence as a connecting factor is not a new phenomenon in European private international law[54] due to the influence of the Hague Conference.[55] Notwithstanding this fact, the meaning of the concept, which was once described as lying 'midway between domicile and residence',[56] remains equivocal.[57] This is because the European legislature has left the concept undefined in its instruments, as it has always been deemed 'a question of fact'[58] to be decided by reference to all the circumstances of any particular case. In line with this practice and in spite of all the arguments raised already during the drafting stage against not providing a definition,[59] the

---

Although the *lex fori* characterisation of connecting factors in Turkish procedural law may have some exceptions, the concept of domicile is certainly not one of these exceptions: Melis Avşar, *Milletlerarası Usul Hukukunda Mahkemelerin Yetkisinin Belirlenmesinde Tarafların İrade Serbestisi* (On İki Levha 2021) 30; Begüm Süzen, 'Milletlerarası Usul Hukukunda Yetki Kurallarında Kullanılan Bağlama Noktalarının Vasıflandırılması' in Sibel Özel and Hatice Selin Pürselim (eds), *Milletlerarası Usul Hukukunda Mahkemelerin Yetkisine İlişkin Güncel Tartışmalar: Ulusal Konferans 20 Şubat 2021* (On İki Levha 2021) 47–48.

[54] See Art 3 and Arts 8–10 of the Brussels IIa Regulation; Art 3(a) and (b), and Art 4(1)(a) of the European Maintenance Regulation; Art 19 of the Rome I Regulation; Art 23 of the Rome II Regulation; Art 5(a) and (b), and Art 8(a) and (b) of the Rome III Regulation as well as most recently Art 5(2) (a) and (b), and Art 6(a), (b) and (c) of the European Matrimonial Property Regulation; and Art 6(a), (b) and (c) of the European Partnership Regulation.

[55] A reference to habitual residence is found in even earlier conventions of the Hague Conference, such as the one relating to civil procedure from 1896 (<https://assets.hcch.net/docs/438b59d0-e6a2-454a-b818-0e3b211fc050.pdf> accessed 21 January 2021), which was later replaced by the 1905 version (<https://www.hcch.net/en/instruments/the-old-conventions/1905-civil-procedure-convention> accessed 21 January 2021). Its use can be traced to the influence of a civil procedure treaty between Germany and France from 1880 (RGBl. 1881 I, 81) referring to the German legal concept of '*gewöhnlicher Aufenthalt*' and its French translation '*résidence habituelle*': Matthijs H. van Hoogstraten, 'La codification par traités en droit international privé dans le cadre de la Conférence de la Haye' (1967) 122 RdC 337, 359; David McClean, 'De Conflictu Legum, Perspectives on Private International Law at the Turn of the Century' (2000) 282 RdC 41, 81.

[56] Graveson, *The Conflict of Laws* (1974) 194.

[57] Schoenblum, *Multistate and Multinational Estate Planning* (2008) § 9-30.

[58] McClean, (2000) 282 RdC 41, 81.

[59] See, for example, Hayton, 'Determination of the Objectively Applicable Law Governing Succession' (2004) 363 ff; Lein, (2009) XI YbPIL 107, 128 ff; House of Lords European Union Committee, 'Minutes of Evidence on the EU's Regulation on Succession – 6th Report of Session' 65–66 (Written Evidence by *Elizabeth Crawford* and *Janeen Car-*

Regulation similarly chose not to define the concept, giving instead some guidance to the courts in its recitals that should be taken into account in complex cases in order to ensure an autonomous interpretation.[60]

As Recitals 23 and 24 stipulate, the courts should make 'an overall assessment of the circumstances of the life of the deceased during the years preceding his death and at the time of his death' in order to determine the place 'in which the centre of interests of his family and social life was located'.[61] Certain key elements of a habitual residence can be deduced from these recitals. According to this, the duration and the regularity of the presence of the deceased in the relevant State; the purpose and the conditions of such presence, such as whether the deceased worked or acquired property in that State, or whether he took his family with him;[62] and the level connection of the deceased to that State,[63] such as being the national of that State or having

---

ruthers); Angelique Devaux, 'The European Regulations on Succession of July 2012: A Path Towards the End of Succession Conflicts of Law in Europe, or Not?' (2013) 47 TIL 229, 232–233; contra Buschbaum and Kohler, [2010] GPR 106, 112; Max Planck Institute for Comparative and International Private Law, (2010) 74 RabelsZ 522, 605 ff.

It is also mostly accepted that the ambiguity of the term could result in problems in the practice. See, for instance, Leipold, 'Die Internationale Zuständigkeit in Erbrechtlichen Verfahren' (2011) 1171; Knut Werner Lange, 'Das Erbkollisionsrecht im neuen Entwurf einer EU-ErbVO' [2012] ZErb 160, 162.

See also, from the perspectives of third States, Kalt and Uhl, 'Die EU-Erbrechtsverordnung und die Schweiz' (2013) 115; Dormann, 'Schweiz und EuErbVO' (2014) 84; Schwander, [2014] AJP 1084, 1090; Lein, 'Die Erbrechtsverordnung aus Sicht der Drittstaaten' (2014) 215–216; Daniel Leu, 'Die EU-Erbrechtsverordnung und ihre Bedeutung aus Schweizer Sicht' [2016] SJZ 441, 443.

[60] Süß, [2009] ZErb 342, 343 ff; Buschbaum and Kohler, [2010] GPR 106, 112; Kunz, [2012] GPR 208, 210; Lorenz, [2012] ErbR 39, 44; Wilke, [2012] RIW 601, 603; Burandt, [2013] FuR 377, 382; Stephanie Herzog, 'Die EU-Erbrechtsverordnung (EU-ErbVO)' [2013] ErbR 2, 6; Kalt and Uhl, 'Die EU-Erbrechtsverordnung und die Schweiz' (2013) 118 ff; Renate Schaub, 'Die EU-Erbrechtsverordnung' in Karlheinz Muscheler (ed), *Hereditare – Jahrbuch für Erbrecht und Schenkungsrecht* (Mohr Siebeck 2013) 112; Maximilian Seibl, 'Objektive und subjektive Anknüpfungen im Internationalen Erbrecht: ein Vergleich der bisherigen Rechtslage und der ErbVO' in Andreas Spickhoff (ed), *Symposium Parteiautonomie im Europäischen Internationalen Privatrecht* (Deutscher NotarVerlag 2013) 133; Heinig, [2014] RNotZ 197, 199; Bonomi, *Bonomi/Wautelet* (2016) ESR Art 4 para 14; Heinrich Dörner, 'Erbauseinandersetzung und Bestellung eines Minderjährigenpflegers nach Inkrafttreten der EuErbVO' [2016] ZEV 117, 118; Astrid Deixler-Hübner, in Astrid Deixler-Hübner and Martin Schauer (eds), *Kommentar zur EU-Erbrechtsverordnung* (2nd edn, Manz 2020) EuErbVO Art 4 paras 13–14; Lein, *Dutta/Weber* (2021) EuErbVO Art 4 para 9.

[61] See Recital 24 of the Regulation.

[62] Solomon, 'Die allgemeine Kollisionsnorm' (2014) 3.

[63] A 'close and stable connection with the State concerned' is needed in order for a place to be regarded as the habitual residence of the deceased: Recital 23 of the Regulation.

his main assets there,[64] should be taken into consideration when determining the habitual residence. These factors play an important role also in the case law of the CJEU, particularly in the context of the Brussels IIa Regulation[65] when determining the habitual residence of the child in question.[66]

It is disputed whether a subjective element, i.e. an intention to stay in the State concerned (*animus manendi*), is also needed when determining the habitual residence of the deceased within the scope of the Regulation. Some commentators argue that only purely objective elements should be decisive for the courts,[67] and hence that neither the intention of the deceased to settle at a place permanently[68] nor the intention to make this place the centre of his interests[69] is relevant for the determination of habitual residence within the scope of the Regulation. On the other hand, it is undeniable, particularly for migrant communities, that there might be circumstances where relying on purely objective elements may not be of much help. For instance, where the deceased always had a desire to return to his national State, a place still could not properly be considered his habitual residence despite its being a long-term place of residence.[70] Thus, the intention of the deceased cannot be com-

---

[64] Recital 24 of the Regulation.

[65] Regulation (EC) No 2201/2003 of 27 November 2003 concerning jurisdiction and the recognition and enforcement of judgments in matrimonial matters and the matters of parental responsibility, repealing Regulation (EC) No 1347/2000 [2003] OJ L 338.

[66] See, for example, C-523/07 A. [2009] ECR I-02805 [38 ff]; C-497/10 PPU Barbara Mercredi v. Richard Chaffe [2010] ECR I-14309 [44 ff]; C-376/14 PPU C v. M [2014] EU:C:2014:2268 [54 ff]; C-499/15 W and V v. X [2017] EU:C:2017:118 [60 ff]; C-111/17 PPU OL v. PQ [2017] EU:C:2017:436 [42 ff].

[67] Max Planck Institute for Comparative and International Private Law, (2010) 74 RabelsZ 522, 605; Kinga M. Weiss and Manuel Bigler, 'Die EU Erbrechtsverordnung – Neue Herausforderungen für die internationale Nachlassplanung aus Schweizer Sicht' [2014] Successio 163, 167; Barbara Graham-Siegenthaler, 'Die EU-Erbrechtsverordnung und deren Auswirkungen auf die Nachlassplanung in der Schweiz' [2015] Jusletter 6.

See, for the argument that objective factors should be given considerable weight, Bettina Heiderhoff, 'Das vertrackte subjektive Element des gewöhnlichen Aufenthalts (zu OLG Düsseldorf, 26.6.2018 – I-3 Wx 214/16)' [2019] IPRax 506; Abbo Junker, 'Die Dogmatik der Aufenthaltszuständigkeit nach der Europäischen Erbrechtsverordnung' in Christoph Althammer and Christoph Schärtl (eds), *Dogmatik als Fundament für Forschung und Lehre – Festschrift für Herbert Roth zum 70. Geburtstag* (Mohr Siebeck 2021) 759–761. See also OLG Frankfurt am Main 14.9.2020 – 21 W 59/20, openJur 2020, 74330 para 45.

[68] Döbereiner, [2013] MittBayNot 358, 362; Reinhold Geimer, 'Die europäische Erbrechtsverordnung im Überblick' in Johannes Hager (ed), *Die neue europäische Erbrechtsverordnung* (Nomos 2013) 25; Odersky, [2013] Notar 3, 5; Müller-Lukoschek, *Die neue EU-Erbrechtsverordnung* (2015) § 2 para 142; Leu, [2016] SJZ 441, 443.

[69] Dörner, [2012] ZEV 505, 510; Weiss and Bigler, [2014] Successio 163, 167. See also BGH 29.10.1980 – IVb ZB 586/80, BGHZ 78, 293, 295.

[70] Anna Junghardt, *Die Vereinheitlichung des Erb- und Testamentrechts im Rahmen einer Europäischen Verordnung – Rom IV – VO* (S. Roderer 2009) 85–86.

pletely disregarded.[71] The CJEU has also stressed that the intention of a permanent stay as manifested through concrete steps such as the purchase or, at least, the leasing of a property in the State of residence could be an 'indicator' when determining the habitual residence.[72]

Despite this guidance, there are nevertheless many cases in which the habitual residence of the deceased at the time of death is a subject of dispute – a situation which has already specifically been acknowledged by the Regulation (Recital 24) – when the deceased had, for instance, changed his habitual residence shortly before death, spent his life as a resident of more than one State at the same time,[73] or never lost his connection to his national State.[74] A number of complex cases, therefore, have already been identified in the litera-

---

[71] Junghardt, *Die Vereinheitlichung des Erb- und Testamentrechts* (2009) 85–86; Kunz, [2012] GPR 208, 211; D. Lehmann, [2012] DStR 2085, 2086–2087; Döbereiner, [2013] MittBayNot 358, 362; Schaub, 'Die EU-Erbrechtsverordnung' (2013) 113; Solomon, 'Die allgemeine Kollisionsnorm' (2014) 24ff; Weiss and Bigler, [2014] Successio 163, 167; Jacopo Re, 'Where Did They Live? Habitual Residence in the Succession Regulation' [2018] RDIPP 978, 980.

See also e.g. OLG Hamm 10.7.2020 – 10 W 108/18, BeckRS 2020, 20439. In this case, the deceased was a German national who died in the Czech Republic where he had lived for an important amount of time and even ran a business in the past. In the years prior to his death, he actually lived in Germany for many years, but almost one year before his death and after being separated from his wife he moved to the Czech Republic again. During this time, he visited Germany many times to consult doctors as well as lawyers, and he never unregistered his residence from Germany and registered himself in the Czech Republic. In the light of these facts alleged by the parties, the Court found that the deceased did not have such an intention for his residence in the Czech Republic, while underlining that the intention to stay in a place is required in addition to actual residence in that place. See, in this regard, particularly paras 21ff.

[72] See, for example, C-523/07 A. [2009] ECR I-02805 [40]; C-497/10 PPU Barbara Mercredi v. Richard Chaffe [2010] ECR I-14309 [51]. In a case that is closely connected to a third State (the U.S.A.), the 1st Civil Chamber of the French Court of Cassation considered the deceased's intention to be buried with his parents in Brooklyn, i.e. a subjective element, along with objective elements, i.e. the U.S. nationality of the deceased and the fact that the majority of his assets were in New York, as indicators of habitual residence: Cass. 1ère civ., 29 mai 2019, n° 18-13383 <https://www.legifrance.gouv.fr/juri/id/JURITEXT000038629401/> accessed 5 March 2022. See, for the comments in this regard, Steffen Kurth, 'Ein Amerikaner in Paris: Zur Bestimmung des gewöhnlichen Aufenthalts eines Weltenbummlers für die Zwecke der EUErbVO? – zugleich Anmerkung zu Cour de cassation, 29.5.2019 – Cass. Civ. 1 Nr. 18–13.383' [2020] ErbR 618, 619–620.

[73] Weiss and Bigler, [2014] Successio 163, 167ff.

It is proposed that in cases where the deceased has the same degree of link with more than one State at the same time, one should look for the 'activating' habitual residence which is located in the place where he lived at the time of death: Pazdan and Zachariasiewicz, (2021) 17 J Priv Int L 74, 87.

[74] Anatol Dutta, 'Das internationale Familien- und Erbrecht in der Rechtsprechung des Gerichtshofs der Europäischen Union – die vergangenen fünf Jahre' [2020] ZEuP 897, 943.

ture which may give rise to concurrent jurisdiction not only between Member State courts but also between Member State courts and third State courts. Such cases which may also arise in the Turkish-European context may be separated into two main groups: temporary residence abroad and multiple residences in different States.

a) Two Complex Case Groups

aa) Temporary Residence Abroad

The first group of cases in which determining habitual residence may prove to be difficult, as Recital 24 of the Regulation has already identified, are cases where the deceased had lived abroad for quite a long time. Such instances are many by virtue of the increased mobility of individuals. International students – whose duration of stay outside their State of origin may nowadays last for years and whose numbers are considerable also from the Turkish perspective[75] – are a textbook example of cases of this kind.[76] One should accept that it is highly unlikely for such students to have property or heirs located at the place of study. In addition, their social or familial integration in that State may often not be comparable to their integration in the State of origin,[77] as they often retain close contacts with their social environment in the origin State and have an intention to return home after the conclusion of their studies.[78] It has, therefore, been rightly pointed out that the habitual residence of students studying abroad should be determined based on their connection to the State of origin regardless of the duration of the stay and the period of study.[79] However, there could be exceptional cases where part of their family already lives in the country in which they choose to study. Or this country may be where, following their studies, they have an intention to find a job and spend their lives; or, perhaps with the help of their families, they have acquired property there. In such cases, a more careful analysis will be needed to identify the habitual residence of the person in question.

---

[75] More than 5,000 residence permits were issued or renewed for Turkish students and researchers in the EU in 2019. See, Eurostat, 'Authorisations for Study and Research by Reason, Type of Decision, Citizenship and Length of Validity (migr_ressrath)' <https://ec.europa.eu/eurostat/web/asylum-and-managed-migration/data/database> (selecting Türkiye as the Country of Citizenship), accessed 24 June 2021.

[76] Solomon, 'Die allgemeine Kollisionsnorm' (2014) 26.

[77] Solomon, 'Die allgemeine Kollisionsnorm' (2014) 26–27.

[78] Döbereiner, [2013] MittBayNot 358, 362; Odersky, [2013] Notar 3, 5; Weiss and Bigler, [2014] Successio 163, 168.

[79] Döbereiner, [2013] MittBayNot 358, 362; Solomon, 'Die allgemeine Kollisionsnorm' (2014) 26; Lein, *Dutta/Weber* (2021) EuErbVO Art 4 para 17; Thorn, *Grüneberg BGB* (2022) EuErbVO Art 21 para 6.

Residence abroad on a temporary basis may also come into play for professional or economic reasons. A scholar, a businessperson, or – as particularly important from the Turkish perspective – an employee ('Gastarbeiter') might, for instance, work abroad for a certain period of time but always with the desire to return to his origin State after the end of this stay. Here again, circumstances proving the connection to each State may be considered by the courts. On the one hand, the temporary nature of the stay, albeit one lasting at times for years, and the intention to return home demand that the habitual residence of the person in question still be designated as being in his State of origin. On the other hand, a level of social and family integration in the State of employment may be relevant for the change of habitual residence. Indeed, the person may acquire a significant amount of property and/or be accompanied by his family in the State of employment.[80] None of these, of course, could be considered as the constituent elements of habitual residence; rather, the facts of each case should be decisive.[81]

Succession cases involving individuals moving abroad for health reasons, i.e. healthcare tourism, are another group of instances in which courts might have difficulties when determining the habitual residence of the deceased. Such cases, though probably small in number, may also arise in the Turkish-European context as Turkey has become a destination for certain medical treatments in recent years.[82] Even though the duration of stay may give rise to doubts as to the determination of the habitual residence of the person in question in these cases, absent other circumstances a temporary residence abroad of this nature will not change the habitual residence.[83]

---

[80] Solomon, 'Die allgemeine Kollisionsnorm' (2014) 27.

[81] Lein, *Dutta/Weber* (2021) EuErbVO Art 4 para 14.

[82] See, for example, Sıdıka Kaya and others, 'Evaluation Report on Medical Tourism in Turkey 2013' (Republic of Turkey, Ministry of Health 2013) <http://dosyasb.saglik.gov.tr/Eklenti/535,turkiye-medikal-turizm-degerlendirme-raporu-2013pdf.pdf> accessed 21 January 2021.

[83] Dutta, *MüKoBGB* (2020) EuErbVO Art 4 para 10.

Though it is not clear based on the summarised facts whether the change of residence was made particularly for medical reasons, the facts of the case V A, Z A v. TP before the CJEU is worth mentioning here. In that case, the deceased was a French national who lived from 1981 to 2012 in the UK. After falling ill in 2012, he moved back to France to live with one of his children, and he eventually died there in 2015, leaving behind his UK national wife and three children as heirs with assets in France as the estate. Upon his death, one of his children applied to a court in France for the appointment of an estate administrator by alleging that the deceased was habitually resident in France. Although the Court found that the deceased was habitually resident in France and confirmed jurisdiction, the Court of Appeal of Versailles, upon appeal, overturned this judgment, stating that the deceased's habitual residence was still located in the UK and jurisdiction cannot be established under Art 4 of the Regulation. The conclusion of the Court is noteworthy in the sense that although the deceased seems to have lived in France for a couple of years prior

One example from legal practice which is relevant in both the guest-worker and medical treatment contexts in the Turkish-EU arena is worth mentioning here. It involves a Turkish-Austrian dual national who came to Austria in 2000 as a guest-worker and who stayed there until 2016. The deceased then returned to Turkey after his retirement and lived there for half a year. Subsequently, he went to Austria at the end of February 2018 due to some serious health problems. In Austria, he underwent an urgent operation and had to stay in the hospital due to his critical health condition. He, therefore, could not return to Turkey and died in Austria after two weeks. On the basis of these factual circumstances, the Austrian local court was of the opinion that the deceased was habitually resident in Austria. The case was then referred to the Supreme Court of Austria. The Supreme Court, however, held that he was not habitually resident in Austria and only came there for medical purposes. The ruling also held that jurisdiction according to Article 10(1) was not possible either, as the deceased – based on the case file – did not have assets in Austria.[84]

It seems that in this Austrian case, as well as in the majority of the aforementioned examples, the deceased maintained a close and stable connection with his State of origin, and thus the centre of interests of his family and social life remained in that State even though the change of residence may have lasted for a long period of time. The courts, however, should not take any single factors as constituent elements of habitual residence and must instead make an overall assessment of the facts when determining this place.

bb) Multiple Residences in Different States

Individuals residing not in a single State but in two or even more States – at the same time – are also not rare nowadays.[85] The typical example of such people are professionals who work in one State but live in another with their families, i.e. cross-border commuters ('Grenzpendler'), their being individuals who

---

to his death, no change of habitual residence was found by the Court from the UK to France. For the summary of the facts and the conclusion of the French courts, see C-645/20 V A, Z A v. TP [2022] ECLI:EU:C:2022:267 [12 ff].

[84] OGH 25.9.2018 – 2 Nc 23/18g, FamRZ 2019, 1010.

A similar example, which this time concerns Germany and another third State (Thailand), may also be given here. In this case, the deceased was a German national who moved to Thailand more than ten years prior to his death. The Court rightly found in its analysis on the law applicable to succession under Art 21(1) of the Regulation that the deceased had his last habitual residence in Thailand, observing that this is where he was residing with his partner, he had become well integrated in Thailand, and he possessed movable and immovable property in Thailand. The court ruled as such even though the deceased died while staying in Germany for a couple of months, was receiving medical treatment in Germany, owned a flat in Germany in order to maintain his ties with his home country, and regularly visited his family members in Germany. For the case, see OLG Hamm 10.8.2021 – 10 W 53/21, BeckRS 2021, 24229 (esp. paras 15 ff).

may also be involved in cases arising in the Turkish-European context. Since the Regulation attaches particular importance to the centre of social and familial interests of the deceased,[86] in a conflict between the State of employment and the State where the familial relationships are located the latter should be given greater weight.[87] This is in line with the traditional understanding of habitual residence in the field of *statut personnel* that a person is habitually resident in the place 'where he rests, where he sleeps'.[88] The nationality of the person or the place where the main assets are located could be used as special factors when making an overall assessment of the facts.[89]

In one case, the Higher Regional Court of Berlin ('Kammergericht') indeed dealt with this question. The case was a typical cross-border commuter case on the succession of *(E)*, who was habitually resident in Wedding/ Germany until 2010, at which time he was 72 years of age. In the last years prior to his death he moved to a flat in Poland, but at the same time he maintained a second residence in Berlin, living as a registered resident on a non-regular basis with his daughter in her flat. He continued working as a contractor and construction consultant at his previous place of business in Berlin. He later died in a hospital in Berlin in 2016. The case filed by his daughter came for review before the Higher Regional Court of Berlin after two local courts declined jurisdiction. The Court underlined that the determination of habitual residence in such cases needs to be made based on where the deceased's centre of gravity was located in terms of his family and social life, and it found that this was in Germany. This is because *(E)*'s family remained in the Berlin area, his level of integration was extremely minimal in Poland (which is actually not far from Germany), he did not speak Polish, he did not have a normal village and community life in Poland apart from some daily conversations with local people, he did not have a new family life in Poland, he maintained his economic activities and accounts in Germany, and he still travelled to Berlin every day for work. The only reason he moved to the flat in Poland was its cheaper rent and its proximity to his business locale in Berlin. There-

---

[85] Ena-Marlis Bajons, 'Zur Interdependenz von IPR und IZVR bei der Schaffung eines europäischen Justizraums für grenzüberschreitende Nachlassangelegenheiten' in DNotI (ed), *Les Successions Internationales dans l'UE* (DNotI 2004) 477.

[86] Recital 24 of the Regulation.

[87] Dörner, [2012] ZEV 505, 510; D. Lehmann, [2012] DStR 2085, 2086; Odersky, [2013] Notar 3, 5; Solomon, 'Die allgemeine Kollisionsnorm' (2014) 30; Weiss and Bigler, [2014] Successio 163, 167–168; Graham-Siegenthaler, [2015] Jusletter 7; cf. Müller-Lukoschek, *Die neue EU-Erbrechtsverordnung* (2015) § 2 para 145.

[88] Schurig, *Soergel BGB* (1996) EGBGB Art 5 para 44 ('wo er zur Ruhe kommt, wo er schläft'); D. Lehmann, [2012] DStR 2085, 2086; Solomon, 'Die allgemeine Kollisionsnorm' (2014) 30.

[89] Recital 24 of the Regulation. See, for example, Cass. 1ère civ., 29 mai 2019, n° 18-13383 <https://www.legifrance.gouv.fr/juri/id/JURITEXT000038629401/> accessed 5 March 2022.

fore, the Court found that *(E)*'s habitual residence remained in Wedding/ Germany, which allowed for the international jurisdiction of the local court there under Article 4 of the Regulation.[90]

Similar situations of multiple residences may also arise as a result of the rising trend of international retirement migration, be it permanent or temporary, to favourable places in the pursuit of a better life.[91] In this sense, the Aegean coast of Turkey as well as the Turkish-Riviera have become favourite destinations in recent years, locations where European pensioners buy summer houses.[92] It appears that the habitual residence of these people in the vast majority of instances is still located in the State of origin where their centre of family and social life are located.[93] Yet complex cases may still exist.[94] Due to the fact that the controversy here does not arise out of the tension between private life and professional life,[95] other factors such as the State of nationality, the place where the main assets are located,[96] or, sometimes, even language skills[97] could be considered as indicators of habitual residence when making an overall assessment.

An example from practice could also be given here. In the succession case of a German national who died in Spain, the Court did not conduct a detailed

---

[90] KG 26.4.2016 – 1 AR 8/16, ZEV 2016, 514.

[91] Balkır and Kırkulak, 'Turkey, the New Destination for International Retirement Migration' (2009) 123.

[92] Balkır and Kırkulak, 'Turkey, the New Destination for International Retirement Migration' (2009) 124; Südaş, 'Lifestyle Migration to Turkey: EU Citizens Living on the Turkish Sunbelt' (2012) 1; Canan Balkır and Bianca Kaiser, 'Türkiye'de Avrupa Birliği Vatandaşları' in Murat Erdoğan and Ayhan Kaya (eds), *Türkiye'nin Göç Tarihi 14. Yüzyıldan 21. Yüzyıla Türkiye'ye Göçler* (İstanbul Bilgi Üniversitesi Yayınları 2015) 225. For German nationals, see also Süß, 'Der Vorbehalt zugunsten bilateraler Abkommen mit Drittstaaten' (2014) 183 (in the context of the Turkish-German Treaty); Barbara Pusch, 'German Retirement Tranquillity that the "Law on Foreigners and International Protection" Cannot Protect' (2015) 29 <http://researchturkey.org/german-retirement-tranquillity-that-the-law-on-foreigners-and-international-protection-cannot-protect/> accessed 2 March 2018.

[93] Burandt, [2013] FuR 377, 383; Herzog, [2013] ErbR 2, 6; Michael von Hinden and Thorsten Müller, 'Die Europäische Erbrechtsverordnung, Aktuelle Auswirkungen auf die Nachfolgeplanung' [2013] ErbStB 97, 99; Odersky, [2013] Notar 3, 5; Rembert Süß, 'Das Europäische Nachlasszeugnis' [2013] ZEuP 725, 733; Weiss and Bigler, [2014] Successio 163, 168; Dutta, *MüKoBGB* (2020) EuErbVO Art 4 para 10; cf. D. Lehmann, [2012] DStR 2085, 2086; Solomon, 'Die allgemeine Kollisionsnorm' (2014) 30–31; Dutta, [2020] ZEuP 897, 922.

[94] Burandt, [2013] FuR 377, 383; Solomon, 'Die allgemeine Kollisionsnorm' (2014) 31.

[95] D. Lehmann, [2012] DStR 2085, 2086; Odersky, [2013] Notar 3, 5; Solomon, 'Die allgemeine Kollisionsnorm' (2014) 30; Weiss and Bigler, [2014] Successio 163, 168.

[96] Recital 24 of the Regulation.

[97] Kunz, [2012] GPR 208, 211; Seibl, 'Objektive und subjektive Anknüpfungen im Internationalen Erbrecht' (2013) 134–135; Solomon, 'Die allgemeine Kollisionsnorm' (2014) 31; Dutta, *MüKoBGB* (2020) EuErbVO Art 4 para 10.

analysis and decided that the habitual residence of the deceased was in Germany. The deceased had four children, two of them being from his first marriage, which ended in 1984 by divorce, and two of them being from his second marriage entered in Spain with a Spanish national, which also ended by divorce in 2003. At the time of death, he was married to this third wife, whom he had lived with in Germany but without any children. The deceased and his wife had lived together in an apartment in Germany which was acquired under joint ownership. He then separated with his wife and moved to Spain without deregistering from his residence in Germany. For medical purposes he visited doctors in Germany rather than in Spain. Some months prior to his death, he filed an application for the early equalisation of accrued gains. In this application, he gave his address in Spain as the current address and stated that he came to Spain in the 1970s as an immigrant. After this application he also made a short visit to Germany. He died when he later returned back to Spain. Two of his daughters applied to the local court in Bad Oeynhausen/Germany for issuance of a succession certificate, but their application was rejected on the basis that the habitual residence of the deceased was in Spain. When the case came before the Higher Regional Court of Hamm, the Court took under consideration the declarations of the deceased in his matrimonial property application, the acquisition of assets in Germany, his residence in Germany, his failure to deregister before moving to Spain, and his medical treatments in Germany; the court found that he was habitually resident in Germany.[98] The Court, however, failed to conduct a thorough analysis and did not consider factors such as the linguistic knowledge of the deceased as well as his social life. It based its decision on evidence such as his registration in Germany and medical treatment received in Germany in connection with previously made appointments. This is a good illustration of the difficulty of determining habitual residence of the deceased and the legal uncertainty attached to it.[99]

The above-mentioned case groups are examples illustrating that the determination of habitual residence may not always be straightforward for the courts.[100] It is evident from those examples that difficult cases of such kind may give rise to jurisdiction conflicts and, in turn, inconsistent decisions among different State courts. Such consequences could be easily prevented between the Member States with the Union-specific tools of the Regulation

---

[98] OLG Hamm 2.1.2018 – I -10 W 35/17, NJW 2018, 2061. For another case concerning Germany and Spain (Gran Canaria), and one probably featuring a better analysis on the last habitual residence of the deceased, see e.g. OLG Düsseldorf 20.11.2020 – 3 Wx 138/20, BeckRS 2020, 33812 (esp. paras 22 ff).

[99] See, in this regard, Steffen Kurth, 'Wechselleben zwischen der spanischen Costa Brava und der ostwestfälischen Provinz – Ermittlung des gewöhnlichen Aufenthalts eines Erblassers, der sich in zwei Staaten abwechselnd aufhält: (zu OLG Hamm, 2.1.2018 – 10 W 35/17)' [2019] IPRax 123, 126–127.

[100] Dutta, *MüKoBGB* (2020) EuErbVO Art 4 para 10.

tailored for this purpose, i.e. Articles 5, 6, 17, and 18 of the Regulation. Yet even before invoking these mechanisms, the courts may tend to decline jurisdiction if most of the elements of the case indicate that the habitual residence of the deceased is located in another Member State or that the situation may be resolved by the higher courts of States or by the CJEU.[101] This is because the cooperation between Member States is and should be closer than the cooperation between Member States and third States thanks to the principle of mutual trust and the judicial network existing between the authorities of Member States.[102] The courts, thus, may apply less strict standards so as to assume jurisdiction when other elements of the case are in a non-Member State.[103] The situation may become even worse when habitual residence is

---

[101] See, for example, C-80/19 E. E. [2020] ECLI:EU:C:2020:569. This was a case in which the habitual residence of the deceased was disputed in the face of circumstances concerning Lithuania and Germany. The deceased was a Lithuanian national who died in Germany. He had heirs in Germany and in Lithuania. His assets were located in Lithuania. The Court held that the deceased can have only *one* habitual residence and this should be determined after a careful analysis of the circumstances (paras 40 ff). See also C-80/19 E. E. [2020] ECLI:EU:C:2020:230, Opinion of *AG Campos Sánchez-Bordona* [40 ff].

[102] Pataut, 'The External Dimension of Private International Family Law' (2016) 118.

[103] See, in the context of conflict rules, for example, Bajons, 'Grenzüberschreitende Nachlassangelegenheiten' (2004) 476 ('the rules of the Regulation should be designed so as to "bring back" many of the possible aspects of estate settlement to the Union').

This, of course, does not always have to be the case. In a Latvian case, as reported, the situation was clarified by the higher court. The deceased was a Russian national who was alleged to be domiciled in Russia, yet he was also an alleged resident of Andorra who was, further, residing in Germany for health reasons in the last year of his life. He owned properties in Russia, Latvia, Andorra, Ukraine, and Spain. Although succession proceedings were opened in Russia, a parallel proceeding for the issue of an ECS was brought before a notary in Latvia. The notary issued the certificate without conducting any analysis. When a challenge procedure took place before the Regional Court of Riga, the Regional Court did not conduct an analysis either. This mistake was, however, later fixed by the Latvian Supreme Court, which overturned the decision of the Regional Court and held that a detailed analysis should be made regarding the habitual residence of the deceased: Krūmiņš, (2019) 15 J Priv Int L 365.

In another case decided in Germany, the deceased was a German national who died in 2017 and who lived since 2004 in China. He only travelled back to Germany during his holidays, but he bought immovable property in Germany in 2007 and, as alleged, he always had the intention to return to Germany permanently in 2018.

After his death, his child applied to a German probate court for the issue of a succession certificate and claimed, due to this intention to return, that his last habitual residence was in Germany. On the other hand, his Chinese wife whom he married in 2014 claimed that his last habitual residence was in China. In this case, both the Probate Court and the Higher Regional Court of Frankfurt am Main held that the last habitual residence of the deceased was in China and that his intention to return to Germany did not change this: OLG Frankfurt am Main 14.9.2020 – 21 W 59/20, openJur 2020, 74330.

Although these disputes could ultimately be resolved by appellate courts – and though jurisdiction was established under Article 10 of the Regulation (and not under Article 4 of

interpreted by the courts in a legal and technical manner. In this regard, it is worth mentioning certain rulings of the European Court in recent years made in the context of Brussels IIa Regulation that encourage such an approach and which may also be used in succession cases.

b) The Approach of the European Court towards the Concept of Habitual Residence

The European Court in its rulings from the past five years has made clear, as in the corresponding Regulation recital, that 'the determination of habitual residence will depend on the analysis of the circumstances in each case',[104] but it has seemingly given much weight to objective factors and interpreted habitual residence in a technical and legal manner.[105]

The case named *W and V v. X*,[106] involved a Lithuanian-Italian dual national child who moved to Italy and then to the Netherlands with his mother (a dual national of the Netherlands and of Argentina) after the separation of the parents, while his father (a Lithuanian national) was in Lithuania. The child had lived together with his parents in the U.S., the Netherlands, Italy, and Canada but not in Lithuania. There were different proceedings regarding divorce, custody of the child, and maintenance before the Canadian, Lithuanian, and Dutch courts. Lithuanian courts referred the issue regarding jurisdiction to the European Court. In this case, the CJEU made clear that habitual residence cannot be established without physical presence (para 60) and went on to state that several years of physical presence in a State (the Netherlands) creates a presumption that habitual residence is already in that State (para 64). Although having the nationality of a State (Lithuania) may be an indicator for the establishment of habitual residence in the home country, it is itself not sufficient unless there are other circumstances in support of that conclusion (para 60).

In another case,[107] the child of an Italian national father and Greek national mother was born in Greece in accordance with couple's prior agreement. Prior to birth the couple had been living in Italy, but they agreed that the birth should occur in Greece so that they could seek support from mother's parents. They had also agreed that the child should later return to Italy together with mother; this, however, did not happen as the infant stayed in Greece with the

---

the Regulation) – they nevertheless illustrate well the jurisdiction conflicts likely to arise at the trial court level due to the complex nature of habitual residence.

[103] Pataut, 'The External Dimension of Private International Family Law' (2016) 118.

[104] C-111/17 PPU OL v. PQ [2017] EU:C:2017:436 [48ff]; C-499/15 W and V v. X [2017] EU:C:2017:118 [60]; C-85/18 PPU CV v. DU [2018] ECLI:EU:C:2018:220 [49]; C-512/17 HR [2018] ECLI:EU:C:2018:513 [49ff].

[105] See, for comments on subsequent cases, Dutta, [2020] ZEuP 897, 918ff.

[106] C-499/15 W and V v. X [2017] EU:C:2017:118.

[107] C-111/17 PPU OL v. PQ [2017] EU:C:2017:436.

mother. The father filed a request for return of the child. In this case, again, the Court gave priority to the physical presence of the child in Greece and did not consider the initial intention of the parents to return to Italy, which, in the Court's view, could only be an indication but not prove habitual residence without the physical presence (paras 49 ff).

Another case[108] that came before the Court was related to an infant girl (a Polish-Belgian dual national) who came to the world in Brussels, being born to a Polish mother and a Belgian father. The little girl travelled many times to Poland with her mother, and even when in Brussels she lived in a social environment populated by people of Polish origin; she also spoke Polish most of the time. The mother later decided to move to Poland permanently. The father objected, and child custody proceedings were initiated. When the case came before the CJEU, the Court again gave greater weight to certain objective criteria, i.e. her regular residence in Belgium, the custody rights of the father (who was also in Belgium), and the mother's continuing presence in Belgium, over cultural ties with Poland (the social environment, certain visits, and the main spoken language), the origins of the child from mother side, and the mother's intention to return to Poland (paras 56 ff).

In its decision titled *UD v. XB*,[109] the Court repeatedly underlined the importance of physical presence for the establishment of habitual residence. The case concerned the custody of a child born in Bangladesh from a Bangladeshi mother and a U.K. father. The couple were living in the U.K. together, but subsequently the father took the pregnant mother to Bangladesh against her alleged will. The mother then gave birth to the child there. The father, however, returned to the U.K. alone after the birth. The Court found that habitual residence cannot be established without physical presence in the U.K. (paras 52 ff); the mother's intention to return there and the father's coercion does not change this (paras 60 ff).[110]

It is argued that these judgments, which are ongoing steps in a systemic edifice mostly lacking a common structure, indicate that the Court's case law considers habitual residence as a technical concept. Furthermore, these rulings of the Court are said to give considerable weight to the needs of the immigrant receiving Member States and to the parallelism between forum and *ius*, rather than focusing on the ties of migrant community members with their origin States.[111] In that the approach towards complex factual scenarios

---

[108] C-512/17 HR [2018] ECLI:EU:C:2018:513.

[109] C-393/18 PPU UD v. XB [2018] ECLI:EU:C:2018:835.

[110] This would mean for the purposes of the Succession Regulation that habitual residence cannot be established with the mere intention (e.g. when the deceased already decided to move to a place and long for his his time there) rather the physical presence in that place is required: Junker, 'Die Dogmatik der Aufenthaltszuständigkeit nach der EuErbVO' (2021) 751.

[111] Dutta, [2020] ZEuP 897, 943.

– involving the migrant community – is of this nature in intra-EU cases, it is highly probable it will also be followed in third-country related cases. As regards a determination of the habitual residence of the deceased in succession cases, it is likely that much weight will be given to intra-EU elements having an objective nature, such as physical presence, duration, and the regularity of residence, as opposed to the parties' connection to their national or origin States, which will thus lead to a conclusion that the habitual residence was in the EU. The same may also be true for third State courts, as they would also declare themselves competent after finding that the deceased was domiciled in that State, regardless of the fact that the case is also connected to another State. Before giving examples of such jurisdiction conflicts in the Turkish-European area, the other side of the coin, i.e. the concept of domicile under Turkish law, should be examined.

2. *The Concept of Domicile under Turkish Law*

Although the concept of habitual residence is not completely unfamiliar to Turkish procedural law,[112] Article 43 of the Turkish Private International Law Act, unlike the Regulation, prefers domicile as the main connecting factor for general jurisdiction on succession issues. Differences may apply between the two concepts, particularly owing to the practice in each legal system.[113] Therefore, the concept of domicile and its meaning in practice should be analysed here.

Unlike European law, which leaves the term of habitual residence intentionally undefined to allow some level of flexibility, domicile is expressly defined in Turkish law, obviously for internal purposes, under Article 19(1) of the Turkish Civil Code. Pursuant to this, a person has his domicile at the place where he resides with the intention to stay permanently. By doing so, the legislature makes explicit that there are two constituent elements of domicile under Turkish law.[114] First, in order to establish a domicile a person must be resident in a place (objective element). Second, such a residence should be

[112] See Art 9(1) and Art 84(1) (a) of the Turkish Code of Civil Procedure and Arts 44, 45, 46 of the Turkish PILA.

[113] See the dissenting opinion to Yargıtay Hukuk Genel Kurulu, T. 6.6.2007, E. 2007/2-331 K. 2007/332 <http://www.kazanci.com> accessed 6 March 2018.

[114] Muammer Raşit Seviğ, 'İkametgâh' (1947) 13 İÜHFM 941, 942; Ferit H. Saymen, *Türk Medeni Hukuku Cilt II – Şahsın Hukuku* (Kenan Matbaası 1948) 170–173; Tuğrul Ansay, 'İkametgâhın Tayininden Doğan Kanunlar İhtilafı' (1953) 10 AÜHFD 666, 666; Tunçomağ, (1961) 26 İÜHFM 153, 156; Burak Huysal, 'Kanunlar İhtilafı Alanında İkametgâh ve Doğurduğu Sorunlar' (2003) 2 MHFD 173, 178–179; Gülşah Vardar Hamamcıoğlu, *Türk Medeni Kanunu'na Göre Yerleşim Yeri* (On İki Levha 2009) 59; Çelikel and Erdem, *Milletlerarası Özel Hukuk* (2021) 571; Şanlı, Esen and Ataman Figanmeşe, *Milletlerarası Özel Hukuk* (2021) 465.

permanent;[115] temporary residences, no matter how long they last, cannot suffice to establish a domicile.[116] Put differently, a domicile cannot be established if the person has no intention to remain in his place of residence permanently (subjective element).[117] Thus, *animus manendi* is not only an indicator but rather an essential component of the domicile,[118] which distinguishes it from habitual residence within the scheme of the Regulation.

An intention to stay in one location permanently is manifested with certain facts, such as when a person makes his place of residence the centre of his personal relations, of his economic and moral interests, and of his familial or professional life.[119] This would be the case, for example, if a person acquires real property in that place,[120] or rents an apartment there and moves into it with his family,[121] or works at the same place.[122] By contrast, the permanent nature of the residence cannot be determined with reference to its duration.[123] Moving abroad for a length period, for example, would not automatically change the domicile.[124]

It has been contended that a firm adherence to the definition of the Turkish Civil Code could sometimes be problematic, as it is not wide enough to cover all circumstances.[125] There could be cases in which the domicile is established, although one of the elements is missing. A person might, for instance, have to reside at a place without an intention to stay there permanently, such

[115] Saymen, *Şahsın Hukuku* (1948) 170–171; T. Ansay, (1953) 10 AÜHFD 666, 666; Tunçomağ, (1961) 26 İÜHFM 153, 165; Zahit İmre, 'İkametgâh Kavramı ve Buna İlişkin Meseleler', *İstanbul Üniversitesi Hukuk Fakültesi'nin 50. Yıl Armağanı: Cumhuriyet Döneminde Hukuk* (Fakülteler Matbaası 1973) 214; Vardar Hamamcıoğlu, *Yerleşim Yeri* (2009) 71.

[116] Saymen, *Şahsın Hukuku* (1948) 170–171; Tunçomağ, (1961) 26 İÜHFM 153, 165–166; Vardar Hamamcıoğlu, *Yerleşim Yeri* (2009) 71.

[117] Hıfzı Veldet Velidedeoğlu, *Türk Medeni Hukuku: Şahsın Hukuku* (6th edn, Nurgök Matbaası 1960) 93–95; Tunçomağ, (1961) 26 İÜHFM 153, 156.

[118] T. Ansay, (1953) 10 AÜHFD 666, 666.

[119] Saymen, *Şahsın Hukuku* (1948) 172; Vardar Hamamcıoğlu, *Yerleşim Yeri* (2009) 62.

[120] See, in the same direction, Yargıtay 2. Hukuk Dairesi, T. 25.6.2003, E. 2003/8088 K. 2003/9483 <http://www.kazanci.com> accessed 8 March 2018.

[121] Vardar Hamamcıoğlu, *Yerleşim Yeri* (2009) 66.

[122] Aybay and Dardağan, *Kanunlar İhtlilafı* (2008) 48; Merve Acun Mekengeç, *Aynî Haklardan Doğan Uyuşmazlıklarda Uygulanacak Hukuk ve Yetkili Mahkeme* (On İki Levha 2016) 309.

[123] Saymen, *Şahsın Hukuku* (1948) 170–171; Tunçomağ, (1961) 26 İÜHFM 153, 165–166; Vardar Hamamcıoğlu, *Yerleşim Yeri* (2009) 71.

[124] Acun Mekengeç, *Aynî Haklar* (2016) 310. See also Yargıtay 2. Hukuk Dairesi, T. 24.2.2005, E. 2005/735 K. 2005/2814 <https://legalbank.net/> accessed 9 March 2018.

[125] Velidedeoğlu, *Şahsın Hukuku* (1960) 90; Tunçomağ, (1961) 26 İÜHFM 153, 156. This, for instance, has already been taken into account in Swiss law. Art 20 of Swiss PILA provides a definition of domicile in the context of private international law and makes clear that the provisions of the Swiss Civil Code on domicile are not applicable in this context.

as individuals who have been taken into custody[126] or applicants for international protection under the Law on Foreigners and International Protection ('Yabancılar ve Uluslararası Koruma Kanunu').[127] There might also be circumstances that the domicile of a person is established without the objective element. For example, a person may have to live apart from his family due to professional reasons.[128] Therefore, it has rightly been argued that the domicile of a person, like the concept of habitual residence in the Regulation, is the place where the centre of a person's social and family life is located.[129] Particularly, in cases with international elements, such an approach seems to be more suitable.[130]

In the light of this, certain issues should be examined. The first issue, in this regard, is the effect of an intention to return to the home State after a certain period of time, which is of utmost significance in *Gastarbeiter* cases. The prevailing opinion is that such an intention has no effect on the domicile[131] if the person has already made this new place the centre of his life.[132]

Another issue is the effect on domicile of a temporary change of residence when done for educational or health reasons. Article 22 of the Turkish Civil Code clarifies that the domicile, like the habitual residence, does not change in such situations. Notwithstanding this, if this new place of residence becomes the centre of social and family life of the person in question,[133] or if there is an intention to stay permanently,[134] domicile is located in this new place.[135]

A further question with regards to the concept of domicile is whether a person can have multiple domiciles. Article 19(2) of the Turkish Civil Code responds to this question and clarifies that natural persons can have only one

---

[126] Tunçomağ, (1961) 26 İÜHFM 153, 156.

[127] *Resmi Gazete* of 11.4.2013, no 28615. See, especially Art 71 of the Law. For the English translation of the Law, see <https://en.goc.gov.tr/kurumlar/en.goc/Ingilizce-kanun/Law-on-Foreigners-and-International-Protection.pdf> accessed 21 January 2021.

[128] Tunçomağ, (1961) 26 İÜHFM 153, 157.

[129] Tunçomağ, (1961) 26 İÜHFM 153, 154.

[130] Erdoğan Göğer, 'Devletler Hususi Hukuku Yönünden İkâmetgah' (1969) 26 AÜHFD 237, 247; Huysal, (2003) 2 MHFD 173, 179.

[131] Velidedeoğlu, *Şahsın Hukuku* (1960) 94; Tunçomağ, (1961) 26 İÜHFM 153, 167.

[132] Vardar Hamamcıoğlu, *Yerleşim Yeri* (2009) 74; cf. İmre, 'İkametgâh' (1973) 220.

[133] Vardar Hamamcıoğlu, *Yerleşim Yeri* (2009) 67.

[134] İmre, 'İkametgâh' (1973) 214; Abdülkadir Arpacı, *Kişiler Hukuku (Gerçek Kişiler)* (2nd edn, Beta 2000) 91; Işıl Özkan, *Devletler Özel Hukukunda İkametgah, Mutad Mesken ve İşyeri Bağlama Noktalarının Yeniden Değerlendirilmesi* (Naturel Yayınları 2003) 69; Acun Mekengeç, *Aynî Haklar* (2016) 311; Mustafa Dural and Tufan Öğüz, *Türk Özel Hukuku Cilt II – Kişiler Hukuku* (22nd edn, Filiz Kitabevi 2021) para 982; Kemal Oğuzman, Özer Seliçi and Saibe Oktay Özdemir, *Kişiler Hukuku (Gerçek ve Tüzel Kişiler)* (20th edn, Filiz Kitabevi 2021) para 482.

[135] See for an example in the context of nursing homes, Yargıtay 20. Hukuk Dairesi, T. 25.9.2017, E. 2017/8211 K. 2017/6839 <http://www.kazanci.com> accessed 9 June 2018.

domicile (the principle of unity of domicile). Hence, in instances where a person has multiple residences in different places at the same time, the court should make an overall assessment of the facts to determine the domicile.[136] In the event of retirement migration, for example, the domicile of the person in question is located in the place where the interests of the social and family life of the person are centred.[137] Nevertheless, in instances where the place of employment and the place of family life are located in different places, the latter, as in the notion of habitual residence, should be considered as the domicile unless there are other circumstances proving the opposite.[138]

Last but not least, a change of domicile can only be possible if the new place already qualifies as a domicile (Article 20(1) of the Turkish Civil Code). This is the consequence of the mandatory nature of domicile under Turkish law. Considering this aspect of domicile, the Turkish legislature also provided that a person's place of temporary residence is deemed to be his domicile if his previous domicile may not be proven or if he was formerly resident abroad and has not yet established a domicile in Turkey (Article 20(2) of the Turkish Civil Code).

The concept of domicile is claimed to have two main differences from the notion of habitual residence. Firstly, domicile is a legal concept which is defined under the law, whereas habitual residence is a question of fact which should be decided by reference to the all circumstances of the case.[139] However, as has already been discussed above, the legal definition of domicile

---

[136] Saymen, *Şahsın Hukuku* (1948) 181; Dural and Öğüz, *Kişiler Hukuku* (2021) para 972.

[137] Acun Mekengeç, *Aynî Haklar* (2016) 310; cf. Oğuzman, Seliçi and Oktay Özdemir, *Kişiler Hukuku* (2021) paras 479–480.

[138] Saymen, *Şahsın Hukuku* (1948) 181; Tunçomağ, (1961) 26 İÜHFM 153, 168; İmre, 'İkametgâh' (1973) 220; Arpacı, *Kişiler Hukuku* (2000) 89; Özkan, *İkametgah, Mutad Mesken ve İşyeri Bağlama Noktaları* (2003) 69; Vardar Hamamcıoğlu, *Yerleşim Yeri* (2009) 67–68; Acun Mekengeç, *Aynî Haklar* (2016) 309; Oğuzman, Seliçi and Oktay Özdemir, *Kişiler Hukuku* (2021) para 477.

[139] David F. Cavers, 'Habitual Residence: A Useful Concept?' (1971) 21 Am U L Rev 475, 487–488; Dietmar Baetge, *Der gewöhnliche Aufenthalt im internationalen Privatrecht* (Mohr Siebeck 1994) 102ff; Rogerson, (2000) 49 ICLQ 86, 89; Akıncı and Demir Gökyayla, *Milletlerarası Aile Hukuku* (2010) 215; İlyas Arslan, *Milletlerarası Özel Hukukta Mutad Mesken Kavramı* (On İki Levha 2014) 40ff and 71; Tekinalp, *Milletlerarası Özel Hukuk* (2020) 57; Nomer, *Devletler Hususî Hukuku* (2021) 121; Şanlı, Esen and Ataman Figanmeşe, *Milletlerarası Özel Hukuk* (2021) 41; Doğan, *Milletlerarası Özel Hukuk* (2022) 218–219; cf. Paul Heinrich Neuhaus, *Die Grundbegriffe des internationalen Privatrechts* (Mohr Siebeck 1976) 226; Burak Huysal, 'Milletlerarası Yetkinin Belirlenmesinde Mutad Meskenin Doğurduğu Sorunlar ve HMK Madde Dokuz Üzerine Bazı Öneriler' in Sibel Özel and Hatice Selin Pürselim (eds), *Milletlerarası Usul Hukukunda Mahkemelerin Yetkisine İlişkin Güncel Tartışmalar: Ulusal Konferans 20 Şubat 2021* (On İki Levha 2021) 98. See also the dissenting opinion to Yargıtay Hukuk Genel Kurulu, T. 6.6.2007, E. 2007/2-331 K. 2007/332 <http://www.kazanci.com> accessed 6 March 2018.

may not be of much help in all cases. Therefore, in order to determine the domicile, the courts should find the centre of social and family interests of the person in question. In this sense, the argued distinction between domicile and habitual residence becomes blurred. This is even more the case given that the European Court is increasingly defining habitual residence in a rather technical and legal manner, like the concept of domicile.[140] The second difference between the two notions is that by virtue of the element of intention, domicile requires an assessment of the facts with an eye toward to the future, unlike habitual residence, which places more importance on the past. Nevertheless, as mentioned above, depending on the facts of the case the intention of the deceased may also be of some relevance when determining habitual residence.[141] Hence, in most cases the domicile of the deceased may coincide with the place of habitual residence.[142] However, in Turkish legal practice the domicile of persons is not always determined in a careful manner, and this may cause a number of instances of friction between the two systems. Therefore, it is also important to look at the Turkish practice on domicile at this point. This should be done in two parts as regards, first, foreigners[143] and, second, Turkish nationals, as the import of the facts may differ for each group in the courts' evaluation.[144]

a) *Domicile of Foreigners*

Whereas Turkish nationals may prove their actual residence in Turkey, i.e. the objective element of domicile, with any kind of evidence, foreigners should hold a residence permit to substantiate their continuous residence in Turkey.[145] Article 19 of the Law on Foreigners and International Protection stipulates that foreigners, unless exemptions are applicable,[146] should apply for a

---

140 See above pp 202–204.

141 Dormann, 'Schweiz und EuErbVO' (2014) 84. It is also argued that even though intention is also important for the habitual residence, in order to establish habitual residence – as opposed to domicile – neither legal capacity nor volition is required: Junker, 'Die Dogmatik der Aufenthaltszuständigkeit nach der EuErbVO' (2021) 749.

142 Kalt and Uhl, 'Die EU-Erbrechtsverordnung und die Schweiz' (2013) 120–121; Dormann, 'Schweiz und EuErbVO' (2014) 84; Schwander, [2014] AJP 1084, 1090; Weiss and Bigler, [2014] Successio 163, 180; Graham-Siegenthaler, [2015] Jusletter 17.

143 According to Art 3(1) (ü) of the Law on Foreigners and International Protection, the term 'foreigner' refers to persons not having citizenship of the Turkish Republic. This, in principle, includes not only nationals of other States but also stateless persons, refugees, and former Turkish nationals who hold a blue card in accordance with Art 28 of the Law on Turkish Citizenship ('Türk Vatandaşlık Kanunu', *Resmi Gazete* of 12.6.2009, no 27256).

144 See, in the same direction, Ekşi, *Milletlerarası Yetki* (2000) 93 ff; Acun Mekengeç, *Aynî Haklar* (2016) 302 ff.

145 Ekşi, *Milletlerarası Yetki* (2000) 93.

146 See Art 20 of the Law on Foreigners and International Protection.

residence permit to stay legally in Turkey beyond the duration of a visa or a visa exemption, or, in any case, when longer than ninety days. In addition, consistent with the Address Registration System[147] and the Central Register of Foreigners,[148] information on the current places of residence and the addresses of foreigners holding a residence permit issued for a minimum six-month period of time is kept electronically.[149] Address registration is made by the written declaration of the person in question, and such a declaration is deemed to be valid unless the contrary is proved.[150] When this is the case, the effect of residence permits and database information on the determination of domicile is questionable in practice. As residence permits are issued for legal residence in Turkey, together with the database information, they are undoubtedly sufficient to prove actual residence in Turkey. However, residence permit holders may not always have the requisite intention to stay in Turkey. When this is the case, holding such permits should not, in principle, be considered as sufficient to establish domicile.[151]

This was reiterated by the Turkish Court of Cassation in a 1998 divorce ruling regarding German spouses. In that case, whilst the spouses lived in Kemer (Antalya) for three years with a valid residence permit, the Court held that holding a valid residence permit is not sufficient to establish domicile.[152] Nevertheless, there have been divergent rulings on the issue after the establishment of such databases.

In a 2009 divorce case brought by a Canadian-Irish national against his Canadian wife, the Istanbul 1st Family Court ruled that the issuance of a residence permit is merely an administrative act and does not indicate *animus manendi* except under the circumstances where the place of residence referred to in the residence permit becomes the centre of life interests of the person in question. In this case, the husband had a two-year residence permit and stayed in Istanbul on a temporary basis. In addition to the residence permit,

---

[147] See Art 8 of the Law on Civil Registration Services ('Nüfus Hizmetleri Kanunu', *Resmi Gazete* of 29.4.2006, no 26153).

[148] See Art 8(1) of the Law on Civil Registration Services. See also By-law on the Registration of Foreigners residing in Turkey ('Türkiyede Oturan Yabancıların Nüfus Kayıtlarının Tutulması Hakkında Yönetmelik', *Resmi Gazete* of 20.10.2006, no 26325).

[149] See Art 1 and Art 10 of the By-Law on the Address Registration System ('Adres Kayıt Sistemi Yönetmeliği', *Resmi Gazete* of 15.12.2006, no 26377).

[150] See Art 13 of the By-Law on the Address Registration System.

[151] Sakmar, *Boşanma* (1976) 73; Ekşi, *Milletlerarası Yetki* (2000) 93; Merve Acun, 'Yabancılık Unsuru Taşıyan Finansal Kiralama (Leasing) Sözleşmelerinde Yetkili Mahkeme' (2013) 19 MÜHF-HAD 441, 458; Acun Mekengeç, *Aynî Haklar* (2016) 313–314; Çelikel and Erdem, *Milletlerarası Özel Hukuk* (2021) 572; Cemile Demir Gökyayla, *Ticarî Uyuşmazlıklarda Türk Mahkemelerinin Milletlerarası Yetkisi* (Vedat Kitapçılık 2021) 116–118; Huysal, *Mutad Mesken* (2021) 102.

[152] Yargıtay 2. Hukuk Dairesi, T. 27.5.1998, E. 1998/4842 K. 1998/6521 <http://www.kazanci.com> accessed 20 January 2021.

he relied on documents related to the Turkish branch of the company of which he claimed to be a shareholder in order to prove his stay in Turkey. However, the Court found that he was just a board member of the company and the documents submitted failed to prove that Istanbul had become the centre of his social and economic relations.[153]

However, in another divorce case from 2011, brought by a foreign national who had been residing in Istanbul for two years against his wife who was resident outside Turkey, the Turkish Court of Cassation erroneously overturned the judgment of the first instance court that had declined to find jurisdiction on the grounds that the claimant was not domiciled in Turkey.[154] In doing so, the Court considered the residence permit of the claimant as presumptive evidence of domicile in Turkey. The approach adopted by the Court in this case does not seem to be appropriate in light of the two constituent elements of domicile required under Turkish law. Whereas the existence of the objective element is undisputed in such cases, an examination of the facts as to the existence of *animus manendi* should be made. Without having undertaken such an examination, the conclusion of the Court therefore seems to be flawed.[155] Notwithstanding this, the courts may tend to rely on the information in databases in determining domicile and assuming jurisdiction as this information can be easily retrieved.[156]

A further question which might be asked here is whether long-term residence permits[157] or family residence permits[158] have any effect on the domicile. It has been argued in academic literature that long-term residence permits or family residence permits are sufficient to establish domicile, unless the contrary is proved.[159] This is because long-term residence permits are issued when the

---

[153] İstanbul 1. Aile Mahkemesi, T. 24.12.2009, E. 2009/372 K. 2009/990 published in Nuray Ekşi, *Milletlerarası Özel Hukuk I Pratik Çalışma Kitabı: Kanunlar İhtilafı Kurallarına ve Milletlerarası Usul Hukukuna İlişkin Seçilmiş Mahkeme Kararları* (2nd edn, Beta 2014) 69 ff.

[154] Yargıtay 2. Hukuk Dairesi, T. 10.5.2011, E. 2010/4537 K. 2011/8105 <http://www.kazanci.com> accessed 6 April 2018.

[155] See the dissenting opinion to the judgment.

[156] This approach is practical but questionable in light of the provisions of the Turkish Civil Code: Rifat Erten, *Türklerin Kişi Hâllerine İlişkin Davalarda Türk Mahkemelerinin Milletlerarası Yetkisi (MÖHUK m. 41)* (Yetkin 2017) 135. For examples of judgments where the Turkish Court of Cassation overruled some first instance court judgments declining jurisdiction without checking the information on the databases, see Yargıtay 2. Hukuk Dairesi, T. 30.3.2009, E. 2009/3778 K. 2009/5884 <http://www.kazanci.com> accessed 6 April 2018; Yargıtay 2. Hukuk Dairesi, T. 27.11.2014, E. 2014/8718 K. 2014/24170 <https://karararama.yargitay.gov.tr> accessed 6 April 2018.

[157] See Arts 42–45 of the Law on Foreigners and International Protection.

[158] See Arts 34–37 of the Law on Foreigners and International Protection.

[159] Acun Mekengeç, *Aynî Haklar* (2016) 315–316. According to *Doğan*, student residence permits also have the same effect: Doğan, *Milletlerarası Özel Hukuk* (2022) 56.

person in question has lived in Turkey for a minimum of eight years.[160] Likewise, family residence permits are issued to enable family members to live together. Hence, it has been contented that *animus manendi* exists in instances where a person resides in Turkey for more than eight years or with his family.[161] There appears to be no court practice on this issue. Giving a direct effect to the residence permit without making an examination as to the existence of *animus manendi* when determining domicile is of course questionable considering the provisions of the Turkish Civil Code.[162] Nevertheless, the courts may be inclined to assume international jurisdiction in these instances on the grounds that the person in question is a long-term resident in Turkey.

The determination of the subjective element of domicile may also be different for foreigners. In a 1977 case regarding the determination of the domicile of German spouses living in Izmir,[163] the Turkish Court of Cassation set a high threshold for the existence of *animus manendi.*[164] In this case, the German couple was resident in Turkey more than ten years and had engaged in trade during this time as the partners of a limited liability company; and they sent their children to Turkish schools. The Court, nonetheless, found none of these facts sufficient to prove *animus manendi* and held that if they had had the intention to stay permanently in Turkey, they would have initiated proceedings to become Turkish nationals. With such a ruling, the establishment of domicile in Turkey becomes particularly difficult and almost amounts to a citizenship requirement for foreigners. It would be then almost impossible to confer jurisdiction on Turkish courts over these individuals.[165] The courts, therefore, as mentioned earlier, should make an assessment only of the facts in order to find whether Turkey has become the centre of life and social interests of the person in question. They may, however, also tend to rely on the information on databases without for practical reasons making an evaluation as to *animus manendi.* When this is the case, it is highly likely that jurisdiction conflicts will arise with European courts when a Member State national dies in Turkey.

b) Domicile of Turkish Nationals

Turkish nationals, unlike foreigners, may prove their domicile in Turkey with any kind of evidence, and determination of the domicile of Turkish nationals who are resident in Turkey will not pose difficult problems from a procedural

---

160 See Art 42(1) of the Law on Foreigners and International Protection.

161 Acun Mekengeç, *Aynî Haklar* (2016) 315–316.

162 See the dissenting opinion to Yargıtay 2. Hukuk Dairesi, T. 10.5.2011, E. 2010/4537 K. 2011/8105 <http://www.kazanci.com> accessed 6 April 2018.

163 Yargıtay 2. Hukuk Dairesi, T. 21.2.1977, E. 1136 K. 1490, 2 MHB 35–36.

164 Ekşi, *Milletlerarası Yetki* (2000) 165.

165 Atâ Sakmar, 'Le nouveau droit international privé turc' (1990) 223 RdC 303, 377; Ekşi, *Milletlerarası Yetki* (2000) 94.

perspective. The domicile of Turkish nationals who have for many years been residing outside of Turkey, in EU Member States for example, may, however, prove a complex issue. Whether such individuals established domicile in their State of residence is indisputably a matter that should be decided in accordance with the laws of that State. On the other hand, the question of whether Turkish courts may assume jurisdiction over these persons in a succession case is of paramount importance here. Despite the fact that objective and subjective elements of domicile should also be present when determining the domicile of Turkish nationals, there seems to be differences in practice.

The Turkish Court of Cassation held in former judgments that Turkish nationals always have a domicile in Turkey. An example of these judgments is a case from 1972 regarding a Turkish guest-worker in Germany where it was held that working in a country is in itself not sufficient to show that the person in question is domiciled in that country. Unless there are other facts to prove *animus manendi*, these individuals are still to be considered as being domiciled at their place of civil registration in Turkey.[166] Likewise, in a 1992 divorce case, it was underlined that the place of civil registration constitutes a legal presumption for the domicile of Turkish nationals and, hence, every Turkish national has a domicile in Turkey.[167] The basis for such an approach was the misinterpretation of Article 4(1) of the former Law on Civil Registration ('Nüfus Kanunu').[168] This provision associates the place of civil registration with domicile and stipulates that each Turkish national is obliged to register himself with the civil registry at his domicile.[169] The Court concluded from this provision that Turkish nationals are deemed to be domiciled at their place of registration in Turkey.[170] This Law was repealed with Article 71 of the Law on Civil Registration Services No 5490. Notwithstanding this development, the Turkish Court of Cassation has maintained its view in certain decisions.[171]

---

[166] Yargıtay 2. Hukuk Dairesi, T. 28.12.1972, E. 7198 K. 7390 published in Ekşi, *Milletlerarası Yetki* (2000) 93 fn 386.

[167] Yargıtay 2. Hukuk Dairesi, T. 21.9.1992, E. 1992/7706 K. 1992/8259 <https://legalbank.net/> accessed 10 June 2018. See also Yargıtay 2. Hukuk Dairesi, T. 18.3.1998, E. 1998/938 K. 1998/3251 <http://www.kazanci.com> accessed 25 June 2018; Yargıtay 2. Hukuk Dairesi, T. 24.6.1999, E. 1999/5494 K. 1999/7289 <https://legalbank.net/> accessed 27 January 2021; Yargıtay 2. Hukuk Dairesi, T. 1.3.2001, E. 2001/1650 K. 2001/3423 <https://legalbank.net/> accessed 25 June 2018; Yargıtay 2. Hukuk Dairesi, T. 9.11.2001, E. 2001/13992 K. 2001/15529 <https://legalbank.net/> accessed 25 June 2018; Yargıtay 2. Hukuk Dairesi, T. 24.2.2005, E. 2005/735 K. 2005/2814 <https://legalbank.net/> accessed 9 March 2018.

[168] *Resmi Gazete* of 16.5.1972, no 14189.

[169] Vardar Hamamcıoğlu, *Yerleşim Yeri* (2009) 21.

[170] The same was also argued by Kuru, *Hukuk Muhakemeleri Usulü/vol 1* (2001) 385 ff.

[171] See, for example, Yargıtay 2. Hukuk Dairesi, T. 11.6.2009, E. 2009/1222 K. 2009/11331 <https://legalbank.net/> accessed 25 June 2018; Yargıtay 20. Hukuk Dairesi, T. 30.5.2016, E. 2016/3863 K. 2016/5917 <https://legalbank.net/> accessed 27 January 2021;

This practice of the Court is rightfully criticised by scholars. Deeming the place of civil registration as the domicile is, in the first place, contrary to the provisions of the Turkish Civil Code. According to the Turkish Civil Code, as stated above, both *animus manendi* and physical residence are *conditio sine qua non* for the establishment of domicile. Where the facts are not clear, the courts should conduct an analysis to locate the centre of life interests of the person in question.[172] In addition, unlike domicile, the place of registration is a factual concept,[173] and attributing it such a meaning is against its essence. This is because registration is done upon the birth of a person, and thus does not reflect an intent to establish domicile.[174] Only on the occasions in which the place of civil registry coincides with the centre of one's life interests can it be considered as the domicile.[175] Yet this would not be the case for Turkish nationals whose centre of social and economic interests is often located in their country of residence. Irrespective of the fact whether they have established domicile in their country of residence, it should be acknowledged that the two requisites of domicile do not exist for them as they have been resident outside Turkey for a significant period of time and no longer have a genuine link with Turkey.[176] Such a broad interpretation of domicile may give rise to forum shopping[177] as well as jurisdiction conflicts in succession cases.

---

contra Yargıtay 3. Hukuk Dairesi, T. 13.10.2014, E. 2014/5251 K. 2014/13083 <https://karararama.yargitay.gov.tr> accessed 27 September 2017. See also Yargıtay 20. Hukuk Dairesi, T. 4.4.2016, E. 2016/1359 K. 2016/3918 <https://legalbank.net/> accessed 25 June 2018. The case is commented on in Tanrıbilir, 'MÖHUK ve Mirasa İlişkin Bağlama Kuralının Uygulanmasında Öne Çıkan Hususlar' (2018) 130.

172 Tunçomağ, (1961) 26 İÜHFM 153, 154; İmre, 'İkametgâh' (1973) 218; Vardar Hamamcıoğlu, *Yerleşim Yeri* (2009) 24; Dural and Öğüz, *Kişiler Hukuku* (2021) para 972; Oğuzman, Seliçi and Oktay Özdemir, *Kişiler Hukuku* (2021) para 479. See also Özkan, *İkametgah, Mutad Mesken ve İşyeri Bağlama Noktaları* (2003) 69.

173 Tunçomağ, (1961) 26 İÜHFM 153, 154; Vardar Hamamcıoğlu, *Yerleşim Yeri* (2009) 19.

174 Sakmar, *Boşanma* (1976) 71; Ekşi, *Milletlerarası Yetki* (2000) 75.

175 Tunçomağ, (1961) 26 İÜHFM 153, 154–155; Sakmar, *Boşanma* (1976) 71; Ekşi, *Milletlerarası Yetki* (2000) 95.

176 Ekşi, *Milletlerarası Yetki* (2000) 96. In a succession case regarding a former Turkish national, the Turkish Court of Cassation found that the last domicile of the person was not in Turkey and jurisdiction should be assumed by the courts of the place where the immovable property was located (Istanbul/Avcılar) in accordance with the subsidiary jurisdiction rule under Article 43 of the Turkish PILA: Yargıtay 3. Hukuk Dairesi, T. 13.10.2014, E. 2014/5251 K. 2014/13083 <https://karararama.yargitay.gov.tr> accessed 27 September 2017. In another succession case involving a non-Turkish deceased, the same was reiterated, and it was held that jurisdiction should belong to the courts of the place where the deceased's bank account was held (Kiraz/İzmir) according to the subsidiary jurisdiction rule under Article 43 of the Turkish PILA: Yargıtay 2. Hukuk Dairesi, T. 7.6.2006, E. 2006/2788 K. 2006/8976 <https://legalbank.net/> accessed 27 January 2021.

177 T. Ansay and Schneider, (1990) XXXVII NILR 139, 148; Ekşi, *Milletlerarası Yetki* (2000) 96 (in the context of actions regarding the personal status of Turkish nationals).

It is apparent that the centre of the person in question's life and social interests is decisive for the concept of both habitual residence in the Regulation and domicile in Turkish law. As a consequence, the courts in both jurisdictions may theoretically reach a consonant conclusion after examining the facts of the case. Notwithstanding this, there might be complex cases in which the courts of both jurisdictions assume that the last habitual residence or the last domicile of the deceased is located in their territories and declare themselves competent to hear the case. The possibility that a Turkish court may in some cases base its domicile analysis on the information in civil registration systems will increase the chance of jurisdiction conflicts and, hence, inconsistent decisions in succession cases arising in the Turkish-European context. Such situations can be exemplified with the help of following case scenarios.

3. Possible Jurisdiction Conflicts: Exemplary Case Scenarios

a) Case No 1

Turkish national (T) from Izmir/Turkey, moves to Lyon/France in 2015 in order to work there. His parents, siblings, and some of his relatives live in Izmir, where he spends four to five months every year. At the same time, he is also well integrated in France, where he has many friends, and some relatives. He speaks French fluently. He has an apartment and some amount of money in the banks in each of the cities. However, he has always retained the intention to return to Turkey where he spent most of his life. He dies in a car accident in Izmir during one of his long visits in 2018.

In this case, the factual circumstances which are significant for the determination of the centre of life and social interests of *(T)* are multifaceted. On the one hand, he worked in Lyon for three years, and he was well integrated there as he had a social environment, owned movable as well as immovable property, and was fluent in French. On the other hand, he spent an important amount of time each year in his hometown, Izmir; his parents, siblings, and some of the relatives were there, and he also acquired movable and immovable property there.

Based on these facts, it seems that *(T)* not only worked but also established close relationships in Lyon during the time he spent there. As a consequence, it is likely that *(T)*'s centre of life and social interests and, hence, his last habitual residence will be considered to be in Lyon from the perspective of the Regulation. Therefore, if the case is brought before the courts of France, they may assume jurisdiction pursuant to Article 4 of the Regulation.

Nevertheless, he maintained close ties with his motherland by spending a considerable amount of time there each year and by owning properties there, and he always had an intention to return home. He also died in Izmir when he was completing one of his long visits. Thus, it is likely that he will be treated by the courts of Turkey as a domiciliary of Izmir in line with the provisions of the Turkish Civil Code. Considering the fact that he is a Turkish national and had civil registry records in Izmir, they may reach the conclusion that Izmir was the last domicile of the deceased and confer jurisdiction in this case according to Article 43 of the Turkish PILA. Although the latter consideration as regards civil registration records will not always come into play and it would be erroneous to reach a conclusion based solely on this information, it is possible that courts would exercise jurisdiction with the intention of making Turkish courts available to heirs of the deceased who are resident in Turkey.

b) *Case No 2*

Dutch national (D) has mainly lived abroad since his early retirement. For the last twenty-five years he has spent the period between September to May every year in his villa in Antalya/Turkey in order to escape cold winter weather in the Netherlands. He has many friends there whom he meets often. He speaks a little Turkish for everyday life. From June to August, however, he lives in his flat in Leiden/Netherlands. Most of his relatives live in Leiden, but he has only few friends there, as many of his friends also moved to Turkey after their retirement. He dies from a sudden heart attack in Antalya.[178]

In this example concerning the senior tourism phenomenon, *(D)* spent an important amount of time each year in Antalya. He had some knowledge of Turkish. He also established a social environment there. However, he maintained his strong bonds with his hometown by spending three months there each year. Leiden is the place where he spent his entire life before retirement and remains the location where the majority of his relatives live.

The duration, regularity, conditions, and reasons for the stay as well as the social environment in this case create the impression that the habitual residence of *(D)* is Antalya. Nonetheless, he does not seem to have particularly close ties with this place. Rather, he continued to maintain a close and stable connection with his country of origin.[179] Based on his attachment to the mother tongue, relatives, culture, and property in Leiden, he could be considered to still have his habitual residence in Leiden.[180] Hence, Dutch courts will have jurisdiction – pursuant to Article 4 of the Regulation – to rule on the succession of *(D)* as a whole.

Should the case be filed in Turkey, Turkish courts may, however, find that *(D)* had his last domicile in Antalya, particularly because of the duration of his recurrent stay in Antalya. The court may also rely on the information on online databases to confirm that *(D)* was domiciled in Antalya prior to his death. Under such an interpretation, Turkish courts will be entitled to hear the case according to Article 43 of the Turkish PILA.

---

[178] This hypothetical example is inspired by Burandt, [2013] FuR 377, 383.

[179] See Recital 24 of the Regulation.

[180] Burandt, [2013] FuR 377, 383.

c) Case No 3

Austrian national (A) is a partner of an international law firm which also has a branch in Istanbul. He, therefore, has been in Istanbul/Turkey many times throughout the years. He buys a mansion by the Bosphorus, an area he has always loved, and moves there with his family before his death, with the intention to settle. However, he often travels back to Vienna/Austria for business purposes and stays there for many days at a time. His parents as well as most of his relatives and friends still live there. He dies in Vienna during one of these visits.[181]

In this example, *(A)* spent many years in Vienna and maintained his close ties with this city even after migration. He had not only parents, relatives, and friends but also significant business relations there. On the other hand, he moved to Istanbul with his family and with the intention to settle. He also had a mansion and business relations in Istanbul.

Should a matter regarding succession arise, Austrian courts, based on these facts, may hold that *(A)* had his last habitual residence in Vienna and, hence, assume jurisdiction in accordance with Article 4 of the Regulation. At the same time, Turkish courts may also declare themselves competent based on the last domicile of the deceased.[182]

d) Case No 4

Turkish national (T) from Istanbul is a famous actor. He moves to Barcelona/Spain for a project but later marries and continues to live there with his Spanish wife and three children. Due to his continuing acting career, however, he visits Istanbul regularly and spends more than half of each year in Istanbul. His parents, his only sister, and most of his relatives live in Istanbul, where he always wants to resettle. He has friends and important amount of properties in each of the cities. He dies in a plane crash when flying from Istanbul to Barcelona.

In this case, *(T)* was well integrated in Barcelona. He had his main family life and friends there as well as an important amount of property. However, albeit primarily for business purposes, he spent more days a year in Istanbul. He also owned properties there. The remainder of his family, relatives, and friends were located there and he always had the intention to resettle.

Under such factual circumstances, Spanish courts will find that the last habitual residence of the deceased is Barcelona and, hence, confer jurisdiction as per Article 4 of the Regulation. Yet when the same dispute is filed in Turkey, Turkish courts may also assume jurisdiction, as *(T)* could be considered as still having had his last domicile in Istanbul. The courts may even consider the place of civil registration (Istanbul) as the domicile of the deceased without undertaking a thorough analysis of the facts.

---

[181] This hypothetical example is inspired by Dormann, 'Schweiz und EuErbVO' (2014) 84.

[182] Dormann, 'Schweiz und EuErbVO' (2014) 84.

Whereas the last habitual residence of the deceased is usually his last domicile, all the above examples – the number of which could even be increased – indicate that the courts in each jurisdiction may interpret the facts differently in complex cases, which will then cause jurisdiction conflicts and, in turn, conflicting decisions on the same matter. However, in some cases, courts may not insist on establishing jurisdiction under the general jurisdiction rule and may instead make use of the subsidiary jurisdiction rule.[183] And within the scope of the Regulation, courts may even do this on their own motion.[184] Therefore, the subsidiary jurisdiction rules of each legal system should also be examined.

II. Subsidiary Jurisdiction: Forum rei sitae

Even if the person in question was not habitually resident or domiciled in their territories, States may still find themselves in a better position to rule over a case. In those instances, they adopt, within the limits of the public international law principle of a genuine link, subsidiary grounds to exercise jurisdiction. Considering the mobility of people in our times, both the Regulation and the Turkish PILA have laid down such a rule of jurisdiction for succession cases. Unsurprisingly, a provision of this kind cannot be found in the Treaty due to its bilateral nature, which deals only with the allocation of jurisdiction between the Contracting States for cases falling within its scope. Therefore, this part should only present a comparison between the Regulation and the Turkish PILA.

1. Subsidiary Jurisdiction under the Regulation

European lawmakers addressed situations in which the last habitual residence of the deceased was located outside the Union, e.g. in Turkey, but where the deceased still had personal links to the Union, as one of the aims was to give individuals such as heirs or other beneficiaries access to 'European justice',[185] even though this may vitiate two important pillars of the Regulation, i.e. *Gleichlauf* and the unity of succession.[186] In line with this aim, Article 10(1) of the Regulation empowers the courts of the Member State 'in which the assets belonging to estate are situated to rule on succession as a whole to extent that the deceased had the nationality of this Member State at the time of death; or, failing that, the deceased had his last habitual residence at this

[183] See, two examples from Turkey in this regard, above n 176, p 213. See also the cases summarised in n 103, p 201.

[184] See, in this regard, above n 7, p 180.

[185] Max Planck Institute for Comparative and International Private Law, (2010) 74 RabelsZ 522, 581.

[186] Buonaiuti, (2016) 12 J Priv Int L 545, 554 ff.

Member State, unless, at the time of the court is seised, no more than five years have passed after the change of habitual residence'. If neither of these criteria can be fulfilled, Member State courts of the *situs* should nevertheless be competent to rule at least on those specific assets (Article 10(2)).

With this provision, only the *forum rei sitae* – which was already being used by some Member States as a ground for jurisdiction in areas not limited to succession matters[187] – may exercise jurisdiction. This is because, in the view of the European legislature, this forum is in the best position to deal with any matter regarding the transfer of succession rights on the assets in terms of proximity, and it is the place which will allow an effective as well expedient exercise of succession rights. The reason for the latter, under the logic of the European side, lies in the fact that the place where the assets are seated is the first place where recognition or enforcement of any decision regarding succession will be sought. Such a process would consequently not need to be engaged in if the courts there have jurisdiction to rule on succession in the first place.[188] However, the deceased may well have assets in different States. Whereas the coordination rules as well as the automatic recognition and enforcement regime of the Regulation might be able to eliminate problems in such a case within the borders of the EU,[189] this may not be the case in outside territories. The only tool of the Regulation that could potentially prevent the difficulties of recognition or enforcement in a third State is the limitation of proceedings under Article 12.[190] The efficiency of this procedure is, however, questionable, as will be discussed below.

Any tangible or intangible assets, and financially quantifiable rights and liabilities of public or private law nature, may in principle constitute the estate as a whole.[191] However, due to the wording of the provision – using 'assets of the estate' instead of just 'the estate' – jurisdiction should be exercised based solely on the assets (active elements of the estate) in order to prevent problems

---

[187] Martha Weser, 'Bases of Judicial Jurisdiction in the Common Market Countries' (1961) 10 AJCL 323, 333–334.

[188] Fabrizio Marongiu Buonaiuti, in Alfonso-Luis Calvo Caravaca, Angelo Davì and Heinz-Peter Mansel (eds), *The EU Succession Regulation – A Commentary* (Cambridge University Press 2016) ESR Art 20 para 5.

[189] It should be noted that such problems are in fact also present within the borders of the Union in relation to the non-participating Member States. See, in this regard, for example, Jürgen Basedow, '"Member States" and "Third States" in the Succession Regulation' (2020) 26 PPPM 15. Such problems, however, obviously fall outside the aim and scope of this study.

[190] Cf. Buonaiuti, *Calvo Caravaca/Davì/Mansel* (2016) ESR Art 10 para 6.

[191] George Panopoulos, in Haris P. Pamboukis (ed), *EU Succession Regulation No 650/2012 – A Commentary* (Nomiki Bibliothiki & C.H. Beck & Hart & Nomos 2017) ESR Art 10 para 6.

of exorbitant jurisdiction.[192] One might question whether the value and the amount of the assets are decisive for the jurisdiction of Member State courts under this provision. The wording of the article does not provide any limitation on its scope. Assume, for instance, a deceased who is habitually resident/domiciled in Turkey and who retains a Belgian bank account holding three hundred euros ever since the time of his postgraduate studies there.[193] Under the wording of the Regulation, this would theoretically be enough for Belgian courts to assume jurisdiction in accordance with Article 10 even if the deceased owns many valuable assets in Turkey. Other extreme cases could also be imaginable, such as where the only estate asset of the deceased in a Member State is a two hundred euro note left in a room safe or a camera left in a hotel. In all these cases, there seems to be a high risk of jurisdiction conflicts as well as exorbitant jurisdiction problems with third States which might not be solved within the system of the Regulation.[194] While it could from a European perspective be claimed that a restriction as to the value or the amount of assets may vitiate legal certainty[195] and that domestic rules, such as the ones relating to abandoned property, e.g. BGB § 959, may be used to handle extreme cases,[196] a third State perspective would suggest that the Member State courts should be competent only in cases where the assets of the estate are of a certain amount or value, thereby precluding jurisdiction conflicts and problems of exorbitant jurisdiction and, at least to a certain extent, the problem of forum shopping with the outside world.[197] Without such an interpretation it would be possible for Member State courts to assume jurisdiction under this provision even in extreme cases, and this would also be against the very objective of the rule, which stipulates a close link with the Union.[198]

The subsidiary rule of jurisdiction under Article 10 refers, first, to the nationality of the deceased under the first paragraph. The nationality of the deceased is indeed easy to determine in most cases and therefore may be seen

---

[192] Johannes Weber, 'Zur Erteilung eines deutschen Erbscheins bei letztem gewöhnlichen Aufenthalt des Erblassers im Ausland – zugleich Besprechung der EuGH-Entscheidung in der Rechtssache Oberle – C-20/17' [2018] RNotZ 454, 459; Dutta, *MüKoBGB* (2020) EuErbVO Art 10 para 5; J. Schmidt, *BeckOGK-EuErbVO* (2022) EuErbVO Art 10 para 8.

[193] See, for a similar opinion, Pürselim, (2021) 9 KHASHFD 179, 191.

[194] Lein, *Dutta/Weber* (2021) EuErbVO Art 10 para 12. Article 10 of the Regulation carries 'the stigma of exorbitant jurisdiction': Wilke, [2012] RIW 601, 604.

[195] Weiss and Bigler, [2014] Successio 163, 170; Weber, [2018] RNotZ 454, 459; Dutta, *MüKoBGB* (2020) EuErbVO Art 10 para 5.

[196] Dutta, *MüKoBGB* (2020) EuErbVO Art 10 para 5.

[197] Kalt and Uhl, 'Die EU-Erbrechtsverordnung und die Schweiz' (2013) 114; Edwin Gitschthaler, in Astrid Deixler-Hübner and Martin Schauer (eds), *Kommentar zur EU-Erbrechtsverordnung (EuErbVO)* (2nd edn, Manz 2020) EuErbVO Art 10 para 3; Lein, *Dutta/Weber* (2021) EuErbVO Art 10 para 12.

[198] Gitschthaler, *Deixler-Hübner/Schauer* (2020) EuErbVO Art 10 para 3.

as advantageous for subsidiary jurisdiction.[199] Problems could arise, however, when the deceased has more than one nationality.[200] This is because there might be cases where the deceased holds the nationality of a third State, e.g. Turkey, in addition to the nationality of one or more Member States. He might also own properties in each of these States.[201] Thus, just which nationality of the deceased should be taken into account under Article 10 may be seen as important from the perspectives of third States.

In a purely EU context, dual or multiple citizenship would not be problematic, as nationalities of Member States, in accord with the decision of the CJEU in *Hadadi*,[202] will be treated equally also for jurisdiction purposes under this provision.[203] In the words of the Court, by choosing nationality as a ground for jurisdiction the rule 'endorses a link that is unambiguous and easy to apply' and, hence, 'does not provide for any other criterion relating to nationality, such as, for example, how effective it is'.[204] Following this reasoning, the heirs may bring their case to the Member State court of their choice when the deceased is a national of different Member States.[205] This may cause conflicts of jurisdiction and forum shopping between the courts of Member States. Yet these could be prevented by declining jurisdiction pursuant to Article 6, by a choice of law, or by mechanisms to avoid parallel proceedings, i.e. Article 17 and Article 18 of the Regulation.[206]

In cases in which the deceased holds passports from a Member State as well as from a third State, neither the equal treatment of nationalities, which

---

[199] Wilke, [2012] RIW 601, 604; Burandt, [2013] FuR 377, 380; Gitschthaler, *Deixler-Hübner/Schauer* (2020) EuErbVO Art 10 para 17.

[200] Bajons, 'Internationale Zuständigkeit und anwendbares Recht in Erbsachen' (2012) 33 fn 10; Süß, [2013] ZEuP 725, 733–734; Müller-Lukoschek, *Die neue EU-Erbrechtsverordnung* (2015) § 2 para 240; Bonomi, *Bonomi/Wautelet* (2016) ESR Art 10 paras 17–18; Volker Grau, in Walter Zimmermann (ed), *Praxiskommentar Erbrechtliche Nebengesetze* (2nd edn, zerb verlag 2017) EuErbVO mit IntErbRVG para 145; Dutta, *MüKoBGB* (2020) EuErbVO Art 10 para 15; Gitschthaler, *Deixler-Hübner/Schauer* (2020) EuErbVO Art 10 para 18; Lein, *Dutta/Weber* (2021) EuErbVO Art 10 para 18.

[201] Müller-Lukoschek, *Die neue EU-Erbrechtsverordnung* (2015) § 2 para 240; Lein, *Dutta/Weber* (2021) EuErbVO Art 10 para 18.

[202] C-168/08 Laszlo Hadadi v. Csilla Marta Mesko [2009] ECR I-06871 [51 ff].

[203] Anatol Dutta, 'Entwicklungen im internationalen Familien- und Erbrecht der Europäischen Union bis Gogova' [2016] ZEuP 427, 439; Lein, *Dutta/Weber* (2021) EuErbVO Art 10 para 20.

[204] C-168/08 Laszlo Hadadi v. Csilla Marta Mesko [2009] ECR I-06871 [51].

[205] Müller-Lukoschek, *Die neue EU-Erbrechtsverordnung* (2015) § 2 para 240; Dutta, [2016] ZEuP 427, 439.

[206] Paul Lagarde, 'Les principes de base du nouveau règlement européen sur les successions' [2012] Rev crit dr int privé 691, 702; Bonomi, *Bonomi/Wautelet* (2016) ESR Art 10 para 18; Dutta, *MüKoBGB* (2020) EuErbVO Art 10 para 15; cf. Lein, *Dutta/Weber* (2021) EuErbVO Art 10 paras 20–22.

leaves the choice to beneficiaries as to which court to apply, nor the application of the effective nationality test, which may normally require European courts to decline jurisdiction in favour of the courts of a non-Member State whose nationality is effective, would make a difference. It is not certain in all the cases whether the third country courts would assume jurisdiction. Depending on their jurisdictional rules, they may not be able to exercise jurisdiction or may only be competent to rule specifically on the assets found in their territories. Article 10 is, thus, a useful tool from the Union's perspective to foreclose problems that could arise in such situations without having recourse to the *forum necessitatis* rule under Article 11.[207] It also aims, as explained above, to open European courts to succession cases that are still closely connected to the Union with the underlying policy of protecting heirs and creditors resident in the EU. Therefore, the courts of the Member State in which the assets of the estate are located and whose nationality the deceased had at the time of death, irrespective of other nationalities from outside of the Union, will exercise jurisdiction under Article 10(1) (a), even if there is a risk of concurrent jurisdiction with third States.[208] The rule may indeed give rise to jurisdiction conflicts and, subsequently, to conflicting decisions with third States, in particular with the State of habitual residence of the deceased.[209]

For example, a Dutch-Turkish dual national who is habitually resident in Turkey and who owns estate assets in both States may well choose Turkish law to govern his succession under Article 22. In this case, even though facts are also closely connected to Turkey, Dutch courts will be competent to hear the case under Article 10(1) (a) of the Regulation and are not permitted to decline jurisdiction under Article 6 in favour of Turkish courts.[210]

Such conflicts may also come into play within the scope of Article 10(1) (b) of the Regulation. In cases where the deceased does not hold the nationality of the Member State in which the assets belonging to the estate are located, the courts of this Member State are still competent to hear the case provided that the deceased had his former habitual residence at this State and, at the time the court was seised, no more than five years have passed since the change of habitual residence (Article 10(1) (b)). With this rule, the European legislature postulates that a previous habitual residence in the Member State where the assets of the estate are located also establishes a substantial connection between the case and the Union, even though the deceased is not a national of that Member State. In order to ensure that the jurisdiction estab-

---

[207] Buonaiuti, (2016) 12 J Priv Int L 545, 555; Buonaiuti, *Calvo Caravaca/Davì/Mansel* (2016) ESR Art 10 paras 19–20.

[208] Lein, *Dutta/Weber* (2021) EuErbVO Art 10 para 19.

[209] Lagarde, [2012] Rev crit dr int privé 691, 702; Lein, 'Die Erbrechtsverordnung aus Sicht der Drittstaaten' (2014) 206; Buonaiuti, (2016) 12 J Priv Int L 545, 555.

[210] See, however, below pp 255 ff.

lished according to this provision is not excessive, it includes a time restriction from the change of habitual residence. The Member State courts at the place of previous habitual residence are able to confer jurisdiction on the case, only where a period of not more than five years has elapsed since that habitual residence changed.[211]

The case of a Turkish national who moves to Turkey after living two years in a tiny apartment in the city centre of Helsinki and who then dies a year later in Istanbul is a hypothetical example of a matter falling in the scope of this provision.[212] In this case, Finnish courts will assume jurisdiction over the entire estate as the State of previous habitual residence in accordance with Article 10(1) (b) of the Regulation. This is because only one year passed after the move. On the other hand, Turkish courts will also assume jurisdiction over the entire estate as the deceased's last domicile is in Istanbul, regardless of the time spent in this city, and no importance will be given to the fact that Finnish courts may also exercise jurisdiction over the case.

To a limited extent, similar problems may also occur with the use of Article 10(2) of the Regulation. The provision provides that the Member State in which the assets are located will nevertheless have jurisdiction to rule on those assets even if the deceased was not a national of that Member State and did not have his previous habitual residence there or where more than five years passed from the change of habitual residence. The aim of the rule, however, is questionable from a third State perspective. This is because, as evident from the first paragraph which is primarily applicable, Article 10 normally operates under the philosophy that the European courts should still have authority over cases that are closely connected to the Union, despite the fact that the deceased is habitually resident in a third State. But in cases falling under the scope of the second paragraph, the case will generally have a much stronger connection to a third State than to a Member State. Hence, the jurisdiction assumed pursuant to this paragraph may be seen as exorbitant by third States,[213] which will result in a rejection of recognition or enforcement of the judgment rendered by Member State courts. With its limited scope, the provision obviously causes fragmentation in terms of jurisdiction, which may not be desirable for the beneficiaries since they may have to go to different courts for the same matter. Finally, it will again pose problems of concurrent jurisdiction and, in turn, conflicting decisions between Union courts and third State courts.[214]

---

[211] Buonaiuti, *Calvo Caravaca/Davì/Mansel* (2016) ESR Art 10 paras 14–15.

[212] This hypothetical example is inspired by Lein, *Dutta/Weber* (2021) EuErbVO Art 10 para 23.

[213] See, for a similar comment generally on the residual jurisdiction rule of the Regulation, Max Planck Institute for Comparative and International Private Law, (2010) 74 RabelsZ 522, 581.

Whilst these problems would normally occur concerning only the assets found in the Member States assuming jurisdiction over those assets, there are certain actions which would affect the entire estate. Actions respecting, for instance, the execution of a testamentary disposition or the reduction of excessive donations made by the deceased during his lifetime as regards the specific assets located in the Member States are limited in their scope and may cause jurisdiction conflicts only with respect to those assets. On the other hand, an action challenging the validity of a will affecting all the assets of the estate, including those located in third States and/or other Member States, is an example of a case which does not have a limited scope. In such a case, problems would be relevant to all assets, including the ones in third States. Unless Member State courts, as recommended by the scholars, restrict themselves to the assets located in their territories, even though the claim is not limited to those assets,[215] the jurisdiction conflicts will again concern all the assets.

It is obvious that by providing a subsidiary jurisdictional rule under Article 10, it has been ensured that the jurisdiction of Member State courts would be exercised on the same grounds also in cases relating to third States and difficulties relating to the delimitation of the scope of application of national and Union rules would not be faced;[216] and EU heirs, legatees, and other beneficiaries would be protected from the exorbitant domestic jurisdiction of Member States.[217] This uniform subsidiary jurisdiction rule is, therefore, more advantageous from the Union's perspective. However, as explained in detail above, it is likely to be problematic for the outside world.

As mentioned at the outset, the *forum rei sitae* has also been used as a subsidiary jurisdiction rule under the Turkish PILA. After explaining the Regulation's use of *forum rei sitae* for the same purposes, the approach of the Turkish PILA should also be explained in detail.

2. *Subsidiary Jurisdiction under the Turkish PILA*

The Turkish PILA, as explained above, adopted the domicile of the deceased as a general ground of jurisdiction in cross-border succession matters in light of the

---

[214] Bonomi, *Bonomi/Wautelet* (2016) ESR Art 10 para 28; Buonaiuti, *Calvo Caravaca/Davì/Mansel* (2016) ESR Art 10 para 19; Lein, *Dutta/Weber* (2021) EuErbVO Art 10 para 36.

[215] Bonomi, *Bonomi/Wautelet* (2016) ESR Art 10 para 26; Buonaiuti, *Calvo Caravaca/Davì/Mansel* (2016) ESR Art 10 para 18; Dutta, *MüKoBGB* (2020) EuErbVO Art 10 para 16; Lein, *Dutta/Weber* (2021) EuErbVO Art 10 para 34.

[216] See Recital 30 of the Regulation. See also Buonaiuti, *Calvo Caravaca/Davì/Mansel* (2016) ESR Art 10 para 3.

[217] Anna-Zoe Steiner, 'EU-Verordnung in Erbsachen sowie zur Einführung eines europäischen Nachlasszeugnisses' [2012] NZ 104, 109.

domestic rules on venue. Nevertheless, the domestic rules concerning venue were silent on the question of allocation of jurisdiction in cases where the deceased was domiciled outside Turkey but owned estate assets there.[218] Such cases could, however, frequently arise in practice, particularly due to the increasing number of Turkish nationals resident abroad, and there was a call for an additional rule in the domestic provisions, especially as regards succession matters on movables.[219] Turkish legislature therefore adopted a subsidiary jurisdiction rule referring to the *forum rei sitae* under Article 43 of the Turkish PILA.

The underlying reason for conferring jurisdiction on the *forum rei sitae* could be the general understanding that the courts of the place where the property is located are in the best position, in terms of proximity, to ascertain facts giving rise to the dispute and, particularly for immovables, to apply the mandatory provisions of that State as the *situs* of the property.[220] In succession cases, the rationale would be that these courts are best placed to rule on the devolution and transfer of the estate assets.[221]

The deceased may have assets in different States, as is prevalent in most international succession cases. For Turkish courts to assert jurisdiction in line with this provision, it will be enough that the deceased has estate assets in Turkey.[222] As the rule refers to 'assets of the estate' ('terekeye dâhil mallar'), it should be understood – in the way that the wording suggests and like in the Regulation – as covering only active elements of the estate. Conferring jurisdiction based solely on the liabilities may indeed give rise to exorbitant jurisdiction.[223]

The wording of the rule is not clear on the question as to which Turkish courts will be competent to hear the case if the deceased has assets in more than one place in Turkey. For example, consider a case where the deceased

---

[218] Vedat Raşit Seviğ, *Hukuk ve Ticaret Davalarında Türk ve Yabancı Mahkemelerinin Devletler Hususi Hukuku Bakımından Yetkisi* (Sulhi Garan Matbaası 1963) 3; İstanbul Üniversitesi Hukuk Fakültesi – Milletlerarası Hukuk ve Milletlerarası Münasebetler Enstitüsü, *MÖHUK Öntasarı Sempozyumu* (1978) 195; Ekşi, *Milletlerarası Yetki* (2000) 160.

[219] İstanbul Üniversitesi Hukuk Fakültesi – Milletlerarası Hukuk ve Milletlerarası Münasebetler Enstitüsü, *MÖHUK Öntasarı Sempozyumu* (1978) 195; 'Danışma Meclisi Tutanakları – Milletlerarası Özel Hukuk ve Usul Hukuku Hakkında Kanun Tasarısı ve Adalet Komisyonu Raporu (1/5)', (1981) 1.

[220] Cf. István Szászy, *International Civil Procedure – A Comparative Study* (A. W. Sijthoff-Leyden 1967) 300. See, in the context of Brussels regime, C-73/77 Theodorus Engelbertus Sanders v. Ronald van der Putte [1977] ECR 02383 [12ff]; C-115/88 Mario P. A. Reichert and others v. Dresdner Bank [1990] ECR I-00027 [10]; Luís Pedro Rocha de Lima Pinheiro, in Ulrich Magnus and Peter Mankowski (eds), *European Commentaries on Private International Law – Brussels Ibis Regulation*, vol 1 (Sellier European Law Publishers 2016) Brussels Ibis Art 24 paras 23–24.

[221] In the context of Regulation, see above p 218.

[222] Ekşi, *Milletlerarası Miras Hukuku* (2013) 29.

[223] Süha Tanrıver, *Medenî Usûl Hukuku*, vol 1 (4th edn, Yetkin 2021) 251 (in the context of Art 9 of the Turkish Code of Civil Procedure).

(A) left, apart from his assets outside Turkey, an apartment in Ankara and a farm in Mersin. The issue arising here is whether the courts of both Mersin and Istanbul are competent to hear the case or whether jurisdiction should belong to one of them. During the drafting of the provision (with Article 30 of the former Turkish PILA as the source of the current rule), it was proposed that more precise statements on this issue such as 'the courts of the place in Turkey where the majority of the estate assets found', 'the courts of the place in Turkey where the immovable estate assets are located', or 'each court of the place in Turkey where the assets are found' could be added to the provision. However, none of these statements was adopted by the Turkish legislature.[224] Notwithstanding this, scholars rightly argue that the rule should be understood so as to grant jurisdiction in such cases to each Turkish court where the assets are found. Therefore, according to this view, in the example both the courts of Mersin and Istanbul will be competent to hear the case.[225]

Here again, the question arises whether Turkish courts will exercise jurisdiction in line with this provision regardless of the value and the amount of the assets. The views on Article 16 of the former Turkish Code of Civil Procedure,[226] which grants jurisdiction to the courts of the place where the assets are located to rule on claims regarding property rights filed against individuals who are not domiciled in Turkey, could be mentioned here. Scholars have argued that the amount and the value of the assets are not taken into consideration by Turkish courts when assuming jurisdiction in line with this article. Turkish courts will take jurisdiction even in cases in which the property in question is non-seisable and of low retail value.[227] However, assuming jurisdiction over an asset with a significantly low value may amount to exorbitant jurisdiction. Therefore, it was contended that things like a shaving kit,[228] clothes,[229] shoes, or a toothbrush[230] left at a hotel should not be enough to

---

224 İstanbul Üniversitesi Hukuk Fakültesi – Milletlerarası Hukuk ve Milletlerarası Münasebetler Enstitüsü, *MÖHUK Öntasarı Sempozyumu* (1978) 215–216.

225 Ekşi, *Milletlerarası Yetki* (2000) 166–167; Aybay and Dardağan, *Kanunlar İhtlilafı* (2008) 60; Tütüncübaşı, *Yabancı Çekişmesiz Yargı Kararlarının Tanınması* (2014) 156; Çelikel and Erdem, *Milletlerarası Özel Hukuk* (2021) 630.

226 It should be noted that the rule was later replaced with Art 9 of the current Turkish Code of Civil Procedure, which grants jurisdiction only to the courts of the place where the disputed property is located.

227 Belgesay, *Şerh* (1939) 34; Sabri Şakir Ansay, *Hukuk Yargılama Usulleri* (7th edn, Güzel Sanatlar Matbaası 1960) 100; Ekşi, *Milletlerarası Yetki* (2000) 140–141; Kuru, *Hukuk Muhakemeleri Usulü/vol 1* (2001) 408–409.

228 The example is given in the scope of Art 10 of the Regulation by Gitschthaler, *Deixler-Hübner/Schauer* (2020) EuErbVO Art 10 para 3.

229 Kuru, *Hukuk Muhakemeleri Usulü/vol 1* (2001) 409.

230 Çelikel and Erdem, *Milletlerarası Özel Hukuk* (2021) 579.

assume jurisdiction according to this article.[231] The same could also be argued in respect of the subsidiary jurisdiction rule in Article 43, and the rule should not be used so as to give rise to exorbitant jurisdiction. Nonetheless, this could come into play only in such extreme cases, and it seems that the courts will assume jurisdiction in the vast majority of the cases without taking into account the value and the amount of the estate assets, as the rule does not restrict its scope. Imagine, for example, that Polish national *(P)* is habitually resident in Warsaw/Poland and dies there intestate, leaving assets in different countries, including Poland, which have a total worth of more than one million euros. In addition to these assets, he also left an old car in Turkey which he used during his business visits. If an issue concerning his succession arises and one of the heirs brings an action in Turkey, it seems that according to the subsidiary jurisdiction rule under Article 43, Turkish courts will consider themselves competent to hear the case regardless of the fact that *(P)* had only an old and financially insignificant car in Turkey.[232]

Another significant question as regards the issue of jurisdiction for the Turkish-EU succession is whether the jurisdiction of Turkish courts in such instances is limited to assets situated in Turkey. This is because Turkish courts in the above example would be able to assume jurisdiction only for the car in Turkey if the rule has a limited scope. A restriction in this regard would have obviously been propitious, thus preventing jurisdiction conflicts to a certain extent. Yet the wording of the provision does not suggest any limitation on its scope. When this is the case, in addition to the potential jurisdiction conflicts, there might be the risk that recognition or enforcement of the decision rendered by Turkish courts may be refused in the State where recognition and/or enforcement is sought. Nevertheless, neither the jurisdiction conflicts nor the recognition and enforcement problems as such are deemed to be sufficient for courts to decline jurisdiction under Turkish international procedural law.[233] In line with this understanding, the subsidiary jurisdictional rule under Article 43 of the Turkish PILA does not seem to be restrictive.

---

[231] Ekşi, *Milletlerarası Yetki* (2000) 141; Kuru, *Hukuk Muhakemeleri Usulü/vol 1* (2001) 277; Nomer, *Devletler Hususî Hukuku* (2021) 470.

[232] Cf. Ekşi, *Milletlerarası Yetki* (2000) 141; Kuru, *Hukuk Muhakemeleri Usulü/vol 1* (2001) 409.

[233] Nomer, *Milletlerarası Usul Hukuku* (2018) 54; Çelikel and Erdem, *Milletlerarası Özel Hukuk* (2021) 578; Şanlı, Esen and Ataman Figanmeşe, *Milletlerarası Özel Hukuk* (2021) 453–454; cf. Kuru, *Hukuk Muhakemeleri Usulü/vol 1* (2001) 633. It has long been argued that assuming jurisdiction particularly over immovable property located in other States could result in recognition and enforcement problems. However, jurisdictional rules are provided regardless of these problems: Nomer, (1974) 40 İÜHFM 393, 419; Nomer, (1981) 1 MHB 61, 62; Nomer, *Milletlerarası Usul Hukuku* (2018) 94–95; contra Kuru, *Hukuk Muhakemeleri Usulü/vol 1* (2001) 635. It cannot be argued that the Turkish legislature never considered these problems when laying down jurisdictional rules. An illustrative

As examples of provisions with a restrictive scope, the relevant rules of the Swiss PILA, as another third State law from the perspective of the Union, could be examined here. The Swiss PILA includes two articles under Section 6 on subsidiary jurisdiction in succession cases.

The first rule is Article 87, carrying the title of 'jurisdiction at the place of origin' ('Heimatzuständigkeit'). In order to prevent jurisdiction conflicts, particularly of a negative nature, with other State courts,[234] the article provides that the Swiss courts and authorities at the place of domicile should be competent over the estate of a Swiss national having his last domicile abroad, unless the courts and authorities of the relevant foreign State, i.e. the State of the last domicile of the deceased,[235] deal with this estate. It is only in the cases in which the deceased submits his entire estate or the assets located in Switzerland, by way of a testamentary disposition, to the jurisdiction or the law of Switzerland that Swiss courts are always competent to hear the case, without prejudice to the exclusive jurisdiction claimed by the courts of the place where the immovable estate are located (i.e. Article 86(2)).

---

example in this regard is Art 9 of the Turkish Code of Civil Procedure, which is applicable also in international cases as a consequence of Art 40 of the Turkish PILA, authorising domestic jurisdictional rules also for the devolution of international jurisdiction. It provides that the courts at the place of habitual residence of the person in question should have jurisdiction to rule on actions filed against persons who are not domiciled in Turkey. Nevertheless, actions regarding property rights could also be brought before the courts of the place where the property that is the subject matter of the dispute is located. That is to say that the case could be brought before the Turkish courts only when the property that is the subject matter of the case is in Turkey. In the preamble of the Law, the rationale behind granting jurisdiction to 'the courts of the place where the relevant property is located' rather than to 'the courts of the places where properties of the person in question are located' is stated as being the prevention of problems regarding recognition and enforcement of Turkish judgments in other States based on exorbitant jurisdiction. In other words, the Turkish legislature clearly justified the restrictive scope of the rule due to potential recognition and enforcement problems that such decisions may encounter outside Turkey. For the preamble of the Law, see <https://www.tbmm.gov.tr/sirasayi/donem23/yil01/ss393.pdf> accessed 27 July 2018. For criticism of this reasoning, see Çelikel and Erdem, *Milletlerarası Özel Hukuk* (2021) 578–579.

234 Botschaft zum IPR-Gesetz vom 10. November 1982, BBl 1982 264, 383 (no 262.2); Andreas Bucher, 'Das neue internationale Erbrecht (Geringfügig geänderte Fassung eines Berichts für die Seminare der Weiterbildungsstufe der Hochschule St. Gallen vom 3. Juni, 3. September und 17. November 1987)' (1988) 69 ZGBR 145, 150; Jolanta Kren Kostkiewicz, *IPRG/LugÜ Kommentar – Bundesgesetz über das Internationale Privatrecht, Lugano-Übereinkommen und weitere Erlasse* (2nd edn, orell füssli 2019) IPRG Art 87 para 2.

235 Bucher, (1988) 69 ZGBR 145, 150; Hans Rainer Künzle, in Markus Müller-Chen and Corinne Widmer Lüchinger (eds), *Zürcher Kommentar zum IPRG: Kommentar zum Bundesgesetz über das Internationale Privatrecht (IPRG) vom 18. Dezember 1987*, vol 1 (3rd edn, Schulthess 2018) IPRG Art 87 para 1; Kren Kostkiewicz, *OFK-IPRG/LugÜ* (2019) IPRG Art 87 para 1.

Imagine, for instance, that Swiss national *(S)* from Zürich is habitually resident in Paris and dies there intestate, leaving a car and a penthouse in Paris as well as a bank account and an apartment in Zürich. In this case, Zürich courts – pursuant to Article 87(1) – will assume jurisdiction on succession only if French courts do not deal with the estate. Hence, a potential jurisdiction conflict with French courts, at least to some extent, can be prevented.[236]

The second rule provided under Article 88 is titled as 'jurisdiction at the place where the property is located' ('Zuständigkeit am Ort der gelegenen Sache'). It grants jurisdiction to the Swiss courts and authorities at the *situs* of the property to rule on this property in succession cases of a foreign national deceased whose last domicile is outside Switzerland. Like the previous one, the aim of the provision is to avoid conflicts of jurisdiction, primarily negative ones,[237] and hence it is also applicable on the condition that the courts and authorities of the respective State, e.g. the State of last domicile or origin of the deceased,[238] decline jurisdiction over the property found in Switzerland.

A hypothetical scenario may be formulated as follows: Spanish businessperson *(S)*, habitually resident in Madrid, has two cars and a house in Madrid. However, he keeps his earnings in his bank account in Switzerland. He dies suddenly in Madrid without making any testamentary dispositions. In this case, Swiss courts will be competent to hear claims concerning succession on the money in *(S)*'s bank account only when the Spanish courts do not assume jurisdiction. Such an instance is however not conceivable on the grounds that Spanish courts, in principle, are sole authorities ruling on succession as a whole within the scope of the Regulation (Article 4).

The above explanations on the similar provisions of Switzerland indicate that the subsidiary jurisdiction rule of the Turkish PILA – conferring jurisdiction on the courts of the place where the property belonging to the estate is located (Article 43) – has a relatively greater likelihood of triggering conflicts of jurisdiction with Member State courts by virtue of its non-restrictive wording. Had the scenarios in the last two examples related to Turkey instead of Switzerland, Turkish courts would be conferred jurisdiction in accordance with this rule, and this could then result in positive conflicts of jurisdiction with Member State courts. Notwithstanding this, as jurisdiction is considered to be within the sovereign powers of a State, it is normal that every legal system determines in which cases its court will have jurisdiction, without considering the jurisdiction rules in other States and without concern about possible conflicts of jurisdiction with other States. Hence, by virtue of the

---

236 For a similar example, see Romano, (2015–2016) XVII YbPIL 253, 273.

237 Botschaft zum IPR-Gesetz vom 10. November 1982, BBl 1982 264, 384 (262.3); Künzle, *Zürcher Kommentar zum IPRG* (2018) IPRG Art 88 para 1; Kren Kostkiewicz, *OFK-IPRG/LugÜ* (2019) IPRG Art 88 para 6.

238 Bucher, (1988) 69 ZGBR 145, 152–153.

rules adopted in the Regulation and in the Turkish PILA, jurisdiction conflicts are likely to arise in Turkish-EU successions. Examples in this regard are examined below with the help of hypothetical scenarios.

3. *Possible Jurisdiction Conflicts: Exemplary Case Scenarios*

After explaining both subsidiary jurisdiction rules concerning succession in the Turkish-EU context, examples should be given to indicate possible jurisdiction conflicts arising out of the interplay between the subsidiary jurisdiction rules and the general jurisdiction rules of each legal system. Such cases could be divided into two groups. The first group of examples will only consider the potential area of conflicts between Article 10 of the Regulation and the general or subsidiary jurisdiction rule under the Turkish PILA. The second group of examples will subsequently focus on the friction between Article 4 of the Regulation and the subsidiary jurisdiction rule of Article 43 of the Turkish PILA.

a) *Article 10 of the Regulation vs. Article 43 of the Turkish PILA*

aa) *Case No 1 – Article 10(1) (a) of the Regulation vs. Article 43 of the Turkish PILA*

(1) *Scenario 1*

Czech national (C) is resident in Istanbul/Turkey, where he has for many years also been a partner in a Turkish subsidiary of a globally-known Czech pharmaceutical company. In addition to his company shares, he has a car, a house, and a significant amount of money held in a bank account in Turkey. At the same time, he has a bank account with 5,000 euros cash in a branch of a Czech bank located in Prague. He dies in Istanbul.

In this case, *(C)* is resident in Turkey for many years where he conducts business. His residence in Turkey, therefore, cannot be seen as temporary. In addition, he has a substantial amount of assets in Turkey. Acquisition of such amounts of movable and immovable property in Turkey may be seen as an indication that he has the intention to stay there permanently. Hence, it could be concluded that *(C)*'s last domicile is located in Turkey, as the two constituent elements of Turkish domicile exist in the case. Turkish courts will then have jurisdiction over the case in accordance with the general jurisdiction rule under Article 43 of the Turkish PILA.

From the Regulation's perspective, however, *(C)*'s Czech nationality establishes a close link between the case and the Czech Republic, and thus Czech courts are competent to hear the case under Article 10(1) (a) as regards his world-wide estate. His residence in Turkey and his owning many assets there will have no effect on the jurisdiction of the Court.

(2) Scenario 2

Czech national (C) is domiciled in London and has most of his assets there. In addition, he has 5,000 euros cash in a branch of a Czech bank located in Prague and a small apartment in Istanbul, where he sometimes visits for business purposes.

This scenario with two non-Member States also portrays the potential conflicts in cross-border succession cases relating to third States, as each State has a different jurisdictional rule.

From the English perspective, English courts will be competent to hear the case. This is because English rules of jurisdiction are traditionally based on territoriality. If a person is in the territorial jurisdiction of an English court, he has impliedly accepted the authority of the English courts. The fact that a person could be served with a writ of the proceedings is sufficient for English courts to assume jurisdiction. This is possible, in the first place, when that person is domiciled in England.[239] Following this approach, the last domicile of the deceased is decisive on the jurisdiction of English courts in succession cases.[240] The courts normally have discretion on the application of these rules due to the fact that assuming jurisdiction in some cases may prove exorbitant or unfair for the defendant in the action; or the case may lack a sufficient link with England; or, quite the contrary, it may be well connected to England even though the defendant or a relevant person is domiciled outside England.[241] In succession cases, the existence of estate assets in England will generally be enough for English courts to exercise jurisdiction, although the deceased is not domiciled in England.[242] Likewise, when the deceased has assets in different States, the courts of foreign States in which those assets are located should be competent to hear the case.[243]

The deceased's small apartment in Turkey will be sufficient to confer jurisdiction on Turkish courts in accordance with the rule of subsidiary jurisdiction under Article 43 of the Turkish PILA. As mentioned earlier, the rule does not suggest any restriction with regards to the value, amount, or location of the estate assets. Therefore, it is highly likely that the courts will exercise jurisdiction over the entire estate if the case is brought before the Turkish courts.

From the perspective of the Regulation, Czech courts will confer jurisdiction over the entire estate, irrespective of the fact that the deceased has left

239 Pippa Rogerson, *Collier's Conflict of Laws* (4th edn, Cambridge University Press 2013) 139ff; Adrian Briggs, *Civil Jurisdiction and Judgments* (7th edn, Routledge 2021) paras 21.01ff.

240 Collins, *Dicey, Morris & Collins the Conflict of Laws* (2012) Rule 131.

241 Rogerson, *Collier's Conflict of Laws* (2013) 139.

242 Miller, *International Aspects of Succession* (2000) 6; Collins, *Dicey, Morris & Collins the Conflict of Laws* (2012) Rule 131.

243 Collins, *Dicey, Morris & Collins the Conflict of Laws* (2012) Rule 132–133.

only five thousand euros cash in a bank account there, since the deceased is a national of the Czech Republic (Article 10(1) (a)).

bb) Case No 2 – Article 10(1) (b) of the Regulation vs. Article 43 of the Turkish PILA

Turkish national (T) is habitually resident in Tallinn/Estonia with his family for many years where he also works as a pilot with an Estonian airline. He has a car, a house, and some amount of money held in an Estonian bank. Due to the financial problems faced by the airline, he loses his job. After searching for a new job for a couple of months, he decides to move to Ankara/Turkey where he was born and spent his childhood. He sells his car and withdraws the money in his bank account, using this money to buy a new house in Ankara. He takes his family with him and they start living in Ankara. After four years, however, (T) has a car accident and dies in Ankara.

This scenario involving Turkey and Estonia is another example of cases in which there exists a clash between the general jurisdiction rule of the Turkish PILA and the subsidiary jurisdiction rule in the Regulation.

When the case is brought before the Turkish courts, Turkish courts will take jurisdiction in line with Article 43, as *(T)* was domiciled in Ankara from the Turkish perspective. Whereas he lived for many years outside Turkey, he moved to Ankara permanently with his family and started living there with the intention to settle. Therefore, it is highly likely that the courts will find that the last domicile of *(T)* is located in Ankara.

Should a succession proceeding be filed before the Estonian courts shortly after his death, the court will also assume jurisdiction over the case by virtue of the fact that *(T)* had his previous habitual residence in Tallinn and not more than five years have elapsed since the change of habitual residence, as required by Article 10(1) (b) of the Regulation.

cc) Case No 3 – Article 10(2) of the Regulation vs. Article 43 of the Turkish PILA

(1) Scenario 1

After living and working in Athens/Greece for many years, Turkish national (T) decides to move to Izmir/Turkey where his parents still live. He sells all his property but keeps the bank account in an Athenian bank upon leaving. In addition to the bank account in Athens he owns an apartment located in the heart of Izmir. After ten years of residence in Izmir, he dies there.

In this case, a jurisdiction conflict between the Turkish courts and Greek courts may arise as a result of Article 10(2) of the Regulation. This is because *(T)* moved to Izmir with the intention to stay permanently and lived there for a significant amount of time prior to his death. These facts amount to his having already established his domicile in Turkey, and, hence, Turkish courts will be competent over the entire estate pursuant to Article 43 of the Turkish PILA.

Whilst the case is more closely connected to Turkey owing to the fact that *(T)* had the nationality of Turkey and was domiciled there, the Athenian court will take jurisdiction in respect of the bank account if the case is brought before Athenian courts. As a consequence, a jurisdiction conflict regarding the money in the Athenian bank account will arise.

(2) Scenario 2

After living and working in Athens for many years, (T) permanently moves to Switzerland and dies there after ten years. He leaves behind a penthouse and a bank account in Athens, a small villa in a village of Switzerland, and a city apartment in Izmir.

In this second version, a potential jurisdiction conflict might arise between two third States and a Member State.

From the Swiss perspective, Swiss courts are competent over the case pursuant to Article 86(1) of the Swiss PILA, as the last domicile of the deceased is in Switzerland. Nevertheless, it is provided in Article 86(2) of the Swiss PILA that the Swiss courts may opt not to rule on the immovable estate assets located in other States as long as the courts of those States have exclusive jurisdiction over these assets. This could be the case for the apartment in Izmir by virtue of the exclusive jurisdiction of Turkish courts for the immovables situated in Turkey.[244] The Regulation, by contrast, does not provide any exclusive head of jurisdiction for immovables. Therefore, Article 86(2) cannot be applied for the penthouse in Athens. The money in the bank account is also not in the scope of Article 86(2) and thus will be subject to the jurisdiction of Swiss courts.

Turkish courts will assume jurisdiction in accordance with Article 43 of the Turkish PILA, as the deceased also left an apartment in Izmir. A rule similar to Article 86(2) of the Swiss PILA, allowing Turkish courts to decline jurisdiction over the immovable and/or movable assets located in other States, does not exist in the Turkish PILA.

Greek courts will also assert jurisdiction over the penthouse and the money in the bank account in Athens according to Article 10(2) of the Regulation.

b) Article 4 of the Regulation vs. Subsidiary Jurisdiction under Article 43 of the Turkish PILA

aa) Case No 1

Turkish national (T) has lived in Stockholm/Sweden since 1992 with his three children and Swedish wife. He works as a civil engineer in a large Swedish construction company. His parents and brothers still live in Turkey, and he therefore spends fifteen days of his vacation each year with his family in Turkey. He has a car accident in Stockholm one day when driving home at late night and dies there intestate. His estate includes two cars, three

[244] On the issue of exclusive jurisdiction, see below, pp 234ff.

houses in Stockholm and a significant amount of money in Swedish banks as well as a summerhouse and a tractor in Turkey, which he bought for his farmer father.

In this case, *(T)* has his family, social, and business life in Stockholm. Although he has ties with Turkey, this is not strong enough as to conclude that he is domiciled in Turkey. Hence, as his last habitual residence is in Stockholm, Swedish courts will be competent over the case. On the other hand, Turkish courts will likewise assume jurisdiction if the case is brought before them, in accordance with the subsidiary jurisdiction rule under Article 43 given that *(T)* had assets in Turkey. A positive conflict of jurisdiction may thus arise between the Turkish and Swedish courts.

The outcome would have actually been the same had *(T)* owned either only the tractor he bought for his father in Turkey along with other assets in Stockholm or, alternatively, only a car in Stockholm along with other assets in Turkey by virtue of the fact that none of the rules have a restrictive scope.

bb) Case No 2

Belgian national (B), who is habitually resident in Antwerp/Belgium, buys a summerhouse in Bodrum/Turkey after his retirement in order to enjoy the sunny weather during the summer months. He comes there each year with his wife for one or two months and keeps in a Turkish bank some money which is enough to pay the bills when he is not there and to cover their expenses during their holiday. On the other hand, he has a significant amount of assets in Antwerp as he spent almost his entire life there. He dies by drowning in the sea during one of his visits to Turkey.

This hypothetical scenario concerning senior tourism is once again another example where the deceased is habitually resident in a Member State but holds properties in Turkey. In this case, courts of both countries will again assume jurisdiction over the matter as the State of habitual residence on the one side (Article 4 of the Regulation) and as the State where an immovable asset is located on the other side (Article 43 of the Turkish PILA).

The above examples also indicate that the jurisdiction rules of Turkey and the European Union are likely to overlap in matters of cross-border succession. Consequently, there will be jurisdiction conflicts between the two legal systems and, in some cases depending on the applicable law, different outcomes at the end of the proceedings. Further, jurisdiction conflicts may result in a refusal to recognise or enforce the decision in the other State if there is a claim of exclusive jurisdiction by one of the States. This may come into play in the Turkish-EU context as the jurisdiction of Turkish courts is deemed to be exclusive for immovables located in Turkey. Although the only group of cases in which a certain level of coherence could be reached is the group covered by the Turkish-German Treaty, the jurisdiction rule of the Treaty also seems to be exclusive, something which – especially for succession matters on movable properties – presents difficulties for Turkish nationals living in

Germany. Therefore, the issue of exclusive jurisdiction should also be analysed from the perspectives of each legal text.

III. Exclusive (Indirect) Jurisdiction?

States may sometimes designate exclusive jurisdiction rules for certain matters – due to their effects on that State's public policy as well as its political and economic interests – so as to assure that the right to adjudicate those matters will be reserved to their courts to the exclusion of all other State courts.[245] Each State, indeed, determines the distribution of jurisdiction between its own courts, and this has no effect on the jurisdiction of the courts of other States. Therefore, it is arguable that creating exclusive heads of jurisdiction, in principle, does not stop other courts located in another corner of the world to proceed with the matter. The importance of exclusive bases of jurisdiction, however, lies in the fact that any decision delivered by a foreign court on matters which falls into the scope of those bases will not be recognised and, hence, will not produce legal effects in the country where those rules exist.[246] Although the plausibility of the reasons underlying exclusivity in such cases may be questionable in today's world,[247] in the vast majority of legal systems matters concerning immovables are commonly afforded exclusive bases of jurisdiction.[248] This also applies to succession matters involving immovable property.[249]

As the Regulation follows a monist approach which does not submit movable and immovable parts of the estate to different regimes, it does not provide a separate exclusive head of jurisdiction for succession matters concerning immovable assets.[250] The exclusive nature of a jurisdiction rule, as men-

---

[245] Szászy, *International Civil Procedure* (1967) 298; Diego P. Fernández Arroyo, 'Compétence exclusive et compétence exorbitante dans les relations privées internationales' (2006) 323 RdC 9, 80–82; Ekşi, *Milletlerarası Miras Hukuku* (2013) 137.

[246] Szászy, *International Civil Procedure* (1967) 299.

[247] See, for example, Peter Hay, 'The Situs Rule in European and American Conflicts Law – Comparative Notes' in Peter Hay and Michael H. Hoeflich (eds), *Property Law and Legal Education – Essays in Honor of John E. Cribbet* (University of Illinois Press 1988) 109 ff; Fernández Arroyo, (2006) 323 RdC 9, 82–83; cf. Szászy, *International Civil Procedure* (1967) 301. Critiques also exist as regards the predominance of the *situs* principle in terms of the law applicable to immovables. See, for example, Russell J. Weintraub, 'An Inquiry Into the Utility of Situs as a Concept in Conflicts Analysis' (1966) 52 Cornell LQ 1; Hay, 'The Situs Rule' (1988) 109 ff.

[248] Szászy, *International Civil Procedure* (1967) 300; Fernández Arroyo, (2006) 323 RdC 9, 84.

[249] Cf. Weintraub, (1966) 52 Cornell LQ 1, 2.

[250] Benoît Chappuis and Julien Perrin, 'Le Règlement (UE) N° 650/2012 du Parlement européen et du Conseil du 4 juillet 2012 relatif à la compétence, la loi applicable, la reconnaissance et l'exécution des décisions, et l'acceptation et l'exécution des actes authentiques en matière de successions et à la création d'un certificat successoral européen'

tioned, is in fact important at the stage of recognition and enforcement. The Regulation does not provide a harmonised mechanism for recognition and enforcement of judgments which emanate from third States. Member States will accordingly refer back to their national rules to decide on whether a decision from a non-Member State country, from Turkey, for example, will produce any effects in their territory. Whereas the jurisdiction of Member State courts under the Regulation (Article 4 et seq.) does not encompass the notion of exclusivity with respect to immovables of the deceased, one might ask whether domestic *indirect*[251] jurisdiction rules of this kind might not give rise to refusals to recognise and enforce a non-Member State decision also concerning immovable assets situated in the Member State (where recognition or enforcement procedures take place). Nevertheless, the Regulation's uniform *direct* rules of jurisdiction leave no room for the national jurisdiction rules of Member States. The courts of Member States will, therefore, examine only their (indirect) jurisdiction in accordance with Article 4 et seq. of the Regulation at the stage of recognition or enforcement, even for decisions from a third State. In line with this, the mere fact that the decision involves immovable assets located in the EU area cannot be a ground for refusing to recognise or enforce the decision.[252]

Thus, it seems that there would be no such problem as regards Turkish judgments involving immovable assets in Member States. If, for example, in a succession case involving a French national domiciled in Turkey, Turkish courts issued a decision on, together with other assets of the deceased, a house

---

[2014] Not@lex 1, 22; Lein, 'Die Erbrechtsverordnung aus Sicht der Drittstaaten' (2014) 216; Pascal Grolimund and Eva Bachofner, 'Schweizer Zuständigkeit über im EU-Raum belegene Liegenschaften im Lichte der EU-Erbrechtsverordnung' in Peter Breitschmid and others (eds), *Tatsachen, Verfahren, Vollstreckung: Festschrift für Isaak Meier zum 65. Geburtstag* (Schulthess 2015) 286; Romano, (2015–2016) XVII YbPIL 253, 267–268; Ilaria Pretelli, in Andrea Bonomi and Patrick Wautelet (eds), *Le droit européen des successions-Commentaire du Règlement n°650/2012 du 4 juillet 2012* (2nd edn, Bruylant 2016) Introduction au Chapitre IV para 10; 'Änderung des Bundesgesetzes über das Internationale Privatrecht (Erbrecht) – Erläuternder Bericht zum Vernehmlassungsentwurf' 12 Art 86(2) <https://www.admin.ch/ch/d/gg/pc/documents/2934/IPRG-Erbrecht_Erl.-Bericht_de.pdf> accessed 19 July 2018; cf. Buonaiuti, (2016) 12 J Priv Int L 545, 559–560.

For a proposal that was made during the drafting process of the Regulation in favour of an exclusive rule of jurisdiction for the courts of the Member State in which the property is situated, see Max Planck Institute for Comparative and International Private Law, (2010) 74 RabelsZ 522, 594–596.

[251] For a brief explanation on the concepts of direct and indirect jurisdiction, see Ralf Michaels, 'Jurisdiction, Foundations' in Jürgen Basedow and others (eds), *Encyclopedia of Private International Law* (Edward Elgar Publishing 2017) 1043.

[252] Buonaiuti, (2016) 12 J Priv Int L 545, 559–560; Pretelli, *Bonomi/Wautelet* (2016) Introduction au Chapitre IV para 10 and fn 20; Romano, (2015–2016) XVII YbPIL 253, 267–268; cf. Chappuis and Perrin, [2014] Not@lex 1, 22.

situated in France, recognition of the decision would not be rejected in France solely because the courts of France have exclusive competence to rule on immovables located within French territories.[253] The Regulation's uniform and unitary approach towards jurisdiction would not allow for such a rejection.[254]

Problems of this kind may, however, occur for judgments of Member States which seek recognition or enforcement in Turkey owing to the fact that the jurisdiction of Turkish courts under Article 43 of the Turkish PILA is regarded as exclusive for succession proceedings which have as their object immovable assets located in Turkey. The jurisdiction rule under the Turkish-German Treaty also seems to have an exclusive nature – different from the Turkish PILA – not only for immovable assets but also for movable assets. Thus, a closer look into these rules is still essential for Turkish-EU successions.

Although there seems to be near unanimity[255] in Turkish legal academia and practice as regards the exclusive character of Article 43 of the Turkish PILA in proceedings concerning succession on immovables located in Turkey, the reasoning behind this exclusivity differs. Some commentators contend that the exclusive nature of Article 43 of the Turkish PILA could be inferred from domestic rules of jurisdiction on succession. Owing to the fact that domestic procedural rules on venue are given, as explained earlier, dual functionality under Article 40 of the Turkish PILA so as to determine also the international jurisdiction of Turkish courts in cases having cross-border elements, they should be determinative for the interpretation of Article 43 of the Turkish PILA. Article 11(1) of the Turkish Code of Civil Procedure, which allocates internal jurisdiction in succession proceedings, explicitly provides that the jurisdiction of the Turkish court in the last domicile of the deceased is *exclusive* in actions for the sharing-out of the estate and for actions for the recovery of inheritance. Therefore, it is concluded that the jurisdiction of Turkish courts under Article 43 of the Turkish PILA is also exclusive, following the wording of Article 11(1) of the Turkish Code of Civil Procedure.[256]

---

[253] This was the case in France before the Regulation: Stefan Stade, 'Die EU-Erbrechtsverordnung Nr. 650/2012 und deren Auswirkungen auf diverse Länder' in DACH Europäische Anwaltsvereinigung e.V. (ed), *Die EU-Erbrechtsverordnung Nr. 650/2012 und deren Auswirkung auf diverse Länder* (Schulthess 2014) 167. For the same example as formulated for Switzerland, see Pretelli, *Bonomi/Wautelet* (2016) Introduction au Chapitre IV para 10-Cas 4.

[254] Pretelli, *Bonomi/Wautelet* (2016) Introduction au Chapitre IV para 10.

[255] See for views arguing the opposite, Demir Gökyayla, 'Mirasçılık Belgeleri' (2006) 575; Tanrıbilir, 'MÖHUK ve Mirasa İlişkin Bağlama Kuralının Uygulanmasında Öne Çıkan Hususlar' (2018) 137–138. It appears to be very difficult to find legal scholars in Turkey who argue against the exclusive head of jurisdiction in cases which have as their object rights *in rem* in immovable properties in general. See, however, Erkan, (2012) 20 SÜHFD 11; cf. Belgesay, *Şerh* (1939) 50–51.

[256] Nomer, *Milletlerarası Usul Hukuku* (2018) 120 and 192 fn 284.

The Turkish Court of Cassation also ruled in one case that the international jurisdiction of Turkish courts located in the last domicile of the deceased is exclusive in cross-border succession cases as is the case in domestic law.[257]

Another view argues that the jurisdiction of Turkish courts under Article 43 is exclusive by virtue not of Article 11(1) but rather of Article 12(1) of the Turkish Code of Civil Procedure, allocating jurisdiction of Turkish courts in proceedings which have as their object rights *in rem* in immovable property.[258] This Article also clearly states that the jurisdiction of the court of the *situs* of the property is *exclusive* in such proceedings. Based on this, it is maintained that the jurisdiction of Turkish courts where an immovable asset of the deceased is situated (which becomes competent through the subsidiary ground of jurisdiction under Article 43 of the Turkish PILA) is also exclusive in a succession proceeding which involves rights *in rem* in that asset.[259] This would be the case, for example, in an action brought by the rightful heir to claim the title of an immovable asset against its current possessor (i.e. an action for the recovery of inheritance), as it is an action concerning a right *in rem* in realty.[260]

Certain scholars, on the other hand, find for the exclusive nature of the jurisdictional rule under Article 43 in cases concerning immovable assets in Turkey as a result of the conflict-of-laws rule applicable to them. As explained in detail in the previous chapter, the general conflict rule under Article 20(1) of the Turkish PILA adopts nationality as the main connecting factor in determining the law applicable to succession matters but submits such matters on immovable assets located in Turkey to the sole authority of Turkish law. Turkish law is the one that should govern those succession issues on immovables because of, among other things, the restrictions applicable in Turkish law for the acquisition of immovable assets by foreign nationals – restrictions which are claimed to affect also the succession rights of these individuals – and because of the fact that any decision rendered will cause the transfer of title on the assets at the public registry of deeds. Thus, it is postulated that the jurisdiction of Turkish courts in cases which have as their objects immovable properties belonging to the estate located in Turkey should

257 Yargıtay 2. Hukuk Dairesi, T. 24.6.1999, E. 1999/5494 K. 1999/7289 <https://legalbank.net/> accessed 27 January 2021.

258 Sargın, *Yetki Anlaşmaları* (1996) 154; Emre Esen, 'Türk Hukukunda Yabancı Mahkeme Kararlarının Tanınması ve Tenfizinde Münhasır Yetki Kavramı' (2002) 22 MHB 183, 190–191; Tütüncübaşı, *Yabancı Çekişmesiz Yargı Kararlarının Tanınması* (2014) 158; Özkan and Tütüncübaşı, *Uluslararası Usûl Hukuku* (2020) 198–199; Çelikel and Erdem, *Milletlerarası Özel Hukuk* (2021) 632; cf. Hacı Can and Ekin Tuna, *Milletlerarası Usul Hukuku* (3rd edn, Adalet Yayınevi 2022) 147.

259 Esen, (2002) 22 MHB 183, 190–191; Çelikel and Erdem, *Milletlerarası Özel Hukuk* (2021) 632; cf. Ergun Önen, 'Gayrimenkul Davalarında Yetki' (1965) 22–23 AÜHFD 567, 588.

260 Cf. Nomer, *Milletlerarası Usul Hukuku* (2018) 192 fn 284.

be exclusive.[261] The Turkish Court of Cassation has also issued a number of judgments in this direction.[262]

Another line of thought holds that jurisdiction of Turkish courts under Article 43 is exclusive in line with its *ratio legis*. According to commentators endorsing this view, the aim of the legislature when providing a residual jurisdiction rule in favour of the *forum rei sitae* is to make sure that Turkish courts should be *exclusively* competent to rule on the assets – even the movable ones – situated in Turkey.[263] According to this line of thought, this conclusion can be reached from the wording of the provision which uses the statement 'shall be heard' ('görülür') instead of 'may be heard' ('görülebilir'), from the purpose and nature of estate proceedings, and from practical considerations. Scholars argue that in regards to assets located in Turkey, it is often impossible for a foreign court to determine the associated succession rights as well as their scope and limits; to take protective measures concerning these assets; and to award possession of those assets to heirs. For these reasons, it

[261] Cemal Şanlı, 'Yabancı Veraset İlamlarının Türk Mahkemelerinde Tanınması veya Delil Olarak Kullanılması', *Prof. Dr. İlhan E. Postacıoğlu'na Armağan* (Bayrak Matbaacılık 1990) 301–302; Ekşi, *Milletlerarası Yetki* (2000) 224–225; Burak Huysal, '6100 Sayılı Hukuk Muhakemeleri Kanunu İle Getirilen Yenilikler Işığında Yabancı Mahkeme Kararlarının Tanınması ve Tenfizi Konusunda Bazı Tespitler' (2012) 32 MHB 71, 85–86; Ekşi, *Milletlerarası Miras Hukuku* (2013) 140–141; Süzen, *Tanıma ve Tenfiz Davalarında Yetki Denetimi* (2016) 65–67; cf. İnci Ataman Figanmeşe, 'Milletlerarası Özel Hukukta Mirasçılık Belgeleri' (Master Thesis, Istanbul University 1998) 52–53; Burak Huysal and Begüm Şermet Süzen, 'Tanıma ve Tenfiz Davalarında Kararı Veren Mahkemenin Yetkisinin İncelenmesi' in Süheyla Balkar Bozkurt (ed), *Yabancı Mahkeme ve Hakem Kararlarının Tanınması ve Tenfizinde Güncel Gelişmeler* (On İki Levha 2018) 53–54. At the time of the Temporary Act, see M. R. Seviğ, *Sentez* (1941) 61; Atâ Sakmar, 'Yabancılık Unsuru Taşıyan Vasiyetnamelerin Tenfizi ve Yargıtay Uygulaması' in İstanbul Üniversitesi Hukuk Fakültesi, Milletlerarası Hukuk ve Milletlerarası Münasebetler Enstitüsü (ed), *Prof. Dr. Hıfzı Timur'un Anısına Armağan* (Fakülteler Matbaası 1979) 733; cf. Işıl Özkan, 'Türk Mahkemelerinin Milletlerarası Yetkisi', *Seha L. Meray'a Armağan*, vol I (T.C. Ziraat Bankası Matbaası 1981) 203.

[262] See, in this regard, Yargıtay 2. Hukuk Dairesi, T. 10.2.1986, E. 1986/808 K. 1986/1284 <http://www.kazanci.com> accessed 20 June 2017; Yargıtay 2. Hukuk Dairesi, T. 11.6.1990, E. 1990/12861 K.1990/5906 published in Sakmar, Ekşi and Yılmaz, *Milletlerarası Özel Hukuk ve Usul Hukuku Hakkında Kanun Mahkeme Kararları* (2001) 354–355; Yargıtay 2. Hukuk Dairesi, T. 22.6.1990, E. 1990/6373 K. 1990/6410 <http://www.kazanci.com> accessed 20 June 2017; Yargıtay 2. Hukuk Dairesi, T. 13.9.1999, E. 1999/6974 K. 1999/8850 published in Ruhi, (2006) 32 YD 265, 292 fn 85; Yargıtay 2. Hukuk Dairesi, T. 12.7.2002, E. 2002/8254 K. 2002/9339 <http://www.kazanci.com> accessed 2 July 2017; Yargıtay 8. Hukuk Dairesi, T. 17.10.2014, E. 2013/23629, K. 2014/18556 <http://www.kazanci.com> accessed 20 June 2017; Yargıtay 14. Hukuk Dairesi, T. 4.4.2016, E. 2015/7541 K. 2016/3995 <http://www.kazanci.com> accessed 20 June 2017.

[263] Aysel Çelikel, 'Yeni Kanuna Göre Yabancı Mahkeme Kararlarının Tenfiz Şartları' (1982) 2 MHB 7, 10; Şanlı, 'Veraset İlamı' (1990) 301; Bilkay, (2021) 41 MHB 905, 926–927; cf. Tekinalp, *Milletlerarası Özel Hukuk* (2020) 411.

is argued, the residual jurisdiction of Turkish courts under Article 43 of the Turkish PILA should be regarded exclusive.[264]

Yet for various reasons it seems difficult to endorse these views. In the first place, as discussed before, succession proceedings are obviously one of the few groups of proceedings which are of paramount practical significance in the international context, and, hence, the legislature felt the need for a separate rule of jurisdiction. Article 43 of the Turkish PILA should, therefore, be considered as a special ground of jurisdiction for cross-border succession matters which prevents a reference back to domestic rules as in other areas. Hence, the nature of the jurisdiction of Turkish courts arising from this provision cannot be determined in the light of domestic rules.[265] Even if one might insist on the use of domestic rules, Article 12(1) of the Turkish Code of Civil Procedure does not address the question of jurisdiction in succession cases, and it rather concerns disputes which have as their object rights *in rem* in immovable property. Moreover, under the domestic jurisdictional rule on succession, i.e. Article 11(1) of the Turkish Code of Civil Procedure, Turkish courts which are vested with exclusive jurisdiction are the ones located at the last domicile of the deceased and not the ones where the assets are located. Like Article 43 of the Turkish PILA, this provision does not adopt a scissionist approach as regards movable and immovable assets. Therefore, it does not seem plausible to contend that the jurisdiction of Turkish courts at the place where the immovable assets are located is exclusive based on Article 11(1) of the Turkish Code of Civil Procedure.[266] Last but not least, as there is a consensus that exclusive jurisdiction within the context of private international law should be different from the understanding of the exclusive jurisdiction within domestic law;[267] exclusive jurisdiction in cross-border cases should be determined in line with the wording and *ratio legis* of the rules.[268]

---

[264] Şanlı, 'Veraset İlamı' (1990) 300–301.

[265] Bilkay, (2021) 41 MHB 905, 926–927; cf. Çelikel and Erdem, *Milletlerarası Özel Hukuk* (2021) 631–632.

[266] Tanrıbilir, 'MÖHUK ve Mirasa İlişkin Bağlama Kuralının Uygulanmasında Öne Çıkan Hususlar' (2018) 137–138.

[267] Çelikel, (1982) 2 MHB 7, 9; Atâ Sakmar, *Yabancı İlamların Türkiye'deki Sonuçları* (Fakülteler Matbaası 1982) 99; Ayfer Uyanık, 'Türk Milletlerarası Usul Hukukunda Yetki Sözleşmeleri' (Master Thesis, Istanbul University 1994) 65; Muktedir Lale, 'Türk Milletlerarası Usul Hukukunda Türk Mahkemelerinin Milletlerarası Yargı Yetkisi' (Master Thesis, Ankara University 1996) 28; Sargın, *Yetki Anlaşmaları* (1996) 152; Bahadır Erdem, 'Hukuki ve Ticari Konularda Mahkemelerin Yetkisi ve Mahkeme Kararlarının Tanınması ve Tenfizi Hakkında 1968 Tarihli Brüksel Antlaşmasının Hükümlerinin Türk Mahkemelerinin Milletlerarası Yetki Kuralları ile Karşılaştırılması' (1997) 17 MHB 183, 205–206; Ekşi, *Milletlerarası Yetki* (2000) 215–216; Esen, (2002) 22 MHB 183, 186; Huysal, (2012) 32 MHB 71, 84–85; Nomer, *Milletlerarası Usul Hukuku* (2018) 195; Tanrıbilir, 'MÖHUK ve Mirasa İlişkin Bağlama Kuralının Uygulanmasında Öne Çıkan Hususlar' (2018) 138; Çelikel and Erdem, *Milletlerarası Özel Hukuk* (2021) 631–632; Şanlı, Esen and Ataman

When the wording of the rule is examined, it cannot be interpreted as an exclusive jurisdiction rule for immovable properties in Turkey even though it reads 'shall be heard'. This is because the rule provides a cascade of grounds for jurisdiction and, as mentioned in the previous paragraph, does not differentiate between movable and immovable property. Hence, it seems that the wording does not suggest that the jurisdiction established based on this provision should in fact be exclusive.[269]

In terms of the *ratio legis* of the rule, although it is true that there are certain restrictions applicable as regards the acquisition of immovables by foreign nationals in Turkey – which is also one of the reasons why the law applicable to succession matters on immovables in Turkey is Turkish law – they do not preclude foreign individuals from inheriting immovable assets in Turkey; rather, they only impose constraints on the use of these rights under certain conditions and are related to the process after the transfer of the estate to the heirs. Indeed, the succession rights of foreign individuals are guaranteed under the Turkish Constitution[270] (Article 35) and cannot be abolished.[271] In

---

Figanmeşe, *Milletlerarası Özel Hukuk* (2021) 660; Doğan, *Milletlerarası Özel Hukuk* (2022) 128.

[268] Sakmar, *Yabancı İlamların Türkiye'deki Sonuçları* (1982) 99; Ekşi, *Milletlerarası Yetki* (2000) 212ff; Özkan and Tütüncübaşı, *Uluslararası Usûl Hukuku* (2020) 191–192; Çelikel and Erdem, *Milletlerarası Özel Hukuk* (2021) 749–750; Şanlı, Esen and Ataman Figanmeşe, *Milletlerarası Özel Hukuk* (2021) 660–661.

[269] Tanrıbilir, 'MÖHUK ve Mirasa İlişkin Bağlama Kuralının Uygulanmasında Öne Çıkan Hususlar' (2018) 138.

[270] *Resmi Gazete (mükerrer)* of 9.11.1982, no 17863.

[271] See, for similar views, Sakmar, 'Yabancılık Unsuru Taşıyan Vasiyetnamelerin Tenfizi ve Yargıtay Uygulaması' (1979) 736–737; Feriha Bilge Tanrıbilir, 'Yabancıların Mirasçılık Sıfatı', *Av. Dr. Faruk Erem Armağanı* (Afşaroğlu Matbaası 1999) 730–731; Baran Çelik, *Ölüme Bağlı Tasarruflar* (2011) 135; Tanrıbilir, 'MÖHUK ve Mirasa İlişkin Bağlama Kuralının Uygulanmasında Öne Çıkan Hususlar' (2018) 140; Baran Çelik, (2019) 24 DÜHFD 439, 489–490. See also Zekeriya Kurşat, *Terekenin Korunması Önlemleri* (Filiz Kitabevi 2010) 351–352; Aysel Çelikel and Günseli Öztekin Gelgel, *Yabancılar Hukuku* (26th edn, Beta 2021) 330ff.

In a judgment rendered in 2020 upon individual application, the Turkish Constitutional Court clearly underlined that restrictions applicable for foreign nationals as regards the acquisition of realty in Turkey should not be interpreted to amount to the violation of property (and succession) rights which are guaranteed under Art 35 of the Turkish Constitution. The dispute in the case is related to the issuance of a succession certificate. The applicants, Syrian nationals, lodged an application for the issuance of a succession certificate to claim their title on a piece of immovable property located in Istanbul. Their application, however, was rejected on the grounds that Syrian nationals had no right to acquire immovable property in Turkey due to restrictions applicable specifically for them (due not least to Syria's failing to satisfy the condition of reciprocity). The Constitutional Court, however, found that the rejection of the issuance of a succession certificate caused the applicants to not be able to benefit from their succession rights and use their disposition

addition, there is no doubt that the meaning of land for the State and the policy towards it have changed over time.[272] The restrictions as to the amount of land that can be owned by foreign natural persons outlined under Article 35 of the Land Registry Law, for example, are no longer as rigid as they used to be in the past.[273] Consequently, these restrictions concerning acquisition of immovable property by foreign nationals do not *per se* require that the jurisdiction of Turkish courts in cross-border succession cases should be exclusive.

Last but not least, the subsidiary jurisdiction rule under Article 43 was laid down by the legislature with the intention of creating a *supplementary* rule for cases in which the deceased was last domiciled outside Turkey but left assets (movable or immovable) in one or more places in Turkey. Therefore, the *forum rei sitae* will only be competent to hear the case when the deceased died while domiciled elsewhere. Thus, with this provision the legislature did not aim to provide that such cases should be exclusively heard by Turkish courts.[274]

Although such an interpretation of the rule would be more in line with the parties' interests – particularly those held by the significant number of Turkish nationals who have for a number of years been resident in locations such as EU Member States – and would give them the opportunity to bring their case also in their country of residence and apply later for recognition in Turkey, the practice as well as the opinions in the literature, as explained, classify this rule as an exclusive head of jurisdiction for succession cases concerning immovables in Turkey. As a consequence, any decision rendered by a Member State court involving immovable assets of the deceased in Turkey cannot be recognised or enforced due to the fact that only judgments on issues which do not fall within the exclusive jurisdiction of Turkish courts are recognisable and enforceable pursuant to Articles 54(1) (b) and 58 of the Turkish PILA.[275]

---

rights on the property, thus violating their property (and succession) rights as ensured under Art 35 of the Turkish Constitution. See, in this regard, Anayasa Mahkemesi, T. 2.6.2020, Antoine Balit ve Diğerleri, no 2017/16211, *Resmi Gazete* of 21.8.2020, no 31220.

[272] The *situs* rule is, indeed, considered as an 'anachronism' from the aspects of both jurisdiction and conflict of laws in a modern world where individuals often change locations and own properties in different parts of the globe. Although land was previously seen as a major of form of wealth and had a territorial importance, this has changed over the years. The most important advantage of the *situs* rule may be that it allows a determination of the title over the property via the recording system, a process that is quicker, easier, and less expensive at the *situs* of the property. However, thanks to international judicial procedures, this could be also done by the courts of other countries: Hay, 'The Situs Rule' (1988) 109–110; Erkan, (2012) 20 SÜHFD 11; cf. Weintraub, (1966) 52 Cornell LQ 1, 3–4.

[273] See above n 510, p 160.

[274] Demir Gökyayla, 'Mirasçılık Belgeleri' (2006) 574–575; cf. Tanrıbilir, 'MÖHUK ve Mirasa İlişkin Bağlama Kuralının Uygulanmasında Öne Çıkan Hususlar' (2018) 138.

[275] Cf. Erkan, (2012) 20 SÜHFD 11, 23–24 and 26.

Article 20(15) of the Treaty does not provide an explicit statement on whether the jurisdiction established by the courts of Contracting Parties is exclusive. However, the legal atmosphere at the time of the Treaty's drafting process and the intention of the drafters seem to suggest that it is an exclusive jurisdiction rule not only for the immovable part of the estate but also for its movable part. The Treaty, as discussed earlier, was a part of the policy of the Ottoman Empire, and later of the newly founded Turkish Republic as its successor, to replace the capitulary system in which the Turkish side had no adjudicatory power over disputes of foreign nationals concerning movable assets, including those related to succession, in its own land with a legal regime which was more in line with the general principles of international law, foremost, with the principle of reciprocity. The lack of jurisdiction on the Turkish side in these matters was, however, preserved with some exceptions even in Article 4 of the Temporary Act, as the first private international law legislation of Turkey, on the premise that Turkish judges did not have enough expertise with the application of foreign law. From the perspective of foreign States, a regime with such rules – as those in the Treaty – also had the advantage of protecting their nationals in such matters from discrimination and from other effects of Islamic law.

This background suggests that jurisdiction under the Treaty is exclusive both for movable and immovable property.[276] Exclusive jurisdiction in the

---

276 V. R. Seviğ, *Mirasla İlgili Devletler Hususi Hukuku Kaideleri* (1963) 191; V. R. Seviğ, *Ahkâmı Şahsiye Davaları – Yetki* (1964) 9; Dörner, [1996] ZEV 90, 96; Atalı, *Internationale Zuständigkeit* (2001) 122; H. Krüger, 'Studien über Probleme des türkischen Internationalen Erbrechts' (2006) 153; Bauer, [2007] FamRZ 1250, 1252ff; Bernd von Hoffmann and Karsten Thorn, *Internationales Privatrecht* (9th edn, C.H. Beck 2007) § 3 para 60; Duygu Damar, 'Deutsch-türkisches Nachlassabkommen: zivilprozess- und kollisionsrechtliche Aspekte' [2012] IPRax 278, 279; Majer, [2012] ZEV 182, 189; Spelsberg-Korspeter, (2017) Deutsch-türkisches Nachlassabkommen para 17; Christiane von Bary, *Gerichtsstands- und Schiedsvereinbarungen im internationalen Erbrecht* (Mohr Siebeck 2018) 13; Nomer, *Milletlerarası Usul Hukuku* (2018) 195 fn 291; Güneş, 'The Relations of Turkey with EU Member States' (2019) 308–309; Looschelders, 'The External Relations of Germany' (2019) 168; Bauer and Süß, *Dutta/Weber* (2021) EuErbVO Art 75 Anhang II-deutsch-türkisches NA para 8; Odersky, *Hausmann/Odersky* (2021) § 15 para 350; Lorenz, *BeckOK BGB* (2022) EGBGB Art 25 aF para 9; Robert Sieghörtner, in Meo-Micaela Hahne, Jürgen Schlögel and Rolf Schlünder (eds), *BeckOK FamFG (Stand: 1.4.2022)* (42nd edn, C.H. Beck 2022) FamFG § 105 para 20.

See also Yargıtay 2. Hukuk Dairesi, T. 27.1.1977, E. 401 K. 665 published and commented on in Nomer, (1981) 1 MHB 61; OLG Köln 30.1.1986 – 12 W 79/85, IPRspr 1986 Nr. 109, 248; LG München I 26.9.2006 – 6 O 15963/05 (rkr.), FamRZ 2007, 1250; OLG Karlsruhe 17.6.2013 – 14 Wx 84/11, ZEV 2014, 158.

For a similar comment as regards the Turkish-Italian Treaty, see Ekşi, *Milletlerarası Miras Hukuku* (2013) 25; Güneş, 'The Relations of Turkey with EU Member States' (2019) 307–309 (also with regards to the Turkish-Hungarian Treaty); contra Franzina, 'The External Relations of Italy' (2019) 198.

context of movables is not consistent with the current understanding of jurisdiction in the law of both Contracting Parties and poses practical problems for Turkish nationals in Germany, who have quite likely spent most of their lives there. In the event of the death of someone from this community who still holds Turkish nationality, his heirs have to travel back to Turkey merely to, for example, claim the money held in a German bank account of the deceased.[277] Whilst a narrow interpretation is desirable in that it allows the Contracting State to assume jurisdiction over the movable property located in its territories[278] when, for example, heirs are resident in Germany[279] or when there is a succession matter between Turkish and German nationals,[280] this decision will be left to the discretion of the courts unless there is a reform or at least the conclusion of interpretation protocols.[281]

The above analysis and examples indicate that it is highly likely there will be jurisdiction conflicts, practical procedural problems, and recognition and enforcement problems in Turkish-EU successions. The question thus arises whether any of the legal texts offer means to avoid such problems. In order to better answer this question, the possible tools and their availability as set out in the legal texts should be examined in detail. The following section will, therefore, focus on coordination tools.

---

[277] Dörner, [1996] ZEV 90, 96; Atalı, *Internationale Zuständigkeit* (2001) 123; H. Krüger, 'Studien über Probleme des türkischen Internationalen Erbrechts' (2006) 152–153; Güneş, 'The Relations of Turkey with EU Member States' (2019) 309; Looschelders, 'The External Relations of Germany' (2019) 168; cf. Göğer, *Devletler Hususi Hukuku* (1977) 336.

It should be noted that the material scope of this jurisdiction rule is interpreted narrowly, at least from the German side. See, in this regard, n 147, p 41 above. Hence, the heirs of a Turkish deceased will need to travel to Turkey only in certain instances where the claim falls within the scope of Article 20(15) of the Treaty.

[278] Dörner, [1996] ZEV 90, 96; Atalı, *Internationale Zuständigkeit* (2001) 124; H. Krüger, 'Studien über Probleme des türkischen Internationalen Erbrechts' (2006) 153; H. Krüger, 'Erbrechtliche Probleme in den deutsch-türkischen Beziehungen' (2010) 46–47; Stürner, *Erman BGB* (2020) EuErbVO Art 75 para 11; Lorenz, *BeckOK BGB* (2022) EGBGB Art 25 aF para 9; Christian Rumpf, 'Türkei' in Murad Ferid, Karl Firsching and Rainer Hausmann (eds), *Internationales Erbrecht* (120th edn, C.H. Beck 2022) para 107; cf. Bauer, [2007] FamRZ 1250, 1256–1257.

[279] Dörner, [1996] ZEV 90, 96.

[280] H. Krüger, 'Studien über Probleme des türkischen Internationalen Erbrechts' (2006) 153.

[281] For a discussion about different options as regards bilateral treaties of Member States, see Wolfgang Wurmnest, 'Comparative Report and Policy Perspectives' in Anatol Dutta and Wolfgang Wurmnest (eds), *European Private International Law and Member State Treaties with Third States – The Case of the European Succession Regulation* (Intersentia 2019) 350–355.

IV. Coordination Tools?

Each legal system, as indicated above, developed its own rules of jurisdiction for cross-border succession matters in line with different policy considerations and backgrounds. However, as beneficiaries exercise their right to a 'day in court' in one country, they should not be allowed to litigate before the courts of another country. Therefore, although the decision to adjudicate an international action is to be made by each State based on its sovereign powers, at least a certain level of coordination to this end between the legal systems is desirable to save public funds and to ensure a proper administration of justice, even beyond the borders.[282] This is also of utmost significance for Turkish-EU successions which involve or – in the future will involve – an important number of people. The alternative tools and their availability in the legal systems should, thus, be analysed here in detail. It is not surprising that no coordination rules are laid down in the Treaty by virtue of its background and bilateral nature. The analysis here will be mostly limited to the Regulation and the Turkish PILA and will concern the Treaty only when relevant.

1. Choice of Court Agreements

The desired coordination of jurisdiction rules can normally be reached by a number of ways. The first is the prorogation of jurisdiction by the parties. The Regulation has actually endorsed this opportunity in its 'all-inclusive' rules. In order to restore *Gleichlauf* between forum and *ius*,[283] Article 5 of the Regulation, as the main exception to the general and subsidiary rules of jurisdiction,[284] enable the parties concerned to make a choice of court agreement in favour of the Member State courts in the event that the deceased chose the law of that Member State pursuant to Article 22. When a choice of this kind is made, the court seised in accordance with Article 4 or Article 10 of the Regulation is under a duty to decline jurisdiction in favour of the Member State court chosen by the parties in parallel to the choice of law by the deceased (Article 6(b)), and the chosen court of the Member State is under the duty to assume jurisdiction over the case (Article 7(a) and (b)). Such a mech-

[282] See, in this regard, Catherine Kessedjian, 'International Jurisdiction and Foreign Judgments in Civil and Commercial Matters' (HCCH 1997) Prel. Doc. No 7 paras 15–16 <https://assets.hcch.net/docs/76852ce3-a967-42e4-94f5-24be4289d1e5.pdf> accessed 2 February 2021.

[283] Hess, 'Die internationale Zuständigkeit nach der Erbrechtsverordnung' (2014) 139; Buonaiuti, *Calvo Caravaca/Davì/Mansel* (2016) ESR Art 5 para 1; Pamboukis, *Pamboukis* (2017) ESR Art 5 para 1; Deixler-Hübner, *Deixler-Hübner/Schauer* (2020) EuErbVO Art 5 para 4; Lein, *Dutta/Weber* (2021) EuErbVO Art 5 para 1. See also Recital 27 of the Regulation.

[284] Dutta, *MüKoBGB* (2020) EuErbVO Art 5 para 1; Lein, *Dutta/Weber* (2021) EuErbVO Art 5 para 1.

anism has obviously a limited scope considering the fact that a prorogation of jurisdiction can be done only by the parties concerned, i.e. all the parties to the proceedings whose rights and duties in regard to the estate are potentially affected by those proceedings, including heirs, forced heirs, and legatees,[285] and not by the deceased himself; the latter is allowed only in cases where the deceased has already made a choice of law to be applicable to his succession, and it is allowed only in favour of the courts of the Member State whose law has been chosen. The rule may be criticised from the Union's perspective due to its limited scope.[286] Nevertheless, the principal shortcoming of this mechanism from an outsider perspective is its intra-Union scope.

Under Article 5, a choice of forum is possible only in favour of Member State courts. This has two different problematic aspects. In the first place, a prorogation of jurisdiction in favour of the courts of a third State will not be sufficient for Member State courts to decline jurisdiction in favour of third State courts pursuant to Article 6(b), even though the deceased has the possibility in accordance with Article 22 to choose his national law, which could well be that of a non-Member State due to the universal nature of the Regulation's conflict rules.[287] What is more, the coveted *Gleichlauf* between forum and *ius* that is achieved with the help of a prorogation of jurisdiction can be reinstated only at the Union level.[288] Such an *inter partes* approach could be seen as a corollary of the fact that the European legislature is not entitled to establish the jurisdiction of third State courts and cannot be sure of the availability of these courts.[289] In addition, it could be argued that there is actually no need to regulate the cases in relation to third States, as the parties themselves may refrain from bringing their case before the Member Courts in

---

[285] Felix Odersky, in Ulf Bergquist and others (eds), *EU Regulation on Succession and Wills – Commentary* (Otto Schmidt 2015) ESR Art 5 para 7; Pamboukis, *Pamboukis* (2017) ESR Art 5 para 15; Dutta, *MüKoBGB* (2020) EuErbVO Art 5 para 6; Lein, *Dutta/Weber* (2021) EuErbVO Art 5 para 13.

[286] See, for example, Hess, 'Die internationale Zuständigkeit nach der Erbrechtsverordnung' (2014) 137ff; Lein, *Dutta/Weber* (2021) EuErbVO Art 5 paras 9 and 18–20.

[287] Robert Magnus, 'Gerichtsstandsvereinbarungen im Erbrecht?' [2013] IPRax 393, 395; Fabrizio Marongiu Buonaiuti, 'Jurisdiction Under the Succession Regulation and Relationships with Third States' in Pietro Franzina (ed), *The External Dimension of EU Private International Law after Opinion 1/13* (Intersentia 2017) 220; von Bary, *Gerichtsstandsvereinbarungen im internationalen Erbrecht* (2018) 66.

[288] Tobias Lübcke, 'EuErbVO: Problemfelder im Rahmen der internationalen Zuständigkeit bei Vorliegen einer Rechtswahl durch den Erblasser' [2015] GPR 111, 112; Buonaiuti, *Calvo Caravaca/Davì/Mansel* (2016) ESR Art 5 para 9.

[289] R. Magnus, [2013] IPRax 393, 394ff; Lübcke, [2015] GPR 111, 112; von Bary, *Gerichtsstandsvereinbarungen im internationalen Erbrecht* (2018) 66; Ioannis K. Somarakis, 'Rethinking EU Jurisdiction in Cross-Border Family and Succession Cases Connected with Non-Member States' (2017–2018) XIX YbPIL 555, 568; Lein, *Dutta/Weber* (2021) EuErbVO Art 5 para 10; cf. Buonaiuti, (2016) 12 J Priv Int L 545, 555.

cases where the deceased has made a *professio iuris* in favour of a third State law as the law of his nationality. This is because the Regulation does not prevent the right of parties to derogate from the jurisdiction of Member State courts intentionally.[290] Notwithstanding this, a purely intra-Union approach with regards to the prorogation of jurisdiction seems to be a missed opportunity for a greater universalism and for *Gleichlauf* within the Regulation and, of course, for the desired coordination on an international level.

A question could be raised here as to whether the parties may have the right to authorise the courts of non-Member States on their succession case under the domestic laws of the Member States.[291] The answer, however, would probably be in the negative owing to two reasons. In the first place, Article 5 allows parties to conclude a prorogation agreement in a very limited way. National rules, on the contrary, may give considerable freedom to parties when making a choice of court agreement in favour of a third State court, which would not be very consistent with the desired harmony in the Regulation.[292] Furthermore, the Regulation leaves no room for domestic rules of Member States in succession matters, and, hence, Member States cannot refer to their national rules to enable parties to make a prorogation agreement in favour of a third State court.[293]

When a solution to the problem cannot be found through the help of domestic laws, one might question whether Article 5 could somehow be extended to third State related cases. In this respect, based on the *Droz*'s doctrine of reflexive effect ('effet réflexe') regarding the Brussels Convention at the time,[294] it is advocated that Article 5 could be applied by analogy by the courts of Member States to decline jurisdiction in favour of a third State court whose law has been chosen by the deceased prior to his death.[295] Such a reflexive application could arguably be adopted either as a typical mirror-image rule – which does not grant

---

[290] Buonaiuti, *Calvo Caravaca/Davì/Mansel* (2016) ESR Art 5 para 9 and fn 20.

[291] Bonomi, *Bonomi/Wautelet* (2016) ESR Art 5 para 4; Dutta, *MüKoBGB* (2020) EuErbVO Art 5 para 12.

[292] Bonomi, *Bonomi/Wautelet* (2016) ESR Art 5 para 4; Buonaiuti, (2016) 12 J Priv Int L 545, 552; Buonaiuti, 'Jurisdiction under the ESR and Third States' (2017) 220.

[293] Bonomi, *Bonomi/Wautelet* (2016) ESR Art 5 para 4; Buonaiuti, (2016) 12 J Priv Int L 545, 552; Buonaiuti, 'Jurisdiction under the ESR and Third States' (2017) 220; Romano, (2015–2016) XVII YbPIL 253, 270; Lein, *Dutta/Weber* (2021) EuErbVO Art 5 para 10.

Even if the Regulation had allowed the application of national rules for choice of court agreements in favour of third States, it is not easy to find Member States having such provisions: Stéphanie Francq and Julie Mary, 'The External Relations of Belgium' in Anatol Dutta and Wolfgang Wurmnest (eds), *European Private International Law and Member State Treaties with Third States – The Case of the European Succession Regulation* (Intersentia 2019) 56 (as regards to Belgium).

[294] Georges A. L. Droz, *Compétence judiciaire et effets des jugements dans le Marché Commun (Etude de la Convention de Bruxelles du 27 septembre 1968)* (Dalloz 1972) paras 164ff.

jurisdiction to third State courts but only derogates the jurisdiction of Member State courts based on the choice of law of the deceased[296] – or as a prerogative rule allowing parties to make a written agreement to submit their case to the court or courts of the third State whose law has already been designated by the deceased as applicable in a succession case.[297] Likewise, the reflexive application of Article 5 for cases related to third States could arguably be invoked on the ground that the choice of court agreement would be valid in the third State[298] and/or that the decision rendered by the third State court can be recognised/enforced in the relevant Member State.[299]

Regardless of the model employed, possible advantages of a reflexive system are obviously manifold. Initially, from the Union's perspective, two important pillars of the Regulation's system, i.e. universality and *Gleichlauf* between forum and *ius*, can be reinforced. Moreover, the desired jurisdictional coordination and decisional harmony could be better accommodated, the risk of forum shopping could be reduced, and an effective cross-border resolution of the succession issues could be ensured – all of which are significant not only in- but also outside the EU.[300] Thus, giving a reflexive effect to Article 5 and, hence, considering the jurisdiction of third State courts in cases where the deceased has chosen the law of that State is beneficial from both the European and the third State perspective.

Such a system, on the other hand, could create doubts for Europeans in two regards. First of all, there might be instances where the third State court does not take jurisdiction over the case despite the existence of a choice of law and/or choice of court agreement. In such a case, there would be the risk of

---

295 R. Magnus, [2013] IPRax 393, 395; Heinig, [2014] RNotZ 197, 226; Dieter Leipold, 'Gerichtsstandsvereinbarungen nach der Europäischen Erbrechtsverordnung' in Karlheinz Muscheler and Reinhard Zimmermann (eds), *Zivilrecht und Steuerrecht, Erwerb von Todes wegen und Schenkung: Festschrift für Jens Peter Meincke zum 80. Geburtstag* (C.H. Beck 2015) 223; Bonomi, *Bonomi/Wautelet* (2016) ESR Art 5 para 4 fn 8; Buonaiuti, (2016) 12 J Priv Int L 545, 553; Buonaiuti, 'Jurisdiction under the ESR and Third States' (2017) 221; von Bary, *Gerichtsstandsvereinbarungen im internationalen Erbrecht* (2018) 65 ff; Somarakis, (2017–2018) XIX YbPIL 555, 568; Dutta, *MüKoBGB* (2020) EuErbVO Art 5 para 12; Lein, *Dutta/Weber* (2021) EuErbVO Art 5 para 10; cf. Geimer, 'Die europäische Erbrechtsverordnung im Überblick' (2013) 20; Francq and Mary, 'The External Relations of Belgium' (2019) 55–56 and 65.

296 Marc Fallon and Thalia Kruger, 'The Spatial Scope of the EU's Rules on Jurisdiction and Enforcement of Judgments: From Bilateral Modus to Unilateral Universality?' (2012–2013) XIV YbPIL 1, 32.

297 For a detailed explanation of the two different systems in the context of succession, see von Bary, *Gerichtsstandsvereinbarungen im internationalen Erbrecht* (2018) 66 ff.

298 Dutta, *MüKoBGB* (2020) EuErbVO Art 5 para 12.

299 An example of a reflexive effect with such a condition is found under Article 7 of the Belgian Private International Law Code.

300 Somarakis, (2017–2018) XIX YbPIL 555, 578–579.

negative jurisdiction conflicts that would then cause denial of justice for the European parties. Furthermore, it is questionable whether such an approach would comport with the claimed 'European standards' underlying the rules of the Regulation, including those relating to jurisdiction. These rules, in the first place, are tailored so as to ensure that the legitimate expectations and rights of persons entitled to a reserved share and of creditors of the estate are met within Europe. In addition, the rules aim to provide for the unity of succession, and in the light of this, fair and equal distribution and transfer of estate assets acquired by the deceased during his lifetime to his heirs. Last but not least, with the help of the rules of the Regulation, the European legislature aspired to a fair, fast, and effective means of dispute resolution in the field of succession law. Therefore, it is argued that the European legislature would face the question of the extent to which those standards are met in the third States which have their own peculiar features and preferences with regards to the conflict as well as to procedural rules in the event that a reflexive effect is given to jurisdictional rules, including but not limited to choice of court rules.[301]

The first issue could actually be addressed with the help of the *forum necessitatis* rule embodied under Article 11 of the Regulation and, therefore, would not pose an important problem for the Union lawmaker.[302] With regards to the 'elusive' standards of Europe which, as claimed, should be safeguarded in any case, the question of whether these may be legitimate reasons arguing extending jurisdictional coordination rules to third State related cases from a pure European point of view is, of course, outside the scope of this book. Notwithstanding this, the effect of a choice of law and a choice of court agreement in Turkey should be examined here not only to provide the general Turkish framework to European scholars in the context of doubts towards third State laws (including Turkey) but also to determine whether it is plausible to support a reflexive application of Article 5 from a Turkish perspective as a third State.

There could well be cases in the Turkish-European context in which there is a choice of law in favour of Turkish law and a choice of court agreement in favour of Turkish courts irrespective of the validity of such choices in both jurisdictions. Imagine, for example, that Turkish national *(T)* habitually resident in Linz/Austria makes a valid choice in favour of Turkish law to govern his succession as a whole pursuant to Article 22 of the Regulation. He has a wife and three children as his heirs, who are all resident in Ankara/Turkey. Most of his estate assets are also located in Ankara. After his death, his heirs make a written choice of court agreement in favour of Ankara courts. In such a case, the extent to which a choice of court agreement made by the parties will be valid under Turkish law is particularly important for the discussion regarding the reflexive application of Article 5 in third State related cases.

---

[301] Somarakis, (2017–2018) XIX YbPIL 555, 579ff.

[302] von Bary, *Gerichtsstandsvereinbarungen im internationalen Erbrecht* (2018) 71.

As discussed in the previous chapter, a *professio iuris* in the field of succession is not allowed under Turkish law, unlike in the Regulation.[303] When this is the case, the choice of law made by *(T)* in favour of Turkish law will not be valid under Turkish law. Nonetheless, this would not cause significant problems in cases such as the above example. This is because the law applicable to succession as a whole on the European side will be Turkish law as a result of the valid choice made pursuant to Article 22 of the Regulation, and the general conflict rule in Turkey would lead us, to a certain extent, to the same result in Turkey. According to Article 20(1) of the Turkish PILA, the law applicable to the succession as a whole is the national law of the deceased, although immovable assets are governed by Turkish law and some issues are excluded from the scope of general rule. The succession of Turkish nationals who have most of their assets in Turkey, as *(T)* in the example, will therefore be governed by Turkish law in line with these rules. It is only for the assets located elsewhere and for the issues falling in the scope of Article 20(2) that the application of the law of the place where those assets are located will come into play. Thus, even though the choice of law is not recognised in Turkey, the decisions rendered both in the Member State and in Turkey would, to a great extent, be in conformity with each other in cases where the deceased is a Turkish national. The underlying 'European standards' regarding the unity of succession, the legitimate expectations of the heirs and legatees, and the fair and equal distribution of the estate would, in principle, also be ensured at the Turkish courts.

The second issue is whether the jurisdiction agreement which was made by the parties would be effective in Turkey. Under Turkish law, prorogation agreements, as a reflection of the party autonomy intrinsic to conflict rules regarding contracts, could be made by the parties either to derogate from the jurisdiction of Turkish courts and instead designate foreign courts as competent over their case or to grant jurisdiction to Turkish courts. The former step is regulated under Article 47 of the Turkish PILA while the latter is addressed under Articles 17 and 18 of the Turkish Code of Civil Procedure.

According to Article 47(1) of the Turkish PILA, except for matters of law that are under the exclusive subject-matter jurisdiction of Turkish courts, parties may conclude forum selection agreements in favour of foreign courts for disputes between them that involve a foreign element and arise from obligations. The agreement is valid on the condition that it is evidenced in writing. The case may be heard by the competent Turkish court only if the foreign court declines jurisdiction or there is no challenge to jurisdiction of the (Turkish) court. After outlining the general prerequisites of jurisdiction agreements, the Article further restricts parties' freedom of prorogation and clarifies that the jurisdiction of Turkish courts regarding employment contracts and rela-

303 See above Chapter 2 under C. pp 70–85, esp. p 76.

tions (Article 44 of the Turkish PILA), consumer contracts (Article 45 of the Turkish PILA), and insurance contracts (Article 46 of the Turkish PILA) cannot be derogated from by the jurisdiction agreement.

In the light of the conditions outlined under Article 47, one might argue that parties may submit their cross-border succession cases – except those involving immovables in Turkey on which there is a claim of exclusive jurisdiction – to the jurisdiction of foreign courts with an agreement which could be evidenced in writing. This is because Article 47 does not include succession cases under its second paragraph enumerating those cases in which the jurisdiction of Turkish courts cannot be derogated from by party agreement. In addition, except cases which have as their objects immovable assets located in Turkey, the jurisdiction of Turkish courts is not considered exclusive in succession cases. Furthermore, the Article refers to disputes arising from obligations between the parties, and, hence, it could be argued that legal relations regarding succession law may also produce obligations between the parties.[304] Therefore, one could assume that parties could make a valid jurisdiction agreement regarding their succession matter in favour of a foreign court of their choice in order to derogate from the jurisdiction of Turkish courts under Article 43 of the Turkish PILA.

It is, however, contended that such an assumption would be inaccurate under Turkish law. Two different reason are given: In the first place, it has in the past been maintained that jurisdiction agreements in favour of foreign courts are inadmissible in the field of succession law because of the mandatory nature of jurisdictional rules in this field.[305] This was arguably true at the time of the former Turkish PILA as Article 31 of the former Turkish PILA provided that parties could make a prorogation agreement in favour of foreign courts regarding disputes with foreign elements that arose out of obligations, unless the jurisdiction of Turkish courts over the dispute was of a compulsory or exclusive nature. But the term compulsory jurisdiction has been removed from the text of the rule in the new version (Article 47 of the Turkish PILA) by virtue of the fact that its function and advantage was not apparent.[306] Thus, within the scope of the current law, it is only for disputes falling into the exclusive jurisdiction of Turkish courts that one could contend jurisdiction agreements are inadmissible.

Nonetheless, the primary reason advanced as to why parties cannot conclude a valid jurisdiction agreement in the field of succession law is that succession disputes are not considered to be disputes arising out of obligations

---

304 Sargın, *Yetki Anlaşmaları* (1996) 153; Aybay and Dardağan, *Kanunlar İhtlilafi* (2008) 76.

305 Sargın, *Yetki Anlaşmaları* (1996) 153.

306 '5718 Sayılı Milletlerarası Özel Hukuk ve Usul Hukuku Hakkında Kanun Tasarısı ve Gerekçe' 17.

within the meaning of Article 47. The term 'disputes arising out of obligations' under Article 47 covers only the disputes arising out of legal relationships in which party autonomy plays an important role, such as disputes arising from contracts, torts, or unjust enrichment. Family and succession law, however, are legal areas in Turkey where party autonomy is traditionally excluded. For this reason, jurisdiction agreements in favour of foreign courts are not allowed in the field of family and succession law.[307] Therefore, a jurisdiction agreement in favour of a Member State court made by the parties, all of whom reside in the EU, will not, for example, be deemed effective from the Turkish perspective. This means that when one of the parties, after concluding a jurisdiction agreement in favour of a Member State court pursuant to Article 5 of the Regulation, brings the case before a Turkish court and a challenge is made to the jurisdiction of the court due to the agreement as to jurisdiction, the court will not decline jurisdiction, as the jurisdiction agreement as such is not effective in Turkey. Nonetheless, when a decision is rendered by that Member State court, the fact that the jurisdiction agreement is not effective in Turkey would not prevent recognition or enforcement of that decision in Turkey, unless the decision involves succession to the immovable property in Turkey. This is because the Turkish court before which the recognition or enforcement is sought will not check whether the rendering court had jurisdiction in accordance with its own rules (Articles 54 and 58 of the Turkish PILA).[308] Consequently, whilst jurisdiction agreements made in favour of Member State courts in accordance with Article 5 of the Regulation will not have any *direct* effect so as to further coordination within the Turkish-EU context, they may have an *indirect* effect in this regard, and hence it may be advisable for Turkish nationals to make use of this opportunity if they do not want to travel back to Turkey to bring their claim.

The second type of prorogation agreement, which is actually more important for the question of the applicability of Article 5 to third State related

---

[307] Yılmaz Altuğ, *Türk Milletlerarası Usul Hukuku (Devletler Hususi Hukukunda Yargı Yetkisi)* (3rd edn, Fakülteler Matbaası 1983) 66; Özlem Canbeldek, 'Hukuk Muhakemeleri Kanunu ve Milletlerarası Özel Hukuk ve Usûl Kanunu Işığında Yetki Sözleşmeleri' (2012) 1 MİHDER 203, 212–213; Giray, (2016) 9 Anali PFZE 235, 236; Demirkol, *Yetki Anlaşmaları* (2018) 136; Nomer, *Milletlerarası Usul Hukuku* (2018) 136; Zeynep Derya Tarman and Meltem Ece Oba, 'Choice of Court Agreements under Turkish Law' (2017–2018) XIX YbPIL 365, 371; Avşar, *Yetki – İrade Serbestisi* (2021) 193–194; Çelikel and Erdem, *Milletlerarası Özel Hukuk* (2021) 646.

Nevertheless, it is claimed that the term 'disputes arising out of obligations' under Article 47 also covers obligations arising in the fields of family and succession law: Aybay and Dardağan, *Kanunlar İhtlilafı* (2008) 76. For a similar view regarding matrimonial property regimes, see also Ersen Perçin, *Milletlerarası Özel Hukuk Bakımından Mal Rejimleri* (2014) 216–217.

[308] Nomer, *Milletlerarası Usul Hukuku* (2018) 139.

cases, is an agreement granting jurisdiction to Turkish courts. There is no specific rule on those kind of agreements under the Turkish PILA, and hence they are regulated under Articles 17 and 18 of the Turkish Code of Civil Procedure. These provisions are also applicable in disputes with cross-border elements due to Article 40 of the Turkish PILA, which provides that the domestic jurisdiction rules on venue should also determine the international jurisdiction of Turkish courts.[309]

Pursuant to Article 17 of the Turkish Code of Civil Procedure, merchants and public entities may bestow competence on one or more Turkish courts for existing or future disputes between them. Unless otherwise agreed by the parties, the case should only be filed before those courts identified in the agreement. Article 18 further clarifies the conditions for the validity of such agreements. According to this, parties are not allowed to make prorogation agreements in favour of a particular Turkish court for legal matters which are not subject to party autonomy and which fall into the exclusive jurisdiction of other Turkish courts. The agreement should be made in writing and indicate the designated court or courts; and the legal relationship which caused the dispute should be identified or identifiable. It is obvious from these conditions that parties are not allowed to make such a jurisdiction agreement in favour of Turkish courts in the field of succession law, as succession and family law matters are not legal matters over which parties enjoy autonomy under Turkish law.[310]

In the light of this, neither a choice of law made by the deceased nor a choice of court agreement drafted by the parties in the field of succession will be effective on the Turkish side. Therefore, in the absence of rules allowing *professio iuris* and *professio fori*, it seems hard, at the first sight, to advocate a reflexive application of Article 5 form the Turkish perspective as it would not be of much help for jurisdiction conflicts in the Turkish-EU context.

The intra-Union scope of Article 5 is, quite certainly, problematic not only from the Turkish side. An example of third State rules which potentially trigger positive jurisdiction conflicts that cannot be solved under the current *inter partes* approach of Article 5 of the Regulation is Article 87(2) of the Swiss PILA.[311] The rule provides that the Swiss courts or authorities at the place of origin will always take jurisdiction if a Swiss national domiciled or habitually resident abroad submits his succession to the authority of the Swiss courts or Swiss law by way of a testamentary disposition. If *(T)* in the above example[312] had been a Swiss national habitually resident in Linz having all his

[309] İstanbul Üniversitesi Hukuk Fakültesi – Milletlerarası Hukuk ve Milletlerarası Münasebetler Enstitüsü, *MÖHUK Öntasarı Sempozyumu* (1978) 196; Sargın, *Yetki Anlaşmaları* (1996) 211.

[310] Tarman and Oba, (2017–2018) XIX YbPIL 365, 382; Güngör, *Türk Milletlerarası Özel Hukuku* (2021) 237.

[311] Lein, *Dutta/Weber* (2021) EuErbVO Art 5 para 10.

[312] See above p 248.

heirs and most of his estate located in Bern/Switzerland and had made a testament stating that he wants Swiss law to govern his succession and Swiss courts to hear any related case, Swiss courts would have taken the jurisdiction according to this provision. On the European side, however, even though the choice in favour of Swiss law had been valid, the prorogation clause would have been disregarded, and Austrian courts would have declared themselves competent over the case pursuant to Article 4 of the Regulation (together with Article 5 et seq.).[313] Reflexive application of Article 5 in such a case would be helpful to prevent a positive jurisdiction conflict. Unlike Turkish rules, Swiss rules allow parties to make a choice of court agreement in favour of foreign courts including Member State courts in succession matters under Article 5 of the Swiss PILA.[314] When this is the case, a choice of court made in favour of a Member State court in a succession case will be valid both in Switzerland and in the EU (Article 5). This would be the situation even where a jurisdiction conflict does not arise between Switzerland and Turkey.

On the Turkish side, however, there is no right of the deceased or the parties to choose the law applicable to succession or the court – be it Turkish or foreign – having jurisdiction over the case. When this is the case, reflexive application of Article 5, especially in the model applicable on the condition that the third State court recognises the jurisdiction agreement, may not be helpful to eliminate the potential jurisdiction conflicts of a positive nature between Turkish and European courts, and hence it does not appear to be arguable. Notwithstanding this, the version of reflexive application of Article 5 which does not stipulate the validity of the jurisdiction agreement in the relevant third country could still presumably be expedient to a certain extent in some cases. Indeed, there is always a possibility, as in the above example, that parties make a jurisdiction agreement in favour of a Turkish court which is normally competent to hear the case under Article 43 of the Turkish PILA. In such a case, the invalidity of the jurisdiction agreement under Turkish law will have no practical importance, and the Turkish courts of – depending on the case – the place of the last domicile of the deceased or the place where the estate assets are located will be competent to hear the case. The reflexive application of Article 5 in such cases would, at least, provide a derogative effect for Member State courts and reduce the risk of potential jurisdiction conflicts.

It should be admitted such an application of Article 5 might be problematic in situations where the parties conclude a prorogation agreement in favour of a Turkish court which does not otherwise have jurisdiction under Article 43 of the Turkish PILA, i.e. where the last domicile of the deceased is located outside Turkey and the deceased has no assets remaining in Turkey. This is because in this second scenario the jurisdiction agreement will again have no

---

[313] See, in this regard, Romano, (2015–2016) XVII YbPIL 253, 268–270.

[314] See, in this regard, Romano, (2015–2016) XVII YbPIL 253, 269 and fn 64.

effect in Turkey; yet this may create a negative jurisdiction conflict when a Member State court declines jurisdiction in favour of the chosen Turkish court based on the theory of reflexive application. The *forum necessitatis* rule under Article 11 of the Regulation would, however, be helpful for such extreme cases. Thus, from the Turkish perspective, extending the application of Article 5 to third State related cases seems viable only where it is not required that the jurisdiction agreement should be valid in the non-Member State whose courts has been chosen, since this would provide at least a certain level of coordination between the jurisdictional rules of Turkey and the Regulation.

Such an uncertainty regarding prorogation agreements in favour of third State courts will not come into play within the scope of bilateral treaties of Member States – which have priority of application under Article 75(1) of the Regulation – if they have provisions enabling or precluding such agreements; or at least if they lead to such a conclusion by way of interpretation.[315] The Turkish-German Treaty has obviously (and, relative to its background, understandably) no explicit rule concerning choice of court agreements. The exclusive nature of Article 20(15) of the Treaty – for disputes falling within its scope –[316] prohibits parties from concluding choice of court agreements and bringing their case before the courts of other Contracting Party, which are normally not competent under this provision.[317] Hence, it is not possible for Turkish nationals living in Germany, or, *vice versa*, for German nationals living in Turkey, to submit a succession case concerning a movable property to the jurisdiction of the courts of the other Contracting Party with a choice of court agreement.

2. *Forum non conveniens*

The second alternative conceivable to avoid jurisdiction conflicts with third States is the use of the *forum non conveniens* doctrine, i.e. the practice by which courts stay or dismiss proceedings upon a determination that another forum is more appropriate for the ends of justice,[318] this being a doctrine

---

[315] Francq and Mary, 'The External Relations of Belgium' (2019) 56; cf. Franzina, 'The External Relations of Italy' (2019) 201.

For a reference to this problem and the prevailing view on it within the scope of the treaties of Poland, see Piotr Rylski, 'The Influence of Bilateral Treaties with Third States on Jurisdiction and Recognition of Decisions in Matters on Succession – Polish Perspective' (2020) 26 PPPM 91, 100–101.

[316] On the scope of the provision, see above n 147, p 41.

[317] LG München I 26.9.2006 – 6 O 15963/05 (rkr.), FamRZ 2007, 1250, 1251; von Bary, *Gerichtsstandsvereinbarungen im internationalen Erbrecht* (2018) 13; cf. Franzina, 'The External Relations of Italy' (2019) 198 and 203–204 (in the context of the Turkish-Italian Treaty).

[318] See, in this regard, Richard Fentiman, 'Forum Non Conveniens' in Jürgen Basedow and others (eds), *Encyclopedia of Private International Law* (Edward Elgar Publishing 2017) 798 ff.

pertaining to common law systems. The possibility of declining jurisdiction in favour of another State court with the rationale of *forum non conveniens*[319] has already been embodied by the Regulation under Article 6(a). Again, with the underlying policy of establishing *Gleichlauf* between forum and *ius* in the absence of a *professio fori* by the parties,[320] Article 6(a) gives a Member State court seised in accordance with Article 4 or Article 10 the discretion to decline jurisdiction at the request of the parties in favour of the courts of the Member State whose law was already chosen by the deceased to govern his succession pursuant to Article 22. Such a declining of jurisdiction will be exercised by the seised court only if it reaches the conclusion that the courts of the Member State whose law governs the succession as a result of the valid choice of law made by the deceased are better placed to hear the case, taking into consideration the relevant facts, such as the last habitual residence of the parties concerned or the location of the assets. Where the court declines jurisdiction, the court at the Member State whose law had been designated by the deceased to rule on his succession will assume jurisdiction according to Article 7(a) of the Regulation.

With these two provisions, the Regulation, like in Article 6(b) and Article 7(b), sets up a mechanism where one Member State court declines jurisdiction with the belief that the court of another Member State is in a better position to hear the case due to the choice of law of the deceased in favour of the law of that State; and with the belief that this latter court will indeed assume jurisdiction. Here again, this mechanism operates only within the Union. Despite the fact that the deceased might have chosen the law of a third State to govern his succession pursuant to Article 22, there is no possibility for the Member State seised to decide that the case is more closely connected with this third State whose law has been chosen and, therefore, decline jurisdiction in favour of the courts of that State. Where, for instance, a Turkish individual has chosen Turkish law to govern his succession while being habitually resident in Spain, a declining of jurisdiction under Article 6(a) will not come into play despite the fact that all his heirs and assets are to be found in Turkey.[321] In such a case, Spanish courts will have to rule on succession by applying Turkish law. This constitutes a crucial restriction to the scope of application and the practical usefulness of the rule, since it cannot be applied as a coordination rule to diminish the jurisdiction conflicts with third States which might

---

[319] Bajons, 'Internationale Zuständigkeit und anwendbares Recht in Erbsachen' (2012) 34; Burandt, [2013] FuR 377, 380; Heinig, [2014] RNotZ 197, 225; Bonomi, *Bonomi/Wautelet* (2016) ESR Art 6 para 4; von Bary, *Gerichtsstandsvereinbarungen im internationalen Erbrecht* (2018) 22; Dutta, *MüKoBGB* (2020) EuErbVO Art 6 para 4; Lein, *Dutta/Weber* (2021) EuErbVO Art 6 para 9.

[320] Buonaiuti, *Calvo Caravaca/Davì/Mansel* (2016) ESR Art 6 para 2.

[321] Lein, *Dutta/Weber* (2021) EuErbVO Art 6 para 5.

arise as a consequence of Article 4 or Article 10.[322] Furthermore, the rule itself may effectuate conflicts of jurisdiction of positive nature with the external world. This would come into play when a non-Member State court exercises jurisdiction on the grounds of a *professio iuris* of the deceased.[323]

The question therefore arises as to whether the application of this rule could also be extended to the cases where there is a choice of law in favour of a third State law based on the theory of reflexive application as in Article 5. This is because the system adopted under Article 6(a) is very similar to Article 5. The only difference here is that the *professio iuris* of the deceased is not accompanied with the parties' *professio fori*.

There are again two opposing views in this regard. On the one hand, some scholars posit that manifold reasons exist to vindicate the *inter partes* scope of Article 6(a). The first reason, as asserted, is again the insurance of 'European standards'. When the jurisdiction is retained within the EU, the access to European justice by the heirs is guaranteed. In the opposite scenario, there could be the jeopardy that the chosen law leads to results that are incompatible with the fundamental values of European States. An example given in this respect is the law of an Islamic country discriminating against some heirs in terms of succession rights based on religion or sex. When the chosen law is applied by a European court, such undesirable effects could be prevented, particularly by way of a public policy exception.[324] Moreover, the European legislature intended with this rule to prevent negative jurisdiction conflicts with third States. In instances where the third State does not recognise the choice made by the deceased or establish jurisdiction over cases in which the deceased is domiciled outside a jurisdiction, conflicts of a negative nature would arise.[325] In the scope of the Regulation, it has been guaranteed that jurisdiction is taken by the court of another Member State when a court of a Member State declines jurisdiction (Article 7). This provides legal certainty in the jurisdictional context. There is no assurance that the jurisdiction would be exercised by the courts of third States in such cases. This argument, in fact, also applies in the context of Article 5, where reflexive application finds support. The difference under Article 6(a), however, is that one party's request is sufficient here for the court to consider the procedure for declining jurisdiction, unlike under Article 5 where all the parties collectively – and with 'open eyes' – take the risk of uncertainty by concluding an agreement of prorogation.[326] Lastly, even though Article 6(a) is based on a valid choice of law of

[322] Bonomi, *Bonomi/Wautelet* (2016) ESR Art 6 para 8.

[323] Article 87(2) of the Swiss PILA could be given again as an example here.

[324] Bonomi, *Bonomi/Wautelet* (2016) ESR Art 6 para 9, cf. Art 35 paras 17ff; Lein, *Dutta/Weber* (2021) EuErbVO Art 6 para 5.

[325] Bonomi, *Bonomi/Wautelet* (2016) ESR Art 6 para 9; Lein, *Dutta/Weber* (2021) EuErbVO Art 6 para 5.

[326] Dutta, *MüKoBGB* (2020) EuErbVO Art 6 para 6.

the deceased, the choice is not always recognised in the third State whose law has been chosen. When this is the case, there is the possibility that jurisdiction will be left to a State where the law chosen by the deceased is not recognised.[327] For these reasons, it is claimed that the application of Article 6(a) cannot be extended to third States.[328]

On the other hand, it is contended that none of these arguments is an entirely convincing argument against the extraterritorial application of Article 6(a) to non-EU States. This is because the court seised has broad discretion under this Article and, hence, can evaluate all the circumstances of a case before rendering its decision to or not to decline jurisdiction. Thus, an option to decline jurisdiction, possibly in the form of a suspension of proceedings, may also be considered in favour of third States.[329]

In the light of these views, the Turkish perspective should be examined here in order to ascertain whether the application of Article 6(a) to Turkish-EU cases would be helpful in providing the desired coordination. As it has already been explained,[330] a choice of law is not allowed with respect to successions upon death under Turkish law. Furthermore, jurisdiction is exercised by Turkish courts only when the deceased's last domicile was in Turkey or the deceased left assets in Turkey (Article 43 of the Turkish PILA). Under these circumstances, it appears difficult to endorse a reflexive application of Article 6(a) in the Turkish-EU context with the belief that it would provide the desired level of coordination between the two systems. Notwithstanding this, as mentioned in the context of Article 5,[331] the two systems considerably coincide with each other with regards to the law applicable to succession in cases where Turkish law has been designated by the deceased to govern his succession under the Regulation, whilst the choice of law is not valid on the Turkish side. In addition, in cases where one of the grounds for the assertion of international jurisdiction by Turkish courts exists, the risk of negative jurisdiction conflicts would not come into existence. In exceptional cases, Article 11 of the Regulation could be invoked. One could still propound the argument regarding the safety valve function of EU courts against a discordant impact of third State laws on 'European standards' in the context of Turkish law. Nonetheless, Turkish substantive succession law, as being based on Swiss law, does not have extreme discrepancies with the laws of EU Member States. Hence, reflexive application of Article 6(a) may still be arguable from the Turkish perspective, considering in particular that staying proceedings is left to the wide discretion of Member States after a careful analysis of the

[327] Bonomi, *Bonomi/Wautelet* (2016) ESR Art 6 para 9.
[328] Dutta, *MüKoBGB* (2020) EuErbVO Art 6 para 6.
[329] Bonomi, *Bonomi/Wautelet* (2016) ESR Art 6 para 9.
[330] See above Chapter 2 under C. pp 70–85, esp. p 76.
[331] See above under A.IV.1. pp 244–254.

facts. However, this could only be useful in certain cases, and thus a reflexive application of Article 6(a) would seemingly not be able to eliminate the vast majority of jurisdiction conflicts arising between Turkish and EU courts. It is also believed that the European side would be unwilling to extend the scope of application of the *forum non conveniens* rule – which is normally unusual for civil law jurisdictions – to third State related cases for reasons of legal uncertainty.[332]

Declining jurisdiction based on *forum non conveniens* is neither regulated nor supported by case law in Turkey. International jurisdiction rules are, indeed, laid down with the consideration that there is some manner of link between the subject matter of a case and the competent court in Turkey. Hence, even if one of the parties challenges the jurisdiction of the court by claiming that there is a court much more closely connected with the case, such a challenge will not be successful. Due to the complexity and uncertainty attached to the application of the doctrine, particularly the process of determining the appropriate forum, and due to the fact that such a practice is not in line with Turkish laws, it does not find support with Turkish commentators either.[333]

The courts of Contracting States are also not allowed to decline jurisdiction in the context of the Treaty based on the fact that the courts of the other Contracting Party are more appropriate to hear the case by virtue of the exclusive and binding nature of Article 20(15) of the Treaty for immovable as well as movable property.

3. *Lis pendens*

Another possible solution to reduce the risk of procedural conflicts between different State courts in succession cases is to use the rule of *lis alibi pendens*. The likelihood of concurrent jurisdictions and, in turn, irreconcilable judgments, thus requiring the use of such a rule, is actually not very high within the Regulation, since jurisdictional rules are drafted so as to ensure that only one Member State court has jurisdiction, unlike in some other instruments.[334]

---

[332] Dutta, *MüKoBGB* (2020) EuErbVO Art 6 para 6.

[333] Ekşi, *Milletlerarası Yetki* (2000) 73–74; Ziya Akıncı, *Milletlerarası Usul Hukukunda Yetki Sözleşmesine Dayanan Yabancı Derdestlik* (Seçkin 2002) 28–30 and 136; Demirkol, *Yetki Anlaşmaları* (2018) 200; Nomer, *Milletlerarası Usul Hukuku* (2018) 142; Şanlı, Esen and Ataman Figanmeşe, *Milletlerarası Özel Hukuk* (2021) 456.

[334] An example in this regard is the Brussels I (recast) Regulation. The Regulation requires that a defendant domiciled in a Member State should be sued at the courts of that State (Art 4). However, when there are other relevant factors, the number of alternative courts at which the defendant may be sued increases. If, for instance, there is a matter relating to a contract, the claimant has the right to bring a claim against the defendant either at his place of domicile or at the place of performance of the obligation in question (Art 7(1) (a)). Under the Brussels I (recast) Regulation, therefore, there is a 'legally allowed kind of forum shopping' for the claimant: Andrew Dickinson and Eva Lein, *The*

Notwithstanding this, divergent interpretations with respect to both the connecting factors as well as the provisions of the governing law may be adopted by the courts of different Member States, and hence irreconcilable judgments could be rendered.[335] These have detrimental effects on the very purposes of European private international law instruments, such as the free and easy movement of judgments, decisional harmony, legal certainty, judicial cooperation and efficacious administration of justice, procedural efficiency, and mutual trust.[336] Considering this, the Regulation adopted Article 17 addressing this issue, in a like manner to other earlier instruments.[337]

Article 17 of the Regulation envisages a scenario where proceedings involving the same cause of action (and between the same parties) are brought before the courts of different Member States. In such a scenario, Member State courts other than the court first seised are compelled to stay and later dismiss proceedings in favour of the court first seised, provided that this court establishes its jurisdiction on the dispute (Article 17).

The problem of parallel proceedings and, subsequently, irreconcilable judgments as addressed in this rule is in fact not specific to the judgments given by Member State courts and may also occur in relation to third countries. This possibility has already been foreseen by the Regulation, which provides that a judgment of a Member State court which is irreconcilable with an earlier judgment rendered by a Member State or third State court in an action involving the same subject matter and between the same parties is not capable of recognition (Article 40(d)).[338] Despite this, the doctrine of *lis pendens* is applicable only within the Union. This is regrettable considering the fact that the potential number of concurrent proceedings which may arise between third State courts and Member State courts is likely to be higher than the number of such proceedings between the Member State courts in the absence of uniform jurisdictional rules.[339] A mechanism to prevent parallel pro-

---

Brussels I Regulation Recast (OUP 2015) para 4.02. When this is the case, the risk of concurrent jurisdiction is higher than under the Succession Regulation: Buonaiuti, *Calvo Caravaca/Davì/Mansel* (2016) ESR Art 17 paras 4–5.

335 Buonaiuti, *Calvo Caravaca/Davì/Mansel* (2016) ESR Art 17 para 3.

336 Dickinson and Lein, *Brussels I Recast* (2015) para 11.02; Buonaiuti, *Calvo Caravaca/Davì/Mansel* (2016) ESR Art 17 paras 2–3.

337 See Art 27 of the Brussels I Regulation (currently Art 29 of the Brussels I (recast) Regulation); Art 12 of the European Maintenance Regulation and Art 19 of the Brussels IIa Regulation. For similar provisions from recent instruments, see Art 17 of the European Matrimonial Property Regulation and Art 17 of the European Partnership Regulation.

338 For similar remarks respecting the Brussels regime, see Fabrizio Marongiu Buonaiuti, 'Lis Alibi Pendens and Related Actions in the Relationships with the Courts of Third Countries in the Recast of the Brussels I Regulation' (2013–2014) XV YbPIL 87, 91.

339 Buonaiuti, *Calvo Caravaca/Davì/Mansel* (2016) ESR Art 17 para 19; Haris P. Meidanis, in Haris P. Pamboukis (ed), *EU Succession Regulation No 650/2012 – A Commen-*

ceedings that is applicable outside the EU – even if it is in a unilateral and discretional form – could also have contributed to the realisation of the above-mentioned objectives of European private international law instruments, particularly the quest for decisional harmony which is of utmost significance for family and succession matters,[340] in the global sense.[341]

When this is the case, it could be questioned again whether a reflexive application of Article 17 may be arguable. In other words, the question is whether an obligation of the Member State courts to suspend or dismiss proceedings in a case where there is already a pending proceeding before a third State court may be derived from these provisions by analogy.[342] This was the discussion regarding the Brussels regime in the aftermath of *Owusu,*[343] which refused to take a stance on the reflexive application of the *lis pendens* rules,[344] an issue on which courts were divided.[345] Decisions rendered within a couple of years after *Owusu* were inclined to opine that such a reflexive application is not possible for *lis pendens* rules,[346] whereas later ones hold the opposite.[347] As the solution has now been provided by Article 33 of the revised version of the Brussels I Regulation, namely the Brussels I (recast) Regulation, which extended the application of *lis pendens* – on a discretionary basis – to cases that are connected to third States, the discussion is not relevant anymore in that context.

---

tary (Nomiki Bibliothiki & C.H. Beck & Hart & Nomos 2017) ESR Art 17 para 5; cf. Álvarez Torné, (2012–2013) XIV YbPIL 409, 423.

340 Pataut, 'International Jurisdiction and Third States' (2008) 143–144.

341 Alegría Borrás, 'Lights and Shadows of Communitarisation of Private International Law: Jurisdiction and Enforcement in Family Matters with Regard to Relations with Third States' in Alberto Malatesta, Stefania Bariatti and Fausto Pocar (eds), *The External Dimension of EC Private International Law in Family and Succession Matters* (CEDAM 2008) 106. For a view arguing that EU regulations should include a provision on *lis pendens* also in favour of courts in third States, see Thalia Kruger, *Civil Jurisdiction Rules of the EU and Their Impact on Third States* (OUP 2008) para 5.27.

342 Bonomi, *Bonomi/Wautelet* (2016) ESR Art 17 para 7; Francq and Mary, 'The External Relations of Belgium' (2019) 57.

343 C-281/02 Owusu v. Jackson and others [2005] ECR I-1445.

344 C-281/02 Owusu v. Jackson and others [2005] ECR I-1445 [48–52].

345 Adrian Briggs, *Civil Jurisdiction and Judgments* (6th edn, Routledge 2015) para 2.311.

346 Goshawk Dedicated Ltd v. Life Receivables Ltd [2009] IESC 7, [2009] ILPr 435; Catalyst Investment Group Ltd v. Lewinsohn [2009] EWHC 1964 (Ch), [2010] Ch 218 [99ff]; cf. Pacific International Sports Clubs Ltd v. Soccer Marketing International Ltd & Ors [2009] EWHC 1839 (Ch) [109].

347 JKN v. JCN [2010] EWHC 843 (Fam), [2011] 1 FLR 826 [115] (in the context of the Brussels II Regulation); Ferrexpo AG v. Gilson Investments Ltd [2012] EWHC 721 (Comm), [2012] 1 Lloyd's Rep 588 [137]; Mittal v. Mittal [2013] EWCA Civ 1255, [2014] Fam 102 (in the context of the Brussels II Regulation).

However, it might still be questionable for the Succession Regulation in the absence of such a rule. With respect to this issue, it is maintained that such a reflexive application cannot be inferred by analogy from Article 17 in favour of third State courts.[348] The reasons for this could be inferred from the discussion regarding the Brussels regime and are manifold. In the first place, for *lis pendens* to be applicable, it is often important that the judgment rendered in another State should be recognisable and enforceable.[349] Under the Regulation, however, there is no such requirement, since the decisions delivered by Member State courts are, in principle, automatically recognisable and enforceable pursuant to Article 39 et seq. For decisions rendered by third States, the national rules of the Member States are applicable, and it is not assured that the decision will be recognised and enforced.[350] Furthermore, recognition and enforcement rules of Member States may also require that the jurisdiction of the court rendering the judgment should be reviewed.[351] Member State courts, on the other hand, are not allowed to examine the jurisdiction of the court first seised when applying Article 17 due to the principle of mutual trust intrinsic to the European judicial area.[352] The principle of mutual trust is not applicable in relation to third States which, as argued, makes it difficult to defend a reflexive application of the tool of *lis pendens* to third States.[353] Last but not least, *lis pendens*, as read in conjunction with Article 40(c), aims to preclude the possibility of irreconcilable judgments on the same proceedings between the same parties. To be more precise, Article 17 necessitates that Member State courts make an analysis as regards the subject matter of the proceedings in the light of recognition and enforcement rules, in particular as regards irreconcilability.[354] Therefore, a reflexive application of *lis pendens* cannot, it is submitted, be

[348] Bonomi, *Bonomi/Wautelet* (2016) ESR Art 17 para 7; Francq and Mary, 'The External Relations of Belgium' (2019) 59.

[349] With respect to Turkey and Germany, for example, see BGH 10.10.1985 – I ZR 1/83, NJW 1986, 2195.

[350] See, in the context of the Brussels I Regulation, Christian A. Heinze and Anatol Dutta, 'Ungeschriebene Grenzen für europäische Zuständigkeiten bei Streitigkeiten mit Drittstaatenbezug' [2005] IPRax 224, 229.

[351] See, for example, § 328(1) 1 of ZPO.

[352] Francq and Mary, 'The External Relations of Belgium' (2019) 59. In the context of the Brussels I Regulation, see, for example, C-116/02 Gasser v. MISAT [2003] ECR I-14693 [44 ff]; C-159/02 Turner v. Grovit, Harada Ltd and Changepoint SA [2004] ECR I-03565 [25 ff].

[353] Francq and Mary, 'The External Relations of Belgium' (2019) 59; cf. Heinze and Dutta, [2005] IPRax 224, 229.

For other considerations on the reflexive effect, see Richard Fentiman, 'National Law and the European Jurisdiction Regime' in Arnaud Nuyts and Nadine Watté (eds), *International Civil Litigation in Europe and Relations with Third States* (Bruylant 2005) 101 ff.

[354] See, with respect to Brussels Convention, C-144/86 Gubisch Maschinenfabrik KG v. Giulio Palumbo [1987] ECR I-04861 [8 ff].

argued given the lack of uniform jurisdiction as well as recognition and enforcement rules *vis-à-vis* third States in the Regulation.[355]

Instead, Member State courts, as contended, may invoke their domestic rules as such to suspend or dismiss proceedings in favour of the courts of non-EU States,[356] unless, of course, the Regulation implicitly provides different rules.[357] The imperative nature of the EU jurisdictional rules, as reinstated in *Owusu*,[358] may cast doubts on the compatibility of applying national rules, since these rules may result in jurisdiction first assumed later being declined under the Regulation in favour of third States.[359] Nevertheless, it is argued that the lack of explicit rules results in the application of national rules to provide coordination with third States and, hence, to achieve European values, particularly the harmony of judgments on a broader scale.[360] Such a line of thought supporting the application of *lis pendens vis-à-vis* third States, albeit by way of national law, is certainly maintainable from the Turkish perspective. Indeed, subject to certain conditions, the vast majority of Member States bound by the Regulation take international *lis pendens* respecting third States into account. Nonetheless, the procedures as well as the conditions of application are divergent among these States. In addition, there are still Member States which do not recognise *lis pendens* in cases of an international na-

---

[355] Heinze and Dutta, [2005] IPRax 224, 229; cf. Bonomi, *Bonomi/Wautelet* (2016) ESR Art 17 para 7; Francq and Mary, 'The External Relations of Belgium' (2019) 59.

[356] Seyfarth, 'Wandel der internationalen Zuständigkeit im Erbrecht' (2012) 167; Bonomi, *Bonomi/Wautelet* (2016) ESR Art 17 para 8; Buonaiuti, *Calvo Caravaca/Davì/Mansel* (2016) ESR Art 17 para 20; Romano, (2015–2016) XVII YbPIL 253, 271; Francq and Mary, 'The External Relations of Belgium' (2019) 60; Mark Makowsky, in Rainer Hüßtege and Heinz-Peter Mansel (eds), *NK-BGB/Rom-Verordnungen*, vol 6 (3rd edn, 2019) EuErbVO Art 17 para 4; Dutta, *MüKoBGB* (2020) EuErbVO Art 17 para 1; Florian Eichel, in Maximilian Herberger and others (eds), *jurisPK-BGB*, vol 6 (9th edn, juris 2020) EuErbVO Art 17 para 3; Lein, *Dutta/Weber* (2021) EuErbVO Art 17 para 15; J. Schmidt, *BeckOGK-EuErbVO* (2022) EuErbVO Art 17 para 27.

[357] It is argued that one of the situations which Member State courts may take into account for the possibility of limitation of proceedings under Article 12(1) of the Regulation is whether there are already proceedings pending before the courts of a third State where a part of the estate is located (see below pp 273–275). Therefore, as contended, for the application of Article 12(1), the Regulation already implicitly provides a *lis pendens* rule against third States, and, hence, a reference back to national rules on *lis pendens* will not be applicable in that context: Dutta, *MüKoBGB* (2020) EuErbVO Art 12 para 10 and Art 17 para 1.

[358] C-281/02 Owusu v. Jackson and others [2005] ECR I-1445 [37 ff].

[359] Kruger, *Civil Jurisdiction Rules of the EU – Third States* (2008) para 5.26; Pataut, 'International Jurisdiction and Third States' (2008) 144; Pippa Rogerson, in Andrew Dickinson and Eva Lein (eds), *The Brussels I Regulation Recast* (OUP 2015) Brussels I Recast Art 33–34 para 11.68; cf. Francq and Mary, 'The External Relations of Belgium' (2019) 59.

[360] Bonomi, *Bonomi/Wautelet* (2016) ESR Art 17 para 8; Buonaiuti, *Calvo Caravaca/Davì/Mansel* (2016) ESR Art 17 para 20; cf. Francq and Mary, 'The External Relations of Belgium' (2019) 60.

ture.[361] These undermine the uniformity of application desired in the Regulation and raise the risk that the needed coordination with third States cannot be provided. It is, thus, unfortunate that the Regulation did not follow the same approach as the Brussels I (recast) Regulation, which was adopted right before it and included a provision on the issue of *lis pendens* with respect to third States.[362] In this regard, the provision in the Brussels I (recast) Regulation could be briefly examined here as a possible model for future amendments to the Succession Regulation.

Under Article 33 of the Brussels I (recast) Regulation a Member State court seised in a matter on which it has a 'general' or 'special' jurisdiction under the Regulation[363] is entitled – on the application of parties or *ex officio* – to take pending actions involving the same cause of action and between the same parties before third State courts into consideration. This is applicable on the condition that the judgment rendered by the third State court is capable of recognition and/or enforcement in the Member State whose court is seised pursuant to the law of that Member State and that such action is consistent with the proper administration of justice. Member State courts have discretion to stay proceedings after making a careful analysis of the factual circumstances of the case in view of a proper administration of justice. Such circumstances may include the connection of the case to the third State concerned, the stage of the proceedings in that State, whether a judgment can be rendered in a reasonable time, whether there is any risk of irreconcilable judgments (only in the context of related actions), whether the continuation of proceedings is necessary for the proper administration of justice, and whether Member State courts and third States claim exclusive jurisdiction on the matter.[364] Where the third State court concludes the proceedings by rendering a judgment capable of recognition and/or enforcement in the Member State seised, the Member State court should dismiss proceedings in a situation of *lis pendens* (Article 33(3)). This provision has been a novelty for EU law and has certain aspects that are different from the intra-EU *lis pendens* rule which dates back to the time of the Brussels Convention.[365] First of all, these rules, unlike the intra-Union ones,

---

361 Nuyts, 'Study on Residual Jurisdiction – Review of the Member States' Rules concerning the "Residual Jurisdiction" of their courts in Civil and Commercial Matters pursuant to the Brussels I and II Regulations (JLS/C4/2005/07-30-CE)0040309/00-37)' (2007) 76ff; Bonomi and Öztürk, (2015) 114 ZVglRWiss 4, 12; Buonaiuti, (2016) 12 J Priv Int L 545, 557–559.

362 Pataut, 'International Jurisdiction and Third States' (2008) 144; Seyfarth, 'Wandel der internationalen Zuständigkeit im Erbrecht' (2012) 168; Lübcke, [2015] GPR 111, 112; Buonaiuti, *Calvo Caravaca/Davì/Mansel* (2016) ESR Art 17 para 20; J. Schmidt, *BeckOGK-EuErbVO* (2022) EuErbVO Art 17 para 27; cf. Francq and Mary, 'The External Relations of Belgium' (2019) 60.

363 See Art 4 and Arts 7, 8, or 9 of the Brussels I (recast) Regulation.

364 See Recitals 23 and 24 of the Brussels I (recast) Regulation.

have a unilateral character. That is to say, the EU legislature only encourages Member State courts to take parallel proceedings into consideration but cannot guarantee that third State courts will also act in the same manner.[366] What is more, the rule has a limited scope, in contrast to the pure Union rules on parallel proceedings, considering that they only apply when the jurisdiction is based on general or special grounds. To put it differently, it does not cover all the cases falling into the scope of the Regulation.[367] Finally, the rule respecting third States is applicable on a discretionary basis as compared to the rigid approach of the rules concerning intra-EU situations.[368] Although all these divergences might have legitimate justifications from the Union's perspective, such as the inability to enact universally applicable rules and the need to strike a balance between the quest for decisional harmony and the protection of the rights of European parties where common values and standards are only applicable inside the EU,[369] such a double-standard approach may be subject to criticism from the third State perspective given that it may not ensure the desired coordination in all cases.[370]

Notwithstanding this, a uniform *lis pendens* rule such as Article 33 of the Brussels I (recast) Regulation might particularly be useful in instances where the relevant third State does not have any rule in this regard. This is the case in Turkey. Whereas rules regarding *lis pendens* exist in the Turkish Code of Civil Procedure (Article 114(1) (ı)) for domestic cases, there is no general provision as such for cross-border cases under the Turkish PILA.[371]

---

[365] Buonaiuti, (2013–2014) XV YbPIL 87, 91; Pietro Franzina, 'Lis Pendens Involving a Third Country under the Brussels I-bis Regulation: An Overview' [2014] RDIPP 23, 24.

[366] Franzina, [2014] RDIPP 23, 24–25.

[367] Buonaiuti, (2013–2014) XV YbPIL 87, 93.

[368] Buonaiuti, (2013–2014) XV YbPIL 87, 94ff.

[369] Buonaiuti, (2013–2014) XV YbPIL 87, 95–96; Franzina, [2014] RDIPP 23, 24–25.

[370] Cf. Tekinalp, *Milletlerarası Özel Hukuk* (2020) 396.

[371] It is contented by certain scholars that *lis pendens* is applicable under the Turkish PILA within the scope of Article 41 concerning actions involving personal status of Turkish nationals and Article 47 on choice of court agreements due to the formulation used in these provisions: Ekşi, *Milletlerarası Yetki* (2000) 202; Akıncı, *Yabancı Derdestlik* (2002) 35, 45 and 47ff; Murat Atalı, 'Beachtung ausländischer Rechtshängigkeit im türkischen Recht' (2005) 10 ZZPInt 417, 429; Ceyda Süral, 'Hukuk Muhakemeleri Kanunu'nun Türk Mahkemelerinin Milletlerarası Yetkisine Etkisi' [2012] TBB Dergisi 167, 178 and 195; Ersin Erdoğan, 'Milletlerarası Derdestlik (Lis Alibi Pendens)' (2014) 16 DEÜHFD 1857, 1861–1862; Nomer, *Milletlerarası Usul Hukuku* (2018) 96; Özkan and Tütüncübaşı, *Uluslararası Usûl Hukuku* (2020) 36; Ebru Şensöz Malkoç, *Türk Milletlerarası Usul Hukukunda Milletlerarası Derdestlik ve Bağlantılı Dava İtirazı* (Beta 2020) 16ff; Tekinalp, *Milletlerarası Özel Hukuk* (2020) 393–394; Çelikel and Erdem, *Milletlerarası Özel Hukuk* (2021) 665–667; Şanlı, Esen and Ataman Figanmeşe, *Milletlerarası Özel Hukuk* (2021) 543–544. See, however, Fügen Sargın, *İnternet Aracılığıyla Gerçekleşen Marka İhlâlleri Hakkında Milletlerarası Yetkiyi Haiz Mahkemeler ve Uygulanacak Hukuk* (Yetkin 2005) 252–253 fn 553; Bilgin Tiryakioğlu, 'Türklerin Kişi Hallerine İlişkin Davalarda Türk

In the absence of a specific legal arrangement, the applicability of *lis pendens* in cross-border cases is contentious in legal academia. Some commentators put forward that due to the lack of a general legal arrangement on the issue, the doctrine of *lis pendens* could not be used in cross-border cases to stay proceedings where there is already a pending case before a foreign court.[372] Different underlying reasons are given for the rejection of the doctrine of *lis pendens*. In the first place, it is argued that not going forward with proceedings pending before Turkish courts based on the claim that the action is already pending before a foreign court would mean the waiver of adjudicatory powers of the State in favour of the courts of a foreign State and hence would be contrary to sovereignty, unless there is a treaty in this regard.[373] Certain scholars, on the other hand, maintain that the party who has already submitted his case to Turkish courts cannot be deprived of the right to sue and the right to legal remedies given the lack of a clear provision in this regard.[374] As a third view, it is also claimed that by virtue of the fact that it is not always certain whether a decision rendered by a foreign court will be recognisable or enforceable in Turkey, proceedings cannot be declined or stayed by a Turkish court based on the plea of parallel proceedings in another country.[375]

Mahkemelerinin Milletlerarası Yetkisi' in Bilgin Tiryakioğlu and Gülin Güngör (eds), *Prof. Dr. Tuğrul Arat'a Armağan* (Yetkin 2012) 1152; Gülüm Bayraktaroğlu Özçelik, *Milletlerarası Usûl Hukukunda Paralel Davalar* (Yetkin 2016) 324 and 329; Gülüm Bayraktaroğlu Özçelik, 'International Lis Pendens as a Contemporary Problem of Turkish International Civil Procedure' (2016–2017) XVIII YbPIL 217, 239–242; Özlem Canbeldek Akın, *Milletlerarası Derdestlik (Lis Pendens)* (On İki Levha 2019) 67–69 and 71–73; cf. Sargın, *Yetki Anlaşmaları* (1996) 189–190 (as regards Art 47); Süral, [2012] TBB Dergisi 167, 196 (as regards Art 47); Mine Tan Dehmen, 'Türk Vatandaşlarının Kişi Hallerine İlişkin Davalar Bakımından 5718 Sayılı MÖHUK'ta Kabul Edilen Yetki Kuralı' (2013) 33 MHB 169, 185–186 (as regards Art 41); Erten, *Türklerin Kişi Hâllerine İlişkin Davalar – Yetki* (2017) 216 (as regards Art 41); Demirkol, *Yetki Anlaşmaları* (2018) 230–232 (as regards Art 47).

As neither of these provisions are relevant for succession cases, this book does not specifically refer to them in the discussion on *lis pendens*.

372 M. R. Seviğ, *Sentez* (1941) 72; Haydar Demirarslan, 'Türk Devletler Hususi Hukukunda Kazai Salâhiyet' (1952) 43 AD 29, 49; V. R. Seviğ, *Devletler Hususi Hukuku – Yetki* (1963) 164–165; Ergin Nomer, 'Milletlerarası Yetki Alanında Derdestlik İtirazı' (1968) 34 İÜHFM 343, 368–369; Altuğ, *Milletlerarası Usul Hukuku* (1983) 219; Akıncı, *Yabancı Derdestlik* (2002) 44–45; Nomer, *Milletlerarası Usul Hukuku* (2018) 95; Şensöz Malkoç, *Milletlerarası Derdestlik ve Bağlantılı Dava İtirazı* (2020) 16ff; Çelikel and Erdem, *Milletlerarası Özel Hukuk* (2021) 666–670; cf. Metin Tuluay, '"Milletlerarası Özel Hukuk ve Usul Hukuku Hakkında Kanun" Üzerine Düşünceler' (1982) 2 MHB 22, 25; Tan Dehmen, (2013) 33 MHB 169, 180–181.

373 M. R. Seviğ, *Sentez* (1941) 72; Demirarslan, (1952) 43 AD 29, 49; Altuğ, *Milletlerarası Usul Hukuku* (1983) 219.

374 V. R. Seviğ, *Devletler Hususi Hukuku – Yetki* (1963) 164–165; Çelikel and Erdem, *Milletlerarası Özel Hukuk* (2021) 667–669.

375 Nomer, (1968) 34 İÜHFM 343, 368–370.

Another line of thought, however, argues that although there is no rule as regards *lis pendens* under the Turkish PILA, this cannot be interpreted as a complete rejection of declining jurisdiction based on *lis pendens*, and, hence, parallel proceedings pending before a foreign court should still be taken into consideration.[376] In the drafting process of the former Turkish PILA (no 2675) preceding the current Turkish PILA no 5718, the drafters, indeed, mentioned that some procedural issues, including *lis pendens*, are not specifically addressed under the international procedural rules of the Turkish PILA and are instead left to the general provisions of the Turkish Code of Civil Procedure or other relevant laws.[377] This supports the idea that the legislature did not intend to reject the doctrine of *lis pendens* but instead consciously refrained from laying down a specific provision on the issue.[378] Some scholars propose that Article 114(1) (ı) of the Turkish Code of Civil Procedure, which regulates *lis pendens* as a procedural requirement for domestic cases, could be directly used to prevent parallel proceedings in cross-border cases.[379] Another view, however, argues that the lack of a provision in the Turkish PILA should be regarded as a legal lacunae.[380] As a solution to the problem, it is maintained that Article 114(1) (ı) could be used by analogy to decline jurisdiction only when there

[376] Mustafa Reşit Belgesay, *Teorik ve Pratik Adliye Hukuku IV – Devletler Hususi Hukukunda Adliye II. Kısım* (İstanbul Üniversitesi Hukuk Fakültesi Yayınları 1938) 92; Vedat Raşit Seviğ and others, *Devletler Hususi Hukuku Pratik Çalışmaları* (Fakülteler Matbaası 1976) 180–181 (*Atâ Sakmar*); Fuat Tiryaki, 'Derdestliğin Şartları' (1979) 36(2) ABD 34, 37; Ersin Şekerci, 'Medeni Usul Hukukunda ve İdari Yargılama Usulünde Derdestlik' (1986) 12 YD 206, 216; Ekşi, *Milletlerarası Yetki* (2000) 204; Saim Üstündağ, *Medeni Yargılama Hukuku* (7th edn, Nesil Matbaacılık 2000) 500; Baki Kuru, *Hukuk Muhakemeleri Usulü*, vol 4 (6th edn, Demir Demir 2001) 4222; Vahit Doğan, 'Türk Hukukunda Yabancı Derdestliğin Nazara Alınması' (2002) 22 MHB 121, 143ff; Sargın, *İnternet Aracılığıyla Gerçekleşen Marka İhlâlleri* (2005) 252; Süha Tanrıver, *Medenî Usul Hukukunda Derdestlik İtirazı* (Adalet Yayınevi 2007) 46; E. Erdoğan, (2014) 16 DEÜHFD 1857, 1870ff; Bayraktaroğlu Özçelik, *Paralel Davalar* (2016) 301ff; Bayraktaroğlu Özçelik, (2016–2017) XVIII YbPIL 217, 229ff; Canbeldek Akın, *Milletlerarası Derdestlik* (2019) 116 and 120–121; Ersin Erdoğan, *Medenî Usûl Hukuku Kurallarının Yer Bakımından Uygulanması* (2nd edn, Yetkin 2020) 177ff; Şanlı, Esen and Ataman Figanmeşe, *Milletlerarası Özel Hukuk* (2021) 545; Doğan, *Milletlerarası Özel Hukuk* (2022) 87ff.

[377] İstanbul Üniversitesi Hukuk Fakültesi – Milletlerarası Hukuk ve Milletlerarası Münasebetler Enstitüsü, *MÖHUK Öntasarı Sempozyumu* (1978) 193.

[378] Canbeldek Akın, *Milletlerarası Derdestlik* (2019) 116.

[379] Belgesay, *Devletler Hususi Hukukunda Adliye* (1938) 92; cf. Doğan, (2002) 22 MHB 121, 143ff; Doğan, *Milletlerarası Özel Hukuk* (2022) 90.

[380] E. Erdoğan, (2014) 16 DEÜHFD 1857, 1877; Bayraktaroğlu Özçelik, *Paralel Davalar* (2016) 301; Canbeldek Akın, *Milletlerarası Derdestlik* (2019) 116; E. Erdoğan, *Yer Bakımından Uygulama* (2020) 183; cf. Sargın, *İnternet Aracılığıyla Gerçekleşen Marka İhlâlleri* (2005) 252.

is already a case pending before a foreign court.[381] A different view, on the other hand, rejects the application of this provision by analogy due to the fact that the objectives of the doctrine of *lis pendens*, i.e. judicial economy and the prevention of contradictory judgments on the same dispute as well as oppressive tactics,[382] could only be realised in cross-border cases when the court first seised renders a judgment which is recognisable and enforceable in Turkey. Therefore, domestic provisions cannot be applicable here. The judge should act as *modo legislatoris* under the authority given by Article 1(2) of the Turkish Civil Code to take parallel proceedings in cross-border cases into account after carefully examining the circumstances of the case pending before him.[383] Although solutions proposed are different from each other, supporters of the doctrine of *lis pendens* all agree that there should be other conditions to stay or dismiss proceedings in favour of a foreign court before which proceedings involving the same subject matter and the same cause of action between the same parties are pending. The suspension or dismissal of proceedings should only come into play, like in the EU rules, if it is expected the judgment to be rendered will be capable of recognition or, where applicable, enforcement in Turkey,[384] and where it appears that the proceedings before the foreign court are likely to be concluded within a reasonable time.[385]

---

[381] Sargın, *İnternet Aracılığıyla Gerçekleşen Marka İhlâlleri* (2005) 252; Bayraktaroğlu Özçelik, *Paralel Davalar* (2016) 302; Bayraktaroğlu Özçelik, (2016–2017) XVIII YbPIL 217, 230; Canbeldek Akın, *Milletlerarası Derdestlik* (2019) 120–121.

[382] See, in this regard, for example, Şekerci, (1986) 12 YD 206, 208–209; Ömer Ulukapı, 'Medeni Usul Hukukunda Derdestlik ve Sonuçları' (1995) 21 YD 395, 400–402; Tanrıver, *Derdestlik* (2007) 20–29.

[383] E. Erdoğan, (2014) 16 DEÜHFD 1857, 1877–1879; E. Erdoğan, *Yer Bakımından Uygulama* (2020) 183–184.

[384] Tiryaki, (1979) 36(2) ABD 34, 37; Şekerci, (1986) 12 YD 206, 216; Ekşi, *Milletlerarası Yetki* (2000) 204–205; Üstündağ, *Medeni Yargılama Hukuku* (2000) 500; Kuru, *Hukuk Muhakemeleri Usulü/vol 4* (2001) 4222; Doğan, (2002) 22 MHB 121, 145–147; Sargın, *İnternet Aracılığıyla Gerçekleşen Marka İhlâlleri* (2005) 253–254; Tanrıver, *Derdestlik* (2007) 46; E. Erdoğan, (2014) 16 DEÜHFD 1857, 1878–1879; Bayraktaroğlu Özçelik, *Paralel Davalar* (2016) 305 ff; Bayraktaroğlu Özçelik, (2016–2017) XVIII YbPIL 217, 232 ff; Canbeldek Akın, *Milletlerarası Derdestlik* (2019) 197 ff; E. Erdoğan, *Yer Bakımından Uygulama* (2020) 184; Şensöz Malkoç, *Milletlerarası Derdestlik ve Bağlantılı Dava İtirazı* (2020) 87–88; Şanlı, Esen and Ataman Figanmeşe, *Milletlerarası Özel Hukuk* (2021) 545; Doğan, *Milletlerarası Özel Hukuk* (2022) 88–89.

[385] Doğan, (2002) 22 MHB 121, 147; Bayraktaroğlu Özçelik, *Paralel Davalar* (2016) 312; Canbeldek Akın, *Milletlerarası Derdestlik* (2019) 216; Şensöz Malkoç, *Milletlerarası Derdestlik ve Bağlantılı Dava İtirazı* (2020) 94–96, 111 and 184 ff; Doğan, *Milletlerarası Özel Hukuk* (2022) 90.

It is also argued that *lis pendens* should only be applicable in cross-border cases if it can be expected that parallel proceedings will be taken into account before a foreign court, in cases where the first-seised courts are Turkish ones and where the judgments from Turkey are capable of recognition/enforcement in that State on a reciprocal basis (Doğan, (2002) 22 MHB 121,

It is undoubted that the growing number of cross-border cases calls for a specific provision generally addressing the phenomenon of *lis pendens* in Turkish law also beyond domestic borders.[386] Until a legal reform to this effect is made, however, *lis pendens* should still be used in practice to prevent parallel proceedings which are already pending before a foreign court at the time when an action involving the same cause of action, the same subject matter, and between the same parties is instituted before a Turkish court, provided that, as articulated by the proponents of *lis pendens*, it is likely that the foreign court first seised will render a judgment that is recognisable/enforceable in Turkey and will conclude the proceedings within a reasonable time. Although the application of *lis pendens* under these conditions will be on a discretionary basis after analysing the circumstances of the case, it will still be useful to a certain extent in eliminating the problems of concurrent litigation and irreconcilable judgments. This is of utmost significance also for succession cases arising in the Turkish-EU context considering the potential number of cases. Apart from the proceedings involving immovable assets in Turkey on which there is a claim of exclusive jurisdiction by the Turkish side, at least a certain level of coordination could be provided between Turkey and Member States with the help of *lis pendens*. Notwithstanding this, courts often do not allow application of *lis pendens* in practice unless there is an explicit provision applicable within the scope of international treaties to which Turkey is a party.[387] Therefore, it is unlikely that a Turkish

---

147; Doğan, *Milletlerarası Özel Hukuk* (2022) 90–91; contra Şensöz Malkoç, *Türk Milletlerarası Usul Hukukunda Milletlerarası Derdestlik ve Bağlantılı Dava İtirazı* (2020) 98); in cases where proper administration of justice is guaranteed in that State (Bayraktaroğlu Özçelik, *Paralel Davalar* (2016) 315) and where there is a genuine link between the dispute and the first-seised court (Ekşi, *Milletlerarası Yetki* (2000) 204; Bayraktaroğlu Özçelik, *Paralel Davalar* (2016) 315; contra Canbeldek Akın, *Milletlerarası Derdestlik* (2019) 220–221).

[386] See, in this regard, Bayraktaroğlu Özçelik, *Paralel Davalar* (2016) 352–354; Bayraktaroğlu Özçelik, (2016–2017) XVIII YbPIL 217, 229; Canbeldek Akın, *Milletlerarası Derdestlik* (2019) 294; Şensöz Malkoç, *Milletlerarası Derdestlik ve Bağlantılı Dava İtirazı* (2020) 106ff.

[387] See, for example, Yargıtay 2. Hukuk Dairesi, T. 15.6.2010, E. 2009/13541 K. 2010/11899 <https://legalbank.net/> accessed 7 February 2021; Yargıtay 2. Hukuk Dairesi, T. 17.5.2011, E. 2010/6713 K. 2011/8635 <https://legalbank.net/> accessed 7 February 2021; Yargıtay 11. Hukuk Dairesi, T. 12.11.2012, E. 2011/9084 K. 2012/17943 <https://www.lexpera.com.tr/> accessed 7 February 2021; Yargıtay 2. Hukuk Dairesi, T. 20.11.2014, E. 2014/12316 K. 2014/23427 <https://kararararama.yargitay.gov.tr> accessed 7 February 2021.

Even though it is rather rare, there are also judgments holding that *lis pendens* could be applicable in cross-border cases. See, for example, Yargıtay 2. Hukuk Dairesi, T. 13.11.1998, E. 10377 K. 12221 published in Kuru, *Hukuk Muhakemeleri Usulü/vol 4* (2001) 4223 (only the relevant part of the judgment has been published); İstanbul Bölge Adliye Mahkemesi, 16. Hukuk Dairesi, T. 15.3.2019, E. 2017/1563 K. 2019/559 <https://www.lexpera.com.tr/> accessed 7 February 2021.

court will suspend or dismiss succession proceedings based on the fact that an action is already pending before a Member State court.

The only exception to the application of *lis pendens* for both sides would come into play in cases falling into the scope of bilateral or multilateral conventions applicable between a Member State and Turkey. Whereas there are agreements between Member States and Turkey containing provisions on *lis pendens* in relation to the recognition and enforcement of judgments,[388] those provisions are related to *lis pendens* only at the recognition/enforcement stage and, hence, do not serve to prevent concurrent succession proceedings in the way that is described here.[389] Treaties which have provisions on jurisdiction will provide such a coordination for Turkish-EU successions.[390] Even though it has no explicit provision on *lis pendens*, the doctrine should be applicable within the scope of the Treaty between Turkey and Germany due to the exclusive and compulsory nature of the rule on jurisdiction.[391] Thus, the desired coordination in Turkish-EU succession will come into play solely in cases between Turkey and German that fall within the ambit of the Treaty.

---

[388] For the provisions as such in the bilateral treaties of Turkey with Member States, see Art 4(1) (b) of the Treaty between Turkey and Austria on Recognition and Enforcement of Judgments of 23.5.1989 (*Resmi Gazete* of 23.9.1991, no 21000); Art 18(1) (e) of the Treaty between Turkey and Croatia on Judicial Cooperation in Civil and Commercial Matters of 10.2.1999 (*Resmi Gazete* of 24.5.2000, no 24058); Art 19(5) of the Treaty between Turkey and Italy on Legal Protection, Judicial Cooperation and Enforcement of Judgments in Civil and Criminal Matters of 19.6.1926 (*Resmi Gazete* of 3.3.1929, no 1133); Art 20(1) (f) of the Treaty between Turkey and Lithuania on Judicial Cooperation in Civil and Commercial Matters of 19.9.1995 (*Resmi Gazete* of 20.4.2004, no 25439); Art 20(1) (f) of the Treaty between Turkey and Poland on Judicial Cooperation in Civil and Commercial Matters of 12.4.1988 (*Resmi Gazete* of 23.7.1990, no 20583); Art 18(1) (4) of the Treaty between Turkey and Romania on Judicial Cooperation in Civil Matters of 28.9.2005 (*Resmi Gazete* of 10.2.2008, no 26783); Art 19(1) (d) of the Treaty between Turkey and Slovakia on Judicial Cooperation in Civil and Commercial Matters of 11.11.2004 (*Resmi Gazete* of 7.12.2007, no 26723).

[389] See, in this regard, Zheng Sophia Tang, *Jurisdiction and Arbitration Agreements in International Commercial Law* (Routledge 2014) 141; Bayraktaroğlu Özçelik, *Paralel Davalar* (2016) 278.

[390] Cf. Francq and Mary, 'The External Relations of Belgium' (2019) 57–58; Andrea Bonomi, 'The Relations of Switzerland with EU Member States' in Anatol Dutta and Wolfgang Wurmnest (eds), *European Private International Law and Member State Treaties with Third States – The Case of the European Succession Regulation* (Intersentia 2019) 279.

[391] V. R. Seviğ, *Devletler Hususi Hukuku – Yetki* (1963) 164 fn 90; Franzina, 'The External Relations of Italy' (2019) 203 (in the context of the Turkish-Italian Treaty). *Franzina*, however, also argues that when there is another Member State involved and the proceedings were brought before the courts of that Member State, Italy should stay proceedings pursuant to Art 17 of the Regulation and this will not amount to a violation of the Treaty: Franzina, 'The External Relations of Italy' (2019) 203.

4. Limitation of Proceedings

A useful coordination rule concerning jurisdiction conflicts between EU courts and third State courts might be a rule enabling courts to limit their proceedings based on a negative recognition or enforcement prognosis. Such a possibility is, unsurprisingly, not applicable in the Treaty, which has already a limited scope, nor in the Turkish PILA, which does not provide under the wording of Article 43 for any limitation of jurisdiction in succession cases and, in general, does not provide that the jurisdiction of Turkish courts in cross-border cases hinges on whether recognition and/or enforcement of the decision will be possible outside Turkey.[392] The Regulation, however, deviates once again from its fundamental principle, the unity of succession,[393] with the rationales of *forum non conveniens*[394] and procedural economy;[395] it addresses the issue of jurisdictional coordination with third States in the context of limitation of proceedings under Article 12.[396]

According to Article 12 of the Regulation, in cases where the estate in question also includes assets in third States, the Member State court seised to rule on succession *may, at the request of one of the parties*, decide not to rule on the assets located in the third State, provided that there is a possibility that the decision rendered at the end of the proceedings may not be recognised and/or enforced in the respective non-EU State. Pursuant to paragraph 2 of this provision, parties may also limit the scope of the proceedings under the law of the Member State of the court seised.

The first – and generally self-evident – condition for Member State courts to limit their proceedings is that they have jurisdiction over the estate assets located in third States. This would be the case under Article 4 or Article 10(1) of the Regulation.[397] If, for example, a Turkish deceased habitually resident in Rotterdam/Netherlands has left assets there as well as in Izmir/Turkey, Dutch

---

[392] An example of a provision of this kind under a third country law is Article 86(2) of the Swiss PILA. However, as explained earlier, this provision cannot be applied in favour of Member States as the Regulation does not have an exclusive jurisdiction rule.

[393] Bajons, 'Internationale Zuständigkeit und anwendbares Recht in Erbsachen' (2012) 35; Buonaiuti, *Calvo Caravaca/Davì/Mansel* (2016) ESR Art 12 para 3; Dutta, *MüKoBGB* (2020) EuErbVO Art 12 para 1; Gitschthaler, *Deixler-Hübner/Schauer* (2020) EuErbVO Art 12 para 1.

[394] Bonomi, *Bonomi/Wautelet* (2016) ESR Art 12 para 10; Giray, (2016) 9 Anali PFZE 235, 235; Dutta, *MüKoBGB* (2020) EuErbVO Art 12 para 1.

[395] Schwander, [2014] AJP 1084, 1089; Lein, *Dutta/Weber* (2021) EuErbVO Art 12 para 11; OGH 26.2.2019 – 2 Ob 124/18a, FamRZ 2019, 1092, 1094.

[396] See also Art 13 of the European Partnership Regulation and the European Matrimonial Property Regulation. A similar provision also exists under Art 5(4) of the EGPIL Proposal for a Convention on Jurisdiction and Enforcement of Family and Succession Matters. See <https://gedip-egpil.eu/wp-content/uploads/1993/10/gedip-documents-3pe.pdf> accessed 3 December 2018.

courts, pursuant to Article 4, will be competent over all assets including those found in Izmir. Article 12(1), therefore, could be invoked in such circumstances. In instances where the jurisdiction of the case is already limited to certain assets which do not include the assets located in third States, the rule has no application. The latter may, however, come into play under Article 10(2) and Article 5 et seq., where parties or the court limit proceedings to certain assets.[398]

A further condition of application for Article 12(1) is that it is only applicable at the request of one of the parties and on a discretionary basis. The Member State court seised on the succession matter cannot restrict its jurisdiction *ex officio* but rather needs the request of one of the parties.[399] In addition, the court is not under a duty to exclude assets located in third States from its ruling. Instead, it is free to make its own decision after a careful analysis of the facts.

Moreover, Article 12(1) is only applicable on the condition of a negative recognition and/or enforcement prognosis. In other words, the Member State courts can decide not to rule on the part of the estate located in third States only if it is expected that their judgment on those assets will not be subject to recognition and/or enforcement. The analysis of the facts of the case, thus, should focus on this issue.[400] An example of such a situation could be the fact that third State courts deem their jurisdiction exclusive, particularly on immovables situated in their territories.[401] This is the case in Turkish law, as explained above.[402] Hence, the judgment of the Rotterdam courts in the above example cannot be considered as recognisable/enforceable in Turkey. This could be a ground for a limitation of proceedings by Rotterdam courts under Article 12(1).[403] The Article is broadly formulated and, thus, scenarios which could lead to the limitation of proceedings are not limited to the cases where there is an exclusive jurisdiction of third State courts. It could also be applied in cases where the recognition and/or enforcement of the Member State

397 It may be claimed that Article 12 has a greater chance of application when the deceased is habitually resident in a third State. For such an opinion expressed in empirical research in Slovenia, see Slađana Aras Kramar and Katarina Vučko, 'A Guide to the Implementation of the Succession Regulation (EU) No 650/2012' (Croatian Law Centre 2020) 32 <https://www.notariesofeurope.eu/wp-content/uploads/2020/07/Guide-to-Succession-Regulation.pdf> accessed 5 March 2022.

398 Panopoulos, *Pamboukis* (2017) ESR Art 12 para 4; Dutta, *MüKoBGB* (2020) EuErbVO Art 12 para 3.

399 OGH 26.2.2019 – 2 Ob 124/18a, FamRZ 2019, 1092, 1096; Dutta, *MüKoBGB* (2020) EuErbVO Art 12 para 2; Gitschthaler, *Deixler-Hübner/Schauer* (2020) EuErbVO Art 12 para 7.

400 Lein, *Dutta/Weber* (2021) EuErbVO Art 12 para 10.

401 Buonaiuti, *Calvo Caravaca/Davì/Mansel* (2016) ESR Art 12 para 9.

402 See above pp 234–243.

403 Giray, (2016) 9 Anali PFZE 235, 236.

judgment is not possible on other grounds, such as, from the Turkish perspective, a violation of either due process (Article 54(1) (ç) of the Turkish PILA) or the *ordre public* (Article 54(1) (c) of the Turkish PILA).[404]

In some cases, nevertheless, the possibility that the decision rendered by the Member State court seised will not be subject to recognition and/or enforcement might not be sufficient for the court to limit its proceedings, as seeking recognition or enforcement in a third State is normally up to parties.[405] In addition, Member State courts are not always well-placed to assess recognition and enforcement rules of third States.[406] In Turkish law, for instance, exclusive jurisdiction is not expressly provided by the legislature but is rather accepted by scholars and through the case law. It is not clear whether the European courts will deem this as a satisfactory ground to limit their proceedings to the assets found in Union territories.[407] This is because a court's mere *presumption* of non-recognition and/or enforcement in a third State is not adequate for the limitation of proceedings; instead, it should be *highly likely* that recognition/enforcement of the decision will be refused.[408] Consequently, in the lack of precise guidance for the exercise of discretion the courts may (or, it is argued,

---

[404] Bonomi, *Bonomi/Wautelet* (2016) ESR Art 12 para 4; Buonaiuti, *Calvo Caravaca/Davì/Mansel* (2016) ESR Art 12 paras 11ff; Panopoulos, *Pamboukis* (2017) ESR Art 12 para 9; Lein, *Dutta/Weber* (2021) EuErbVO Art 12 para 8.

For an interpretation of *ordre public* from Turkish perspective within the scope of Article 12(1) of the Regulation, see below n 419, p 274.

[405] Dutta, [2013] FamRZ 4, 7; Dutta, *MüKoBGB* (2020) EuErbVO Art 12 para 10; Gitschthaler, *Deixler-Hübner/Schauer* (2020) EuErbVO Art 12 para 8.

[406] Bonomi, *Bonomi/Wautelet* (2016) ESR Art 12 para 9; Dutta, *MüKoBGB* (2020) EuErbVO Art 12 para 10.

[407] Under Art 5(4) of the EGPIL's proposal, for instance, it is provided that the declaration of incompetence by the courts is only possible in cases where the third State rules at the place of *situs* of the immovable property assert exclusive jurisdiction. Even though there is no clarity on the issue under Art 12(1) of the Regulation, it is questionable whether the same could be applicable for this provision and whether the Member State courts will limit their jurisdiction to certain assets in a Turkish-EU case where the Turkish rules are not explicit on the issue of exclusive jurisdiction. See, however, Buonaiuti, (2016) Art 12 para 10, stating that exclusive jurisdiction may also be established in the third State through case-law. The author, however, lists common law countries where domestic rules are established by precedents. It is, therefore, still questionable whether the same would be applicable in the Turkish context.

[408] Bonomi, *Bonomi/Wautelet* (2016) ESR Art 12 para 8; Makowsky, *NK-BGB/Rom-Verordnungen* (2019) EuErbVO Art 12 para 5; Dutta, *MüKoBGB* (2020) EuErbVO Art 12 para 7; Gitschthaler, *Deixler-Hübner/Schauer* (2020) EuErbVO Art 12 para 9; Lein, *Dutta/Weber* (2021) EuErbVO Art 12 para 9; J. Schmidt, *BeckOGK-EuErbVO* (2022) EuErbVO Art 12 para 10; cf. Bajons, 'Internationale Zuständigkeit und anwendbares Recht in Erbsachen' (2012) 36; Michael Kränzle, *Heimat als Rechtsbegriff?* (Mohr Siebeck 2014) 201.

See also OGH 26.2.2019 – 2 Ob 124/18a, FamRZ 2019, 1092, 1094.

should) be reluctant to apply this provision,[409] especially considering the fact that the limitation of proceedings would amount to a scission of succession, something whose avoidance is the very purpose of the Regulation.[410]

Nonetheless, this unilateral coordination rule – one which did not exist in the Commission Proposal but was later inserted into the Regulation and which is the only rule in this regard – should be welcomed from a third State perspective by virtue of the fact that it may be useful to prevent jurisdiction conflicts and, hence, at least to a certain extent promote decisional harmony between the EU and outside world.[411] Even though it will give rise to scission and potentially associated problems – the parties will, for instance, have to institute different proceedings in- and outside the EU concerning different assets – jurisdiction conflicts with third States seem to represent a bigger problem.[412]

Furthermore, it is argued that one of the factors to be considered under Article 12(1) when deciding not to rule on the assets found in third States is whether there are already proceedings pending before the courts of the relevant third State.[413] In such cases, Article 12(1) will function as a *lis pendens* rule for the assets located in third States[414] where such a situation (i.e. the fact that identical proceedings are already pending or have already been closed in the State where the recognition and/or enforcement is sought) is a ground for the refusal of recognition of enforcement of a judgment in the law of those third States.[415] Indeed, the Austrian Supreme Court of Justice decided in 2019 that the already concluded succession proceedings of an Austrian deceased in Switzerland should be a reason for the court in Austria, upon application of parties, not to rule on assets situated in Switzerland since such a situation is a ground for the refusal of recognition/enforcement of a judgment.[416]

---

[409] Dutta, [2013] FamRZ 4, 7; Bonomi, *Bonomi/Wautelet* (2016) ESR Art 12 para 9; Dutta, *MüKoBGB* (2020) EuErbVO Art 12 para 10; Gitschthaler, *Deixler-Hübner/Schauer* (2020) EuErbVO Art 12 para 8.

[410] Cf. Lein, *Dutta/Weber* (2021) EuErbVO Art 12 para 11.

[411] Schwander, [2014] AJP 1084, 1089; Bonomi and Öztürk, (2015) 114 ZVglRWiss 4, 11.

It is claimed that it is also useful for Member States which did not conclude international agreements concerning recognition and enforcement of judgments with third States: Francq and Mary, 'The External Relations of Belgium' (2019) 63.

[412] Lein, *Dutta/Weber* (2021) EuErbVO Art 12 para 11.

[413] Bonomi, *Bonomi/Wautelet* (2016) ESR Art 12 para 11; Dutta, *MüKoBGB* (2020) EuErbVO Art 12 para 10; Lein, *Dutta/Weber* (2021) EuErbVO Art 12 para 10.

See also OGH 26.2.2019 – 2 Ob 124/18a, FamRZ 2019, 1092, 1094.

[414] Gabriele Meusburger-Hammerer and Alexander Wittwer, 'OGH, 26.2.2019 – 2 Ob 124/18 a: Beschränkung des Verlassenschaftsverfahrens bei Nachlass in der Schweiz' [2019] ErbR 353, 359; Dutta, *MüKoBGB* (2020) EuErbVO Art 12 para 13; cf. Bonomi and Öztürk, (2015) 114 ZVglRWiss 4, 11.

[415] OGH 26.2.2019 – 2 Ob 124/18a, FamRZ 2019, 1092, 1094 ff; Meusburger-Hammerer and Wittwer, [2019] ErbR 353, 359.

This will also be useful in providing a level coordination in Turkish-EU successions. The Turkish PILA does not indicate that the existence of a judgment rendered by a Turkish court and having the effect of substantive *res judicata*[417] is a ground for the refusal of recognition or enforcement of foreign judgments. However, Article 114(1) (i) of the Turkish Code of Civil Procedure enumerates such a situation as a procedural requirement. As the Turkish Code of Civil Procedure should be decisive for procedural issues in recognition and enforcement cases which are not specifically addressed within the Turkish PILA,[418] the fact that there is already a final judgment of a Turkish court on the issue will prevent recognition and enforcement of the judgment rendered by a Member State court, if they are on the same issue, the same cause of action and between the same parties.[419] Such a ground for the refusal of recognition and enforcement also exists in most of the bilateral treaties concluded between Turkey and Member States.[420] Yet if the proceedings before the Turkish courts are still pending, this will not be a ground to reject the recognition or enforcement of a judgment rendered by a Member State court.[421] Notwithstanding this, here again the provisions of existing bilateral

---

416 OGH 26.2.2019 – 2 Ob 124/18a, FamRZ 2019, 1092.

417 See below under B.II. pp 293–318.

418 Musa Aygül, 'Yabancı Mahkeme Kararlarının Tanınması ve Tenfizinde Bazı Usul Hukuku Problemleri (Harç–İspat Yükü ve Deliller–Vasıflandırma)' (2011) 31 MHB 83, 85 and 114; Cemal Şanlı, *Uluslararası Ticari Akitlerin Hazırlanması ve Uyuşmazlıkların Çözüm Yolları* (7th edn, Beta 2019) 256.

419 Nuray Ekşi, *Yabancı Mahkeme Kararlarının Tanınması ve Tenfizi* (2nd edn, Beta 2020) 318; Nomer, *Devletler Hususî Hukuku* (2021) 538; Şanlı, Esen and Ataman Figanmeşe, *Milletlerarası Özel Hukuk* (2021) 680; cf. Canbeldek Akın, *Milletlerarası Derdestlik* (2019) 244. For judgments of the Turkish Court of Cassation in the same direction, see Ekşi, *Tanıma ve Tenfiz* (2020) 318ff; Şanlı, Esen and Ataman Figanmeşe, *Milletlerarası Özel Hukuk* (2021) 606 fn 436.

Certain scholars, however, contend that the recognition or enforcement of a foreign judgment on an issue on which a Turkish Court already rendered a judgment should be refused, as this will be a manifest violation of *ordre public*, which is a ground for the refusal of recognition and enforcement under Article 54(1) (c) of the Turkish PILA: Sakmar, *Yabancı İlamların Türkiye'deki Sonuçları* (1982) 80; Şeref Ertaş, 'Yabancı İlamların Tanınması ve Tenfizi' (1987) 3 DEÜHFD 365, 396; Demir Gökyayla, *Tanıma ve Tenfiz'de Kamu Düzeni* (2001) 261–262; Özkan and Tütüncübaşı, *Uluslararası Usûl Hukuku* (2020) 213; Çelikel and Erdem, *Milletlerarası Özel Hukuk* (2021) 767. For a decision of the Turkish Court of Cassation in this direction, see Şanlı, Esen and Ataman Figanmeşe, *Milletlerarası Özel Hukuk* (2021) 680 fn 469.

As the result would be the same in both views and a foreign judgment will not recognised or enforced in Turkey for the reason that there is already a judgment given by a Turkish court on the issue, the issue will not be treated in detail here.

420 This is the case in all the treaties mentioned above in n 388, p 269.

421 Nomer, (1968) 34 İÜHFM 343, 372; Altuğ, *Milletlerarası Usul Hukuku* (1983) 220.

treaties concerning recognition and enforcement of judgments between some Member States and Turkey may be helpful. If the Member State whose courts are seised of the dispute and before which a request for the limitation of proceedings under Article 12(1) of the Regulation has been made by the parties has a bilateral treaty with Turkey as such, it will decide not to rule on the assets of the deceased located in Turkey.

It is, further, put forward that Article 12(1) will be a ground for Member State courts to refer back to their national *lis pendens* rules for assets located in the European Union. When proceedings in the third State are not limited to assets of the deceased found there but also include assets in the Union, the Member State court may also decline proceedings also as regards the European part of the estate with the help of national *lis pendens* rules. This will not be in conflict with the purpose of Article 12(1).[422] As the wording of Article 43 of the Turkish PILA does not suggest limiting succession proceedings merely to the assets located in Turkey, such an extensive interpretation of Article 12(1) will be of much help in preventing jurisdiction conflicts in the Turkish-EU context, particularly considering the fact that there is no mechanism to provide the desired coordination under the Turkish PILA.

The second paragraph of Article 12 is also useful in the Turkish-EU context as it enables parties to limit the scope of the proceedings with the help of national rules of Member States in this regard. Parties may use this possibility by agreement not only in contentious proceedings but also in non-contentious proceedings, such as proceedings for the issue of a succession certificate.[423]

Therefore, although Article 12 has a limited scope and may not provide the desired coordination with third States in all the cases, it is still of paramount

---

However, it is argued that recognition and enforcement of a foreign judgment in such cases could still be refused based on *ordre public*: V. R. Seviğ and others, *Pratik Çalışmalar* (1976) 191 (*Atâ Sakmar*).

There are views in Turkish literature which propose that a provision on this issue should be drafted in a future reform of the Turkish PILA: Uğur Tütüncübaşı, 'Türk Hukukuyla Karşılaştırmalı Olarak Alman Hukukunda Yabancı Yargı Kararlarının Tanınması ve Tenfizi' (2014) 16 DEÜHFD 1525, 1547; Canbeldek Akın, *Milletlerarası Derdestlik* (2019) 245–247.

422 Dutta, *MüKoBGB* (2020) EuErbVO Art 12 para 13.

423 Dutta, *MüKoBGB* (2020) EuErbVO Art 12 para 12. See also OGH 26.2.2019 – 2 Ob 124/18a, FamRZ 2019, 1092, 1094.

From the German perspective, an example of such a rule is said to be § 352c of FamFG: Grau, *Praxiskommentar Erbrechtliche Nebengesetze* (2017) EuErbVO mit IntErbRVG para 151; Dutta, *MüKoBGB* (2020) EuErbVO Art 12 para 12; contra Kurt Siehr, 'Erbrechtliche Probleme um den Nachlass eines Schweizer Bürgers, der mit letztem gewöhnlichen Aufenthalt ausserhalb der Schweiz verstorben ist – Erbrecht im schweizerischen-deutschen-US-amerikanischen Rechtsverkehr' in Alexander R. Markus, Stephanie Hrubesch-Millauer and Rodrigo Rodriguez (eds), *Zivilprozess und Vollstreckung national und international – Schnittstellen und Vergleiche, Festschrift für Jolanta Kren Kostkiewicz* (Stämpfli Verlag 2018) 287.

significance for Turkish-EU successions as it is the only tool in this regard, a conclusion that is amplified by the lack of coordination tools in Turkey.[424]

Procedural issues in relation to Turkish-EU successions are, of course, relevant in terms of beyond jurisdiction. The Regulation also adopts rules on a uniform succession certificate that is to be applicable within the Union, and there may also be procedural issues in relation to the European Certificate of Succession which are important in Turkish-EU successions. Accordingly, after having discussed the jurisdictional rules in three legal texts, those issues should also be examined below.

B. Procedural Issues in Relation to the European Certificate of Succession

The most innovative aspect of the Regulation is undoubtedly the introduction of the ECS.[425] Alongside the classical rules of private international and procedural law, the European legislature has established under the Regulation rules on the ECS (Article 62 et seq.) with the aim of a speedy, smooth, and efficient settlement of cross-border succession issues within the Union.[426] The ECS is conceived as a 'sui generis legal instrument'[427] to be used by heirs, legatees, testamentary executors, or estate administrators in all Member States.[428]

The idea of a succession certificate is of course not peculiar to the Regulation. Every legal system has a certificate or a comparable document to that effect. The differences between the national systems in terms of the nature, form, content, procedure, and effects of their respective instruments as well as their recognition outside the State issuing them are, however, likely to trigger problems within the Union.[429] Hence, the ECS was created in addition to the national certificates.[430]

---

[424] Bonomi and Öztürk, (2015) 114 ZVglRWiss 4, 11.

[425] Dörner, [2010] ZEV 221, 222. See also Devaux, (2013) 47 TIL 229, 230 ('a real innovative European tool'); Mihaela Pătrăuş and Ionita Maria Ofrim, 'European Certificate of Succession' [2019] AGORA Int'l J Jurid Sci 78, 79 and 87 ('a major innovation').

[426] Recital 67 of the Regulation.

[427] Knut Werner Lange, 'Das geplante Europäische Nachlasszeugnis' [2012] DNotZ 168, 170.

[428] Recital 67 and Art 63(1) of the Regulation.

[429] Andreas Fötschl, 'The Relationship of the European Certificate of Succession to National Certificates' (2010) 18 ERPL 1259, 1260; Jens Kleinschmidt, 'Optionales Erbrecht: Das Europäische Nachlasszeugnis als Herausforderung an das Kollisionsrecht' (2013) 77 RabelsZ 723, 727ff; Anatol Dutta, 'The European Certificate of Succession: A New European Instrument between Procedural and Substantive Law' (2015) 5 IJPL 38, 42.

[430] Recital 67, Art 62, and Art 63 of the Regulation.

The ECS can be requested and used by heirs and legatees having direct succession rights or by testamentary executors and administrators of the estate in order to invoke their status or to exercise their rights or powers in another Member State (Articles 63(1) and 65(1)). It is issued by the courts or competent authorities of the Member State, e.g. notaries, having jurisdiction under Article 4 et seq. of the Regulation (Article 64). The issuing authority should use the pre-established form[431] and issue the ECS without delay once the status, rights, and powers of the requesting parties have been established under the law applicable to the succession or under the law governing specific issues (Article 67(1)). The information to be included in the ECS is enumerated under Article 68 of the Regulation. It covers in particular the relevant information regarding the deceased, regarding all the beneficiaries and their respective shares as well as their rights/assets and regarding the law applicable to succession.

The issuing authority would be competent to rectify, modify, or withdraw the ECS (Article 71). Third parties could also challenge the decisions taken by the issuing authority before a judicial authority of the issuing Member State pursuant to law of that State (Article 72). Both the issuing authority or the judicial authority where the challenge procedure is brought may suspend the effects of the ECS until the final decision is made in the challenge, modification, or withdrawal procedure (Article 73).

The ECS will produce its effects immediately in all Member States (Article 69(1)). This means that there is no recognition or control procedure over the ECS even where it violates the *ordre public* of the Member State in which it is presented.[432] The uniform effects of the ECS are clarified under Article 69 of the Regulation. First, it creates a rebuttable[433] 'presumption of accuracy'[434] for the elements included in it. It is presumed, in particular, on the face of the ECS that

---

[431] Annex 5 in the Commission Implementing Regulation (EU) No 1329/2014 of 9 December 2014 establishing the Forms referred to in Regulation (EU) No 650/2012 of the European Parliament and of the Council on jurisdiction, applicable law, recognition and enforcement of decisions and acceptance and enforcement of authentic instruments in matters of succession and on the creation of a European Certificate of Succession [2014] OJ L 359/30.

[432] Dutta, (2015) 5 IJPL 38, 47; Christine Budzikiewicz, in Alfonso-Luis Calvo Caravaca, Angelo Davì and Heinz-Peter Mansel (eds), *The EU Succession Regulation – A Commentary* (Cambridge University Press 2016) ESR Art 69 para 2; Wautelet, *Bonomi/Wautelet* (2016) ESR Art 69 para 8; Stamatiadis, *Pamboukis* (2017) ESR Art 69 para 4; Carl Friedrich Nordmeier, in Rainer Hüßtege and Heinz-Peter Mansel (eds), *NK-BGB/Rom Verordnungen*, vol 6 (3rd edn, Nomos 2019) EuErbVO Art 69 para 4; Matteo Fornasier, in Anatol Dutta and Johannes Weber (eds), *Internationales Erbrecht* (C.H. Beck 2021) EuErbVO Art 69 para 2.

[433] Kleinschmidt, (2013) 77 RabelsZ 723, 726; Wautelet, *Bonomi/Wautelet* (2016) ESR Art 69 paras 33 ff; Köhler, *NK/Nachfolgerecht* (2019) EuErbVO Art 69 para 3; Dutta, *MüKoBGB* (2020) EuErbVO Art 69 para 11; Fornasier, *Dutta/Weber* (2021) EuErbVO Art 69 para 7.

[434] Dutta, (2015) 5 IJPL 38, 47.

the heir, legatee, executor of a will, or administrator of the estate holds the status indicated in it (Article 69(2)). Moreover, the ECS carries a 'legitimation effect'[435] for the relevant registry of Member States in the process of recording the assets belonging to the estate (Article 69(5)). Last but not least, it has a 'good faith effect'[436] on third parties, especially on creditors and on individuals to whom succession property has been transferred by the persons certified in the ECS, unless they know or ought to have known that the contents of the ECS are not accurate. Any creditor who makes a payment or passes property to a person mentioned in the ECS will be considered as having validly transacted with this person (Article 69(3)). In the same vein, a disposition made in favour of third parties by a person certified in the ECS will be valid (Article 69(4)).

The ECS, which has been equipped with such uniform effects, could, of course, only produce those effects, and hence, ensure a harmony of decisions with respect to the legal positions of the persons indicated (in all participating Member States) when issued in accordance with the uniform conflict-of-laws rules.[437] Indeed, the harmonised conflict rules of the Regulation are also applicable for the determination of the legal status, rights, and obligations of the persons certified in the ECS, as Article 67(1) stresses. Notwithstanding this, a full of harmony of decisions within the Union regarding the certified legal positions in the ECS seems to be a utopia. One of the fundamental reasons[438] for this is the existing bilateral treaties of the Member States with certain non-Member States which prevail over the Regulation pursuant to Article 75(1) of the Regulation. Because of these treaties, an important number of succession cases arising in the Union fall outside the scope of the Regulation and the harmonised system it creates.[439] This is obviously problematic under the European perspective and may be considered as of no practical im-

---

[435] Dörner and others, [2005] IPRax 1, 8; Dutta, (2015) 5 IJPL 38, 48.

[436] Dörner and others, [2005] IPRax 1, 8; Dutta, (2015) 5 IJPL 38, 48.

[437] Dörner and others, [2005] IPRax 1, 8; Mansel, 'Vereinheitlichung des Internationalen Erbrechts in der EG' (2006) 222; Wilke, [2012] RIW 601, 608; Kleinschmidt, (2013) 77 RabelsZ 723, 751; Süß, 'Der Vorbehalt zugunsten bilateraler Abkommen mit Drittstaaten' (2014) 191; Dutta, (2015) 5 IJPL 38, 48; Konvalin, *Das Europäische Nachlasszeugnis* (2018) 6; Fornasier, *Dutta/Weber* (2021) EuErbVO Vorb. Art 62ff para 19.

[438] For other reasons, see Konvalin, *Das Europäische Nachlasszeugnis* (2018) 38ff; Duy Tuong Huynh, *Internationale Nachlassabwicklung im Lichte des Europäischen Nachlasszeugnisses* (Mohr Siebeck 2021) 469ff.

[439] Christian Kohler, 'Die künftige Erbrechtsverordnung der Europäischen Union und die Staatsverträge mit Drittstaaten' in Gerte Reichelt and Walter H. Rechberger (eds), *Europäisches Erbrecht: Zum Verordnungsvorschlag der Europäischen Kommission zum Erb- und Testamentsrecht* (Jan Sramek Verlag 2011) 116ff; Daniel Lehmann, 'Der Referentenentwurf für ein Begleitgesetz zur EuErbVO' [2014] ZEV 232, 235; Süß, 'Der Vorbehalt zugunsten bilateraler Abkommen mit Drittstaaten' (2014) 186ff; Döbereiner, [2015] NJW 2449, 2453; Dutta, (2015) 5 IJPL 38, 49; Müller-Lukoschek, *Die neue EU-Erbrechtsverordnung* (2015) § 2 paras 412 and 414; Stamatiadis, *Pamboukis* (2017) ESR Art 67 para 12; Konvalin, *Das*

portance from the third State perspective. The missing harmony of decisions within the Union by virtue of the bilateral treaties may, however, also give rise to legal issues for third country nationals when proving their legal status or rights and powers in other Member States. This, in turn, makes the issue significant also for non-Member States having nationals in the European Union. This is the case for Turkish nationals living in Germany whose succession matters are governed by the Turkish-German Treaty. In this respect, the issue of the ECS for Turkish nationals should be examined.

Moreover, the fact that the ECS is designed to be used in all Member States does not mean that it cannot be used in a third State. The statement '[the ECS] shall be issued for use in another Member State' under Article 63(1) of the Regulation would not prevent third States from allowing the extension of its effects to their territories on the basis of their rules on recognition under domestic law or a treaty.[440] This may particularly come into play if certified persons look to invoke their legal position, rights, and powers with an ECS before an authority in a third State[441] or if a third State court is to determine the effects of the ECS, especially the good faith effects for third parties (Article 69(3) and (4)) in accordance with the law of a Member State.[442] Such instances may also be relevant for Turkey. Therefore, the recognition and possible effects of the ECS in Turkey, both in the scope of the Turkish PILA and the Treaty, should also be discussed here.

Europäische Nachlasszeugnis (2018) 30 ff; R. Magnus, *NK-BGB/Rom-Verordnungen* (2019) EuErbVO Art 75 para 4; Fornasier, *Dutta/Weber* (2021) EuErbVO Vorb. Art 62 ff para 20.

440 Budzikiewicz, *Calvo Caravaca/Davì/Mansel* (2016) ESR Art 69 para 4; Wautelet, *Bonomi/Wautelet* (2016) ESR Art 62 para 40; Nordmeier, *NK-BGB/Rom-Verordnungen* (2019) EuErbVO Art 69 para 10; Dutta, *MüKoBGB* (2020) EuErbVO Art 69 para 6. See also Huynh, *Internationale Nachlassabwicklung* (2021) 422 and 432. For an overview from the Turkish perspective, see Giray, (2016) 9 Anali PFZE 235, 242 ff; Sedat Sirmen, 'AB Mirasçılık Tüzüğü ile Getirilen Avrupa Mirasçılık Belgesi ve Belge'nin Üçüncü Devletlerde Etkisi' in Bilgin Tiryakioğlu and others (eds), *Milletlerarası Özel Hukukta Güncel Konular Sempozyumu* (Yetkin 2016) 559 ff. The recognition and possible effects of the ECS have been much discussed from the Swiss perspective. See, for example, Schwander, [2014] AJP 1084, 1103 ff; Weiss and Bigler, [2014] Successio 163, 192 ff; Romano, (2015–2016) XVII YbPIL 253, 285–287; Alexander Wittwer, 'Praxisfragen des Europäischen Nachlasszeugnisses, insbesondere im Verhältnis zu Drittstaaten' in Helmut Heiss (ed), *Europäische Erbrechtsverordnung – Auswirkungen auf das Fürstentum Liechtenstein und Schweiz* (Dike & Facultas 2016) 130 ff (also with respect to Liechtenstein); Urs Bürgi, *Internationales Erbrecht Schweiz* (3rd edn, C.H. Beck & Helbin Lichtenhahn 2017) paras 878 ff; Huynh, *Internationale Nachlassabwicklung* (2021) 433 ff.

441 Martin Schauer, 'Europäisches Nachlasszeugnis' in Martin Schauer and Elisabeth Scheuba (eds), *Europäische Erbrechtsverordnung (2012/650/EU vom 4. Juli 2012)* (Manz 2012) 94–95; Budzikiewicz, *Calvo Caravaca/Davì/Mansel* (2016) ESR Art 69 para 4; Dutta, *MüKoBGB* (2020) EuErbVO Art 69 para 6.

442 Budzikiewicz, *Calvo Caravaca/Davì/Mansel* (2016) ESR Art 69 para 4; Dutta, *MüKoBGB* (2020) EuErbVO Art 69 para 6.

I. Issuance of an ECS within the Scope of the Treaty?

The mere fact that an overriding treaty – which has no rules on the ECS but has jurisdictional and conflict-of-laws rules that deviate from those of the Regulation – is applicable between Turkey and Germany should not normally prevent German authorities from issuing an ECS for Turkish nationals.[443] The Regulation's uniform procedural and applicable law rules, however, aspire to impede, or at least minimise, contradictory results among the Member States in order to ensure the 'harmonious functioning of justice'.[444] Therefore, it is potentially problematic for Member States which are party to the treaties falling within the scope of Article 75(1) of the Regulation, and hence have priority of application, to issue an ECS when requested by the nationals of Contracting third States in cases covered by those treaties. To this end, the question of whether Turkish nationals could obtain an ECS in Germany to be used in the entire Union should be considered here.

Such a discussion requires, first of all, a closer look into the rules, especially those concerning the procedure of the Treaty in terms of succession certificates. No less important are, from the Union's perspective, the potential problems or, more precisely, frictions which may arise when an ECS that is issued by German courts in favour of a Turkish national (whose succession case is within the scope of application of the Turkish-German Treaty) presumably overrides the relevant rules of the Regulation. In this light, this section first focuses on these two issues before then discussing the right of the Turkish nationals to obtain an ECS in a case in which the Treaty is applicable.

1. Jurisdiction to Issue Succession Certificates under the Treaty

Article 20(15) of the Treaty, as has already been analysed in detail above, prescribes that all lawsuits concerning the entitlement to an estate, claims for the recovery of an inheritance, claims arising out of dispositions of property upon death, and claims to a reserved share are to be filed – where the movable part of the estate is concerned – before the courts of the Contracting State whose nationality the deceased possessed at the time of death; and when it is the immovable part of the estate that is at issue, before the courts of the Contracting State where the estate is found.

One may contend that the term 'lawsuit' in this provision should be understood in a broad manner. This is because the provision includes a list of law

---

[443] Stamatiadis, *Pamboukis* (2017) ESR Art 67 para 12; Dutta, *MüKoBGB* (2020) EuErbVO Art 75 para 5; Huynh, *Internationale Nachlassabwicklung* (2021) 472. On the issuance of the ECS by the Member States in cases falling within the scope of treaties, see Huynh, *Internationale Nachlassabwicklung* (2021) 423 ff.

[444] See Recitals 34 and 37 of the Regulation.

suits regarding succession which clarifies that the determination of heirs and legatees and their respective shares will fall within the ambit of this provision. A succession certificate is a document issued upon the request of heirs and legatees demonstrating their status and rights on the estate left by the deceased (Article 598(1) and (2) of the Turkish Civil Code). The respective shares on the estate are also indicated in the succession certificate.[445] Therefore, it could be concluded that the issuing of succession certificates is also a 'lawsuit' regarding succession within the meaning of Article 20(15) of the Treaty. In line with this, the jurisdiction of the courts to issue succession certificates should be determined according to this Article.[446]

Nevertheless, it is obvious that the Treaty adopts the term 'lawsuits' ('Klagen' or 'davalar') in this provision and clarifies the scope of the rule by giving a list of those types of proceedings which are intended. The given examples, thus, seem to suggest that the term covers only contentious proceedings, with the word 'lawsuit' referring to contentious proceedings which involve a legal dispute between different parties.[447] The issue of succession certificates is, however, in principle,[448] a non-contentious proceeding in both jurisdictions,[449] and hence it may not be considered as a 'lawsuit' that is governed by this provision.[450] A more important reason arguing in favour of a restrictive interpretation is that a rule which makes a distinction between movable and immovable elements of the assets for the issue of jurisdiction is in contrast

[445] Serozan and Engin, *Miras Hukuku* (2021) § 5 paras 81 ff.

[446] Pürselim, (2011) 31 MHB 243, 253 ff.

[447] Art 382(1) of the Turkish Code of Civil Procedure lays down three criteria for a proceeding to be of a non-contentious nature. A proceeding is a non-contentious in circumstances where there is no dispute between the concerned persons, and/or the concerned persons have no claim to make, and/or the judge should act *ex officio*. On the meaning of lawsuit and non-contentious proceedings, see Baki Kuru, *Nizasız Kaza* (Ajans Türk Matbaası 1961) 16; Süha Tanrıver, 'Türk Hukuku Bağlamında Çekişmesiz Yargı ve Noterlik', *Makalelerim II (2006–2010)* (Adalet Yayınevi 2011) 347; Aslı Aras, 'Çekişmesiz Yargı İşlerinde Görev ve Yetki' (2016) 7 İnÜHFD 65, 65–66; Hakan Pekcanıtez, in Hakan Pekcanıtez and others (eds), *Pekcanıtez Usûl: Medenî Usûl Hukuku*, vol 2 (15th edn, On İki Levha 2017) § 9. Dava Hakkında Genel Bilgiler, 923–924.

[448] It is noteworthy that in a judgment concerning an application by a Greek national for the issuance of a succession certificate for an immovable asset located in Istanbul, the Turkish Court of Cassation held that proceedings for the issuance of certificates are of a contentious nature: Yargıtay 3. Hukuk Dairesi, T. 29.5.2012, E. 2012/8111 K. 2012/13537, 8–23 MİHDER 2012/3 142. The relevant part of the judgment is also published in Murat Atalı, in Hakan Pekcanıtez and others (eds), *Pekcanıtez Usûl: Medenî Usûl Hukuku*, vol 3 (15th edn, On İki Levha 2017) § 18. Çekişmesiz Yargı, 2111–2112.

[449] See Art 382(1) (c) (6) of the Turkish Code of Civil Procedure. The proceedings for the issuance of succession certificates in Germany are also of a non-contentious nature and are regulated under the Act on Court Procedure in Family and Non-litigious Matters (FamFG – BGBl. I 2008, 2586–2587): Herbert Grziwotz, in Franz Jürgen Säcker and others (eds), *MüKoBGB*, vol 11 (8th edn, C.H. Beck 2020) Vorb. BGB § 2353 para 9.

with the modern jurisdictional rules of both States and, as explained above,[451] is likely to give rise to difficulties for some persons, especially for the large Turkish migrant community in Germany. If a broader interpretation is adopted, these individuals will even have to travel to Turkey to get a succession certificate to prove their hereditary rights on the movable property in Germany. By considering that succession certificates have more practical relevance than any other succession matters,[452] it should be concluded that the jurisdiction to issue succession certificates is a matter that does not fall within the scope of the Treaty and that such certificates should thus be issued in accordance with the national jurisdictional rules of the States.[453]

A dispute may arise here as to whether jurisdiction for certificates concerning the immovable part of the estate should be an exception to this interpretation. This arises from Article 20(12) (1) of the Treaty, which states that the competent authorities of the State where immovable assets are situated are exclusively entitled and obliged to take all the appropriate measures respecting those assets. This clause, according to one line of thought, also allocates jurisdiction for the issuance of succession certificates, and hence it constitutes an exception to the interpretation that the Treaty does not regulate jurisdiction for non-contentious proceedings.[454] The provision was, however, introduced by the drafters in the part of the Treaty dealing with the powers of the consular staff over (movable) property of the nationals of the Sending State found in the Receiving State. Its sole purpose is, presumably, to underscore that local authorities of the State where the assets are located are exclusively

---

[450] See, for similar views respecting Art 43 of the Turkish PILA, Tekinalp, *Milletlerarası Özel Hukuk* (2020) 411; Çelikel and Erdem, *Milletlerarası Özel Hukuk* (2021) 632–633; Şanlı, Esen and Ataman Figanmeşe, *Milletlerarası Özel Hukuk* (2021) 495.

[451] See above p 189.

[452] Şanlı, Esen and Ataman Figanmeşe, *Milletlerarası Özel Hukuk* (2021) 265.

[453] Jurisdiction in non-contentious proceedings fall outside the scope of the Treaty: Gerhard Kremer, 'Die Bedeutung des deutsch-türkischen Konsularvertrags für Nachlaßverfahren in der Bundesrepublik Deutschland' [1981] IPRax 205, 206; Dörner, [1996] ZEV 90, 96; Bauer, [2007] FamRZ 1250, 1252; Philipp Sticherling, 'Türkisches Erbrecht und deutscher Erbschein (zu LG Braunschweig, 18.5.2009 – 8 T 344/09)' [2010] IPRax 234, 236; Ralf Wittkowski, 'Die Beantragung und Erteilung von Erbscheinen in Erbfällen mit Auslandsberührung nach dem FamFG' [2010] RNotZ 102, 105 fn 35; Kohler, 'Die künftige EuErbVO und die Staatsverträge mit Drittstaaten' (2011) 115 and 117; Christian Rumpf, 'Erbrechtsfälle im deutsch-türkischen Rechtsverkehr' (2018) 27 Informationsbrief der DTJV 25, 31; Konvalin, *Das Europäische Nachlasszeugnis* (2018) 135; Looschelders, 'The External Relations of Germany' (2019) 168; Odersky, *Hausmann/Odersky* (2021) § 15 para 350; Sieghörtner, *BeckOK FamFG* (2022) FamFG § 105 para 20; cf. Güneş, 'The Relations of Turkey with EU Member States' (2019) 307. See also LG Braunschweig 18.5.2009 – 8 T 344/09, IPRax 2010, 255; DNotI, [2016] DNotI-Report 103, 105.

[454] Christian Bachmayer, 'Ausgewählte Problemfelder bei Nachlasssachen mit Auslandsberührung' [2010] BWNotZ 146, 149–150; Z. Kaya, [2015] ZEV 208, 212.

competent to take measures as to those assets when the assets are of an immovable nature and, hence, to draw the line between the powers of the consul and of the local authorities.[455] For this reason, it is believed that this cannot be regarded as an exception to the conclusion reached above.

For the German side, the applicable rules on the issuance of an ECS, in accordance with the references made in Article 64, are found in Article 4 et seq. of the Regulation. Nevertheless, there is no clarity in the Regulation as to which rules, i.e. those of the Regulation or of national legislation, should govern when the courts or authorities of Member States are to assess whether they have jurisdiction when a request is made for the issuance of a national certificate.[456] The topic has been contentious in German legal academia and practice.

Some commentators argue that jurisdiction to issue national certificates of succession is not governed by the Regulation and that national rules should apply.[457] The primary reason for this is that the issuance of a German 'Erbschein', in their view, is not a decision ('Entscheidung') within the meaning of Article 3(1) (g) and Article 4 et seq. of the Regulation since the action has, like the ECS, only a declaratory character concerning the findings of fact and projects no *res judicata* effect, especially that of a substantive nature.[458] Article 4 et seq. of the German version of the Regulation on determining the jurisdiction of the courts refers to 'decisions in succession matters' ('Entscheidungen in Erbsachen') – this being different from the English text that uses the phrase 'to rule on the succession'. As a consequence, it is argued that this phrase does not cover succession certificates.[459] In this line of thought,

---

455 Looschelders, 'The External Relations of Germany' (2019) 169.

456 Weber, [2018] RNotZ 454, 454.

457 See, for example, Fabian Wall, 'Richtet sich die internationale Zuständigkeit zur Erbscheinserteilung künftig ausschließlich nach Artt. 4 ff EU-ErbVO?' [2015] ZErb 9, 14 ff; Nordmeier, *NK-BGB/Rom-Verordnungen* (2019) EuErbVO Art 62 para 33; and from practice, KG 10.1.2017 – 6W 125/16, ZEV 2017, 213.

458 Wall, [2015] ZErb 9, 11; Christoph Dorsel, in Reinhold Geimer and Rolf A. Schütze (eds), *Europäische Erbrechtsverordnung (EuErbVO) – Internationales Erbrechtsverfahrensgesetz (IntErbRVG) – Kommentar zur VO(EU) Nr. 650/2012 (Sonderdruck aus Geimer/Schütze (Hg.), Internationaler Rechtsverkehr in Zivil- und Handelssachen)* (C.H. Beck 2016) EuErbVO Art 69 para 6; Heinrich Dörner, 'Die internationale Zuständigkeit zur Ausstellung eines deutschen Erbscheins – Zugleich Anmerkungen zum Beschl. des KG v. 10.1.2017 – 6 W 125/16 –' [2017] DNotZ 407, 408; von Bary, *Gerichtsstandsvereinbarungen im internationalen Erbrecht* (2018) 79.

On the declaratory character of the ECS, see also Markus Buschbaum and Marius Kohler, 'Vereinheitlichung des Erbkollisionsrechts in Europa Zweiter Teil' [2010] GPR 162, 168; Knut Werner Lange, 'Das Europäische Nachlasszeugnis' in Anatol Dutta and Sebastian Herrler (eds), *Die Europäische Erbrechtsverordnung, 20 Jahre DNotI 1993–2013* (C.H. Beck 2014) 168.

459 Wall, [2015] ZErb 9, 10–12; Makowsky, *NK-BGB/Rom-Verordnungen* (2019) EuErbVO Art 4 para 13. However, it is argued that this is a problem not only in the German

the Act on Court Procedure in Family and Non-litigious Matters (hereinafter referred to with the abbreviation used in Germany, 'FamFG') § 105 should then be applicable and consequently German courts should have jurisdiction when a German court has territorial jurisdiction. Territorial jurisdiction in matters of succession is governed by FamFG § 343, which provides that the court in the district in which the deceased had his habitual residence at the time of death should have territorial jurisdiction. If the deceased has no habitual residence in Germany at the time of death, the court at the district where he had his last habitual residence should have territorial jurisdiction. In cases in which the jurisdiction can still not be established, the Local Court ('Amtsgericht') of Schöneberg in Berlin should be competent if the deceased is a German national or a part of the estate is located in Germany.

Others, by contrast, defend the opposite view and advocate that the Regulation should apply also for the issuing of national certificates in order to avoid any conflict between the Regulation and national rules and to safeguard decisional harmony within the Union.[460] According to these commentators, the term 'decision' ('Entscheidung') under Article 3(1) (g) and Article 4 et seq. of the Regulation should be interpreted broadly, consistent with the phrasing in the English text, so as to comprise the proceedings for the issuing of national succession certificates.[461] The CJEU, following the opinion of Advocate General *Szpunar*,[462] has rather recently taken a stance in favour of this view by clarifying that the application of national rules would be contrary to two of the main pillars of the Regulation: coordination between forum and *ius* (Recital 27) and decisional harmony within the Union (Recital 34); and thus it held that the jurisdiction of the courts and the competent authorities of Member States in proceedings for the issuance of national succession certificates is to be assessed in accordance with the Regulation.[463] In the Court's understanding, the jurisdictional rules of the Regulation, or in particular the word 'to rule' in the English version of these rules, do not specifically refer to decisions which are of a judicial character but rather apply to all proceedings respecting the succession as a whole, including, in particular, the issuing of national certificates of succession.

---

version of the Regulation, rather it is relevant also in texts of the Regulation in other languages. In English, for example, the phrase 'to rule' cannot be interpreted to cover all acts of a court: Weber, [2018] RNotZ 454, 456.

460 See, for example, Jessica Schmidt, 'Der Erbnachweis in Deutschland ab 2015: Erbschein vs. Europäisches Nachlasszeugnis' [2014] ZEV 389, 391; Süß, 'Der Vorbehalt zugunsten bilateraler Abkommen mit Drittstaaten' (2014) 190; Konvalin, *Das Europäische Nachlasszeugnis* (2018) 22–23; Dutta, *MüKoBGB* (2020) EuErbVO Vorb. Art 4 para 5; Fornasier, *Dutta/Weber* (2021) EuErbVO Art 62 paras 15 ff; and from practice, OLG Hamburg 16.11.2016 – 2 W 85/16, FGPrax 2017, 129.

461 Dutta, *MüKoBGB* (2020) EuErbVO Vorb. Art 4 paras 8–9.

462 C-20/17 Oberle [2018] ECLI:EU:C:2018:89, Opinion of *AG Szpunar* [102 ff].

463 C-20/17 Oberle [2018] ECLI:EU:C:2018:485 [44 ff].

Article 13 of the Regulation – which regulates jurisdiction for declarations for the acceptance or waiver of the succession, of a legacy, or of a reserved share – also vindicates this. Such declarations indeed do not qualify as judicial decisions but still fall under the scope of the Regulation.[464]

Whereas the judgment of the Court may not be found satisfactory by all,[465] it elucidates that Articles 4 et seq. of the Regulation determine the jurisdiction to issue a succession certificate, irrespective of whether an application is made for an ECS or an 'Erbschein'. The question would then arise whether this will also be applicable in cases falling into the scope of the Treaty. Here again two contradictory standpoints are possible. The ruling of the Court could first be construed to include all cases regardless whether the case at issue is covered by a Treaty whose rules supersede the Regulation.[466] This would mean that, for example, when a Turkish 'guest worker' who is habitually resident in Munich/Germany dies and leaves behind there a car and a flat, German courts will be competent to issue the succession certificate requested by his heirs in accordance with Article 4 of the Regulation.

One could, on the other hand, hold that the conclusion of the Court applies only in purely European cases and, hence, does not apply to those cases in which an overriding Treaty finds application under Article 75(1) of the Regulation.[467] Pursuant to this view, for instance, in the succession case of a Turkish national deceased who was habitually resident in France but had an immovable in Germany at the time of death, German courts would be competent to hear the case according to FamFG § 105 and § 343.[468]

It is highly likely that German courts would adopt the first interpretation to avoid the risk of conflicting decisions within the EU.[469] It is important to note that in any of the cases, the territorial jurisdiction of the courts is determined in accord with FamFG § 343, which was explained above. In contrast to some other Member States,[470] probate courts are the only competent authorities for the issuing of succession certificates in Germany (BGB § 2353).

---

464 C-20/17 Oberle [2018] ECLI:EU:C:2018:485 [34 ff].

465 For some of the critics, see Heinrich Dörner, 'Anerkennung mitgliedstaatlicher Nachlasszeugnisse (im Lichte von „Oberle")' [2018] DNotZ 661, 681 ff; Weber, [2018] RNotZ 454, 456 ff.

466 Looschelders, 'The External Relations of Germany' (2019) 168–169; Wolfgang Wurmnest and Benedikt Wössner, 'Kollisionsrechtliche Staatsverträge mit Drittstaaten in Europa: Ein Blick auf die "Achillesferse" der EuErbVO' [2019] ZVglRWiss 449, 473; cf. Dutta, *MüKoBGB* (2020) EuErbVO Vorb. Art 4 para 28 and Art 75 para 5.

467 Weber, [2018] RNotZ 454, 462; cf. D. Lehmann, [2014] ZEV 232, 234 ff; Süß, 'Der Vorbehalt zugunsten bilateraler Abkommen mit Drittstaaten' (2014) 191; R. Magnus, *NK-BGB/Rom-Verordnungen* (2019) EuErbVO Art 75 paras 20–22.

468 Weber, [2018] RNotZ 454, 462.

469 Wurmnest and Wössner, [2019] ZVglRWiss 449, 472.

470 See, for example, Art 730-1 of the *Code Civil*, which states that notaries are competent to issue succession certificates. On this issue, see below p 300.

After analysing the matter of jurisdiction to issue succession certificates from the German perspective, one could question why the issue of an ECS is disputed in the scope of the Treaties. The following part, thus, will concentrate on the possible problems which may arise when an ECS is issued in a case in which the Treaty is applicable.

2. *Possible Problems Relating to the Issue of an ECS under the Treaty*

One of the most important questions arising from the situation that the Treaty, like other such treaties of Member States, continues to apply alongside the Regulation despite not having coordinated rules is, as pointed out above, whether Turkish nationals whose succession cases are governed by the Treaty can obtain an ECS which is issued for the entire estate of the deceased irrespective of their location. Given that the ECS is created to enable heirs, legatees, estate administrators, and executors of wills to invoke their status, rights, and powers in other Member States easily for the sake of a speedy, smooth, and efficient settlement of cross-border succession issues,[471] Turkish nationals, when required, should normally be able to apply for and obtain such a certificate.[472] Notwithstanding this, the fact that the law of the Treaty is not coordinated with the Regulation causes friction with regard to the ECS, particularly in terms of its functionality and simplifying effect,[473] and it makes us reconsider the use of an ECS in such cases. Such potential conflicts could be exemplified here through two hypothetical scenarios.

In the first place, friction between the Regulation and the Treaty might come into play due to the territorial scope of application (*ratione loci*) of the Treaty. As highlighted in the first chapter,[474] different provisions of the Treaty refer to different terms, i.e. either to the 'Contracting State' (Articles 20 and 20(1)) or to the 'State' (Article 20(14) (2)), and this causes dissension among commentators regarding the territorial scope of the Treaty. The prevailing view holds that the Treaty is applicable only to assets located in Contracting States in accordance with Article 20 of the Consular Treaty, to which succession rules are annexed. An opposite interpretation, as rightly indicated, would run counter to the bilateral nature of the Treaty, which vests consular staff

---

[471] Recital 67 of the Regulation.

[472] The case is similar with respect to Swiss nationals, see Kalt and Uhl, 'Die EU-Erbrechtsverordnung und die Schweiz' (2013) 130–131.

For the argument that the issuance of an ECS is within the scope of Polish bilateral treaties, see Rylski, (2020) 26 PPPM 91, 102.

[473] Wurmnest, 'Comparative Report and Policy Perspectives' (2019) 342–343; Wurmnest and Wössner, [2019] ZVglRWiss 449, 471; Dutta, *MüKoBGB* (2020) EuErbVO Art 67 para 11; Jens Kleinschmidt, in Maximilian Herberger and others (eds), *jurisPK-BGB*, vol 6 (9th edn, juris 2020) EuErbVO Art 69 para 4.

[474] See above pp 46–48.

with broad powers over the estate of the deceased and creates a special private international law regime between the Contracting States that is different from the normally applicable rules found in the national law of the States without an explicit *ordre public* exception.

With this interpretation, therefore, the application of the Treaty would be territorially limited to the assets located in the Contracting States. Hence, in a scenario where a Turkish national who was habitually resident in Germany at the time of death dies intestate and leaves assets there as well as in, for example, France,[475] only the part of the assets found in Germany would be governed by the succession regime of the Treaty. As a consequence, a problem will arise when the heirs of the deceased request an ECS from the German courts pursuant to their jurisdiction based on Article 64 and Article 4 of the Regulation. This is because the Court will determine the law applicable to succession differently for the part of the estate found in Germany as opposed to the portion in France when issuing the ECS. While the conflict-of-laws provision of the Treaty (Article 20(14)) becomes applicable for the assets found in Germany, the Regulation governs the assets located in France. Thus, in the document which is issued for the entire estate, different regimes become applicable, and the desired uniformity within the EU through the Regulation would be negated. This becomes especially important as the ECS issued by German probate courts should produce its effects also in France *ipso iure*, without any special procedure being required (Article 69(1) of the Regulation). This means that France, which is not bound by the Treaty between Turkey and Germany and has no treaty to that effect with Turkey, would have to accept the application of a law to the succession determined in accordance with the Treaty that is different from the one in the Regulation. Hence, there will be a 'difference' with the result reached in Germany and the result which would have normally been reached in France. In other words, the ECS issued by German courts would be inaccurate in France with respect to the law applicable to succession.[476]

A further problem ensues when the last habitual residence of the deceased is in a Member State which is not party to the Treaty.[477] In the above-men-

---

[475] See, for similar examples, Kohler, 'Die künftige EuErbVO und die Staatsverträge mit Drittstaaten' (2011) 116–117; Süß, 'Der Vorbehalt zugunsten bilateraler Abkommen mit Drittstaaten' (2014) 186–187.

[476] Kohler, 'Die künftige EuErbVO und die Staatsverträge mit Drittstaaten' (2011) 116–117; D. Lehmann, [2014] ZEV 232, 235; Süß, 'Der Vorbehalt zugunsten bilateraler Abkommen mit Drittstaaten' (2014) 186–187; Looschelders, 'The External Relations of Germany' (2019) 170–171; Wurmnest and Wössner, [2019] ZVglRWiss 449, 471–472; Fornasier, *Dutta/Weber* (2021) EuErbVO Vorb. Art 62 ff para 33.

[477] Kohler, 'Die künftige EuErbVO und die Staatsverträge mit Drittstaaten' (2011) 116–117; D. Lehmann, [2014] ZEV 232, 234; Süß, 'Der Vorbehalt zugunsten bilateraler Abkommen mit Drittstaaten' (2014) 189–190; Lechner, 'EU Regulation 650/2012' (2015)

tioned case scenario, when the Turkish national dies in France instead of Germany where he was habitually resident, the French notary to which the relevant parties apply for the issue of an ECS will draw up the certificate for all the assets of the deceased and will certify the status of heirs and their respective shares or rights in accordance with French law (as the law of the last habitual residence of the deceased within the scope of Article 21(1) of the Regulation). The Treaty between Turkey and Germany which should normally be applicable, at least for the assets in Germany, will obviously not be taken into account by the French notary, as it does not bind France.[478] Notwithstanding this, the issued ECS will produce the same effects in Germany automatically without a recognition or similar procedure according to Article 69(1) of the Regulation. In the event that a party takes the ECS to Germany to seek the registration of an immovable on his behalf before the German Land Registry, the question would follow whether the Land Registry is entitled or obliged – pursuant to § 35 of the German Real Estate Registry Act ('GBO')[479] – to make the registration or to refuse it due to the fact that the ECS certifying the status of the heir was issued in accordance with the 'wrong' law from the German perspective.[480]

It is obvious from these examples that the priority of the Treaty over the Regulation creates a crucial potential of conflicts for the use of the ECS – in addition to other areas of conflict already noted – and raises the question of whether German probate courts will issue the ECS in such cases. These problems might have possibly been avoided, at least to some extent, if the German legislature had laid down rules to this end, particularly in the Act on International Procedure in Succession Matters ('IntErbRVG').[481] The German legislature, however, left the issue unresolved. Hence, proposals have been made

---

144; Looschelders, 'The External Relations of Germany' (2019) 171; Wurmnest and Wössner, [2019] ZVglRWiss 449, 472–473.

[478] See similarly R. Magnus, *NK-BGB/Rom-Verordnungen* (2019) EuErbVO Art 75 para 12.

[479] BGBl I 1994, 1114.

[480] Kohler, 'Die künftige EuErbVO und die Staatsverträge mit Drittstaaten' (2011) 116–117; D. Lehmann, [2014] ZEV 232, 234; Süß, 'Der Vorbehalt zugunsten bilateraler Abkommen mit Drittstaaten' (2014) 190; Markus Buschbaum and Ulrich Simon, 'Beantragung und Erteilung eines Europäischen Nachlasszeugnisses sowie Verwendung eines ausländischen Europäischen Nachlasszeugnisses in Deutschland' [2015] Rpfleger 444, 453; R. Magnus, *NK-BGB/Rom-Verordnungen* (2019) EuErbVO Art 75 para 11; cf. Looschelders, 'The External Relations of Germany' (2019) 171; Wurmnest and Wössner, [2019] ZVglRWiss 449, 473.

[481] Looschelders, 'The External Relations of Germany' (2019) 170. See, for a proposal in this regard, D. Lehmann, [2014] ZEV 232; Daniel Lehmann, 'Der Regierungsentwurf für ein Gesetz zum Internationalen Erbrecht' [2015] ZEV 138. See, for the Act, BGBl. I 2015, 1042.

by scholars to restrict the use of the ECS within the scope of the Treaty. The details of these proposals are examined below.

3. The Solution: Restricting the Use of the ECS within the Scope of the Treaty?

The solution for the potential conflicts outlined above is contended to be the restriction of the use of the ECS to the part of the estate located in Member States which are not bound by the Treaty. For the part of the estate located in Germany, therefore, a German 'Erbschein' could be issued.[482] Such a proposal may be seen as plausible owing to the fact that the Regulation allows for the co-existence and parallel use of national certificates and the ECS.[483] An evaluation from the Turkish perspective, however, should still be made here. To this end, the proposal should be examined in detail for both possible situations.

In the first scenario, i.e. the succession of a Turkish national who left properties in both Germany and France, German probate courts, according to the view supporting the partial use of the ECS, will issue two certificates: a German 'Erbschein' for the assets located in Germany in accordance with the conflict-of-laws provisions of the Treaty and an ECS for the assets found in France pursuant to Chapter III of the Regulation. In such a case, it is contended that in order to avoid a conflict between the effects of the ECS and the national certificate, the ECS should include an explanation indicating that it is only valid for the assets located outside the issuing Member State,[484] even though the Regulation itself does not restrict the use of the ECS to certain assets.[485] Even the authorities of non-Contracting Member States, as argued, could be obliged to issue such a restrictive statement on the ECS upon considering the fact that a part of the estate is located in a Member State party to

[482] D. Lehmann, [2014] ZEV 232, 234ff; Süß, 'Der Vorbehalt zugunsten bilateraler Abkommen mit Drittstaaten' (2014) 187ff; D. Lehmann, [2015] ZEV 138, 140; Looschelders, 'The External Relations of Germany' (2019) 170–171; contra Stürner, *Erman BGB* (2020) EuErbVO Art 75 para 13.

It should be noted that Art 39 of the Commission Proposal allowed for the application for and the issuance of a partial certificate. The Regulation lacks such an explicit provision. Notwithstanding this, it is held that parties can still apply for and obtain a partial certificate: Kleinschmidt, (2013) 77 RabelsZ 723, 749.

[483] Wurmnest and Wössner, [2019] ZVglRWiss 449, 471–472. On the co-existence and parallel use of both certificates, see Bernhard Kreße, in Alfonso-Luis Calvo Caravaca, Angelo Davì and Heinz-Peter Mansel (eds), *The EU Succession Regulation – A Commentary* (Cambridge University Press 2016) ESR Art 62 paras 15ff; Nordmeier, *NK-BGB/Rom-Verordnungen* (2019) EuErbVO Art 62 paras 31ff; Dutta, *MüKoBGB* (2020) EuErbVO Art 62 paras 9ff; contra Kleinschmidt, (2013) 77 RabelsZ 723, 749.

[484] Süß, 'Der Vorbehalt zugunsten bilateraler Abkommen mit Drittstaaten' (2014) 192.

[485] Wurmnest and Wössner, [2019] ZVglRWiss 449, 472.

a bilateral treaty with a third State.[486] For this purpose, the European Ministry of Justice has been advised to prepare a handbook for the ECS which includes a list of treaties between Member States and non-Member States which have a priority of application under Article 75(1) of the Regulation.[487]

It might be arguable that this will not pose complications for Turkish nationals for the time being in the vast majority of the cases, as succession cases arising in the Turkish-German context often have no relation to other Member States.[488] It is highly likely that a Turkish national who is habitually resident in Germany will generally have properties in Germany and/or in Turkey but not in other Member States. Accordingly, the need for obtaining multiple certificates will seldom arise. However, one cannot neglect the effect of the increasing mobility of individuals within the EU, where free movement and residence of persons is guaranteed (Article 21 of the TFEU). Undoubtedly, the upward trend in the mobility of individuals among the Member States will eventually culminate in instances in which Turkish nationals who are already resident in an EU country own properties scattered around Europe.[489] Imagine, for instance, that there is a Turkish couple, both of whom are migrant workers in Austria where they also acquired a house. Their children later move to Germany because of their jobs. The elder couple may then follow their children and also move to Germany to be together with them. In such scenarios, which may currently be seen as rare instances, the possibility of owning assets in more than one Member State is not particularly small.[490] Considering the number of Turkish nationals residing in Germany, and hence the practical relevance of succession cases of this kind in the near future, Turkish nationals should not be deprived of the opportunity to easily invoke their legal status and succession rights as heirs, legatees, executors of wills, and estate administrators with the ECS in all Member States.[491] An opposite interpretation would obviously create harmony within the Union but would give rise to difficulties for the nationals of Turkey, and in so doing subvert the purposes of the Treaty.[492] It is, there-

[486] Süß, 'Der Vorbehalt zugunsten bilateraler Abkommen mit Drittstaaten' (2014) 192; Dutta, *MüKoBGB* (2020) EuErbVO Art 75 para 5.

[487] Süß, 'Der Vorbehalt zugunsten bilateraler Abkommen mit Drittstaaten' (2014) 192.

[488] Süß, 'Der Vorbehalt zugunsten bilateraler Abkommen mit Drittstaaten' (2014) 197; Looschelders, 'The External Relations of Germany' (2019) 172.

[489] Wurmnest, 'Comparative Report and Policy Perspectives' (2019) 343.

[490] See, for the same example in the Iranian-German context, Wurmnest, 'Comparative Report and Policy Perspectives' (2019) 343.

[491] See, in this regard, Dutta, *MüKoBGB* (2020) EuErbVO Art 75 para 5; cf. Anatol Dutta, 'Die Europäische Erbrechtsverordnung vor ihrem Anwendungsbeginn: Zehn ausgewählte Streitstandsminiaturen' [2015] IPRax 32, 39; Looschelders, 'The External Relations of Germany' (2019) 171.

[492] Cf. Süß, 'Der Vorbehalt zugunsten bilateraler Abkommen mit Drittstaaten' (2014) 197–198.

fore, hoped that this will be considered and Turkish nationals will be able to obtain and use the ECS to demonstrate their status and rights or powers within the entire Union, like all other citizens living in the Union.

The restrictive use of the ECS may also avoid the problem in the second scenario, in which an heir applies to the German Land Registry with an ECS issued in France to be registered as the rightful owner of the inherited immovable property. The power/duty of the Land Registry to refuse registration in such a case could be advocated, so that Germany does not violate international law by acting contrary to the Treaty.[493] The ECS, thus, will once again be applicable only for the assets located outside Germany. A German 'Erbschein' will be drawn up for the rest of the assets found in Germany. Such a solution could perhaps be justified by the rebuttable nature[494] of the presumptions as regards the elements of the ECS under Article 69(2) of the Regulation.[495] This view seems to have found support from the Austrian legislature.[496] The Austrian legislature stressed in a reform process that ECSs issued or decisions on succession concerning assets in Austria rendered by the courts and authorities of other Member States which are based on the Regulation (Chapter III on applicable law) but which disregard the private international law provisions of the treaties applicable between Austria and third States cannot be recognised.[497]

In such a case, however, the land registry should make a detailed evaluation of the applicable conflict-of-laws and substantive provisions on succession (of the States whose laws are applicable) in order to identify differences.

---

[493] See, in this regard, Kohler, 'Die künftige EuErbVO und die Staatsverträge mit Drittstaaten' (2011) 116–117; D. Lehmann, [2014] ZEV 232, 234; Süß, 'Der Vorbehalt zugunsten bilateraler Abkommen mit Drittstaaten' (2014) 190; Buschbaum and Simon, [2015] Rpfleger 444, 453; R. Magnus, *NK-BGB/Rom-Verordnungen* (2019) EuErbVO Art 75 para 11; cf. Looschelders, 'The External Relations of Germany' (2019) 171; Wurmnest and Wössner, [2019] ZVglRWiss 449, 473.

[494] See, in this regard, Bonomi, *Bonomi/Wautelet* (2016) ESR Art 69 paras 33 ff; Budzikiewicz, *Calvo Caravaca/Davì/Mansel* (2016) ESR Art 69 para 9; Nordmeier, *NK-BGB/Rom-Verordnungen* (2019) EuErbVO Art 69 para 13; Dutta, *MüKoBGB* (2020) EuErbVO Art 69 para 11.

[495] Fornasier, *Dutta/Weber* (2021) EuErbVO Vorb. Art 62 ff para 21; cf. Süß, 'Der Vorbehalt zugunsten bilateraler Abkommen mit Drittstaaten' (2014) 192; contra Dutta, *MüKoBGB* (2020) EuErbVO Art 69 para 5. *Dutta* seems to suggest a different view in Dutta, *MüKoBGB* (2020) EuErbVO Art 69 para 24. See also, general on this issue, Looschelders, 'The External Relations of Germany' (2019) 171; Wurmnest and Wössner, [2019] ZVglRWiss 449, 472–473.

[496] Thomas Traar, in Alfred Burgstaller and others (eds), *Die EU-Erbrechtsverordnung* (LexisNexis 2016) EuErbVO Art 75 para 7; Rudolf, 'The External Relations of Austria' (2019) 36.

[497] Regierungsvorlage 17.6.2015, 688 der Beilagen XXV. GP 48 (§ 106 JN). JN: RGBl. Nr. 111/1895.

Nonetheless, the ECS is equipped with a 'good faith effect' (Article 69(3) and (4)), which means that any person certified in the document will be considered as the right holder with whom one can make any relevant transaction.[498] Thus, it is criticised that land registries have no such power or obligation to verify the information certified by the ECS as to its consistency with the law determined according to the Treaty.[499] The priority of application of the Treaty, in the view of these authors, cannot be construed to entitle or oblige the local authorities to restrict the use of the ECS in Germany.[500]

Furthermore, when the ECS issued by another Member State is rejected, heirs (or any other beneficiaries) have to apply for an 'Erbschein' in Germany to be able to assert their succession rights. This seems however to be very difficult – if not entirely impossible – under the Regulation given that the CJEU has recently rejected in *Oberle*[501] the right of Member States to have recourse to national rules on jurisdiction when issuing national certificates. This means that German probate courts cannot confer jurisdiction when the deceased, as in the example, is habitually resident in another Member State. The only option for German courts to be competent to issue an 'Erbschein' would be the exceptional circumstances of *forum necessitatis* under Article 11 of the Regulation.[502] Consequently, the ECSs issued by other Member States will, in principle, be used in Germany, even though the issuing authority did not take the provisions of the Treaty into account when determining the beneficiaries and their respective succession rights.

The discussion above clearly demonstrates the potential problems concerning the ECS given the continuing application of the Treaty regime within the Union. The solution proposed is a restrictive use of the ECS in cases falling within the scope of the Treaty, not only for the purposes of safeguarding decisional harmony in the EU but also to prevent the possibility of a violation of the Treaty by Germany. Both of the problems exemplified here, however, do not seem to justify such a restriction. Turkish nationals should thus have the

---

498 Wurmnest and Wössner, [2019] ZVglRWiss 449, 473.

499 Looschelders, 'The External Relations of Germany' (2019) 171–172; Wurmnest and Wössner, [2019] ZVglRWiss 449, 473; Harald Wilsch, in Stefan Hügel (ed), *BeckOK GBO (Stand: 1.3.2022)* (45th edn, C.H. Beck 2022) GBO § 35 para 41; cf. Konvalin, *Das Europäische Nachlasszeugnis* (2018) 66–67. See also Wilsch, *BeckOK GBO* (2022) GBO § 35 para 51; OLG München 21.12.2015 – 34 Wx 245/15, RNotZ 2016, 185, 187. It is highlighted that third parties are generally not in a position to verify whether the issuing authority correctly determined the law applicable to the succession: Nordmeier, *NK-BGB/Rom-Verordnungen* (2019) EuErbVO Art 69 para 22; Fornasier, *Dutta/Weber* (2021) EuErbVO Art 69 para 26.

500 Looschelders, 'The External Relations of Germany' (2019) 172.

501 C-20/17 Oberle [2018] ECLI:EU:C:2018:485. On the Court´s conclusion, see above pp 284–285.

502 Wurmnest and Wössner, [2019] ZVglRWiss 449, 473; Kohler, 'Die künftige EuErbVO und die Staatsverträge mit Drittstaaten' (2011) 116–117.

right to obtain an ECS like the citizens of other States living in the EU, and they should not be in a different position just because a bilateral treaty and not the Regulation governs their cases.

It is highly likely in the given hypothetical examples that the deceased will also own property in Turkey. This will also be the case in the vast majority of succession cases arising in the Turkish-European context. Although the ECS is designed for use within the Union, as explained earlier, nothing will prevent relevant persons from attempting to use it outside the Union, including in Turkey. When this is the case, the question will arise whether the ECS could be recognised in Turkey. The following part will, hence, focus on this question.

II. Recognition of an ECS in Turkey?

In a succession case with cross-border elements, one of the momentous questions, maybe even more important than the questions surrounding jurisdiction and applicable law in practice, is whether heirs or any other beneficiaries will be able to establish their title and succession rights in Turkey with the help of a certificate of succession issued by the courts or other authorities of a foreign State.[503] All the transactions regarding succession – such as the collection of debts, the transfer of immovables, the transfer of money and other assets which are kept at banks, and claiming rights before the social security authorities – will indeed only be made with a valid certificate of succession.[504] When the requisite certificate has been issued in a State outside Turkey, the question will arise as to which steps the parties should take to use the certificate before Turkish authorities.

This is also relevant with respect to the ECS. The Regulation normally provides a limitation for the use of the ECS: '[it] is for use by heirs, legatees having direct rights in the succession and executors of wills or administrators of the estate who, *in another Member State*, need to invoke their status or to exercise respectively their rights […]' (Article 63(1)). Such a circumscription, however, does not seem realistic under real-life circumstances. Once it has been issued by a competent court or authority of a Member State, nothing will prevent an heir or a beneficiary from seeking to use it also before Turkish authorities, particularly in cases where the estate of the deceased includes assets located in Turkey.[505] If, for example, French authorities draw up an ECS to be used in Italy, the heir of the deceased may try to use it not only before Italian banks but also before Turkish banks as long as the deceased also left some

[503] See, for similar remarks with respect to Swiss law, Romano, (2015–2016) XVII YbPIL 253, 284.

[504] Dural and Öz, *Miras Hukuku* (2021) para 1674.

[505] See, in this regard, Weiss and Bigler, [2014] Successio 163, 193; Romano, (2015–2016) XVII YbPIL 253, 285–286; Dutta, *MüKoBGB* (2020) EuErbVO Art 69 para 6.

money there.[506] In such instances, of course, the question of whether the Turkish side would allow recognition of the ECS in Turkey is crucial.

Here at the outset, it is important to mention Article 37 of the Land Registry Law, which could also be relevant regarding the ECS. The Article prescribes that the transfer of immovable assets to foreign nationals by way of succession can be made only with succession certificates issued by Turkish courts or such certificates issued by the competent authorities of foreign States that have been *authenticated* by Turkish courts as being in conformity with succession procedure under Turkish law. The provision makes a reference to *authentication* ('tasdik') and not to *recognition* ('tanıma'), and hence it creates an impression that foreign succession certificates concerning immovable assets of the deceased could be used in Turkey after an *authentication* process before Turkish courts. Nevertheless, there is no authentication process under Turkish law, and thus it should be understood as meaning recognition.[507] Hence we are left with the question of how a foreign succession certificate should be examined within the light of recognition rules.

An ECS issued by an authority of a Member State has no immediate effect in Turkey. This is an inevitable corollary of the fact that Turkey is not a part of the Regulation's uniform system. Such a consequence, however, is obviously unsatisfactory for the beneficiaries, particularly in cases where a part of the estate is located in Turkey. Therefore, they may seek before Turkish courts the recognition of the ECS they hold in order to prove their entitlement to the relevant part of the estate. To this end, the rules of the Turkish PILA, which are applicable in the absence of special arrangements on recognition between Turkey and the issuing Member State, should be examined. After this examination of the rules of the Turkish PILA, the role of the Treaty as a special arrangement between Turkey and Germany, should also be briefly analysed for the recognition of an ECS.

1. Recognition of an ECS under the Turkish PILA?

The Turkish PILA does not provide a special recognition procedure for succession certificates. Therefore, one may doubt whether the general procedure for the recognition of judgments (Articles 50–58) are also applicable for the

---

[506] For a similar example, see Romano, (2015–2016) XVII YbPIL 253, 286.

[507] Ergin Nomer, 'Yabancı Verâset İlamlarının Tanınmasında Yargıtay Kararları' (1991) 65 İBD 789, 795 fn 14; Demir Gökyayla, 'Mirasçılık Belgeleri' (2006) 560–561; Ekşi, *Milletlerarası Miras Hukuku* (2013) 109ff; Nomer, *Devletler Hususî Hukuku* (2021) 304; cf. Şanlı, 'Veraset İlamı' (1990) 303ff; Pürselim, (2021) 9 KHASHFD 179, 185; Şanlı, Esen and Ataman Figanmeşe, *Milletlerarası Özel Hukuk* (2021) 495 fn 161. See, however, Ataman Figanmeşe, 'Mirasçılık Belgeleri' (1998) 40–42; Miray Altınkaya, *Medeni Usul Hukuku Açısından Mirasçılık Belgesine İlişkin Talep* (On İki Levha 2021) 31; Güngör, *Türk Milletlerarası Özel Hukuku* (2021) 302.

recognition of succession certificates. Due to the fact that procedural issues are governed by the *lex fori* under Turkish law,[508] the characterisation of an ECS from the Turkish perspective is important in determining the applicability of these rules.

A succession certificate is a formal deed issued for heirs upon request by civil courts of peace or, in purely domestic cases,[509] by notaries in order for heirs to prove succession rights and the power to dispose over inherited property. Legatees, for the same purposes, may also request the issue of such certificates from civil courts of peace. The validity of a succession certificate can be challenged at any time (Article 598 of the Turkish Civil Code).[510] This means that succession certificates under Turkish law merely create rebuttable presumptions for succession rights and for the powers of disposition of heirs and legatees. Hence, they are not final.[511]

Another important aspect of succession certificates under Turkish law is that they are issued in non-contentious proceedings (Article 382(2) (c) (6) of the Turkish Code of Civil Procedure). The proceeding will, however, be contentious when the validity of the succession certificate is subsequently challenged along with a request to redress or modify the certificate.[512] In other words, the issue of a succession certificate is normally a declaratory judgment[513] of the

---

[508] Nomer, *Milletlerarası Usul Hukuku* (2018) 17 ff; Çelikel and Erdem, *Milletlerarası Özel Hukuk* (2021) 503 ff.

[509] See below p 304–305.

[510] Köksal Kocaağa, 'Mirasçılık Belgesi (MK 598)' (2005) IX GÜHFD 83; Nuri Erişgin, *Mirasçılık Belgesi* (Turhan Kitabevi 2013); Ahmet Cemal Ruhi and Canan Ruhi, *Mirasçılık Belgesi, İptali ve Yeni Mirasçılık Belgesi Verilmesi* (Seçkin 2015); Serozan and Engin, *Miras Hukuku* (2021) § 5 paras 81 and 84–85.

[511] Kuru, *Nizasız Kaza* (1961) 87; Kocaağa, (2005) IX GÜHFD 83, 85; Erişgin, *Mirasçılık Belgesi* (2013) 141 ff; Serozan and Engin, *Miras Hukuku* (2021) § 5 para 84. The Preamble to Art 598(3) of the Turkish Civil Code states that a succession certificate does not acquire the force of *res judicata*. See, for the preamble of the relevant part, <https://www.tbmm.gov.tr/sirasayi/donem21/yil01/ss723_Madde_Gerekceleri_3.pdf> accessed 7 April 2020.

[512] Atalı, *Pekcanıtez Usûl* (2017) § 18. Çekişmesiz Yargı, 2114–2115.

[513] Judgments can be classified in different ways. One important classification is differentiating between condemnatory judgments ('eda kararları'), declaratory judgments ('tespit kararları'), and constitutive judgments ('inşaî kararlar'). A condemnatory judgment refers to the order of a court requiring the defendant to do or not to do something. A declaratory judgment means the determination of a legal right or relationship between the parties. Finally, a constitutive judgment is a judgment that creates, changes, or terminates a legal right or status between parties: Baki Kuru, *Hukuk Muhakemeleri Usulü*, vol 3 (6th edn, Demir Demir 2001) 3004 ff; Pekcanıtez, *Pekcanıtez Usûl* (2017) § 9. Dava Hakkında Genel Bilgiler, 960 ff.

See similarly for Germany, Christian A. Heinze, 'The Effect in the European Community of Judgments in Civil and Commercial Matters: Recognition, Res Judicata and Abuse of Process – Germany' (BIICL 2006) 9 <https://www.biicl.org/files/3482_germany_final_c.pdf> accessed 19 March 2020. The issue of succession certificates, therefore, is a declaratory judgment: Kuru, *Nizasız Kaza* (1961) 86–88.

court issued in non-contentious proceedings in Turkey. Whereas different procedures apply in some legal systems for the recognition of judgments based on non-contentious jurisdiction and on contentious jurisdiction, there is no difference between the two under Turkish law. Article 58(2) of the Turkish PILA reiterates this by stating that the recognition of foreign non-contentious judgments is subject to the same provisions. Therefore, Articles 50–58 of the Turkish PILA also cover recognition of succession certificates issued in other States. The conditions provided in these provisions should be analysed for the ECS.

Pursuant to Article 58(1) of the Turkish PILA, a foreign judgment may be recognised as conclusive evidence or a final judgment once the court confirms that it fulfils the conditions applicable for enforcement. Subparagraph (a) of Article 54(1) on reciprocity[514] will not apply for recognition. This suggests that the conditions for enforcement, except for the principle of reciprocity, have a dual function and also serve as conditions for recognition. These conditions are regulated under Article 50 and Article 54 of the Turkish PILA.[515] From these provisions, Article 50 clarifies which types of judgments are recognisable un-

[514] The principle of reciprocity in the field of recognition and enforcement of judgments requires that a State will grant recognition and/or enforcement only to the judgments of another State which already recognises/enforces the former State's judgments: Ralf Michaels, 'Recognition and Enforcement of Foreign Judgments' in Rüdiger Wolfrum (ed), *Max Planck Encyclopedia of Public International Law* (OUP 2009) para 9; Béligh Elbalti, 'Reciprocity and The Recognition and Enforcement of Foreign Judgments: A Lot of Bark but Not Much Bite' (2017) 13 J Priv Int L 184, 186–187. Reciprocity is a condition for the enforcement of a foreign judgment in Turkey under Article 54(1) (a) of the Turkish PILA.

[515] A dispute exists as to the applicability of Article 50 of the Turkish PILA to the recognition of judgments. This is because Article 58, when determining the conditions of recognition makes a reference to conditions of enforcement under Article 54 and not to Article 50, which also focuses on conditions of enforcement. Notwithstanding this, scholars rightly argue that recognition would only be granted to judgments satisfying all these conditions, though Article 58 is not clear on the applicability of Article 50 for recognition. On the issue in the context of succession certificates, see Şanlı, 'Veraset İlamı' (1990) 296; Demir Gökyayla, *Tanıma ve Tenfiz'de Kamu Düzeni* (2001) 561; Ekşi, *Milletlerarası Miras Hukuku* (2013) 106ff; Tütüncübaşı, *Yabancı Çekişmesiz Yargı Kararlarının Tanınması* (2014) 127; Ruhi and Ruhi, *Mirasçılık Belgesi* (2015) 48; cf. Ergin Nomer, 'Yabancı Çekişmesiz Yargı Kararlarının Tanınmasında Kesinleşme Şartı' in Hayri Domaniç (ed), *Prof. Dr. Erdoğan Moroğlu'na 65. Yaş Günü Armağanı* (2nd edn, Beta 2001) 910.

Generally on the issue, see also Sakmar, *Yabancı İlamların Türkiye'deki Sonuçları* (1982) 112; Bilgin Tiryakioğlu, *Yabancı Boşanma Kararlarının Türkiye'de Tanınması ve Tenfizi* (Yetkin 1996) 34; Aybay and Dardağan, *Kanunlar İhtlilafı* (2008) 296; Fügen Sargın and Rifat Esen, 'MÖHUK Hükümleri Dairesinde Tanımanın Hukuki Niteliği, Usûlü ve Karşılaşılan Bazı Sorunlar: "Yeni Bir Düzenleme Yapma Gereği"' (2014) 3 UTTDER 37, 79–80; Ebru Şensöz Malkoç, *Aile Hukukuna İlişkin Yabancı Kararların Tanınması* (On İki Levha 2017) 258ff; Çelikel and Erdem, *Milletlerarası Özel Hukuk* (2021) 717ff; Şanlı, Esen and Ataman Figanmeşe, *Milletlerarası Özel Hukuk* (2021) 628ff; Doğan, *Milletlerarası Özel Hukuk* (2022) 117ff.

der Turkish law, or, as described by commentators,[516] it describes the preconditions of recognition. Article 54, on the other hand, lists the grounds for non-recognition. Both provisions should be examined in detail for the ECS.

a) *Judgments Eligible for Recognition under Article 50 of the Turkish PILA*

Article 50 of the Turkish PILA stipulates three important requirements for foreign judgments to be eligible for recognition under Turkish law. According to this provision, only judgments rendered by foreign courts in civil law matters that are final under the laws of the State of their origin may be eligible for recognition in Turkey. These requirements should now be evaluated for the ECS.

aa) Judgments Rendered by Foreign Courts in Civil Matters

Article 50 of the Turkish PILA first provides that only judgments rendered by foreign courts in civil matters are recognisable in Turkey. Succession matters evidently fall within the scope of civil matters. There are, then, two elusive issues that are worthy of consideration here: the scope of the terms 'judgment' and 'court' from the perspective of succession certificates, particularly of the ECS.

Based on this provision, it is opined by some scholars that succession certificates issued outside Turkey are not recognisable due to the fact that they do not qualify as 'judgments'. This is because succession certificates are often issued in non-contentious proceedings, and, hence, they are not judgments which have *res judicata* effect.[517] Although a generic term 'judgment' is used to describe judicial decisions, there are of course different types of judgments. It is particularly important to make a distinction between 'hüküm/ilâm'[518] and 'karar' under Turkish law. The former, which may be translated into English as 'judgment', refers to a decision of the court which *finally* resolves the dispute on the merits between the parties. By contrast, the latter, which might be named as 'decision' in English, has a much broader meaning, one which refers

---

[516] Sakmar, *Yabancı İlamların Türkiye'deki Sonuçları* (1982) 112; Tiryakioğlu, *Yabancı Boşanma Kararlarının Tanınması ve Tenfizi* (1996) 34; Aybay and Dardağan, *Kanunlar İhtlilafı* (2008) 296; Ekşi, *Tanıma ve Tenfiz* (2020) 117; Güngör, *Türk Milletlerarası Özel Hukuku* (2021) 288; Özkan and Tütüncübaşı, *Uluslararası Usûl Hukuku* (2020) 176; Şanlı, Esen and Ataman Figanmeşe, *Milletlerarası Özel Hukuk* (2021) 628; Doğan, *Milletlerarası Özel Hukuk* (2022) 117.

[517] See, for example, Ali Naim İnan, Şeref Ertaş and Hakan Albaş, *Miras Hukuku* (11th edn, Seçkin 2022) para 1593.

[518] Although both terms are used interchangeably, they are, in fact, different. '*ilâm*' is only a copy of '*hüküm*', which is the final judgment of the court, served on parties (Art 301(2) of the Turkish Code of Civil Procedure). See, in this regard, Kuru, *Hukuk Muhakemeleri Usulü/vol 3* (2001) 3146; Nilüfer Boran Güneysu, *Medenî Usûl Hukukunda Karar* (Adalet Yayınevi 2014) 10; Tütüncübaşı, *Yabancı Çekişmesiz Yargı Kararlarının Tanınması* (2014) 69 fn 276.

to all types of decisions made by a court irrespective of whether they are procedural or on the merits and also of the fact whether they are final or not (Article 294(1) of the Turkish Code of Civil Procedure).[519] In non-contentious proceedings, there is in fact no real conflict, and hence a decision rendered at the end would have obviously not have the function of putting an end to a dispute. Therefore, such judgments are not qualified as 'ilâm' (judgment) in this sense.[520] Succession certificates drawn up in non-contentious proceedings also fall within this group. They are not final and cannot acquire the force of *res judicata*.[521] Article 50 of the Turkish PILA, however, uses the term 'ilâm' (judgment), and thus, as claimed, it could be interpreted as to exclude succession certificates issued in non-contentious proceedings due to their nature. In this interpretation, solely succession certificates granted in contentious proceedings would be subject to recognition in Turkey.[522]

The issuing procedure for the ECS under the Regulation is mostly non-contentious. This is apparent from different provisions. The first provision to this end is Article 66(1), whereby the European legislature gives the issuing authority the power to act *ex officio* to establish the facts in the procedure. Moreover, pursuant to Article 66(4), it is the duty of the issuing authority to make sure that all the beneficiaries are informed, that any person involved is heard, and that other possible beneficiaries are given the opportunity to invoke their status and rights through the help of public announcements. The non-contentious nature of the issuing procedure is further iterated with Article 67(1) (a). The provision states that the Certificate will not be issued in the event that the content to be certified is being challenged. Lastly, Article 67(1) (b) provides that the possible non-conformity of the Certificate with a former decision on the same elements also constitutes a ground for refusing to issue the Certificate. All these provisions prove that the issuing procedure under the Regulation contains a number of elements unique to non-contentious procedure.[523]

---

[519] Kuru, *Hukuk Muhakemeleri Usulü/vol 3* (2001) 2997ff; Atalı, *Pekcanıtez Usûl* (2017) § 16. Karar ve Hüküm, 1965ff; Boran Güneysu, *Karar* (2014) 6 and 10ff; Tütüncübaşı, *Yabancı Çekişmesiz Yargı Kararlarının Tanınması* (2014) 68. For a short explanation on a similar distinction under German law, see Heinze, 'The Effect in the European Community of Judgments in Civil and Commercial Matters: Recognition, Res Judicata and Abuse of Process – Germany' (2006) 5–6.

[520] Kuru, *Nizasız Kaza* (1961) 173–174 and 174 fn 7; Ali Cem Budak, 'Türk Hukukunda Çekişmesiz Yargı', *Medenî Usûl ve İcra-İflâs Hukukçuları Toplantısı IV – Medenî Usûl Hukukunda Çekişmesiz Yargı – İcra ve İflâs Kanunu'nda Yapılan Değişikliklerin Değerlendirilmesi* (Türkiye Barolar Birliği 2006) 174; Tütüncübaşı, *Yabancı Çekişmesiz Yargı Kararlarının Tanınması* (2014) 68.

[521] Kuru, *Nizasız Kaza* (1961) 87; cf. Budak, 'Çekişmesiz Yargı' (2006) 159–160 fn 150.

[522] Cf. İnan, Ertaş and Albaş, *Miras Hukuku* (2022) paras 1593–1594.

[523] Dutta, (2015) 5 IJPL 38, 45. On the similar particularities of non-contentious procedure in Turkey, see for example, Atalı, *Pekcanıtez Usûl* (2017) § 18. Çekişmesiz Yargı, 2107ff.

The non-contentious nature of the Certificate's issuing procedure has no significant impact within the Union owing to the help of an automatic system enabling it to produce its effects in other Member States without any special procedure being required (Article 69). In Turkey, however, the aforementioned reading of Article 50 of the Turkish PILA may mean that an ECS issued in a Member State cannot be recognised due to the fact that it is issued at the end of a non-contentious procedure. Notwithstanding this, such an interpretation would be against the *ratio legis* of Article 58(2) of the Turkish PILA on the recognition of decisions issued at the end of non-contentious proceedings, which clarifies that they are also governed by the general regime of recognition (Articles 50 and 54) under the Turkish PILA. Even without this specific provision, the scope of Article 50 should be broadly interpreted to govern any type of decision rendered by a foreign court on the claims concerning substantive law by disregarding the differences in domestic law. With such a broad interpretation, succession certificates issued by courts outside Turkey, including the ECS, would be considered as judgments.[524]

Despite the fact that a wide interpretation of the term 'judgment' is favoured, it should be noted that the word's use would cover only decisions made by 'courts'. Therefore, only succession certificates issued by courts outside Turkey, subject to other conditions, may be recognised in Turkey. Succession certificates issued by other authorities of foreign States, such as notaries, cannot be recognised.[525]

By introducing the ECS, the Regulation leaves the matter of determining the competent authorities to issue succession certificates to the internal legislation of Member States (Article 64, Recital (70)). Depending on the national legislations of Member States, it could be issued by courts or other authorities, e.g. notaries or registry offices.[526]

---

[524] Ekşi, *Milletlerarası Miras Hukuku* (2013) 128; Sirmen, 'Avrupa Mirasçılık Belgesi' (2016) 572; cf. Demir Gökyayla, 'Mirasçılık Belgeleri' (2006) 562; Giray, (2016) 9 Anali PFZE 235, 242–243.

[525] Şanlı, 'Veraset İlamı' (1990) 295; Demir Gökyayla, 'Mirasçılık Belgeleri' (2006) 563; Kurşat, *Terekenin Korunması Önlemleri* (2010) 356; Ekşi, *Milletlerarası Miras Hukuku* (2013) 112; Ahmet Cahit İyilikli, 'Mirasçılık (Veraset) Belgesinin Hukuk Yargılamasındaki Görünümü' (2017) 5 UMD 281, 340; Nomer, *Milletlerarası Usul Hukuku* (2018) 225 fn 339; İnan, Ertaş and Albaş, *Miras Hukuku* (2022) paras 1590 ff.

See, in the context of the ECS, Ekşi, 'Comparison of the Turkish PILA with the ESR' (2014) 151; Giray, (2016) 9 Anali PFZE 235, 244.

The Turkish Court of Cassation is also of the same opinion. In one of its judgments, for example, it held that a succession certificate issued by a French notary cannot be recognised in Turkey: Yargıtay 2. Hukuk Dairesi, T. 12.7.2002, E. 2002/8254 K. 2002/9339 <http://www.kazanci.com> accessed 2 July 2017. The case is also published and reviewed in Ekşi, *Milletlerarası Miras Hukuku* (2013) 112–113.

[526] Art 78 of the Regulation requires Member States to communicate relevant information in national law to the Commission. This also covers the information regarding the

In Germany, for instance, pursuant to § 34(4) of the Act on International Procedure in Succession Matters ('IntErbRVG'), the local courts ('Amtsgericht') are competent as probate courts ('Nachlassgericht') to issue ECSs. In these courts, senior judicial officers ('Rechtspfleger') are in charge of issuing an ECS in accordance with § 3(2) (i) of the Act on Senior Judicial Officers ('RPflG').[527] Unless otherwise provided under the domestic legislation of the relevant German States, the judge should issue the Certificate when there is a testamentary disposition or – even though the likelihood of such cases is very little considering the 'Gleichlauf' between forum and *ius* in the Regulation – when the law applicable to succession is foreign law. Despite the existence of a testamentary disposition, the judge may leave the issuing of an ECS to senior judicial officers in cases in which intestate succession rules are still applicable and the governing law is that of Germany (§ 16(2), (3) (2) and § 19(1) (5) RPflG).[528]

An example of a Member State which assigns competence to notaries for the issuance of the Certificate is France.[529] In French law, heirs/beneficiaries can prove their status by any means (Article 730-1 of the French Civil Code ('Code Civil')). Notwithstanding this, in practice they often seek from a notary a statutory declaration ('acte de notoriété') indicating their status and respective shares.[530] In line with this national procedure, the power to issue an

---

authorities competent to issue the Certificate in each Member State under Art 64. The information communicated to the Commission is published in the Official Journal of the European Union and made available to the public by other communication means, especially through the European Judicial Network in civil and commercial matters (Art 79). See, for the information on the Network, <https://e-justice.europa.eu/content_succession-380-en.do?clang=en> accessed 25 March 2020.

For a general information on the national legislation of Member States, see also Lucia Ruggeri, Ivana Kunda and Sandra Winkler (eds), *Family Property and Succession in EU Member States: National Reports on the Collected Data* (Sveučilište u Rijeci, Pravni fakultet 2019) <https://www.euro-family.eu/documenti/news/psefs_e_book_compressed.pdf> accessed 26 March 2020.

A communication from the Member States to the Commission on the authority competent to issue succession certificates creates a presumption that the designated authority qualifies as a 'court' within the meaning of Article 3(2) of the Regulation. On the other hand, the failure of a Member State to designate the authority does not, in principle, mean that the competent authority under national legislation is not a 'court' pursuant to Article 3(2) of the Regulation: C-658/17 WB [2019] ECLI:EU:C:2019:444 [44 ff].

527 BGBl. I 1969, 2065.

528 See, for more information, Anatol Dutta, in Anatol Dutta and Johannes Weber (eds), *Internationales Erbrecht* (2nd edn, C.H. Beck 2021) IntErbRVG § 34(4) paras 12 ff.

529 Other examples would be Poland and Lithuania, see below n 535, p 301.

In fact, as reported, this is the situation in most of the Member States: Sjef van Erp, 'Inheritance Certificates and EU Law: Less European "Effet Utile" Implies More National "Pratique Utile"' (2020) 9 EPLJ 67, 69.

530 Frank Lipworth, Jean-Pierre Le Bouffo and Jérôme Le Bouffo, 'France' in Louis Garb and John Wood (eds), *International Succession* (4th edn, OUP 2015) para 16.75;

ECS has also been given to notaries (Article 1381-1 of the French Code of Civil Procedure ('Code de procédure civile')).[531]

It is believed that ECSs, which are issued by courts or other authorities subject to the national legal arrangements of Member States as shown in the examples, are identical to other certificates used in different jurisdictions for the same purpose in Turkey. Therefore, only ECSs issued by courts of Member States can be recognised under the Turkish PILA.[532] It is inconsequential whether the Certificate, as in the example of Germany, has actually been issued by an official at the court other than the judge so long as that individual acts on behalf of the court in the procedure.[533] In a similar vein, with respect to succession certificates (including the ECS) drawn up by other competent authorities, such as notaries or registry offices, outside Turkey, before the application for recognition is lodged the Turkish court should make an assessment to determine their powers under the law of the State of origin. It is likely that under that law those authorities or legal professionals are empowered with judicial functions (like courts) or delegated authority by courts in succession cases. If this is the case, these persons or entities may still be considered as falling within the meaning of 'court', and hence the recognition of succession certificates issued by them may not be rejected based solely on this ground.[534]

The Regulation acknowledges under Article 3(2) and Recital 20 that such circumstances might be possible in Member States, but it stresses that they are rather rare.[535] From the Member States, the law of Austria is an example of a

---

Maria Virginia Maccari, 'France' in Lucia Ruggeri, Ivana Kunda and Sandra Winkler (eds), *Family Property and Succession in EU Member States: National Reports on the Collected Data* (Sveučilište u Rijeci, Pravni fakultet 2019) 248 <https://www.euro-family.eu/documenti/news/psefs_e_book_compressed.pdf> accessed 26 March 2020.

531 Maccari, 'France' (2019) 256–257.

532 Ekşi, 'Comparison of the Turkish PILA with the ESR' (2014) 151; Giray, (2016) 9 Anali PFZE 235, 242; Sirmen, 'Avrupa Mirasçılık Belgesi' (2016) 571.

533 See, for Germany, Dutta, *MüKoBGB* (2020) EuErbVO Art 64 para 11. See also Emre Esen, 'Alman Hukukunda İhtarlı Basit Dava Usulü (Mahnverfahren) Çerçevesinde Verilen Kararların Türk Hukukunda Tenfizi' (2007) 27 MHB 21, 51–52; Tütüncübaşı, *Yabancı Çekişmesiz Yargı Kararlarının Tanınması* (2014) 135–136.

534 Ekşi, *Milletlerarası Miras Hukuku* (2013) 113; cf. Demir Gökyayla, 'Mirasçılık Belgeleri' (2006) 565. See also Ertaş, (1987) 3 DEÜHFD 365, 380.

535 In two cases, the CJEU has already discussed the meaning of judicial functions for notaries in Poland and in Lithuania. In the *WB* case (C-658/17 WB [2019] ECLI:EU:C:2019:444), the Court clarified that it should be examined whether the authority has the power to act on its own motion, without a mutual request by parties, to hear a legal matter and to decide on it (paras 55–56). In that case, the Court considered that Polish notaries could issue a succession certificate only with the unanimous request of parties, and they were self-employed professionals only within the limits of the parties' agrement and for a certain renumaration. The Court therefore found that they cannot be considered as exercising judicial functions (paras 57 ff).

case where a notary, normally a non-judicial authority, exercises judicial functions when issuing a succession certificate. Under Austrian law, district courts ('Bezirksgerichte') in principle have competence for non-contentious proceedings (§ 104a 'JN'). The competence to issue the ECS, however, belongs to notaries as court commissioners ('Gerichtskommissäre') according to § 1(1) (d) of the Court Commissioners Act ('GKG').[536] Only in cases where the elements to be certified are challenged should the issue be dealt with by the Court (§ 181b(2) Non-Contentious Proceedings Act ('AußStrG')).[537] It could be said that Austrian notaries exercise judicial functions in the process due to the fact that they are under the duty of impartiality (§ 6 GKG) and are charged with the protection of the right to a fair hearing between the parties (§ 15 AußStrG). Their acts are subject to the review of the Court (§ 7a(2) GKG).[538] Thus, the recognition of an ECS issued by an Austrian notary should not be refused in Turkey based solely on the ground that it is a notarial succession certificate.

Should the issuing authority have no judicial powers under its own law, it is not possible to file for recognition of a succession certificate in Turkey, be it a national certificate of succession or an ECS. Such certificates could then simply be used as evidence in relevant legal actions pending before Turkish courts, provided that they have been translated into Turkish and, unless an international treaty is in force between Turkey and the State of origin abolishing the requirement, duly legalised with the procedure applicable under Article 224(1) of the Turkish Code of Civil Procedure. According to this, legalisation can be done by the issuing authority or the Turkish Consulate in the State of issue. If an international treaty to this effect is applicable between Turkey and the State of origin, no such legalisation is needed for certificates to be presented to Turkish courts. The most prominent international treaty in this regard is the Convention of 5 October 1961 Abolishing the Requirement of Legalisation for Foreign Public Documents (the so-called 'Apostille Convention').[539] Under the Convention, an 'apostille' placed on the certificate would

---

Likewise, in the *E.E.* case (C-80/19 E. E. [2020] ECLI:EU:C:2020:569), the Court underlined that only authorities which can decide on disputed matters between the parties may be regarded as exercising judicial powers and, hence, found that Lithuanian notaries lack such powers and do not qualify as courts under Article 3(2) of the Regulation (paras 53 ff).

[536] BGBl. Nr. 343/1970.

[537] BGBl. I Nr. 111/2003.

[538] Astrid Deixler-Hübner and Martin Schauer, in Astrid Deixler-Hübner and Martin Schauer (eds), *Kommentar zur EU-Erbrechtsverordnung* (2nd edn, Manz 2020) EuErbVO Art 3 paras 43 ff; Alice Perscha, in Astrid Deixler-Hübner and Martin Schauer (eds), *Kommentar zur EU-Erbrechtsverordnung* (2nd edn, Manz 2020) EuErbVO Art 64 paras 35 ff.

[539] For the full text of the Convention, see <https://www.hcch.net/en/instruments/conventions/full-text/?cid=41> accessed 31 March 2020. This is an important convention with respect to the use of public documents in other States and is in force more than 100 States, including all EU Member States. See, in this regard, <https://www.hcch.net/en/instru

suffice. There could be also other treaties, such as those on mutual legal assistance, concluded between Turkey and the State of issue, the provisions of which abolish the legalisation procedure and give automatic effect to a public document in the other Contracting State.[540] Succession certificates issued by administrative authorities exercising no judicial functions can have only evidentiary effects in Turkey under this procedure.[541]

Notwithstanding this, divergent solutions have been proposed in Turkish academic literature so as to allow recognition of certificates of this kind pursuant to this condition. It is argued, first of all, that a succession certificate issued by a competent non-judicial authority of a foreign State may be considered as a 'judgment' for the purposes of a recognition procedure in Turkey after having been legalised by the competent court of that State.[542] One may contend, as an alternative solution, that there is no need for court legalisation and the recognition procedure; instead, such certificates could have immediate effects in Turkey after being duly legalised by either the issuing authority or the Turkish Consulate in that State (Article 224(1) of the Turkish Code of Civil Procedure), or even without such a legalisation in cases where an international treaty lifts the prerequisite legalisation procedure. This could, however, be subject to dispute, since notaries became competent with the amendments made in 2011[543] to issue succession certificates under Article 598(1) of the Turkish Civil Code. Although the authority of notaries in this respect is limited to issuing succession certificates for heirs, such a key amendment might be seen as a good reason to defend the extension of the effects of foreign notarial succession certificates to Turkey without a recognition process. They could be used for the transfer of assets before the Turkish authorities competent once the procedure for the use of public documents is completed.[544]

It appears that neither of these proposals is plausible. The first option may work only if, under the law of the State of origin, courts are competent on the legalisation of a succession certificate and the certificate gains a similar force and effect as a decision of a judicial authority after being legalised by a court.

---

ments/conventions/status-table/?cid=41> accessed 31 March 2020. The Convention entered into force in Turkey on 29.9.1985. See, for Turkey, *Resmi Gazete* of 16.9.1984, no 18517.

540 See, for example, Art 7 of The Treaty of 19.9.1995 on Mutual Legal Assistance in Civil and Commercial Matters between Turkey and Lithuania, *Resmi Gazete* of 20.4.2004, no 25439.

541 Şanlı, 'Veraset İlamı' (1990) 305–306; Ekşi, *Milletlerarası Miras Hukuku* (2013) 114; Ruhi and Ruhi, *Mirasçılık Belgesi* (2015) 50; Bilkay, (2021) 41 MHB 905, 922. In the context of the ECS, see Ekşi, 'Comparison of the Turkish PILA with the ESR' (2014) 151; Giray, (2016) 9 Anali PFZE 235, 244; cf. Sirmen, 'Avrupa Mirasçılık Belgesi' (2016) 573.

542 Şanlı, 'Veraset İlamı' (1990) 295–296; contra Demir Gökyayla, 'Mirasçılık Belgeleri' (2006) 565–566; Ekşi, *Milletlerarası Miras Hukuku* (2013) 115.

543 See Art 19 of the Law no 6217 of 31.3.2011, *Resmi Gazete* of 14.4.2011, no 27905.

544 Ekşi, *Milletlerarası Miras Hukuku* (2013) 116.

This seems rather a small probability.[545] In addition, even if this is the case under the law of the State of issue, this would not be enough to make the certificate a 'judgment' in Turkey, as the judicial character of a decision should also be determined by Turkey as the State where the recognition is sought.[546]

The second proposal – i.e. to treat foreign succession certificates issued by non-judicial authorities, especially by notaries, as other public documents and to allow their direct use before relevant authorities, such as at a registry of deeds, without any recognition procedure pursuant to the procedure for the use of public documents – is not plausible either by virtue of two reasons.

Firstly, this will result in a contradiction in practice. Under this proposition, while foreign succession certificates issued by judicial authorities will produce effects in Turkey only after a successful recognition procedure, those drawn up by non-judicial authorities would bypass a recognition procedure and have effects in Turkey in an easier manner. In addition, as will be explained below,[547] the recognition of foreign succession certificates, in particular those concerning immovable property in Turkey, is refused owing to the fact that legal matters concerning such property are considered to be within the exclusive jurisdiction of Turkish courts. The outcome would then be that succession certificates of foreign judicial authorities can produce effects only for movable properties in Turkey, although certificates of foreign administrative authorities – which, as proposed, do not require recognition procedure – could be used both for movable and immovable assets. This contradiction is obviously unacceptable.[548]

Moreover, despite the fact that notaries became competent on the issuance of succession certificates under Article 598(1) of the Turkish Civil Code, which is the main justification for the second solution, their competence is limited to domestic cases which involve no foreign elements. This is evident from the relevant provisions of the Law on Notaries[549] and the By-law on the Issuance of Succession Certificates by Notaries[550] as well as from Article 37 of the Land Registry Law. Amendments made in 2011 also introduced three new provisions to the Law on Notaries regarding this new area of notary competence.[551] Article 71/A of the Law reiterates the authority of notaries to issue succession certificates in parallel with Article 598(1) of the Turkish

---

545 Cf. Demir Gökyayla, 'Mirasçılık Belgeleri' (2006) 565; Ekşi, *Milletlerarası Miras Hukuku* (2013) 115.

546 Tuğrul Arat, 'Yabancı İlamların Tanınması ve Tenfizi' (1964) 21 AÜHFD 421, 500; Işıl Özbakan, *Türk Hukukunda Yabancı Mahkeme Kararlarının Tanınması ve Tenfizi* (Kazancı 1987) 144; Nomer, *Milletlerarası Usul Hukuku* (2018) 177; Şanlı, Esen and Ataman Figanmeşe, *Milletlerarası Özel Hukuk* (2021) 634–635.

547 See below pp 313 ff.

548 Ekşi, *Milletlerarası Miras Hukuku* (2013) 116.

549 *Resmi Gazete* of 5.2.1972, no 14090.

550 *Resmi Gazete* of 4.10.2011, no 28074.

551 See Art 14 of the Law no 6217 of 31.3.2011, *Resmi Gazete* of 14.4.2011, no 27905.

Civil Code. The subsequent provision, i.e. Article 71/B, however, provides under its paragraph (3) that they have no authority when succession certificates are requested by foreign nationals. Article 37 of the Land Registry Law and Article 5 of the By-law on the Issuance of Succession Certificates by Public Notaries take the restriction of authority a step further and express that notaries are not competent to issue succession certificates when the dispute involves a foreign element. Consequently, when only courts are competent to draw up a succession certificate and even Turkish notaries do not have such a power in cases where cross-border elements are involved, it is seemingly implausible to defend the idea of granting immediate effects to foreign succession certificates issued by non-judicial authorities.[552]

Therefore, succession certificates, also ECSs, issued by non-judicial authorities cannot be recognised under the Turkish PILA. They can only produce evidentiary effects in relevant lawsuits. It is, however, advisable that a new provision be inserted into the legislation in the future, a provision which would allow recognition and, where applicable, allow the enforcement of foreign administrative documents, including succession certificates.[553]

bb) Judgments which are Final under the Law of the State of Their Origin

Article 50 of the Turkish PILA also stipulates that only final judgments can be recognised in Turkey. The provision clarifies that the finality of the judgment should be determined by the law of its State of origin. It is not difficult for the courts of Turkey to ascertain whether the judgment has become final in its country of origin. The reason is that the application for recognition should include 'a statement or a document duly authenticated by the authorities of the country where the judgment is rendered indicating that the judgment has become final and by an authenticated translation of it' (Article 53(1)(b) of the Turkish PILA).[554] The procedure to prove the finality of the decision and to establish its authenticity will also be decided in accordance with the procedural law of the State where the judgment was delivered.[555] Hence, as long as the application file includes a statement or a document duly proving that the foreign judgment, or the succession certificate, is final under the law of the origin State, one would expect no further problems as regards to

---

552 Ekşi, *Milletlerarası Miras Hukuku* (2013) 116ff.

553 Ekşi, *Milletlerarası Miras Hukuku* (2013) 115; Ruhi and Ruhi, *Mirasçılık Belgesi* (2015) 49; cf. Tütüncübaşı, *Yabancı Çekişmesiz Yargı Kararlarının Tanınması* (2014) 134; Özkan and Tütüncübaşı, *Uluslararası Usûl Hukuku* (2020) 179.

554 Tütüncübaşı, *Yabancı Çekişmesiz Yargı Kararlarının Tanınması* (2014) 140; Çelikel and Erdem, *Milletlerarası Özel Hukuk* (2021) 722; Güngör, *Türk Milletlerarası Özel Hukuku* (2021) 290.

555 Güngör, *Türk Milletlerarası Özel Hukuku* (2021) 290; Şanlı, Esen and Ataman Figanmeşe, *Milletlerarası Özel Hukuk* (2021) 645.

finality.[556] This is because it is the Turkish PILA itself which explicitly states that the finality should be determined in accordance with the law of the State where it was delivered, and this will be proved in Turkey by a document or statement to this effect.[557]

Nonetheless, the exact meaning of finality is contentious in Turkish legal academia and practice. The underlying reason for this is that the finality of judgments is assured by the doctrine of *res judicata*[558] under Turkish procedural law. In spite of being a universally recognised doctrine, every legal system undoubtedly has its own understanding of *res judicata*. As in certain other civilian legal traditions,[559] the effects of *res judicata* are two-fold, being procedural (or formal) and substantive pursuant to Article 303 of the Turkish Code of Civil Procedure. Although both aspects serve public and private interests of legal certainty and predictability and the need for an end to litigation;[560] their scopes are somewhat different. The former refers to a procedural-bar against re-opening the dispute. A judgment acquires the force of procedural or formal *res judicata* when there is no ordinary legal remedy against the judgment[561] that is available to the parties; or failing that, the parties ne-

---

[556] It is well established in the case law of the Turkish Court of Cassation that if the document or the statement indicating the finality of the judgment whose recognition or enforcement is sought before a Turkish court is not included, the application is not dismissed immediately; rather, a reasonable time is granted to the plaintiff to submit it. See, for example, Yargıtay 2. Hukuk Dairesi, T. 21.3.2019, E. 2019/744 K. 2019/3219 <https://www.lexpera.com.tr/> accessed 18 April 2020.

[557] Ekşi, *Milletlerarası Miras Hukuku* (2013) 130–133.

[558] In its Turkish original, the phrasing which is used to refer to the Latin term of *res judicata* is '*kesin hüküm*'. Nevertheless, it is claimed that '*kesin hüküm*' is not actually a full equivalent of the *res judicata*. See, in this regard, Kemal Gözler, 'Res Iudicata'nın Türkçesi Üzerine' (2007) 56 AÜHFD 45, 49 ff. In this paper, however, the term *res judicata* is used to present discussions on the concept of finality regardless of whether it is fully captured by '*kesin hüküm*' in Turkish law.

[559] See, for instance, § 322 and § 705 ZPO in Germany. Such a distinction exists in domestic laws, with some nuances, and Italy could be another example in this regard: Niccolò Ridi, 'Precarious Finality? Reflections on Res Judicata and the Question of the Delimitation of the Continental Shelf Case' (2018) 31 Leiden J Int Law 383, 385 and fn 7.

[560] See, for example, Yargıtay Hukuk Genel Kurulu, T. 9.4.2003, E. 2003/20-266 K. 2003/285 <https://legalbank.net/> accessed 9 April 2020.

[561] Legal systems often provide for remedies against judgments. There could be different classifications as regards such remedies. From these classifications, the most widely used distinction under Turkish procedural law is that between ordinary and extraordinary legal remedies. Ordinary legal remedies are possible against judgments which are not yet final, and the use of such legal remedies in fact prevents the finality of the judgment. These are first-degree appeal procedures ('istinaf'), appeal procedures before the Turkish Court of Cassation ('temyiz'), and rectification procedures ('karar düzeltme'). Extraordinary legal remedies, on the other hand, are retrial procedures ('yargılamanın yenilenmesi') which come into play only against judgments which have acquired a procedural *res judica-*

glect to make use of the available legal remedy in a timely manner, or they waive their rights in this regard, or they do appeal against the judgment but the appeal is dismissed. On the other hand, substantive *res judicata* means that the judgment granted by the court on the subject matter of the dispute is final and binding on the parties. In other words, a judgment will bar the relitigation of a dispute before any court if the parties, subject matter, and cause of action are identical in subsequent proceedings. In order to gain such an effect, a judgment should first acquire the force of procedural or formal *res judicata*. Therefore, this latter effect of *res judicata* is much broader than its procedural effect.[562]

It is this two-sided characteristic of *res judicata* that precipitates debate in academia and court practice in Turkey. Since foreign judgments, subject to other conditions, should be final to be recognisable and/or enforceable in Turkey, an uncertainty arises whether this signifies 'finality' in the sense of the procedural/formal concept of *res judicata* or the substantive concept of *res judicata*.[563] This is particularly important in the context of judgments rendered at the end of non-contentious proceedings, as they can acquire the force of *res judicata* only in a procedural sense but not in substantive sense under Turkish law (Article 388 of the Turkish Code of Civil Procedure). As explained above, succession certificates lack substantive finality under Turkish law due to the fact that any person showing a legitimate interest may request the modification or withdrawal of the certificate from the court at any time. The same apparently applies for the ECS. It has a declaratory character and, hence, is not final in the substantive sense.[564] Therefore, it is of uppermost significance to determine the scope of the term 'finality' under Article 50 of the Turkish PILA and to answer the question of whether succession certificates meet this requirement in the light of the views expressed by legal scholars and found in the case law.

Some scholars contend that the meaning of the term 'finality' in the context of recognition of foreign judgments is an allusion to the concept of *res judicata*

---

ta effect. For more information on the issue, see Muhammet Özekes, in Hakan Pekcanıtez and others (eds), *Pekcanıtez Usûl: Medenî Usûl Hukuku*, vol 3 (15th edn, On İki Levha 2017) § 19. Kanun Yolları, 2149 ff.

562 Baki Kuru, *Hukuk Muhakemeleri Usulü*, vol 5 (6th edn, Demir Demir 2001) 4981 ff; Atalı, *Pekcanıtez Usûl* (2017) § 16. Karar ve Hüküm, 2054 ff. On the concept of *res judicata*, see also Ersin Erdoğan, *Hakem Kararlarının Kesin Hüküm Etkisi* (2nd edn, Yetkin 2020) 61 ff.

563 Şanlı, 'Veraset İlamı' (1990) 296; Demir Gökyayla, *Tanıma ve Tenfiz'de Kamu Düzeni* (2001) 566; Ekşi, *Milletlerarası Miras Hukuku* (2013) 122; Tütüncübaşı, *Yabancı Çekişmesiz Yargı Kararlarının Tanınması* (2014) 138; Çelikel and Erdem, *Milletlerarası Özel Hukuk* (2021) 720; Şanlı, Esen and Ataman Figanmeşe, *Milletlerarası Özel Hukuk* (2021) 643.

564 See above p 283.

as a whole. That is to say, only judgments which have the force of procedural/formal as well as substantive *res judicata* in their country of origin might be subject to recognition under Turkish law.[565] This is justified on the grounds of legal certainty and predictability. A judgment which has not yet become final in a real sense, i.e. has not yet acquired the force of substantive *res judicata*, in the country where it has been rendered should not have any effect in Turkey. This is because there is a risk that the judgment will be later reversed in the origin country. This is especially important regarding judgments given at the end of non-contentious proceedings, which are not considered final on the merits and, hence, have no substantive *res judicata* effect.[566] Even though Article 58(2) of the Turkish PILA states that recognition of non-contentious judgments is also governed by the same provisions, this, in the view of some scholars, refers only to such judgments having a constitutive nature, e.g. those on correction of age or name, declaration of absence, or appointment of a guardian. Only these types of judgments of a non-contentious nature can acquire the force of substantive *res judicata* and can be recognised in Turkey, providing that they also meet the other conditions of recognition.[567] Succession certificates do not fall into this category and should not be subject to recognition, unless they are drawn up in contentious proceedings.[568]

---

[565] Uluocak, *Milletlerarası Özel Hukuk Dersleri* (1987) 149–150; Şanlı, 'Veraset İlamı' (1990) 296–297; Ataman Figanmeşe, 'Mirasçılık Belgeleri' (1998) 34–35; Nomer, 'Yabancı Çekişmesiz Yargı Kararlarının Tanınmasında Kesinleşme Şartı' (2001) 909ff; Bilkay, (2021) 41 MHB 905, 922–923; Şanlı, Esen and Ataman Figanmeşe, *Milletlerarası Özel Hukuk* (2021) 644.

[566] Göğer, *Devletler Hususi Hukuku* (1977) 386; Şanlı, 'Veraset İlamı' (1990) 297; Nomer, 'Yabancı Çekişmesiz Yargı Kararlarının Tanınmasında Kesinleşme Şartı' (2001) 912 fn 8 and 916–917; Çelikel and Erdem, *Milletlerarası Özel Hukuk* (2021) 720; contra Sakmar, *Yabancı İlamların Türkiye'deki Sonuçları* (1982) 58; Demir Gökyayla, *Tanıma ve Tenfiz'de Kamu Düzeni* (2001) 568; Tütüncübaşı, *Yabancı Çekişmesiz Yargı Kararlarının Tanınması* (2014) 143.

[567] Şanlı, 'Veraset İlamı' (1990) 296–298; Ataman Figanmeşe, 'Mirasçılık Belgeleri' (1998) 35–36; Nomer, 'Yabancı Çekişmesiz Yargı Kararlarının Tanınmasında Kesinleşme Şartı' (2001) 917ff; Ahmet Cemal Ruhi, *Milletlerarası Özel Hukuk ve Usul Hukuku Hakkında Kanun – Gerekçeli, Kısa Açıklamalı, Yargıtay İçtihatlı* (4th edn, Seçkin 2014) 415; Çelikel and Erdem, *Milletlerarası Özel Hukuk* (2021) 801; cf. Çelikel, (1982) 2 MHB 7, 13.

[568] Ertaş, (1987) 3 DEÜHFD 365, 384ff; Uluocak, *Milletlerarası Özel Hukuk Dersleri* (1987) 149–150; Şanlı, 'Veraset İlamı' (1990) 298; Ataman Figanmeşe, 'Mirasçılık Belgeleri' (1998) 36–37; Nomer, 'Yabancı Çekişmesiz Yargı Kararlarının Tanınmasında Kesinleşme Şartı' (2001) 918–919; Ruhi and Ruhi, *Mirasçılık Belgesi* (2015) 50; İyilikli, (2017) 5 UMD 281, 338–339; İnan, Ertaş and Albaş, *Miras Hukuku* (2022) paras 1593–1594; Tekinalp, *Milletlerarası Özel Hukuk* (2020) 236 fn 7; Çelikel and Erdem, *Milletlerarası Özel Hukuk* (2021) 720–721 and 801–802; Pürselim, (2021) 9 KHASHFD 179, 196; Şanlı, Esen and Ataman Figanmeşe, *Milletlerarası Özel Hukuk* (2021) 641 fn 405; Doğan, *Milletlerarası Özel Hukuk* (2022) 151; cf. Çelikel, (1982) 2 MHB 7, 13. With respect to the ECS, see Giray, (2016) 9 Anali PFZE 235, 243–244.

Another line of thought, on the other hand, finds procedural/formal *res judicata* effect adequate for the purposes of recognition (and enforcement) of foreign judgments,[569] thereby contending that non-contentious judgments, and also succession certificates which belong to this category, could also be recognised.[570] According to the proponents of this view, there are numerous grounds vindicating it. First, legal certainty and predictability could not justify the condition that foreign judgments, and succession certificates, should have acquired also substantive *res judicata* effect in their countries of origin.[571] This is because, as explained earlier, succession certificates are issued by civil courts of peace or notaries upon the application of heirs under Turkish law. The issuing procedure is non-contentious; they do not have the force of substantive *res judicata*, and they could be declared invalid at any time after a successful challenge by the persons whose rights are affected (Article 598 of the Turkish Civil Code, Articles 382(2)(c)(6) and 388 of the Turkish Code of Civil Procedure). Despite this, the heirs mentioned in the certificate are entitled to request the transfer of the assets on their behalf or to dispose of any property belonging to the estate to other persons. In the same way as the succession certificate itself, any transaction made on the basis of the information certified in it could be declared invalid at any time by the court if it is established that the certificate or the elements thereof are not accurate.[572] It seems that the Turkish legislature did not take legal certainty and predictability into account even in purely domestic cases.[573] In

See also V. R. Seviğ, *Mirasla İlgili Devletler Hususi Hukuku Kaideleri* (1963) 192–193; cf. O. Işık Nazikioğlu, 'Yabancı Memleket Mahkemelerinden Verilen Kararların Tanınması ve Tenfizi' (1950) 7 AÜHFD 468, 485; O. F. Berki, *Miras* (1960) 94.

[569] Sakmar, *Yabancı İlamların Türkiye'deki Sonuçları* (1982) 57–58 and 112–113; Tiryakioğlu, *Yabancı Boşanma Kararlarının Tanınması ve Tenfizi* (1996) 38; Sargın and Erten, (2014) 3 UTTDER 37, 79–80 fn 94; Tütüncübaşı, *Yabancı Çekişmesiz Yargı Kararlarının Tanınması* (2014) 141–142; Özkan and Tütüncübaşı, *Uluslararası Usûl Hukuku* (2020) 186–187; Altınkaya, *Mirasçılık Belgesi* (2021) 33; cf. Baki Kuru, *Hukuk Muhakemeleri Usulü*, vol 6 (6th edn, Demir Demir 2001) 5771; Günseli Öztekin, 'Recognition and Enforcement of Foreign Court Judgments Within the Framework of the Application of the Supreme Court of Appeals', *Prof. Dr. Tahir Çağa'nın Anısına Armağan* (Beta 2000) 391.

[570] Demir Gökyayla, 'Mirasçılık Belgeleri' (2006) 568–569; Kurşat, *Terekenin Korunması Önlemleri* (2010) 358; Ekşi, *Milletlerarası Miras Hukuku* (2013) 128 ff; Tütüncübaşı, *Yabancı Çekişmesiz Yargı Kararlarının Tanınması* (2014) 143 ff; Özkan and Tütüncübaşı, *Uluslararası Usûl Hukuku* (2020) 186–187; Güngör, *Türk Milletlerarası Özel Hukuku* (2021) 301; cf. Özbakan, *Tanıma ve Tenfiz* (1987) 130.

[571] Sakmar, *Yabancı İlamların Türkiye'deki Sonuçları* (1982) 58; Demir Gökyayla, 'Mirasçılık Belgeleri' (2006) 568–569; Tütüncübaşı, *Yabancı Çekişmesiz Yargı Kararlarının Tanınması* (2014) 144; Özkan and Tütüncübaşı, *Uluslararası Usûl Hukuku* (2020) 186.

[572] Ekşi, *Milletlerarası Miras Hukuku* (2013) 128; Demir Gökyayla, 'Mirasçılık Belgeleri' (2006) 568–569; Tütüncübaşı, *Yabancı Çekişmesiz Yargı Kararlarının Tanınması* (2014) 144; Özkan and Tütüncübaşı, *Uluslararası Usûl Hukuku* (2020) 186.

[573] Demir Gökyayla, 'Mirasçılık Belgeleri' (2006) 568–569; Kurşat, *Terekenin Korunması Önlemleri* (2010) 358 fn 1291.

addition, recognition gives *res judicata* effect to a foreign judgment. Although the scope of *res judicata* effect should be determined in accordance with the law of the State where the judgment was rendered, it is argued that it cannot produce a broader effect than a judgment rendered in Turkey.[574] This applies for succession certificates too. Thus, persons presenting legitimate interests may request before Turkish courts the rectification, modification, or invalidation of a foreign succession certificate already recognised in Turkey.[575] When this is the case, it does not seem plausible to declare foreign succession certificates unrecognisable for the sake of legal certainty and predictability simply because they lack substantive *res judicata* effects.[576]

Furthermore, the latter view is said to be more in line with the intention of the legislature when laying down the rules regarding recognition and enforcement of foreign judgments. Before the enactment of the former Turkish PILA (Law no 2675), which is considered as the first *actual* private international law code of Turkey, recognition and enforcement of foreign judgments was regulated under Articles 537–545 of the former Turkish Code of Civil Procedure (Law no 1086). The relevant provision there was Article 537, and it provided that only judgments rendered in foreign countries which are 'final' and have 'the force of *res judicata*' could be enforced and recognised in Turkey. Though a distinction is made between procedural/formal and substantive effects of judgments in Turkish academic literature, commentators often mean the substantive effect of judgments with reference to the term *res judicata*. This is the effect which a judgment presents the (legal) truth. Finality, on the other hand, refers in their understanding only to procedural effects of a judgment. Hence, references to both terms in the then Article 537 of the Turkish Code of Civil Procedure could be interpreted as the legislature having desired that a foreign judgment be recognisable in Turkey only after having acquired both procedural / formal and

574 Sakmar, *Yabancı İlamların Türkiye'deki Sonuçları* (1982) 182; Ertaş, (1987) 3 DEÜHFD 365, 369–370; Tiryakioğlu, *Yabancı Boşanma Kararlarının Tanınması ve Tenfizi* (1996) 64; Demir Gökyayla, 'Mirasçılık Belgeleri' (2006) 569; Tütüncübaşı, *Yabancı Çekişmesiz Yargı Kararlarının Tanınması* (2014) 145 fn 144; Nomer, *Milletlerarası Usul Hukuku* (2018) 172; Özkan and Tütüncübaşı, *Uluslararası Usûl Hukuku* (2020) 187. See also Yargıtay 7. Hukuk Dairesi, T. 23.1.2013, E. 2012/7173 K. 2013/366 <https://www.lexpera.com.tr/> accessed 19 April 2020.

575 Demir Gökyayla, 'Mirasçılık Belgeleri' (2006) 569; Tütüncübaşı, *Yabancı Çekişmesiz Yargı Kararlarının Tanınması* (2014) 145; Özkan and Tütüncübaşı, *Uluslararası Usûl Hukuku* (2020) 187. See also Nomer, 'Yabancı Çekişmesiz Yargı Kararlarının Tanınmasında Kesinleşme Şartı' (2001) 917 fn 20. From practice, see also Yargıtay 7. Hukuk Dairesi, T. 23.2.2012, E. 2011/6691 K. 2012/1100 <https://www.lexpera.com.tr/> accessed 19 April 2020.

576 Demir Gökyayla, 'Mirasçılık Belgeleri' (2006) 569; cf. Tütüncübaşı, *Yabancı Çekişmesiz Yargı Kararlarının Tanınması* (2014) 145; Özkan and Tütüncübaşı, *Uluslararası Usûl Hukuku* (2020) 186–187.

substantive forces of *res judicata*.[577] This wording, however, was changed later by the legislature under Article 34 of the former Turkish PILA (Law no 2675), which is identical to Article 50 of the current Turkish PILA (Law no 5718) and in which pre-conditions of recognition and enforcement of foreign judgments are embodied. The legislature preferred the term 'final' in this provision and explained in the preamble to the Article that it refers to procedural/formal *res judicata*.[578] It is additionally important to note that the legislature also included a rule regarding recognition of judgments delivered at the end of non-contentious proceedings and clarified that they will be governed by the same regime as judgments of a contentious nature (Article 42(2) of the former Turkish PILA (Law no 2675) and Article 58(2) of the current Turkish PILA (Law no 5718)). An interpretation that would lead to rejection of non-contentious judgments merely because they do not have the force of substantive *res judicata* would obviously render this provision unenforceable. Consequently, it is suggested that the condition of finality should be understood as procedural/formal *res judicata*, and hence non-contentious judgments should be considered final for the purposes of recognition.[579]

Consistent with the discord among commentators, the case law of the Turkish Court of Cassation on the issue does not seem to be settled. To illustrate this, two decisions of the 7th Civil Chamber of the Court, rendered in 2012 and in 2013, can be summarised here. In the former decision, the plaintiff lodged a request before a first instance court in Turkey for recognition of the succession certificate proving his title that had been issued by a court in Nürnberg/Germany. The Court dismissed the request on the grounds that the certificate did not have the force of *res judicata*. The Turkish Court of Cassation, however, overturned the decision and held that Article 58(2) of the Turkish PILA provides that the recognition of non-contentious judgments is subject to the same provisions of recognition as other judgments, and it is stipulated nowhere in the Turkish PILA that the judgment whose recognition is sought should have acquired a substantive *res judicata* effect in order to be

[577] It is argued that the two terms refer to different concepts: İstanbul Üniversitesi Hukuk Fakültesi – Milletlerarası Hukuk ve Milletlerarası Münasebetler Enstitüsü, *MÖHUK Öntasarı Sempozyumu* (1978) 279–280 (*İlhan E. Postacıoğlu*). However, it could be contended that the use of both terms is merely a translation mistake, as the Code was adapted from the civil procedural code of the Swiss Canton of Neuchâtel at the time: Sakmar, *Yabancı İlamların Türkiye'deki Sonuçları* (1982) 56–57.

[578] 'Danışma Meclisi Tutanakları – Milletlerarası Özel Hukuk ve Usul Hukuku Hakkında Kanun Tasarısı ve Adalet Komisyonu Raporu (1/5)', (1981) 10.

[579] Sakmar, *Yabancı İlamların Türkiye'deki Sonuçları* (1982) 175; Tiryakioğlu, *Yabancı Boşanma Kararlarının Tanınması ve Tenfizi* (1996) 37–38; Sargın and Erten, (2014) 3 UTTDER 37, 79–80 fn 94; Tütüncübaşı, *Yabancı Çekişmesiz Yargı Kararlarının Tanınması* (2014) 142; Özkan and Tütüncübaşı, *Uluslararası Usûl Hukuku* (2020) 184–185; Altınkaya, *Mirasçılık Belgesi* (2021) 33; Güngör, *Türk Milletlerarası Özel Hukuku* (2021) 301.

recognised in Turkey. The Higher Court further explained that this applies to succession certificates too, and they could always be challenged in Turkey even after recognition. Therefore, there is no reason to reject requests seeking their recognition in Turkey.[580]

In the following year, on the other hand, the same chamber set aside another judgment from a first instance court by arguing the exact opposite. In that case, the deceased was a U.S. national, and his spouse and children – all U.S. nationals – filed an application with a Turkish court for the issuance of a succession certificate certifying their heirship. Their application was rejected, and it was held by the Court that they could have submitted a succession certificate to be duly drawn up by the competent U.S. court. Such a certificate, in the Court's understanding, would be subject to recognition in Turkey, and hence there was no need for its issuance by the presiding Court. The Turkish Court of Cassation, however, disagreed with the reasoning of the first instance court on appeal and ruled that the Court should have issued the certificate requested in accordance with the relevant legislation. It also held that foreign succession certificates cannot be recognised in Turkey due to their rebuttable legal character, i.e. the lack of a substantive *res judicata* force, as with all other types of non-contentious judgments.[581]

Even though the Turkish Court of Cassation has issued other judgments in favour of both interpretations, the number of cases where it takes an anti-recognition stance seems to be higher on account of the declaratory and rebuttable legal nature of succession certificates.[582] In light of this approach,

---

[580] Yargıtay 7. Hukuk Dairesi, T. 23.2.2012, E. 2011/6691 K. 2012/1100 <https://www.lexpera.com.tr/> accessed 19 April 2020. See also, for example, Yargıtay 2. Hukuk Dairesi, T. 10.2.1986, E. 1986/808 K. 1986/1284 <http://www.kazanci.com> accessed 20 June 2017.

[581] Yargıtay 7. Hukuk Dairesi, T. 23.1.2013, E. 2012/7173 K. 2013/366 <https://www.lexpera.com.tr/> accessed 19 April 2020. See also, for example, Yargıtay 2. Hukuk Dairesi, T. 10.7.2001, E. 2001/3841 K. 2001/10889 <https://legalbank.net/> accessed 21 June 2019; Yargıtay 2. Hukuk Dairesi, T. 12.7.2002, E. 2002/8254 K. 2002/9339 <http://www.kazanci.com> accessed 2 July 2017; Yargıtay 2. Hukuk Dairesi, T. 27.5.2004, E. 8671 K. 10023 published in Ali İhsan Özuğur, *Türk Medeni Kanunundan Önce ve Sonra Miras Hukuku*, vol 1 (4th edn., Seçkin 2016) 719; Yargıtay 2. Hukuk Dairesi, T. 21.12.2004, E. 2004/13533 K. 2004/15443 <http://www.kazanci.com> accessed 5 January 2018; Yargıtay 2. Hukuk Dairesi, T. 13.6.2006, E. 2006/2290 K. 2006/9327 <https://karararama.yargitay.gov.tr> accessed 7 February 2021; Yargıtay 2. Hukuk Dairesi, T. 19.7.2006, E. 2006/4387 K. 2006/11476 <http://www.kazanci.com> accessed 20 April 2020; Yargıtay 2. Hukuk Dairesi, T. 6.12.2006, E. 2006/17733 K. 2006/17107 <http://www.kazanci.com> accessed 20 April 2020; Yargıtay 11. Hukuk Dairesi, T. 7.4.2014, E. 2014/4823 K. 2014/6777 <http://www.kazanci.com> accessed 20 April 2020; Yargıtay 14. Hukuk Dairesi, T. 12.12.2016, E. 2016/14569 K. 2016/10281 <http://www.kazanci.com> accessed 20 April 2020; Yargıtay 3. Hukuk Dairesi, T. 6.7.2017, E. 2016/16615 K. 2017/11258 <http://www.kazanci.com> accessed 20 April 2020.

[582] See the judgments cited in the two previous footnotes.

which reiterates the views in academic literature, a foreign succession certificate will not be recognised in Turkey due to the fact that the condition of finality under Article 50 is not met.[583] It is highly likely that this will be the same for the ECS. Notwithstanding this, it is believed that the requests for recognition of foreign succession certificates should not be refused on the ground of finality. This is because the Law states that finality should be determined according to the law of the State of origin. If the case file includes a document or a statement to this effect, as stipulated by Article 53(1) (b) of the Turkish PILA, the certificate should be considered final. Nevertheless, recognition of succession certificates could still be refused on other grounds. As is explained below, succession certificates concerning immovable property in Turkey are not subject to recognition based on the exclusive jurisdiction of Turkish courts over these matters.[584]

b) Conditions for Recognition under Article 58 and Article 54 of the Turkish PILA: Exclusive Jurisdiction of Turkish Courts to Issue Succession Certificates?

Article 58 of the Turkish PILA addressing recognition of foreign judgments states in its first paragraph that a foreign judgment may be treated as a final judgment or as conclusive evidence in Turkey provided that the conditions of enforcement (under Article 54 of the Turkish PILA) are satisfied. Regarding recognition, Article 54(1) (a) should not apply. This clarifies that recognition of a foreign judgment should, in principle, be governed by the conditions of enforcement with the exception of the reciprocity condition under subparagraph (a).[585]

There are then three conditions applicable for recognition of a foreign judgment according to Article 54 of the Turkish PILA, which are as follows: (a) the foreign judgment should not be on a matter falling within the scope of exclusive jurisdiction of Turkish courts or, subject to a challenge to jurisdiction raised by the defendant, have been granted by a State court exercising its jurisdiction despite there being a lack of a genuine connection between that State and either the parties or the dispute (i.e. so-called exorbitant jurisdiction); (b) the foreign judgment should not be manifestly contrary to the *ordre public*; (c) where the person against whom the recognition is sought was not

[583] Even the supporters of this view sometimes criticise the wording of Art 50 and propose an amendment to it in favour of a broader one so as to include decisions that cannot become final by their nature but are still valid according to the law of the country of their origin. See, in this regard, Ruhi and Ruhi, *Mirasçılık Belgesi* (2015) 50.

[584] Ekşi, *Milletlerarası Miras Hukuku* (2013) 133.

[585] 'Danışma Meclisi Tutanakları – Milletlerarası Özel Hukuk ve Usul Hukuku Hakkında Kanun Tasarısı ve Adalet Komisyonu Raporu (1/5)', (1981) 12 (See specifically the Preamble to Art 42 which was identical to the current Art 58).

duly summoned to the court that pronounced the judgment or was not represented at that court in accordance with the law of that State, or the judgment was given in default of his/her appearance contrary to the law of that State and this person failed to oppose the request for recognition before the Turkish court dealing with the request on the basis of these grounds. It is only where the defendant raised corresponding objections that the circumstances regarding exorbitant jurisdiction in point (a) and the violation of the right of a defence in point (c) can be considered as grounds for the refusal of recognition by the court. Other conditions should be examined by the court *ex officio*, and where they are not satisfied the request for recognition should be refused.

All of these requirements similarly apply to the recognition of foreign judgments of a non-contentious nature and, hence, succession certificates, which in principle belong to this group (Article 58(2) of the Turkish PILA). The recognition of a foreign succession certificate could be refused when any of these mandatory conditions is not satisfied. However, in practice, courts often refuse to recognise succession certificates issued outside Turkey based on the exclusive jurisdiction for immovable assets situated in Turkey.

In the first place, it should be discussed here whether jurisdiction to issue succession certificates is also governed under Article 43 of the Turkish PILA. The reason for this is that the issuance of succession certificates, as explained above, is a non-contentious proceeding in Turkish law (Article 382(1) (c) (6) of the Turkish Code of Civil Procedure), unless there was a subsequent challenge to the certificate seeking redress or modification of the certificate.[586] As Article 43, like Article 20(15) of the Treaty, refers to 'legal suits', it is accordingly argued that the issuance of succession certificates – which is in principle a non-contentious proceeding in Turkish law – is not governed under this provision and that the jurisdiction to issue succession certificates should be determined in accordance with the domestic rule of jurisdiction for non-contentious proceedings, i.e. Article 384 of the Turkish Code of Civil Procedure. Therefore, for the issuance of succession certificates, Turkish courts at the place where one of the applicants or the concerned persons are domiciled will have jurisdiction. Article 43 of the Turkish PILA will be applicable only if the proceedings concerning the succession certificate is of a contentious nature.[587]

Nevertheless, Article 43 of the Turkish PILA employs a broad formulation and does not seem to limit its scope to contentious proceedings. The jurisdic-

---

[586] Art 11(3) of the Turkish Code of Civil Procedure.

[587] Toker and Ruhi, *Milletlerarası Özel Hukuk ve Usul Hukuku Hakkında Kanun* (2019) 316–317; Özkan and Tütüncübaşı, *Uluslararası Usûl Hukuku* (2020) 85 and 197; Bilkay, (2021) 41 MHB 905, 920; Çelikel and Erdem, *Milletlerarası Özel Hukuk* (2021) 632–633; Can and Tuna, *Milletlerarası Usul Hukuku* (2022) 148; Doğan, *Milletlerarası Özel Hukuk* (2022) 67; cf. Şanlı, Esen and Ataman Figanmeşe, *Milletlerarası Özel Hukuk* (2021) 495. For a similar view, see Demir Gökyayla, 'Mirasçılık Belgeleri' (2006) 579–580; Demirkol, *Yetki Anlaşmaları* (2018) 23–24; Tekinalp, *Milletlerarası Özel Hukuk* (2020) 411.

tion to issue succession certificates in cases with foreign elements should also be covered under this provision.[588] When the last domicile of the deceased was located outside Turkey and he did not have assets in Turkey, opening the jurisdiction of Turkish courts (which are situated in places where one of the applicants or concerned persons are domiciled) to issue a succession certificate may result in exorbitant jurisdiction. This place has, indeed, no genuine link with the dispute. It is often the case in practice that even the applicants in such proceedings are outside Turkey.[589] Thus, the jurisdiction to issue succession certificates in cross-border cases should also be determined pursuant to Article 43 of the Turkish PILA.

Although it is discussed within the context of Article 43 of the Turkish PILA whether Turkish courts have exclusive jurisdiction in succession cases, particularly for succession matters on immovable properties located in Turkey, as noted above,[590] this is also considered to be the case for the issuance of succession certificates.[591]

As explained above, it is believed that the exclusivity of a jurisdictional rule in cross-border cases should be determined particularly under the guidance of its *ratio legis*. Thus, a jurisdictional rule in a transnational context is often considered exclusive when it has been laid down with the purpose of making Turkey the sole forum for a particular matter based on the importance of that matter, notwithstanding the absence of express wording to that effect. In the light of this, it is believed that the *raison d'être* of Article 43 of the Turkish PILA is to confer jurisdiction to Turkish courts in transnational suc-

---

[588] Ekşi, *Milletlerarası Miras Hukuku* (2013) 28; Baran Çelik, (2019) 24 DÜHFD 439, 450–451; Güngör, *Türk Milletlerarası Özel Hukuku* (2021) 258; Pürselim, (2021) 9 KHASHFD 179, 187; Tanrıbilir, 'Kişi Halleri ve Mirasa İlişkin Milletlerarası Yetki Kurallarının Kapsamı' (2021) 93 ff; cf. Tütüncübaşı, *Yabancı Çekişmesiz Yargı Kararlarının Tanınması* (2014) 159; Süzen, *Tanıma ve Tenfiz Davalarında Yetki Denetimi* (2016) 60.

See also, at the time of the former Turkish PILA, Şanlı, 'Veraset İlamı' (1990) 300; Demir Gökyayla, 'Mirasçılık Belgeleri' (2006) 575 and 581.

See, in the same direction, Yargıtay 14. Hukuk Dairesi, T. 1.6.2015, E. 2015/1997 K. 2015/6013 <https://karararama.yargitay.gov.tr> accessed 13 February 2021; cf. Yargıtay 20. Hukuk Dairesi, T. 4.4.2016, E. 2016/1359 K. 2016/3918 <https://legalbank.net/> accessed 25 June 2018.

[589] Tanrıbilir, 'MÖHUK ve Mirasa İlişkin Bağlama Kuralının Uygulanmasında Öne Çıkan Hususlar' (2018) 135.

Even domestic rules of jurisdiction are criticised for being too broad: Kurşat, *Terekenin Korunması Önlemleri* (2010) 275.

[590] See above pp 234–243.

[591] See, particularly in the context of succession certificates, Şanlı, 'Veraset İlamı' (1990) 300–301; Ekşi, *Milletlerarası Miras Hukuku* (2013) 140 ff; Tütüncübaşı, *Yabancı Çekişmesiz Yargı Kararlarının Tanınması* (2014) 159; Süzen, *Tanıma ve Tenfiz Davalarında Yetki Denetimi* (2016) 60 and 65–67; Özkan and Tütüncübaşı, *Uluslararası Usûl Hukuku* (2020) 199; Bilkay, (2021) 41 MHB 905, 923; Pürselim, (2021) 9 KHASHFD 179, 190–191.

cession proceedings involving properties situated in Turkey, and, hence, it does not be interpreted as an exclusive rule of jurisdiction. This also applies for the jurisdiction to issue succession certificates.[592]

However, in practice, the first view is adopted and recognition of foreign succession certificates concerning immovable properties situated in Turkey is also refused due to the fact that the jurisdiction of Turkish courts in succession matters involving immovables in the territory is exclusive.[593]

Under these conditions, therefore, even if the parties seek the recognition of an ECS, or a national certificate to this effect, recognition in Turkey will be refused because either the issuing authority is not a court; such a certificate is not final; or, particularly when the certificate relates to an immovable part of the estate located in Turkey, Turkish courts are the courts exclusively empowered to deal with succession matters on these assets, including the issuing of a succession certificate. Therefore, the parties should apply for the issuance of a succession certificate in Turkey.

As explained before, notaries are not competent to issue succession certificates for cases involving foreign elements. Thus, the application should, pursuant to Article 43 of the Turkish PILA, be lodged before the courts of the place where the deceased had his last domicile in Turkey, or failing that, before the courts of the place (or one of the places) where the assets of the deceased are situated.[594] In terms of subject-matter jurisdiction, provisions of the Turkish Code of Civil Procedure will find application. As the issuance of a succession certificate is a proceeding of a non-contentious nature, civil courts of peace ('Sulh Hukuk Mahkemeleri') have subject-matter jurisdiction according to Article 383 of the Turkish Code of Civil Procedure and Article 598(1) of the Turkish Civil Code.[595] When the validity of a succession

---

[592] See, particularly in the context of succession certificates, Demir Gökyayla, 'Mirasçılık Belgeleri' (2006) 575; Tanrıbilir, 'MÖHUK ve Mirasa İlişkin Bağlama Kuralının Uygulanmasında Öne Çıkan Hususlar' (2018) 137–138.

[593] Yargıtay 2. Hukuk Dairesi, T. 10.2.1986, E. 1986/808 K. 1986/1284 <http://www.kazanci.com> accessed 20 June 2017; Yargıtay 2. Hukuk Dairesi, T. 11.6.1990, E. 1990/12861 K. 1990/5906 published in Sakmar, Ekşi and Yılmaz, *Milletlerarası Özel Hukuk ve Usul Hukuku Hakkında Kanun Mahkeme Kararları* (2001) 354–355; Yargıtay Hukuk Genel Kurulu, T. 24.10.2001, E. 2001/2-922 K. 2001/746 <http://www.kazanci.com> accessed 22 June 2021; Yargıtay 2. Hukuk Dairesi, T. 12.7.2002, E. 2002/8254 K. 2002/9339 <http://www.kazanci.com> accessed 2 July 2017; Yargıtay 8. Hukuk Dairesi, T. 17.10.2014, E. 2013/23629, K. 2014/18556 <http://www.kazanci.com> accessed 20 June 2017.

[594] See, for views advocating the applicability of Art 11 of the Turkish Code of Civil Procedure, above p 184.

[595] According to Article 25(1) of the Cadastral Law (*Resmi Gazete* of 9.7.1987, no 19512), when there is a succession case involving an immovable pending before a cadastral court, the succession certificate may also be requested from this court. See, for more information on this, İyilikli, (2017) 5 UMD 281, 292–293; Baran Çelik, (2019) 24 DÜHFD 439, 446.

certificate is challenged and its content will be of contentious nature, first instance civil courts ('Asliye Hukuk Mahkemeleri') will be competent.[596]

Succession certificates issued outside Turkey, whether issued by courts or by other authorities, are authentic instruments and, hence, could be submitted as *rebuttable* evidence to prove kinship and succession rights during the proceedings taking place in Turkey – after they have been duly legalised in line with the procedure applicable.[597] The Turkish court will then not need to order parties to bring civil registration records to prove their status.[598] This should also be applicable for an ECS obtained from Member State courts.[599] Although Article 74 of the Regulation provides that for the use of the ECS in other Member States neither legalisation nor any other formality is needed, Member States should apply legalisation procedures when there is a request from the parties to use to the ECS in Turkey or, in general, outside the EU.[600]

2. *Recognition of an ECS under the Treaty?*

When examining the recognition of an ECS, or even of a German 'Erbschein', it is also appropriate to mention the role of the Treaty in this context. This is because Article 20(17) of the Treaty provides that 'a certificate of a legal relationship relating to succession (on the movable part of the estate), particularly on the status as well as the rights (or powers) of an heir, legatee or an executor of the will, issued by the national State of the deceased in accordance with the law applicable in that State, is sufficient to prove this legal relationship in the other Contracting State. The attestation by a consul or a diplomatic representative of the national State of the deceased should be sufficient to prove the authenticity of the certificate'.

It is opined that this provision does not state that the succession certificates issued by one Contracting State will be *recognised* in the other Contracting State. It rather speaks for the extension of the evidentiary effects of a succession certificate on the movable part of the estate in the other Contracting State without going to a recognition procedure. The meaning of this is that a succession certificate or a comparable document issued in Germany or, *vice versa*, in Turkey (as the national State of the deceased) by the competent authorities could be used before the Turkish courts or authorities regarding this estate to invoke the status, rights, and/or powers of his heirs, legatees,

---

[596] Aras, (2016) 7 İnÜHFD 65, 68; İyilikli, (2017) 5 UMD 281, 327; Baran Çelik, (2019) 24 DÜHFD 439, 452–453.

[597] For the procedure, see above pp 302–303.

[598] V. R. Seviğ, *Mirasla İlgili Devletler Hususi Hukuku Kaideleri* (1963) 192–193; Şanlı, 'Veraset İlamı' (1990) 305–306; cf. Kurşat, *Terekenin Korunması Önlemleri* (2010) 356.

[599] Ekşi, 'Comparison of the Turkish PILA with the ESR' (2014) 151; Giray, (2016) 9 Anali PFZE 235, 244.

[600] Cf. Sirmen, 'Avrupa Mirasçılık Belgesi' (2016) 573.

and executors of testaments on movable properties before the courts of the other Contracting Party, after being authenticated by the consular staff or the diplomatic representatives of the national State of the deceased. The certificate will only have evidentiary effects, and the scope of this will be decided in accordance with the law of the State where the certificate is presented. A succession certificate from Germany can only be considered as rebuttable evidence in Turkey, as Turkish succession certificates have the same status (Article 598(3) of the Turkish Civil Code).[601]

It seems that this rule can also be used for the ECS, as the provision speaks of succession certificates issued by the national State of the deceased pursuant to *the laws in force* in that State. As the Regulation is now part of the German legal system, an ECS issued in Germany could be used in Turkey.[602] However, only ECSs for the movable property of a German national in Turkey would fall into the scope of this provision. Although the ECS is equipped with wider effects within the EU under Article 69 of the Regulation, it will have evidentiary effects with a rebuttable nature in Turkey.

C. Concluding Remarks on Procedural Issues

Jurisdiction rules of States adopt, in the light of their policy interests, a wide range of grounds to assert jurisdiction over private law matters, based on the territorial or personal connections that the parties or the subject matter of the dispute has with that State. As an inevitable corollary of such distinct approaches, we often face problems of overlapping jurisdiction in the international arena unless there are universal rules or, at least, rules that are uniformly applicable in more than one State.[603] This is also the situation with respect to succession matters arising in the Turkish-EU context.

---

[601] LG München I 25.10.2011 – 28 O 243/10, ZEV 2012, 596; H. Krüger, 'Studien über Probleme des türkischen Internationalen Erbrechts' (2006) 155; Ekşi, *Milletlerarası Miras Hukuku* (2013) 95–96; Nomer, *Milletlerarası Usul Hukuku* (2018) 224–225; Atalı, *Internationale Zuständigkeit* (2001) 123; Pürselim, (2011) 31 MHB 243, 254–255; cf. Altınkaya, *Mirasçılık Belgesi* (2021) 36; Bilkay, (2021) 41 MHB 905, 910; Spelsberg-Korspeter, (2017) Deutsch-türkisches Nachlassabkommen para 35.

See also Dörner, *Staudinger BGB* (2007) EGBGB Vorb. zu Art 25 f para 189; Kurt Siehr, 'Ausländischer Erbschein für Nachlass in Deutschland? (zu LG München, 25.10.2011 – 28 O 243/10)' [2013] IPRax 241, 244; Looschelders, 'The External Relations of Germany' (2019) 169; Katharina Dorth, *Das Verhältnis von Erbschein und Europäischem Nachlasszeugnis* (Nomos 2019) 95–96; Dutta, *MüKoBGB* (2020) EuErbVO Art 75 para 29.

[602] Dutta, *MüKoBGB* (2020) EuErbVO Art 69 para 6; contra Z. Kaya, [2015] ZEV 208, 214.

[603] Mills, (2014) 84 BYIL 187, 208.

In order to achieve full-fledged uniform rules within the Union, the Regulation leaves no room for national jurisdiction rules of Member States – which, in the view of the Union, could have caused friction and difficulties – and regulates the allocation of jurisdiction between the Member State courts not only for succession cases that are closely connected to the territory of the Member States but to the world beyond the Union.[604] As a novelty in the field of succession, especially in comparison to the domestic rules of the vast majority of the Member States which were subsequently replaced, the Regulation adopts habitual residence, based on the principle of unity of succession (just as in the conflict of laws), as a general head of jurisdiction under Article 4.[605] However, with an eye to the underlying policy of opening the doors of 'European justice' to its citizens in all possible scenarios, it deviates from its key concept, i.e. the unity of succession, and adopts subsidiary grounds of jurisdiction under Article 10 for cases where the deceased's last habitual residence was in a third State but he remained closely connected to the Union due either to his national bonds with a Member State, his previous habitual residence in a Member State, or even his assets in a Member State.[606]

It is obvious from the above analysis that the European side pursues a purely European policy to achieve a full harmonisation of its jurisdictional rules for succession. The Turkish side, on the other hand, changed its traditional approach of jurisdiction based on nationality and a differentiation of the movable and immovable parts of the deceased's estate (Article 4 of the Temporary Act). It now follows the solution of its national civil procedure law and espouses domicile as the general head of jurisdiction for succession as a whole under Article 43 of the Turkish PILA. However, the experience with the approach of national civil procedure law showed, over the years, that the exercise of jurisdiction in cross-border succession matters was not possible in cases where the deceased had not established a domicile in Turkey or where he had changed it long before his death but still had a close link to Turkey by having assets there. Therefore, the Turkish legislature also laid down a residual ground of jurisdiction under the same provision and provided that the *forum rei sitae* should have jurisdiction in such cases.[607]

Although this approach, first introduced in 1982 as part of the former Turkish PILA, is obviously different from the traditional one found in the Temporary Act, that latter era's notion that jurisdiction to rule on immovable assets found within the territory of Turkey should rest exlusively with Turkish

---

[604] Davì, *Calvo Caravaca/Davì/Mansel* (2016) Introduction para 23.

[605] Re, [2018] RDIPP 978, 978–979.

[606] Davì, *Calvo Caravaca/Davì/Mansel* (2016) Introduction para 31.

[607] İstanbul Üniversitesi Hukuk Fakültesi – Milletlerarası Hukuk ve Milletlerarası Münasebetler Enstitüsü, *MÖHUK Öntasarı Sempozyumu* (1978) 194–195.

courts is an idea that continues to be embraced by the majority of legal scholars and put into practice by the courts.

The interplay between the approaches of both sides may unsurprisingly trigger an overlap of jurisdiction in different scenarios. Although the Regulation and the Turkish PILA adopt two similar connecting factors for the general head of jurisdiction in cross-border succession disputes, there may often be complex cases in which both sides consider themselves competent. The conflicts may also arise as a result of one side exercising jurisdiction based on its general jurisdiction rule while the other side assumes jurisdiction on a subsidiary ground of jurisdiction, for instance, in the case of a deceased who was habitually resident in an EU State but who left assets in Turkey or, *vice versa*, a deceased who was domiciled in Turkey but who owned assets in the Union. It is even possible that subsidiary grounds of jurisdiction may themselves give rise to overlaps in some scenarios. Particularly considering that the European side even covers cases which are more closely connected to a third State and requires Member State courts to assume jurisdiction in such cases under its Article 10, the number of conflicts may be high.[608] Further, the problem becomes much more complicated due to the Turkish side's claim of exclusive (indirect) jurisdiction over immovables located in Turkey.[609]

These conflicts may be important for legal practice due to the mobility of people between the Union and Turkey, especially the Turkish migrants who have connections to both sides. For this reason, it may be desirable, at least to a certain extent, to avoid such conflicts with the help of coordination rules. International procedural law has, indeed, developed coordination rules to overcome or at least to minimise the problem of overlapping jurisdictions by allowing the relevant parties to choose the jurisdiction where they may want to bring their case, by deferring action in favour of another jurisdiction where the case is more appropriately heard, or by staying proceedings because a court of another jurisdiction was first seised of the dispute.[610] The Regulation actually adopted such rules but only from an *internal* perspective which do not apply in relation to third States. In the same vein, no rules to this end exist on the Turkish side. The only rule which could be of some help for Turkish-EU successions is the potential limitation of proceedings under Article 12 of the Regulation. Despite the fact that it may not eliminate all possible jurisdictional conflicts, it is still be considered as a positive development from the Turkish perspective, particularly in the absence of any coordination rules in Turkey. Article 12 could at least provide a solution for recognition and enforcement problems which may possibly arise as a consequence of the exclusive jurisdiction

---

608 Bonomi, 'Switzerland' (2019) 279.

609 See above pp 234–243.

610 Mills, (2014) 84 BYIL 187, 208.

of Turkish courts for immovable estate assets in Turkey, and it could even function as a *lis pendens* rule when there are parallel proceedings.

A single rule is undoubtedly insufficient to overcome all issues respecting jurisdiction in the Turkey-EU context. To this end, it could be proposed that the Member State courts should reflexively apply Article 5 and Article 6 of the Regulation in third State related cases. Due to the fact that Turkish law neither recognises the right of the deceased to choose the law applicable to succession nor allows parties to designate the court to hear their succession matter, such a reflexive application will have an effect only where Turkish courts already have jurisdiction over the case under Article 43 of the Turkish PILA, and thus it does not seem defensible from the Turkish (and, hence, from the Union) perspective. Another means to bring coordination between the rules of both jurisdictions may be *lis pendens* and related actions rules. Whilst the Regulation, unlike the Brussels I (recast) Regulation, contains no rules of those kind *vis-à-vis* third States, it is maintained that Member States may refer to their national rules to prevent parallel proceedings with third States. This would indeed be helpful in bringing a level of coordination to the rules of both jurisdictions from the Turkish perspective, which does not have any rule on international *lis pendens* and related actions rules. However, express provisions as in the Brussels I (recast) Regulation seem to be much more desirable to guarantee a uniform application, and it is hoped that the European legislature will introduce such rules in the further amendments.

On the other side of the picture, from the aspect of coordination rules, a rule on *lis pendens* should be introduced in a future amendment of the Turkish PILA. Until that time, however, taking parallel proceedings into account on a case-by-case basis is advisable if it is expected that the judgment to be rendered by the foreign court will be subject to recognition and, if applicable, enforcement in Turkey; and if the proceedings before the foreign court are likely to be concluded within a reasonable time. This is obviously important in overcoming the difficulties arising as a result of concurrent jurisdiction in succession cases, but, in a more general sense, it is important for all private law cases arising in cross-border context. Another recommendation for the Turkish side, particularly for succession cases, should be to not consider jurisdiction over immovables as exclusive, which, as will be seen below, is much more problematic as regards succession certificates.[611]

The only full coordination between the two systems is currently reached through the bilateral treaties between Turkey and, from the Member States, Germany, Italy, and Hungary. As the most practically relevant, we have examined the jurisdiction rule of the Turkish-German Treaty. The Treaty follows a

---

[611] For a view arguing that there is a need for a legal reform or a change of interpretation (by the Court of Cassation) which will clarify the exclusive nature of Article 43 of the Turkish PILA, see Bilkay, (2021) 41 MHB 905, 928.

very traditional approach, one different from the jurisdictional rules of the Regulation and the Turkish PILA, and submits issues of succession on movable property to the courts of the national State of the deceased, and on immovable property to the *forum rei sitae*. Based on the historical and legal background of the rule, both heads of jurisdiction have an exclusive nature. It is obvious that especially in terms of jurisdiction, the scissionist approach is outdated in the face of the current rules in both legal systems. Furthermore, the size of the group which could be possibly affected from the exclusive nature of the jurisdiction rule, particularly in the context of movables, is undoubtedly larger today than at the time when the Treaty was concluded. Turkish nationals who have spent most of their lives in Germany – representing a substantial number of people – must travel back to Turkey merely to claim, for instance, an amount of money in a bank account that was inherited from a recently deceased close relative. Thus, at least a reform on this rule is needed considering the current legal and social situation.

Within its 'all-inclusive' rules, the Regulation also creates a uniform succession certificate, namely the ECS, for the free circulation of succession titles, rights, and powers throughout the Union. Whereas it is designed to be an intra-Union document, it seems to raise two important questions from a Turkish perspective. In the first place, what will occur when Turkish nationals in Germany, whose succession cases are covered by the Turkish-German Succession Treaty, avail themselves of the Certificate to certify their status, rights, and powers in other Member States. This is of utmost significance given that the approach of the Treaty is starkly different from that of the Regulation. When an ECS is issued in Germany for Turkish nationals to be used in other Member States, the law applicable to assets in Germany will be determined in accordance with the Treaty, whilst succession matters for assets located in other Member States will be governed by the rules of the Regulation. The part of the estate situated in Germany, therefore, will be under the authority of a 'wrong' law within the eyes of other Member States. Should the ECS be issued in another European State, the law applicable to the succession as a whole is to be determined pursuant to the Regulation without taking into account the rules of the Treaty, as the Treaty between Turkey and Germany does not bind that State. The law governing the German part of the estate, in this case, will be 'wrong' from the perspective of Germany. To eliminate such friction within the borders of the Union, it is highly likely that two different certificates, i.e. a German 'Erbschein' for the part of the case falling within the scope of the Treaty and an ECS for the part which is not covered by the Treaty, will need to be issued. Turkish nationals would then have to deal with two different procedures in such cases. This seems to be an area in which the existence of the Treaty poses problems for Turkish nationals, and neither the European legislature nor the German legislature, as the Contracting Party of the Treaty, have clarified the setting.

The second question within the context of the ECS is whether the ECS will be subject to recognition in Turkey. This is a question to be evaluated in line with the recognition and enforcement rules of the Turkish PILA. Under the Turkish PILA, Turkish courts can only recognise judgments issued by *courts* that are *final*; and that are on the *matters* not falling within the *exclusive* jurisdiction of Turkish courts. Thus, under these conditions, an ECS issued by a Member State court or an authority will not be recognised in Turkey. The parties have to make another application for the issuing of a Turkish succession certificate to prove their titles, rights, and powers in Turkey. The only effect that can be given to the ECS – or to any other comparable documents of Member States – in Turkey is to receive them as *rebuttable* evidence in the relevant proceedings when parties submit them.

In terms of finality, a problem potentially arises in that a succession certificate can be challenged at any time even in a purely domestic context. However, in the presence of Article 58(2) of the Turkish PILA, in which the legislature clearly provided that court orders of a non-contentious nature are to be *recognised* in accordance with the same procedure for decisions rendered at the end of contentious proceedings, it does not seem plausible to argue that the recognition of succession certificates is foreclosed by virtue of their not being final. Therefore, consistent with the aim of Article 58(2) of the Turkish PILA, in which the legislature also emphasised that procedural finality is sufficient for recognition under the preamble to Article 54 of the Turkish PILA, succession certificates issued by courts outside Turkey, including the ECS, should be considered subject to recognition provided that the other prerequisites for recognition under the Turkish PILA are satisfied.

As explained earlier, it is believed that the recognition of such certificates, in particular those certifying succession rights on immovable property in Turkey, cannot be refused on the grounds that all the matters concerning immovable properties, even the issuance of a succession certificate, are within the exclusive jurisdiction of Turkish courts. This is first because the *ratio legis* of Article 43 of the Turkish PILA does not suggest that jurisdiction under this provision should be exclusive, given that it sets out cascading grounds for jurisdiction and does not differentiate between succession matters on movable and immovable properties. Even though there are restrictions applicable for foreign nationals on the *acquisition* of immovables in Turkey, they do not directly deprive them of their *capacity* to inherit. It is also obvious, at least when comparing the earlier versions of Article 35 of the Land Registry Law to its current wording, that there has been a change of the policy of the Turkish State towards this issue. Thus, the fact that restrictions apply on the acquisition of immovable property by foreign nationals does not constitute a strong argument for the exclusive nature of jurisdiction.

Allowing recognition of succession certificates – which, in our view, would be the correct interpretation of the rules of the Turkish PILA – may give rise to forum (and law) shopping if the law applicable under the Regulation is more favourable for a party than the law applicable under the Turkish PILA. Such a possibility, however, is not very high for the ECS. This is because in most of the Member States other authorities, e.g. notaries, have competence to issue succession certificates,[612] and their recognition is not possible under the current rules of the Turkish PILA. Yet the lack of a provision in this regard would seem to be problematic for legal practice. Therefore, it is advisable that a future reform include a general recognition mechanism for authentic instruments which could also be applied for succession certificates of this kind.[613] Although this may, within the context of the ECS and other foreign succession certificates, extend the potential scope of forum shopping, the risk of forum shopping should not be an argument for recognition antagonism in a general sense.

For cases within the scope of the Treaty, the situation is different. Article 20(17) of the Treaty creates a possibility whereby the heirs, legatees, and testamentary executors of a German deceased can prove their status in succession matters with a German 'Erbschein' or with an ECS in Turkey. These certificates, nevertheless, can produce only evidentiary effects of a rebuttable nature in Turkey.

---

[612] See above n 529, p 300.

[613] Ekşi, *Milletlerarası Miras Hukuku* (2013) 115; Sirmen, 'Avrupa Mirasçılık Belgesi' (2016) 573.

Conclusion

European private international law was once described as a 'jungle that can confuse even Europeans and an outsider without guidance may easily become lost'.[1] It is undoubted that the existence of divergent conflict-of-laws rules in Member States was among the reasons that turned European private international law into a 'jungle'. Harmonisation efforts, therefore, have been initiated in order to eliminate difficulties that are faced in cross-border cases by virtue of this diversity. One of the latest areas subject to harmonisation has been the law of succession.[2] The diversity, however, still exists with the outside world because the bilateral treaties of Member States preceding the Succession Regulation are still applicable and because the harmonising effect of the Regulation is limited to the Member States. The above analysis indicates that this disconsonant state also describes Turkish-EU successions.

If there is for the sake of decisional harmony a wish to avoid the divergence (at least to a certain degree), the first solution may be to eliminate the treaties – such as the Turkish German Treaty on which the present study has mainly focussed. Indeed, the discussion above clearly demonstrates that the Treaty, which is a reflection of the time in which it was drafted, has outdated rules from the perspective of the Regulation – and, to some extent, from the perspective of the Turkish PILA as well. It perpetuates the scissionist approach, the exclusive jurisdiction approach (even for succession matters involving movable property), and it has rules which do not take into account all aspects of succession cases arising today, as is the case, for example, with the rule on the law applicable to the formal validity of testamentary dispositions, a rule having a considerably limited scope in comparison with the Hague Form Convention. There is no doubt that the Treaty presents certain challenges for the people covered by it. Nonetheless, it still guarantees a level coordination within Turkish-EU successions (between Turkey and Germany), particularly considering that Turkey still continues to retain its traditional under-

[1] Mathias Reimann, *Conflict of Laws in Western Europe: A Guide through the Jungle* (Transnational Publishers 1995) xxi.

[2] Although the adoption of the Regulation has been an important development for the Union, there is also need for the harmonisation of substantive succession law within the EU for full integration. In this regard, see for example, Załucki, 'The Future of Succession Law in the EU' (2018) 581 ff.

standing regarding the applicable law and jurisdiction for succession on immovable property situated in its territory. In addition, it should not be forgotten that the Succession Treaty is an annex of the Consular Treaty between Turkey and Germany, which addresses many issues regarding consular rights and functions. Accordingly, one can ask whether it would be a wise political decision to terminate the Treaty on account of its possessing a handful of annexed succession law provisions that are inconsistent with the EU's Succession Regulation and its harmonised rules on private international law and civil procedure – and that are inconsistent with certain rules of Turkish law.[3] A reform of the Treaty rules, however, should be considered so as to make them more suitable for the circumstances of our world today.[4]

In terms of the tension between the Regulation and Turkish private international law on succession, it is argued above that there some elements that should be reformed in the Turkish PILA. In the first place, it is believed that there needs to be a reassessment of the *situs* rule, both in terms of its use in finding the law applicable to succession and in concluding that the jurisdiction to rule on succession should exclusively belong to Turkish courts when the proceedings involve realty in Turkey, this being a rule which, though rooted in the feudal era, 'has firmly been imbedded into the conscience of [every Turkish judge]'[5] for decades. Although the State has a legitimate interest in terms of realty, particularly as regards its acquisition and transfer, this does not justify that every matter, even the issuance of a succession certificate, should be *exclusively* governed by Turkish law and settled by Turkish courts. Furthermore, the interest of the State in preserving the integrity of the recording system, which is argued to be one of the main reasons behind the exclusive jurisdiction rule, will be satisfied by the conducting of recognition procedures before Turkish courts as well as by the subsequent procedures undertaken at the Turkish title registry, where decisions will be made on the face of a recognised judgment or certificate of succession.[6] During the recognition procedures, the restrictions applicable to foreign nationals on the acquisition of immovables, which are considered as overriding mandatory provisions,

---

[3] Kohler, 'Die künftige EuErbVO und die Staatsverträge mit Drittstaaten' (2011) 126; Wurmnest, 'Comparative Report and Policy Perspectives' (2019) 351.

It is also argued that a complete termination of the treaties may not be a wise solution from the perspective of the Member States which are party to them, as their citizens will no longer be able to enjoy the protection attributed to them in Contracting third States with these treaties: Rylski, (2020) 26 PPPM 91, 97 (in relation to the treaties of Poland).

[4] Güneş, 'The Relations of Turkey with EU Member States' (2019) 315–316; cf. Dutta, 'The Perspective of the European Union' (2019) 323 ff; Wurmnest, 'Comparative Report and Policy Perspectives' (2019) 353 ff; Bilkay, (2021) 41 MHB 905, 910–911. In relation to the treaties of Poland, see also Rylski, (2020) 26 PPPM 91, 103.

[5] Symeonides, (1987) 47 La L Rev 1029, 1092.

[6] Cf. Symeonides, (1987) 47 La L Rev 1029, 1091.

could be evaluated within the light of the *ordre public* exception.[7] It should also be borne in mind that these restrictions are related only to the transfer of title on these assets and not to the right to inherit. The policy of the State concerning these restrictions has also liberalised over time, which is evident in the current version of the provisions in the Land Registry Law. All these facts require that the traditional understanding be re-evaluated. Decisional harmony, not only within the Union but also with other States, can only be provided when States do not insist on the application of the forum's law and exclusive jurisdiction.[8] This could be achieved with a change of interpretation and practice as regards procedural issues, i.e. a change related to jurisdiction and the recognition of succession certificates as well as judgments.[9] In terms of conflict-of-laws rules, however, a reform is needed.

Moreover, a change of interpretation as to the *finality* requirement on the recognition and enforcement of non-contentious decisions would also eliminate the problem at the stage of recognition of foreign succession certificates. The only step that needs to be taken is to interpret the rule in accordance with the intent of the legislature, which is clearly indicated under Article 58 of the Turkish PILA, providing that decisions of a non-contentious nature should be governed by the same procedure as set out in the preamble of the Turkish PILA. For the recognition of succession certificates issued by other authorities, however, the Turkish PILA needs a general provision allowing for the recognition of all administrative documents, including succession certificates.

Last but not least, another aspect of the Turkish PILA which calls for an introduction of a new provision relates to *lis pendens*. This is not only of practical significance for Turkish-EU successions but rather for all cross-border cases. *Lis pendens* is a very important tool to provide a level coordination of the cross-border cases which frequently arise in today's world.

One may expect that the adoption of the Regulation and its increasing implementation may put pressure on third States to reconsider their positions.[10] The Regulation, in fact, prompted a reform of the provisions of Section 6 of the Swiss PILA in order to bring a certain level of harmonisation between the rules in pursuit of decisional harmony.[11] The harmonisation created by the Regulation was seen as an opportunity by the Swiss legislature to minimise conflicts in the field of cross-border Swiss-EU successions and thereby to

---

7 Demir Gökyayla, 'Mirasçılık Belgeleri' (2006) 577–578.
Judgments which violate overriding mandatory provisions of Turkey cannot be recognised in Turkey if they also violate public policy: Demir Gökyayla, *Tanıma ve Tenfiz'de Kamu Düzeni* (2001) 278–280.

8 Cf. Tanrıbilir, *Kanuni Mirasçılıktan Doğan Kanunlar İhtilafı* (2000) 99.

9 Cf. Bilkay, (2021) 41 MHB 905, 928.

10 Cf. Dutta, (2009) 73 RabelsZ 547, 564.

11 'Änderung des Bundesgesetzes über das Internationale Privatrecht (Erbrecht) – Erläuternder Bericht zum Vernehmlassungsentwurf', (2018) 8, no 1.3.

achieve a higher degree of legal certainty and foreseeable estate planning for Swiss nationals or domiciliaries.[12] First of all, a possible EU-Swiss convention on the issue was debated.[13] However, this was rejected in the Swiss parliament on the grounds that such a solution in the field of succession law did not seem to be feasible at the time.[14] After the refusal, there commenced a reform process on the provisions of Section 6 of the Swiss PILA concerning succession.[15]

It is a truism that legal developments in the European Union have also been a catalyst a truism during the enactment process of new laws and contributed to the legal discussions in Turkish academic literature. Nevertheless, in the field of succession law, an area which is coded in the culture and history of the society and which often involves immovable estate assets located in Turkey, such a change cannot easily be made. This is also evident from the fact that no plans to reform the Turkish PILA have as yet been announced. The Regulation did not arouse much interest in the literature. Nonetheless, in today's globalised world, it is a common practice even for non-professionals to possess multiple nationalities or domiciles and to acquire properties in different countries. As a consequence, it is undoubted that the number of succession cases having connections to more than one State has increased and that it will continue to increase in the near future, and this will eventually require a change in, among other areas, the field of private international law on succession. It is hoped that in realising such changes, a level of convergence can be achieved with other States – more importantly with European States – in cross-border successions.

Instead of putting pressure on third States and waiting for each of them to bring their laws in line with the Regulation, it would be more desirable that the Union, which acts on behalf of an important number of States, should take the initiative in this regard and attempt to bring about a level of harmony also with third States. This is because the decisional harmony which once existed between the Member States and the Turkish PILA – through the prevalence of the nationality connecting factor in the field of succession – seems to have

---

[12] 'Änderung des Bundesgesetzes über das Internationale Privatrecht (Erbrecht) – Erläuternder Bericht zum Vernehmlassungsentwurf', (2018) 8 no 1.1.4.

[13] For such a view, see Romano, (2015–2016) XVII YbPIL 253, 287 ff.

[14] For more information on the process, see <https://www.parlament.ch/centers/kb/Documents/2014/Kommissionsbericht_RK-N_14.4285_2015-08-28.pdf> accessed 20 July 2018. See also Romano, (2015–2016) XVII YbPIL 253, 289 fn 146.

[15] For more information on the process and its motives, see 'Änderung des Bundesgesetzes über das Internationale Privatrecht (Erbrecht) – Erläuternder Bericht zum Vernehmlassungsentwurf', (2018). For the text of the draft, see Entwurf des Bundesamts für Justiz für das Bundesgesetz über das Internationale Privatrecht (IPRG), BBl 2020 3353. For the general content and a short critique of Working Paper no COO.2180.109.7.164594/233.1/2015/00008, preceding the preliminary draft, see Peter Picht and Goran Studen, 'Die Schweiz will ihre Rechtsregeln für grenzüberschreitende Erbfälle reformieren – Anpassung an die EU-Rechtslage' [2016] Successio 318.

been distorted with the new regime of the Regulation, which puts the connecting factor of habitual residence at the centre. A level of harmony in Turkish-EU successions can be provided only through *renvoi* under Article 34(1) of the Regulation – if, of course, it is applied correctly by the Member State courts[16] – and by a *professio iuris* made by the deceased (particularly but not limited to Turkish nationals) pursuant to Article 22 of the Regulation, although such a choice will not be valid in Turkey. At the conflict-of-laws level, these are the only possibilities to safeguard the harmony between Turkey and the EU and, hence, should be seen as positive developments.

More important, however, is the harmony which is needed at the procedural level, which in fact opens the door to conflict-of-laws provisions in the first place. Although the habitual residence factor in general jurisdiction is a policy choice of the Union which should be respected, it is highly likely that it may give rise to jurisdiction conflicts with third States in cases having third country elements. The situation seems to be more complex between Turkey and the EU, given the approach of the Turkish side to the interpretation of domicile and given the adherence to a legal and technical interpretation of habitual residence in recent case law of the EU.[17] Even if the Member State courts conclude that the habitual residence of the deceased at the time of death was outside the EU, the courts of the Member States where the assets of the estate are located will still have jurisdiction to rule on the succession *as a whole* (even on assets located in third States) according to Article 10(1) of the Regulation. This is another and even more important source of possible jurisdiction conflicts between third States, Turkey in our case, and Member States. Notwithstanding this, the coordination rules of the Regulation place much weight on preventing internal conflicts and mostly disregard such conflicts with the outside world. The only provision in this regard is Article 12 of the Regulation, but it only applies upon the application of the parties and on a discretionary basis which may not guarantee coordination.

Other coordination possibilities, choice of court agreements (Article 5), *forum non conveniens* (Articles 6 and 7), and *lis pendens* along with related rules (Articles 17 and 18) are unfortunately not applicable – at least not according to the wording of the rules[18] – in cases related to third States. Even though neither a *professio iuris* nor a *professio fori* is possible for succession cases in Turkey, an extension of the rules for choice of court agreements and *forum non conveniens* (Articles 5–7) *vis-à-vis* third State courts could have provided a level of convergence in Turkey-related cases. In the absence of rules to avoid parallel proceedings on the Turkish side, a more important

---

[16] See above p 154, n 486.

[17] See above pp 202–204.

[18] For comments advocating a reflexive application of these rules, see above pp 246 ff, 256 ff, and 260 ff.

level of coordination could have been guaranteed if the EU side had adopted such rules, especially the *lis pendens* rule, also within the context of third-country related cases. It is believed that these rules of the Regulation call for a reconsideration from a third State perspective in future amendments. It seems that this would also further the interests of the EU as judicial cooperation would be improved by its extension to third countries. Such a third-country-friendly approach by the Union may also be more influential in encouraging judicial reforms in third countries.[19]

[19] Cf. Alexander Trunk and Nikitas Hatzimihail, 'Conclusions' in Alexander Trunk and Nikitas Hatzimihail (eds), *EU Civil Procedure Law and Third Countries* (Nomos 2021) 279.

Bibliography

Abadan Unat, Nermin, 'Turkey: Late Entrant into Europe's Work Force' in Daniel Kubat (ed), *The Politics of Migration Policies: Settlement and Integration – The First World into the 1990s* (2nd edn, Center for Migration Studies 1993), 307–336.

– *Turks in Europe: From Guest Worker to Transnational Citizen* (Berghahn Books 2011).

Acar, Faruk, *Aile Konutu, Mal Rejimleri, Eşin Yasal Miras Payı* [Matrimonial Home, Matrimonial Property Regimes, The Succession Share of the Surviving Spouse] (6th edn, Seçkin 2021).

Acun, Merve, 'Yabancılık Unsuru Taşıyan Finansal Kiralama (Leasing) Sözleşmelerinde Yetkili Mahkeme' [The Competent Court in Financial Lease Contracts with Foreign Elements] (2013) 19 MÜHF-HAD 441–482.

Acun Mekengeç, Merve, *Aynî Haklardan Doğan Uyuşmazlıklarda Uygulanacak Hukuk ve Yetkili Mahkeme* [Applicable Law and Competent Court for Disputes Arising from Rights *in rem*] (On İki Levha 2016).

Aiwanger, Felix, 'Alte Lieder auf neuen Instrumenten: Die europäischen Güterrechtsverordnungen und das Erbrecht' [2019] ErbR 202–209.

Akıncı, Ziya, *Milletlerarası Usul Hukukunda Yetki Sözleşmesine Dayanan Yabancı Derdestlik* [Lis Pendens Based on Jurisdiction Agreements in International Civil Procedural Law] (Seçkin 2002).

Akıncı, Ziya and Demir Gökyayla, Cemile, *Milletlerarası Aile Hukuku* [International Family Law] (Vedat Kitapçılık 2010).

Akkan, Mine, in Hakan Pekcanıtez and others (eds), *Pekcanıtez Usûl: Medenî Usûl Hukuku* [Pekcanıtez Procedure: Civil Procedural Law], vol 1 (15th edn, On İki Levha 2017).

Akkermans, Bram, 'Lex Rei Sitae and the EU Internal Market – Towards Mutual Recognition of Property Relations' (Social Science Research Network 2018) SSRN Scholarly Paper ID 3289625 <https://papers.ssrn.com/abstract=3289625> accessed 5 September 2020.

Aksoy, Muammer, *Mukayeseli Hukuk Açısından Karı Koca Mal Rejimi ve Miras Hukuku İle Bağı* [Matrimonial Property Regime in Comparative Law and Its Relation to Succession Law] (Ankara Üniversitesi Basımevi 1964).

Allarousse, Veronique, 'A Comparative Approach to the Conflict of Characterization in Private International Law' (1991) 23 Case W Res J Int'l L 479–516.

Altınkaya, Miray, *Medeni Usul Hukuku Açısından Mirasçılık Belgesine İlişkin Talep* [The Application for a Certificate of Inheritance from the Perspective of Civil Procedural Law] (On İki Levha 2021).

Altıparmak, Ayşe Kübra, *İngiliz, Avrupa Birliği ve Türk Hukukunda Mirasa Uygulanacak Hukuk* [Applicable Law to Succession in English, European Union and Turkish Law] (On İki Levha 2017).

Altuğ, Yılmaz, *Yabancıların Hukukî Durumu* [The Legal Status of Foreigners] (3rd edn, Sermet Matbaası 1968).
– 'Âmme İntizamı ve Tesirleri (Bir Özet)' [Public Policy and Its Effects (A Summary)] (1972) XXVII AÜSBFD 371–385.
– *Yabancıların Arazi İktisabı Meselesi* [The Issue of Acquisition of Land by Foreigners] (4th edn, Sulhi Garan Matbaası 1976).
– *Türk Milletlerarası Usul Hukuku (Devletler Hususi Hukukunda Yargı Yetkisi)* [International Civil Procedural Law (Jurisdiction in Private International Law)] (3rd edn, Fakülteler Matbaası 1983).
Álvarez Torné, Maria, 'Key Points on the Determination of International Jurisdiction in the New EU Regulation on Succession and Wills' (2012–2013) XIV YbPIL 409–423.
Ansay, Sabri Şakir, *Hukuk Yargılama Usulleri* [Civil Procedure] (7th edn, Güzel Sanatlar Matbaası 1960).
Ansay, Tuğrul, 'İkametgâhın Tayininden Doğan Kanunlar İhtilafı' [Conflict of Laws Arising from the Determination of Domicile] (1953) 10 AÜHFD 666–687.
– 'Law of Succession' in Tuğrul Ansay, Don Wallace Jr and Işık Önay (eds), *Introduction to Turkish Law* (7th edn, Wolters Kluwer 2020), 149-161.
Ansay, Tuğrul and Schneider, Eric, 'The New Private International Law of Turkey' (1990) XXXVII NILR 139–161.
Apaydın, Bahadır, *Kapitülasyonların Osmanlı-Türk Adli ve İdari Modernleşmesine Etkisi* [The Effect of Capitulations on Ottoman-Turkish Judicial and Administrative Modernisation] (3rd edn, Adalet Yayınevi 2017).
Aras, Aslı, 'Çekişmesiz Yargı İşlerinde Görev ve Yetki' [Competence and Venue in Non-Contentious Matters] (2016) 7 İnÜHFD 65–86.
Aras Kramar, Slađana and Vučko, Katarina, 'A Guide to the Implementation of the Succession Regulation (EU) No 650/2012' (Croatian Law Centre 2020) 32 <https://www.notariesofeurope.eu/wp-content/uploads/2020/07/Guide-to-Succession-Regulation.pdf> accessed 5 March 2022.
Arat, Tuğrul, 'Yabancı İlamların Tanınması ve Tenfizi' [Recognition and Enforcement of Foreign Judgments] (1964) 21 AÜHFD 421–527.
Arıkan, Zeki, 'Mahmut Esat Bozkurt ve Kapitülasyonlar' [Mahmut Esat Bozkurt and Capitulations] (1994) 2 ÇTTAD 217–231.
Arpacı, Abdülkadir, *Kişiler Hukuku (Gerçek Kişiler)* [Law of Persons (Natural Persons)] (2nd edn, Beta 2000).
Arslan, İlyas, *Milletlerarası Özel Hukukta Mutad Mesken Kavramı* [The Concept of Habitual Residence in Private International Law] (On İki Levha 2014).
Artigot i Golobardes, Mireia, 'Will Regulation 650/2012 Simplify Cross-Border Successions in Europe?' (2015) 4 EPLJ 22–55.
Atalı, Murat, *Internationale Zuständigkeit im deutsch-türkischen Rechtsverkehr* (Peter Lang 2001).
– 'Beachtung ausländischer Rechtshängigkeit im türkischen Recht' (2005) 10 ZZPInt 417–431.
– in Hakan Pekcanıtez and others (eds), *Pekcanıtez Usûl: Medenî Usûl Hukuku* [Pekcanıtez Procedure: Civil Procedural Law], vol 3 (15th edn, On İki Levha 2017).
Ataman Figanmeşe, İnci, 'Milletlerarası Özel Hukukta Mirasçılık Belgeleri' [Succession Certificates in Private International Law] (Master Thesis, Istanbul University 1998).
– 'Çifte Vatandaşlık Halinde MÖHUK'un 4. Maddesinin b ve c Bentlerinin Uygulama Alanı' [Scope of Application of Subpragraphs b and c of Article 4 of the PILA in Case of Dual Natioality] (2000) 19–20 MHB 95–114.

Atamer, Yeşim M., 'Rezeption und Weiterentwicklung des schweizerischen Zivilgesetzbuches in der Türkei' (2008) 72 RabelsZ 723–754.

Avşar, Melis, *Milletlerarası Usul Hukukunda Mahkemelerin Yetkisinin Belirlenmesinde Tarafların İrade Serbestisi* [Party Autonomy in Determining the International Jurisdiction of Courts] (On İki Levha 2021).

Aybay, Rona and Dardağan, Esra, *Uluslararası Düzeyde Yasaların Çatışması (Kanunlar İhtilafı)* [Conflict of Laws at the International Level] (2nd edn, İstanbul Bilgi Üniversitesi Yayınları 2008).

Aybay, Rona, Özbek, Nimet and Ersen Perçin, Gizem, *Vatandaşlık Hukuku* [Citizenship Law] (Siyasal Kitabevi 2019).

Aydın, Esen, 'Maddi Hukuk ve Milletlerarası Özel Hukuk Açısından Eşcinsel Evliliklerin Değerlendirilmesi' [Evaluation of Same-Sex Marriages in terms of Substantive Law and Private International Law] in Günseli Öztekin Gelgel and Faruk Kerem Giray (eds), *Milletlerarası Aile ve Çocuk Hukukuna İlişkin Seçilmiş Makaleler* [Selected Articles on International Family and Child Law] (Beta 2017), 103–136.

Aydoğmuş, Ayşe Yasemin, *AİHS'E Ek 1 No'lu Protokole Göre Yabancıların Türkiye'de Taşınmaz Edinmesi* [Foreigners' Right to Acquire Real Estate in Turkey According to Protocol No 1 of the ECHR] (On İki Levha 2016).

Aygül, Musa, 'Yabancı Mahkeme Kararlarının Tanınması ve Tenfizinde Bazı Usul Hukuku Problemleri (Harç–İspat Yükü ve Deliller–Vasıflandırma)' [Some Procedural Issues in Recognition and Enforcement of Foreign Judgments (Fees–Burden of Proof and Evidence-Qualification)] (2011) 31 MHB 83–121.

Aygün, Mesut and Altıparmak, Ayşe Kübra, '650/2012 Sayılı Avrupa Birliği Miras Tüzüğü'nde Mirasa Uygulanacak Hukukun Tespiti' [The Determination of Applicable Law to Succession in The European Succession Regulation No 650/2012] (2016) 11 BAÜHFD 29–56.

Ayiter, Nuşin and Kılıçoğlu, Ahmet, *Miras Hukuku* [Succession Law] (3rd edn, Savaş Yayınevi 1993).

Bachmayer, Christian, 'Ausgewählte Problemfelder bei Nachlasssachen mit Auslandsberührung' [2010] BWNotZ 146–178.

Baetge, Dietmar, *Der gewöhnliche Aufenthalt im internationalen Privatrecht* (Mohr Siebeck 1994).

Bajons, Ena-Marlis, 'Zur Interdependenz von IPR und IZVR bei der Schaffung eines europäischen Justizraums für grenzüberschreitende Nachlassangelegenheiten' in DNotI (ed), *Les Successions Internationales dans l'UE* (DNotI 2004), 465–484.

– 'Internationale Zuständigkeit und anwendbares Recht in Erbsachen' in Martin Schauer and Elisabeth Scheuba (eds), *Europäische Erbrechtsverordnung (2012/650/EU vom 4. Juli 2012)* (Manz 2012), 29–41.

Balkar Bozkurt, Süheyla, 'Uluslararası Özel Hukukta Bitmeyen Tartışma: Atıf (Renvoi) Teorisi, Uygulaması ve Değerlendirilmesi' [Never Ending Issue of Private International Law: The Renvoi Theory – Its Application and Evaluation] [2014] GSÜHFD 795–861.

Balkır, Canan and Kaiser, Bianca, 'Türkiye'de Avrupa Birliği Vatandaşları' [European Union Nationals in Turkey] in Murat Erdoğan and Ayhan Kaya (eds), *Türkiye'nin Göç Tarihi 14. Yüzyıldan 21. Yüzyıla Türkiye'ye Göçler* [Turkey's Migration History Migrations to Turkey from the 14th Century to the 21st Century] (İstanbul Bilgi Üniversitesi Yayınları 2015), 221–238.

Balkır, Canan and Kırkulak, Berna, 'Turkey, the New Destination for International Retirement Migration' in Heinz Fassmann, Max Haller and David Lane (eds), *Migration and Mobility in Europe: Trends, Patterns and Control* (Edward Elgar Publishing 2009), 123–143.

von Bar, Christian and Mankowski, Peter, *Internationales Privatrecht: Allgemeine Lehren*, vol 1 (2nd edn, C.H. Beck 2003).

– *Internationales Privatrecht: Besonderer Teil*, vol 2 (2nd edn, C.H. Beck 2019).

Baran Çelik, Neşe, *Milletlerarası Unsurlu Ölüme Bağlı Tasarruflara Uygulanacak Hukukun Tayini* [Determination of the Applicable Law to International Testamentary Dispositions] (Yetkin 2011).

– 'Milletlerarası Özel Hukuk Alanındaki Gelişmeler Işığında Mirasa Uygulanacak Hukuk Bağlamında İrade Muhtariyeti İlkesinin Değerlendirilmesi' [Evaluation of the Party Autonomy as Regards the Law Applicable to Succession in the Light of Developments in Private International Law], *Prof. Dr. İlhan Unat'a Armağan* [Liber Amicorum Prof. Dr. İlhan Unat] (Mülkiyeliler Birliği Vakfı Yayınları 2012), 115–134.

– 'Türkiye'de Yabancılık Unsuru İçeren Mirasçılık Belgelerinin Düzenlenmesi' [Issuing of Certificate of Succesion Involving Foreign Elements in Turkey] (2019) 24 DÜHFD 439–511.

Bärmann, Johannes, 'Das neue Ehegüterrecht' (1958–1959) 157 AcP 145–214.

Barnard, Catherine, *The Substantive Law of the EU: The Four Freedoms* (6th edn, OUP 2019).

von Bary, Christiane, *Gerichtsstands- und Schiedsvereinbarungen im internationalen Erbrecht* (Mohr Siebeck 2018).

Basedow, Jürgen, '"Member States" and "Third States" in the Succession Regulation' (2020) 26 PPPM 15–25.

Basedow, Jürgen and Diehl-Leistner, Barbara, 'Das Staatsangehörigkeitsprinzip im Einwanderungsland' in Erik Jayme and Heinz-Peter Mansel (eds), *Nation und Staat im Internationalen Privatrecht* (C.F. Müller 1990), 13–44.

Batiffol, Henri, 'La neuvième session de la Conférence de la Haye de droit international privé' [1961] Rev crit dr int privé 461–476.

– 'Rapport Explicatif' in Le Bureau Permanent de la Conférence de La Haye de droit international privé (HCCH) (ed), *Actes et Documents de la Neuvième Session – TOME III Forme des Testaments* (Imprimerie Nationale 1961), 159–174.

Bauer, Frank, 'Anmerkung zur Entscheidung LG München v. 26.9.2006 – 6 O 15963/05' [2007] FamRZ 1250–1257.

Bauer, Frank and Fornasier, Matteo, in Anatol Dutta and Johannes Weber (eds), *Internationales Erbrecht* (2nd edn, C.H. Beck 2021).

Bauer, Frank and Schmidt, Jan Peter, in Anatol Dutta and Johannes Weber (eds), *Internationales Erbrecht* (2nd edn, C.H. Beck 2021).

Bauer, Frank and Süß, Rembert, in Anatol Dutta and Johannes Weber (eds), *Internationales Erbrecht* (2nd edn, C.H. Beck 2021).

Bauer, Frank and Weber, Johannes, in Anatol Dutta and Johannes Weber (eds), *Internationales Erbrecht* (2nd edn, C.H. Beck 2021).

Baykal, Sanem, 'Turkey's EU Accession Process: Current State of Play in Accession Negotiations' in Paul Beaumont and Burcu Yüksel (eds), *Turkish and EU Private International Law – A Comparison* (On İki Levha 2014), 1–29.

Bayraktaroğlu Özçelik, Gülüm, 'Kanunlar İhtilafı Hukukunda Olumlu Vatandaşlık İhtilaflarının Çözümü ve MÖHUK m. 4(1)(b) ve (c) Hükümlerinin Değerlendirilmesi' [Resolving the Positive Conflicts of Nationality in Conflict of Laws and Assessment of Articles 4 (1)(b) and (c) of the Turkish PILA] (2015) 19 GÜHFD 111–150.

– *Milletlerarası Usûl Hukukunda Paralel Davalar* [Parallel Proceedings in International Procedural Law] (Yetkin 2016).

– 'International Lis Pendens as a Contemporary Problem of Turkish International Civil Procedure' (2016–2017) XVIII YbPIL 217–247.

Beaumont, Paul and Holliday, Jayne, 'Some Aspects of Scots Private International Law of Succession Taking Account of the Impact of the EU Succession Regulation' (2015) <https://www.abdn.ac.uk/law/documents/CPIL_Working_Paper_No_6_Beaumont_and_Holliday.pdf> accessed 22 June 2021.

Beckett, William E., 'The Question of Classification (Qualification) in Private International Law' (1934) 15 BYIL 46–81.

Belgesay, Mustafa Reşit, *Teorik ve Pratik Adliye Hukuku IV – Devletler Hususi Hukukunda Adliye II. Kısım* [Theoretical and Practical Procedural Law IV – Procedure in Private International Law Part II] (İstanbul Üniversitesi Hukuk Fakültesi Yayınları 1938).

– *Hukuk Muhakemeleri Kanunu Şerhi* [Commentary of the Code of Civil Procedure], vol I (Güven Basımevi 1939).

Bell, Andrew S., *Forum Shopping and Venue in Transnational Litigation* (OUP 2003).

Bentwich, Norman, *The Law of Domicile in Its Relation to Succession and the Doctrine of Renvoi* (Sweet & Maxwell 1911).

Berki, Osman Fazıl, 'Türk Devletler Özel Hukukunda Vasiyet' [Testament in Turkish Private International Law] (1944) 2 AÜHFD 175–190.

– *Kanuni Miras ve Ölüme Bağlı Tasarruflardan Doğan Kanun İhtilafları* [Conflict-of Laws Arising from Intestacy and Dispositions of Property Upon Death] (Güzel Sanatlar Matbaası 1960).

Berki, Osman Fazıl and Ergüney, Hilmi, *Yabancılar Hukuku ve Kanun İhtilafları İle İlgili Yargıtay Kararlarının Tahlil ve İzahı* [Analysis of and Comments on the Judgments of the Court of Cassation Regarding the Law on Foreigners and Conflict of Laws] (Banka ve Ticaret Hukuku Araştırma Enstitüsü 1963).

Berki, Şakir, *Tatbîkî Devletler Hususî Hukuku* [Practical Private International Law] (Nur Matbaası 1950).

Bierce, Ambrose, *Complete Works of Ambrose Bierce* (ePUB, Delphi Classics 2013) <https://www.delphiclassics.com> accessed 13 January 2021.

Bilkay, Musab, 'Miras Hukukuna İlişkin Dava ve İşlerde Türk Mahkemelerinin Milletlerarası Yetkisi' [International Jurisdiction of Turkish Courts in Cases and Affairs Related to Inheritance Law] (2021) 41 MHB 905–929.

Bilsel, Cemil, *Lozan* [Lausanne], vol 2 (Sosyal Yayınlar 1998).

Bogdan, Michael, *Private International Law as Component of the Law of the Forum* (Ail-Pocket 2012).

Bonomi, Andrea, in Andrea Bonomi and Patrick Wautelet (eds), *Le droit européen des successions-Commentaire du Règlement n°650/2012 du 4 juillet 2012* (2nd edn, Bruylant 2016).

– 'The Relations of Switzerland with EU Member States' in Anatol Dutta and Wolfgang Wurmnest (eds), *European Private International Law and Member State Treaties with Third States – The Case of the European Succession Regulation* (Intersentia 2019), 267–282.

Bonomi, Andrea and Öztürk, Azadi, 'Das Statut der Verfügung von Todes wegen (Art. 24 ff EuErbVO)' in Anatol Dutta and Sebastian Herrler (eds), *Die Europäische Erbrechtsverordnung, 20 Jahre DNotI 1993–2013* (C.H. Beck 2014), 47–69.

– 'Auswirkungen der Europäischen Erbrechtsverordnung auf die Schweiz unter besonderer Berücksichtigung deutsch-schweizerischer Erbfälle' (2015) 114 ZVglRWiss 4–40.

Boran Güneysu, Nilüfer, *Medenî Usûl Hukukunda Karar* [Judgment in Civil Procedural Law] (Adalet Yayınevi 2014).

Borgen, Christopher J., 'Resolving Treaty Conflicts' (2005) 37 Geo Wash Int'l L Rev 573–648.

Borrás, Alegria, 'Lights and Shadows of Communitarisation of Private International Law: Jurisdiction and Enforcement in Family Matters with Regard to Relations with Third States' in Alberto Malatesta, Stefania Bariatti and Fausto Pocar (eds), *The External Dimension of EC Private International Law in Family and Succession Matters* (CEDAM 2008), 99–121.

Briggs, Adrian, *Civil Jurisdiction and Judgments* (6th edn, Routledge 2015).

– *Civil Jurisdiction and Judgments* (7th edn, Routledge 2021).

Bruns, Manfred, 'Eingetragene Lebenspartnerschaften im Rahmen der EU-Erbrechtsverordnung' [2014] ZErb 181–184.

Bucher, Andreas, 'Das neue internationale Erbrecht (Geringfügig geänderte Fassung eines Berichts für die Seminare der Weiterbildungsstufe der Hochschule St. Gallen vom 3. Juni, 3. September und 17. November 1987)' (1988) 69 ZGBR 145–159.

Buckland, William Warwick and McNair, Arnold Duncan, *Roman Law and Common Law* (2nd edn, Cambridge University Press 1965).

Budak, Ali Cem, 'Türk Hukukunda Çekişmesiz Yargı' [Non-Contentious Jurisdiction in Turkish Law], *Medenî Usûl ve İcra-İflâs Hukukçuları Toplantısı IV – Medenî Usûl Hukukunda Çekişmesiz Yargı – İcra ve İflâs Kanunu'nda Yapılan Değişikliklerin Değerlendirilmesi* [Meeting of Civil Procedure and Execution and Bankruptcy Law Jurists IV – Non-Contentious Jurisdiction in Civil Procedural Law – Evaluation of Amendments to the Execution and Bankruptcy Law] (Türkiye Barolar Birliği 2006), 128–187.

Budzikiewicz, Christine, in Alfonso-Luis Calvo Caravaca, Angelo Davì and Heinz-Peter Mansel (eds), *The EU Succession Regulation – A Commentary* (Cambridge University Press 2016).

Buonaiuti, Fabrizio Marongiu, 'Lis Alibi Pendens and Related Actions in the Relationships with the Courts of Third Countries in the Recast of the Brussels I Regulation' (2013–2014) XV YbPIL 87–111.

– 'Jurisdiction Under the Succession Regulation and Relationships with Third States' in Pietro Franzina (ed), *The External Dimension of EU Private International Law after Opinion 1/13* (Intersentia 2017), 211–226.

– 'The EU Succession Regulation and Third Country Courts' (2016) 12 J Priv Int L 545–565.

– in Alfonso-Luis Calvo Caravaca, Angelo Davì and Heinz-Peter Mansel (eds), *The EU Succession Regulation – A Commentary* (Cambridge University Press 2016).

Burandt, Wolfgang, 'Die EU-ErbVO – Das europäische Erbrecht im Wandel (Teil 2)' [2013] FuR 377–388.

Buschbaum, Markus and Kohler, Marius, 'Vereinheitlichung des Erbkollisionsrechts in Europa Eine kritische Würdigung des Kommissionsvorschlags zur Erbrechtsverordnung Erster Teil' [2010] GPR 106–113.

– 'Vereinheitlichung des Erbkollisionsrechts in Europa Zweiter Teil' [2010] GPR 162–170.

Buschbaum, Markus and Simon, Ulrich, 'Beantragung und Erteilung eines Europäischen Nachlasszeugnisses sowie Verwendung eines ausländischen Europäischen Nachlasszeugnisses in Deutschland' [2015] Rpfleger 444–454.

Bürgi, Urs, *Internationales Erbrecht Schweiz* (3rd edn, C.H. Beck & Helbin Lichtenhahn 2017).

Caamiña Domínguez, Celia M., in Alfonso-Luis Calvo Caravaca, Angelo Davì and Heinz-Peter Mansel (eds), *The EU Succession Regulation – A Commentary* (Cambridge University Press 2016).

Calvo Caravaca, Alfonso-Luis, in Alfonso-Luis Calvo Caravaca, Angelo Davì and Heinz-Peter Mansel (eds), *The EU Succession Regulation – A Commentary* (Cambridge University Press 2016).

Can, Hacı and Tuna, Ekin, *Milletlerarası Özel Hukuk* [Private International Law] (5th edn, Adalet Yayınevi 2021).

– *Milletlerarası Usul Hukuku* [International Civil Procedural Law] (3rd edn, Adalet Yayınevi 2022).

Canbeldek, Özlem, 'Hukuk Muhakemeleri Kanunu ve Milletlerarası Özel Hukuk ve Usûl Kanunu Işığında Yetki Sözleşmeleri' [Juristiction Agreements in the Light of Turkish Code of Civil Procedure and Turkish Act on Private International and Procedural Law] (2012) 1 MİHDER 203–238.

Canbeldek Akın, Özlem, *Milletlerarası Derdestlik (Lis Pendens)* [International Lis Pendens] (On İki Levha 2019).

Casswell, Donald G., 'The Conflict of Laws Rules Governing the Formal Validity of Wills: Past Developments and Suggested Reform' (1977) 15 Osgoode Hall LJ 165–214.

Castellanos Ruiz, Esperanza, in Alfonso-Luis Calvo Caravaca, Angelo Davì and Heinz-Peter Mansel (eds), *The EU Succession Regulation – A Commentary* (Cambridge University Press 2016).

Cavers, David F., 'Habitual Residence: A Useful Concept?' (1971) 21 Am U L Rev 475–493.

Chappuis, Benoît and Perrin, Julien, 'Le Règlement (UE) N° 650/2012 du Parlement européen et du Conseil du 4 juillet 2012 relatif à la compétence, la loi applicable, la reconnaissance et l'exécution des décisions, et l'acceptation et l'exécution des actes authentiques en matière de successions et à la création d'un certificat successoral européen' [2014] Not@lex 1–37.

Coester, Michael, 'Das Erbrecht registrierter Lebenspartner unter der EuErbVO' [2013] ZEV 115–117.

Collins, Lawrence (ed), *Dicey, Morris & Collins the Conflict of Laws*, vol 1 (15th edn, Sweet & Maxwell 2012).

– *Dicey, Morris & Collins the Conflict of Laws*, vol 2 (15th edn, Sweet & Maxwell 2012).

Coudert, Frederic R., 'Some Considerations in the Law of Domicil' (1927) 36 YLJ 949–965.

Currle, Edda, 'Theorieansätze zur Erklärung von Rückkehr und Remigration' [2006] soFid – Migration und ethnische Minderheiten 7–23.

Czubik, Paweł, 'Polish Consular Law and Practice after Regaining Independence in 1918 – the Selected Key Issues of the Interwar Period' (2020) 9 Pol Int Eur Law 49–72.

Çabri, Sezer, *Miras Hukuku Şerhi (TMK m. 495-574)* [Commentary of Succession Law (Turkish Civil Code Art. 495-574)], vol I (2nd edn, On İki Levha, 2022).

Çekin, Mesut Serdar, 'Mal Rejimi Hukukunda Gerçekleştirilen Tasarrufların Miras Hukukuna Etkisi' [The Effect of the Savings Made in the Law of Matrimonial Property Regime on the Law of Inheritance] (2017) 4 İ MHFD 189–207.

Çelikel, Aysel, 'Yeni Kanuna Göre Yabancı Mahkeme Kararlarının Tenfiz Şartları' [Conditions of Enforcement of Foreign Judgments According to New (Private International Law) Code] (1982) 2 MHB 7–13.

Çelikel, Aysel and Erdem, Bahadır, *Milletlerarası Özel Hukuk* [Private International Law] (17th edn, Beta 2021).

Çelikel, Aysel and Öztekin Gelgel, Günseli, *Yabancılar Hukuku* [Law on Foreigners] (26th edn, Beta 2021).

Çörtoğlu Koca, Sema and Yücer Aktürk, İpek, 'Yabancı Unsurlu Miras İlişkilerinden Doğan Uyuşmazlıklarda Mirasın Reddine Uygulanacak Hukuk' [Applicable Law to the Renunciation of Inheritance in Disputes Arising From Succession Relations with Foreign Elements] (2018) 4 BÜHFD 11–32.

Damar, Duygu, 'Deutsch-türkisches Nachlassabkommen: zivilprozess- und kollisionsrechtliche Aspekte' [2012] IPRax 278–281.

Dannemann, Gerhard, 'Adjustment/Adaptation (Anpassung)' in Jürgen Basedow and others (eds), *Encyclopedia of Private International Law* (Edward Elgar Publishing 2017), 8–13.

Dardağan Kibar, Esra, 'Güncel Gelişmeler Işığında Atıf Sorununa Bakış Denemesi' [An Attempt to Look into the Problem of Renvoi in the Light of Current Developments] in Feriha Bilge Tanrıbilir and Gülce Gümüşlü Tunçağıl (eds), *10. Yılında MÖHUK Sempozyumu – 7–8 Aralık 2017, Ankara* [Symposium on the 10th Anniversary of the PILA – 7–8 December 2017, Ankara] (Adalet Yayınevi 2018), 26–46.

Davì, Angelo, in Alfonso-Luis Calvo Caravaca, Angelo Davì and Heinz-Peter Mansel (eds), *The EU Succession Regulation – A Commentary* (Cambridge University Press 2016).

Dayınlarlı, Kemal K, 'Milletlerarası Özel Hukukta Kamu Düzeni' [Public Policy in Private International Law], *Prof. Dr. Yaşar Karayalçın'a 65 inci Yaş Armağanı* [Liber Amicorum Prof. Dr. Yaşar Karayalçın in Honour of his 65th Birthday] (Türkiye İş Bankası Kültür Yayınları 1988), 653–692.

de Lima Pinheiro, Luís Pedro Rocha, in Ulrich Magnus and Peter Mankowski (eds), *European Commentaries on Private International Law – Brussels Ibis Regulation*, vol 1 (Sellier European Law Publishers 2016).

de Waal, Marius J., 'A Comparative Overview' in Kenneth G. C. Reid, Marius J. de Waal and Reinhard Zimmermann (eds), *Exploring the Law of Succession* (Edinburgh University Press 2007), 1–26.

de Winter, Louis I., 'Nationality or Domicile? The Present State of Affairs' (1969) 128 RdC 346–503.

Deixler-Hübner, Astrid, in Astrid Deixler-Hübner and Martin Schauer (eds), *Kommentar zur EU-Erbrechtsverordnung* (2nd edn, Manz 2020).

Deixler-Hübner, Astrid and Schauer, Martin, in Astrid Deixler-Hübner and Martin Schauer (eds), *Kommentar zur EU-Erbrechtsverordnung* (2nd edn, Manz 2020).

Demir Gökyayla, Cemile, *Yabancı Mahkeme Kararlarının Tanınması ve Tenfizde Kamu Düzeni* [Public Policy in Recognition and Enforcement of Foreign Judgments] (Seçkin 2001).

– 'Yabancı Mahkemelerden Alınan Mirasçılık Belgelerinin Türkiye'de Hüküm ve Sonuç Doğurması' [Effectiveness and Consequences of Succession Certificates Obtained from Foreign Courts in Turkey] in Mehmet Ünal (ed), *Prof. Dr. Fikret Eren'e Armağan* [Liber Amicorum Prof. Dr. Fikret Eren] (Yetkin 2006), 559–581.
– 'Yeniden Kamu Düzeni' [Public Policy Revisited] in Feriha Bilge Tanrıbilir and Gülce Gümüşlü Tunçağıl (eds), *10. Yılında MÖHUK Sempozyumu – 7–8 Aralık 2017, Ankara* [Symposium on the 10th Anniversary of the PILA – 7–8 December 2017, Ankara] (Adalet Yayınevi 2018), 85–98.
– *Ticarî Uyuşmazlıklarda Türk Mahkemelerinin Milletlerarası Yetkisi* [International Jurisdiction of Turkish Courts in Commercial Disputes] (Vedat Kitapçılık 2021).
Demirarslan, Haydar, 'Türk Devletler Hususi Hukukunda Kazai Salâhiyet' [Jurisdiction in Private International Law] (1952) 43 AD 29–63.
Demirkol, Berk, 'Uluslararası Hukukta Dikkate Alınan Vatandaşlık: Gerçek Kişilerde "Etkin Vatandaşlık" Sorunsalı' [Nationality Under International Law: Questioning the "Effective Nationality" Requirement for Natural Persons] [2015] GSÜHFD 159–193.
– *Milletlerarası Yetki Anlaşmaları* (Vedat Kitapçılık 2018).
Devaux, Angelique, 'The European Regulations on Succession of July 2012: A Path Towards the End of Succession Conflicts of Law in Europe, or Not?' (2013) 47 TIL 229–248.
Dickinson, Andrew and Lein, Eva, *The Brussels I Regulation Recast* (OUP 2015).
Diederichsen, Uwe, 'Teilhabegerechtigkeit in der Ehe' [1992] FamRZ 1–12.
DNotI, 'Deutsch-türkisches Nachlassabkommen; EUErbVO, Türkei: Gesetzliche Erbfolge nach einem türkischen Staatsangehörigen' [2016] DNotI-Report 103–105.
DNotI, 'BGB § 1371 Abs. 1; EuErbVO Art. 1 Abs. 1 Erbrechtliche Qualifikation des zusätzlichen Erbteils des überlebenden Ehegatten aus § 1371 Abs. 1 BGB' [2018] DNotI-Report 54–547.
DNotI (in collaboration with Heinrich Dörner and Paul Lagarde), 'Rechtsvergleichende Studie der erbrechtlichen Regelungen des Internationalen Verfahrensrechtes und Internationalen Privatrechts der Mitgliedsstaaten der Europäischen Union (2002)' in DNotI (ed), *Les Successions Internationales dans l'UE* (DNotI 2004), 169-330.
Doğan, Vahit, 'Miras Hukukundan Doğan Kanunlar İhtilafı' [Conflict of Laws Arising from Succession] (1990) 3 SÜHFD 181–214.
– 'Atıf Teorisindeki Gelişmeler ve Türk Hukuku' [Developments in the Theory of Renvoi and Turkish Law] (1998) 6 SÜHFD 821–849.
– 'Türk Hukukunda Yabancı Derdestliğin Nazara Alınması' [Applicability of International Lis Pendens in Turkish Law] (2002) 22 MHB 121–147.
– *Milletlerarası Özel Hukuk* [Private International Law] (8th edn, Savaş Yayınevi 2022).
Dormann, Agnes, 'Das schweizerische internationale Privatrecht und die europäische Erbrechtsverordnung im Vergleich' in DACH Europäischen Anwaltsvereinigung e.V. (ed), *Die EU-Erbrechtsverordnung Nr. 650/2012 und deren Auswirkungen auf diverse Länder* (Schulthess 2014), 79–122.
Dorsel, Christoph, in Reinhold Geimer and Rolf A. Schütze (eds), *Europäische Erbrechtsverordnung (EuErbVO) – Internationales Erbrechtsverfahrensgesetz (IntErbRVG) – Kommentar zur VO(EU) Nr. 650/2012 (Sonderdruck aus Geimer/Schütze (Hg.), Internationaler Rechtsverkehr in Zivil- und Handelssachen)* (C.H. Beck 2016).
Dorth, Katharina, *Das Verhältnis von Erbschein und Europäischem Nachlasszeugnis* (Nomos 2019).
Döbereiner, Christoph, 'Das internationale Erbrecht nach der EU-Erbrechtsverordnung (Teil I)' [2013] MittBayNot 358–366.

– 'Das internationale Erbrecht nach der EU-Erbrechtsverordnung (Teil II)' [2013] MittBayNot 437–446.
– '(Bindende?) Rechtswahlen nach der EU-Erbrechtsverordnung' [2014] DNotZ 323–340.
– 'Vindikationslegate unter Geltung der EU-Erbrechtsverordnung: Praktische Anmerkungen aus notarieller Sicht' [2014] GPR 42–44.
– 'Das Gesetz zum Internationalen Erbrecht und zur Änderung von Vorschriften zum Erbschein' [2015] NJW 2449–2455.
Dölle, Hans, 'Die Rechtswahl im Internationalen Erbrecht' (1966) 30 RabelsZ 205–240.
Dörner, Heinrich, 'Das deutsch-türkische Nachlaßabkommen' [1996] ZEV 90–96.
– in Jan Kropholler (ed), *Staudinger BGB – EGBGB/IPR Einführungsgesetz zum Bürgerlichen Gesetzbuche – Art. 25, 26 EGBGB (Internationales Erbrecht)* (Sellier & de Gruyter 2007).
– 'Der Entwurf einer europäischen Verordnung zum Internationalen Erb- und Erbverfahrensrecht – Überblick und ausgewählte Probleme' [2010] ZEV 221–228.
– 'Die Verordnung zum Internationalen Erb- und Erbverfahrensrecht ist in Kraft!' [2012] ZEV 505–513.
– 'Erbauseinandersetzung und Bestellung eines Minderjährigenpflegers nach Inkrafttreten der EuErbVO' [2016] ZEV 117–123.
– 'Die internationale Zuständigkeit zur Ausstellung eines deutschen Erbscheins – Zugleich Anmerkungen zum Beschl. des KG v. 10.1.2017 – 6 W 125/16 –' [2017] DNotZ 407–417.
– 'Anerkennung mitgliedstaatlicher Nachlasszeugnisse (im Lichte von „Oberle")' [2018] DNotZ 661–686.
– 'Erbrechtliche Qualifikation des § 1371 Abs. 1 BGB durch den EuGH: Konsequenzen und neue Fragen' [2018] ZEV 305–310.
Dörner, Heinrich and others, 'Auf dem Weg zu einem europäischen Internationalen Erb- und Erbverfahrensrecht' [2005] IPRax 1–8.
Dreher, Karin, *Die Rechtswahl im internationalen Erbrecht* (Peter Lang 1999).
Drobnig, Ulrich, *American-German Private International Law* (2nd edn, Oceana Publications 1972).
Droz, Georges A. L., *Compétence judiciaire et effets des jugements dans le Marché Commun (Etude de la Convention de Bruxelles du 27 septembre 1968)* (Dalloz 1972).
Duchek, Alfred and Schwind, Fritz, *Internationales Privatrecht* (Manz 1979).
Dural, Mustafa, 'İsviçre Türk Hukukunda Ortak (Müşterek) Vasiyetnameler' [Joint Wills in Swiss Turkish Law] (1969) 3 MHAD 165–173.
Dural, Mustafa and Öğüz, Tufan, *Türk Özel Hukuku Cilt II – Kişiler Hukuku* [Turkish Private Law Volume II – Law of Persons] (22th edn, Filiz Kitabevi 2021).
Dural, Mustafa, Öğüz, Tufan and Gümüş, Mustafa Alper, *Türk Özel Hukuku Cilt III – Aile Hukuku* [Turkish Private Law Volume III – Family Law] (17th edn, Filiz Kitabevi 2022).
Dural, Mustafa and Öz, Turgut, *Türk Özel Hukuku Cilt IV – Miras Hukuku* [Turkish Private Law Volume IV – Succession Law] (17th edn, Filiz Kitabevi 2021).
Durugönül, Esma, 'Turkish Return Migration from Europe' (2013) 21 Eur Rev 412–421.
Dutta, Anatol, 'Succession and Wills in the Conflict of Laws on the Eve of Europeanisation' (2009) 73 RabelsZ 547–606.

– 'Die Rechtswahlfreiheit im Künftigen internationalen Erbrecht der Europäischen Union' in Gerte Reichelt and Walter H. Rechberger (eds), *Europäisches Erbrecht: Zum Verordnungsvorschlag der Europäischen Kommission zum Erb- und Testamentsrecht* (Jan Sramek Verlag 2011), 57–84.
– 'Das neue internationale Erbrecht der Europäischen Union – Eine erste Lektüre der Erbrechtsverordnung' [2013] FamRZ 4–15.
– *Warum Erbrecht?* (Mohr Siebeck 2014).
– 'Die Europäische Erbrechtsverordnung vor ihrem Anwendungsbeginn: Zehn ausgewählte Streitstandsminiaturen' [2015] IPRax 32–39.
– in Franz Jürgen Säcker and others (eds), *MüKoBGB*, vol 11 (6th edn, C.H. Beck 2015).
– 'The European Certificate of Succession: A New European Instrument between Procedural and Substantive Law' (2015) 5 IJPL 38–50.
– 'Das neue internationale Güterrecht der Europäischen Union – ein Abriss der europäischen Güterrechtsverordnungen' [2016] FamRZ 1973–1985.
– 'Entwicklungen im internationalen Familien- und Erbrecht der Europäischen Union bis Gogova' [2016] ZEuP 427–463.
– 'The Perspective of the European Union' in Anatol Dutta and Wolfgang Wurmnest (eds), *European Private International Law and Member State Treaties with Third States – The Case of the European Succession Regulation* (Intersentia 2019), 319–328.
– 'Das internationale Familien- und Erbrecht in der Rechtsprechung des Gerichtshofs der Europäischen Union – die vergangenen fünf Jahre' [2020] ZEuP 897–943.
– 'EuErbVO' in Franz Jürgen Säcker and others (eds), *MüKoBGB*, vol 12 (8th edn, C.H. Beck 2020).
– 'Pauschalierter Zugewinnausgleich nach § 1371 Abs. 1 BGB bei ausländischem Güterstatut? – Vom praktischen Nutzen der funktionalen Rechtsvergleichung' [2020] ErbR 304–305.
– in Anatol Dutta and Johannes Weber (eds), *Internationales Erbrecht* (2nd edn, C.H. Beck 2021).
Dutta, Anatol and Weber, Johannes (eds), *Internationales Erbrecht* (2nd edn, C.H. Beck 2021).
Dutta, Anatol and Wurmnest, Wolfgang, *European Private International Law and Member State Treaties with Third States – The Case of the European Succession Regulation* (Intersentia 2019).
– 'Introduction' in Anatol Dutta and Wolfgang Wurmnest (eds), *European Private International Law and Member State Treaties with Third States – The Case of the European Succession Regulation* (Intersentia 2019), 1–4.

Eagleton, William L., 'Joint and Mutual Wills Mutual Promises to Devise as a Means of Conveyancing' (1930) 15 Cornell LQ 358–389.
Eichel, Florian, in Maximilian Herberger and others (eds), *jurisPK-BGB*, vol 6 (9th edn, juris 2020).
Ekşi, Nuray, *Türk Mahkemelerinin Milletlerarası Yetkisi* [International Jurisdiction of Turkish Courts] (2nd edn, Beta 2000).
– *Yabancıların Türkiye'de Taşınmaz İktisabı* [Acquisition of Immovable Property by Foreigners in Turkey] (2nd edn, Beta 2012).
– *Yargıtay Kararları Işığında Milletlerarası Miras Hukuku* [International Succession Law in the Light of the Judgments of the Court of Cassation (*Yargıtay*)] (Beta 2013).

– *Milletlerarası Özel Hukuk I Pratik Çalışma Kitabı: Kanunlar İhtilafı Kurallarına ve Milletlerarası Usul Hukukuna İlişkin Seçilmiş Mahkeme Kararları* [Private International Law I Practice Workbook: Selected Judgments on Conflict-of-Laws Rules and International Civil Procedural Law] (2nd edn, Beta 2014).
– 'Comparison of Articles 20 and 43 of the Turkish Private International Law and Procedural Law Act ('PILA') with the EU Succession Regulation' in Paul Beaumont and Burcu Yüksel (eds), *Turkish and EU Private International Law – A Comparison* (On İki Levha 2014), 117–152.
– *Yabancı Mahkeme Kararlarının Tanınması ve Tenfizi* [Recognition and Enforcement of Foreign Judgments] (2nd edn, Beta 2020).
Elbalti, Béligh, 'Reciprocity and The Recognition and Enforcement of Foreign Judgments: A Lot of Bark but Not Much Bite' (2017) 13 J Priv Int L 184–218.
Emmerich, Julian, *Probleme der Anknüpfung im Rahmen der EuErbVO* (Duncker & Humblot 2016).
Emmerling de Oliveira, Nicole and Heggen, Marc, 'Türkische Mandanten im Notariat' [2011] Notar 39–46.
Ercan, Bergü, 'Deutsch-Türkische erbrechtliche Probleme' (1996) 5 Informationsbrief der DTJV 6–11.
Erdem, Bahadır, 'Hukuki ve Ticari Konularda Mahkemelerin Yetkisi ve Mahkeme Kararlarının Tanınması ve Tenfizi Hakkında 1968 Tarihli Brüksel Antlaşmasının Hükümlerinin Türk Mahkemelerinin Milletlerarası Yetki Kuralları ile Karşılaştırılması' [Comparison of the Provisions of the Brussels Convention of 1968 on Jurisdiction and Recognition and Enforcement of Judgments in Civil and Commercial Matters and the Rules on International Jurisdiction of Turkish Courts] (1997) 17 MHB 183–216.
Erdoğan, Ersin, 'Milletlerarası Derdestlik (Lis Alibi Pendens)' [Lis Alibi Pendens in International Civil Procedure] (2014) 16 DEÜHFD 1857–1884.
– *Hakem Kararlarının Kesin Hüküm Etkisi* [Res Judicata Effect of Arbitral Awards] (2nd edn, Yetkin 2020).
– *Medenî Usûl Hukuku Kurallarının Yer Bakımından Uygulanması* [Territorial Application of the Rules of Civil Procedural Law] (2nd edn, Yetkin 2020).
Erişgin, Nuri, *Mirasçılık Belgesi* [Certificate of Succession] (Turhan Kitabevi 2013).
Erkan, Mustafa, 'Bir Tabu: Taşınmazın Aynına İlişkin Davalarda Münhasır Yetki' [A Taboo: Exclusive Jurisdiction over Immovable Property] (2012) 20 SÜHFD 11–51.
– 'Türk Milletlerarası Özel Hukuk Sisteminde Yabancı Hukukun Tatbiki: Olan vs. Olması Gereken' [Application of Foreign Law in Turkish Private International Law: De Lege Lata vs. De Lege Ferenda] in Bilgin Tiryakioğlu and others (eds), *Milletlerarası Özel Hukukta Güncel Konular Sempozyumu* [Symposium on Current Issues in Private International Law] (Yetkin 2016), 543–555.
Ersen Perçin, Gizem, *Milletlerarası Özel Hukuk Bakımından Mal Rejimleri: Uygulanacak Hukuk, Milletlerarası Yetki, Tanıma ve Tenfiz* [Matrimonial Property Regimes in Private International Law: Applicable Law, Jurisdiction, Recognition and Enforcement] (On İki Levha 2014).
Ertaş, Şeref, 'Yabancı İlamların Tanınması ve Tenfizi' [Recognition and Enforcement of Foreign Judgments] (1987) 3 DEÜHFD 365–438.
Erten, Rifat, *Türklerin Kişi Hâllerine İlişkin Davalarda Türk Mahkemelerinin Milletlerarası Yetkisi (MÖHUK m. 41)* [International Jurisdiction of Turkish Courts in Cases Concerning the Personal Status of Turkish Nationals (Art. 41 of the PILA) (Yetkin 2017).

Esen, Emre, 'Türk Hukukunda Yabancı Mahkeme Kararlarının Tanınması ve Tenfizinde Münhasır Yetki Kavramı' [The Concept of Exclusive Jurisdiction in the Recognition and Enforcement of Foreign Court Judgments under Turkish Law] (2002) 22 MHB 183–206.
– 'Alman Hukukunda İhtarlı Basit Dava Usulü (Mahnverfahren) Çerçevesinde Verilen Kararların Türk Hukukunda Tenfizi' [Recognition and Enforcement of Decisions Rendered in Accordance with Mahnverfahren of German Law in Turkish Law] (2007) 27 MHB 21–80.

Fallon, Marc and Kruger, Thalia, 'The Spatial Scope of the EU's Rules on Jurisdiction and Enforcement of Judgments: From Bilateral Modus to Unilateral Universality?' (2012–2013) XIV YbPIL 1–35.
Fassmann, Heinz and İçduygu, Ahmet, 'Turks in Europe: Migration Flows, Migrant Stocks and Demographic Structure' (2013) 21 Eur Rev 349–361.
Fentiman, Richard, 'National Law and the European Jurisdiction Regime' in Arnaud Nuyts and Nadine Watté (eds), *International Civil Litigation in Europe and Relations with Third States* (Bruylant 2005), 83–128.
– 'Forum Non Conveniens' in Jürgen Basedow and others (eds), *Encyclopedia of Private International Law* (Edward Elgar Publishing 2017), 797–806.
Ferid, Murad, 'Le Rattachement Autonome de la Transmission Successorale en Droit International Privé' (1974) 142 RdC 71–202.
Fernández Arroyo, Diego P., 'Compétence exclusive et compétence exorbitante dans les relations privées internationales' (2006) 323 RdC 9–260.
Fetsch, Johannes, 'Auslandsvermögen im Internationalen Erbrecht – Testamente und Erbverträge, Erbschein und Ausschlagung bei Auslandsvermögen –' [2006] RNotZ 77–117.
Firsching, Karl, *Deutsch-Amerikanische Erbfälle* (C.H. Beck 1965).
Fischer-Czermak, Constanze, in Astrid Deixler-Hübner and Martin Schauer (eds), *Kommentar zur EU-Erbrechtsverordnung* (2nd edn, Manz 2020).
Flam, Harry, 'Turkey and the EU: Politics and Economics of Accession' (2004) 50 CESifo Econ Stud 171–210.
Fornasier, Matteo, '§ 1371 I BGB: Qualifikation des güterrechtl. Viertels in deutsch-türk. Erbfällen – Anmerkung – OLG Karlsruhe 27.02.2018 – 14 W 113/16 (Wx)' [2018] FamRZ 860–862.
– 'Anmerkung – EuGH 01.03.2018, Art. 1 I EUErbVO, § 1371 I BGB: Erbrechtl. Qualifikation des güterrechtl. Viertels' [2018] FamRZ 634–635.
– in Anatol Dutta and Johannes Weber (eds), *Internationales Erbrecht* (2nd edn, C.H. Beck 2021).
Fötschl, Andreas, 'The Relationship of the European Certificate of Succession to National Certificates' (2010) 18 ERPL 1259–1271.
Francescakis, Phocion, 'Quelques précisions sur les "lois d'application immédiate" et leurs rapports avec les règles sur les conflits de lois' [1966] Rev crit dr int privé 1–18.
Francq, Stéphanie and Mary, Julie, 'The External Relations of Belgium' in Anatol Dutta and Wolfgang Wurmnest (eds), *European Private International Law and Member State Treaties with Third States – The Case of the European Succession Regulation* (Intersentia 2019), 39–65.
Franzina, Pietro, 'Lis Pendens Involving a Third Country under the Brussels I-bis Regulation: An Overview' [2014] RDIPP 23–42.

– 'The External Relations of Italy' in Anatol Dutta and Wolfgang Wurmnest (eds), *European Private International Law and Member State Treaties with Third States – The Case of the European Succession Regulation* (Intersentia 2019), 175–206.

Fröhler, Oliver, 'Die erbrechtliche Stellung des längstlebenden Ehegatten in deutsch-schweizerischen Erbfällen' [2008] BWNotZ 38–47.

Gaida, Martin, Hille, Holger and Mendl, Patricia, Vermögensnachfolge in der Finanzberatung: Erb-, Steuer- und Gesellschaftsrecht — systematisch, fallorientiert, anlagegerecht (Gabler 2001).

Gärtner, Franz, *Die Behandlung ausländischer Vindikationslegate im deutschen Recht* (C.H. Beck 2014).

Gebauer, Martin, '§ 1371 Abs. 1 BGB und das deutsch-türkische Nachlassabkommen im Sog der erbrechtlichen Qualifikation' [2018] IPRax 586–588.

– 'Das deutsch-türkische Nachlassabkommen im Sog des Europäischen Kollisionsrechts' [2018] IPRax 345–351.

– 'Erbrechtliche Fragen im deutsch-türkischen Rechtsverkehr' (2018) 27 Informationsbrief der DTJV 18–24.

Geimer, Reinhold, 'Die europäische Erbrechtsverordnung im Überblick' in Johannes Hager (ed), *Die neue europäische Erbrechtsverordnung* (Nomos 2013), 9–38.

Giray, Faruk Kerem, 'Possible Impacts of EU Succession Regulation No 650/2012 on Turkish Private International Law' (2016) 9 Anali PFZE 235–247.

– 'Milletlerarası Özel Hukuk Hakkaniyetinin 5718 Sayılı MÖHUK Kapsamında Değerlendirilmesi' [Evaluation of Private International Law Justice within the Scope of the PILA No 5718] (2012) IX YÜHFD 555–577.

Gitschthaler, Edwin, in Astrid Deixler-Hübner and Martin Schauer (eds), *Kommentar zur EU-Erbrechtsverordnung (EuErbVO)* (2nd edn, Manz 2020).

Göğer, Erdoğan, 'Devletler Hususi Hukuku Yönünden İkâmetgah' [Domicile in Private International Law] (1969) 26 AÜHFD 237–252.

– *Devletler Hususi Hukuku (Kanunlar İhtilafı)* [Private International Law (Conflict of Laws)] (4th edn, Ankara Üniversitesi Hukuk Fakültesi Yayınları 1977).

– 'Çifte Vatandaşlık' [Dual Nationality] (1995) 44 AÜHFD 127–181.

Gönensay, Samim and Birsen, Kemalettin, *Miras Hukuku* [Succession Law] (2nd edn, Ahmed Said Matbaası 1963).

Gözler, Kemal, 'Res Iudicata'nın Türkçesi Üzerine' [On the Turkish (Equivalent) of the Term Res Iudicata] (2007) 56 AÜHFD 45–61.

Graham-Siegenthaler, Barbara, 'Die EU-Erbrechtsverordnung und deren Auswirkungen auf die Nachlassplanung in der Schweiz' [2015] Jusletter.

Grau, Volker, in Walter Zimmermann (ed), *Praxiskommentar Erbrechtliche Nebengesetze* (2nd edn, zerb verlag 2017).

Graue, Eugen Dietrich, 'The Rights of Surviving Spouses under Private International Law' (1966) 15 AJCL 164–194.

Graveson, Ronald Harry, *The Conflict of Laws* (7th edn, Sweet & Maxwell 1974).

Gray, Jacqueline, 'Identifying the Impetus behind the Europeanization of the Private International Law Rules on Family Matters and Succession' (2015) 17 Eur J L Reform 341–351.

Greeske, Marion, *Die Kollisionsnormen der neuen EU-Erbrechtsverordnung* (Peter Lang 2014).

Grolimund, Pascal and Bachofner, Eva, 'Schweizer Zuständigkeit über im EU-Raum belegene Liegenschaften im Lichte der EU-Erbrechtsverordnung' in Peter Breitschmid and others (eds), *Tatsachen, Verfahren, Vollstreckung: Festschrift für Isaak Meier zum 65. Geburtstag* (Schulthess 2015), 279–291.

Grziwotz, Herbert, in Franz Jürgen Säcker and others (eds), *MüKoBGB*, vol 11 (8th edn, C.H. Beck 2020).

Gubenko, Elena, *Die Abgrenzung des Erbstatuts vom Sachstatut in der EuErbVO* (Mohr Siebeck 2021).

Gugu Bushati, Aida, 'The Albanian Private International Law of 2011' (2013–2014) XV YbPIL 509–528.

Gümüş, Mustafa Alper, 'Edinilmiş Mallara Katılma Rejiminin Tasfiyesinden Kaç Tane "Katılma Alacağı" Doğar? – TMK m.236/I Kapsamında Bir İnceleme' [How Many "Participation Claim(s)" Arise from the Liquidation of the Regime of Participation in Acquired Property – An Analysis within the Scope of Art. 236/I of the Turkish Civil Code (TMK)] (2009) VI YÜHFD 91–115.

Güneş, Biset Sena, 'The Relations of Turkey with EU Member States' in Anatol Dutta and Wolfgang Wurmnest (eds), *European Private International Law and Member State Treaties with Third States – The Case of the European Succession Regulation* (Intersentia 2019), 283–316.

Güngör, Gülin, *Tâbiiyet Hukuku: Gerçek Kişiler – Tüzel Kişiler – Şeyler* [Nationality Law: Natural Persons – Legal Persons – Things] (9th edn, Yetkin 2021).

– *Türk Milletlerarası Özel Hukuku* [Turkish Private International Law] (2nd edn, Yetkin 2021).

Gürzumar, Aydanur, 'Türk Devletler Özel Hukuku Açısından Boşanma Davalarında Kamu Düzeninin Etkileri' [The Effects of Public Policy in Divorce Cases in Terms of Turkish Private International Law] (1994) 14 MHB 21–54.

Guterman, Simeon L., 'The Principle of the Personality of Law in the Early Middle Ages: A Chapter in the Evolution of Western Legal Institutions and Ideas' (1966) 21 U Miami L Rev 259–348.

Güven, Pelin, 'Yabancıların Vasiyetname Yapma Ehliyetine, Vasiyetin Şekline ve Esasına Uygulanacak Hukuk ile Bu Kapsamda Yabancı Gerçek Kişilerin Miras Hakkı' [The Law Applicable to the Testamentary Capacity of Foreigners, to the Form and Substance of a Will and Succession Rights of Foreign Nationals within this Scope] (2006) X AÜEHFD 341–360.

Harris, Jonathan, 'The Proposed EU Regulation on Succession and Wills: Prospects and Challenges' (2008) 22 Tru L I 181–235.

Hartley, Trevor C., *International Commercial Litigation: Text, Cases and Materials on Private International Law* (3rd edn, Cambridge University Press 2020).

Hausmann, Rainer, in Dieter Henrich (ed), *Staudinger BGB – EGBGB/IPR Einführungsgesetz zum Bürgerlichen Gesetzbuche – Art. 3–6 EGBGB (IPR – Allgemeiner Teil)* (Sellier & de Gruyter 2013).

– *Internationales und Europäisches Familienrecht* (2nd edn, C.H. Beck 2018).

Hay, Peter, 'The Situs Rule in European and American Conflicts Law – Comparative Notes' in Peter Hay and Michael H. Hoeflich (eds), *Property Law and Legal Education – Essays in Honor of John E. Cribbet* (University of Illinois Press 1988), 109–132.

Hayton, David, 'Determination of the Objectively Applicable Law Governing Succession to Deceaseds' Estates' in DNotI (ed), *Les Successions Internationales dans l'UE* (DNotI 2004), 359–369.

Hedemann-Robinson, Martin, 'An Overview of Recent Legal Developments at Community Level in Relation to Third Country Nationals Resident within the European Union, with Particular Reference to the Case Law of the European Court of Justice' (2001) 38 CML Rev 525–586.

Heiderhoff, Bettina, 'Das vertrackte subjektive Element des gewöhnlichen Aufenthalts (zu OLG Düsseldorf, 26.06.2018 – I-3 Wx 214/16)' [2019] IPRax 506–510.

von Hein, Jan, in Franz Jürgen Säcker and others (eds), *MüKoBGB*, *vol* 12 (8th edn, C.H. Beck 2020).

Heinig, Jens, 'Rechtswahlen in Verfügungen von Todes wegen nach der EU-Erbrechts-Verordnung' [2014] RNotZ 197–229.

Heinze, Christian A., 'The Effect in the European Community of Judgments in Civil and Commercial Matters: Recognition, Res Judicata and Abuse of Process – Germany' (BIICL 2006) <https://www.biicl.org/files/3482_germany_final_c.pdf> accessed 19 March 2020.

Heinze, Christian A. and Dutta, Anatol, 'Ungeschriebene Grenzen für europäische Zuständigkeiten bei Streitigkeiten mit Drittstaatenbezug' [2005] IPRax 224–230.

Hertel, Christian, in Thomas Rauscher (ed), *EuZPR/EuIPR*, vol V (4th edn, Otto Schmidt 2016).

Herweg, Cornelia, *Die Vereinheitlichung des Internationalen Erbrechts im Europäischen Binnenmarkt* (Nomos 2004).

Herzog, Stephanie, 'Die EU-Erbrechtsverordnung (EU-ErbVO)' [2013] ErbR 2–14.

Hess, Burkhard, 'Die internationale Zuständigkeit nach der Erbrechtsverordnung' in Anatol Dutta and Sebastian Herrler (eds), *Die Europäische Erbrechtsverordnung, 20 Jahre DNotI 1993–2013* (C.H. Beck 2014), 131–142.

Hill, Jonathan and Shúilleabháin, Máire Ní, *Clarkson & Hill's Conflict of Laws* (5th edn, OUP 2016).

von Hinden, Michael and Müller, Thorsten, 'Die Europäische Erbrechtsverordnung, Aktuelle Auswirkungen auf die Nachfolgeplanung' [2013] ErbStB 97–103.

von Hoffmann, Bernd, 'The Relevance of European Community Law' in Bernd von Hoffmann (ed), *European Private International Law* (Ars Aequi Libri 1998), 19–37.

von Hoffmann, Bernd and Thorn, Karsten, *Internationales Privatrecht* (9th edn, C.H. Beck 2007).

Hohloch, Gerhard, in Harm Peter Westermann, Barbara Grunewald and Georg Maier-Reimer (eds), *Erman BGB*, vol 2 (14th edn, Otto Schmidt 2014).

Huber, Eugen, *Schweizerisches Zivilgesetzbuch, Expertenkommission*, vol II (1902).

Huynh, Duy Tuong, *Internationale Nachlassabwicklung im Lichte des Europäischen Nachlasszeugnisses* (Mohr Siebeck 2021).

Huysal, Burak, 'Kanunlar İhtilafı Alanında İkametgâh ve Doğurduğu Sorunlar' [Domicile in the field of Conflict of Laws and Problems Attached to It] (2003) 2 MHFD 173–205.

– '6100 Sayılı Hukuk Muhakemeleri Kanunu İle Getirilen Yenilikler Işığında Yabancı Mahkeme Kararlarının Tanınması ve Tenfizi Konusunda Bazı Tespitler' [Some Observations on the Recognition and Enforcement of Foreign Judgements in the Light of the Reforms Introduced by the (Turkish) Code of Civil Procedure No 6100] (2012) 32 MHB 71–101.

– 'Milletlerarası Yetkinin Belirlenmesinde Mutad Meskenin Doğurduğu Sorunlar ve HMK Madde Dokuz Üzerine Bazı Öneriler' [Problems Arising from Habitual Residence in Determining International Jurisdiction and Some Suggestions on Art. 9 of the (Turkish) Code of Civil Procedure (HMK)] in Sibel Özel and Hatice Selin Pürselim (eds), *Milletlerarası Usul Hukukunda Mahkemelerin Yetkisine İlişkin Güncel Tartışmalar: Ulusal Konferans 20 Şubat 2021* [Current Debates on the Jurisdiction of Courts in International Civil Procedural Law: National Conference 20 February 2021] (On İki Levha 2021), 97–109.

Huysal, Burak and Şermet Süzen, Begüm, 'Tanıma ve Tenfiz Davalarında Kararı Veren Mahkemenin Yetkisinin İncelenmesi' [Examination of the Jurisdiction of the Court of Origin in Recognition and Enforcement Cases] in Süheyla Balkar Bozkurt (ed), *Yabancı Mahkeme ve Hakem Kararlarının Tanınması ve Tenfizinde Güncel Gelişmeler* [Current Developments in the Recognition and Enforcement of Foreign Judgments and Arbitral Awards] (On İki Levha 2018), 47–67.

İmre, Zahit, 'İkametgâh Kavramı ve Buna İlişkin Meseleler' [The Concept of Domicile and Related Issues], *İstanbul Üniversitesi Hukuk Fakültesi'nin 50. Yıl Armağanı: Cumhuriyet Döneminde Hukuk* [Liber Amicorum in Honour of the 50th Anniversary Istanbul University Faculty of Law: Law in the Republican Era] (Fakülteler Matbaası 1973), 205–231.

İmre, Zahit and Erman, Hasan, *Mıras Hukuku – Yasal Mirasçılık, Ölüme Bağlı Tasarruflar, Mirasın Geçmesi, Mirasın Taksimi* [Succession Law – Intestacy, Dispositions of Property Upon Death, Transfer of Succession, Sharing-Out of Succession] (15th edn, Der Yayınları 2021).

İnalcık, Halil, 'Imtiyāzāt – The Ottoman Empire' in Bernard Lewis and others (eds), *The Encyclopaedia of Islam*, vol III (H-Iram) (2nd edn, J Brill 1986), 1179–1189.

İnan, Ali Naim, Ertaş, Şeref and Albaş, Hakan, *Miras Hukuku* [Succession Law] (11th edn, Seçkin 2022).

İrge Erdoğan, Burcu, '5718 Sayılı MÖHUK Uyarınca Tenkis Davasında Uygulanacak Hukukun Kamu Düzeni Bakımından Değerlendirilmesi ve Yetkili Mahkeme' [Evaluation of the Applicable Law in the Action for Reduction in Terms of Public Policy and the Competent Court Pursuant to the (Turkish) PILA No 5718] (2018) 20 DEÜHFD 397–430.

İstanbul Üniversitesi Hukuk Fakültesi – Milletlerarası Hukuk ve Milletlerarası Münasebetler Enstitüsü, *Milletlerarası Özel Hukuk ve Milletlerarası Usul Hukuku Kanunu Öntasarı Sempozyumu, 22–24 Kasım 1976* [Symposium on the Preliminary Draft for the (Turkish) Private International and Procedural Law Act, 22–24 November 1976] (Fakülteler Matbaası 1978).

İyilikli, Ahmet Cahit, 'Mirasçılık (Veraset) Belgesinin Hukuk Yargılamasındaki Görünümü' [The Certificate of Succession in Civil Proceedings] (2017) 5 UMD 281–382.

Jaeschke, Gotthard, 'Türk Hukukunda Evlenme Aktinin Şekli: Devletler Hususi Hukukunda bir Araştırma' [The Form of the Marriage in Turkish Law: An Examination of Private International Law] (1953) 19 İÜHFM 400–431.

Jayme, Erik, 'Identité Culturelle et Intégration: Le Droit International Privé Postmoderne' (1995) 251 RdC 9–267.

– 'Party Autonomy in International Family and Succession Law: New Tendencies' (2009) XI YbPIL 1–10.

Jayme, Erik and Kohler, Christian, 'Europäisches Kollisionsrecht 1997 – Vergemeinschaftung durch "Säulenwechsel"?' [1997] IPRax 385–401.
Jeremias, Christoph and Schäper, Eva, 'Zugewinnausgleich nach § 1371 BGB bei Geltung ausländischen Erbrechts (zu OLG Stuttgart, 08.03.2005 – 8 W 96/04)' [2005] IPRax 521–526.
Jud, Brigitta, 'Rechtswahl im Erbrecht: Das Grünbuch der Europäischen Kommission zum Erb- und Testamentsrecht' [2005] GPR 133–139.
Juenger, Friedrich K., 'Jurisdiction, Choice of Law and the Elusive Goal of Decisional Harmony' (1992) 39 NILR 137–147.
– 'What's Wrong with Forum Shopping?' (1994) 16 Sydney L Rev 5–13.
Junghardt, Anna, *Die Vereinheitlichung des Erb- und Testamentrechts im Rahmen einer Europäischen Verordnung – Rom IV – VO* (S Roderer 2009).
Junker, Abbo, 'Die Dogmatik der Aufenthaltszuständigkeit nach der Europäischen Erbrechtsverordnung' in Christoph Althammer and Christoph Schärtl (eds), *Dogmatik als Fundament für Forschung und Lehre – Festschrift für Herbert Roth zum 70. Geburtstag* (Mohr Siebeck 2021), 747–762.

Kahn, Franz M., Ueber Inhalt, Natur und Methode des internationalen Privatrechts (G Fischer 1899).
Kalss, Susanne, *Company Law and the Law of Succession* (Springer 2015).
Kalt, Michelle and Uhl, Matthias, 'Die EU-Erbrechtsverordnung und die Schweiz' in Lukas Fahrländer and Reto A. Heizmann (eds), *Europäisierung der schweizerischen Rechtsordnung* (Dike 2013), 103–133.
Kaya, Zekiye, 'Der Nachlass eines deutsch-türkischen Doppelstaaters' [2015] ZEV 208–215.
Kegel, Gerhard and Schurig, Klaus, *Internationales Privatrecht* (9th edn, C.H. Beck 2004).
Kern, Christoph A. and Glücker, Daniela, 'Das neue Europäische Erbstatut und seine Aufnahme in der deutschen Literatur' (2014) 78 RabelsZ 294–314.
Kessedjian, Catherine, 'International Jurisdiction and Foreign Judgments in Civil and Commercial Matters' (HCCH 1997) Prel. Doc. No 7 <https://assets.hcch.net/docs/76852ce3-a967-42e4-94f5-24be4289d1e5.pdf> accessed 2 February 2021.
Kindler, Peter, 'Vom Staatsangehörigkeits- zum Domizilprinzip: das künftige internationale Erbrecht der Europäischen Union' [2010] IPRax 44–50.
Kılıç, Memet, 'Türkei' in Rembert Süß (ed), *Erbrecht in Europa* (4th edn, zerb verlag 2020), 1511–1546.
Kleinheisterkamp, Jan, 'Overriding Mandatory Laws in International Arbitration' (2018) 67 ICLQ 903–930.
Kleinschmidt, Jens, 'Optionales Erbrecht: Das Europäische Nachlasszeugnis als Herausforderung an das Kollisionsrecht' (2013) 77 RabelsZ 723–785.
– 'Anmerkung – § 1371 Abs. 1 BGB ist erbrechtlich zu qualifizieren' [2018] ErbR 327–330.
– in Maximilian Herberger and others (eds), *jurisPK-BGB*, vol 6 (9th edn, juris 2020).
Knur, Alexander, 'Zugewinngemeinschaft, Ehevertrag und Verfügung von Todes wegen' [1957] DNotZ 451–483.
Kocaağa, Köksal, 'Mirasçılık Belgesi (MK 598)' [Certificate of Succession (Turkish Civil Code (MK) Art. 598] (2005) IX GÜHFD 83–105.
Kocayusufpaşaoğlu, Necip, *Miras Hukuku* [Succession Law] (3rd edn, Filiz Kitabevi 1987).
Koch, Elisabeth, in Franz Jürgen Säcker and others (eds), *MüKoBGB*, vol 9 (8th edn, C.H. Beck 2019).

Kohler, Christian, 'Auf dem Weg zu einem europäischen Justizraum für das Familien- und Erbrecht' [2002] FamRZ 709–714.

– 'Die künftige Erbrechtsverordnung der Europäischen Union und die Staatsverträge mit Drittstaaten' in Gerte Reichelt and Walter H. Rechberger (eds), *Europäisches Erbrecht: Zum Verordnungsvorschlag der Europäischen Kommission zum Erb- und Testamentsrecht* (Jan Sramek Verlag 2011), 109–128.

– 'Application of the Succession Regulation by German Courts – Selected Issues' (2020) 26 PPPM 27–43.

Kohler, Christian and Pintens, Walter, 'Entwicklungen im Europäischen Personen- und Familienrecht 2010–2011' [2011] FamRZ 1433–1440.

Köhler, Andreas, *Eingriffsnormen – Der 'unfertige Teil' des europäischen IPR* (Mohr Siebeck 2013).

– in Ludwig Kroiß, Claus-Henrik Horn and Dennis Solomon (eds), *NK/Nachfolgerecht: Erbrechtliche Spezialgesetze* (2nd edn, Nomos 2019).

– 'Teil 1 EuErbVO' in Walter Gierl and others (eds), *Internationales Erbrecht: EuErbVO, IntErbRVG, DurchfVO, Länderberichte* (3rd edn, Nomos & Manz 2020).

Konan, Belkıs, 'Osmanlı Devletinde Protégé (Koruma) Sistemi' [Protégé (Protection) System in the Ottoman Empire] (2009) 58 AÜHFD 169–188.

– *Osmanlı Devleti'nde Yabancıların Hukuki Statüsü* [Legal Status of Foreigners in the Ottoman Empire] (Statü Yayıncılık 2013).

Konvalin, Linus, *Das Europäische Nachlasszeugnis ohne europäischen Entscheidungseinklang* (Wolfgang Metzner Verlag 2018).

Kränzle, Michael, *Heimat als Rechtsbegriff?* (Mohr Siebeck 2014).

Kremer, Gerhard, 'Die Bedeutung des deutsch-türkischen Konsularvertrags für Nachlaßverfahren in der Bundesrepublik Deutschland' [1981] IPRax 205–206.

Kren Kostkiewicz, Jolanta, *IPRG/LugÜ Kommentar – Bundesgesetz über das Internationale Privatrecht, Lugano-Übereinkommen und weitere Erlasse* (2nd edn, orell füssli 2019).

Kreße, Bernhard, in Alfonso-Luis Calvo Caravaca, Angelo Davì and Heinz-Peter Mansel (eds), *The EU Succession Regulation – A Commentary* (Cambridge University Press 2016).

Kroiß, Ludwig, in Thomas Heidel and others (eds), *NK-BGB/EGBGB*, vol 1 (3rd edn, Nomos 2016).

– in Ludwig Kroiß and Claus-Henrik Horn (eds), *NK-BGB/Erbrecht*, vol 5 (6th edn, Nomos 2022).

Kropholler, Jan, *Internationales Einheitsrecht* (Mohr Siebeck 1975).

– *Internationales Privatrecht* (6th edn, Mohr Siebeck 2006).

Kruger, Thalia, *Civil Jurisdiction Rules of the EU and Their Impact on Third States* (OUP 2008).

Krüger, Hilmar, 'Studien über Probleme des türkischen Internationalen Erbrechts' in Sabih Arkan and Aynur Yongalık (eds), *Festschrift Liber Amicorum Tuğrul Ansay – Zum 75. Geburtstag/in Honour of his 75th Birthday* (Kluwer Law International 2006), 131–158.

– 'Erbrechtliche Probleme in den deutsch-türkischen Beziehungen' in Hilmar Krüger and Yasemin Körtek (eds), *Beiträge zum türkischen Recht – Erbrecht und Sozialrecht* (BWV 2010), 39–59.

– 'Neues zum deutsch-türkischen Nachlassabkommen – Zu einer Initiative des nordrhein-westfälischen Justizministers –' (2013) 22 Informationsbrief der DTJV 4–7.

Krūmiņš, Toms, 'Application of the EU Succession Regulation in Practice: The case of Latvia and Beyond' (2019) 15 J Priv Int L 365–392.

Kunz, Lena, 'Die neue Europäische Erbrechtsverordnung – ein Überblick (Teil I)' [2012] GPR 208–212.

– 'Die neue Europäische Erbrechtsverordnung – ein Überblick (Teil II)' [2012] GPR 253–257.

Kurdakul, Necdet, *Osmanlı Devleti'nde Ticaret Anlaşmaları ve Kapitülasyonlar* [Trade Agreements and Capitulations in the Ottoman Empire] (Döler Neşriyat 1981).

Kurşat, Zekeriya, *Terekenin Korunması Önlemleri* [Estate Preservation Measures] (Filiz Kitabevi 2010).

Kurth, Steffen, 'Wechselleben zwischen der spanischen Costa Brava und der ostwestfälischen Provinz – Ermittlung des gewöhnlichen Aufenthalts eines Erblassers, der sich in zwei Staaten abwechselnd aufhält: (zu OLG Hamm, 02.01.2018 – 10 W 35/17)' [2019] IPRax 123–127.

– 'Ein Amerikaner in Paris: Zur Bestimmung des gewöhnlichen Aufenthalts eines Weltenbummlers für die Zwecke der EUErbVO? – zugleich Anmerkung zu Cour de cassation, 29.5.2019 – Cass. Civ. 1 Nr. 18–13.383' [2020] ErbR 618–620.

Kuru, Baki, *Nizasız Kaza* [Non-Contentious Proceedings] (Ajans Türk Matbaası 1961).

– *Hukuk Muhakemeleri Usulü* [Civil Procedure], vol 1 – 3 – 4 – 5 – 6 (6th edn, Demir Demir 2001).

Küçükgüngör, Erkan, 'Roma ve Türk Hukukunda Muayyen Mal Vasiyeti' [Legacy in Roman and Turkish Law] (1996) 45 AÜHFD 505–531.

Kühne, Gunther, *Die Parteiautonomie im internationalen Erbrecht* (Gieseking 1973).

Künzle, Hans Rainer, in Markus Müller-Chen and Corinne Widmer Lüchinger (eds), *Zürcher Kommentar zum IPRG: Kommentar zum Bundesgesetz über das Internationale Privatrecht (IPRG) vom 18. Dezember 1987*, vol 1 (3rd edn, Schulthess 2018).

Küpe, Bahar, *Milletlerarası Özel Hukukta Şekil* [Form in Private International Law] (Adalet Yayınevi 2021).

Lagarde, Paul, 'Public Policy' in Kurt Lipstein (ed), *International Encyclopedia of Comparative Law – Vol III: Private International Law* (Mohr Siebeck & Martinus Nijhoff Publishers 2011), Chapter 11 (1994).

– 'Les principes de base du nouveau règlement européen sur les successions' [2012] Rev crit dr int privé 691–732.

– in Ulf Bergquist and others (eds), *EU Regulation on Succession and Wills – Commentary* (Otto Schmidt 2015).

Lale, Muktedir, 'Türk Milletlerarası Usul Hukukunda Türk Mahkemelerinin Milletlerarası Yargı Yetkisi' [International Jurisdiction of Turkish Courts in Turkish International Civil Procedural Law] (Master Thesis, Ankara University 1996).

Lange, Knut Werner, 'Das Erbkollisionsrecht im neuen Entwurf einer EU-ErbVO' [2012] ZErb 160–165.

– 'Das geplante Europäische Nachlasszeugnis' [2012] DNotZ 168–179.

– 'Das Europäische Nachlasszeugnis' in Anatol Dutta and Sebastian Herrler (eds), *Die Europäische Erbrechtsverordnung, 20 Jahre DNotI 1993–2013* (C.H. Beck 2014), 161–178.

Lechner, Kurt, 'EU Regulation 650/2012 on successions and the creation of a European Certificate of Succession' in European Parliament, Directorate-General for Internal Policies, Policy Department C: Citizens' Rights and Constitutional Affairs – Legal Affairs (ed), *Cross-border activities in the EU, Making life easier for citizens – Workshop for the JURI Committee – PE 510.003* (2015) <http://www.europarl.europa.eu/RegData/etudes/STUD/2015/510003/IPOL_STU(2015)510003_EN.pdf> accessed 17 January 2017, 113–149.

– 'Die Europäische Erbrechtsverordnung' [2016] DNotZ-Sonderheft 102–114.
– in Reinhold Geimer, Rolf A. Schütze and Wolfgang Hau (eds), *Internationaler Rechtsverkehr in Zivil- und Handelssachen* (63rd edn, C.H. Beck 2021).
Lehmann, Daniel, 'Stellungnahme zum Grünbuch der Kommission der Europäischen Gemeinschaften zum Erb- und Testamentsrecht' [2005] ZErb 320–327.
– *Die Reform des Internationalen Erb- und Erbprozessrechts im Rahmen der geplanten Brüssel – IV Verordnung* (zerb verlag 2006).
– 'Internationale Reaktionen auf das Grünbuch zum Erb- und Testamentsrecht' [2006] IPRax 204–207.
– 'Die EU-Erbrechtsverordnung zur Abwicklung grenzüberschreitender Nachlässe' [2012] DStR 2085–2089.
– 'Der Referentenentwurf für ein Begleitgesetz zur EuErbVO' [2014] ZEV 232–236.
– 'Der Regierungsentwurf für ein Gesetz zum Internationalen Erbrecht' [2015] ZEV 138–141.
Lehmann, Walther, *Die Kapitulationen* (Kiepenheuer 1917).
Lein, Eva, 'A Further Step Towards a European Code of Private International Law – The Commission Proposal for a Regulation on Succession' (2009) XI YbPIL 107–141.
– 'Die Erbrechtsverordnung aus Sicht der Drittstaaten' in Anatol Dutta and Sebastian Herrler (eds), *Die Europäische Erbrechtsverordnung, 20 Jahre DNotI 1993–2013* (C.H. Beck 2014), 199–220.
– in Anatol Dutta and Johannes Weber (eds), *Internationales Erbrecht* (2nd edn, C.H. Beck 2021).
Leipold, Dieter, 'Wandlungen in den Grundlagen des Erbrechts?' (1980) 180 AcP 160–237.
– 'Europa und das Erbrecht' in Gerhard Köbler, Meinhard Heinze and Wolfgang Hromadka (eds), *Europas universale rechtsordnungspolitische Aufgabe im Recht des dritten Jahrtausends – Festschrift für Alfred Söllner zum 70. Geburtstag* (C.H. Beck 2000), 647–668.
– 'Die internationale Zuständigkeit in erbrechtlichen Verfahren (nach deutschem Recht und nach dem Kommissionsvorschlag für eine Europäische Erbrechtsverordnung)' in Jacek Gudowski and Karol Weitz (eds), *Aurea Praxis Aurea Theoria: Księga Pamiątkowa ku Czci Profesora Tadeusza Erecińskiego*, vol 1 (LexisNexis 2011), 1155–1182.
– 'Ist der Wegfall des Zugewinnausgleichs bei Vorversterben des Ehegatten mit dem geringeren Zugewinn verfassungsgemäß?' [2011] NJW 1179–1182.
– 'Gerichtsstandsvereinbarungen nach der Europäischen Erbrechtsverordnung' in Karlheinz Muscheler and Reinhard Zimmermann (eds), *Zivilrecht und Steuerrecht, Erwerb von Todes wegen und Schenkung: Festschrift für Jens Peter Meincke zum 80. Geburtstag* (C.H. Beck 2015), 219–235.
– in Franz Jürgen Säcker and others (eds), *MüKoBGB*, vol 11 (8th edn, C.H. Beck 2020).
Leitzen, Mario, 'Die Rechtswahl nach der EuErbVO' [2013] ZEV 128–132.
Leu, Daniel, 'Die EU-Erbrechtsverordnung und ihre Bedeutung aus Schweizer Sicht' [2016] SJZ 441–449.
Li, Haopei, 'Some Recent Developments in the Conflict of Laws of Succession' (1990) 224 RdC 9–121.
Lipworth, Frank, Le Bouffo, Jean-Pierre and Le Bouffo, Jérôme, 'France' in Louis Garb and John Wood (eds), *International Succession* (4th edn, OUP 2015), 275–296.
Liu, Yin, 'Recognition of Foreign Same-Sex Unions in China' (2019–2020) XXI YbPIL 425–456.

Löhnig, Martin, in Dagmar Kaiser and others (eds), *NK-BGB/Familienrecht*, vol 4 (4th edn, Nomos 2021).

Looschelders, Dirk, 'Anwendbarkeit des § 1371 Abs. 1 BGB nach Korrektur einer ausländischen Erbquote wegen Unvereinbarkeit mit dem ordre public' [2009] IPRax 505–509.

– 'Die allgemeinen Lehren des Internationalen Privatrechts im Rahmen der Europäischen Erbrechtsverordnung' in Katharina Hilbig-Lugani and others (eds), *Zwischenbilanz – Festschrift für Dagmar Coester-Waltjen zum 70. Geburtstag* (Gieseking 2015), 531–542.

– 'The External Relations of Germany' in Anatol Dutta and Wolfgang Wurmnest (eds), *European Private International Law and Member State Treaties with Third States – The Case of the European Succession Regulation* (Intersentia 2019), 149–173.

– 'Treaty 19: Germany-Turkey' in Anatol Dutta and Wolfgang Wurmnest (eds), *European Private International Law and Member State Treaties with Third States – The Case of the European Succession Regulation* (Intersentia 2019), 427–429.

– in Rainer Hüßtege and Heinz-Peter Mansel (eds), *NK-BGB/Rom-Verordnungen, vol* 6 (3rd edn, Nomos 2019).

– in Franz Jürgen Säcker and others (eds), *MüKoBGB*, vol 11 (8th edn, C.H. Beck 2020).

Lorenz, Stephan, 'Erbrecht in Europa – Auf dem Weg zu kollisionsrechtlicher Rechtseinheit' [2012] ErbR 39–49.

– in Wolfgang Hau and Roman Poseck (eds), *BeckOK BGB (Stand: 1.2.2022)* (61st edn, C.H. Beck 2022).

Lorenzen, Ernest G., 'The Qualification, Classification, or Characterization Problem in the Conflict of Laws' (1941) 50 YLJ 743–761.

Loussouarn, Yvon, 'The IXth Session of the Hague Conference on Private International Law' (1961) 88 JDI 655–673.

Lowenfeld, Andreas F., 'International Litigation and the Quest for Reasonableness: General Course on Private International Law' (1994) 245 RdC 9–319.

Ludwig, Ingo, 'Notariat II Villingen: Zuständigkeit deutscher Gerichte im Einantwortungs- und Erbscheinsverfahren nach einem österreichischen Erblasser' [2013] ZEV 150–152.

– in Maximilian Herberger and others (eds), *jurisPK-BGB*, vol 6 (7th edn, juris 2015).

– in Maximilian Herberger and others (eds), *jurisPK-BGB*, vol 6 (9th edn, juris 2020).

Lübcke, Tobias, 'EuErbVO: Problemfelder im Rahmen der internationalen Zuständigkeit bei Vorliegen einer Rechtswahl durch den Erblasser' [2015] GPR 111–118.

Lüttringhaus, Jan D., 'Substitution' in Jürgen Basedow and others (eds), *Encyclopedia of Private International Law* (Edward Elgar Publishing 2017), 1675–1682.

Maccari, Maria Virginia, 'France' in Lucia Ruggeri, Ivana Kunda and Sandra Winkler (eds), *Family Property and Succession in EU Member States: National Reports on the Collected Data* (Sveučilište u Rijeci, Pravni fakultet 2019) <https://www.euro-family.eu/documenti/news/psefs_e_book_compressed.pdf> accessed 26 March 2020, 234–257.

Maggiolo, Marcello, 'The Decedent' in Ulrich Drobnig and Karl Heinz Neumayer (eds), International Encyclopedia of Comparative Law – Vol V: Succession (Mohr Siebeck & Martinus Nijhoff Publishers 2018), Chapter 1 (1992).

Magnus, Robert, 'Gerichtsstandsvereinbarungen im Erbrecht?' [2013] IPRax 393–398.

– in Rainer Hüßtege and Heinz-Peter Mansel (eds), *NK-BGB/Rom-Verordnungen*, vol 6 (3rd edn, Nomos 2019).

Majer, Christian Friedrich, 'Das deutsch-türkische Nachlassabkommen: ein Anachronismus' [2012] ZEV 182–186.

Makarov, Alexander N., *Grundriß des internationalen Privatrechts* (Alfred Metzner Verlag 1970).

Makowsky, Mark, in Rainer Hüßtege and Heinz-Peter Mansel (eds), *NK-BGB/Rom-Verordnungen, vol* 6 (3rd edn, 2019).

Mankowski, Peter, in Dieter Henrich (ed), *Staudinger BGB – EGBGB/IPR Einführungsgesetz zum Bürgerlichen Gesetzbuche – Art. 13–17b EGBGB (Internationales Eherecht)* (Sellier & de Gruyter 2010).

– 'Gelten die bilateralen Staatsverträge der Bundesrepublik Deutschland im Internationalen Erbrecht nach dem Wirksamwerden der EuErbVO weiter?' [2013] ZEV 529–534.

– 'Das erbrechtliche Viertel nach § 1371 Abs. 1 BGB im deutschen und europäischen Internationalen Privatrecht' [2014] ZEV 121–129.

– 'Der gewöhnliche Aufenthalt des Erblassers unter Art. 21 Abs. 1 EuErbVO' [2015] IPRax 39–46.

– 'Europäische Reversion: Das erbrechtliche Viertel ist im europäischen IPR Erbrecht! – Kritik, Umschau und Folgen zur EuGH-Entscheidung Mahnkopf' [2018] ErbR 295–305.

Mansel, Heinz-Peter, *Personalstatut, Staatsangehörigkeit und Effektivität* (C.H. Beck 1988).

– 'Vereinheitlichung des Internationalen Erbrechts in der Europäischen Gemeinschaft – Kompetenzfragen und Regelungsgrundsätze' in Sabih Arkan and Aynur Yongalık (eds), *Prof. Dr. Tuğrul Ansay'a Armağan* [Liber Amicorum Prof. Dr. Tuğrul Ansay] (Turhan Kitabevi 2006), 183–226.

Max Planck Institute for Comparative and International Private Law, 'Comments on the European Commission's Proposal for a Regulation of the European Parliament and of the Council on Jurisdiction, Applicable Law, Recognition and Enforcement of Decisions and Authentic Instruments in Matters of Succession and the Creation of a European Certificate of Succession' (2010) 71 RabelsZ 522–570.

McClean, David, 'De Conflictu Legum, Perspectives on Private International Law at the Turn of the Century' (2000) 282 RdC 41–227.

McLean, James A., 'The UK and the European Succession Regulation: Fog over the Channel – Potential Pitfalls for the Unwary?' (2018) 22 Edinburgh L Rev 86–93.

von Mehren, Arthur Taylor, 'Special Substantive Rules for Multistate Problems: Their Role and Significance in Contemporary Choice of Law Methodology' (1974) 88 Harv L Rev 347–371.

Meidanis, Haris P., in Haris P. Pamboukis (ed), *EU Succession Regulation No 650/2012 – A Commentary* (Nomiki Bibliothiki & C.H. Beck & Hart & Nomos 2017).

Meijers, Eduard Maurits, 'Erfrechtelijke moeilijkheden op het gebied van het internationaal privaatrecht' (1936) 67 WPNR 609–612 (I); 621–625 (II); 633–636 (III); 641–645 (IV, *slot*).

Meray, Seha L., *Lozan Barış Konferansı – Tutanaklar, Belgeler* [Lausanne Peace Conference – Minutes, Documents] (3rd edn, Yapı Kredi Yayınları 2001).

Mesci, Barış, 'Milletlerarası Özel Hukukta Atıf (Renvoi)' [Renvoi in Private International Law] (2017) 16 İKÜHFD 311–370.

Metallinos, Alexander S., in Haris P. Pamboukis (ed), *EU Succession Regulation No 650/2012 – A Commentary* (Nomiki Bibliothiki & C.H. Beck & Hart & Nomos 2017).

Meusburger-Hammerer, Gabriele and Wittwer, Alexander, 'OGH, 26.02.2019 – 2 Ob 124/18 a: Beschränkung des Verlassenschaftsverfahrens bei Nachlass in der Schweiz' [2019] ErbR 353–360.

Meyer-Sparenberg, Wolfgang, *Staatsvertragliche Kollisionsnormen* (Duncker & Humblot 1990).
Michaels, Ralf, 'Recognition and Enforcement of Foreign Judgments' in Rüdiger Wolfrum (ed), *Max Planck Encyclopedia of Public International Law* (OUP 2009).
– 'Comparative Law and Private International Law' in Jürgen Basedow and others (eds), *Encyclopedia of Private International Law* (Edward Elgar Publishing 2017), 417–425.
– 'Jurisdiction, Foundations' in Jürgen Basedow and others (eds), *Encyclopedia of Private International Law* (Edward Elgar Publishing 2017), 1043–1051.
Miller, Gareth, *International Aspects of Succession* (Ashgate 2000).
Mills, Alex, 'Rethinking Jurisdiction in International Law' (2014) 84 BYIL 187–239.
Morris, John Humphrey Carlile, 'Intestate Succession to Land in the Conflict of Laws' (1969) 85 LQR 339–371.
Müller-Freienfels, Wolfram, 'Kernfragen des Gleichberechtigungsgesetzes' [1957] JZ 685–696.
Müller-Lukoschek, Jutta, *Die neue EU-Erbrechtsverordnung: Leitfaden mit Erläuterungen für die notarielle Praxis* (2nd edn, Deutscher NotarVerlag 2015).
Murakami, Haruki, *Norwegian Wood* (Jay Rubin tr, The Harvill Press 2001).
Musielak, Hans-Joachim, in Franz Jürgen Säcker and others (eds), *MüKoBGB*, vol 11 (8th edn, C.H. Beck 2020).

Nadelmann, Kurt H., 'The Hague Conference on Private International Law Ninth Session' (1960) 9 AJCL 583–595.
– 'The Formal Validity of Wills and the Washington Convention 1973 Providing the Form of an International Will' (1974) 22 AJCL 365–383.
Naumann, Hanno, 'Grundzüge des neuen türkischen Ehegüter- und Erbrechts' [2003] RNotZ 344–370.
Nazikioğlu, O. Işık, 'Yabancı Memleket Mahkemelerinden Verilen Kararların Tanınması ve Tenfizi' [Recognition and Enforcement of Foreign Country Judgments] (1950) 7 AÜHFD 468–500.
Neuhaus, Paul Heinrich, 'Legal Certainty versus Equity in the Conflict of Laws' (1963) 28 Law & Contemp Probs 795–807.
– *Die Grundbegriffe des internationalen Privatrechts* (Mohr Siebeck 1976).
Nietner, Sarah, *Internationaler Entscheidungseinklang im europäischen Kollisionsrecht* (Mohr Siebeck 2016).
Nomer, Ergin, 'Milletlerarası Yetki Alanında Derdestlik İtirazı' [Objection of Lis Pendens in International Jurisdiction] (1968) 34 İÜHFM 343–374.
– 'Yabancıların "Ahkamı Şahsiyesi" (Statut Personnel) ve Terekesi ile İlgili İhtilaflarda Türk Kanunlar İhtilafı Sisteminin Gelişimi' [The Development of the Turkish Conflict-of-Laws System in Disputes Concerning Foreigners' Personal Status (Statut Personnel) and Succession], *İstanbul Üniversitesi Hukuk Fakültesi'nin 50. Yıl Armağanı: Cumhuriyet Döneminde Hukuk* [Liber Amicorum in Honour of the 50th Anniversary Istanbul University Faculty of Law: Law in the Republican Era] (Fakülteler Matbaası 1973), 495–527.
– 'Devletler Hususi Hukukunda Milletlerarası Yetki Mefhumu' [The Concept of Jurisdiction in Private International Law] (1974) 40 İÜHFM 393–426.
– 'Ehliyetsizlik Sebebi ile Almanya'daki Gayrimenkul Mallar İçin Vasiyetin İptali' [Invalidation of a Will for Immovable Properties in Germany Due to Incapacity] (1981) 1 MHB 61–63.

– 'Yabancı Verâset İlamlarının Tanınmasında Yargıtay Kararları' [Judgments of the Turkish Court of Cassation (Yargıtay) on the Recognition of Foreign Certificates of Succession] (1991) 65 İBD 789–796.
– 'Türk Devletler Özel Hukukunda Çifte Vatandaşlık' [Dual Nationality in Turkish Private International Law] (1994) 14 MHB 55–62.
– 'Yabancı Çekişmesiz Yargı Kararlarının Tanınmasında Kesinleşme Şartı' [Condition of Finality for the Recognition of Foreign Decisions Rendered in Non-Contentious Proceedings] in Hayri Domaniç (ed), *Prof. Dr. Erdoğan Moroğlu'na 65. Yaş Günü Armağanı* [Liber Amicorum Prof. Dr. Erdoğan Moroğlu in Honour of his 65th Birthday] (2nd edn, Beta 2001), 909–922.
– *Milletlerarası Usul Hukuku* [International Civil Procedural Law] (2nd edn, Beta 2018).
– *Devletler Hususî Hukuku* [Private International Law] (23rd edn, Beta 2021).
– *Türk Vatandaşlık Hukuku* [Turkish Nationality Law] (29th edn, Filiz Kitabevi 2021).
Nordlund, Lisa, 'Sweden' in Lucia Ruggeri, Ivana Kunda and Sandra Winkler (eds), *Family Property and Succession in EU Member States: National Reports on the Collected Data* (Sveučilište u Rijeci, Pravni fakultet 2019) <https://www.euro-family.eu/documenti/news/psefs_e_book_compressed.pdf> accessed 14 December 2020, 657–677.
Nordmeier, Carl Friedrich, 'Erbverträge und nachlassbezogene Rechtsgeschäfte in der EuErbVO – eine Begriffsklärung' [2013] ZEV 117–124.
– 'Grundfragen der Rechtswahl in der neuen EU-Erbrechtsverordnung – Eine Untersuchung des Art. 22 ErbRVO' [2013] GPR 148–155.
– in Rainer Hüßtege and Heinz-Peter Mansel (eds), *NK-BGB/Rom Verordnungen*, vol 6 (3rd edn, Nomos 2019).
Nuyts, Arnaud, 'Study on Residual Jurisdiction – Review of the Member States' Rules concerning the "Residual Jurisdiction" of their courts in Civil and Commercial Matters pursuant to the Brussels I and II Regulations (JLS/C4/2005/07 30 CE)0040309/00-37)' <https://gavclaw.files.wordpress.com/2020/05/arnaud-nuyts-study_residual_jurisdiction_en.pdf> accessed 15 January 2021.

Odendahl, Hanswerner, 'Edinilmiş Mallara Katılma Rejiminin Alman Yasal Mal Rejimi ile Karşılaştırılması ve Alman Milletlerarası Özel Hukukunda Mal Rejimi' [Comparison of the Regime of Participation in Acquired Property with the German Default Matrimonial Property Regime and the Matrimonial Property Regime in German Private International Law] in Şükran Şıpka, Barış Özbilen and Ebru Şensöz (eds), *Uygulamalı Aile Hukuku Sertifika Programı III. Dönem 17–18 Kasım 2006 – Edinilmiş Mallara Katılma Rejimi ve Uygulama Sorunları* [Practical Family Law Certificate Programme III. Term 17–18 November 2006 – The Regime of Participation in Acquired Property and Problems in Practice] (İstanbul Ticaret Üniversitesi Yayınları 2007), 113–122.
– 'Die Bedeutung neuer internationaler IPR-Normen im Familien- und Erbrecht für Fälle mit Türkeibezug' [2018] IPRax 450–455.
– *Die Auseinandersetzung der Errungenschaftsbeteiligung in der Rechtsprechung des türkischen Kassationshofs* (Peter Lang 2020).
Odersky, Felix, 'Die Europäische Erbrechtsverordnung in der Gestaltungspraxis' [2013] Notar 3–9.
– in Ulf Bergquist and others (eds), *EU Regulation on Succession and Wills – Commentary* (Otto Schmidt 2015).
– in Felix Odersky and Rainer Hausmann (eds), *Internationales Privatrecht in der Notar- und Gestaltungspraxis* (4th edn, C.H. Beck 2021).

Odman Boztosun, N. Ayşe, 'The 2007 Turkish Code on Private International Law and International Civil Procedure' (2007) IX YbPIL 583–604.

Oğuzman, Kemal, Seliçi, Özer and Oktay Özdemir, Saibe, *Kişiler Hukuku (Gerçek ve Tüzel Kişiler)* [Law of Persons (Natural and Legal Persons)] (20th edn, Filiz Kitabevi 2021).

Ongley, Frederick Oliver Jones, *The Ottoman Land Code* (W Clowes 1892).

Ökçün, Gündüz, *Devletler Hususî Hukukunun Kaynakları ve Kamu Düzeni* [Sources of Private International Law and Public Policy] (Sevinç Matbaası 1967).

Önen, Ergun, 'Gayrimenkul Davalarında Yetki' [Jurisdiction in Real Estate Litigation] (1965) 22–23 AÜHFD 567–663.

Özbakan, Işıl, *Türk Hukukunda Yabancı Mahkeme Kararlarının Tanınması ve Tenfizi* [Recognition and Enforcement of Foreign Court Judgments in Turkish Law] (Kazancı 1987).

Özdemir Kocasakal, Hatice, *Doğrudan Uygulanan Kurallar ve Sözleşmeler Üzerindeki Etkileri* [Overriding Mandatory Rules and Their Effects on Contracts] (Galatasaray Üniversitesi Yayınları 2001).

Özekes, Muhammet, in Hakan Pekcanıtez and others (eds), *Pekcanıtez Usûl: Medenî Usûl Hukuku* [Pekcanıtez Procedure: Civil Procedural Law], vol 3 (15th edn, On İki Levha 2017).

Özkan, Işıl, 'Türk Mahkemelerinin Milletlerarası Yetkisi' [International Jurisdiction of Turkish Courts], *Seha L. Meray'a Armağan* [Liber Amicorum Seha L. Meray], vol I (TC Ziraat Bankası Matbaası 1981), 176–222.

– *Devletler Özel Hukukunda İkametgah, Mutad Mesken ve İşyeri Bağlama Noktalarının Yeniden Değerlendirilmesi* [Reassessment of the Connecting Factors of Domicile, Habitual Residence and Place of Employment in Private International Law] (Naturel Yayınları 2003).

Özkan, Işıl and Tütüncübaşı, Uğur, *Uluslararası Usûl Hukuku* [International Procedural Law] (2nd edn, Adalet Yayınevi 2020).

Öztan, Bilge, *Miras Hukuku (Tablolar ve Örneklerle)* [Succession Law (With Tables and Examples)] (12th edn, Yetkin 2021).

Öztekin, Günseli, 'Recognition and Enforcement of Foreign Court Judgments Within the Framework of the Application of the Supreme Court of Appeals', *Prof. Dr. Tahir Çağa'nın Anısına Armağan* [Limer Amicorum in Memory of Prof. Dr. Tahir Çağa] (Beta 2000), 389–396.

Öztürk, Necla, 'Miras Statüsünün Belirlenmesinde İrade Muhtariyetinin Rolü' [The Role of Party Autonomy in Determining Succession Statute] (2015) 5 AkdHFD 177–208.

– *Milletlerarası Özel Hukukta Aile Kurma Amaçlı Evlilik Benzeri Yaşam Modelleri* [Marriage-like Relationships for the Purpose of Establishing a Family in Private International Law] (Adalet Yayınevi 2016).

Özuğur, Ali İhsan, *Türk Medeni Kanunundan Önce ve Sonra Miras Hukuku* [Succession Law Before and After the Turkish Civil Code], vol 1 (4th edn, Seçkin 2016).

Panopoulos, George, in Haris P. Pamboukis (ed), *EU Succession Regulation No 650/2012 – A Commentary* (Nomiki Bibliothiki & C.H. Beck & Hart & Nomos 2017).

Pamboukis, Haris P., in Haris P. Pamboukis (ed), *EU Succession Regulation No 650/2012 – A Commentary* (Nomiki Bibliothiki & C.H. Beck & Hart & Nomos 2017).

Pataut, Etienne, 'International Jurisdiction and Third States: A View from the EC in Family Matters' in Alberto Malatesta, Stefania Bariatti and Fausto Pocar (eds), *The External Dimension of EC Private International Law in Family and Succession Matters* (CEDAM 2008), 123–148.

– 'The Public-Policy Exception and the Proposal for a Regulation of the European Parliament and of the Council on Jurisdiction, Applicable Law, Recognition and Enforcement of Decisions and Authentic Instruments in Matters of Succession and the Creation of a European Certificate of Succession (COM(2009)154)' in European Parliament, Directorate-General for Internal Policies, Policy Department C: Citizens' Rights and Constitutional Affairs – Legal Affairs (ed), *Note PE 432.741* (2010) <http://www.europarl.europa.eu/thinktank/en/document.html?reference=IPOL-JURI_NT(2010)432741> accessed 31 July 2019.

– 'The External Dimension of Private International Family Law' in Marise Cremona and Hans-W. Micklitz (eds), *Private Law in the External Relations of the EU* (OUP 2016), 107–124.

Pătrăuş, Mihaela and Ofrim, Ionita Maria, 'European Certificate of Succession' [2019] AGORA Int'l J Jurid Sci 78–88.

Patzina, Reinhard, in Wolfgang Krüger and Thomas Rauscher (eds), *MüKoZPO*, vol 1 (6th edn, C.H. Beck 2020).

Pazdan, Maksymilian and Zachariasiewicz, Maciej, 'The EU Succession Regulation: Achievements, Ambiguities, and Challenges for the Future' (2021) 17 J Priv Int L 74–113.

Pekcanıtez, Hakan, in Hakan Pekcanıtez and others (eds), *Pekcanıtez Usûl: Medenî Usûl Hukuku* [Pekcanıtez Procedure: Civil Procedural Law], vol 2 (15th edn, On İki Levha 2017).

Pérès, Cécile, 'Compulsory Portion in France' in Kenneth G. C. Reid, Marius J. de Waal and Reinhard Zimmermann (eds), *Comparative Succession Law – Volume III: Mandatory Family Protection* (OUP 2020), 78–107.

Perscha, Alice, in Astrid Deixler-Hübner and Martin Schauer (eds), *Kommentar zur EU-Erbrechtsverordnung* (2nd edn, Manz 2020).

Pfeiffer, Magdalena, 'Choice of Law in International Family and Succession Law' (2012) 2 TLQ 291–305.

– 'Legal Certainty and Predictability in International Succession Law' (2016) 12 J Priv Int L 566–586.

Picht, Peter Georg and Studen, Goran, 'Die Schweiz will ihre Rechtsregeln für grenzüberschreitende Erbfälle reformieren – Anpassung an die EU-Rechtslage' [2016] Successio 318–323.

Piltz, Detlev J., in Hans Flick and Detlev J. Piltz (eds), *Der internationale Erbfall: Erbrecht, Internationales Privatrecht, Erbschaftssteuerrecht* (2nd edn, C.H. Beck 2008).

Pintens, Walter, 'Foreword' in Anatol Dutta and Wolfgang Wurmnest (eds), *European Private International Law and Member State Treaties with Third States – The Case of the European Succession Regulation* (Intersentia 2019), v–vii.

Pretelli, Ilaria, in Andrea Bonomi and Patrick Wautelet (eds), *Le droit européen des successions-Commentaire du Règlement n°650/2012 du 4 juillet 2012* (2nd edn, Bruylant 2016).

Pusch, Barbara, 'German Retirement Tranquillity that the "Law on Foreigners and International Protection" Cannot Protect' (2015) <http://researchturkey.org/german-retirement-tranquillity-that-the-law-on-foreigners-and-international-protection-cannot-protect/> accessed 2 March 2018.

Pürselim, Hatice Selin, 'Almanya'da Tescil Edilmiş Eşcinsel Hayat Ortaklığında Veraset İlamının Alınması ve bu İlama Dayanılarak Türkiye ve Almanya'da Bulunan Terekenin Paylaşılması' [Obtaining A Certificate of Succession for a Registered Same-Sex Partnership in Germany and Sharing-out of the Estate Situated in Turkey and in Based on This Certificate] (2011) 31 MHB 243–266.

– 'Uygulanacak Hukuk, Yetkili Mahkeme ve Tanıma Davası Kapsamında Mirasçılık Belgesinin İncelenmesi' [Examination of Certificate of Inheritance with Respect to Applicable Law, International Jurisdiction and Action for Recognition] (2021) 9 KHASHFD 179–197.

Rabel, Ernst, *The Conflict of Laws: A Comparative Study*, vol I (Callaghan & Company 1945).

Re, Jacopo, 'Where Did They Live? Habitual Residence in the Succession Regulation' [2018] RDIPP 978–1009.

Reid, Kenneth G. C., de Waal, Marius J. and Zimmermann, Reinhard, 'Intestate Succession in Historical and Comparative Perspective' in Kenneth G. C. Reid, Marius J. de Waal and Reinhard Zimmermann (eds), *Comparative Succession Law – Volume II: Intestate Succession* (OUP 2015), 442–512.

Reimann, Mathias, *Conflict of Laws in Western Europe: A Guide through the Jungle* (Transnational Publishers 1995).

Remde, Julia, 'Die Europäische Erbrechtsverordnung nach dem Vorschlag der Kommission vom 14. Oktober 2009' [2012] RNotZ 65–85.

Rheinstein, Max, 'European Methods for the Liquidation of the Debts of the Deceased Persons' (1935) 20 Iowa L Rev 431–475.

Ridi, Niccolò, 'Precarious Finality? Reflections on Res Judicata and the Question of the Delimitation of the Continental Shelf Case' (2018) 31 Leiden J Int Law 383–401.

Rittner, Fritz, 'Zur Auslegung des § 1371 Abs. 2 BGB n. F.' [1958] DNotZ 181–200.

Rodríguez Rodrigo, Juliana, in Alfonso-Luis Calvo Caravaca, Angelo Davì and Heinz-Peter Mansel (eds), *The EU Succession Regulation – A Commentary* (Cambridge University Press 2016).

Rogerson, Pippa, 'Habitual Residence: The New Domicile?' (2000) 49 ICLQ 86–107.

– *Collier's Conflict of Laws* (4th edn, Cambridge University Press 2013).

– in Andrew Dickinson and Eva Lein (eds), *The Brussels I Regulation Recast* (OUP 2015).

Romano, Gian Paolo, 'Remarks on the Impact of the Regulation No 650/2012 on the Swiss-EU Successions' (2015–2016) XVII YbPIL 253–289.

Rudolf, Claudia, 'The External Relations of Austria' in Anatol Dutta and Wolfgang Wurmnest (eds), *European Private International Law and Member State Treaties with Third States – The Case of the European Succession Regulation* (Intersentia 2019), 11–38.

Ruggeri, Lucia, Kunda, Ivana and Winkler, Sandra (eds), *Family Property and Succession in EU Member States: National Reports on the Collected Data* (Sveučilište u Rijeci, Pravni fakultet 2019) <https://www.euro-family.eu/documenti/news/psefs_e_book_compressed.pdf> accessed 26 March 2020.

Ruhi, Ahmet Cemal, 'Mirasçılık Belgesi ve Yabancı Ülke Mahkemelerinden Verilen Mirasçılık Belgelerinin Türkiye'de Tanınması' [Certificate of Inheritance and Recognition of Certificates of Succession Issued by Foreign Courts in Turkey] (2006) 32 YD 265–300.

– *Milletlerarası Özel Hukuk ve Usul Hukuku Hakkında Kanun – Gerekçeli, Kısa Açıklamalı, Yargıtay İçtihatlı* [Act on Private International and Procedural Law – With Preamble, Brief Expalanations, Case Law of the Turkish Court of Cassation (Yargıtay)] (4th edn, Seçkin 2014).

Ruhi, Ahmet Cemal and Ruhi, Canan, *Mirasçılık Belgesi, İptali ve Yeni Mirasçılık Belgesi Verilmesi* [Certificate of Succession, Its Revocation, and the Issuance of a New Certificate of Succession] (Seçkin 2015).

Rumpf, Christian, 'Erbrechtsfälle im deutsch-türkischen Rechtsverkehr' (2018) 27 Informationsbrief der DTJV 25–38.

– 'Türkei' in Murad Ferid, Karl Firsching and Rainer Hausmann (eds), *Internationales Erbrecht* (120th edn, C.H. Beck 2022).

Rylski, Piotr, 'The Influence of Bilateral Treaties with Third States on Jurisdiction and Recognition of Decisions in Matters on Succession – Polish Perspective' (2020) 26 PPPM 91–105.

Sakka, Samy, 'Der pauschalierte Zugewinnausgleich und das Europäische Nachlasszeugnis' [2018] MittBayNot 4–9.

Sakmar, Atâ, *Devletler Hususi Hukukunda Boşanma* [Divorce in Private International Law] (İstanbul Üniversitesi Hukuk Fakültesi Yayınları 1976).

– 'Yabancılık Unsuru Taşıyan Vasiyetnamelerin Tenfizi ve Yargıtay Uygulaması' [Execution of Testaments with a Foreign Element and the Case Law of the Turkish Court of Cassation (Yargıtay)] in İstanbul Üniversitesi Hukuk Fakültesi, Milletlerarası Hukuk ve Milletlerarası Münasebetler Enstitüsü (ed), *Prof. Dr. Hıfzı Timur'un Anısına Armağan* [Liber Amicorum in Memory of Prof. Dr. Hıfzı Timur] (Fakülteler Matbaası 1979), 729–745.

– *Yabancı İlamların Türkiye'deki Sonuçları* [Effects of Foreign Judgments in Turkey] (Fakülteler Matbaası 1982).

– 'Le nouveau droit international privé turc' (1990) 223 RdC 303–416.

Sakmar, Atâ, Ekşi, Nuray and Yılmaz, İlhan, *Milletlerarası Özel Hukuk ve Usul Hukuku Hakkında Kanun Mahkeme Kararları* [Judgments on the Private International and Procedural Law Act] (3rd edn, Beta 2001).

Salomon, Lourdes, 'The Acquisition of Possession in Legacies per vindicationem in Classical Roman Law and Its Influence in the Modern Civil Codes' (2006) 3 Roman LT 65–78.

Saner Gönen, Yasemin, 'Osmanlı İmparatorluğunda Yabancıların Adli Ayrıcalıkları' [Judicial Privileges of Foreigners in the Ottoman Empire] (DPhil thesis, Marmara University 1998).

– 'Osmanlı Konsolosluk Sözleşmeleri – II' [Ottoman Consular Conventions – II] [1999] Toplumsal Tarih 36–41.

Sargın, Fügen, *Milletlerarası Usul Hukukunda Yetki Anlaşmaları* [Jurisdiction Agreements in International Civil Procedural Law] (Yetkin 1996).

– *Yabancı Gerçek Kişilerin Türkiye'de Taşınmaz Mal Edinmeleri ve Sınırlı Aynî Haklardan Yararlanmaları* [Acquisition of Immovable Property and the Use of Limited Real Rights by Foreign Natural Persons in Turkey] (Yetkin 1997).

– *İnternet Aracılığıyla Gerçekleşen Marka İhlâlleri Hakkında Milletlerarası Yetkiyi Haiz Mahkemeler ve Uygulanacak Hukuk* [Jurisdiction and Applicable Law for Trademark Infringements on the Internet] (Yetkin 2005).

Sargın, Fügen and Erten, Rifat, 'MÖHUK Hükümleri Dairesinde Tanımanın Hukuki Niteliği, Usûlü ve Karşılaşılan Bazı Sorunlar: "Yeni Bir Düzenleme Yapma Gereği"' [The Legal Nature of and Procedure for Recognition under the Turkish Private International Law and Procedural Law Act (PILA) and Some Problems Encountered: "The Need for a New Regulation"] (2014) 3 UTTDER 37–136.

von Savigny, Friedrich Carl, *System des heutigen Römischen Rechts*, vol 8 (Veit & Comp 1849).

Saymen, Ferit H., *Türk Medeni Hukuku Cilt II – Şahsın Hukuku* [Turkish Civil Law Volume II – Law of Persons], vol II (Kenan Matbaası 1948).

von Schack, Wilfried, 'Neue Kollisionsnormen für die Form von Testamenten: Das Haager Übereinkommen über das auf die Form letztwilliger Verfügungen anzuwendende Recht' [1966] DNotZ 131–146.

Schaub, Renate, 'Die EU-Erbrechtsverordnung' in Karlheinz Muscheler (ed), *Hereditare – Jahrbuch für Erbrecht und Schenkungsrecht* (Mohr Siebeck 2013), 91–131.

Schauer, Martin, 'Europäisches Nachlasszeugnis' in Martin Schauer and Elisabeth Scheuba (eds), *Europäische Erbrechtsverordnung (2012/650/EU vom 4. Juli 2012)* (Manz 2012), 73–98.

– in Astrid Deixler-Hübner and Martin Schauer (eds), *Kommentar zur EU-Erbrechtsverordnung* (2nd edn, Manz 2015).

Scherpe, Jens M., 'The Financial Consequences of Divorce in a European Perspective' in Jens M. Scherpe (ed), *European Family Law Volume III – Family Law in a European Perspective* (Edward Elgar Publishing 2016), 146–208.

Schmidt, Jessica, 'Der Erbnachweis in Deutschland ab 2015: Erbschein vs. Europäisches Nachlasszeugnis' [2014] ZEV 389–395.

– in Christine Budzikiewicz, Marc-Philippe Weller and Wolfgang Wurmnest (eds), *BeckOGK-EuErbVO (Stand: 1.2.2022)* (C.H. Beck 2022).

Schmidt, Jan Peter, 'Transfer of Property on Death and Creditor Protection: The Meaning and Role of "Universal Succession"' in Andrew JM Steven, Ross Gilbert Anderson and John Keith Macleod (eds), *Nothing so Practical as a Good Theory: Festschrift for George L Gretton* (Avizandum 2017), 323–337.

– 'Challenged Legacies – First Decision of the European Court of Justice on the EU Succession Regulation (ECJ, 12 October 2017, C-218/16 (Kubicka))' (2018) 7 EPLJ 4–31.

– 'Abschied von alten Gewissheiten: Die EU-Erbrechtsverordnung in der Rechtsprechung' [2020] ErbR 91–98.

– 'Trying to Square the Circle: Comparative Remarks on the Rights of the Surviving Spouse on Intestacy' (2020) 24 Edinburgh L Rev 123–131.

– 'The Interplay between Succession and Matrimonial Property Regimes from a Comparative Perspective – Abstract', *ELI The Family and Succession Law SIG* (2020) <https://www.europeanlawinstitute.eu/fileadmin/user_upload/p_eli/SIGs/Family_Law/Webinar_2020/JP_Schmidt.pdf> accessed 4 January 2021.

– in Anatol Dutta and Johannes Weber (eds), *Internationales Erbrecht* (2nd edn, C.H. Beck 2021).

Schmidt, Michael, in Harm Peter Westermann, Barbara Grunewald and Georg Maier-Reimer (eds), *Erman BGB*, vol I (16th edn, Otto Schmidt 2020).

Schoenblum, Jeffrey A., *Multistate and Multinational Estate Planning*, vol 1 (CCH 2008).

Schols, Freek and Reijnen, Theo, 'The Netherlands' in Lucia Ruggeri, Ivana Kunda and Sandra Winkler (eds), *Family Property and Succession in EU Member States: National Reports on the Collected Data* (Sveučilište u Rijeci, Pravni fakultet 2019) <https://www.euro-family.eu/documenti/news/psefs_e_book_compressed.pdf> accessed 20 December 2020, 478–506.

Schömmer, Hans-Peter and Kesen, Nebi, *Internationales Erbrecht Türkei* (C.H. Beck 2004).

Schotten, Günther and Schmellenkamp, Cornelia, *Das Internationale Privatrecht in der notariellen Praxis* (2nd edn, C.H. Beck 2007).

Schotten, Günther and Wittkowski, Ralf, 'Das deutsch-iranische Niederlassungsabkommen im Familien- und Erbrecht' [1995] FamRZ 264–269.

Schurig, Klaus, in Gerhard Kegel (ed), *Soergel BGB*, vol 10 (Einführungsgesetz) (12th edn, Kohlhammer 1996).

Schwab, Martin T., in Christopher Keim and Daniel Lehmann (eds), *BeckFormB ErbR* (4th edn, C.H. Beck 2019).

Schwander, Ivo, 'Die EU-Erbrechtsverordnung' [2014] AJP 1084–1113.

Schwartze, Andreas, in Astrid Deixler-Hübner and Martin Schauer (eds), *Kommentar zur EU-Erbrechtsverordnung* (2nd edn, Manz 2020).

Schweizerisches Civilgesetzbuch, Vorentwurf des Eidgenössischen Justiz- und Polizeidepartements – Code Civil Suisse, Avant-Projet des Département Fédéral de Justice et Police (Buchdruckerei Büchler & Co 1900).

Schwenzer, Ingeborg and Keller, Tomie, 'The Changing Concept of "Family" and Challenges for Family Law in Switzerland' in Jens M. Scherpe (ed), *European Family Law Volume II – The Changing Concept of 'Family' and Challenges for Domestic Family Law* (Edward Elgar Publishing 2016), 309–334.

Schwimmer, Walter, 'The Effects of Globalisation on Law: The Impact on the Council of Europe' (2000) 2 FORUM 227–229.

Schwind, Michael A., 'Liability for Obligations of the Inheritance' in Ulrich Drobnig and Karl Heinz Neumayer (eds), *International Encyclopedia of Comparative Law – Vol V: Succession* (Mohr Siebeck & Martinus Nijhoff Publishers 2002), Chapter 8 (1995).

Scoles, Eugene F., 'The Hague Convention on Succession' (1994) 42 AJCL 85–123.

Seibl, Maximilian, 'Objektive und subjektive Anknüpfungen im Internationalen Erbrecht: ein Vergleich der bisherigen Rechtslage und der ErbVO' in Andreas Spickhoff (ed), *Symposium Parteiautonomie im Europäischen Internationalen Privatrecht* (Deutscher NotarVerlag 2013), 123–143.

Serozan, Rona and Engin, Baki İlkay, *Miras Hukuku ve Uygulama Çalışmaları* [Succession Law and Case Studies] (7th edn, Seçkin 2021).

Seviğ, Muammer Raşit, *Devletler Hususi Hukuku: Tabiiyet – Yabancılar Hukuku – Kanunlar İhtilafı* [Private International Law: Nationality – Law on Foreigners – Conflict of Laws], vol I (Bozkurt Basımevi 1937).

– *Türkiye Cumhuriyeti Kanunlar İhtilafı Kaidelerinin Sentezi* [Synthesis of Turkish Conflict-of-Laws Rules] (Fakülteler Matbaası 1941).

– 'İkametgâh' [Domicile] (1947) 13 İÜHFM 941–958.

Seviğ, Muammer Raşit and Seviğ, Vedat Raşit, *Devletler Hususi Hukuku* [Private International Law] (3rd edn, İsmail Akgün Matbaası 1962).

Seviğ, Vedat Raşit, *Hukuk ve Ticaret Davalarında Türk ve Yabancı Mahkemelerinin Devletler Hususi Hukuku Bakımından Yetkisi* [International Jurisdiction of Turkish and Foreign Courts in Civil and Commercial Matters] (Sulhi Garan Matbaası 1963).

– *Mirasla İlgili Devletler Hususi Hukuku Kaideleri* [Principles of Private International Law Related to Succession] (Sulhi Garan Matbaası 1963).

– *Ahkâmı Şahsiye Davalarında Türk Mahkemesinin Yetkisi* [Jurisdiction of Turkish Courts in Personal Status Cases] (Sermet Matbaası 1964).

– *Kanunlar İhtilafı (Yasama ve Yargılama Çatışmaları)* [Conflict of Laws (Conflicts of Legislation and Procedure)] (2nd edn, Sulhi Garan Matbaası 1974).

– *Devletler Hususi Hukuku Pratik Çalışmaları* [Case Studies on Private International Law] (Fakülteler Matbaası 1976).

– 'Yabancı Gerçek Kişilerin Türkiye'de Miras Hakları' [Succession Rights of Foreign Natural Persons in Turkey], *Prof. Dr. Hıfzı Timur'un Anısına Armağan* [Liber Amicorum Prof. Dr. Hıfzı Timur] (Fakülteler Matbaası 1979), 783–814.

Seyfarth, Stefan Georg, 'Wandel der internationalen Zuständigkeit im Erbrecht' (DPhil Thesis, Universität Konstanz 2012) <http://kops.uni-konstanz.de/handle/123456789/19299> accessed 17 January 2017.

Sieghörtner, Robert, in Meo-Micaela Hahne, Jürgen Schlögel and Rolf Schlünder (eds), *BeckOK FamFG* (*Stand: 1.4.2022*) (42nd edn, C.H. Beck 2022).

Siehr, Kurt, 'Connecting Factors, Party Autonomy and Renvoi' in Alberto Malatesta, Stefania Bariatti and Fausto Pocar (eds), *The External Dimension of EC Private International Law in Family and Succession Matters* (CEDAM 2008), 251–267.

– 'Ausländischer Erbschein für Nachlass in Deutschland? (zu LG München, 25.10.2011 – 28 O 243/10)' [2013] IPRax 241–245.

– 'Erbrechtliche Probleme um den Nachlass eines Schweizer Bürgers, der mit letztem gewöhnlichen Aufenthalt ausserhalb der Schweiz verstorben ist – Erbrecht im schweizerischen-deutschen-US-amerikanischen Rechtsverkehr' in Alexander R. Markus, Stephanie Hrubesch-Millauer and Rodrigo Rodriguez (eds), *Zivilprozess und Vollstreckung national und international – Schnittstellen und Vergleiche, Festschrift für Jolanta Kren Kostkiewicz* (Stämpfli Verlag 2018), 283–306.

Simon, Ulrich and Buschbaum, Markus, 'Die neue EU-Erbrechtsverordnung' [2012] NJW 2393–2398.

Sirmen, Sedat, 'Eş Cinsel Birliktelikler ve Bunların Kanunlar İhtilâfı Hukukunda Düzenlenişi' [Same-Sex Unions and Their Regulation in Conflict of Laws] (2009) 58 AÜHFD 825–879.

– 'AB Mirasçılık Tüzüğü ile Getirilen Avrupa Mirasçılık Belgesi ve Belge'nin Üçüncü Devletlerde Etkisi' [European Certificate of Succession Introduced by the European Succession Regulation and the Effect of the Certificate in Third States] in Bilgin Tiryakioğlu and others (eds), *Milletlerarası Özel Hukukta Güncel Konular Sempozyumu* [Symposium on Current Issues in Private International Law] (Yetkin 2016), 559–573.

Solomon, Dennis, 'Die Renaissance des Renvoi im Europäischen Internationalen Privatrecht' in Ralf Michaels and Dennis Solomon (eds), *Liber Amicorum Klaus Schurig zum 70. Geburtstag* (Sellier European Law Publishers 2012), 237–263.

– 'Die allgemeine Kollisionsnorm (Art. 21, 22 EuErbVO)' in Anatol Dutta and Sebastian Herrler (eds), *Die Europäische Erbrechtsverordnung, 20 Jahre DNotI 1993–2013* (C.H. Beck 2014), 19–45.

Somarakis, Ioannis K., 'Rethinking EU Jurisdiction in Cross-Border Family and Succession Cases Connected with Non-Member States' (2017–2018) XIX YbPIL 555–584.

Sonnenberger, Hans Jürgen, 'Anerkennung der Staatsangehörigkeit und effektive Staatsangehörigkeit natürlicher Personen im Völkerrecht und im internationalen Privatrecht' (1988) 29 BerGesVR 9–36.

Sonnentag, Michael, 'Die erbrechtliche Qualifikation des güterrechtlichen Viertels durch den EuGH und ihre Konsequenzen' [2019] JZ 657–666.

Sonyel, Salahi R., 'The Protégé System in the Ottoman Empire' (1991) 2 J Islam Stud 56–66.

Spelsberg-Korspeter, Ullrich, in Walter Zimmermann (ed), *Praxiskommentar Erbrechtliche Nebengesetze* (2nd edn, zerb verlag 2017).

Stade, Stefan, 'Die EU-Erbrechtsverordnung Nr. 650/2012 und deren Auswirkungen auf diverse Länder' in DACH Europäische Anwaltsvereinigung e.V. (ed), *Die EU-Erbrechtsverordnung Nr. 650/2012 und deren Auswirkung auf diverse Länder* (Schulthess 2014), 162–185.

Stamatiadis, Dimitrios, in Haris P. Pamboukis (ed), *EU Succession Regulation No 650/2012 – A Commentary* (Nomiki Bibliothiki & C.H. Beck & Hart & Nomos 2017).

Steiner, Anna-Zoe, 'EU-Verordnung in Erbsachen sowie zur Einführung eines europäischen Nachlasszeugnisses' [2012] NZ 104–113.

Sticherling, Philipp, 'Türkisches Erbrecht und deutscher Erbschein (zu LG Braunschweig, 18.05.2009 – 8 T 344/09)' [2010] IPRax 234–236.

Stürner, Michael, 'Die Bedeutung des ordre public in der EuErbVO' [2014] GPR 317–325.

– in Harm Peter Westermann, Barbara Grunewald and Georg Maier-Reimer (eds), *Erman BGB*, vol 2 (16th edn, Otto Schmidt 2020).

Stürner, Michael and Wendelstein, Christoph, 'Eine deutsch-türkische Erbschaft mit Tücken' [2014] JURA 707–717.

Südaş, İlkay, 'Lifestyle Migration to Turkey: EU Citizens Living on the Turkish Sunbelt' <https://lifestylemigrationhub.files.wordpress.com/2012/09/lifestyle_migration_turkey.pdf> accessed 22 June 2021.

Süral, Ceyda, 'Hukuk Muhakemeleri Kanunu'nun Türk Mahkemelerinin Milletlerarası Yetkisine Etkisi' [The Effect of the Code of Civil Procedure on the International Jurisdiction of Turkish Courts] [2012] TBB Dergisi 167–216.

– 'Avrupa Birliği'nin Milletlerarası Özel Hukuka İlişkin Düzenlemelerinin Türk Hukukuna Etkileri' [The Effects of the European Union Private International Law Rules on Turkish Law] (2013) 12 MHFD 31–62.

Süß, Rembert, 'Die Wahl deutschen Güterrechts für inländische Grundstücke' [1999] ZNotP 385–394.

– 'Das Vindikationslegat im Internationalen Privatrecht' (2001) 65 RabelsZ 245–263.

– 'Notarieller Gestaltungsbedarf bei Eingetragenen Lebenspartnerschaften mit Ausländern' [2001] DNotZ 168–176.

– 'Der Vorschlag der EG-Kommission zu einer Erbrechtsverordnung (Rom IV Verordnung) vom 14. Oktober 2009' [2009] ZErb 342–348.

– 'The Proposed EU Regulation on Succession and German Law' in European Parliament, Directorate General for Internal Policies, Policy Department C: Citizens' Rights and Constitutional Affairs – Legal Affairs (ed), *Workshop on the Proposal for a Regulation on Succession – Some National Analysis – 22 March 2010 – PE 419.629* (2010) <http://www.europarl.europa.eu/RegData/etudes/STUD/2010/419629/IPOL-JURI_DV(2010)419629_EN.pdf> accessed 10 October 2017.

– 'Das Europäische Nachlasszeugnis' [2013] ZEuP 725–750.

– 'Der Vorbehalt zugunsten bilateraler Abkommen mit Drittstaaten' in Anatol Dutta and Sebastian Herrler (eds), *Die Europäische Erbrechtsverordnung, 20 Jahre DNotI 1993–2013* (C.H. Beck 2014), 181–198.

– in Rembert Süß (ed), *Erbrecht in Europa* (3rd edn, zerb verlag 2015).

– 'Die Entscheidung des EuGH in der Rechtssache Mahnkopf: Folgen für das gesetzliche Erbrecht des überlebenden Ehegatten in internationalen Ehen und neue Gestaltungsmöglichkeiten' [2018] DNotZ 742–757.

– 'Erste Konsequenzen aus der Mahnkopf-Entscheidung des EuGH – und Rechtsermittlung zweiter Klasse für türkische Witwen? Anmerkungen zur Entscheidung des OLG Hamm vom 21. März 2019' [2019] ZErb 249–254.

– in Anatol Dutta and Johannes Weber (eds), *Internationales Erbrecht* (2nd edn, C.H. Beck 2021).

Sütçü, Filiz, 'Deutsch-türkische Erbrechtsfälle in der Anwaltspraxis' [2015] ZErb 43–52.

Süzen, Begüm, *Tanıma ve Tenfiz Davalarında Kararı Veren Mahkemenin Yetkisinin Denetimi* [Review of the Jurisdiction of the Court of Origin in Recognition and Enforcement Cases] (On İki Levha 2016).

– *Milletlerarası Özel Hukukta Hukuki İşlemlerin Şekline Uygulanacak Hukuk* [Law Applicable to Form of Legal Acts] (On İki Levha 2020).

– 'Milletlerarası Usul Hukukunda Yetki Kurallarında Kullanılan Bağlama Noktalarının Vasıflandırılması' [Characterisation of the Connecting Factors used in Rules of Jurisdiction in International Civil Procedural Law] in Sibel Özel and Hatice Selin Pürselim (eds), *Milletlerarası Usul Hukukunda Mahkemelerin Yetkisine İlişkin Güncel Tartışmalar: Ulusal Konferans 20 Şubat 2021* [Current Debates on the Jurisdiction of Courts in International Civil Procedural Law: National Conference 20 February 2021] (On İki Levha 2021), 47–61.

Symeonides, Symeon C., 'Exploring the "Dismal Swamp": The Revision of Louisiana's Conflicts Law on Successions' (1987) 47 La L Rev 1029–1104.

Szászy, István, *International Civil Procedure – A Comparative Study* (A. W. Sijthoff-Leyden 1967).

Szilágyi, Ferenc, 'The Option to Choose the Law Applicable to Succession Under the EU Succession Regulation' (2021) XVII IAS 149–190.

Şanlı, Cemal, 'Yabancı Veraset İlamlarının Türk Mahkemelerinde Tanınması veya Delil Olarak Kullanılması' [Recognition or Use of Foreign Certificates of Succession as Evidence in Turkish Courts], *Prof. Dr. İlhan E. Postacıoğlu'na Armağan* [Liber Amicorum Prof. Dr. İlhan E. Postacıoğlu] (Bayrak Matbaacılık 1990), 291–307.

– *Uluslararası Ticari Akitlerin Hazırlanması ve Uyuşmazlıkların Çözüm Yolları* [Drafting International Commercial Contracts and Dispute Resolution] (7th edn, Beta 2019).

Şanlı, Cemal, Esen, Emre and Ataman Figanmeşe, İnci, *Milletlerarası Özel Hukuk* [Private International Law] (9th edn, Beta 2021).

Şekerci, Ersin, 'Medeni Usul Hukukunda ve İdari Yargılama Usulünde Derdestlik' [Lis Pendens in Civil and Administrative Procedural Law] (1986) 12 YD 206–226.

Şensöz, Ebru, '27.11. 2007 Tarih ve 5718 Sayılı MÖHUK Uyarınca Yabancılık Unsuru Taşıyan Evlilik Mallarına İlişkin İhtilaflarda Uygulanacak Hukuk' [Law Applicable to Disputes Concerning Matrimonial Property Having a Foreign Element Pursuant to the PILA No 5718 dated 27.11.2007] (2009) 8 İTİCÜSBD 173–211.

Şensöz Malkoç, Ebru, *Aile Hukukuna İlişkin Yabancı Kararların Tanınması* [Recognition of Foreign Judgements on Family Law] (On İki Levha 2017).

– *Türk Milletlerarası Usul Hukukunda Milletlerarası Derdestlik ve Bağlantılı Dava İtirazı* [Lis Pendens and Parallel Proceedings Objection in Turkish International Civil Procedural Law] (Beta 2020).

Şıpka, Şükran, *Türk Hukukunda Edinilmiş Mallara Katılma Rejimi ve Uygulamaya İlişkin Sorunlar* [The Regime of Participation in Acquired Property in Turkish Law and Problems Related to Practice] (3rd edn, On İki Levha 2013).

Şıpka, Şükran and Özdoğan, Ayça, *Yargı Kararları Işığında Soru ve Cevaplarla Eşler Arasındaki Malvarlığı Davaları* [Property Cases between Spouses with Questions and Answers in the Light of Judgments] (2nd edn, On İki Levha 2017).

Takavut, İbrahim Doğan, *Milletlerarası Ticari Tahkimde Doğrudan Uygulanan Kurallar* [Mandatory Rules of Law in International Commercial Arbitration] (On İki Levha 2018).

Tan Dehmen, Mine, 'Türk Vatandaşlarının Kişi Hallerine İlişkin Davalar Bakımından 5718 Sayılı MÖHUK'ta Kabul Edilen Yetki Kuralı' [The Rule of Jurisdiction Adopted in the PILA No 5718 in Respect of Cases Concerning the Personal Status of Turkish Citizens] (2013) 33 MHB 169–211.

Taner, Tahir, *Kapitülasyonlar Nasıl İlga Edildi?* [How Were the Capitulations Abolished?] (İsmail Akgün Matbaası 1956).

– 'Lozan Muahedesi ve Kapitülasyonların İlgası' [Treaty of Lausanne and The Abolition of Capitulations], *Devletler Hususi Hukuku Ordinaryüs Profesörü Muammer Raşit Seviğ'e Armağan* [Liber Amicorum Ordinarius Professor of Private International Law Muammer Raşit Seviğ] (İsmail Akgün Matbaası 1956), 723–730.

Tang, Zheng Sophia, *Jurisdiction and Arbitration Agreements in International Commercial Law* (Routledge 2014).

Tanrıbilir, Feriha Bilge, 'Yabancıların Mirasçılık Sıfatı' [Foreigners' Entitlement to Succession], *Av. Dr. Faruk Erem Armağanı* [Liber Amicorum Adv. Dr. Faruk Erem] (Afşaroğlu Matbaası 1999), 695–731.

– *Kanuni Mirasçılıktan Doğan Kanunlar İhtilafı* [Conflict of Laws Arising from Intestacy] (Gazi Üniversitesi İletişim Fakültesi Basımevi 2000).

– 'MÖHUK ve Mirasa İlişkin Bağlama Kuralının Uygulanmasında Öne Çıkan Hususlar' [The Prominent Issues in the Application of the PILA and the Conflict-of-Laws Rule on Succession] in Feriha Bilge Tanrıbilir and Gülce Gümüşlü Tunçağıl (eds), *10. Yılında MÖHUK Sempozyumu – 7–8 Aralık 2017, Ankara* [Symposium on the 10th Anniversary of the PILA – 7–8 December 2017, Ankara] (Adalet Yayınevi 2018), 125–147.

– 'Kişi Halleri ve Mirasa İlişkin Milletlerarası Yetki Kurallarının Kapsamı' [The Scope of International Jurisdiction Rules on Personal Status and Succession] in Sibel Özel and Hatice Selin Pürselim (eds), *Milletlerarası Usul Hukukunda Mahkemelerin Yetkisine İlişkin Güncel Tartışmalar: Ulusal Konferans 20 Şubat 2021* [Current Debates on the Jurisdiction of Courts in International Civil Procedural Law: National Conference 20 February 2021] (On İki Levha 2021), 75–96.

Tanrıver, Süha, *Medenî Usul Hukukunda Derdestlik İtirazı* [Lis Pendens Objection in Civil Procedural Law] (Adalet Yayınevi 2007).

– 'Türk Hukuku Bağlamında Çekişmesiz Yargı ve Noterlik' [Non-Contentious Jurisdiction and Notary Public in the Context of Turkish Law], *Makalelerim II (2006–2010)* [My Articles II (*2006–2010)*] (Adalet Yayınevi 2011), 345–358.

– *Medenî Usûl Hukuku* [Civil Procedural Law], vol 1 (4th edn, Yetkin 2021).

Tarman, Zeynep Derya, 'Die eherechtlichen Kollisionsnormen im türkischen Recht' [2013] StAZ 206–211.

Tarman, Zeynep Derya and Oba, Meltem Ece, 'Choice of Court Agreements under Turkish Law' (2017–2018) XIX YbPIL 365–394.

Tekinalp, Gülören, 'Türk "Milletlerarası Özel Hukuk ve Milletlerarası Usul Hukuku Tasarısı"' [Draft Bill for the Turkish "Private International and Procedural Law Act"] (1978) 44 İÜHFM 91–121.

– *Türk Yabancılar Hukuku* [Turkish Law on Foreigners] (8th edn, Beta 2003).

– 'The 2007 Turkish Code Concerning Private International Law and International Civil Procedure' (2007) IX YbPIL 313–341.

– *Milletlerarası Özel Hukuk: Bağlama ve Usul Hukuku Kuralları* [Private International Law: Conflict-of-Laws and Procedural Law Rules] (13th edn, Beta 2020).

Tekinalp, Gülören, Nomer, Ergin and Odman Boztosun, Ayşe, *Private International Law in Turkey* (Wolters Kluwer 2012).

Tereszkiewicz, Piotr and Wysocka-Bar, Anna, 'Legacy by Vindication Under the EU Succession Regulation No 650/2012 Following the Kubicka Judgment of the ECJ' (2019) 27 ERPL 875–894.

Terner, Paul, 'Perspectives of a European Law of Succession' (2007) 14 Maast J Eur & Comp L 147–178.

Thiele, Burkhard, in Christian von Bar (ed), *Staudinger BGB – Buch 4: Familienrecht – §§ 1363–1407 (Eheliches Güterrecht 1 – Gesetzliches Güterrecht)* (Sellier & de Gruyter 2017).

Thorn, Karsten, in Christian Grüneberg (ed), *Grüneberg BGB* (81st edn, C.H. Beck 2022).

Thorn, Karsten and Varón Romero, Karen, 'Die Qualifikation des pauschalisierten Zugewinnausgleichs im Todesfall gemäß § 1371 Abs. 1 BGB nach der EuErbVO' [2020] IPRax 316–323.

Tiryaki, Fuat, 'Derdestliğin Şartları' (1979) 36(2) ABD 34–40.

Tiryakioğlu, Bilgin, *Yabancı Boşanma Kararlarının Türkiye'de Tanınması ve Tenfizi* [Recognition and Enforcement of Foreign Divorce Judgments in Turkey] (Yetkin 1996).

– 'Multiple Citizenship and its Consequences in Turkish Law' (2006) 3 Ankara L Rev 1–16.

– 'Türklerin Kişi Hallerine İlişkin Davalarda Türk Mahkemelerinin Milletlerarası Yetkisi' [International Jurisdiction of Turkish Courts in Cases on Personal Status of Turkish Nationals] in Bilgin Tiryakioğlu and Gülin Güngör (eds), *Prof. Dr. Tuğrul Arat'a Armağan* [Liber Amicorum Prof. Dr. Tuğrul Arat] (Yetkin 2012), 1141–1165.

Toker, Ali Gümrah and Ruhi, Ahmet Cemal, *Milletlerarası Özel Hukuk ve Usul Hukuku Hakkında Kanun – Gerekçeli, Açıklamalı, İçtihatlı* [Act on Private International and Procedural Law – With Preamble, Brief Expalanations, Case Law] (On İki Levha 2019).

Tomkins, Frederick J. and Jencken, Henry D., *A Compendium of the Modern Roman Law: Founded Upon the Treatises of Puchta, Von Vangerow, Arndts, Franz Moehler, and the Corpus Juris Civilis* (Butterworth 1870).

Torremans, Paul and Fawcett, James J. (eds), *Cheshire, North and Fawcett Private International Law* (15th edn, OUP 2017).

Traar, Thomas, in Alfred Burgstaller and others (eds), *Die EU-Erbrechtsverordnung* (LexisNexis 2016).

Trunk, Alexander and Hatzimihail, Nikitas, 'Conclusions' in Alexander Trunk and Nikitas Hatzimihail (eds), *EU Civil Procedure Law and Third Countries* (Nomos 2021), 271–306.

Tuluay, Metin, '"Milletlerarası Özel Hukuk ve Usul Hukuku Hakkında Kanun" Üzerine Düşünceler' [Reflections on the Private International and Procedural Law Act] (1982) 2 MHB 22–30.

Tunçomağ, Kenan, 'İkametgâh' [Domicile] (1961) 26 İÜHFM 153.

Tütüncübaşı, Uğur, 'Türk Hukukuyla Karşılaştırmalı Olarak Alman Hukukunda Yabancı Yargı Kararlarının Tanınması ve Tenfizi' [Recognition and Enforcement of Foreign Judgments under German Law in Comparison with Turkish Law] (2014) 16 DEÜHFD 1525–1551.

– *Yabancı Çekişmesiz Yargı Kararlarının Türk Hukukunda Tanınması* [Recognition of Foreign Decisions Rendered in Non-Contentious Proceedings in Turkey] (Adalet Yayınevi 2014).

Ulukapı, Ömer, ‘Medeni Usul Hukukunda Derdestlik ve Sonuçları’ Lis Pendens in Civil Procedural Law and Its Consequences] (1995) 21 YD 395–445.

Uluocak, Nihal, *Kanunlar İhtilafı (Yasama Yetkisi Kuralları)* [Conflict of Laws (Conflict Rules)] (Fakülteler Matbaası 1971).

– *Milletlerarası Özel Hukuk Dersleri (Kişisel Statü – Miras Statüsü)* [Private International Law Lectures (Personal Statute – Succession Statute) (Filiz Kitabevi 1987).

Ulusu Karataş, A. Elif, ‘Türk Miras Hukukunda Mirasın Kazanılmasında Halefiyet Türleri ve Türk Milletlerarası Özel Hukukundaki Yansımaları’ [Types of the Transfer of Succession in Turkish Succession Law and Their Reflections in Turkish Private International Law] (2015) 73 İÜHFM 357–390.

Unat, İlhan, *Türk Vatandaşlık Hukuku (Metinler – Mahkeme Kararları)* [Turkish Nationality Law (Texts – Judgments] (Sevinç Matbaası 1966).

Uyanık, Ayfer, ‘Türk Milletlerarası Usul Hukukunda Yetki Sözleşmeleri’ [Jurisdiction Agreements in Turkish International Civil Procedural Law] (Master Thesis, Istanbul University 1994).

Uyar, Turgut, ‘Ölüme Dair Konuşmalar 2’ [Conversations about Death 2] in Bedirhan Toprak (ed), *Büyük Saat* [The Big Clock] (11th edn, Yapı Kredi Yayınları 2011).

Üstündağ, Saim, *Medeni Yargılama Hukuku* [Civil Procedural Law] (7th edn, Nesil Matbaacılık 2000).

van Boxstael, Jean-Louis, ‘Succession internationale, double nationalité et renvoi’ [2021] JT 339–341.0

van Erp, Sjef, ‘The New Succession Regulation: The Lex Rei Sitae Rule in Need of Reappraisal?’ (2012) 1 EPLJ 187–190.

– ‘Inheritance Certificates and EU Law: Less European “Effet Utile” Implies More National “Pratique Utile”’ (2020) 9 EPLJ 67–72.

van Hoogstraten, Matthijs H., ‘La codification par traités en droit international privé dans le cadre de la Conférence de la Haye’ (1967) 122 RdC 337–425.

van Meegen, Patricia, *Das gemeinschaftliche Testament im europäischen Kontext* (JWV Jenaer Wissenschaftliche Verlagsgesellschaft 2021).

Vardar Hamamcıoğlu, Gülşah, *Türk Medeni Kanunu’na Göre Yerleşim Yeri* [Domicile according to the Turkish Civil Code] (On İki Levha 2009).

Vasileva, Katya, ‘Population and Social Conditions’ (2011) 34 Eurostat-Statistics in Focus <https://ec.europa.eu/eurostat/documents/3433488/5579176/KS-SF-11-034-EN.PDF/63cebff3-f7ac-4ca6-ab33-4e8792c5f30c> accessed 27 November 2020.

Vékás, Lajos, ‘Zur Konkurrenz zwischen Erbstatut und Güterrechtsstatut’ [1985] IPRax 24–25.

– ‘Objektive Anknüpfung des Erbstatuts’ in Gerte Reichelt and Walter H. Rechberger (eds), *Europäisches Erbrecht: Zum Verordnungsvorschlag der Europäischen Kommission zum Erb- und Testamentsrecht* (Jan Sramek Verlag 2011), 41–56.

Velidedeoğlu, Hıfzı Veldet, *Türk Medeni Hukuku: Şahsın Hukuku* [Turkish Civil Law: Law of Persons] (6th edn, Nurgök Matbaası 1960).

Verbeke, Alain-Laurent and Leleu, Yves-Henri, ‘Harmonisation of the Law of Succession in Europe’ in Arthur S Hartkamp and Others (eds), *Towards A European Civil Code* (4th edn, Kluwer Law International 2011), 459–479.

Vischer, Frank, ‘General Course on Private International Law at the Hague Academy of International Law’ (1992) 232 RdC 9–255.

Vural Çelenk, Belkıs, 'A Promising Shift to Limit Ordre Public Intervention of Applicable Foreign Law Before Turkish Supreme Court' in Juana Vasella (ed), *Von A wie Arbitration über T wie Transport bis Z wie Zivilprozess: Liber discipulorum für Professor Dr. Andreas Furrer zum 55. Geburtstag* (Stämpfli Verlag 2018), 129–140.

– *Application of Third Country Overriding Mandatory Rules – Analytical Comparison of Swiss, Turkish and EU Law* (Schulthess 2018).

Wagner, Rolf, 'Der Kommissionsvorschlag vom 14.10.2009 zum internationalen Erbrecht: Stand und Perspektiven des Gesetzgebungsverfahrens' [2010] DNotZ 506–519.

– 'Aktuelle Entwicklungen in der justiziellen Zusammenarbeit in Zivilsachen' [2012] NJW 1333–1338.

Wall, Fabian, 'Richtet sich die internationale Zuständigkeit zur Erbscheinserteilung künftig ausschließlich nach Artt. 4 ff EU-ErbVO?' [2015] ZErb 9–16.

Wansbrough, John, 'Imtiyāzāt' in Bernard Lewis and others (eds), *The Encyclopaedia of Islam*, vol III (H-Iram) (2nd edn, J Brill 1986), 1178–1179.

Wautelet, Patrick, in Andrea Bonomi and Patrick Wautelet (eds), *Le droit européen des successions-Commentaire du Règlement n°650/2012 du 4 juillet 2012* (2nd edn, Bruylant 2016).

Weber, Johannes, 'Die Europäischen Güterrechtsverordnungen: Eine erste Annäherung' [2016] DNotZ 659–697.

– 'Ein Klassiker neu aufgelegt Die Qualifikation des § 1371 BGB unter dem Regime der Europäischen Erbrechtsverordnung' [2018] NJW 1356–1358.

– 'Zur Erteilung eines deutschen Erbscheins bei letztem gewöhnlichen Aufenthalt des Erblassers im Ausland – zugleich Besprechung der EuGH-Entscheidung in der Rechtssache Oberle – C-20/17' [2018] RNotZ 454–463.

– in Anatol Dutta and Johannes Weber (eds), *Internationales Erbrecht* (2nd edn, C.H. Beck 2021).

Weintraub, Russell J., 'An Inquiry Into the Utility of Situs as a Concept in Conflicts Analysis' (1966) 52 Cornell LQ 1–42.

Weiss, Kinga M. and Bigler, Manuel, 'Die EU Erbrechtsverordnung – Neue Herausforderungen für die internationale Nachlassplanung aus Schweizer Sicht' [2014] Successio 163–193.

Weller, Matthias, in Alfonso-Luis Calvo Caravaca, Angelo Davì and Heinz-Peter Mansel (eds), *The EU Succession Regulation – A Commentary* (Cambridge University Press 2016).

Wenckstern, Manfred, 'Inheritance, Acceptance and Disclaimer' in Jürgen Basedow and others (eds), *The Max Planck Encyclopedia of European Private Law*, vol I (OUP 2012), 884–888.

Werner, Olaf, in Gerhard Otte (ed), *Staudinger BGB – Buch 4: Erbrecht – §§ 1922–1966 (Einleitung zum Erbrecht – Erbfolge)* (Sellier & de Gruyter 2017).

Weser, Martha, 'Bases of Judicial Jurisdiction in the Common Market Countries' (1961) 10 AJCL 323–344.

Wilderspin, Michael, 'Overriding Mandatory Provisions' in Jürgen Basedow and others (eds), *Encyclopedia of Private International Law* (Edward Elgar Publishing 2017), 1330–1336.

Wilke, Felix M., 'Das internationale Erbrecht nach der neuen EU-Erbrechtsverordnung' [2012] RIW 601–609.

Wilsch, Harald, in Stefan Hügel (ed), *BeckOK GBO (Stand: 1.3.2022)* (45th edn, C.H. Beck 2022).

Wittkowski, Ralf, 'Die Beantragung und Erteilung von Erbscheinen in Erbfällen mit Auslandsberührung nach dem FamFG' [2010] RNotZ 102–132.

Wittwer, Alexander, 'Praxisfragen des Europäischen Nachlasszeugnisses, insbesondere im Verhältnis zu Drittstaaten' in Helmut Heiss (ed), *Europäische Erbrechtsverordnung – Auswirkungen auf das Fürstentum Liechtenstein und Schweiz* (Dike & Facultas 2016), 115–139.

Wolf, Stephan and Spichiger, Bettina, 'Zum Erbvertrag – Einführung und Überblick' in Stephan Wolf and others (eds), *Der Erbvertrag aus rechtsvergleichender Sicht: Rechtsvergleichendes Symposium an der Rechtswissenschaftlichen Fakultät der Universität Bern vom 17./18. Mai 2018 / Il contratto Successorio, aspetti di diritto comparato: Convegno di diritto comparato alla Facoltà di Giurisprudenza dell'Università di Berna, 17/18 maggio 2018* (Stämpfli Verlag 2018), 1–34.

Wolff, Martin, *Das internationale Privatrecht des Deutschlands* (3rd edn, Springer 1954).

Wurmnest, Wolfgang, 'Comparative Report and Policy Perspectives' in Anatol Dutta and Wolfgang Wurmnest (eds), *European Private International Law and Member State Treaties with Third States – The Case of the European Succession Regulation* (Intersentia 2019), 329–356.

Wurmnest, Wolfgang and Wössner, Benedikt, 'Kollisionsrechtliche Staatsverträge mit Drittstaaten in Europa: Ein Blick auf die "Achillesferse" der EuErbVO' [2019] ZVglRWiss 449–483.

Wysocka, Anna, 'How Can a Valid Professio Iuris Be Made under the EU Succession Regulation?' [2012] NIPR 569–575.

Yasan, Candan, *Milletlerarası Özel Hukukta Aynı Cinsiyetten Kişilerin Birliktelikleri* [Relationships between Persons of the Same-Sex in Private International Law] (On İki Levha 2013).

Yaşar, Hakkı, 'Konsoloslara İlişkin Adli Ayrıcalıklar ve Bağışıklıklar (I)' [Judicial Privileges and Immunities of Consuls (I)] (1982) 8 YD 37–49.

Yaşar, Tuğçe Nimet, 'Türk Mahkemelerinde Yabancı Hukukun Uygulanması' [Application of Foreign Law in Turkish Courts] (2013) 33 MHB 75–114.

Yazıcı, Hilmi and Atasoy, Hasan, *Şahıs, Aile ve Miras Hukuku ile İlgili Yargıtay Tatbikatı 1952–1970* [Case Law of the Court of Cassation (Yargıtay) on the Law of Persons, Family and Succession Law 1952–1970] (Kardeş Matbaası 1970).

Yeazell, Stephen C. and Schwartz, Joanna C., *Civil Procedure* (10th edn, Wolters Kluwer 2019).

Yetano, Toni Marzal, 'The Constitutionalisation of Party Autonomy in European Family Law' (2010) 6 J Priv Int L 155–173.

Yöney, Can, *Yabancı Hukukun Uygulanması* [Application of Foreign Law] (On İki Levha 2018).

Yörük, Abdülhak Kemal, *Nazari ve Ameli Devletler Hususi Hukuku* [Theoretical and Practical Private International Law] (2nd edn, İsmail Akgün Matbaası 1950).

Załucki, Mariusz, 'Attempts to Harmonize the Inheritance Law in Europe: Past, Present, and Future' (2018) 103 Iowa L Rev 2318–2338.

– 'The Future of Succession Law in the EU. A Proposal' in Catarina Santos Botelho and Fábio da Silva Veiga (eds), *Future Law* (Universidade Católica Editora 2018), 581–588.

Zeytin, Zafer, *Edinilmiş Mallara Katılma Rejimi ve Tasfiyesi* [The Regime of the Participation in Acquired Property and Its Liquidation] (5th edn, Seçkin 2021).

Zimmermann, Reinhard (ed), *Freedom of Testation – Testierfreiheit* (Mohr Siebeck 2012).
– 'Intestate Succession in Germany' in Kenneth G. C. Reid, Marius J. de Waal and Reinhard Zimmermann (eds), *Comparative Succession Law – Volume II: Intestate Succession* (OUP 2015), 181–223.
– 'Das Ehegattenerbrecht in historisch-vergleichender Perspektive' (2016) 80 RabelsZ 39–92.
– 'Pflichtteil und Noterbenrecht in historisch-vergleichender Perspektive' (2020) 84 RabelsZ 465–547.
Zoumpoulis, Christos G., in Haris P. Pamboukis (ed), *EU Succession Regulation No 650/ 2012 – A Commentary* (Nomiki Bibliothiki & C.H. Beck & Hart & Nomos 2017).
Zweigert, Konrad, 'Einige Auswirkungen des Gemeinsamen Marktes auf das internationale Privatrecht der Mitgliedstaaten' in Ernst von Caemmerer, Hans-Jürgen Schlochauer and Ernst Steindorff (eds), *Probleme des europäischen Rechts, Festschrift für Walter Hallstein zu seinem 65. Geburtstag* (Klostermann 1966), 559–569.

Other Sources

Arno, Peter, 'Now read me the part again where I disinherit everybody' *The New Yorker* (7 December 1940) 29.

BAMF, 'Wohnen und innerstädtische Segregation von Migranten in Deutschland – Working Paper 21' <https://www.bamf.de/SharedDocs/Anlagen/DE/Forschung/WorkingPapers/wp21-wohnen-innerstaedtische-segregation.pdf?__blob=publicationFile&v=12> accessed 22 June 2021.

Bericht der Kommission für Rechtsfragen des Nationalrates über die Motion von Ständerat Luc Recordon vom 28. August 2015 — Internationales Übereinkommen über Erbsachen <https://www.parlament.ch/centers/kb/Documents/2014/Kommissionsbericht_RK-N_14.4285_2015-08-28.pdf> accessed 20 July 2018.

Council of the European Union, 'Presidency Conclusions (Helsinki, 10 and 11 December 1999)' <https://www.consilium.europa.eu/ueDocs/cms_Data/docs/pressData/en/ec/ACFA4C.htm> accessed 22 June 2021.

– 'Conclusions of the Presidency (Copenhagen, 12 and 13 December 2002)' <https://www.consilium.europa.eu/ueDocs/cms_Data/docs/pressData/en/ec/72921.pdf> accessed 22 June 2021.

– 'Negotiating Framework (Luxembourg, 3 October 2005)' <http://ec.europa.eu/enlargement/pdf/turkey/st20002_05_tr_framedoc_en.pdf> accessed 22 June 2021.

– General Affairs Council, 'Council Conclusions on Enlargement and Stabilisation and Association Process as adopted by the Council on 26 June 2018 – No. 10374/18' <https://www.consilium.europa.eu/media/35863/st10555-en18.pdf> accessed 22 June 2021.

– 'Council Conclusions on Enlargement and Stabilisation and Association Process from 18 June 2019' <http://www.consilium.europa.eu/en/press/press-releases/2019/06/18/council-conclusions-on-enlargement-and-stabilisation-and-association-process/> accessed 22 June 2021.

Denkschrift zu dem Konsularvertrag von 1917, Reichstagsdrucksache Nr. 755, 13. Legislaturperiode, 11. Session (1914–1917) 171.

Denkschrift zu dem Konsularvertrag von 1929, Reichstagsdrucksache Nr. 1584, 4. Wahlperiode (1928) 29.

Deutscher Notarverein, 'Stellungnahme – Entwurf eines Gesetzes zum Internationalen Güterrecht und zur Änderung von Vorschriften des Internationalen Privatrechts' <https://www.bmjv.de/SharedDocs/Gesetzgebungsverfahren/Stellungnahmen/2018/Downloads/070618_Stellungnahme_Notarverein_RefE_Intern.Gueterrecht_intern.Privatrecht.pdf;jsessionid=47C4BB3655C2B0237A9C997515C8C1D7.2_cid324?__blob=publicationFile&v=4> accessed 7 June 2021.

Erläuternder Bericht zum Vernehmlassungsentwurf über die Änderung des Bundesgesetzes über das Internationale Privatrecht (Erbrecht) <https://www.fedlex.admin.ch/filestore/fedlex.data.admin.ch/eli/dl/proj/6018/12/cons_1/doc_2/de/pdf-a/fedlex-data-admin-ch-eli-dl-proj-6018-12-cons_1-doc_2-de-pdf-a.pdf> accessed 19 July 2018.

European Commission, Directorate-General for Neighbourhood and Enlargement Negotiations, 'Screening Report Turkey, Chapter 24 – Justice, Freedom and Security (6 June 2006)' <http://www.ab.gov.tr/files/ardb/evt/2_turkiye_ab_iliskileri/2_2_adaylik_sureci/2_2_6_muzakere_sureci/2_2_6_2_tarama_raporlari/Screening_Report-Chapter_24_-_Justice_Freedom_and_Security-TR.pdf> accessed 22 June 2021.

– `Responses to Green Paper on Successions and Wills` <http://europa.eu.int/comm/justice_home/news/consulting_public/successions/news_contributions_successions_en.htm> accessed 21 September 2016.

European Parliament, 'Legislative resolution of 13 March 2012 on the proposal for a regulation of the European Parliament and of the Council on jurisdiction, applicable law, recognition and enforcement of decisions and authentic instruments in matters of succession and the creation of a European Certificate of Succession (COM(2009)0154 – C7-0236/2009 – 2009/0157(COD)) – P7_TA(2012)0068' <http://www.europarl.europa.eu/sides/getDoc.do?type=TA&reference=P7-TA-2012-0068&language=EN> accessed 21 September 2016.

– ´European Parliament resolution of 19 May 2021 on the 2019-2020 Commission Reports on Turkey (2019/2176(INI))` <https://www.europarl.europa.eu/delegations/en/d-tr/documents/ep-resolutions> accessed 22 June 2021.

Eurostat, *People in the EU: Who Are We and How Do We Live?* (Publications Office of the European Union 2015) <http://ec.europa.eu/eurostat/documents/3217494/7089681/KS-04-15-567-EN-N.pdf/8b2459fe-0e4e-4bb7-bca7-7522999c3bfd> accessed 22 June 2021.

– 'Migration and Migrant Population Statistics – Statistics Explained' <https://ec.europa.eu/eurostat/statistics-explained/index.php/Migration_and_migrant_population_statistics#Migrant_population:_21.8_million_non-EU-27_citizens_living_in_the_EU-27_on_1_January_2019> accessed 30 July 2020.

– 'Acquisition of Citizenship by Age Group, Sex and Former Citizenship (Migr_acq)' <https://ec.europa.eu/eurostat/databrowser/view/migr_acq/default/table?lang=en> accessed 14 March 2022.

– 'All Valid Permits by Age, Sex and Citizenship on 31 December of Each Year (MIGR_RESVAS)' <https://ec.europa.eu/eurostat/databrowser/view/MIGR_RESVAS__custom_2278646/default/table?lang=en> accessed 14 March 2022.

– 'Authorisations for Study and Research by Reason, Type of Decision, Citizenship and Length of Validity (migr_ressrath)' <https://ec.europa.eu/eurostat/web/asylum-and-managed-migration/data/database> accessed 24 June 2021.

– 'First Permits by Reason, Length of Validity and Citizenship (MIGR_RESFIRST)' <https://ec.europa.eu/eurostat/databrowser/view/MIGR_RESFIRST__custom_2279549/default/table?lang=en> accessed 14 March 2022.

– 'Population on 1 January by Age Group, Sex and Citizenship (Migr_pop1ctz)' <https://ec.europa.eu/eurostat/databrowser/view/MIGR_POP1CTZ__custom_2278307/default/table?lang=en> accessed 14 March 2022.

European Union, `Succession – National information and online forms concerning Regulation No. 650/2012´ <https://e-justice.europa.eu/content_succession-380-en.do?clang=en> accessed 25 March 2020.

European Union Agency for Fundamental Rights, ´Entering into a same-sex marriage´ <https://fra.europa.eu/en/publication/2017/mapping-minimum-age-requirements/same-sex-marriage> accessed 20 December 2020.

GEDIP, ′Proposal for a Convention concerning jurisdiction and the enforcement of judgments in family and succession matters' <https://gedip-egpil.eu/wp-content/uploads/1993/10/gedip-documents-3pe.pdf> accessed 3 December 2018.

Gesamte Rechtsvorschrift für Niederlassungsvertrag (Türkei), Fassung vom 23.5.2023 <https://www.ris.bka.gv.at/GeltendeFassung.wxe?Abfrage=Bundesnormen&Gesetzesnummer=10000075> accessed 5 March 2021.

Hariciye Nazırı Halil Beyin Almanya Devleti ile Muamele-i Mütekabile Esası Üzerine Konsolosluk, İkâmet-i Tebea ve Müzaheret-i Adliyye Mukavelenamesi ve İade-i Mücrimin Muahedenamesi Yapıldığına Dair Beyanatı [Speech of the Minister of Foreign Affairs Halil Bey as Regards the Conclusion of Consular, Residence, Judicial Assistance and Extradition Treaties with Germany based on Reciprocity], Meclis-i Mebusan Zabıt Ceridesi [Minutes of Proceedings of the First Turkish Parliament], Cilt 1 [1916 – Devre: 3 İçtima Senesi: 3] (T.B.M.M. Basımevi 1991).

House of Commons – Home Affairs Committee, Implications for the Justice and Home Affairs Area of the Accession of Turkey to the European Union: Tenth Report of Session 2010–12 (The Stationery Office 2011).

House of Lords European Union Committee, 'Minutes of Evidence on the EU's Regulation on Succession – 6th Report of Session' 2009–2010 HL 75 <https://publications.parliament.uk/pa/ld200910/ldselect/ldeucom/75/75.pdf> accessed 22 June 2021.

Hukuk Muhakemeleri Kanunu Tasarısı ve Adalet Komisyonu Raporu (1/574) [Draft Bill for the Code of Civil Procedure Act the Report of the Justice Commission (1/574)] <https://www.tbmm.gov.tr/sirasayi/donem23/yil01/ss393.pdf> accessed 27 July 2018.

İktisadi Kalkınma Vakfı [Economic Development Foundation], 'Türkiye Kamuoyunda Avrupa Birliği Desteği ve Avrupa Algısı Araştırması' [Survey on the European Union Support and Perception of Europe in Turkish Public Opinion] (Anadolu Basın Merkezi 2019) <https://www.ikv.org.tr/images/files/%C4%B0KV%20Kamuoyu%20ara%C5%9Ft%C4%B1rmas%C4%B1(1).pdf> accessed 22 June 2021.

Jenard, Paul, 'Report on the Convention on Jurisdiction and the Enforcement of Judgments in Civil and Commercial Matters (Signed at Brussels, 27 September 1968)' (1979) OJ C 59/1.

Kaya, Sıdıka and others, 'Evaluation Report on Medical Tourism in Turkey 2013' (Republic of Turkey, Ministry of Health 2013) <http://dosyasb.saglik.gov.tr/Eklenti/535,turkiye-medikal-turizm-degerlendirme-raporu-2013pdf.pdf> accessed 21 January 2021.

Lausanne Conference on Near Eastern Affairs (1922–1923) – Records of Proceedings and Draft Terms of Peace [With Map] (His Majesty's Stationery Office 1923).

Milletlerarası Özel Hukuk ve Usul Hukuku Hakkında Kanun Tasarısı ve Adalet Komisyonu Raporu (1/5) [Draft Bill for the Private International and Procedural Law Act and the Report of the Justice Commission (1/5)] <https://www.tbmm.gov.tr/tutanaklar/TUTANAK/DM__/d02/c004/dm__02004071ss0100.pdf> accessed 29 November 2020.

Statistisches Bundesamt (Destatis) (ed), *Statistisches Jahrbuch 1990 für die Bundesrepublik Deutschland* (Metzler-Poeschel Verlag 1990).

– *Bevölkerung und Erwerbstätigkeit: Natürliche Bevölkerungsbewegung 2015 (Fachserie 1, Reihe 1.1)* (Statistisches Bundesamt 2017) <https://www.destatis.de/DE/Themen/Gesellschaft-Umwelt/Bevoelkerung/Geburten/Publikationen/Downloads-Geburten/bevoelkerungsbewegung-2010110157004.pdf;jsessionid=67375A0636B645667895767CFE2B7D90.live722?__blob=publicationFile> accessed 5 March 2022.

– *Migration und Integration – Integrationsindikatoren* (Statistisches Bundesamt (Destatis) 2019) <https://www.destatis.de/DE/Themen/Gesellschaft-Umwelt/Bevoelkerung/Migration-Integration/_inhalt.html#sprg228898> accessed 22 June 2021.

– Bevölkerung und Erwerbstätigkeit: Ausländische Bevölkerung Ergebnisse des Ausländerzentralregisters 2020 (Fachserie 1, Reihe 2) (Statistisches Bundesamt (Destatis) 2021) <https://www.destatis.de/DE/Themen/Gesellschaft-Umwelt/Bevoelkerung/Migration-Integration/Publikationen/Downloads-Migration/auslaend-bevoelkerung-2010200207004.pdf?__blob=publicationFile> accessed 14 March 2022.
– 'Entwicklung der Lebenserwartung bei Geburt in Deutschland nach Geschlecht in den Jahren von 1950 bis 2060' <https://www-genesis.destatis.de/genesis/online?operation=ergebnistabelleDownload&levelindex=3&levelid=1622738269859&option=xml> accessed 3 June 2021.
T.C. Adalet Bakanlığı, Adli Sicil ve İstatistik Genel Müdürlüğü, Adalet İstatistikleri 2020 [Republic of Türkiye, Ministry of Justice, General Directorate of Judicial Record and Statistics, Judicial Statistics 2020] (Resmi İstatistik Programı 2020) 41 <https://adlisicil.adalet.gov.tr/Resimler/SayfaDokuman/1692021162011adalet_ist-2020.pdf> accessed 14 March 2022.
T.C. Dışişleri Bakanlığı [Republic of Türkiye, Ministry of Foreign Affairs], ′Vatandaş Sayısı Tablosu′ [Table on the Number of Citizens] <https://www2.tbmm.gov.tr/d27/7/7-2838sgc.pdf> accessed 22 June 2021.
– `Yurtdışında Yaşayan Türk Vatandaşları` [Turkish Citizens Living Abroad] <http://www.mfa.gov.tr/yurtdisinda-yasayan-turkler_.tr.mfa> accessed 14 March 2021.
T.C. Dışişleri Bakanlığı, Avrupa Birliği Başkanlığı [Republic of Türkiye, Ministry of Foreign Affairs, Directorate for EU Affairs], ′Türkiye-European Union Relations′ <http://www.ab.gov.tr/index.php?p=4&l=2> accessed 22 June 2021.
T.C. İçişleri Bakanlığı, Göç İdaresi Başkanlığı [Republic of Türkiye, Ministry of Interior, Presidency of Migration Management], ′Geçici Korumamız Altındaki Suriyeliler′ [Syrians under Temporary Protection] <https://www.goc.gov.tr/gecici-korumamiz-altindaki-suriyeliler> accessed 18 February 2021.
Toprak Koruma ve Arazi Kullanımı Kanunu ve Türk Medeni Kanununda Değişiklik Yapılması Hakkında Kanun Tasarısı [Draft Bill on Amendments to the Law on Soil Conservation and Land Use and Turkish Civil Code] <https://www5.tbmm.gov.tr/tutanaklar/TUTANAK/TBMM/d24/c076/tbmm24076082ss0564.pdf> accessed 25 July 2019.
Turkstat, 'Foreign Population by Country of Citizenship' <https://data.tuik.gov.tr/Bulten/Index?p=The-Results-of-Address-Based-Population-Registration-System-2021-45500> accessed 14 March 2022.
– 'House Sales Statistics, December 2021' <https://data.tuik.gov.tr/Bulten/Index?p=House-Sales-Statistics-December-2021-45672> accessed 14 March 2022.
– 'Tourism Statistics, Quarter IV: October-December and Annual, 2021' <https://data.tuik.gov.tr/Bulten/Index?p=Tourism-Statistics-Quarter-IV:-October-December-and-Annual,-2021-45785> accessed 14 March 2022.
Türkiye Cumhuriyeti ile Almanya Hükûmeti Arasında Akdolunan Konsolosluk Mukavelesinin Tasdikine Dair 1/601 Numaralı Kanun Lâyihası ve Hariciye Encümeni Mazbatası [Bill of law Numbered 1/601 on the Ratification of the Consular Agreement between the Republic of Turkey and the Government of Germany and the Report of the Foreign Affairs Committee] <https://www.tbmm.gov.tr/tutanaklar/TUTANAK/TBMM/d03/c019/tbmm03019062ss0163.pdf> accessed 7 October 2020.
Türk Kanunu Medenisinde Değişiklik Yapılması Hakkında Kanun Tasarısı – Madde Gerekçeleri Bölüm 3 [Draft Law on the Amendment of the Turkish Civil Code – Preamble to Articles Part 3] <https://www.tbmm.gov.tr/sirasayi/donem21/yil01/ss723_Madde_Gerekceleri_3.pdf> accessed 7 April 2020.

Zentrales Testamentsregister der Bundesnotarkammer, Jahresbericht 2020 (2020) <https://www.testamentsregister.de/fileadmin/user_upload_ztr/dokumente/Jahresbericht_2020.pdf> accessed 14 March 2022.

5718 Sayılı Milletlerarası Özel Hukuk ve Usul Hukuku Hakkında Kanun Tasarısı ve Gerekçe [Draft Bill for the Private International and Procedural Law Act No. 5718 and Its Preamble] <http://www2.tbmm.gov.tr/d23/1/1-0337.pdf> accessed 22 June 2021.

Table of Cases

Austria

Germany

European Union

Turkey

United Kingdom

Others

Index